Wissenschaftliche Untersuchungen
zum Neuen Testament · 2. Reihe

Herausgegeben von
Martin Hengel und Otfried Hofius

100

Timo Eskola

Theodicy and Predestination in Pauline Soteriology

Mohr Siebeck

Die Deutsche Bibliothek – CIP-Einheitsaufnahme

Eskola, Timo:
Theodicy and predestination in Pauline soteriology / Timo Eskola.
– Tübingen : Mohr Siebeck, 1998
   (Wissenschaftliche Untersuchungen zum Neuen Testament : Reihe 2 ; 100)
   ISBN 3-16-146894-5

This book was printed by Gulde-Druck in Tübingen on acid-free paper from Papier-
fabrik Niefern and bound by Heinr. Koch in Tübingen.

Printed in Germany.

ISSN 0340-9570

To Martin Hengel and Peter Stuhlmacher

Preface

Ever since 1992, after completing my doctoral dissertation on Pauline Christology, I have had the opportunity to investigate Paul's soteriology and the theology of Second Temple Judaism in my capacity as a New Testament scholar and lecturer at the Theological Institute of Finland (Helsinki). During my research the problem of theodicy constantly recurred in the texts under investigation. This led me to make a closer assessment of Paul's theology of predestination, which also appeared to be one of the areas of his teaching which had received little attention. As my research proceeded, the texts began to lead me towards surprising conclusions. They were rather different from those commonly drawn in the context of the popular "new perspective" on Paul and the question of "Paul and Palestinian Judaism". For this reason the present work suggests some new solutions to the problems concerning the relation of Paul to Second Temple Judaism – as well as the problem of the fundamental structure of Paul's soteriology.

The research was made possible by the research project of the Institute, for which I am truly grateful. I am especially indebted to my colleague, Rev. Eero Junkkaala, General Secretary of the Theological Institute, who has inspired and encouraged me and taught me much of what I know of the history and archaeology of Israel. My thanks also go to the staff of the Institute, our librarians Olavi Komu and Erkki Hanhikorpi, who have been of invaluable assistance in acquiring relevant literature, as well as to our secretary, Mrs. Kirsi Sell, who has taken care of all practical everyday matters.

I should also like to thank several friends of mine and "fellows" of the Institute: Docent Lauri Thurén (Åbo/Joensuu) for his suggestions and helpful comments concerning the manuscript, and Docent Antti Laato (Åbo/Helsinki), an Old Testament scholar with whom I have spent hours discussing the relation of the Testaments and the nature of biblical interpretation. Dr. Timo Laato has been a helpful 'partner in dialogue' as regards the question of Paul and the law, and my thanks go also to Dr. Erkki Koskenniemi for his inspiration in the area of classical literature.

Not least, I am deeply indebted to Mr. Michael Cox, Lic. Theol., Kerava for his indispensable labours in undertaking the language revision of my manuscript. I should also like to record my gratitude to Prof. Heikki Räisänen and the Department of Biblical Studies at the Faculty of Theology (University of Helsinki), for financial assistance with the language revision.

This is furthermore a fitting place to thank my lovely wife Tiina and our daughters Eeva and Elisa for their compassion and care during these years of study. Thank you for all this.

Finally, I wish to express my sincere thanks to Professors Martin Hengel and Otfried Hofius of Tübingen for their kind acceptance of my study for publication in this distinguished series, as well as the editorial staff of J.C.B. Mohr (Paul Siebeck) for their highly professional assistance in preparing the manuscript for publication.

Timo Eskola
Theological Institute of Finland
Kaisaniemenkatu 13 A 4. krs
FIN-00100 Helsinki
Finland
e-mail: teolinst@clinet.fi

Unless otherwise indicated, biblical quotations in English are taken from the New Revised Standard Version.

Contents

Preface VII

Abbreviations XII

Introduction 1

§ 1 Theodicy and Predestination in New Testament Exegesis 1
    1.1. Occasion and purpose of the study 1
    1.2. How to define predestination: on methodology 3
    1.3. Predestination in the context of the problem of theodicy 6
§ 2 Different 'History-of-Religions' Approaches and the
    Context of Paul's Soteriology 8
    2.1. The traditional 'history-of-religions' approach
        (W. Bousset, A. Deissmann) 8
    2.2. Paul the mystic (A. Schweitzer) 11
    2.3. The gnostic hypothesis (R. Bultmann) 12
    2.4. New emphasis on Paul's Jewish background
        (W.D. Davies, H.-J. Schoeps, P. Stuhlmacher) 15
    2.5. Paul and Rabbinic Judaism: a new pattern (E.P. Sanders) 18
    2.6. Locating Paul in the diversity of Second Temple
        Jewish theology (J.Chr. Beker, B.W. Longenecker,
        G. Schimanowski, M.A. Seifrid, et al.) 22

Chapter I: God's Chosen People in Crisis 27

§ 3 The Problem of Theodicy in Second Temple Sapiential Theology 28
    3.1. A theology of crisis 29
    3.2. Soteriological dualism 41
    3.3. An era of synergistic nomism 44
Excursus: The Theory of Covenantal Nomism 52
§ 4 The Solution of Apocalyptic: The Judgment of God 61
    4.1. The desecration of the Temple 63
    4.2. The decline of the Hasmoneans 65
    4.3. The destruction of Jerusalem 69

4.4. Judgment and the Day of Wrath 74
§ 5 The Ambivalent Concept of Predestination at Qumran 79
    5.1. Cosmic predestination 79
    5.2. The call to repentance 84
    5.3. Atonement by obedience 87
Summary 93

*Chapter II: The Problem of Theodicy and Predestination in
Paul's Soteriology* 95

§ 6 Will God Still Help His People? 95
    6.1. The faithfulness of God has not failed (Rom. 3:3-4) 96
    6.2. The righteous shall live by faith (Rom. 1:16-17) 101
    6.3. The Day of Wrath will come (Rom. 1:18) 116
    6.4. God's judgment will bring justice 122
§ 7 The Radical Anthropology of Paul's Soteriology 125
    7.1. The total domination of sin 125
    7.2. The dynamics of Adam typology 129
    7.3. The principle of paradoxical polarization in soteriology 137
§ 8 Mankind Imprisoned Under the Power of Sin 143
    8.1. Sold into slavery 143
    8.2. The hardening of Israel 149
    8.3. The predestination of judgment 160
§ 9 Predetermination and Election 165
    9.1. Calling and election 166
    9.2. Christocentric predestination 177
    9.3. The problem of double predestination 180
Summary 186

Chapter III: Predestination, Law and Justification 189

§ 10 The Paradoxical Function of the Law 190
    10.1. The Law which brings death 191
    10.2. Does the law produce sin? 201
    10.3. Avodat Israel and the "works of the law" 208
§ 11 The Principle of "Counting as Loss" in Paul 221
    11.1. Abandoning the old religious identity (Gal. 2:15-16) 221
    11.2. Denying human efforts (Phil. 3:4-8) 225
    11.3. Denying religious achievements (Rom. 3:27-28) 230

§ 12 Two Kinds of Righteousness 235
        12.1. Submitting to God's righteousness (Rom. 10:2-3) 235
        12.2. "As if based on works" (Rom. 9:31-32) 241
        12.3. The righteousness of Christ (Rom. 3:21-26) 246
Summary 250

Chapter IV: Paul's Universalist Soteriology 252

§ 13 The Christological Argument in Soteriology 252
        13.1. Paul and his Jewish heritage 253
        13.2. The centre of salvation history 259
        13.3. The principle of contemporary application 262
§ 14 A Solution Before the Plight? 267
        14.1. Paul and the alleged "covenantal nomism" 267
        14.2. Paul's consistency questioned 275
        14.3. What is the "plight" of man? 282
Excursus: A Hermeneutical Problem – Lutherans, Calvinists, and
        Dispensationalists study Jewish Christianity 287
§ 15 The Principles of Predestinarian Soteriology 293
        15.1. Providing a solution to the problem of theodicy 293
        15.2. Paul's apocalyptic eschatology 299
        15.3. Divine coercion and Christocentric universalism 302

Conclusion 307

Bibliography 315
Index of Passages 333
Index of Authors 343
Index of Subjects 348

Abbreviations

1. Periodicals, Series, Reference Works

AGJU	Arbeiten zur Geschichte des antiken Judentums und des Urchristentums
ALGHJ	Arbeiten zur Literatur und Geschichte des hellenistischen Judentums
AncB	Anchor Bible
ABD	Anchor Bible Dictionary
AGSU	Arbeiten zur Geschichte des Spätjudentums und Urchristentums
AnBib	Analecta Biblica
ANFa	Ante-Nicene Fathers
ASOR	American Schools of Oriental Research
ATD	Altes Testament Deutsch
AThANT	Abhandlungen zur Theologie des Alten und Neuen Testaments
AThD	Acta Theologica Danica
AzTh	Arbeiten zur Theologie
BA	Biblical Archaeologist
BBB	Bonner Biblische Beiträge
BBR	Bulletin for Biblical Research
BDR	Blass/Debrunner/Rehkopf, Grammatik des neutestamentlichen Griechisch
BEThL	Bibliotheca Ephemeridum Theologicarum Lovaniensium
BEvTh	Beiträge zur Evangelischen Theologie
Bib	Biblica
BK	Biblischer Kommentar
BKAT	Biblischer Kommentar. Altes Testament
BNTC	Black's New Testament Commentaries
BZ	Biblische Zeitschrift
BZAW	Beihefte zur Zeitschrift für die alttestamentliche Wissenschaft
BZNW	Beihefte zur Zeitschrift für die neutestamentliche Wissenschaft
CB	Coniectanea Biblica
CB.NT	Coniectanea Biblica. New Testament Series
CBQ	Catholic Biblical Quarterly
CCWJCW	Cambridge Commentaries on Writings of the Jewish and Christian World 200 BC to AD 200
DJD	Discoveries in the Judaean Desert (of Jordan)
EETh	Einführung in die evangelische Theologie
EHS.T	Europäische Hochschulschriften. Reihe 23, Theologie
EJ	Encyclopedia Judaica
EJTh	European Journal of Theology
EKK	Evangelisch-Katholischer Kommentar

EQ	Evangelical Quarterly
EvTh	Evangelische Theologie
EWNT	Exegetisches Wörterbuch zum Neuen Testament, ed. H. Balz, G. Schneider
ExpT	Expository Times
FzB	Forschung zur Bibel
FRLANT	Forschungen zur Religion und Literatur des Alten un Neuen Testaments
GCS	Die griechischen christlichen Schriftsteller der ersten drei Jahrhunderte
GTA	Göttinger Theologische Arbeiten
HAT	Handbuch zum Alten Testament
HNT	Handbuch zum Neuen Testament
HR	History of Religions
HThK	Herders Theologischer Kommentar
HTR	Harvard Theological Review
ICC	International Critical Commentary
Interp.	Interpretation
IVP	InterVarsity Press
JBL	Journal of Biblical Literature
JJS	Journal of Jewish Studies
JR	Journal of Religion
JSJ	Journal for the Study of Judaism
JSNT	Journal for the Study of the New Testament
JSNTS	Journal for the Study of the New Testament, Supplement Series
JSOT	Journal for the Study of the Old Testament
JSOTS	Journal for the Study of the Old Testament, Supplement Series
JThS	Journal of Theological Studies
Jud	Judaica
KAT	Kommentar zum Alten Testament
KEK	Kritisch-Exegetischer Kommentar
KuD	Kerygma und Dogma
LCC	Library of Christian classics
LCL	Loeb Classical Library
MNTC	Moffatt New Testament commentary
MS	Monograph Series
MSSNTS	Monograph Series. Society for New Testament Studies
NF	Neue Folge
NICNT	New international commentary on the New Testament
NIGTC	New International Greek Testament Commentary
NT	Novum Testamentum (=NovT)
NTA	Neutestamentliche Abhandlungen
NTD	Neues Testament Deutsch

NTS	New Testament Studies
NT.S	Novum Testamentum. Supplements
OTL	Old Testament library
PVTG	Pseudepigrapha veteris testamenti Graece
RB	Revue biblique
RGG	Religion in Geschichte und Gegenwart
RQ	Revue de Qumran
SBL	Society of Biblical Literature
SBL.DS	SBL Dissertation Series
SBLMS	SBL Monograph Series
SBLSBS	SBL Sources for Biblical Study
SBL.SP	SBL Seminar Papers
SBM	Stuttgarter Biblische Monographien
SBS	Stuttgarter Bibelstudien
SBT	Studies in Biblical Theology
SESJ	Suomen eksegeettisen seuran julkaisuja
SEÅ	Svensk Exegetisk Årsbok
SJLA	Studies in Judaism in Late Antiquity
SJT	Scottish Journal of Theology
SMBen.BE	Serie monografica di 'Benedictina'. Sezione biblico-ecumenica
SNT	Schriften des Neuen Testaments
SNTS	Society for New Testament Studies
SSN	Studia semitica Neerlandica
StTDJ	Studies on the texts of the desert of Judah
StTh	Studia theologica (Lund)
StUNT	Studien zur Umwelt der Neuen Testaments
SUTS	Suomalainen Uuden testamentin selitys
SVT	Supplements to Vetus Testamentum
SVTP	Studia in Veteris Testamenti Pseudepigrapha
TAik	Teologinen Aikakauskirja
TANZ	Texte und Arbeiten zum neutestamentlichen Zeitalter
TBLNT	Theologisches Begriffslexikon zum Neuen Testament
TEH	Theologische Existenz heute
THAT	Theologisches Handwörterbuch zum Alten Testament
ThBeitr	Theologische Beiträge
ThLZ	Theologische Literaturzeitung
ThR	Theologische Rundschau
ThSt	Theological Studies
ThW	Theologische Wissenschaft
ThWAT	Theologisches Wörterbuch zum Alten Testament
ThWNT	Theologisches Wörterbuch zum Neuen Testament
ThZ	Theologische Zeitschrift
TRE	Theologische Realenzyklopädie
TPI	Trinity Press International
TS	Theological studies

TSAJ	Texte und Studien zum Antiken Judentum
TToday	Theology Today (=ThTo)
TyndB	Tyndale Bulletin
USF	University of South Florida
UTB	Uni-Taschenbücher
VT	Vetus Testamentum
WBC	Word Biblical Commentary
WTJ	Westminster theological journal
WMANT	Wissenschaftliche Monographien zum Alten und Neuen Testament
WUNT	Wissenschaftliche Untersuchungen zum Neuen Testament
ZAW	Zeitschrift für die alttestamentliche Wissenschaft
ZNW	Zeitschrift für die neutestamentliche Wissenschaft
ZThK	Zeitschrift für Theologie und Kirche

2. Technical and Other Abbreviations

AV	Authorized Version
cf.	confer
col.	columna
ed(s).	editor(s)
ET	English Translation
f	fragment
FS	Festschrift (Studies in Honour of, etc.)
H	Hebrew text of Sirach
KJV	King James Version
LXX	Septuagint
m	Mishnah tractate
MS(S)	manuscript(s)
MT	Masoretic text
n	footnote
n.d.	no date
NEB	New English Bible
NIV	New International Version
NRSV	New Revised Standard Version
NT	New Testament
o.c.	opus citatum
OT	Old Testament
RSV	Revised Standard Version
v(v)	verse(s)
vol.	volume

Introduction

Paul's theology is a real challenge to scholars. His uniqueness is evident even from the fact that scholars have been completely unable to reach a consensus concerning the nature of his teaching or the structure of his soteriology. The direction of interpretation has changed over and over again. One scholar considers Paul a mystic and another sees him as a rationalistic Christian Pharisee. As regards soteriology, there has been a lengthy battle between those who define his soteriology as participationist eschatology and those who emphasize a juridical theology of justification. In such a situation it is more than interesting to make an attempt at finding a new approach and a new way of interpretation.

§ 1 Theodicy and Predestination in New Testament Exegesis

1.1. Occasion and purpose of the study

At the key point of the first chapter of Romans Paul introduces the heart of his message concerning the election and salvation which God has prepared for human beings. The gospel is the power of God, because in the gospel the righteousness of God is disclosed to this world, and it alone can bring salvation to those who believe (Rom. 1:16-17). Paul's description of the gospel is good predestinarian language. It contains all the elements needed: a criterion for eschatological salvation and a criterion for eternal damnation.

The aspect of predestination has not aroused great interest among scholars, however. Paul's soteriology has been studied from quite another perspective and with different premises. Thus there is room for a fresh start, especially as the texts themselves bring out the dynamics of predestinarian theology. This is true throughout Paul's letters, and especially as concerns Romans. In the history of New Testament scholarship this theme is not unknown, however.[1] For example, during the time of the Reformation it was considered one of the

---

[1] For some modern treatments of the subject see e.g. B. Mayer, *Unter Gottes Heilsratschluss. Prädestinationsaussagen bei Paulus;* and G. Röhser, *Prädestination und Verstockung. Untersuchungen zur frühjüdischen, paulinischen und johanneischen Theologie.* Questions concerning the Protestant tradition of interpretation have been discussed, for example, in P.K. Jewett, *Election and Predestination.*

most important features of Pauline (!) theology, and it greatly influenced the formulation of Protestant soteriology.

Due to the Protestant tradition this subject is also rather loaded with dogmatic presuppositions and hermeneutical premises. Ever since Calvin, and actually even since Augustine earlier, the idea of double predestination has had considerable influence on the interpretation of this theme in general, and the interpretation of Paul's letters in particular. The basic belief was that God has foreordained and elected some individuals to salvation, and left some unelected or even foreordained them to damnation.

Such a teaching can be found in the writings of Calvin:[2]

"We call predestination God's eternal decree, by which he compacted with himself what he willed to become of each man. For all are not created in equal condition; rather, eternal life is foreordained for some, eternal damnation for others. Therefore, as any man has been created to one or the other of these ends, we speak of him as predestined to life or to death."

Since this kind of teaching was based on the interpretation of certain passages in the letters of Paul, and especially Romans, Calvin's views have remained influential in Pauline studies and in commentaries on Romans. No study of the subject can be made without an analysis of and comment on this tradition.

An exegetical analysis of Paul's theology of predestination must not be dependent on dogmatics, however. We must concentrate on the texts themselves and further analyze Paul's tradition-historical background in Judaism. This leads us to undertake an investigation of the theology of predestination in Second Temple Jewish literature. This is the proper religious and theological context of Paul's teaching. Through the analysis we are able to pay attention to the problems and tensions between Paul and his Jewish contemporaries.

As the study concerns the theological dynamics of Jewish teaching during the Second Temple period, we are led to investigate the problem of theodicy. This is the context in which the theology of predestination was formulated in the time of Paul himself.

Such a context leads us to the primary task of this study. *In this work we shall investigate the relation between Jewish predestinarian theology and Paul's soteriology.* As the former originated in the context of the problem of theodicy, we must assess the relevance of this question in the theology of Paul, too.

There are several points of contact between Jewish predestinarian theology and the letters of Paul. Both write about the coming judgment of God. The election of God is a key subject as regards the anticipation of the end. And apocalyptic

---

[2] Calvin, *Institutes*, 3.21.5. See also McGrath, *Theology*, 451f.

eschatology naturally focusses its proclamation on the message of eternal salvation.

The investigation of Jewish theology can naturally be no more than a survey, because the emphasis is on the analysis of Paul's teaching. The purpose of chapter 3 is to penetrate to the question, how general and common the problem of theodicy was in the Second Temple period. This investigation also leads us to present criticism of the theory of covenantal nomism elaborated by E.P. Sanders, which is a leading paradigm in the study of this subject.

As regards the theology of Paul, we shall investigate especially the question how predestinarian themes occur in his soteriology (part II). This also comprises analyses of Pauline anthropology and the occurrence of the problem of theodicy itself. On the basis of these foundational subjects we can then in part III assess how Paul's predestinarian theology affected his conceptions of the status of the law and the nature of justification. In the last part (IV) of the book we shall assess and outline the overall picture of Paul's soteriology and discuss the value of the results in relation to other main interpretations of Paul's soteriology.

1.2. How to define predestination: on methodology

The word "predestination" refers to some kind of decree, but this does not yet help us to define the concept itself. When we pay attention to the meaning of the word we immediately encounter a great number of questions. What has been decreed and how did it happen? Is the decree unconditional or not? What is the goal of the one who has been predested? What is the relation of man's will to the decree of God?

In academic scholarship there have been several attempts to provide a definition and all of them have both advantages and faults.

1. Definition according to the terminology. One could naturally investigate predestinarian theology by analysing the words which denote divine foreordination. In Greek the most important of these words is προορίζω, which occurs in several interesting contexts, for example in Romans 8. The same semantic field contains words such as πρόθεσις (< προτίθημι). It has a meaning which concerns God's plan and Paul uses it when speaking of God's election (Rom. 9:11). Words denoting election belong to the same group. This concerns, for example, the word ἐκλογή.[3]

The investigation of such words is not only possible but necessary. This is an essential element of the study, even though we are dealing with quite a

---

[3] A definition based on relevant terminology is typical of dictionary articles. For an example, see Dinkler, *RGG* 5 (1986) 481-483. He does not over-simplify this approach, however, but also takes the tradition history into account.

simple point of departure. One of the problems in this line of study is, however, that we have few occurrences of relevant words in the New Testament. Thus it is not easy to construct a consistent interpretation merely on that basis.

The semantic aspect has its dangers, too, and we must beware of one-sidedness here. The use of Latin carries a danger, since the word *praedestino* has a somewhat deterministic teleological meaning. The verb *destino* relates to ordination and decreeing, and *destinatum* denotes a goal. It is quite natural that predestination is easily interpreted as a deterministic decreeing of a person's destiny.

In the analysis of Second Temple Jewish theology and Paul's teaching we cannot assume beforehand that the concept of predestination must be deterministic. Quite on the contrary, we must investigate the texts as they are and attempt to define the concept of predestination according to the available evidence. In this work we need to take seriously the demands of both modern semantics and contextual theological analysis.

2. A classical problem of Romans 9-11. As regards the theology of Paul, the problem of predestination has often been analysed by concentrating on the special section of Romans, i.e. chapters 9-11. This section has sometimes been considered an excursus on the problem of divine election. Thus the answer to the dilemma concerning Paul's theology of predestination has been sought in an analysis of these chapters.[4]

The advantage of this approach is that there is a clearly defined section which is easily subjected to investigation. One cannot neglect this section in any analysis of the problem of predestination. There is a danger, however, as regards the usefulness of this approach. If the section is separated from its context in Romans, it can lead to a one-sided conclusion once again. This is what has happened during the history of research. These chapters have been separated from the other parts of the letter, and they have been considered an independent essay on the subject of divine hardening. Such a treatment should not be welcomed in modern research.

3. The dogmatic approach: the question of double predestination. In the Protestant tradition we have had a strong tendency to use the concept of double predestination in the study of Paul's theology. This is primarily due to the influence of Calvinist theology, to which we referred above. In this tradition salvation has been prepared only for the elect, and others will be left unsaved.

---

[4] For example, Röhser has studied the theme of predestination by concentrating on these chapters. This is why the problem arising from Romans is for him primarily the problem concerning divine hardening. Röhser, *Prädestination,* 1ff. This question is naturally part of the question concerning the status of Israel in God's plan of salvation, but as regards the theology of predestination in general it is merely a part of the whole subject.

This kind of conception is completely deterministic. The fate of the individual has been foreordained even before he or she was born. During his or her lifetime he or she cannot really alter his or her fate, even though the gospel must be proclaimed to the elect.[5]

It is naturally tempting to make use of a clear concept of predestination in the interpretation of a difficult issue. We must resist this temptation, however, and attempt to find an unprejudiced approach instead. The danger of anachronistic interpretation is too great in the dogmatic assessment. On the contrary, we must attempt to find the basic dynamics of Second Temple Jewish theology and compare them with the teaching of Paul. Jewish theologians were convinced that God would sentence sinners to eternal damnation. This is common knowledge. But the conditions and nature of this kind of predestination are not evidently clear.

4. Predestination as an election of grace. There is furthermore a tradition beginning from Augustine where predestination is defined as an *electio gratiae*, God's divine decree of salvation. As regards a dogmatic analysis this is actually not clearly a separate approach from that of the concept of double predestination. Here the emphasis is on grace, however.

It is good to note that predestination can also be evaluated as a question of how God has prepared salvation for human beings. In our investigation of the subject we are here interested in God's election and the realization of that election in this world.[6] This is not a denial of the critical remark as to whether this conception as such is not similar to the concept of double predestination. If the elect are predestined to salvation, others must be predestined to damnation.

This approach has its advantages, too. One must not forget the aspect of election when the descriptions of judgment seem to be prevalent. It seems to be clear, however, that when the overall picture of Paul's theology of predestination is outlined, it must comprise all possible aspects of the question. Too narrow a description results in a distorted picture and does not resolve the problems of Pauline soteriology.

---

[5] The concept of double predestination occurs, for example, in the monographs of Schweitzer, *Mystik,* 102-104; and Sanders, *Paul,* 446f. The greatest problem in this tradition of interpretation is that after a scholar has accepted this approach he no longer questions the premises of the theology of predestination – even though the texts themselves point to a different conception.

[6] This is the primary aspect on which Mayer concentrated in his monograph, Mayer, *Heilsratschluss.* He concentrated on Pauline passages where God's act of election is perceptible This approach is good as regards the Christological texts of Paul. Mayer has presented an interesting analysis of them, even though his interpretation of Paul's soteriology in its entirety is rather narrow.

1.3. Predestination in the context of the problem of theodicy

There are some important conclusions which we can draw from previous attempts at defining the concept of predestination. Firstly, we must note that we should beware of an anachronistic approach in the analysis of Second Temple Jewish theology and the teaching of Paul. The contextual analysis itself should bring forth those features which form the basic structure of each concept of predestination.

It is clear that predestination must mean the decreeing of a person's eternal destiny or fate in one way or another. Predestinarian theology treats above all the question of how God sentences sinners to damnation or how he elects the righteous to salvation. This is why the term predestination belongs in the context where terms such as sin, judgment, grace and salvation occur. At this stage we do not need to define the concept more accurately. It is not good to restrict the analysis and lay out too many conditions in advance. An explanation of Paul's theology of predestination must be based on the texts themselves. In the analysis we must be cautious about the dogmatic premises because they can easily lead the explanation away from the intentions of the material studied.

In the analysis we must take the section Rom. 9-11 into account, but the analysis cannot centre solely on this. In the assessment of the theology of predestination we must consider Paul's teaching in its entirety. As regards the other subjects mentioned above, namely the idea of divine hardening and God's election, they must be regarded as important aspects of this study. They too, however, must be assessed in the context of the overall picture which is drawn by contextual tradition-historical analysis and theological construction.

In Jewish theology the problem of theodicy dictates the framework for the theology of predestination. The theme of predestination occurs in texts where the despotic power of ungodly rulers and the sinfulness of Israel are criticized. This point of departure directs the investigation of the subject of predestination. It also brings to the fore two methodological details. We must pay attention to the conception of sin and the respective anthropology of each writer. This helps us to define how they think God will solve the problem of Israel or the problem of the whole of humankind.

The problem of theodicy is actually the problem of sin. For this reason the same problem reaches a climax in the questions concerning the will and omnipotence of God. If sin prevails the omnipotence of God is called into question. If ungodly despots rule, the faithfulness of God is called into question. Thus it is the history of Israel itself which generates the basic problems which demand the solutions given in the theology of predestination.

This is methodically a proper context for the assessment of predestinarian theology. This definition also outlines the purpose of the investigation as regards the other traditions of interpretation referred to above. There is an evident relation between the problem of theodicy and the theology of predestination, both in Jewish theology and in Paul's soteriology. The aim of this study is to find an answer to the question concerning the basic dynamics of this relation.

§ 2 *Different 'History-of-Religions' Approaches and the Context of Paul's Soteriology*

The long history of the study of Pauline soteriology is full of significant changes. This is why no proper discussion with earlier research is possible without a thorough overview of that history. One cannot bypass old studies since the views and explanations which were conceived at the beginning of the century have had a surprisingly strong influence, "Wirkungsgeschichte", for a long time. Only when we know these theories can we properly understand modern scholarship and discern its details.

2.1. The traditional 'history-of-religions' approach (W. Bousset, A. Deissmann)

In early Protestant Pauline studies there was a tension between the traditional, systematic approach and that of the emerging study of the history of religions. For a long time the study of Paul's theology had concentrated mostly on his "dogmatics". The analysis of Paul's theology was interested only in details of dogma. Great emphasis was naturally laid on the subject of justification, which at the Reformation had become the centre of theology. According to the prevailing method, theology was believed to be solved when the right "centre" was found.

This traditional view was popular in Germany until the end of the nineteenth century, as is shown in A. Schweitzer's history of Pauline studies. A change in scholarship took place when the school of 'history of religions' presented its own theories about the genealogy of Paul's thinking. New ideas were introduced, especially by R. Reitzenstein in his study of Paul's letters.[1]

This new school of the history of religions soon became a rival for the dogmatic tradition. Paul's theology was approached from quite a new direction. Paul was no longer regarded as a systematic theologian, "the first Christian dogmatist", but as a religious thinker and even a meditative mystic. The object of study was Paul's "religion". According to W. Bousset, Paul was the founder of a cultic religion, and H. Weinel, in turn, regarded him as a religious mystic.[2]

The ideas of the 'history-of-religions' school were built on the foundation laid by F.C. Baur. He had introduced a pattern for the history of the early

---

[1] See the ET of Schweitzer, *Paul and His Interpreters.* A presentation of Reitzenstein e.g. in Kümmel, *History,* 268-269.

[2] See Bousset, *Kyrios Christos,* 104ff. This description of Bousset and Weinel is presented by Beker, who emphasizes that the history-of-religions approach was a reaction against earlier dogmatic study. Beker, *Paul,* 13.

Church. According to Baur, Paul was an opponent of Peter and formed an antithesis to an alleged conservative Palestinian Jewish Christianity.[3] According to the history-of-religions school, Paul belonged in the sphere of Hellenistic thinking. This is why his theology and "mysticism" was explained in the context of Hellenistic philosophy and Hellenistic religions.[4]

For Bousset the Hellenistic mystery religions were a key to Paul's soteriology. In this phase of study the idea of divine election was not considered an important feature in soteriology. According to Bousset, salvation meant merely a mystical union with a divine heavenly being. He thought that the soteriology of Paul, as well as the soteriology of Hellenistic Christian theology in general, was based on a Hellenistic cult of the *kyrios*. The proclamation of Jesus as a heavenly Lord was thus of Greek origin.[5] And further, when baptism and the Holy Communion were explained against a similar background, the whole outlook of Christianity was that of a mystery religion.[6]

A. Deissmann was also familiar with the interpretation of the history-of-religions school, but he shifted the emphasis from pagan Hellenism to Hellenistic Judaism. He disagreed with his predecessors and did not attempt to explain the structure of Paul's theology according to Hellenistic mystery religions. He rejected Bousset's conception and focused on Hellenistic Jewish theology, instead. In this sense he protected the link between Paul and early Jewish Christianity.[7] The core of Paul's theology, however, was again found in a concept of mystical relationship with Christ ("being in Christ") – a feature that is rather easy to understand against Deissmann's background in the scholarship of the history-of-religions school. In this way he supported and strengthened the idea of the "spiritual" nature of Paul's soteriology. According to Deissmann, the Hellenistic element in Paul's thinking can be detected in his way of describing faith as "being in Christ" and Christ himself as "Spirit".[8]

---

[3] This is also evident in Baur's concept of Christology, see Baur, *Paulus*, 620ff. The ideas of Baur are presented in general by Kümmel, *History,* 127ff.

[4] See Bousset, *Kyrios Christos*, 75ff. For critical assessments of Baur's scheme, see e.g. Vielhauer, *EvTh 25* (1965) 24-72, and Balz, *Methodische Probleme,* 23-24.

[5] Berger has detected the backgrounds of this kind of hermeneutics which concentrates on the idea of a cultic hero. According to his analysis, Bousset has been linked to German Idealism through Fichte and Carlyle. In this Idealism history was seen as a playground of great personalities, "heroes", who gave form to the great intentions and "ideas" of the transcendent. When this kind of Idealism was connected with the theory of the history of religions it produced the conception of a cultic hero. Berger, *Exegese und Philosophie,* 90-93.

[6] Bousset, *Kyrios Christos*, 57, 99. See the analysis of Colpe, *Die religionsgeschichtliche Schule,* 194-195. A critique of Bousset's influence is given in an article by Hurtado, bearing a similar title, *TS 40* (1979) 306-317.

[7] Deissmann, *Paulus*, 100, 101.

[8] Deissmann, *Paulus*, 107ff. The origins of an interpretation of participatory soteriology

Deissmann, too, was one of those scholars who desired to get rid of the dogmatic "Paulinismus" of German scholarship.[9] He proposed to replace it with history in the manner of Bousset and other predecessors. Furthermore, Deissmann is important for his assessment of the nature of Paul's thinking. For Deissmann, Paul was in fact not a real theologian. He was more a man of prayer than a thinker and learned exegete.[10]

Dogmatic Pauline scholarship was thus replaced by a history-of-religions paradigm, where Paul was regarded as a mystic concentrating on subjective experience. He was distanced from both systematic thinking and Second Temple Jewish theology. As far as the latter was concerned there were two interpretations, though. The earlier history-of-religions school was interested in the mystery religions of the Hellenistic world. Later the emphasis was on Jewish theology, and apocalyptic literature in particular.

A tension between the dogmatic approach and the history-of-religions scholarship seems to be somewhat over-emphasized. Traditional "Paulinismus" belonged in a sense to the pre-critical period and after the birth of historico-critical study it is only natural to consider its views rather time-bound. It is, however, justified to search for a systematic structure in any writer's presentation.

Not only dogmatic studies but also nearly all the human sciences are based on such a "common-sense" presupposition. The denial of this starting-point would result in a kind of post-modern eclecticism, according to which it is even theoretically impossible to obtain factual knowledge from cultural objects.[11] Furthermore, one should not forget the linguistic level of study.

---

can thus be detected in the history-of-religions school. I would not make precise claims about the innovator of the interpretation, though, since – as it seems – several scholars presented it simultaneously at the beginning of the century.

[9] Deissmann, *Paulus*, 2.

[10] "Mit seinem Besten gehört Paulus nicht in die Theologie, sondern in die Religion." Deissmann, *Paulus*, 4. For the analysis see Beker, *Paul*, 15.

[11] In the area of Pauline studies there has been an ongoing debate over the question whether in Paul's theology it is possible to discern a doctrinal core which would explain his thinking. For the discussion see Beker, *Paul*, 13f. Räisänen has rightly criticized previous efforts at searching for this kind of doctrinal centre in the footsteps of J.P. Gabler, i.e. trying to separate "timeless" dogma from time-bound material. Räisänen, *Beyond*, 3ff. At the same time, however, he unfortunately serves as an example for a view which abandons the task of making a systematic analysis in theological hermeneutics. In the footsteps of W. Wrede (New Testament theology does not differ from a history of religion) – and Deissmann in principle – he treats Paul as an incoherent writer. Räisänen, *Beyond*, 16, 105, 126; Räisänen, *Law*, 201

Ideological writings have a conceptual structure even on the grounds of common linguistics.

The history-of-religions approach did undoubtedly answer some questions left open in earlier research. In practice it turned out to be too reactive, however. For this reason several scholars began to correct its views later on. Naturally history-of-religions scholarship bore some good fruit. One of the most important of these is the question how the analysis of the doctrinal content and the significance of the religious context of Paul's teaching should be brought into a right relation. Even if we are not content with the answer given by that school, we cannot ignore the problem.

2.2. Paul the mystic (A. Schweitzer)

Somewhat more serious criticisms of the approach of the old history-of-religions school were made by A. Schweitzer, who had already gained fame with his book on the history of the study of Paul's theology. In his monograph "Die Mystik des Apostels Paulus" Schweitzer applied his "consequent eschatology" to the interpretation of Paul's soteriology. The teaching of Paul, according to Schweitzer, was not based on Hellenistic mythology but on Jewish tradition. It was novel Jewish eschatology which contained a bold re-interpretation of the old teaching.[12] In his new approach Schweitzer used several Second Temple apocalyptic texts, such as 1 Enoch, the Psalms of Solomon and 4 Ezra.[13]

There evidently remains a link between Deissmann and Schweitzer, as the latter interprets the theology of Paul. To him Paul's soteriology was still an example of eschatological mysticism, which is of a sacramental nature.[14] The core of this mysticism was "being in Christ". It meant a mystic unity in his death and resurrection.[15] According to Schweitzer, this new relationship with Christ could not be based on Hellenistic religious ideas, because it lacks the idea of man's deification (Vergottung).[16]

---

[12] Schweitzer, *Mystik,* 40-41.

[13] Schweitzer, *Mystik,* 56.

[14] Schweitzer, *Mystik,* 13; 22; 252; 367. The uniqueness of Schweitzer's theory can be seen in his way of defining the mystic. He makes a distinction between Paul's mysticism and primitive magic. In a similar way he treats mystery religions which search after deification and consider the material world merely as a manifestation of spiritual reality. The mysticism of Paul is something quite different. It is centred on Christ and offers unity with him and a relationship to his death and resurrection. See pp. 1-3.

[15] Schweitzer, *Mystik,* 110, 122-124.

[16] Schweitzer, *Mystik,* 16. "Sicher aber ist, dass diese Mystik als Ganzes sich nicht aus hellenistischen Ideen zusammenflicken lässt, sondern nur aus der Eschatologie begreiflich wird." p. 139.

Unity with Christ had produced a new state of being, instead, which was dependent on the resurrection. Schweitzer thought that Paul expected the imminent end of the world. A great process of change was in motion. This also meant that a new mode of existence was achieved by union with Christ. This is why Schweitzer abandoned the old view, according to which the content of sacraments had been borrowed from the Hellenistic mystery cults. They too had to be interpreted against the background of Jewish eschatology.[17]

Interest in Jewish texts and Jewish soteriology led Schweitzer to undertake an examination of the question of predestination. He noted that in Judaism the concept of God's election had undergone a change due to the fact that Israel had fallen into sin. In several texts it becomes evident that, according to the writer, the whole nation as such could not be regarded as the redeemed people of God. Salvation was prepared only for those who had not fallen from the will of God. Schweitzer thought that this dilemma in Jewish theology was resolved by a concept of double predestination. He assumed that Paul's teaching about the election of God must also have been directed by predestinarian theology: God would call those whom he had predetermined to salvation.[18]

Schweitzer's approach did not gain adherents immediately, since the older history-of-religions school still had a leading role in the study of Paul's theology. In history-of-religions scholarship the theology of Paul was merely a question of abstract ideology and subjective religious contemplation. Schweitzer's theories provided scholarship with one important distinction, though. We must consider to what extent the theology of Paul can be described as participatory Christ-mysticism and to what extent it is controlled by an objective, systematic content. This concerns many crucial elements in Paul's theology, such as the concepts of justification and faith.

2.3. The gnostic hypothesis (R. Bultmann)

Subjective interpretation was raised to a new level in the theology of R. Bultmann. He was not content with merely describing different features in the mysticism of Paul. Bultmann wanted to find a method for defining theology in the context of this new setting. Mediums for interpretation were found in the programme of "Entmythologisierung" and in existential interpretation. As regards Paul's theology, it was explained with the help of a gnostic mystery religion – a theme easily conceivable in the context of his background in the history-of-religions school.

In his New Testament theology Bultmann defined Paul's soteriology above

[17] Schweitzer, *Mystik,* 111, 139; concerning the sacraments, see pp. 270-275.
[18] Schweitzer, *Mystik,* 102-104.

all as a function of Christology.[19] According to Bultmann, Paul's soteriology was Christology and Christology was soteriology. As regards Paul's Christology, its nature was primarily mythic. Bultmann thought that it had been coined with the aid of a Redeemer-myth prevailing in the gnostic mystery religion of Paul's time. This is why the essence and structure of Paul's soteriology was gnostic.[20]

The world-view of Paul was mythic, thought Bultmann, just as that of other writers of the New Testament had been. This became a question of principle in Biblical scholarship. According to Bultmann, a modern scholar could no longer accept the previous world-view with its concept of three-stage reality. Neither was the apocalyptic concept of history acceptable to modern man. For this reason mythic theology, Paul's "mysticism", had to be re-interpreted, it should be criticized by the "Entmythologisierung" programme, and be given a new content. [21]

The right assessment of Paul's theology was to be achieved, according to Bultmann, with the aid of existential interpretation. He was certain that the existential philosophy of M. Heidegger provided an unquestioned truth of the ontological structure of all existence.[22] This is why the interpretation of Paul's theology must also be based on existential interpretation. Theological sentences were understood properly only when their nature as referring to the self-assurance ("Selbstverständnis") of man was realized. Such an interpretation might easily lead to plain anthropology, but Bultmann wanted to preserve the concept of God in this theory. The "authentic" existence of man was considered dependent on divine reality. According to Bultmann, existential self-assurance was a part of understanding the essence of God and his world.[23]

As an heir of the history-of-religions school, Bultmann also wished to free the religious personality from the chains of dogmatism. In performing this task

---

[19] It is well known that, according to Bultmann, there was little similarity in content between the proclamation of Jesus and the teaching of Paul. See e.g. Bultmann, *Theologie*, 190.

[20] Bultmann, *Theologie*, 192; his presentation of gnostic Christology p. 298. This kind of concept of the nature of theology was based on a dualistic epistemology. As God could not be an object of perception, knowledge concerning God must be sought for in the existence of man. The basis of this epistemology was in neo-Kantian philosophy. Thiselton, *Two Horizons*, 210-211; Berger, *Exegese und Philosophie*, 130ff,; see also my ideas in *EQ 68* (1996) 334-337.

[21] In his book *Neues Testament und Mythologie*, see pp. 12ff., 39ff., 54ff.

[22] Cf. Gruenler, *Meaning*, 88-89.

[23] Bultmann, *Theologie*, 587. Thiselton has been analyzing the dynamics of Bultmann's theory and remarks that, according to the existentialist, the real intention behind myth is to express self-understanding, and that its "objectifying pseudo-hypostatizing form is misleading as to its true function". Thiselton, *Two Horizons*, 290.

he no longer applied simple psychology, where the teaching of Paul would be assessed only by a hypothesis about his personality. Bultmann was assured that the actual message of the Bible was *kerygma,* divine truth about man.

Behind the concept of *kerygma* there was a comprehensive theory of ontology, which Bultmann had learnt from M. Heidegger. According to Bultmann, *kerygma* inevitably correlated with man's anthropological reality. *Kerygma* is not something found in the texts of the Bible. It has a different status. *Kerygma* precedes the new understanding of man and even precedes faith. It is something between God and man. This is why the theory of interpretation must have a method for distinguishing kerygmatic statements from theological statements.[24]

Bultmann proposed this kind of method in his book. The reader "must interpret the theological thoughts as the unfolding of the self-understanding awakened by the kerygma."[25] Existential interpretation revealed that doctrinal statements in the Bible were also actually descriptions of "authentic existence".[26]

Even though Bultmann did not want to reduce theology to anthropology, his theory inevitably led in this direction. For example, the essence of Paul's theology was to be found by means of anthropology. Christological soteriology had turned out to be mythical and so proper interpretation had to reveal its true essence behind the myth. In this respect the theology of Paul was significant only when it could "unfold the self-understanding" of man. In his New Testament Theology Bultmann analysed Paul's theology with the aid of anthropology. This was the means by which the existential tension between freedom and determination could be solved.[27]

Bultmann's existential interpretation of Pauline theology remained in the tradition of the history-of-religions school, however. For him Paul's soteriology was but one part of gnostic mystery religion. A historical survey of Paul's life and work cannot find anything but this in his writings. For this reason the questions of soteriology were resolved by using hermeneutics.

---

[24] Bultmann, *Theologie,* 587-588.

[25] Quotation from the English translation, see Bultmann, *Theology,* 240.

[26] See also my analysis of the ontology of Bultmann's hermeneutics in *EQ 68* (1996) 334-337. The main problem with Bultmann is that according to his theory the New Testament can never be a direct source for modern theology. Furthermore, theology cannot really have a propositional content because every statement is merely an explication of some kind of experience which alone is real. This is due to a somewhat mystical nature of his basic concept of kerygma.

[27] See Bultmann, *Theologie,* 204, 227. In a certain way Bultmann's theory is related to Second Temple Jewish sapiential theology, where the freedom of man was made the basis of his responsibility.

Existential interpretation was no longer interested in the content of Paul's theology. It concentrated on its intention, instead, and produced new theology on this premise.

In research on Paul's theology the inheritance of Bultmann left room for both an existential and a dogmatic interpretation. In German theology both branches have survived to some extent. There has been criticism, naturally, of his premises in the history-of-religions field of study. Furthermore, his interpretation of Paul's theology as a form of gnosticism has been abandoned by most scholars.[28]

Even though Bultmann's gnostic hypothesis has not been popular among scholars, his existential interpretation has influenced the study of Paul for several decades. The reason for this is mostly the fact that his influential book on New Testament theology was primarily interested in the "anthropological" theology of Paul.

2.4. *New emphasis on Paul's Jewish background (W.D. Davies, H.-J. Schoeps, P. Stuhlmacher)*

After Bultmann there was a significant change in research on Pauline theology. Paul's letters were compared with Second Temple Jewish literature to a greater extent than had been done before. Paul's relationship with Jewish literature and rabbinic traditions had naturally been studied by independent scholars even earlier. For example, the Jewish scholar C. Montefiore and A. Deissmann, mentioned above, had explained Paul's theology in the context of Judaism of the Diaspora. A. Schweitzer, of course, had directed Pauline research into this area at the beginning of the century.[29] After Bultmann there was a reaction against existentialist research, and an emphasis on Jewish theology was often part of it.[30] In spite of this, however, the discussion also included traits from

---

[28] In fact an original "Bultmannian" approach can in my view be found in modern literature only in monographs such as Schmithals' commentary, *Der Römerbrief*. This does not mean, however, that the fact of the immense influence of Bultmann and even an unconscious acceptance of several themes in his theology should be ignored. We should instead try to become more and more aware of them.

[29] The relationship of earlier Pauline studies to Jewish studies is well dealt with in Schoeps, *Paulus*, 14, 27. The dating of Schweitzer's study is a little difficult. He published the book in the middle of the century but the main theses are said to have been completed after the publication of Schweitzer's history of Pauline research, at the beginning of the century.

[30] This kind of change is evident e.g. in Jüngel's study *Paulus und Jesus,* see 14ff.

the old controversy. Scholars wrote against the Hellenistic mythology theory.[31]

The new discussion was inaugurated in 1948 by W.D. Davies. In his book "Paul and Rabbinic Judaism" Davies drew a parallel between Paul and Jewish rabbinic theology in order to discern the characteristic features of Pauline teaching. Davies wanted to show that Paul had simply been a rabbi who had converted to Christianity. This is why his theology was full of themes typical of Pharisaic teaching.[32]

Despite the fact that Davies criticized Schweitzer's conclusions in several details, he actually learned more from him than he would probably have admitted. When Davies eventually defined the nature of Paul's soteriology, his theory resembled that of Schweitzer's concept of Paul's mysticism. The most significant soteriological theme in Paul, according to Davies, is "being in Christ", i.e. the participatory element which Schweitzer too had emphasized.[33]

According to Davies, the concept of participation contained, in the sense of proper Jewish theology, both an individualistic feature and a corporative feature. "There is a parallel twofold strain in Paul's view of redemption; the individual 'dies and rises' with Christ, but this experience is also of necessity a corporate one in that it involves participation in the death and resurrection of a community, the Israel of God."[34]

Also in Germany the new approach soon gained several adherents. The title of the Pauline study of H.-J. Schoeps reveals the essential content of this direction: "Die Theologie des Apostels im Lichte der jüdischen Religions-geschichte". He walked in the steps of Schweitzer and explained Paul's soteriology in the context of Jewish theology.[35] Schoeps wanted to find a new solution to the problematic relationships between Jewish theology, Hellenistic Judaism and Hellenistic (pagan) religions.

According to Schoeps, there are certain inalienable elements in the theology of Paul. We are not allowed to disregard Paul's cultic concept of the vicarious

---

[31] There were undoubtedly several factors behind the development of the study and it is impossible to mention them all. There is, however, one detail still worth mentioning: the monumental commentary of Strack and Billerbeck, presenting most of the relevant parallels between the New Testament and rabbinic literature. The publication of this work began in 1922. See Strack-Billerbeck, *Kommentar.* In Finnish scholarship this commentary produced one interesting consequence. In 1928 A.F. Puukko, Professor of Old Testament, published a lengthy article "Paulus und das Judentum" (in: *Studia Orientalia*). Here he maintains that Paul, when writing about Christ, was using the Old Testament in accordance with methods he had learnt in rabbinical schools. Puukko, *Studia Orientalia,* 86-87.

[32] Davies, *Paul,* 16.

[33] Davies, *Paul,* 99, 102.

[34] Davies, *Paul,* 109-110.

[35] Schoeps, *Paulus,* 37; 85f.

atonement of Christ. And when this theme is analyzed, it turns out to be a most typical Jewish feature of his theology.[36]

When interpreting the basic structure of Paul's theology, Schoeps did not follow Schweitzer, however, despite his interest in Jewish theology. Perhaps due to his ties with the Bultmann school Schoeps concluded that the mythical part of Paul's soteriology, namely themes such as incarnation, sacrificial death and exaltation, were radically un-Jewish. Paul, who normally argued with Jewish concepts, had in his Christology adopted the soteriological pattern of Hellenistic mystery religions ("heidnische Prämisse"). This concerned above all the 'Son of God' Christology.

Furthermore, this soteriological pattern affected every element connected with Christology, such as the meaning of sacraments.[37] In this way Schoeps abandoned Schweitzer's "Jewish" Christ-mysticism and called the mysticism in fact Hellenistic. The Jewish element in Paul's theology remained something vague.

Interest in Jewish theology was eventually gaining ground at several universities and appeared in various studies. We can take L. Goppelt, for example, who wrote his extensive monograph on New Testament Theology. In this work he wished to explain the connection between Jewish theology and the teaching of Paul.[38] One can also see the importance of the context of Jewish studies in some studies of predestinarian theology published at that time, in such books as the monographs of G. Maier and B. Mayer. The former wrote on Sirach, sapiential theology and Qumran, as he was studying the problem of free will in Jewish theology and the letters of Paul. The latter, in turn, focused on Paul's theology of predestination in his monograph "Unter Gottes Heilsratschluss". [39]

Another scholar who set Paul in the context of Jewish theology was P. Stuhlmacher. Both his dissertation on the righteousness of God and his monograph on Paul's gospel contained a thorough comparison of Paul and Jewish theology. The perspective of the study was that of tradition-history. Stuhlmacher abandoned the old "Bultmannian" approach and no longer tried to locate Paul in a Hellenistic environment. He searched for a Jewish context, instead. In this way a methodological solution was arrived at, where central concepts were studied systematically in the consistent setting of a novel

---

[36] Schoeps, *Paulus,* 127f. This aspect had not been completely abandoned, even though it had often been classified under other themes. For example Schweitzer considered it a "main" feature in Paul's theology, Schweitzer, *Mystik,* 64f.

[37] Schoeps, *Paulus,* 160, 163.

[38] Goppelt, *Theologie,* 372.

[39] See e.g. Maier, *Mensch und Freier Wille,* 24ff., 165ff; Mayer, *Heilsratschluss,* 57ff., 70ff.

religion of history. This interpretation was later developed further by Stuhlmacher in his 'Biblical Theology of the New Testament'.[40]

Stuhlmacher made the righteousness of God the centre of Paul's theology. He thought that, for Paul, the righteousness of God was not merely the idea of God's being a righteous judge. In the Old Testament the righteousness of God was often connected with God's saving acts, too. Stuhlmacher detected this theme in the Psalms and in the texts of Qumran. In the Old Testament, God's saving acts were usually connected with the Torah and with the life Torah was to bring. Paul, however, in his original teaching, would define the righteousness of God "without the law". This is why, according to Stuhlmacher, the soteriology of Paul could be best explained by his concept of righteousness by faith.[41]

The new emphasis on Jewish theology led research in two different directions, which was already apparent in earlier scholarship. On the one hand, the interpretation of participatory soteriology gained new adherents. On the other hand, there was a growing interest in tradition history and in theological links between Jewish theology and Paul. These two elements persisted in scholarship for several decades.

2.5. Paul and Rabbinic Judaism: a new pattern (E.P. Sanders)

A consistent methodical comparison between Jewish theology and Paul's letters reached a new level in the book by E.P. Sanders, entitled "Paul and Palestinian Judaism". His comparison was carried out on a large scale, on the level of "patterns of religion". Behind this task there was also a criticism of the traditional picture of Judaism given by German scholarship.

Judaism was regarded by most New Testament scholars as a legalistic religion until Sanders defined it as a covenantal religion based on the mercy of God.[42] He contested a distorted picture of Judaism given by a long tradition of

---

[40] Stuhlmacher, *Gerechtigkeit,* 113ff., 145ff; Stuhlmacher, *Paulinische Evangelium,* 109ff.

[41] A general presentation in Stuhlmacher, *Biblische Theologie,* 315-320, 326-330. His views were accepted and developed later e.g. by S. Kim, *The Origin of Paul's Gospel,* 269ff, especially 288. Cf. also Hofius, *Paulusstudien,* 35ff.

[42] The idea of a legalistic Judaism was a commonplace in the writings of Weber, Schürer and Bousset, says Sanders, but already such scholars as Montefiore and Moore thought that it was a problematic identification. See Sanders, *Paul,* 2-6, 33-34. For example W. Bousset, in his *Die Religion des Judentums,* describes Early Judaism as "eine Religion der Observanz" (p. 85, cf. 409). This kind of attitude was no doubt a living one and it must have directed research for a long time. "Durch den engen Zusammenhang mit dem Gesetz ist der jüdischen Sittlichkeit ferner der Charakter der Uneinheitlichkeit und kleinlichen Kasuistik aufgeprägt." Bousset, *Religion,* 137.

Protestant Biblical criticism.[43] According to Sanders, Jewish theology was covenantal. The concept of keeping the law was always included under the category of the covenant of grace. Obedience to the law was "merely" obedience within this covenant of grace.[44]

This new approach was applied especially to Pauline studies. According to Sanders, Paul did not think that Judaism was legalistic in itself. The law could never have been primarily a problem to Paul. This theory certainly made a difference in biblical criticism and shifted the general line of interpretation significantly.[45]

Paul's theology too was studied as a "pattern of religion". Sanders thought that Paul did not oppose covenantal nomism in his soteriology. In fact he had even adopted it himself.[46] For this reason Paul's theology had to be interpreted without earlier polarizations. There was yet another consequence. Since nomism was no longer in the centre of Pauline theology, one had to find the core of his teaching elsewhere. Here the aspect of religious experience found its place.

Here we encounter the impact of Schweitzer once again. Sanders, when tracing the soteriology of Paul, takes up his thesis concerning Christ-mysticism.[47] Sanders thinks that the subjective element is crucial for Paul and prevails over other features. This is why the theology of "being in Christ" is, for Sanders, "participationist eschatology".[48] The concept of predestination too has a role to play in Sanders' evaluation of Jewish theology. On the one hand, he assesses Jewish teaching according to a concept of a rather deterministic double predestination. On the other hand, he has to admit the important role of free will in sapiential theology, because in the source texts there is evidently room for independent human action and responsibility.[49]

---

[43] "Thus the general Christian view of Judaism, or of some part of it, as a religion of legalistic works-righteousness goes on, unhindered by the fact that it has been sharply – one would have thought, devastatingly criticized by scholars who have known the material far better than any of its proponents. One of the intentions of the present chapter, to put the matter clearly, is to destroy that view." Sanders, *Paul*, 59; c.f. xiii.

[44] Sanders did not claim that this view was his own invention. He refers e.g. to Moore, as we saw above, who already in 1921 published his study "Christian Writers on Judaism", *HTR 14* (1921) 197-254. In this article Moore wrote that Judaism was not a religion marked by a constant need to earn salvation by legalistic observation of the law. Cf. a review of the history of scholarship in this question in Tomson, *Paul*, 7f.

[45] For further comments, see the excursus below.

[46] See Sanders, *Law*, 46-47, also note 142.

[47] Sanders, *Paul*, 459.

[48] Sanders, *Paul*, 552.

[49] Sanders' concept of predestination will be studied later in chapter 14.1.

T. Laato, who wrote a critical dissertation on Sanders' theory, accepts his point of departure. Even though all the features of covenantal nomism cannot be found in every Jewish text, he considers this theory a valid description of Second Temple nomism.[50] There are some details, however, which Laato wishes to adjust. He thinks that the "Palestinian-Jewish pattern of religion" does not contain the aspect of eternity.

Laato's most negative criticism is directed against the anthropological premises of the pattern of religion. He thinks that Jewish covenantal nomism cannot be parallelled or identified with Paul's soteriology. The reason for this is the profound difference in the structure of these "patterns". Jewish soteriology, according to Laato, is synergistic. Even though Jewish theology builds on covenant and the mercy of God, there is always a very positive attitude towards man's capability to effect his salvation.[51] One attains covenant grace by an act of free will. [52]

Paul's soteriology, according to Laato, is monergistic. Salvation is dependent solely on the gospel. Paul says that obedience to the law will follow, after the gospel has first brought new life by faith. There is the fruit of the Spirit, but this too is produced by God. It is God who effects all man's willing and doing.[53]

Concerning negative criticism of Sanders we should mention S. Westerholm. In his book "Israel's Law and Church's Faith" he presented a detailed analysis of both modern Pauline studies and Sanders' theory. Westerholm's book is a valuable tool as an overview of the modern discussion and it also contains some clear insights about the theory of covenantal nomism.

One of the most important claims of Westerholm is that in Paul, as well as in Jewish theology, the law has a soteriological function. He says that even according to Paul, the law *does* have positive significance as regards salvation. Paul is not merely blaming the Jews for having such a view but accepts it himself, too. They both promise life to the one who fulfils the law. If anyone is able to do this, he will also be made righteous by it. What Paul actually claims, then, is that the concept of righteousness by law is common to both him and the traditionalist Jews.

Secondly, Westerholm remarks here that, for Paul, the idea of righteousness

---

[50] Laato, *Paulus,* 81-82. According to Laato, the features of covenantal nomism cannot be found e.g. in Sirach.

[51] Laato, *Paulus,* 210.

[52] Laato, *Paulus,* 194. In his criticism Laato could have, in fact, gone even further, as several other scholars have done. See the more detailed discussion concerning the consequences of a thoroughgoing criticism in chapter 14.1.

[53] Laato, *Paulus,* 210.

by the law is a Biblical theme. He never uses concepts such as "Pharisaic theology" or the "teachings of the sages" as an argument. Paul appeals to Moses. In this way he is able to use an argument which every Jew can accept.[54]

In the books of Moses Jews are told to choose between life and death. So it should be obvious that the keeping of the law has a function of maintaining life. When salvation was later interpreted in an eschatological context concerning "the age to come", the same exhortation to obedience prevailed as an essential part of theology. This is why, according to Westerholm, the law most evidently had a soteriological function.[55]

Westerholm wanted to re-introduce some previously abandoned views in the interpretation of Pauline theology. When trying to correct our view of the nature of Jewish theology Sanders had, by his theory, given birth to a new one-sided explanation of Judaism. Simple covenantal nomism based on God's grace did not correspond to the reality of Jewish theology in the Second Temple period.

This critical front was joined by F. Thielman. He thought that Paul was very aware of the "plight" of man in Jewish theology and intentionally desired to provide a solution to it. According to Thielman, the most important question of contemporary Jewish theology was the problem of the unfaithfulness of Israel, because it brought God's punishment on the people. Faith in Christ was to be the answer to a huge problem in contemporary Jewish theology. This is why the roots of Paul's theology were deep in Second Temple Jewish thought.[56]

Sanders' theory had a strong impact on Pauline studies. B.W. Longenecker commences his dissertation with the words: "It may not be too much to say that New Testament scholarship is currently working in a 'post-Sanders' environment".[57] An emphasis on rabbinic theology and Jewish nomism gave birth to a new paradigm where the keys to Paul's theology, and soteriology in particular, were sought after in his concept of nomism.[58]

---

[54] Westerholm, *Law,* 145.

[55] Westerholm, *Law,* 149. Westerholm has been accused of a return to the Lutheran interpretation. This can hardly be true as regards the direct references to the Old Testament and Jewish theology.

[56] Thielman, *Law,* 49, 53, 239.

[57] Longenecker, *Eschatology and the Covenant,* 14. Also in the new edition of S. Neill's *The Interpretation of the New Testament,* edited by N.T. Wright, Sanders' book is said to have changed the whole trend of Pauline studies – permanently. Neill-Wright, *Interpretation,* 424.

[58] Concerning the literature see e.g. Dunn, *Law;* Gaston, *Torah;* Martin, *Law;* Thielman, *Plight;* Schreiner, *Law;* Räisänen, *Law;* Winger, *Law.* More literature is given for example

After Sanders different scholars applied his theory in several, rather different ways. J.D.G. Dunn, for example, followed Sanders and accepted his theory. As regards the theology of Paul, he went even further. Dunn thought that Paul intentionally set his gospel in opposition to the Jewish way of conducting covenantal nomism by using the works of law as "identity markers".[59] H. Räisänen, in turn, thought that with the aid of the theory of covenantal nomism we are now able to prove that Paul has given us a distorted picture of Judaism.[60] Paul's theology was biassed and polemical. All Paul endeavoured to do was to present a soteriology with a Christological premise.[61]

After the relationship between Paul and the Jewish theology of Second Temple Judaism had permanently come into the focus of scholarship, Sanders' theory has directed the discussion in a significant way. This is why a modern study cannot avoid assessing the real applicability of the theory of covenantal nomism in the explanation of contemporary Jewish theology. The same concerns Sanders' assessment of Paul's soteriology.

2.6. Locating Paul in the diversity of Second Temple Jewish theology (J. Chr. Beker, B.W. Longenecker, G. Schimanowski, M.A. Seifrid, et al.)

Sanders' theory of covenantal nomism has had a strong impact on the study of Pauline soteriology ever since it was published.[62] The interpretation of Paul's theology was based on a fixed concept of Jewish nomism. In this context heavy arguments and even accusations were directed against Paul, who was no longer an object of study but more like a defendant. The main problem with this tradition of interpretation was that it was based on a too homogenous concept of Jewish soteriology. It was dominated by rabbinistic theology,

---

in the book by Westerholm, *Law;* and in the new introduction of the second edition of Räisänen's book, where the author gives detailed comments on almost every reaction against his first edition, see Räisänen, *Law (2nd ed.).*

[59] In the prologue of the commentary on Romans, Dunn, *Romans,* lxv-lxxii; cf. Dunn, *Law,* 195-196. Dunn emphasizes that in this procedure covenantal nomism is not called into question and not denied. Dunn's explanation will be treated in chapter 10.3.

[60] Räisänen, *Law,* 179f., 187. An assessment of the ideas of Räisänen will be given in chapter 14.2.

[61] Räisänen, *Law,* 201. Räisänen follows the tradition of Deissmann in this sense (see above). Paul was not considered a coherent thinker or even a theologian but just an eager preacher with a rather unsystematic mind. This kind of interpretation of Paul was quite early in scholarship taken to the final extreme by F. Overbeck, see the description of Kümmel in *History,* 199-205.

[62] For example, new general overviews on early Christianity were written from the point of view of Sanders' theory, see e.g. Rowland, *Christian Origins,* 25-27.

which in turn had been studied from a rather narrow point of view.[63] Furthermore, the diversity of Second Temple Jewish literature and theology was not given proper appreciation.[64]

The scholarly tradition where rabbinic theology was given priority was gradually in the 80's provided with balance by a group of studies where the letters of Paul were compared and parallelled directly with other Second Temple texts. In the 90's this kind of research has grown significantly. Even though some of these scholars still remain in the "school" of Sanders, the focus of research has changed.

Studies include analyses of texts such as Sirach (= Ecclesiasticus) and sapiential literature (E.J. Schnabel, G. Schimanowski, D.B. Garlington; and thematically T. Laato),[65] 4 Ezra (B.W. Longenecker),[66] Qumran, e.g. 1QS (M.A. Seifrid), [67] and the Psalms of Solomon (M. Winninge, M. A. Seifrid).[68] The new perspective has significantly changed our understanding of the tradition history behind Paul's theology. We can now better place Paul in the context of Second Temple Jewish theology.[69]

In the study of predestinarian theology the new emphasis has been seen especially in the recent work of G. Röhser, whose monograph dealt with the theme of hardening in Romans 9-11. In his research Röhser compares Paul's theology with 1 Enoch and the texts of Qumran, where the themes of the Old Testament are interpreted in a novel way.[70]

---

[63] See a thorough and excellent analysis in a recent book by Avemarie, *Tora und Leben,* 34ff., 579-583. According to his research, there are several examples in rabbinic sources where the new life promised by God is a direct result of the obedient life of the righteous. The concept of covenant was not used in order to displace this conviction. In this respect the theory of Sanders was one-sided.

[64] For negative criticism against Sanders' theory in general, see Overman-Green, *ABD III* (1992) 1038. Sanders had established G.F. Moore's notion of Rabbinic Judaism as 'normative Judaism'. Modern Jewish studies have later made this approach untenable.

[65] See Schnabel, *Law and Wisdom;* Schimanowski, *Weisheit und Messias;* Garlington, *Obedience of Faith,* Laato, *Paulus.*

[66] Longenecker, *Eschatology and the Covenant.*

[67] Seifrid, *Justification.*

[68] Winninge, *Sinners and the Righteous,* Seifrid, *Justification.*

[69] There is also a certain ambivalence in the writing of some scholars of this new trend. For example, Longenecker has accepted the diversity of Second Temple Judaism, and he has also criticised Sanders for a one-sided interpretation of Jewish theology. Further, he has at least partly abandoned the concept of covenantal nomism and talked about "ethnocentric covenantalism" with an emphasis on anthropology in the study of soteriology. In spite of this he still praises the theory of Sanders in his monograph. Whatever the reason, it is obvious that the impact of Sanders is enormous and it has also homogenized the results of modern studies. See Longenecker, *Eschatology and the Covenant,* 32, 34, 36-37.

[70] Röhser, *Prädestination.*

Another field has been the study of Jewish apocalyptic, which has also enriched Pauline studies by opening new perspectives. A. Schweitzer already focused his research on the themes of eschatology and Jewish apocalyptic, even though he interpreted most themes according to his concept of mysticism. Later E. Käsemann took these themes and developed them into a thesis: apocalyptic is the "mother" of Christian theology.[71] After these early notions the study of apocalyptic has grown significantly in the field of Jewish studies. Scholars have engaged in intensive study of the apocalyptic writings, the texts of Qumran and the Merkavah literature. This has provided new insights for the explanation of Paul's theology, too.[72]

One of the best adherents of this line of study in the area of Pauline studies is J. Chr. Beker with his monograph "Paul the Apostle, The Triumph of God in Life and Thought". According to Beker, the whole basic structure of Paul's soteriology was remarkably apocalyptic. For Paul, the death of Christ and the cross of Christ marked the defeat of the apocalyptic powers and signified the final judgment of the old age. Furthermore, this theology was centred on the resurrection, which was an apocalyptic-cosmic event that inaugurated the cosmic triumph of God.[73]

For Beker the study of apocalyptic was also of methodological significance. He thought that in the study of Paul we must distinguish between a primary and secondary level of language and avoid identifying a particular symbol (such as righteousness, justification) with the whole of the symbolic structure. As the whole symbolic structure is studied so too the significance of apocalyptic becomes evident.[74]

One of the most important features of Pauline research after the appearance of

---

[71] Käsemann, "Zum Thema der urchristlichen Apokalyptik" *(Exegetische Versuche und Besinnungen II)*, 110f., 120-121. For detailed studies see e.g. H-H. Schade, *Apokalyptische Christologie*.

[72] Here a selection of relevant studies could be mentioned, such as the collection *Königsherrschaft Gottes und himmlischer Kult im Judentum, Urchristentum un in der hellenistischen Welt* (Hengel - Schwemer, eds.); *Le Trône de Dieu* (Philonenko, ed.); and the outstanding article by Hengel, "Psalm 110 und die Erhöhung des Auferstandenen zur Rechten Gottes" (in: *Anfänge der Christologie,* the theme was developed further in *Le Trône de Dieu,* 108-194); see also: Hurtado, *One God, one Lord*; concerning apocalyptic: Collins, *Apocalyptic Imagination*; on Qumran: Martínez, *Qumran and Apocalytic*; on Merkavah literature: Gruenwald, *Apocalyptic and Merkavah Mysticism*; Schäfer, *Hekhalot–Studien*.

[73] Beker, *Paul,* 189.

[74] Beker, *Paul,* 16. There is an element of structuralism in his methodology. After Beker the aspect of apocalyptic has found its place in several monographs, see e.g. Kreitzer, *Jesus and God*; Segal, *Paul the Convert*.

Sanders' theory has been the emphasis on the investigation of various Second Temple Jewish texts. This has opened new insights into the context of Paul's theology. At the same time it has provided scholars with new tools for a better comparison between Paul and contemporary Jewish thought.

We can summarize the results of previous chapters as follows. Firstly, the new history-of-religions approach will be welcomed warmly. The new emphasis on Jewish theology and a contextual approach do make real progress in the investigation of the background of Paul's theology. The scope of the old history-of-religions approach was too narrow and quite subjective. It further resulted in regarding Paul's theology as abstract, Hellenistic thinking with little connection to Second Temple Jewish theology.

The gnostic hypothesis of Bultmann, with its ontological theory of religion has turned out to be rather valueless, as well. Hardly anyone accepts any longer his history-of-religions approach. Furthermore, his interpretation was based on Heidegger's existentialist philosophy. This is why an adherent of Bultmann's theory should accept its implicit premises, too. In reality the theory of Bultmann has lost its attraction at the same time as continental existentialism has fallen out of fashion.

The new history-of-religions approach is also free from Baur's biased pattern of the history of the early church. The problem of Hellenism is assessed today from quite another perspective. The division between Jewish Christianity and Hellenistic Christianity does not depend on the theological separateness of the Judaism of the Diaspora. Interest is focused today on branches of tradition, instead. There is diversity in the multiplicity of Jewish theology, but it cannot be explained by Baur's theories.

The growth of the study of apocalyptic has also revitalized research in a positive way. Schweitzer began a novel approach towards Jewish theology and this line of investigation has later resulted in several fruitful consequences in Pauline studies, one of these being Beker's theory of the "triumph of God". Schweitzer himself was unfortunately restricted by an old concept of mysticism, which he had learnt from the history-of-religion school. This is why he ended up defining Paul's theology in a rather abstract way.

One positive contribution made by Sanders has been the growth of the investigation of larger patterns in both Jewish theology and Pauline theology. The flaw of Sanders' theory was that his analysis was directed by pragmatic and sociological purposes. For example Beker has improved this setting substantially by emphasizing the pattern of content.

In Pauline research we must further maintain the perspective of tradition-history. Paul's presentations of soteriology must not be cut off from their consequent connections with earlier tradition. Paul must be considered a part of Jewish theology. His soteriology grew in dynamic dialogue with the multiplicity of Second Temple Jewish theology.

This assessment is of value when we turn to the investigation of the problem of theodicy and predestinarian theology in Second Temple Judaism and in Paul. We need a consistent explanation of the nature of Jewish theology. Here the question concerning the theory of covenantal nomism becomes an important one, because it has been so popular in Pauline research. In the analysis of Paul's thinking, later, we must assess to what extent the Christological principle really affects his soteriology. And finally we must consider the claim made in previous research that participatory mysticism should satisfactorily explain the heart of Paul's soteriology.

Chapter 1

God's Chosen People in Crisis

The teaching of Paul is an essential part of Second Temple Jewish theology. His relationship to his Jewish background is especially interesting and important for a study of the problem of theodicy. Paul was well acquainted with the literature of his time and was a sincere heir of the theological heritage of his Jewish predecessors. As the problem of theodicy was a common theme in this literature, Paul was certainly familiar with it, too. Speculations over theodicy arose in the context of different historical disasters. The era in which Paul was living ensured the occurrence of this theme in a vivid way.

When we examine Paul's relation to the theology of his time we must study the latter in its own right. The problem of theodicy must first be approached by considering its features in Second Temple Judaism, and only thereafter is a comparison with Paul's writings possible. This is necessary because there is a trend in contemporary scholarship which has accepted a rather monolithic conception of the nature of Jewish theology. In this tradition several important features of Jewish theology have been left out of consideration.[1]

As regards Paul, his personal history has been the focus of a growing interest among scholars over the last few years. After several decades of study where the emphasis had been on the Hellenistic context of Paul's life, scholars have now paid attention to his Jewish background,[2] which Paul himself

---

[1] Above we have become acquainted with the criticism of Sanders' views. While he emphasized new aspects of Jewish soteriology, he happened to replace the old paradigm with a rather one-dimensional concept of covenantal nomism. That is why he did not discover the diversity and richness which is to be found in the literature of Second Temple Judaism. (On Sanders see the excursus below, and chapter 14.1.) This kind of study has been partly dependent on the old division between Palestinian Judaism and Hellenistic Judaism which was quite popular in Biblical studies from Baur to Bultmann. A thorough re-assessment of this division was made in later scholarship, and it will be noted in the course of this study.

[2] The biography and Jewish background of Paul has been the subject of several recent studies. See e.g. Hengel, *Der Vorchristliche Paulus;* Riesner, *Die Frühzeit;* the article of Lührmann ("Paul and the Pharisaic Tradition"), *JSNT 36* (1989) 75-94; Jeremias ("Paulus als Hillelit") in: *Neotestamentica et semitica,* 88-94; Haacker ("War Paulus Hillelit?") in: *Institutum Judaicum,* 106-120. A good overview with literature is provided by Betz, *ABD V* (1992) 186-201.

describes in his letters. This has helped us to locate Paul in his Jewish environment. He was a Pharisee and had received an education of a high standard in Jerusalem.[3] He was a teacher and an expert in Jewish law. This is why we need to study the theology of Paul in its most natural context – Second Temple Jewish literature.[4]

§ 3   The Problem of Theodicy in Second Temple Sapiential Theology

In the Second Temple period the problem of theodicy occurs in nearly every theological tradition we can find. The manner of treating the question differs, however, since there is a remarkable diversity among the traditions. Sapiential theology was often associated with social issues, as is very much the case in Ben Sira. His non-eschatological interpretation flourished later in Sadducean conservatism. Already in sapiential theology there is, however, a strong emphasis on apocalyptic interpretation. Here eschatological thought is prominent and life in this world is said to have a connection and interplay with heavenly powers. Apocalyptic soteriology, in turn, is far from political eschatology – even though there was often some idea of interplay even there. The writers of apocalyptic constantly attempted to solve the problem of how God could vindicate the suffering righteous. Furthermore, this subject is familiar to the theologians of the Qumran community, too. Their apocalyptic eschatology actually forms the basis for their religious identity.[5]

On the other hand, we could say that there are several uniting features in Jewish theology behind the diversity described above.[6] Jewish belief included,

---

[3] Tomson too, who has studied *halakha* in the letters of Paul, concludes that in spite of his Hellenistic environment, Paul is on several issues "rather much at one with Palestinian, Pharisaic-Rabbinic Judaism". Tomson, *Paul*, 53. He defines Paul eventually as a "Hellenistic Pharisee".

[4] Lührmann has noted that in the interpretation of the history-of-religions school, as in that of Bultmann, Paul was located in Hellenistic Judaism. In this way the "traditional" Paul was abandoned, as well as Paul's own references to his Jewish background and his connections to the Pharisaic party. In opposition to this, he was made an opponent of "Palestinian" Judaism and Jewish Christianity. Lührmann, *JSNT 36* (1989) 75-76. Instead of such an opposition Paul's close contact with Second Temple Judaism is today emphasized.

[5] The diversity of Jewish theology is nowadays noted widely in modern study. The new attitude becomes clear from the characterizations which scholars use, such as: "multiform Jewish heritage" (Kraft, *Christianity,* 188-191, 197-199), "internal diversification" (Talmon, *Jewish Civilization,* 16), or merely "diversity" (Porton, *Early Judaism,* 57).

[6] As Overman and Green put it: "The model of multiple Judaisms depicts them as distinct but not disparate." Overman-Green, *ABD III* (1992) 1038.

without exception, the concepts of God's dominion, theocracy, covenant, the rejection of idols and then, of course, the high esteem of *torah,* the Law, which had been given solely to the chosen people.[7] Another uniting factor was the nature of the age in which the people were living. Difficult conditions forced every Jewish group to consider how their tradition provided answers to the situation in which they were living. It was this kind of context which gave birth to the burning issue in theology, the question of theodicy, where the goodwill, power and faithfulness of God were the subjects at issue.

3.1. A theology of crisis

The basic dilemma of Jewish theology in the Second Temple period was simple but severe: Israel should have been *the* Chosen People of God, but it drifted into crises century after century. Promises given by the faithful Lord were supposed to be steadfast – but the experience of even pious Jews seemed to prove the contrary. There was a contradiction between God's promises and the tribulations which the course of history had brought. The reality of the crisis was so strong that it gave substance to most theological writings at that time.[8]

This kind of experience brought up the question whether God was still just and whether he was still willing to help and guide his people. For example, in Wisdom literature this theme occurs repeatedly. On the other hand, it is a central idea behind the proclamation of apocalyptic.

The theology of Second Temple Judaism is thus primarily *theology concerning the problem of theodicy.* Israel as a nation was in crisis and Judaism was experiencing an inner struggle.[9] It is only natural that in theology the question arose whether the Almighty was actually able to lead his people or not. Mostly,

---

[7] This kind of analysis is common, for example, in the discussion about the theme of the "partings of the ways" theme which J. Dunn has re-inaugurated. There the characteristic features of each religion are considered in detail. See Dunn, *Partings of the Ways,* 18ff.

[8] This point of departure has been observed in scholarship for a long time. For example, Nickelsburg, in his introduction to Second Temple literature, describes most writings as a reaction to some kind of crisis or tension in the history of Israel. See e.g. Nickelsburg, *Literature,* 52, 76, 86, 205; cf. Eissfeldt, *Introduction,* 598, 607, 612, 616, 619, 626.

[9] This question is also a watershed as regards the explanation of the primary nature of Second Temple Judaism. Sanders, who rightly recognizes the "context of conflict" in that period, still refuses to draw conclusions concerning the multiplicity of the Jewish theology of that time. He depreciates the importance of crisis and concentrates on a monolithic "common" Judaism instead. Sanders, *Judaism,* 35-36, 241ff. He considers the conflict as having been mostly political and presents the Zealots as an example of resistance to the Romans, pp. 280ff.

however, this question took another form. It was more a question why God allowed power to the oppressors of his people.[10]

A model answer had been given already in the time of the kings. The problem of apostate kings had been one of the most burning issues of that time. This was the case e.g. in the time of Manasseh. The answer of the prophets was simple and clear: God is just and his wrath will fall on the unfaithful in the end.[11]

During this kind of period of transition the prophets also gave answers to the problem of the people's suffering. This can be seen clearly in *Habakkuk,* where the prophet preaches against the decadence of the time of the kings and anticipates the rise of Babylon.[12]

The proclamation of the prophet begins with an exclamation over the problem of theodicy (Hab. 1:2-3):

"O Lord, how long shall I cry for help, and you will not listen? Or cry to you 'Violence!' and you will not save? Why do you make me see wrong-doing and look at trouble?"

A theology which is born under siege asks two burning questions: how long and why?[13]

The despair of the righteous and even doubt as to the justice of God is expressed in quite a classical manner in Habakkuk. The righteous are suffering while godless people meet with success: "Why do you look on the treacherous, and are silent when the wicked swallow those more righteous than they?" (Hab. 1:13).[14]

The answer of the prophet which follows these desperate cries reminds one of the answers of his famous predecessors in the history of Israel. God is not

---

[10] General features of the problem of theodicy are presented in Crenshaw *ABD VI* (1992) 444-445. The theme of crisis is examined in modern study especially by Scott, *EQ 64* (1992) 199-200. Hengel, in turn, has shown that Jewish theology, in controversy with Hellenistic ideology, quite commonly formulated the theological dilemma as a problem of theodicy. This can be seen in several texts from Ben Sira to Essene apocalyptic. Hengel, *Judentum,* 262, 357, 395, 457.

[11] On the literature of the times of the kings, see von Rad, *Theologie II,* 271-273, 286. Eichrodt connects trust in the acts of God, which is seen in the Old Testament, with the concept of providence. Eichrodt, *Faith,* 20-24.

[12] In Habakkuk it is not clear whom the prophet is speaking against. The best solution might be that he has two targets. Firstly, the exhortation is directed against the sins of the people. After that the Chaldeans, i.e. Babylonians, are brought into the picture. They are not solely executors of God's judgment in a positive sense. They are rather the cause of another agony for Israel, to which the prophet needs to seek a solution. See Sweeney, *ABD III* (1992) 1-6.

[13] Rudolph, *Habakuk,* 201. See also Crenshaw, *ABD VI* (1992) 445. The text of Habakkuk is of special importance because of its later influence on several passages (1QpHab; Rom. 1:17; Heb. 10:38).

[14] Smith, *Micah-Malachi,* 103-104.

powerless. Now it is time for Israel to suffer, but punishment will also reach the godless in due time. God Almighty is above the incidents of this world and there is no change in him. "But the Lord is in his holy temple; let all the earth keep silence before him!" (Hab. 2:20). No one can make God responsible for the injustice committed by man himself.[15]

According to Habakkuk, God heard the cry of his people and would grant them his help and his grace. The real climax of the prophecy is a verse which became important in later Jewish theology as well as in the New Testament: "Look at the proud! Their spirit is not right in them, but the righteous live by their faith/faithfulness." (Hab. 2:4, NRSV). Only faithfulness to the Lord and his law, in other words separation from the wicked, will bring life to Israel.[16]

Under the siege of Babylon the fears of Israel were realized. In this context the idea of theodicy was unavoidable, especially when the crisis of the exile had to be explained in theological terms. The break had been severe. The independence of Judah had been lost in the exile and it seemed that it would never be restored again.

Nearly all Jewish theology endeavoured to solve this problem. The solutions can be seen already in the thundering proclamation of the major prophets. The chosen people were living in sin and as a result were under the wrath of God. The suffering of the people was a consequence of sin.[17] Especially the sins of the leaders of Israel had been grave. That is why the whole nation had to suffer. But no sinner could escape his responsibility before God. This was the crisis of all Israel.[18]

Later the returning Jews were able to rebuild the Temple and to restore the feasts and sacrifices, but politically the people lived under foreign rulers.

---

[15] Rudolph, *Habakuk,* 230; von Rad, *Theologie I,* 404-405. We have a similar situation in the book of Zephaniah. The officials and judges of Jerusalem are called wolves and the prophets faithless. The priests have profaned the temple and led the people astray (3:3,4). In spite of this there is no reason to blame God and bring up the problem of theodicy: "The Lord within it is righteous; he does no wrong" (3:5).

[16] Habakkuk speaks of the faithfulness of the righteous ones. The basis for this kind of piety was in deuteronomistic teaching, and later it became a prominent feature of Second Temple sapiential theology as well. The translation "faith" might possibly lead us astray here because of its possible anachronistic connotations. Discussion concerning the later interpretation of this verse will be dealt with in chapter 6.2.

[17] This feature is rightly referred to by Pauline scholars too, see e.g. Thielman, *Law,* 239.

[18] This is naturally the atmosphere of the Psalms too. Most of Psalms 1-37, 52-73, 97-109 and 123-144 were written from the point of view of a suffering pious Jew. There are several statements, in addition, where the righteous ask for justice on the ground of their righteousness (see e.g. Pss. 1:5; 4:4; 7:9; 31:24, 32:10: 64:11; 97:10; 103:6; 109:31; 140:17). Cf. Kraus, *Psalmen I,* xlv-lii.

Furthermore, it seemed that God allowed godless kings to oppress the "chosen people" time after time. A tension between the glory of the time of the kings and the shame of post-exilic Judah was evident.[19]

The prophets of the Exile discussed the problem of theodicy in the same manner as Habakkuk had done. For *Ezekiel* the problem of determinism yielded the answer (Ezek. 18:2-4).[20]

"What do you mean by repeating this proverb concerning the land of Israel, 'The parents have eaten sour grapes, and the children's teeth are set on edge'?... Know that all lives are mine; the life of the parent as well as the life of the child is mine: it is only the person who sins that shall die."

One should not doubt the righteousness of God because his judgment will fall on every sinner without injustice.[21]

According to Ezekiel, the word of admonition is directed to the whole nation. There is a clear demand for repentance. "Have I any pleasure in the death of the wicked, says the Lord God, and not rather that they should turn from their ways and live?" (Ezek. 18:23).[22] Everyone who turns from his sins and obeys the commandments of God, shall live. "If a man is righteous and does what is lawful and right... and is careful to observe my ordinances, acting faithfully – such a one is righteous; he shall surely live, says the Lord God." (18:5, 8).

The admonitions and warnings of Ezekiel are accompanied by a promise. Israel will have to face punishment for its sins and this means the agony of the exile. New mercy is promised to the nation, however. God will raise up a new shepherd for Israel (34:23), and wash the people with a new baptism (36:25). He will raise dead bones and make them alive by his Spirit (37:5).

In *Second Isaiah*, as well, the doubts which had been raised by the problem of theodicy are dispelled. There is no uncertainty as to God's faithfulness and power (Isa. 50:1-2).[23]

"Where is your mother's bill of divorce with which I put her away? Or which of my creditors is it to whom I have sold you? No, because of your sins you were sold, and for your transgressions your mother was put away... Is my hand shortened, that is cannot redeem? Or have I no power to deliver?"

---

[19] For example, Scott, *EQ 64* (1992) 198-199; cf. Talmon, *Jewish Civilization,* 28.

[20] Fear for the burden of the sins of the fathers is evident, for example, in Lamentations: "Our ancestors sinned; they are no more, and we bear their iniquities" (5:7).

[21] Eichrodt, *Ezekiel,* 237; Greenberg, *Ezekiel,* 339-340.

[22] Here we can see a pattern of individualization. Every person is responsible for his own sins. See Crenshaw, *Old Testament,* 222; cf. von Rad, *Theologie II,* 275.

[23] Cf. Westermann, *Isaiah,* 224. The metaphor of the bill of divorce was effective when God's faithfulness was explained. A woman was not able to divorce her husband by herself. She always needed a bill of divorce from him (Deut. 24:1). On the metaphors see McKenzie, *Second Isaiah,* 114.

The hope of the book of Isaiah is based on the power of God Almighty. This is repeatedly proclaimed by the prophet: "I am the Lord, your Holy One, the Creator of Israel, your King" (43:15; cf. 40:9; 41:17; 42:24; 44:6). God is a King who guides the fate of all nations. This is why he is also able to renew Israel and lead it back to its own country.[24]

A similar hope for a renewal after the punishments of God can be seen in the prayer of *Ezra*. Here a repentant sinner is calling upon God in fear and trembling (Ezra 9:13-14).[25]

"After all that has come upon us for our evil deeds and for our great guilt, seeing that you, our God, have punished us less than our iniquities deserved and have given us such a remnant as this, shall we break your commandments again and intermarry with peoples who practise these abominations?"

We can say that there are two important poles in early Second Temple Jewish theology. On the one hand, theology is governed by the ever recurring problem of theodicy. On the other hand, we can see ongoing trust in God in the midst of severe difficulties. Hope is never totally abandoned.[26]

The repentance preached by Ezra was not the only solution to the problem of theodicy, however. We must note that the focus was usually not on men but on God. For example, in Isaiah faith in the Lordship of God Almighty is steadfast. The righteous were certain that godless people could not endlessly avoid God's punishment. There was a judgment appointed for them. Justice would be done for the suffering pious. And the hope of the righteous was in salvation: it was prepared for the elect. This is why the suffering would not endure eternally.[27]

In Second Temple texts righteous Jews constantly search for reasons for the agony and suffering of Israel. This theme occurred over and over again, because after the Exile there certainly were crises which made the question a topical one. Godless rulers took over Israel time after time. The crisis did not slacken even though people, according to the texts, often lived in open repentance and had decided to change their way of living.[28]

This was probably the reason why the pattern of interpretation, developed

---

[24] The theme of God's power is emphasized by von Rad, *Theologie II*, 255-256.

[25] Cf. Neh. 9; Dan. 9:4-19; Bar. 1:15-20. There is a causal relationship between repentance and restoration.

[26] Schrey, *RGG VI* (1986) 741.

[27] See Eichrodt, *Theodicy*, 33. Concerning eschatology and the idea of judgment as a solution to the problem of theodicy, see Crenshaw, *JBL 94* (1975) 56. According to Berger's sociological analysis, this connection might even be of a universal nature. Berger, *Sacred Canopy*, 68-69.

[28] A good overview of this era is given by Schürer, *History I*, 138f.

under the Exile, prevailed in Jewish theology from century to century. The sins
of Israel were the reason why God punished the people again and again. These
punishments did not prevent the Temple from functioning, and this provided a
certain security for Jewish identity. But it was not enough to keep Israel on the
right path.[29]

The next significant crisis came with Alexander the Great and his politics. It
was he who brought Hellenism to Israel.[30] Hellenism changed Jewish theology
in a profound and substantial way despite the fact that the change in political
rule seems to have taken place rather easily. Alexander replaced Persian rule in
Israel. If we are to believe Josephus, the conquest took place without violence
and the elite of the nation welcomed the new tyrant in a good spirit. The
peaceful change may naturally be true in the sense that the suffering that took
place under Alexander was probably not greater than it had been under the
Persians.

One doubts the reliability of Josephus, however, when he emphasizes the
keen and positive relationship between Alexander and the high priest in
Jerusalem.[31] It may be that Alexander did not interfere in the activities of the
Temple and that he secured for himself the acceptance of the leading
priesthood.[32] On the other hand, Josephus places the authority of Alexander
behind the temple at Gerizim and makes him in this way the upholder of a
constant schism.[33]

The politics of Alexander the Great were not always welcomed in a positive
way. In *Daniel*, for example, his acts are condemned severely. Here Alexander
is a "warrior king" who destroys the country and takes action "as he pleases"

---

[29] According to Josephus, the Temple was desecrated in the Persian period, for example by
an incident of murder among the priests. A high priest called John killed his brother Jesus in
the Temple. The Persian general Bagoses took over and used this as an excuse to enter the
Temple. Jos. Ant. 11.297-301.

[30] Concerning Hellenism in particular, see Hengel, *Judentum*, 191-195; Marböck,
Weisheit, 170-173; Betz, *ABD III* (1992) 127-128.

[31] According to Hengel, Alexander was treated in a positive way, especially among the
Hellenist Jews of Alexandria. There the conqueror was turned into a monotheist and a servant
of the God of Israel. Hengel, *Political and Social History*, 44.

[32] Jos. Ant. 11.304ff.; Tcherikover, *Political Situation*, 57-58. On the grounds of Greek
sources Tcherikover thinks that Alexander hardly had time to visit Jerusalem. After capturing
Gaza he marched to Pelusium in seven days.

[33] According to Josephus, a brother of the high priest Jaddua of Jerusalem, Manasseh,
began the building of the temple of Samaria. After marrying the daughter of the Persian
Sanballat, Manasseh was in danger of being driven out of the temple by the elders of
Jerusalem. Manasseh appealed to Sanballat, who saw a political opportunity in this
situation. He joined Alexander and received permission to build a new temple in Samaria.
Manasseh, naturally, was made the high priest by Alexander and Sanballat (Jos. Ant. 11.321-
328). Historical records do not reveal the actual date of the building of the temple, however.

(Dan. 11:3). His "fourth kingdom" was an embodiment of violence and godlessness (Dan. 7:7; 8:5-21).[34] In the same way the writer of 1 Maccabees describes the conquests of Alexander: "He fought many battles, conquered strongholds, and put to death the kings of the earth... When the earth became quiet before him, he was exalted, and his heart was lifted up" (1 Macc. 1:2-3).[35] The most significant threat to Jewish tradition was posed by Hellenism, however, which was a result of Alexander's politics. Also, it later met with resistance in Israel in many different ways.

After the death of Alexander several political crises arose. The consequences of the battle between the Ptolemaic dynasty and the Seleucids also affected the lot of Israel.[36] Israel had fallen between Egyptian and Syrian rule and had to face the endless struggles of the Diadochi.[37] We can see written reactions to these struggles in the oldest part of *1 Enoch* (especially 1 Enoch 6-11), where the acts of the warrior-kings are described as a battle between "giants". Military expeditions brought a constant crisis, and in Enoch it is resolved by God's divine intervention to save Israel.[38]

In the giant-story of 1 Enoch there are not many features, however, to help one to date the text accurately. Assuming that the alleged dating is appropriate, the interpretation nicely fits the details. Here we have a typical example of how the agony of a crisis is expressed in the language of the problem of theodicy. In this sequence the giants maintain tyrannous rule over Israel. They destroyed some of the people and compelled others to practice magic and astrology (1 Enoch 7:1-5; 8:3-4), until the "earth brought an accusation against the oppressors" (7:6).[39]

Heaven is not indifferent to the sufferings of the people, however. Their pain is seen and their cries are heard, and vindication is promised. The guardian angels communicate the information of the fate of the martyrs to the King of kings (9:3-5), who also gives his answer. The earth "and everything" will be destroyed and judgment will fall because of the ungodly giants (10:2-4). Sinners will be punished when the last day arrives (10:12-13).

The problem of theodicy is clearly at issue in the giant-story. The people are

---

[34] Cf. 1 Enoch 90:2; Sib.Or. 4:80-96. Hengel, *Political and Social History*, 44.

[35] Hengel, *Political and Social History*, 45.

[36] See Whitehorne, *ABD* V (1992) 541.

[37] Tcherikover, *Political Situation*, 63-68. In twenty years there were five different rulers in the region.

[38] See Nickelsburg, *Literature*, 50-52.

[39] On the dating, see Isaac, *Enoch*, 6-7; Nickelsburg, *JBL 96* (1977) 389-395, especially 391; Nickelsburg, *Literature*, 48. Cf. Milik, *Books of Enoch*, 28-35; and Black, *Enoch*, 13-15.

suffering under oppression and this provokes the question of how God will deal with the tyrants. The answer is simple, though. God's Lordship and Kingship are emphasized above all (9:4-5). The people's sufferings will not escape the Lord's notice. God's answer to the problem of suffering is full of authority: "And the Deluge is about to come upon all the earth; an all that is in it will be destroyed" (10:2). Godless people will be bound until the last judgment (10:12), but the righteous are given the promise of salvation and peace (10:16-17).

In the imagery of the giant-story in 1 Enoch the problem of theodicy is described in figurative language using archaic metaphors. The application itself, however, is quite fitting and effective, as regards the crises of the era. In the sufferings of the people it is God Almighty who has the final word.[40]

After the wars of succession there followed a rather peaceful century under Ptolemaic rule – despite the fact that the loyalty of the people was being ensured by a strong military power.[41] In 200 B.C. Israel saw a new crisis when Antiochus III the Great defeated young Ptolemy V Epiphanes. This brought Ptolemaic control to an end, and Israel was transferred to Seleucid domination. The conquests brought destruction above all to northern Israel and Samaria. Military governors and a system of tax farming were introduced throughout Judaea.[42] There were many kinds of problems in Israel, and Josephus writes that at that time the Jews "suffered greatly". Their land was "sorely harassed", even though the temple of Jerusalem was guaranteed inviolability. In this ambivalent situation, according to Josephus, the high priest of Jerusalem (apparently Simon II) welcomed Antiochus warmly.[43]

The book of *Jesus, the son of Sirach,* belongs to the period after this incident. It is a foremost example of sapiential theology in the Second Temple period. Most of his life the writer had lived under rather peaceful circumstances, under Ptolemaic rule. He was a teacher of the law and probably

---

[40] Cf. Hanson, *JBL 96* (1977) 219: "Though the concern with theodicy, wedded to a pessimistic view regarding the possibilities inherent within historical processes, has moved the problem of alienation to the lofty plane of cosmic events, traces of the concrete social matrix have not been completely obliterated. Under circumstances within which the victims of oppression find themselves powerless to eradicate the evil they see engulfing them, they give expression both to their bitter frustrations and their fervent hopes by creating a new myth."

[41] Tcherikover, *Political Situation,* 72-73.

[42] Whitehorne, *ABD I* (1992) 270.

[43] Jos. Ant. 12.129-144; Tcherikover, *Political Situation,* 82-83; Hengel, *Political and Social History,* 70-72.

even had a school in Jerusalem.[44] Behind the teaching of Sirach we have again the problem of the suffering of the righteous. Sirach is a theologian of theodicy *par excellence*. It is not easy, however, to discern all the factors which affected the development of his theology.[45]

As a teacher of the law, Sirach was concerned with the lawlessness and ungodly life prevailing in his time. Ptolemaic Hellenism was a threat to Jewish identity. On the other hand, Sirach writes of the crises which Israel was facing under the threat of foreign oppression. Some godless rulers, such as Antiochus III in his time, kept strict control over the Jews and there was no hope of independence in Israel.

What Sirach desired to do was to remind the people of the appropriate fear of God (1:11-20). Even the rulers had no right to abandon the principles of Jewish faith. When Sirach wrote against the abuse of power in Israel, he seems to have commented on incidents that took place in his own time: "Sovereignty passes from nation to nation on account of injustice and insolence and wealth. How can dust and ashes be proud? Even in life the human body decays" (10:8-9).

The danger of stumbling naturally threatened all Jews in their everyday lives. And furthermore, the godless were not allowed to be confident about their lives, since they had already been subjected to God's wrath: "Do not be so confident of forgiveness (Gk: atonement) that you add sin to sin... for both mercy and wrath are with him, and his anger will rest on sinners" (5:5-6).

Even though the theology of Sirach had not grown as a reaction to any national catastrophe, his thought was built around the problem of theodicy. He considered his time a godless one, and his reasons may have been many. The influence of Hellenism was growing and threatened to alter Jewish identity. On the other hand, even the peaceful period of two generations may have raised many of the ideas against which Sirach was preaching: that God's blessings in material wealth give security, that his power robs man of the freedom to act decisively to avoid sinful conduct, and that his blindness makes evil profitable.[46]

When opposing such assertions Sirach took up the problem of theodicy. No one had permission to appeal to it as an excuse for his sins. His answer must

---

[44] The dating of the book is dependent on the fact that the high priest Simon II of Jerusalem is not mentioned in the text. On the other hand, the rule of Antiochus Epiphanes had not yet begun. On Sirach, see Di Lella, *ABD VI* (1992) 931ff.

[45] The problem of theodicy in Sirach has been studied e.g. by Hengel, *Judentum*, 262-263; Maier, *Mensch und freier Wille*, 106-112; Prato, *Teodicea;* Murphy, *Tree of Life*, 74-76; and especially Crenshaw, *JBL 94* (1975) 47ff.

[46] This list is given by Crenshaw, *JBL 94* (1975) 47.

be a typical theme of a teacher of the law. The world is not deterministic. Man himself is responsible for his acts. "Do not say, 'It was he who led me astray'; for he has no need of the sinful" (15:12).

This verse presents the problem of theodicy in almost its classical form. Godlessness is not identified here with any foreign ruler but with the common Jew. One cannot escape the problem of evil. It must be dealt with in accordance with the law. And this is where it becomes a problem for man. Man must assume responsibility.[47]

The solution to the problem of theodicy is found in Sirach along the lines of creation theology. First of all, God's creation is good and everything has its place in good harmony. If man spoils this harmony he must be considered responsible because he had been given dominion over everything (Sirach 17:1-6). In this creation theology there is probably also some influence from Hellenism, because there evidently is confidence that a rationalistic world-view is able to solve the problem of theodicy.[48]

In the book of Sirach we have a further problem concerning eschatology, and it has interested scholars for several decades. In the Hebrew text we cannot find any trace of a judgment after death. According to Sirach himself, the wages of sin are paid in this world. The hour of death seems to be especially important in this respect. This is, of course, somewhat surprising, since Sirach is interested indeed in the problem concerning the success of the godless and the suffering of the righteous. In the Greek version the problem of theodicy is later solved quite clearly in the context of eschatology. There is a judgment after death and that moment will reveal divine justice. This question will be dealt with in detail below.[49]

In the sapiential tradition we can find a similar concept later in the *Wisdom of Solomon*. Here the question remains the same. According to the writer, godless people "summon death" when they abandon the precepts of the Lord. They pretend that God will not take notice of their actions (Wisd. 1:15-2:1):[50]

"For they reasoned unsoundly, saying to themselves, 'Short and sorrowful is our life, and there is no remedy when a life comes to its end... for we were born by mere chance"

The righteous have to suffer under the oppression of the wicked. "Let us lie in wait for the righteous man, because he is inconvenient to us and opposes our actions; he reproaches us for sins against the law" (2:12). This shows that in

---

[47] Cf. DiLella, *Sirach*, 499; Murphy, *Tree of Life*, 75. Sirach also demanded strict nomism, see Marböck, *Weisheit*, 110.

[48] See Sirach 39:16; cf. 40:10. On the relationship between creation theology and Hellenism, see Hengel, *Judentum*, 262, 265.

[49] Here especially Skehan-DiLella, *Ben Sira*, 86.

[50] Winston, *Wisdom*, 58, 113-114.

the Wisdom of Solomon too the problem of theodicy is a prominent feature and directs the interpretation of the controversy in question. The writer's hope of final justice is strong, however: "the ungodly will be punished as their reasoning deserves, those who disregarded the righteous and rebelled against the Lord" (3:10).[51]

In the Hasmonean era, too, sapiential theology remained alive and affected the theological interpretation of history. This was a time when crises created quite distinctive situations in Israel. Answering these crises became unique events in several respects, and we shall return to these themes later when investigating apocalyptic. In spite of new aspects in theology, the sapiential tradition remained strong in Jewish literature. This is easily seen in the first reactions to the Roman invasion in the first century B.C.

In 63 the last significant siege of the Second Temple era began. Roman power had been increasing for some time, and once again Israel was to be a pawn in a political game. With the invasion of Pompey, Jerusalem was captured and the Temple defiled. Probably for political reasons the temple service was allowed to continue, however, under Hyrcanus II.[52]

Roman power was resisted with zeal, both in Israel and in the Diaspora. In the *Psalms of Solomon* the ungodly Roman rule is criticized vehemently. The theology of these psalms follows the dualistic pattern of their predecessors. The people's agony has its reason: God is punishing Israel for its sins.[53] The punishment of God is not restricted solely to the unfaithful of Israel, however. The rule of the ungodly tyrants, too, will come to an end. God's judgment will come and fall on the oppressors of Israel (PsSol. 2; 8).[54]

In PsSol. 2, which is evidently commenting on the invasion of Pompey, the setting is similar to that of other Second Temple texts. The Temple has been desecrated and godless warriors have entered its places of sacrifice. The reason for this destruction was the offence of the priests who had abandoned God's law and this is why the offerings were profaned "with lawless acts". It were they who had, according to the writer, "defiled the sanctuary of the Lord"(PsSol. 2:1-5). The writer is not totally desperate, though. He will not

---

[51] Cf. Winston, *Wisdom*, 125, 128; Wright, *Wisdom*, 514.

[52] Schürer, *History I*, 244f., 267f. The Proconsul Gabinius deprived Hyrcanus II of his political power and granted him only the leadership of the temple. Israel was divided into five districts, and each of these had a capital of its own.

[53] "Pss.Sol. interpret God's acts within history, the catastrophic experience under Pompei in particular, as divine judgments upon sin." Seifrid, *Justification*, 118; cf. Bruce, *New Testament History*, 11ff.

[54] Nickelsburg dates the psalms to the time of Pompey, Nickelsburg, *Literature*, 205-206.

doubt the power of God. "And the earth shall know all your righteous judgments, O God" (2:10).[55]

The crisis brought by the Romans is also commented on by Josephus, who, because of his personal situation, is inclined to write from the point of view of the Romans. In spite of this tendency he writes that the sufferings under the Romans are a direct consequence of the sin of the people. This time only the Roman power was to be the whip of God (Jos. Bell. 5,398; Jos. Ant. 14.176). In this respect Josephus, too, stands in the sapiential tradition when he interprets the punishment as a result of Israel's sins. He says nothing further about the problem of theodicy nor does he consider how much of a problem the status of Rome actually was.[56]

Second Temple Jewish theology thus consists of both old tradition and current interpretation. Soteriology developed and new features were attached to it. The causal connection between sin and punishment is similar to that of the proclamation of the major prophets centuries earlier. On the other hand, the point of view is even more dramatic than before. The problem of theodicy is acute, since the suffering of the people can always be interpreted as implying either their having broken the covenant or the unfaithfulness of God.

It seems to be clear that a simple "deuteronomistic" concept of covenant does not fit in very well with Second Temple Jewish theology. The status of covenantal promises is no longer the same as it was before the Exile. A deep consciousness of the reality of the crises changed the concept of covenant in most groups. At the same time the concept of the future of Israel underwent a change. This resulted in the growth of eschatology and the strengthening of soteriological dualism, which was closely connected with it.[57]

The first seeds of this kind of thinking are found already in the sapiential theology of Sirach and the Wisdom of Solomon. The main issues in their theology were the problem of the suffering of the pious, and a desire for justice. Since Israel was constantly subject to the rule of godless people – even Jews – the covenant could not concern all Jews. The covenant could not be used as an excuse for everything. Salvation was promised only to the "remnant". So the situation resembled the times of the prophets. The "faithful remnant" was the true Israel which kept the law of God. There was hope for

---

[55] Winninge pays attention to the fact that in PsSol. 2 Jews from several stages of the society are condemned as sinners. Winninge, *Sinners and the Righteous*, 34-35.

[56] Concerning the locating of Josephus in contemporary theology, see Thielman, *Law*, 53.

[57] This kind of description of Jewish theology is in open disagreement with the theory of covenantal nomism. According to Sanders' theory Jewish soteriology had to be interpreted in terms of traditional covenantalism. In this case the crucial factor would be trust in God's mercy. We shall later assess in detail the applicability of Sanders' theory in the interpretation of respective texts.

the oppressed and the martyrs; it was to be found in the future life which God would give.[58]

So the "remnant" was not merely *one* link in God's salvation history. It was always *the* group of the saved. This kind of eclectic election was clearly eschatological in nature.

According to the sapiential tradition, the pious had to keep the law since they knew that it was the only way to life. They did not need to worry about godless oppressors since their rule was only temporary and transient. In sapiential theology the problem of suffering was solved by emphasizing historical dualism. God would punish the godless in the end and the keepers of the law would inherit life.[59]

The soteriological dualism of sapiential theology is an important feature in Jewish theology. It will be analyzed more closely in the next chapter. With the aid of this dualism theologians were able to give a profiled answer to the problem of theodicy. As a result they ended up with a soteriology which was to be crucial for nearly every religious party in Second Temple Judaism.

3.2. Soteriological dualism

In the earliest sapiential literature the problem of theodicy was considered mainly from the perspective of this temporal world. Eventually the eschatological aspect became prevalent, however, and moulded the answer given by sapiential theology. In this process a soteriological dualism developed. Actually this theme was not new in the long history of Jewish theology, as we have already seen in the previous chapter. In the harsh proclamation of the great prophets of Israel and Judah the people were often divided into two groups according to their obedience to God.

The early roots of soteriological dualism can be seen in the (Hebrew) text of *Sirach*, where the problem of sin is dealt with without any eschatological context.[60] Sirach describes the whole creation as antithetical pairs. In this scheme the problem of sin could also be resolved.[61] "Good is the opposite of evil, and life the opposite of death, so the sinner is the opposite of the godly. Look at all the works of the Most High; they come in pairs, one the opposite of the other" (Sirach 33:14-15).

---

[58] This theme will be analyzed below, in chapter 4.1.

[59] Scott thinks that the prominent status of the problem of theodicy during the Exile, leads to the strengthening of nomism. Scott, *EQ 64* (1992) 199. In addition, we must note that the theme of God's judgment became inalienable in theology.

[60] This concerns the original Hebrew Sirach, see Skehan-DiLella, *Ben Sira,* 86. The problem of the eschatology of the book of Sirach will be dealt with elsewhere.

[61] Marböck, *Weisheit,* 152-153; Crenshaw, *Wisdom,* 168; Murphy, *Tree of Life,* 75.

Sirach explained the question of evil by exploiting creation theology. This further led to the problem of determinism, which is to be discussed in the next chapter. Sirach did not find it difficult, however, to define dualism, since in his view the responsibility for evil was always in the hands of men.

According to Sirach, the most severe mistake made by sinners is to forsake the Lord.

"The beginning of pride is to forsake the Lord, when the human heart revolts against its Maker; as its beginning is sin, so persistence in it brings on a deluge of depravity. Therefore the Lord inflicts signal punishments on the proud and brings them to utter disaster" (Sirach 10:12-13).

Sirach is certain that the wickedness of humankind will not escape the punishment of God.

"Even if there were but one stubborn person, it would be a miracle for him to escape punishment, for mercy and anger belong to the Lord: he shows his power now in forgiveness, now in overflowing anger. His mercy is great, but great also his condemnation; he judges each by what he has done. He does not let the wrongdoer escape with his plunder or try the patience of the godly too long" (Sirach 16:11-12).

There is a punishment for godless people, but this punishment is not deterministic. Every wrongdoer should repent and return to his God. "Return to the Lord and have done with sin; make your prayer in his presence and lessen your offence. Come back to the Most High, renounce wrongdoing, and hate intensely what he abhors" (Sirach 17:25-26).

In Sirach the fate of man is bound up with his willingness to keep God's commands.[62] If one transgressed the commandments one's relationship to the covenant was at stake. We should perhaps not speak of expulsion. It is more a question of a warning of the final judgment. Wrongdoers could not avoid the consequences which transgression against the order of creation would inevitably involve.

As regards its teaching on the fate of man, the book of Sirach is somewhat inconsistent. In the Hebrew Sirach blessings and curses fall on men in this life.[63] This concept is based on the nomism of the Old Testament. Everything ends in death, which will confront everyone equally: "Do not rejoice over any one's death; remember that we must all die" (8:7). The wrath of God will be experienced in this life, and for Ben Sira it is "the day of calamity" (5:8). After

---

[62] Sanders admits this feature in the theology of Sirach, even though it speaks against his theory of covenantal nomism. For some reason he claims, however, that in Sirach the question whether a Jew could sin so severely that he would be expelled from the covenant, is never brought up. Sanders, *Paul,* 333.

[63] This has been noted e.g. by DiLella, *ABD VI* (1992) 942-943. He thinks that the eschatology was introduced when the nephew of Jesus ben Sira translated the book into Greek, cf. Murphy, *Tree of Life,* 74.

death, judgment can be seen merely in the state of a man's reputation. The righteous have a good reputation (11:28), but "the bad name of sinners will be blotted out" (41:11).[64]

In the redaction of the book of Sirach, eschatology becomes more prominent. Now sin will be punished after death and sinners will be re-paid according to their works. "Humble yourself to the utmost, for the punishment of the ungodly is fire and worms" (7:17). Dualism is perfect since the righteous will be granted the glory of heaven: "You who fear the Lord, hope for good things, for lasting joy and mercy" (2:9).[65]

In sapiential theology, soteriological dualism was hardly ever immanent. In the *Wisdom of Solomon* the point of view was eschatological, and the writer believed that the judgment of God would reach even beyond death.

"Death has no sovereignty on earth, for justice is immortal; but the godless by their deeds and words have death for his company. Thinking him their friend and pining for him, they have made a pact with him because they are fit members of his party" (Wisd. 1:15).

According to the writer, every sinner will be punished for his wrongdoings. Here the proclamation is rather juridical in nature. "So, on the day of reckoning for their sins, they will come cringing, convicted to their face by their own lawless actions" (Wisd. 4:19-20).[66]

It is very typical of sapiential theology to contrast the temporal power and success of the ungodly and the suffering of the righteous. The divine determination of God will eventually provide salvation for the suffering pious (Wisd. 4:17). "For they will see the end of the wise, and will not understand what the Lord purposed for them, and for what he kept them safe."

In the *Psalms of Solomon,* too, soteriological dualism is prominent. In PsSol. 2, which was mentioned above, the division between the ungodly and righteous had to be made even among the Temple priests (PsSol. 2:3-5). In Psalm 8 the writer assesses the history of Israel and points to the judgments of God (e.g. 8:6-17). In Psalm 12 the opposition is between a vocal criminal and a silent righteous man. God's punishment is meant for the ungodly, but the righteous who suffer in silence will be granted salvation (12:4-6).[67]

In sapiential literature eschatology affects soteriology and eventually becomes quite dualistic. This became one of the main features of Second

---

[64] Skehan-DiLella, *Ben Sira,* 84-85; Crenshaw, *JBL 94* (1975) 62.

[65] Cf. Skehan-DiLella, *Ben Sira,* 86. In the commentary the new eschatology is explained by the fact that, in Alexandria, where the nephew of Jesus ben Sira translated the work, apocalyptic was popular and the book of Daniel had become a standard work of eschatology.

[66] Wright, *Wisdom,* 515.

[67] PsSol. 12 presents a typical example of a dualism which focuses on the hope of the just judgment of God at the end of days. See Winninge, *Sinners and the Righteous,* 118.

Temple Jewish theology. Salvation has its conditions, and this cannot all be reduced to simple covenantalism. The problem of theodicy is too difficult to be solved merely by appealing to ethnocentricism. We see a novel soteriology, instead. Here the Lordship of God provides a basis for the salvation of the righteous.

3.3. An era of synergistic nomism

Even though the demand for repentance and the exhortation to keep the precepts of the Lord were of utmost importance in Jewish theology, this does not mean that we are justified in calling this kind of religious behaviour mere legalism. In this respect the critics of the approach adopted by older continental scholarship have been on the right track. Without exception Jewish theology contained a concept of God's mercy and providence. In the temple cult the rite of atonement perpetually provided forgiveness for those who had transgressed against God's will.

We may use the word "legalism" only in the sense that obedience was set in an eschatological context. The keeping of the commandments of God was believed to affect people's salvation in the future. In scholarship, however, another name is normally given to this kind of "pattern" of soteriology.

Jewish soteriology can be defined as synergism. This means simply that man's own actions, i.e. keeping the law, affect his salvation. In the context of the temple cult and covenantal theology, nomism can never be the only condition for salvation, however. According to the basic principles of synergism, God always plays a prominent role in the salvation of man.[68]

Behind the discussion concerning synergism we have the opposition between predestination and free will. This theme is evident in the theology of *Sirach,* even though his soteriology is quite immanent. The creation theology in Sirach resulted in a major problem as regards the responsibility of man, as we saw in the previous chapter. Sirach attempted to explain both good and evil under the Lordship of God. A world created in pairs was God's creation in every detail. Man is "like clay in the hand of the potter" and is unable to choose his lot (Sirach 33:11-15).

There is naturally the danger that a creation theology that is this comprehensive makes God responsible for evil. Sirach, however, does not accept such determinism. According to Sirach, sin is always the responsibility of man himself. "Do not say, 'It was the Lord's doing that I fell away'; for he does not do what he hates" (Sirach 15:11).[69]

---

[68] Several scholars regard synergism as a central feature in Jewish soteriology, see Gundry, *Bib 66* (1985) 36; Laato, *Paulus,* 210; Hagner, *BBR 3* (1993) 122.

[69] Cf. Marböck, *Weisheit,* 139-142.

Thereafter the problem of determinism is solved by positing creation as a premise. Man was created responsible in this world. "When in the beginning God created the human race, he left them free to take their own decisions (διαβούλιον): if you choose, you can observe the commandments; you can keep faith if you are so minded" (Sirach 15:14-15).[70]

In the theology of Sirach the keeping of the commandments becomes identified with the working out of the basic order of creation. Man is expected to observe God's law in everyday life.[71] This has been made possible by the free will of man.[72]

In principle, soteriological synergism is possible only in an eschatological theology. If we speak of being saved and of affecting that salvation, we need to have a concept of judgment. There has to be something by which earthly life is to be assessed. In this sense the exhortation of Sirach which appears in the context of creation theology, is non-eschatological. This is why it resembles rather closely the nomism defined in the theory of covenantal nomism. Man has free will and is capable of fulfilling the purpose of creation in his life. If then death is the end of everything, any concept of judgment or hope must be included in the categories of earthly life.

Accordingly we may note that Adam's fall does not have any significant place in the theology of Sirach. His anthropology is dependent on creation, and it is quite optimistic. "Discretion (διαβούλιον) and tongue and eyes, ears and a mind for thinking he gave them. He filled them with knowledge and understanding, and showed them good and evil" (Sirach 17:6-7). This means that even the knowledge of good and evil is understood in a positive sense. It is a condition of being able to make moral judgments.[73]

This kind of nomism rests naturally on the teaching of the books of Moses, and of Deuteronomy in particular. And this is also the Scripture which Sirach uses in this connection. "He has placed before you fire and water; stretch out your hand for whichever you choose. Before each person are life and death, and whichever one chooses will be given" (15:16-17). These allusions remind one of the blessings dependent on the keeping of the law (Deut. 30).[74]

This passage in Deuteronomy begins with a promise:

---

[70] Cf. Prato, *Teodicea*, 385.

[71] See the thorough analysis of Maier, *Mensch und freier Wille*, 93-94.

[72] See Skehan-DiLella, *Ben-Sira*, 271; cf. Laato, *Paulus*, 83, 91.

[73] Cf. Skehan-DiLella, *Ben-Sira*, 282. Concerning the ethical dimension, Schnabel, *Law and Wisdom*, 82-83.

[74] See Hengel, *Judentum*, 255.

"When all these things have happened to you, the blessings and the curses that I have set before you, if you call them to mind among all the nations where the Lord your God has driven you, and return to the Lord your God, and you and your children obey him with all your heart and with all your soul, just as I am commanding you today, then the Lord your God will restore your fortunes and have compassion on you..." (Deut. 30:1-3).

Writing after the Exile, Sirach desired to bring people back to their Lord and make them keep his commandments, in order to inherit the promised restoration.

These verses in Deuteronomy were significant indeed for Sirach. He also quotes some later clauses in the same chapter. "See, I have set before you today life and prosperity, death and adversity. If you obey the commandments of the Lord your God... then you shall live" (Deut. 30:15-16). A choice between life and death, according to Sirach, was possible on the grounds of free will. This is why men could live a righteous life if they so wished. Ungodly people had chosen death instead of life. This made them guilty without excuse.[75]

One of the evident consequences of the anthropology of Sirach is that no man is hopelessly bound to sin. A condition for free will is responsibility. This is especially emphasized by the writer. "He has not commanded anyone to be wicked, and he has not given anyone permission to sin" (15:20). Men have no doubt resisted God, but as a result of pride (10:12) and hypocrisy (1:25-30).[76]

Ben Sira's theology of free will gives hope to the righteous, as well as to fallen Israelites. Even though the wrath of God is at hand, everyone can return to God and find mercy. This is what Sirach explicitly proclaims. "Turn back to the Lord and forsake "your sins; pray in his presence and lessen your offence" (17:25). "Have you sinned, my child? Do so no more, but ask forgiveness for your past sins... Those who hate reproof walk in the sinner's steps, but those who fear the Lord repent in their heart" (21:1, 6).[77]

Besides these strong nomistic clauses we must remember that, in synergism, God's mercy and forgiveness are freely offered to every repentant person. Returning to God was only possible because of God's compassion. Sirach expresses this as follows: "You who fear the Lord, wait for his mercy... For the Lord is compassionate and merciful; he forgives sins and saves in time of distress"(Sirach 2:7, 11).

If creation extends to all things, we unavoidably seem to arrive at a certain

---

[75] Skehan-DiLella, *Ben-Sira,* 272. According to Hengel, Sirach must have criticized some kind of deterministic ideology, such as astrology, which was popular in Jerusalem at that time. Hengel, *Judentum,* 255.

[76] Sirach does not question here man's ability to be obedient. Maier, *Mensch und freier Wille,* 105.

[77] Cf. DiLella, *ABD VI* (1992) 942.

determinism, which would be in disagreement with the idea of free will.[78] This problem has led to voluntarism, the teaching that in the creation God also gave man will-power. In this case the judgments of the free will would in a sense be produced by God.[79] The problem itself, however, does not need to be as difficult as depicted here. In a philosophical sense, a scholar can naturally claim that, in theory, predetermination excludes any possibility of free choice.[80] But then we must admit that, in the theology of Sirach, we do not find such a polarity. There is a distinction between determinism and predestination.

In Sirach the theology of free will is actually a solution to the problem of theodicy – and as such it avoids the danger of determinism. Sirach thinks that God created everything in pairs, but men have been left "free to take their own decisions". Creation theology does not result in determinism or a concept of double predestination. Creation is rather the basis for free will. According to Sirach, man as a creature is autonomous. He has not been given "permission" to sin.[81]

Anthropology is of prime importance in the theology of Sirach. There is no philosophical contradiction between free will and predestination. Anthropology solves every problem by placing certain conditions on soteriology. Predestination concerns the ungodly, but Sirach is speaking of a conditional predestination. We might equally call it *prospective predestination*. If man sins, he will be under God's wrath. If he repents and becomes obedient to the law, his end will be good.

In the immanent soteriology of Ben Sira the hope of the righteous concerned this life and the good reputation of the pious one. The book of Sirach itself is a good example of the development of eschatological soteriology in the Second Temple period. In the stage of the Greek redaction the theology of free will

---

[78] Murphy thinks that Sirach does not even make an attempt to solve this problem. It seems, however, that he does not follow the logic of Sirach far enough. Murphy, *Tree of Life,* 75. G. von Rad is content with assuming that the problem will be solved by Sirach's ambivalent concept of the nature of things: even evil becomes good eventually, and men can interpret God's just acts as negative in different situations; von Rad, *Wisdom,* 253-254. This remark hardly covers the whole theology of Sirach.

[79] In this way Winston, *Wisdom,* 48, 57. His explanation is based on a comparison with Stoic determinism.

[80] In this sense some scholars have said, especially in respect to Qumran texts, that there is a philosophical contradiction between the themes of free will and predestination. Ringgren, *Faith,* 74; Merrill, *Predestination,* 42. This question will be dealt with in detail in chapter 5.

[81] Against Sanders, who constantly maintains that, in Jewish piety, "God's grace preceded the requirement of obedience". Sanders, *Judaism,* 275. In his explanation anthropology is not given due importance.

was set in an eschatological soteriology. This is how the Greek version of
Sirach became a watershed in the theology of its time. Its soteriology is an
early example of the synergistic concept of salvation.[82]

It is also possible that we are witnessing here the very birth of soteriological
synergism. In the context of eschatology the theology of free will becomes a
part of soteriology. According to sapiential anthropology, synergism means
simply that by exercising his free will man affects his eschatological future, i.e.
salvation. Synergism, in the very best sense of the word, is the result of
joining together sapiential anthropology and eschatological soteriology.

In this sense predestination is a matter of consequence. The simple pattern of
sin-punishment is valid for both this life and the coming day of judgment. The
life of an individual is not deterministic, however. This is where the idea of
free will comes in. Man has not been permanently predetermined to be under
the power of good or evil. This is why synergism is almost the only means by
which a sinner can be offered a new chance of salvation. Only repentance and
new obedience can free men from the prescribed judgment.

In later literature we can see the influence of Sirach and its eschatological
synergism, especially in the *Wisdom of Solomon*. In this text wisdom means
keeping the commandments, and it results in eternal life. "The beginning of
wisdom is the most sincere desire for instruction, and concern for instruction is
love of her, and love of her is the keeping of her laws, and giving heed to her
laws is assurance of immortality, and immortality brings one near to God"
(Wisd. 6:17-19). Salvation is bound up with the keeping of the law, because
this is the main purpose of sapiential parenesis.[83]

The hope of salvation is, in this document too, based on repentance: "you
have filled your children with good hope, because you give repentance for
sins" (12:19). Determinism can be avoided by emphasizing that God leaves
former sins unpunished. "But you are merciful to all, for you can do all things,
and you overlook people's sins, so that they may repent" (11:23).

Furthermore, we meet the problem of theodicy in the brief passages in
Josephus where the teaching of the *Pharisaic movement* is presented.[84] He
writes about Pharisaic soteriology as follows:

"[T]he Pharisees, who are considered the most accurate interpreters of the laws, and hold the
position of the leading sect, attribute everything to Fate and to God; they hold that to act

---

[82] What is meant here is the question of the relationship between the Hebrew Sirach and
the Greek translation. This has been discussed above. See DiLella, *ABD VI* (1992), 943;
Skehan-DiLella, *Ben Sira*, 86.

[83] On the soteriology of the Wisdom of Solomon, see Winston, *Wisdom,* 46ff.

[84] Sources are assessed e.g. in Nickelsburg-Stone, *Faith and Piety*, 25ff. A general
overview in Jeremias, *Jerusalem*, 246-267; Bruce, *New Testament History*, 69ff.

rightly or otherwise rests, indeed, for the most part with men, but that in each action Fate co-operates. Every soul, they maintain, is imperishable, but the soul of the good alone passes into another body, while the souls of the wicked suffer eternal punishment" (Jos. Bell. 2.162-163).

The Pharisees, at least according to Josephus, carefully defined the relationship between man's free will and fate, the deterministic destiny of man.[85] They solved this problem by emphasizing the omnipotent Lordship of God. The problem of theodicy, however, was solved in a different way. Here they followed the sapiential tradition by underlining man's responsibility. Evil gains power in this world, but only when men abandon the observance of the law. This is why sinners must renounce evil and commit themselves to the observance of God's precepts.[86]

"Though they postulate that everything is brought about by fate, still they do not deprive the human will of the pursuit of what is in man's power, since it was God's good pleasure that there should be a fusion and that the will of man with his virtue and vice should be admitted to the council-chamber of fate. They believe that souls have power to survive death and that there are rewards and punishments under the earth for those who have led lives of virtue or vice: eternal imprisonment is the lot of evil souls, while the good souls receive an easy passage to a new life" (Jos. Ant. 18.12-15).

The Pharisees seem to have accepted the soteriological dualism which is so typical of the theology of the Second Temple period. Trust in circumcision and the Jewish tradition did not suffice for them, either, as regards the securing of salvation for Israel. Neither could one place one's hope solely in the service of the Temple in this respect. Salvation was provided only for those who had lived by "virtuous conduct". Evil souls were to enter eternal damnation.[87]

At this moment we must note that in Jewish theology the concept of predestination and the problem of free will differ from the teachings of modern theology. The Jewish concept is based on the idea that God has predetermined a future for men who act in a certain way. If one is unfaithful to God, one will face God's punishment. It is prescribed for him in an unconditional way. God is just and he will punish all ungodly people.

According to sapiential theology, the ungodly have not, however, been

---

[85] Saldarini, *Pharisees,* 116, 121; Stemberger, *Jewish Contemporaries,* 68-69.

[86] Josephus is right, as Hengel writes, when he says that the basic difference between the Essenes and the Pharisees is in their attitude to the (deterministic) power of fate. Jos. Ant. 13.172. See Hengel, *Judentum,* 398.

[87] This has also been noted by Saldarini. "The Pharisees probably held positions on eschatology, divine providence, and human responsibility which were different enough from traditional Jewish teachings... In this the Pharisees were not unusual, as the great diversity of outlook in Second Temple apocryphal and pseudepigraphical literature shows." Saldarini, *ABD V* (1992) 302. As we have seen above, we do not need to restrict their views even to apocryphal literature.

predetermined to eternal damnation. Sinners have themselves brought about their fate by abandoning the Lord and his commandments. In this pattern, predestination is not the opposite of the theology of free will, but rather a necessary addition to it. If one has been unfaithful, instead of being obedient by free choice, one will face the appropriate punishment.[88]

This is why the Jewish concept of predestination is not totally deterministic in the sense that man is unable to alter his future. In practice all people have the opportunity to repent and live in obedience. In this they are helped by the mercy of God, which is an inseparable part of synergistic soteriology. The choice of free will and an obedient life could never save man, without resorting to the grace of God.

The development of predestinarian theology also reflects some processes which were in progress in the Second Temple period. Firstly, the theology has been seen to change from theocentricism to anthropocentricism.[89] Apparently in this connection we can also speak of a change in focus from cult to Torah, and from ceremonies to morals.[90] As a common feature behind these processes there is the growth of individualism and the emergence of a soteriological anthropology. These traits, in turn, are related to the rise of eschatology, which is one of the most obvious features of that period.[91]

The theme of acute crisis remained in the centre of theology for both political and cultural reasons. It created a situation which can be described in several ways. In addition to certain changes and developments in Second Temple Jewish theology, we can detect a dynamic process between reactive separation and gradual assimilation. The Jewish élite were usually pressured to conform to the political changes in the country. At the same time, however, they jealously endeavoured to maintain their restricted power in religious affairs. On the other hand, the religious counter-reaction, such as sapiential theology, also contained features from the opposing ideology. Assimilation had taken place gradually over a long period.[92]

In the midst of such a dynamic process the answer to the problem of theodicy, too, found several forms of expression. At the end of the period of

---

[88] Westerholm remarks that even though Judaism was not a legalistic religion in a self-confident sense, the law was in any case considered a way to life. The Jewish concept of salvation always left room for man's own actions and also expected some action to be taken. Westerholm, *Law,* 142, 147,148.

[89] Crenshaw, *Theodicy,* 5.

[90] In this way, Scott, *EQ 64* (1992) 201; cf. Saldarini, *Pharisees,* 303.

[91] These features are important to Hengel, *Judentum,* 369.

[92] The idea of assimilation was important in Hengel's study of the influence of Hellenism in Israel: "*auch das palästinische Judentum als 'hellenistisches' Judentum bezeichnet werden muss*". Hengel, *Judentum,* 459 (italics his); cf. pp. 561-563.

the kings, theologians were afraid that Almighty God had abandoned his chosen people. Later in sapiential theology, teachers of the law believed that constant obedience would certainly lead Israel back to a harmonious unity with the Creator of the world and the giver of the Torah. The response of sapiential theology to the crisis was in this sense a "theology of survival".[93]

Synergistic nomism is a characteristic feature of sapiential theology. It is based on the concept of free will. Israel was living in sin, at least this was frequently the case, but there was a remedy provided. Every sinner had an opportunity to repent and return to his God. Here we are actually talking about returning to God's grace or, one might remark, against Sanders, "getting in" the covenant. Already in sapiential eschatology, however, we find features of soteriological dualism. The keeping of the law led directly to salvation. In this sense the categories of "getting in" the covenant and "staying in" the covenant are not distinct categories in soteriology. In the context of predestinarian theology, repentance and returning to the covenant were crucial events as regards salvation.

---

[93] Cf. Crenshaw, *Wisdom,* 149f.

Excursus: The Theory of Covenantal Nomism

When we survey the discussion of Pauline soteriology over the last two decades we must acknowledge the unique status of E.P. Sanders' theory of "covenantal nomism". He has inspired an enormous amount of research and almost no writer dares to publish a study without commenting on his work. Sanders' theory was basically a thesis about the nature of the soteriology of Second Temple Judaism.[1]

The criticism that Sanders directed against many New Testament scholars was that Judaism had been wrongly regarded as a legalistic religion, as we have seen above.[2] Sanders shifted the emphasis to covenantal religion and the mercy of God. This critique concerned Protestant, primarily Lutheran, Biblical criticism.[3]

The debate over soteriology has been animated ever since but it has, nevertheless, almost totally lacked an antithesis. Corrections have been made to the theory of covenantal nomism but the idea has been accepted quite generally. This results in the danger of Sanders' contribution remaining unfruitful in the long run. It is due time for a reassessment of the theory. We must ask afresh: is Sanders doing justice to the texts we know from the Second Temple period?

In his book *Paul and Palestinian Judaism* Sanders analysed the soteriological structure of Judaism – working back from the Mishnah and Talmud – and came to the conclusion that its theology was covenantal. Jewish writers and teachers did not expect to gain salvation on the basis of their deeds. Only God could give salvation. Thus nomism, too, had to be understood in terms of this structure.[4]

As regards Paul, Sanders thought that he had known Judaism as covenantal nomism. In his soteriology Paul naturally changed the basis of salvation, which could come only through Christ, but he did not alter the concept of covenantal nomism.[5] In Pauline studies the conclusions reached by other scholars did not always follow Sanders. Since Paul is obviously speaking of

---

[1] Evaluations and reviews of this theory have been numerous, see e.g. Caird, *JTS 29* (1978) 538-543; Cooper, *WTJ 44* (1982) 123-139; Garnet, *Pauline Studies,* 19-32; Gundry, *Bib 66* (1985) 1-38; Hooker, *Paul and Paulinism,* 47-56; McNamara, *JSNT 5* (1979) 67-73; Moo, *STJ 40* (1987) 287-307; Murphy-O'Connor, RB 85 (1978) 122-126; Moule, *Tradition,* 43-52; Saldarini, *JBL 98* (1979) 299-303.

[2] See the general presentation of Sanders in chapter 2.5.

[3] This feature, which we have already noted, is only natural, since mainstream scholarship in the field was primarily German.

[4] Sanders, *Paul,* 422ff.

[5] Sanders, *Paul,* 497, 514, 552.

the self-righteousness of the Jews, there must be something strange in his thinking. Is his teaching consistent with Jewish covenantal nomism, or is he actually giving a distorted picture instead? Some scholars arrived at the latter conclusion.[6]

By its very nature, covenantal nomism is a sociological theory. It is based on a dichotomy between two sociological categories which are called practically the aspects of "getting in" and "staying in". These terms concern the conditions of "getting into" a group and "staying in" it.[7]

"A pattern of religion, defined positively, is the description of how a religion is perceived by its adherents to function. 'Perceived to function' has the sense not of what an adherent does on a day-to-day basis, but of how getting in and staying in are understood: the way in which a religion is understood to admit and retain members is considered to be the way it 'functions'... A pattern of religion thus has largely to do with the items which a systematic theology classifies under 'soteriology'."

A critical examination of the theory of covenantal nomism is necessary if we wish to gain a clear picture of Sanders' main ideas. Covenantal nomism means for him that the keeping of the law is a response to the mercy and election of God. It takes place within God's covenant. Nomism as such cannot be a condition for "getting in".

Sanders has defined his theory in detail:[8]

"The 'pattern' or 'structure' of covenantal nomism is this: (1) God has chosen Israel and (2) given the law. The law implies both (3) God's promise to maintain the election and (4) the requirement to obey. (5) God rewards obedience and punishes transgression. (6) The law provides for a means of atonement, and atonement results in (7) maintenance or re-establishment of the covenantal relationship. (8) All those who are maintained in the covenant by obedience, atonement and God's mercy belong to the group which will be saved".

We have seen above that Sanders uses sociological concepts when speaking about soteriology. Now these sociological concepts are filled with substance. Covenantal nomism is a sociological key to the understanding of Jewish soteriology.[9] As a starting-point Sanders uses the Old Testament teaching of Israel as a chosen people led by God throughout history.

---

[6] This question will be treated in detail elsewhere, but it deserves to be mentioned here, as well. Unlike Sanders, Räisänen finds the problem even in the theology of Paul. The new approach of Sanders is said to prove Paul's thinking to be inconsistent and intentional (in a negative sense). Räisänen, *Law*, 187. See also above, chapter 2.5.

[7] Sanders, *Paul*, 17.

[8] Sanders, *Paul*, 422.

[9] This methodological problem has been noted e.g. by Saldarini, *JBL 98* (1979) 302, and Gundry, *Bib 66* (1985) 2f. Saldarini remarks that soteriology is not yet sufficient for a total "pattern of religion". This is why Sanders lacks a proper holistic comparison (see p. 300).

This kind of definition is near the ideal presented in the books of Moses. Furthermore, it must resemble, at least to some extent, the ideas concerning the relationship between God and his people that were current in the period of the kings. In this respect Sanders can indeed provide arguments to support his theory. It is also easy to find the words "election" and "covenant" in almost every text in the Second Temple period. One could say that there is a formal justification for covenantal nomism. The "getting in" of the covenantal election seems to precede any possible theology concerning the law.[10]

At the time of the Second Temple period the "normative" religion of Israel, at least the conservative one centred around the temple of Jerusalem, was thus based on some kind of theology of covenantal nomism. Israel was the "elect" of God. Every male child was circumcised eight days after birth. With this election they were members of the people of God, and as they matured they were taught the Torah of God. All this is part of our general knowledge and we do not need to question it. When this kind of ideal was identified with rabbinic Judaism, the theory seemed valid and acceptable.[11]

In this respect there is but one problem in Sanders' theory. According to the knowledge we have from the contemporary sources of Judaism, the religion of Israel was not always eschatological. Salvation had to do more with this day ("that you might live") than the future. There was perhaps the hope of a new paradise on earth, but we must remember that not all adherents of the temple cult even believed in resurrection.

This is why the justification of the theory of covenantal nomism is valid only when the idealized picture of Judaism is considered. When we deal with other sources of Jewish theology where the aspect of "getting in" is questioned, the theory of Sanders runs into problems. We should widen the horizon of Jewish soteriology more than Sanders has done.

When criticizing Sanders' theory we need to note that for the most part the piety of Second Temple Judaism did not resemble the idealistic view of Judaism. Jewish theology was not uniform and the old tradition does not

---

[10] This is perhaps the reason why several modern writers who analyze the Second Temple literature have accepted the theory of covenantal nomism, see Seifrid, *Justification,* 132-133; Winninge, *Sinners and the Righteous,* 2-3, 219.

[11] It is no wonder that Sanders' theory was also accepted by several scholars in the field of Jewish studies, especially as regards research on rabbinic Judaism. This encouraged Räisänen to say that even Sanders' opponents have accepted the basic thrust of his theory, Räisänen, *Jesus, Paul and Torah,* 266. He means especially the disagreement between J. Neusner and Sanders over the nature of rabbinic Judaism. Neusner, too, accepted the theory of covenantal nomism in principle.

explain all the features in the complex reality of post-exilic Israel.[12] We have e.g. the traditions of Wisdom literature (Sirach, Wisdom of Solomon, Baruch), the apocalyptic literature (1 Enoch, Pseudepigraphic Testaments, Sibyllines) and the library of Qumran.[13] Some of these movements were living in strict opposition to the temple. [14]

Even so-called normative Jewish theology was not coherent.[15] Sadducean deuteronomistic theology was covenantal and traditional but our view of e.g. the Pharisaic movement, based on information given by Josephus, is different. This movement had adopted many "sectarian" ideas in its teaching and theology. There is a terminological unity in Second Temple Judaism, due to the Old Testament background and the exilic and post-exilic tradition, but the views of the movements were quite different from each other in detail.[16]

Another feature which one cannot clearly separate from the previous ones is the Hellenization of Judaism in the Second Temple period. Many features in Jewish theology have a counterpart in Greek philosophy. Some themes are in fact taken directly from it, others again are reactions against it. This is best seen in the theology of Philo, but it would be a mistake to limit this merely to the Diaspora. [17]

Texts of the Second Temple period are mainly eschatological in nature. Sanders claims that these texts, too, are based on the general idea of covenantal nomism.[18] We should note, however, that in these texts obedience is usually the criterion and condition for eschatological salvation.

It is no wonder that severe criticism has been levelled at Sanders' one-sided

---

[12] The discussion concerning the diversity of Second Temple Judaism and its theology is presented in Porton, *Early Judaism,* 73.

[13] This is the reason for a negative criticism of Sanders by e.g. Saldarini, *JBL 98* (1979) 302. He mentions especially 1 Enoch and the texts of Qumran.

[14] Collins suspects that Sanders has neglected the aspect of apocalypticism: "Since he begins his study with the rabbinic literature (which is chronologically later), it is difficult to avoid the suspicion that the apocalyptic literature is not being studied in its own right, but only checked for evidence of covenantal nomism." Collins, *Apocalyptic,* 359-360.

[15] Cfr. Talmon, *Jewish Civilization,* 30, 34-35.

[16] We need to remind ourselves here of the analysis by Avemarie. Rabbinic Judaism was not merely a religion of coherent covenantalism, as Sanders has attempted to show. Avemarie, *Tora und Leben,* 34ff., 579-583

[17] We have noted this earlier, see Hengel, *Judentum,* 275ff.; in addition to this see also e.g. Porton, *Early Judaism,* 57f.

[18] Sanders, *Paul,* 423ff.

approach.[19] In fact, another kind of tradition of interpretation has emerged, where the diversity of Second Temple Judaism is emphasized.[20] This explanation usually speaks of "multiple Judaisms" in order to describe truthfully the nature of Jewish theology at that time.[21]

In several Jewish texts salvation is not promised to the circumcised without reservations. It is a little astonishing that Sanders himself has actually said this explicitly, too, as we have seen above: "All those who are maintained in the covenant by obedience... will be saved" (with a reference to the mercy of God, naturally).[22] This is why the question concerning the content of the concept of obedience is a crucial one for our discussion.

It seems evident that Sanders has problems in defining his concept of obedience. He has not been able to explain why covenantal nomism was not legalism. *If legalism means that keeping the law affects eschatological salvation, then covenantal nomism is legalistic nomism by definition.*[23] The reason for this is the fact that his theory does not deny nomism but only gives it a new status.[24]

The result of this is the common theory of synergistic religion. Man's actions, such as keeping the law ('staying in'), affect his salvation. This concept is naturally rooted in the context of covenantal theology. So it is not

---

[19] J.J. Scott, for example, thinks that with his one-sided theory Sanders does injustice to the diversity of intertestamental Judaism. Scott, *EQ 64* (1992) 197-212; especially p. 211; cf. Nickelsburg and Kraft, *Early Judaism,* 20. "Clearly Sanders is justified in criticizing the interpretation that early Judaism was legalistic... Nonetheless, like all harmonizing approaches, his own synthesis obscures the dynamic variety in the documents and material remains that have been preserved for us" (on sapiential theology see p. 21).

[20] This disagreement concerning the diversity can be seen already in early comments on Sanders' theory, see e.g. Garnet, *Pauline Studies,* 20; Gundry, *Bib 66* (1985) 3; Moo, *STJ 40* (1987) 292; Murphy-O'Connor, *RB 85* (1978) 123; Moule, *Tradition,* 48; Saldarini, *JBL 98* (1979) 300. Even Cooper, who accepts Sanders' basic idea, ends up noting that "certain elements of Palestinian Judaism" evidence a re-thinking of this scheme. Cooper, *WTJ 44* (1982) 129; cf. McNamara, *JSNT 5* (1979) 72.

[21] In addition to the references in the notes above, see the general presentation in Overman-Green, *ABD III* (1992) 1038f.

[22] Sanders, *Paul,* 422.

[23] Legalism has not been easy to define in this new "covenantal" tradition of interpretation. For example, Räisänen tries to distinguish between 'hard' and 'soft' legalism – the former denoting conscious self-righteousness and the latter merely neutral Torah observance without boasting. Of these, the latter can be found in Jewish literature, but only in 4 Ezra. Räisänen, *Paulinische Literatur,* 63-64. This distinction by Räisänen is rather a fruitless one, however. Treating legalism merely as an attitude is bound to lead one's reasoning astray.

[24] Sanders, for example, constantly maintains that "the conception of *obedience* is distinctive in the apocalyptic literature" (italics his) without questioning this feature as regards the covenantal idea. Sanders, *Paul,* 424.

legalism alone which brings salvation. In a synergistic religion it is, of course, God who works for the benefit of men. [25]

As a conclusion to the notions outlined above we end up with the following thesis: *In the theory of covenantal nomism Sanders defines a synergistic nomism.* This is why the theory cannot properly deal with the legalistic features of Jewish theology.[26] When examining his theory we must consider how Sanders applies it in the interpretation of individual texts in the Second Temple period.

Sanders' theory seems to imply a strange ambivalence. He uses two syllogisms which are not at all consistent with each other. The first one is used in order to deny legalism and to confirm the idea that the law has no relevance in eschatological salvation. The second one, in turn, talks about the keeping of the law as obedience.

The first syllogism runs as follows:
- the law cannot affect the "getting in"
- salvation is based on election and covenant
- the law is kept only within the covenant
so: the acts of "staying in" do not affect eschatological salvation (Judaism is not a legalistic religion).

The second syllogism also concerns eschatological salvation:
- God expects obedience from his people
- transgressors are punished and they cannot attain salvation
so: keeping the law is necessary for eschatological salvation.

This ambivalence in Sanders' theory becomes evident in the theoretical analysis. Should his theory be regarded as a description of the synergistic nature of Second Temple Jewish soteriology it would be useful. This, however, would result in a need to reassess his claims about the theology of Paul.

Why did Sanders end up with such a concept of covenant? His conception reminds one of a great ontological theory, such as that of the theory of double

---

[25] For example, Cooper, who was "disposed to adopt Sanders' characterization", eventually reached rather critical conclusions. "Judaism laid the law's demand for obedience at the door of each individual." And: "Judaism grounded salvation upon a combination of God's grace in establishing the covenant, and man's response of obedience, repentance." This definition falls undoubtedly in the category of synergism. Cooper, *WTJ 44* (1982) 124, 137; cf. Gundry, *Bib 66* (1985) 36. Concerning the teaching of Qumran, Garnet noted that: "There is no salvation without obedience, even for the members of the covenant". Garnet, *Pauline Studies,* 20.

[26] Moule defined the problem sharply: "I am asking whether 'covenantal nomism' itself is so far from implicit 'legalism'." Moule, *Tradition,* 48.

predestination.[27] This concept is clearly in disagreement with the teaching of the Old Testament. There the concept of covenant is relational. Covenant is a relation and there are conditions by which this covenant is fulfilled.

In Sanders' covenantal religion there is not much room for the seriousness of the law. In sapiential theology and at Qumran, however, obedience to the law is a matter of life and death. It is not merely a matter of polite covenantal symbiosis in mutual loving-kindness.[28]

We can agree with Sanders on many features of Second Temple Judaism. He has rightly pointed out the pious reliance of all the differing groups on the sovereignty of God. What should be reconsidered is the structure of the soteriology of Jewish revivalism, which in turn covers practically all the texts we know from that period. As regards nomism, it was not "covenantal". *Eschatological soteriology was synergistic.*

The ambivalence in Sanders' theory becomes explicit in the fact that despite his underlining of the necessity of obedience he totally denies any legalistic features in Jewish theology. We have stated above that in fact Sanders himself had defined covenantal nomism by making good use of a synergistic element. According to Sanders, obedience was necessary in order to attain salvation. Strictly speaking, we should say that he has never actually even defined pure "covenantal nomism" but a "synergistic nomism".[29]

Also, the methodological starting-point in sociology is open to criticism. As we saw earlier, Sanders was interested in the functioning of a religion: "the way in which a religion is understood to admit and retain members is considered to be the way it 'functions'." [30] As Sanders evaluates religious concepts by their "functioning" in the dynamics of a group, his theory must be called *functional.* "Dogma" has a function in life. Sanders is, however, at the same time speaking about salvation. This reveals the fact that "getting in" has an eschatological context and meaning. Considering this starting-point, we can

---

[27] The similarities between Sanders' theory and Calvinist soteriology, as well as that of dispensationalism, will be analyzed later in an excursus in chapter 14.

[28] Cf. for example Gundry, *Bib 66* (1985) 6; Saldarini, *JBL 98* (1979) 300.

[29] At the end of his book Sanders maintains that it is actually the relationship of grace and works that is in question. Judaism cannot be *merely* casuistic legalism: "the Judaism of before 70 kept grace and works in the right perspective, did not trivialize the commandments of God and was not especially marked by hypocrisy... By consistently maintaining the basic framework of *covenantal nomism,* the gift and demand of God were kept in a healthy relationship with each other, the minutiae of the law were observed on the basis of the large principles of religion..." Sanders, *Paul,* 427. In a systematic analysis this would mean synergism.

[30] Sanders, *Paul,* 17.

make our second statement about his theory: *Sanders believes that soteriology can be understood according to the categories of sociology.*

Sanders has attempted to solve the implicit problem that arises between eschatology and a sociological approach by emphasizing the aspect of function, perhaps in order to make the theory more "abstract". The group of the saved is, however, the same sociological group of the covenant which has been "elected" by circumcision. This idea lies behind the following definition, too:[31]

"A pattern of religion... does have to do with thought, with the understanding that lies behind religious behaviour, not just with the externals of religious behaviour. Thus from cultic practice one may infer that the cult of a given religion was perceived by its adherents to have a certain function in their religious life."

This kind of reasoning is rather problematic, since a sociological method restricts the study of texts so that it becomes one-sided. The themes of soteriology are all analysed by their consistency with "getting in" or "staying in" a group. When a text happens to be talking about eschatological salvation, Sanders' method becomes invalid and fails to recognize the very nature of the text.[32]

The first problem of the theory of covenantal nomism is that it explains the themes of eschatological salvation in sociological categories.[33] We might pose the question, on what grounds would the sociological "staying in" (keeping the law in order to stay in a group) not be an eschatological "getting in" (keeping the law in order to attain salvation) at the same time?

Even before analyzing apocalyptic texts we may remark that in Second Temple theology the judgment of God is said to fall on the people of the covenant. No idealistic view of a covenant can in that situation explain salvation in too simple terms. In the soteriology of Jewish theology most writers do not ask who is "getting in" a group or who is "staying in" it. They ask who will endure the coming judgment of God.[34]

Sanders seems to have used sociological categories because he wishes to explain the status of nomism in Jewish theology in that way. In that case the covenant would be an eschatological concept and the keeping of the law a sociological activity. This, however, is not very consistent with Jewish thinking of the Second Temple period. In Jewish eschatology the law has a

---

[31] Sanders, *Paul*, 18.

[32] This has to do with the methodological problem of Sanders. McNamara says that there is a danger of "over-concentrating on the pattern of religion" and other overtones may thus be lost sight of. "There is more in a religious system than the overall pattern of religion." McNamara, *JSNT* 5 (1979) 72.

[33] Sanders himself says that as regards soteriology, this item is not important, Sanders, *Paul*, 424.

[34] Cf. Garnet, *Pauline Studies*, 20-21.

clear and important eschatological role and it is not merely a sociological factor, as we shall see later.

We could summarize the results of this excursus in a few sentences. Sanders' theory has been inspiring and it has focused the attention of scholars on an important theme. The theory itself has some severe weaknesses, though. The sociological starting-point creates problems as regards soteriology – and soteriology in itself is not yet a "pattern" of religion, as Saldarini has pointed out. There is further a problematic inconsistency in the theory as regards the function of keeping the law. And lastly, the description of Judaism is rather narrow and one-sided. More recognition should be given to the diversity of Second Temple Judaism. As we began by noting that this theory has been left without a detailed antithesis, now is the proper time for one. In the course of this study we shall examine several Jewish texts from the perspective of the discussion presented in this chapter and compare the results with the interpretations which have been made in the context of the theory of covenantal nomism.

§ 4   The Solution of Apocalyptic: The Judgment of God

The theology of crisis was especially significant among apocalyptic movements. Apocalyptic as such did not enter Jewish theology in connection with any distinctive, dramatic historical event. It was a result of a longer development during the Second Temple period.[1] The theology of apocalyptic literature, such as 1 Enoch or Jubilees, is mainly of a traditional Jewish nature. In addition, sapiential insights are common in this tradition. In spite of this we must pay attention to a certain theological radicalism and a new world-view which give these texts quite an original flavour. And lastly, soteriological dualism was strained to the very utmost in these writings.[2]

The problem in formulating a proper definition of Jewish apocalyptic has been an acute one for decades. It is rather difficult to classify texts merely according to some of their individual features, because normally most of the alleged features appear in some form in almost all of Second Temple literature. This does not prevent us from discerning some features of apocalyptic. Rather, it reminds us that the basic nature of apocalyptic is a way of thinking instead of a genre or a pile of key-words.[3]

Jewish apocalyptic in the Second Temple period was part of the tradition of producing theology in a crisis, and there surely was no lack of suitable incidents. Theological comments, made in different historical situations, were characterized by several common themes. In apocalyptic thinking there was a strict dualism between sinners and the righteous. The writers were interested in the fate of both groups and attempted to solve the problem of the relationship between them.

We need to note, however, that apocalyptic was not merely an ideology of doom. The "revealed" message was one of consolation. It was a message of hope. The writers desired to strengthen the faith of the faithful when they encountered crises in their lives.[4]

---

[1] Examples are numerous, beginning with the old section of 1 Enoch (1 Enoch 6-11, which was analyzed earlier in chapter 3.1) all the way to 4 Ezra, which dates from the post-70 period, after the destruction of Jerusalem. Hanson has traced the roots even further back and underlines the connection between apocalyptic and prophetic literature. Hanson, *Apocalyptic,* 9-10.

[2] Especially in the area of apocalyptic studies the problem of theodicy has been considered an important feature of the theology of the period, see e.g. Mundle, *ZAW 47* (1929) 236; Mattern, *Verständnis,* 13; Thompson, *Theodicy,* 296-297; cf. Moore, *Judaism,* 377.

[3] Concerning the definition cf. Collins, *Apocalyptic Imagination,* 4-10; and *ABD I* (1992) 283; Hanson, *Apocalyptic,* 6ff.; a methodological approach is presented by Müller, *TRE III* (1978) 207-210.

[4] "Freilich will auch diese Offenbarung eine Botschaft vermitteln: sie will den

Furthermore, we may note that the theme of God's heavenly rule was prominent in apocalyptic writings. Even though there was a temple in Jerusalem, God did not actually appear to act on the earth. His dwelling is in heaven. Criticism of the Temple was implicit in several writings.[5] In apocalyptic texts, soteriological dualism is not merely historical. God has abandoned Israel, and she lives under God's wrath. Here we can see a significant change in traditional Jewish theology. According to the new message, Israel cannot find a proper connection with God solely through the temple cult.[6]

In several texts world history is divided into periods or aeons. God's actions are seen as deterministic and believed to progress in periods until the end comes.[7] The final aeon is, probably without exception, an age of salvation. Then God will raise the righteous to a new paradise. In many texts this salvation is described in a traditional way as a renewal of the Davidic dynasty.[8] The turning-point of history is the judgment of God, the Day of Wrath. The suffering of the righteous will be avenged and justice will be done. The godless will be sentenced to eternal death.[9]

It is easy to see that many of these features occurred already in the earlier message of the prophets. Afterwards they found their way into sapiential theology. On the other hand, we can say that none of these features can be found in the entire corpus of Second Temple literature. Some of the theology was centred around the Temple. Messianic expectations include a variety of emphases as well. Some of the hopes entertained in this area were of quite a political and "earthly" nature. This did not, however, always imply a devaluation of eschatology.[10]

Glaubensmut der Frommen in schweren Zeiten stärken (zB Dan in der Verfolgung unter Antiochus IV., 4Esr nach dem Fall Jerusalems)." Ringgren, *RGG I* ([3]1986) 465.

[5] Transcendent features are already evident in 1 Enoch, but in the Testaments of the Twelve Patriarchs (TLev. 18) they find their clearest expressions. In the texts from Qumran criticism of the Temple took its sharpest form, see 1QpHab VIII,8-13; IX,4-6; 1QS IX, 3-6.

[6] The wrath of God is a theme which grows out of the strict dualism of apocalyptic writings. On the dualistic nature of the soteriology of these texts see Collins, *Dead Sea Sect*, 34. The respective texts include Jubilees 22-23 and 36; cf. 1 Enoch 94-102.

[7] Several texts, such as Jubilees and 1 Enoch, divide history into periods and aeons. On determinism, see Ringgren, *RGG I* ([3]1986) 465.

[8] For example, in the Testament of Levi the appearance of a messianic priest is described in the context of cosmic dualism (TLev. 18:10-11). The allegedly Christian nature of this text is under discussion, however (see the analysis in chapter 4.4.).

[9] Descriptions of judgment are prominent material in apocalyptic literature. See 1 Enoch 98:8-16; SibOr. 3, 670-700; 741-750; 4 Ezra 7:60; 9:15-25. These texts will be treated in detail later.

[10] The definition of apocalyptic has been under discussion for a long time. Some of the

When attempting to define apocalyptic we could well follow Collins, who introduced the idea of "apocalyptic imagination". We are really facing an ideology which in one way or another had influenced and fertilized a wide variety of beliefs and traditions in different contexts.[11]

4.1. The desecration of the Temple

Many of the concrete historical events and crises of Israel which were commented upon in apocalyptic, were quite dramatic in character. A special place in this gallery of horrors was assigned to Antiochus IV Epiphanes. His oppression gave birth to a crisis which was one of the most shocking experiences in the entire history of the nation.

Antiochus plundered the Temple in 167. He also prohibited the performing of the sacrifices. According to Josephus, the Temple remained desolate for three years. Only after Judah had conquered the troops of Antiochus, was the Temple re-consecrated in 164 BC. Menelaus was the reigning high priest according to the proper succession. The successor of Antiochus, Antiochus Eupator, secured his death, however, and in his stead (in 161) appointed Alcimus, who was not even a member of a priestly family.[12]

In Daniel we can see shocked reactions to the siege of Antiochus. The king of Syria desecrates the Temple and sets up an idol, "the abomination that makes desolate".[13] He also seduces covenant-breakers into committing apostasy and forces them join him. The righteous, in turn, suffer captivity and having their goods plundered (Dan. 11:31-33). There is hope for the persecuted, however. God will grant his help, and Michael, the great prince, will arise to bring deliverance to Israel (12:1-3).[14]

In 1 Enoch the attack that is commented on in the Dream Visions ("animal visions") in chapters 85-90, is most evidently that of Antiochus. The identification of the hero is uncertain, naturally, but the "great horn" that

---

main features of this discussion can be read in an article by Sanders, written for a symposium on this theme, Sanders, *Apocalypticism,* 447f., 458. Even though the subject is a difficult one, it should not lead to the basic aim being abandoned. Sanders did not relinguish the attempt in frustration, but placed apocalyptic literature in a context where the hope of the restoration of Israel was steadfast.

[11] See Collins, *Apocalyptic Imagination,* 28.

[12] Jos. Ant. 12.248-256, 319, 386; Avi-Yonah, *Hasmonean Revolt,* 171-174; Schiffman, *From Text to Tradition,* 76-77.

[13] Cf. 1 Macc. 1:41-54; 2 Macc. 6:5; Jos. Ant. 12.253; Collins, *Daniel,* 384-385; Whitehorne, *ABD I* (1992) 270.

[14] See Nickelsburg - Stone, *Faith and Piety,* 126-127.

sprouts could be Judah the Maccabee (1 Enoch 90:9).[15] This vision ends in a typical way with a description of God's judgment (90:20ff.).

In Jubilees, Antiochus is not directly criticised, but it seems that most of his acts of oppression are mentioned and the writer opposes them vigorously. The writer condemns the people's breaking of the covenant and their idolatry. He further admonishes the Jews for obeying the restrictions which Antiochus had prescribed. The most glaring of these was the prohibition of circumcision. Here the writer of Jubilees declares his severe condemnation.[16] His condemnation is directed both against the tyrant who issued the order and against those Jews who had left their children uncircumcised. Their fate is considered hopeless – even more hopeless than in traditional sapiential theology. They have made themselves "like the Gentiles". There is therefore "for them no forgiveness or pardon so that they might be pardoned and forgiven from all of the sins of this eternal error." All that is left is the "great wrath from the Lord" (Jubilees 15:33-34).

Soteriological dualism plays a significant role in the book of Jubilees. The names of those who break the covenant will be wiped out of the heavenly books and they will be treated as enemies. This threat is a warning to the righteous, who must keep the law and refrain from sin (Jubilees 30:21-23). In Jubilees, as well as in 1 Enoch, the seriousness of eschatology is especially underlined.[17]

"In those days, they will cry out and call and pray to be saved from the hand of the sinners, the gentiles, but there will be none who will be saved... And in those days, children will begin to search the law, and to search the commandments and to return to the way of righteousness... And then the Lord will heal his servants, and they will rise up and see great peace. And they will drive out their enemies, and the righteous ones will see and give praise, and rejoice forever and ever with joy" (Jubilees 23:24, 26, 30).

The Damascus Document (CD), a Qumranic and possibly a more broadly Essene writing, also preserves some reactions to the attack by Antiochus IV. The interpretation of the writer holds even here to the tradition of the theology of theodicy. The time of Antiochus was a time of wrath when God was punishing Israel for its sins (CD I, 7-11).[18]

---

[15] So e.g. Müller, *TRE III* (1978) 213.

[16] Cf. 1 Macc. 1:48. It is related that, during his expeditions, the rebel Mattathias forcibly circumcised all the uncircumcised male children he could find. 1 Macc. 2:64.

[17] Jubilees 23:24–30. According to Nickelsburg, this passage about the time of Antiochus has a clear pattern: sin, punishment, turning-point and salvation. See Nickelsburg, *Literature,* 77.

[18] In this way Jeremias, *Lehrer der Gerechtigkeit,* 159; the discussion of earlier decades is described on pp. 151-166. In modern scholarship this perspective has not been totally abandoned. See Davies, *Damascus Covenant,* 61-69, especially p. 67.

Antiochus Epiphanes' fierce attack soon met with stiff resistance. This was the beginning of the Maccabean revolt, to which the Hasmoneans responded with all their military might. The Maccabees were fighting to protect the land of their fathers and the faith of Israel (1 Macc. 2:39-48). The theological interpretation given by the writer of 1 Maccabees here too contains all the features of a theodicy. The fate of those who had suffered as martyrs under the oppression was interpreted eschatologically.

This eschatological answer to the problem of theodicy was centred on hope and restoration. In this the martyrs had a key role to play. According to the writers, God would raise them from the dead and grant them a new life. Their persecutors would be destroyed, and nothing awaited them but God's wrath.[19] These were the roots from which the eschatological theology of martyrdom was eventually developed into the concept of an apocalyptic holy war.[20]

Under the persecution of Antiochus Epiphanes the eschatological soteriology in Jewish theology was polarized into a strict dualism, a true apocalyptic. The problem of theodicy was alive because of the rule of godless tyrants. A solution to this difficult problem was found now even more clearly than previously in the coming judgment of God. Israel had sinned and would face the punishment of God in history. But this was only the beginning. God's final word and the real judgment would fall on the oppressors and the kings who had defiled the Temple. In the last day God would avenge all injustice and bring forth righteousness. This is why the hope of the persecuted was placed in God's renewing mercy. The martyrs would be resurrected and obtain their reward in the glory of heaven.

4.2. *The decline of the Hasmoneans*

After the Hasmonean counter-offensive the situation in Israel was an altered one. In order to understand the tensions between different groups we must remember how political power had been distributed both in society and in the Temple. After Alcimus' death the priesthood was probably given to Judas Maccabaeus (Jos. Ant. 12.414). He was not officially authorized, though, since, according to Josephus, the Temple had to function without a high priest for 7-8 years. In these uncertain circumstances the priesthood began to slide into the hands of the Hasmoneans.[21]

---

[19] So in 2 Macc. 7:9-19; about the raising of the persecuted cf. SapSol. 2:19-20; 4:7-11; 5:15-16; Nickelsburg, *Resurrection,* 48f.; Nickelsburg - Stone, *Faith and Piety,* 117, 131ff.

[20] The idea of a holy war was also important in the Zealot movement. Hengel, *Zealots,* 271ff., especially 273. Further it had a prominent role in the texts of Qumran, which will be analysed below (see 5.3.).

[21] See Rajak, *ABD III* (1992) 68.

At this time the high priest was appointed by the Seleucid ruler. So Judah's brother, Jonathan, received the priesthood from Alexander Balan in 152 BC. Even though Jonathan was not a member of a priestly family, he was appointed high priest with great ceremony.[22]

Eventually the priesthood underwent a dramatic change when Simon, the brother of Jonathan, was installed in office in 143 BC. He acted both as an ethnarch and as high priest. In Simon's time there was a degree of independence in the country, and as 1 Maccabees puts it: "The yoke of the Gentiles was removed from Israel, and the people began to write in their documents and contracts, 'In the first year of Simon the great high priest and commander and leader of the Jews'" (1 Macc. 13:41-42).[23]

With the help of priests and leading members of society Simon ordered a decree to be written, giving the high priesthood to the Hasmoneans, i.e. the sons of Simon. This decree "on bronze tablets" was placed on pillars on Mount Zion. The rejection of this decree was declared a criminal offence: "Whoever acts contrary to these decisions or rejects any of them shall be liable to punishment" (1 Macc. 14:30-39).[24]

The change in the priesthood is of importance for our attempt to understand the theology of crisis. It created and established strong tensions within Jewish society. We would automatically have expected that in spite of the admiration there was also negative criticism of the Hasmoneans in Israel. Without the discovery of the texts of Qumran, however, we would never have known the extent and severity of this opposition.[25]

The incidents described above were most probably reasons why the now famous Teacher of Righteousness headed for a conflict with most of the Temple priests. And this was to lead to the founding of the community at

---

[22] Jos. Ant. 13.46.; Klausner, *Hasmonean rulers*, 183-185. Jeremias remarks that "the Hasmoneans had not even a claim to full membership of a priestly course, not to mention the title of high priest." Jeremias, *Jerusalem*, 189.

[23] Rajak, *ABD III* (1992) 69; Bruce, *New Testament History,* 5f.

[24] Schürer, *History I,* 189-195.

[25] Several groups opposed the Hasmoneans and in this sense the crisis shown by the Qumran texts is merely one example. Cf. Schiffman: "Opposition to the Hasmonean house came from a variety of corners. First, they had never made peace with remnants of the old-line Hellenizers among the landed aristocracy. Second, the Pharisees... opposed the concentration in Hasmonean hands of both temporal and religious power... Third, other groups, whose point of view is represented in some of the Dead Sea Scrolls, accepted the legitimacy of the Hasmoneans as high priests but condemned them for also holding political power." Schiffman, *From Text to Tradition,* 102; see also Fischer, *ABD IV* (1992) 439ff.

Qumran.[26] In the texts of Qumran the Zadokite priesthood is held in great honour, and it is evident that precisely this high-priestly lineage had been displaced by Hasmonean rule. It is no wonder that in the Qumran texts the new priesthood in Jerusalem was considered godless, and conservative Jews (Essenes) had totally withdrawn from it.

In the texts of Qumran we find a conflict which had confronted the Teacher of Righteousness in the Temple. It is often quite difficult to explain the texts, since the persons involved are not directly identified. We may conclude, however, that the "Wicked Priest" who opposed the Teacher of Righteousness was the high priest in Jerusalem around the year 150 BC.[27] The Teacher of Righteousness himself must have been a prominent member of the group of the chief priests.

The conflict itself is documented rather clearly in the commentary on Habakkuk: [They] "did not help him against the Man of Lies, *Blank* who rejected the Law in the midst of their whole Community" (1QpHab. V, 11-12, Martínez).[28] There was disagreement over interpretation of the law. This can be concluded from other Qumran sources, as well. The matter on which there was disagreement was under discussion in the council, i.e. the Sanhedrin, which was the proper place for adjudging such a quarrel.

The situation of the Teacher of Righteousness was a rather hopeless one, according to the documents. He was left practically alone among the leading priests. In the Temple there was a group of other priests, however, who sympathized with his views and joined him. The earliest documents of the Qumran group give the impression that in the earliest days the community consisted mainly of priests. A controversy concerning the application of the law thus resulted in a division among the Temple priests.

The interpretation by the Qumran community of the situation into which it

---

[26] "Der Hohepriester Jonathan suchte erneut mit den gottlosen Seleukiden engere Verbindungen zu knüpfen. Die Essener waren diesen Bestrebungen gegenüber der Meinung, dass nur die rigorose Scheidung von allem gottlosen Wesen der nahen Heilszeit gerecht werden könnte." Hengel, *Judentum,* 414.

[27] The dating is rather difficult due to the lack of detailed information. Arguing from the content, Jeremias identifies the actual opponent of the Teacher of Righteousness with Jonathan, and dates the incident to 153-143 BC. Jeremias, *Lehrer der Gerechtigkeit,* 75-76. Cross, in turn, suggested Simon instead, since his biographical details seem to fit some features in the Qumran texts. Cross, *Qumran,* 115.

[28] On the commentary on Habakkuk in general, see VanderKam, *Dead Sea Scrolls,* 46-48. The famous document 4QMMT (4Q394-399) has been connected with the incident in question. This letter contains several questions concerning proper interpretation of the law and aims at restoring tradition in the Temple of Jerusalem. This question is treated in detail below, see 10.3. I have here accepted the identification of the Wicked Priest with the Man of Lies, cf. discussion in Collins, *ABD II* (1992) 98.

had been driven, followed eschatological and apocalyptic lines. There is a very strict soteriological dualism in the texts. The righteous ones of Qumran were convinced that the Temple had been left in the hands of godless apostates. This conviction resulted in a polarization. The Temple had been desecrated. Now it was the task of the remnant to build a new temple.[29] According to the texts, the community was in the wilderness "preparing a way for the Lord" and gathering together those left untainted in the age of temptation.[30]

This historical situation must be the reason why soteriological dualism, which elsewhere, too, was produced by attempting to solve the problem of theodicy, was so strict at Qumran. Israel was divided into two groups, the children of light and the children of darkness. The godless were ruling in the Temple, but in reality they were already living under God's wrath – and judgment was prepared for them. Ultimately God was in control.

The basis of this dualism was creation theology, and so it was of a cosmic nature. On the other hand, in practice this concept was applied in a rather ambivalent way. This ambivalence will be treated in detail below.[31]

The concept of a holy war, which had been emerging in the time of the Maccabees, was quite clear at Qumran. The solution may have been military because the very problem, i.e. doubting God's power, had arisen due to the mental agony experienced in the face of military invasions by foreign armies. The theology of theodicy found its climax in the concept of an eschatological war, and the Dead Sea Sect was making preparations for such a war. The pattern as such, of course, was familiar from the writings of the prophets of the Exile.[32]

The Temple continued to function in Jerusalem, despite such incidents. Some priests had become rebellious, but others had accepted a non-eschatological interpretation of Jewish tradition. Our information on the Sadducees, for example, tells us that they endeavoured to strike a balance between pragmatic accommodation and conservative preservation of the tradition. The group probably embraced the Zadokite priesthood, but in spite of this they did not react to the change in the high priesthood. From some sporadic information we

---

[29] See 1QS VIII, 6-8. A detailed analysis below in chapter 5.3. On the religious nature of the community see Gärtner, *Temple*, 4-10; Black, *Scrolls*, 194.

[30] 1QS VIII, 14-15; 1QM.

[31] Dualism is discussed in Osten-Sacken, *Gott und Belial*, 85, 116ff.,170-174; Ringgren, *Faith*, 68ff.; Cross, *Qumran*, 83; Hengel, *Qumrân*, 355. The soteriology of the community and tensions within the dualistic pattern will be analyzed in chapter 5.

[32] This soon becomes evident when one reads the War Scroll, see 1QM I, 1ff. Cf. Osten-Sacken, *Gott und Belial*, 84-86.

know that the Sadducean party had been Hellenized and accepted most of the views of their foreign rulers.[33]

Due to their rigid conservatism, the Sadducees were careful to preserve tradition.[34] This is why the books of Moses were given primacy. They represented "real" Judaism which was free from later interpretations. The so-called eschatology of the Sadducees was immanent in character. The religion of Israel was centred around the Temple. The doctrine of resurrection was pure apocalyptic, and as such could not be accepted. This is a feature of Sadducean theology which both the New Testament and other Jewish literature are acquainted with.[35] In this respect it is easy to understand why predestinarian theology did not bother the Sadducees. According to Josephus, they claimed that God is not interested in whether men do good or evil. The choice was left to man himself (Jos. Bell. 2.164-166).

A prominent example of the theology of the Hasmonean period is the community of Qumran. Its assessment of Israel as regards the keeping of the law, was rather harsh. The problem of theodicy which clearly directed the thoughts of the community, led to a soteriological dualism. The group became exclusive, and the righteous ones of Qumran considered themselves the last, holy "remnant" of true Israel among the fallen nation.

4.3. The destruction of Jerusalem

When the destiny of Israel was sealed by the destruction of Jerusalem in 70 A.D., the theologians once again faced a terrible situation. Israel's hope was gone when the Temple and the whole city was torn down. The crisis facing the Chosen People was the most severe one since the times of the Exile. This is perhaps also the reason why the character of *4 Ezra* is so dark. The call to repentance is uncompromising and the condemnation of sins unconditional – perhaps more so than previously. At the same time the questions arising were connected with the problem of theodicy with unprecedented clarity.[36]

In the opening scene, Ezra is given a mission to inveigh against the sins of Israel.

---

[33] Schiffman has proposed that the roots of the Qumran community were in the Sadducean party. This is not acceptable, at least as far as eschatology is concerned. Schiffman, *From Text to Tradition,* 110; on Sadducean views in general, pp. 107-112.

[34] The short description of the Sadducees given here is merely a general overview. For the ideas cf. Jeremias, *Jerusalem,* 229ff., Bruce, *New Testament History,* 74ff., Porton, *ABD V* (1992) 892-893.

[35] On the belief in resurrection see Nickelsburg - Stone, *Faith and Piety,* 31; Stemberger, *Jewish Contemporaries,* 70-72.

[36] The problem of theodicy in 4 Ezra has been analysed e.g. by Mundle, *ZAW 47* (1929) 222-249; Thompson, *Theodicy;* Harnisch, *Verhängnis;* Brandenburger, *Verborgenheit Gottes;* and Longenecker, *Eschatology and Covenant.*

"The word of the Lord came to me, saying, 'Go and declare to my people their evil deeds, and to their children the iniquities which they have committed against me, so that they may tell their children's children that the sins of their parents have increased in them, for they have forgotten me and have offered sacrifices to strange gods" (4 Ezra 1:4-6).

Fear that God would abandon Israel brings up the problem of theodicy. It drives the writer to compare the Chosen People with other nations. As a sapiential theologian, the writer constantly asks why Israel has not found mercy in God's eyes.[37]

"Are the deeds of Babylon better than those of Zion? Or has another nation known you besides Israel? Or what tribes have so believed your covenants as these tribes of Jacob? Yet their reward has not appeared and their labour has borne no fruit. For I have travelled widely among the nations and have seen that they abound in wealth, though they are unmindful of your commandments." (4 Ezra 3:32-33).

The wealth and success of other nations, which is primarily at issue, is not the sole problem of the writer. It is much more difficult for him to understand the oppression by tyrant kings and their freedom to exploit Israel.[38]

"And now, O Lord, behold, these nations, which are reputed as nothing, domineer over us and devour us. But we your people, whom you have called your first-born, only begotten, zealous for you, and most dear, have been given into their hands. If the world has indeed been created for us, why do we not possess our world as an inheritance? How long will this be so?" (4 Ezra 6:57-59).

There are a number of methodological problems concerning the assessment of the problem of theodicy in 4 Ezra. The first of these is the question whether the thoughts of Ezra, who is speaking, can be identified with the writer or not. Is he speaking through the writer's mouth, or is he instead perhaps presented as an example of a false interpretation of the fate of Israel? Some scholars have concluded that in the story related in the book the character of Ezra is a heretic.[39] This kind of solution seems to rest on weak arguments, however. As a historical exemplar, Ezra is naturally a positive prototype.

Furthermore, the eschatology of the character of Ezra in the book conforms

---

[37] The first scholar to write about the problem of theodicy in 4 Ezra was W. Mundle, in his article "Das religiöse Problem des IV. Esrabuches". "Sehen wir, wie es in dieser Studie beabsichtigt ist, von dem Interesse des Verfassers an den eigentlichen eschatologischen Fragen ab, so ist es im Grunde nur ein Problem, um das sich das Denken des Apokalyptikers bewegt und das von ihm in immer neuen Wendungen wieder aufgenommen wird: das Problem der Theodizee." Mundle, *ZAW* 47 (1929) 236. One weakness in Mundle's analysis is that he separates the problem of theodicy from apocalyptic. See Lohmeyer, *Probleme*, 48.

[38] See Thompson, *Theodicy*, 258.

[39] In this way Harnisch, *Verhängnis*, 60ff., and Brandenburger, *Adam*, 36.

with that of other apocalyptic books in the Second Temple period.[40] We must note once again that the Ezra who speaks does not doubt either God's ability to act or God's power. He merely wonders why God does not wish to use His power against godless rulers. Israel is once again in a situation where she must suffer under the rule of foreign nations. In this situation God seems to withdraw and keep silent.[41]

The writer of 4 Ezra responds to this difficult problem in many ways. Firstly, he uses a traditional way, as almost any Old Testament writer would have done, and emphasizes that God is sovereign and incomprehensible. Man can never find a final answer to the problem of evil, because the will of God is beyond the thoughts of men. (4 Ezra 4:7-12). This is why human beings must accept their fate and believe that it is in the hands of God.

Even though the mind of God is unreachable, the writer does not advocate fatalism. Many acts of God are known to the righteous. The book is full of apocalyptic eschatology, according to which justice will be done on the day of judgment. Sin will ultimately be punished.

In 4 Ezra the judgment of God is concerned with two separate groups of sinners. The idea is similar to that of other apocalyptic literature. On the one hand, the sins of Israel will be punished (4 Ezra 2:1-14). On the other hand, justice will be done to righteous Israelites and their oppressors will receive their punishment (7:37).

Knowledge of the coming judgment thus gives hope to Israel.[42] Those who endure the temptations and the siege of sinners "shall be saved and shall see… salvation" on the day when truth will be revealed (6:25-28). The day of God's judgment will come and everyone will be rewarded according to their deeds (7:33-35).[43]

The soteriology of 4 Ezra appears to be rather legalistic. Salvation depends almost entirely on one's ability to obey the law of God. According to the writer, the law was given in order to bring life, as the Old Testament testifies

---

[40] Cf. Thompson, *Theodicy,* 269. Sanders tried to find a solution by changing the setting: the view of the main author was that of the angel in the dialogues. Sanders, *Paul,* 418. This perspective is evidently needed, but it does not solve the above problem. Ezra as a person must be important, too.

[41] "So Ezra has no worries about God's power; he just cannot fathom why God does not use his power to hinder evil-doers (3:8), to take away the evil heart so that the law can bear fruit (3:20), to restore his people and thereby rescue his own reputation (4:25), and to punish his people himself rather than handing them over to his enemies (5:30)." Thompson, *Theodicy,* 297.

[42] These themes are common in apocalyptic writings commenting on the destruction of Jerusalem, cf. 2 Bar. 78:5-7.

[43] Cf. 2 Bar. 5:2-4; 13:2-6; Apoc.Abr. 31:2-8.

(4 Ezra 7:19-22). The importance of the giving of the law is emphasized repeatedly, despite the fact that the fathers had abandoned proper obedience a long time since (9:30-34). On this basis, several scholars who accept the theory of covenantal nomism have considered 4 Ezra an exception to normative Jewish theology.[44]

Some scholars have even considered the book to be a story of repentance. In this case the character of Ezra would be a tool with which the writer was able to describe how Jewish theology changed from old ethnocentric soteriology to a new, individualistic legalism.[45] This would separate the book from previous literature of the period.

We must note, however, that there is little difference between 4 Ezra and other apocalyptic writings. The problem of theodicy is treated here in a familiar way. In 4 Ezra, too, predestinarian theology leads to a nomism which is synergistic.[46] This leads to an exclusivist soteriology. True Israel is merely a remnant which is granted the promises and covenants of God.[47]

Synergism which is linked to the nomism of the writer, is neatly defined in chapter 9. "And it shall be that everyone who will be saved and will be able to escape on account of his works, or on account of the faith [*per opera sua vel per fidem*] by which he has believed, will survive the dangers that have been predicted, and will see my salvation in my land and within my borders, which I have sanctified for myself from the beginning" (4 Ezra 9:7-8). Righteousness and faithfulness are the true cornerstones on which any Jew can rely. These cannot be separated from the saving acts of God, however. The basis of salvation is the mercy of God.

As regards the origin of sin, 4 Ezra explains it in accordance with the sapiential tradition. On the one hand, there is the argument which is based on

---

[44] See Sanders, *Paul*, 409, 422, and especially 418: "One has here the closest approach to legalistic works-righteousness which can be found in the Jewish literature of the period." The problem is discussed in Longenecker, *Eschatology and Covenant*, 18, 150-152.

[45] See especially Longenecker, *Eschatology and Covenant*, 149-150.

[46] This horizon has been totally lost in the tradition of interpretation where covenantal nomism is accepted. For example, Räisänen summarized his conviction as follows: "The exception is IV Ezra, where the framework of covenant has collapsed and one really has to earn one's salvation by perfect obedience to the law." Räisänen, *Paulinische Literatur*, 67. Gundry sees the problem in his criticism, but is restricted by the influence of the theory and does not find any real solution to it. "Here, indeed, a crack opens in the pattern of Palestinian Judaism." Gundry, *Bib 66* (1985) 4-5. We should not speak merely of a "crack" in a pattern. There is a whole new horizon in the interpretation of the synergistic nomism of 4 Ezra. This nomism is part of the Second Temple synergism which had already begun in sapiential literature and 1 Enoch.

[47] This feature is accepted by Longenecker, even though he does not draw any further conclusions from it. Longenecker, *Eschatology and Covenant*, 150. Cf. Thompson, *Theodicy*, 298.

creation theology, and God's omnipotence is assured thereby. On the other hand, the idea of creation again justifies the concept of free will, and the responsibility is transferred to man himself (9:19). In the theology of 4 Ezra the fall of Adam has a significant status. The first Adam had an evil heart (*cor malignum*) and he transgressed against the will of God (3:21). An evil seed had been planted in his heart from the very beginning (4:30).[48]

The fall of Adam changed God's plans for the fate and salvation of men (7:10-15). This is why Adam became the father of the sinfulness of all mankind, and Ezra constantly bewails this wickedness. "For what good is it to all that they live in sorrow now and expect punishment after death? O Adam, what have you done? For though it was you who sinned, the fall was not yours alone, but ours also who are your descendants" (7:117-118). Previous promises given to the chosen people could not give hope, since the burden of evil deeds would eventually bring death. "For what good is it to us, if an eternal age has been promised to us, but we have done deeds that bring death?" (7:118).

The problem of theodicy is a burning issue in 4 Ezra. The writer does believe the promises of God, but for him there is a difficulty which prevents these promises from being fulfilled. They remain powerless because no one is able to reach the moral standard which is a condition for salvation.[49] Fatalism is not the answer the writer espouses, however. He wishes to give his readers hope. Not every Jew will be sentenced to eternal damnation. God has prepared salvation for the righteous, and he will execute justice for those who have suffered oppression.

4 Ezra, too, belongs to the tradition so common in Second Temple Jewish theology, where the problem of theodicy dictates most of the features in soteriology. The book is dated to the end of the era. As it commented on the greatest catastrophe of them all, it was a document that provided a summary of Jewish predestinarian theology. The crises of Israel had led people to question God's faithfulness towards his people. As a herald of hope, Ezra responded to this repeated problem in quite a traditional way. The suffering had been a punishment for the sins of the people. At the same time it had, however, produced agony for the righteous. This age of oppression will come to an end. The final judgment will bring justice. Then the righteous will obtain their reward and attain eternal salvation.

---

[48] According to Longenecker, it is precisely the anthropological significance of Adam's fall which reveals a change in soteriology. He says that the writer resists the ethnocentricism of traditional Judaism. It is now replaced by individualistic legalism. Longenecker, *Eschatology and Covenant*, 270.

[49] Thompson, *Theodicy*, 288.

4.4. Judgment and the Day of Wrath

Apocalyptic texts have preserved similar aspects of the problem of theodicy to those we have met already in sapiential theology. In addition, apocalyptic developed an eschatology which goes far beyond that of wisdom literature. The history of the world is now approaching its final moments. When the last aeon comes, God will enter this world and call people to account for their evil deeds. On this occasion the idea of a holy war is often introduced. In this war the ungodly will be destroyed. The climax of the period is the predestined judgment, in which the godless will be punished according to their deeds.[50]

A thematic analysis will show the generality of this kind of eschatology and the richness of the description of the last judgment. Especially in the time just before that of the New Testament and during the first Christian century, apocalyptic literature contains endless descriptions of the Day of Wrath. The best examples can be found in 1 Enoch, the Sibyllines and 4 Ezra. Despite the fact that these texts contain covenantal terminology, they present a strong demand for repentance, too.[51]

In sapiential tradition it was common to teach that the punishments of God occur in the course of history. We can take *Baruch*, for example, where the righteous judgments of God are praised, even though they have fallen on Israel. "The Lord our God is in the right, but there is open shame on us and our ancestors this very day. All those calamities with which the Lord threatened us have come upon us" (Bar. 2:6-7).[52] This perspective further contained the ideas of revealing justice and bringing the righteous to the resurrection of life (2 Macc. 7:14).

In apocalyptic texts, such as *1 Enoch*, this kind of presentation is accompanied by straightforward descriptions of eschatological judgment. This document echoes the powerful proclamation of the Old Testament prophets and even goes beyond their visions. At the beginning of the book, in chapters 1-5, the last judgment is described as a horrible, cosmic event. The earth moves and people are horrified at meeting the Holy God.[53] A similar atmosphere can be found in later prophecies in the collection. There their juridical nature is underlined in a clear way.

---

[50] Cf. Schiffman, *From Text to Tradition,* 127ff.

[51] On the descriptions of the day of judgment in related texts, see Hiers, *ABD II* (1992) 79-80; Nickelsburg - Stone, *Faith and Piety,* 117-123, 139ff.; Stuhlmacher, *Römer,* 44-45 (an excursus "Das Endgericht nach den Werken"); Stuhlmacher, *Theologie,* 260-261.

[52] Cf. the doxologies of judgment in Gk. Dan. 3:26-46 and the Prayer of Esther, Addns. to Esth. 4:6f. See Garnet, *Qumran,* 20-21.

[53] These chapters are dated to the third century B.C. and they represent early apocalyptic of the Second Temple period. Nickelsburg - Stone, *Faith and Piety,* 122.

"And now do know that you are ready for the day of destruction. Hope not that you shall live, you sinners, you who shall depart and die, for you know for what (reason) you have been ready for the day of the great judgment, for the day of anguish and great shame for your spirits."(1 Enoch 98:10).

God himself will raise his hand against sinners:

"And the Most High will arise on that day of judgment in order to execute a great judgment upon all the sinners. He will set a guard of holy angels over all the righteous and holy ones, and they shall keep them as the apple of the eye until all evil and all sin are brought to an end. From that time on the righteous ones shall sleep a restful sleep, and there shall be no one to make them afraid." (1 Enoch 100:4-5).

In 1 Enoch the day of judgment is described as a meeting of a heavenly court. All people, good and evil, are gathered in front of the heavenly judge, and they will be sentenced according to their deeds. In the *Psalms of Solomon*, as well, the difference between sinners and the righteous is emphasized.[54] In the descriptions of doom also the result of the judgment is painted in vivid colours. Faithful people will gain the glory of heaven as a reward: "The Lord is faithful to those... who live in the righteousness of his commandments, in the Law... The Lord's devout shall live by it forever... they shall not be uprooted as long as the heavens shall last." (Ps.Sol. 14:1-4).[55]

The fate of sinners, in turn, is Hades, the kingdom of death, the place of their eternal punishment. "But not so are sinners and criminals... their inheritance is Hades, and darkness and destruction; and they will not be found on the day of mercy for the righteous." (Ps.Sol. 14:6-9).[56]

Similar descriptions concerning the judgment of God and the Day of Wrath are to be found in several later texts. In *4 Ezra* a general resurrection takes place and God puts the whole of mankind on trial (4 Ezra 7:28-42).[57] In the *Sibyllines* the judgment of God is a cosmic event where the collapse of the whole created world sets the scene for the punishment of sinners.[58] "And God will speak... and judgment will come upon them from the great God, and all will perish at the hand of the Immortal. Fiery swords will fall from heaven on the earth" (Sib.Or. 3, 669-673).

---

[54] This also leads to the concept of judgment, see e.g. PsSol. 3:1-12. Schüpphaus, *Psalmen Salomos,* 92-93; Lührmann, *JSNT 36* (1989) 82; Winninge, *Sinners and the Righteous,* 42-43; Seifrid, *Justification,* 118-119.

[55] Winninge, *Sinners and the Righteous,* 119.

[56] On the nature of the Psalm, Schüpphaus, *Psalmen Salomos,* 60. Cf. PsSol. 15:10-13.

[57] Cf. TestAbr. 12-14. Nickelsburg - Stone, *Faith and Piety,* 142-144.

[58] The description in the Sibyllines is rather similar to that in the New Testament. Both the apocalyptic words of Jesus and the imagery of the book of Revelation present such a cosmic scene behind the final judgment.

In the fourth book of the Sibyllines, too, the execution of the judgment is described in a vivid way (Sib.Or. 4, 40-43).[59]

"But when the judgment of the world and of mortals has already come, which God himself will perform, judging impious and pious at once, then he will also send the impious down into the gloom in fire."

The multiplicity of the eschatology of Jewish apocalyptic led to the working out of the judgment being described in different ways. In many texts the executor is a messianic figure. He often resembles the Davidic Messiah, but in most writings the character himself stands far from traditional, political messianology.[60]

In certain apocalyptic texts the eschatological Messiah is clearly a royal figure. In these texts he is a Davidide, even though he hardly ever is called the Son of David. We meet the Son of Man, instead, a character who is quite significant, for example, in the eschatology of the *Book of Daniel*. In a vision the Son of Man comes to the Ancient One (God). "To him was given dominion and glory and kingship, that all peoples, nations, and languages should serve him. His dominion is an everlasting dominion that shall not pass away, and his kingship is one that shall never be destroyed" (Dan. 7:14).[61]

In a section of *1 Enoch* ("Similitudes", 37-71) that is dated rather late, the Son of Man will judge the world together with God:[62]

"and pain shall seize them when they see that Son of Man sitting on the throne of his glory... On that day, all the kings, the governors, the high officials, and those who rule the earth shall fall down before him on their faces, and worship and raise their hopes in that Son of Man" (1 Enoch 62:5-9).

The idea of eschatological atonement is connected with a priestly Messiah, who brings salvation to the faithful. This kind of teaching is prominent in the *Testament of Levi*, especially in chapter 18.

"And then the Lord will raise up a new priest to whom all the words of the Lord will be revealed. He shall effect the judgment of truth over the earth for many days. And his star shall rise in heaven like a king; kindling the light of knowledge as day is illumined by the sun. And he shall be extolled by the whole inhabited world" (TLev. 18:2-3).

The messianic figure here is a priest who brings salvation to Israel. He is not merely a priest (as would be the case in the eschatology of Qumran). We can

---

[59] Cf. Sib.Or. 3, 741-750; 4, 180-190; 4 Ezra 7:60; 9:15-25.

[60] On Christology see e.g. Hengel, *Le Trône de Dieu*, 161ff.; Hurtado, *One God, one Lord*, 77ff.; Collins, *Scepter and the Star*, 34f., 136ff.

[61] Collins, *Scepter and the Star*, 36.

[62] Hurtado, *One God, one Lord*, 53f.; Collins, *Scepter and the Star*, 180.

see that he has the status of a king, as well.[63] The Messiah is seen both as a priest and a king. He will be the judge of the nations. Such a function can be attached only to a king, to whom all people have been subjected.[64]

Together with the belief in an eschatological judgment we find a strong confidence in the inauguration of the age of salvation. The righteous will be granted eternal life. According to some texts, they will be taken to Paradise together with their Lord. For example, in the Testament of Levi the arrival of the messianic priest is set in the context of a cosmic dualism. After the expulsion from Paradise only the Messiah will re-open the gates. "And he shall open the gates of paradise; he shall remove the sword that has threatened since Adam, and he will grant to the saints to eat of the tree of life. The spirit of holiness shall be upon them" (TLev. 18:10-11).

In the *Testament of Naphtali* the rivalry between the tribes of Levi and Judah concerning their messianic role is settled in favour of Judah.[65]

"Command your children that they be in unity with Levi and Judah, for through Judah will salvation arise for Israel, and in him will Jacob be blessed. Through his kingly power God will appear... to save the race of Israel" (TNaph. 8:2-3).

In the apocalyptic texts of *Qumran* we find both a Davidic Messiah and a priestly Messiah. These two clearly exercise a different function and role in eschatology.[66] As regards judgment, we have further the figure of Melchizedek, who is an agent of salvation – but not in a priestly sense, as is the case in the New Testament. In 11QMelch. the figure of Melchizedek is described as an eschatological saviour who will bring peace on earth. This era is described as the last year of Jubilee in Israel (11QMelch. 1-5).

Melchizedek is even called *Elohim* (11QMelch. 25), though he is not a divine

---

[63] Qumran as a priestly community taught more conservatively of a priestly Messiah. The "Messiah of Aaron" was to end the power of the "Wicked Priest" in Jerusalem (1QSa II, 17-21). He was to take over the service of atonement (4QAaronA). At Qumran it would have been a sacrilege to teach that a royal Messiah could have a priestly function. Qumran will also be treated below. On the origins of priestly messianism, see Collins, *Scepter and the Star*, 83.

[64] In TLev. 18 the royal Messiah has a priestly title but the function of a judge. This dualism might be explained by the fact that the Hasmoneans had attempted to unite the roles of the ruler and the High Priest. Due to historical uncertainty several scholars have concluded, however, that in this text we see evidence of Christian influence. See the discussion in Becker, *Testamente*, 291-293. Christian influence is proposed e.g. in the commentary Hollander - de Jonge, *Testaments*, 76, 179.

[65] van der Woude, *Die messianischen Vorstellungen*, 195, 200f.

[66] A royal Messiah occurs in several texts, such as 1QS IX, 9-11; 4QPatr. 1-4; 4QFlor. 10-13; 4Q285. See van der Woude, *Die messianischen Vorstellungen*, 75f., 172f. A priestly Messiah was connected solely with the Temple cult, 1QSa II, 11ff.; Collins, *Scepter and the Star*, 75-77.

person. He is Michael the archangel, who will act as a judge at the end of days.[67] He will also be the one who rescues people from the power of Belial. He must be regarded as an important heavenly agent, because the scriptural proof of Isa. 52:7 actually talks about the Lordship of God himself. At Qumran the salvation of Zion concerned the chosen of the community who kept the covenant of God (11QMelch. 15-16).[68]

The theme of eschatological judgment expresses one of the main features in the tradition of Second Temple theology. The coming judgment will reveal the Lordship of God to all nations. There is a simple answer to the problem of theodicy. The Lord God is the King of Israel and he will execute righteousness in the land. Every one who is disobedient will be cut off from the nation and placed under the judgment of God.

In Jewish apocalyptic the concept of eschatological salvation is based on a strong dualistic soteriology. Israel – besides the whole world – is under the power of sin and ruled by godless people. This produces agony for the righteous, but God will listen to their woes. On the day of judgment he will parade all the world before him. The leading theme of this theology is not new as such. In apocalyptic, traditional eschatology is applied to a developed world-view. Eschatological salvation is defined in detail. Only the righteous will survive before God and attain Paradise. Godless people will be punished in a horrible way when the wrath of God falls on them.

The soteriology of apocalyptic is also synergistic. In this respect, too, it follows the tradition of sapiential theology. It is possible to escape the coming wrath – if one does what one is expected to do. Most apocalyptic writers think that the most severe problem of Israel is their abandoning of the Law. This is why the day of justice will appear as a day of judgment. Then their willingness to obey will be measured. Salvation is dependent on the mercy of God, but it has a condition: repentance and a commitment to observing the law of Moses.

---

[67] Hurtado thinks that the divine title is used because "this figure was so highly exalted and so closely identified with divine purposes that the community could see him referred to in quite exalted terms such as 'Elohim' and in passages where one could more easily see God himself as the referent." Hurtado, *One God, one Lord*, 79.

[68] Hurtado, *One God, one Lord*, 77ff.; Collins, *Scepter and the Star*, 162.

§ 5   The Ambivalent Concept of Predestination at Qumran

The theology of the Qumran community is so rich in themes and details that we are justified in examining it again as a separate subject. While it was useful to locate the Dead Sea Sect in the context of Second Temple apocalyptic in order to describe one important Jewish reaction to apostasy in the Hasmonean period, it is interesting, as well, to analyze the individual features of the soteriology of the sect. We can discern both sapiential and apocalyptic traditions and themes in the Qumran texts. In addition, the theology of the community has independent features which often emerge from the unique historical situation of the group.

5.1. Cosmic predestination

The Dead Sea Sect was still living within the contemporary sapiential tradition, even though it employed it in an eschatological context and even for an apocalyptic purpose. Their tradition naturally had unique features due to their exclusiveness. We should, however, not be too hasty in separating Qumran from other movements of that period.

We must remember that the founders of the Qumran movement came from the very heart of Jewish religion and theological tradition – the temple of Jerusalem. Qumran theology was elaborated by Zadokite priests. For this reason the teaching of the sect, for the most part, is consonant with the general Jewish theology of the Second Temple period.[1]

The problem of theodicy was of great importance at Qumran, as it was among the other movements of that time. When attempting to solve the problem of suffering, the priests of Qumran were in fact concerned to maintain their belief in their God as Omnipotent and Almighty. In fulfilling this task the concept of predestination assumed importance.[2] The dilemma of the community had become crystallized in its opposition to the Temple in Jerusalem. Even though God was leading his people, his chosen ones, godless rulers seemed to have usurped power both in politics and in the Temple.

Actually, it was for this reason that the founders of the community at Qumran

---

[1] On the priestly nature of the community see Gärtner, *Temple*, 4ff.; Cross, *Qumran*, 118; Klinzing, *Umdeutung*, 50ff.; Collins, *ABD II* (1992) 99.

[2] It is interesting that some comments by Josephus concerning the Essenes deal with the same subject. "The sect of Essenes, however, declares that Fate (εἱμαρμένη) is mistress of all things, and that nothing befalls men unless it be in accordance with her decree." Jos. Ant. 13.172.

were obliged to leave the Jerusalem Temple.[3] We can say that the trauma of the Dead Sea Sect concerned the very core of Jewish piety and faith. The great Temple had fallen into the hands of godless priests. This had many consequences. The cult and sacrifices could no longer be recognized as a legitimate channel of forgiveness and salvation. This, in turn, led to a totally new interpretation of the fate and future of Israel. Here the warnings and admonitions of sapiential theology were most applicable. It was easy to conceive of the world as governed by great spiritual powers and so violent confrontation was likely to occur.[4]

In early Qumran texts, such as the book of Hymns (Hodayot), dualistic soteriology is presented harshly and in a very polarized manner. The events leading to the founding of the community naturally explain the unusual strictness of these views. The dualism between the devout and sinners was experienced in the sect at an existential level. In fact, the identity of the community was based on this dualism. The texts have many features which might lead one to assume that the main teaching of Qumran theologians was built upon a concept of double predestination. There are sections, indeed, which seem to teach that the whole of mankind has been divided into two by God from the very beginning.[5]

In Hodayot the idea of predestination is based on a theology of creation.[6] In the manner of sapiential theology the writer of the hymns believes that the whole world is in the hands of the Almighty. God has created both the pious and sinners:[7]

---

[3] The concept of predestination in the theology of Qumran has aroused much interest among scholars. Some scholars think that the sect taught double predestination (Kuhn, *Scrolls,* 98; Flusser, *Spiritual History,* 49). There are others, however, who speak of determinism in a general sense (Cross, *Qumran,* 152-153; cf. Ringgren, *Faith,* 74; VanderKam, *Dead Sea Scrolls,* 76-77, 109). In Qumran's concept of predestination some see tensions, the dynamics of which will be assessed later (Ringgren, *Faith,* 110; Marx, *RQ 6/22* (1967) 180-181; Merrill, *Predestination,* 27). Older discussion and literature is presented in Marx, *RQ 6/22* (1967) 163-164; modern discussion in Lange, *Prädestination,* 30-32).

[4] The origin of the community has been studied e.g. by Cross, *Qumran,* 100ff.; Milik, *Discovery,* 44ff.; Jeremias, *Lehrer der Gerechtigkeit,* 36ff.; VanderKam, *Dead Sea Scrolls,* 71ff.

[5] The book of Hymns probably comes from the hand of the Teacher of Righteousness, see e.g. Dupont-Sommer, *Essene Writings,* 200. This would explain the existential nature of the presentation of dualism. In addition, Holm-Nielsen has noted that the Hymns were written for communal use. This is why they cannot be interpreted merely from a subjective angle, Holm-Nielsen, *Hodayot,* 340-341.

[6] Here we have, according to several scholars, the basic difference vis-à-vis the dualism of Persian religions, Kuhn, *Scrolls,* 98; cf. Ringgren, *Faith,* 68-70; Merrill, *Predestination,* 25.

[7] Cf. 1QH II, 23-24.

"I know through the understanding which comes from Thee that righteousness in not in a hand of flesh, [that] man [is not master of] his way and that it is not in mortals to direct their step... Thou alone didst [create] the just and establish him from the womb for the time of goodwill, that he might hearken to Thy Covenant and walk in all [Thy ways]... But the wicked Thou didst create for [the time] of Thy [wrath], Thou didst vow them from the womb to the Day of Massacre, for they walk in the way which is not good" (1QH XV, 12-21; Vermes).

Behind the dualism of the soteriology was a concept of two spirits or angels which govern the world. Especially in the Rule of the Community (1QS) the fate of men is said to be determined by these spirits. They are called the spirit of truth and the spirit of falsehood. All people have a portion of both these spirits.

"He has created man to govern the world, and has appointed for him two spirits in which to walk until the time of his visitation... All the children of righteousness are ruled by the Prince of Light and walk in the ways of light, but all the children of falsehood are ruled by the Angel of Darkness and walk in the ways of darkness." (1QS III, 17-21; Vermes).

The spirit of falsehood had been predestined to rule this world. Those who walk in this spirit will face "everlasting damnation by the avenging wrath of the fury of God" (1QS IV, 12; Vermes). The sinfulness of men was so overwhelming that it had to be predestined.[8] "The nature of all the children of men is ruled by these (two spirits)" (IV, 15; Vermes).[9]

The cosmic dualism of the Qumran texts is so strongly determined by the idea of God's predestination that in a general sense we are justified in speaking of the existence of a strict predestination in the theology of the sect.[10] The godless are condemned to eternal damnation and they no longer have the opportunity of repentance. This is especially evident in the Hodayot hymns (1QH II, 23-24; XV 17).

The theme of predestination is a dominant feature in the soteriology of Qumran. It is not a simple theme to explain, however. Scholars disagree on its

---

[8] The purpose of the writers, here as well, is evidently to formulate a theodicy. They wish to explain the origin of evil in the context of the creation by God. Cf. Hengel, *Judentum*, 395.

[9] On the dualism implied in the teaching of the two spirits, see especially Osten-Sacken, *Gott und Belial*, 185ff.; Milik, *JJS 23* (1972) 96ff., 124ff.; also Davies, *Scrolls*, 157ff., especially 171-172. Lange considers dualism a pre-existent order, and describes its nature as follows: "sie ist von einem Dualismus der sich kosmisch, ethisch und antropologisch realisiert, geprägt". Lange, *Prädestination*, 169.

[10] Cf. Martínez-Barrera, *The People*, 73. This kind of conclusion will also be reached when the teaching of Qumran is compared, for example, with the Stoic concept of predestination. See Hengel, *Qumrân*, 354, 355; cf. Pohlenz, *Die Stoa*, 101-104, 153ff., 164-165. According to Hengel, this is not the result of a direct influence by the Stoa but we are facing more or less a contemporary trend, Hengel, *Qumrân*, 357.

nature and many identify it with (dogmatic) double predestination. In this view, God predestined some to salvation and others to eternal damnation.[11] The theology of the community does not, however, seem to be that simple. The main starting-point is in the detail that men possess a different portion of the two spirits. They are in fact under the influence of both spirits at the same time. This creates a tension which scholars have attempted to solve in many different ways.[12]

When we read the Qumran texts more closely it is difficult to avoid the impression that the strict dualism in soteriology is, however, rather theoretical. One suspects that it must be dependent on a theological tradition. On the practical level, in turn, the writers of the community describe in a quite optimistic manner the fate of the Israelites and their opportunity of being saved. In theory, the logical implication of a concept of predestination would be that all Israelites were determined either to eternal damnation or to salvation. In practice, however, this is not the case. The writers of the texts do not describe the situation of the people in this way. Not all Israelites were predestined to eternal damnation. Here we have the original feature of the theology of Qumran.

There were naturally some godless rulers who had no hope and would not receive forgiveness (see e.g. 1QH II, 23-24; XV, 17). Most people were somewhere in between, however. They belonged to a third group. There was a distinction between the children of Light and the children of Darkness, but there were Israelites who were not children of Darkness, but who still could not be saved without performing certain actions. Thus most Israelites were considered potential children of Light, but they were not automatically members of the elect. Soteriological dualism seems to be interpreted in accordance with synergistic sapiential theology.[13]

As regards the practical conclusions of the soteriology of the Qumran community, we seem to have reached the core of their teaching. They did not make a distinction between people who came to their group in search of salvation. Nothing in these texts indicates that they classified men as children of Darkness because they had received some kind of insight, or by employing a particular method. Only the godless rulers of Jerusalem and the Temple were consigned to damnation by the pious Qumran monks. They were real apostates

---

[11] A concept of double predestination in this sense has been used by Flusser in his analysis, *Dead Sea Scrolls,* 28-29.

[12] On the tension, see Merrill, *Predestination,* 27.

[13] Lange says that this setting is an attempt to express the fact that the struggle between cosmic powers also affects the lives of men. People live in the middle of the battle of the spirits and at the same time they have a share of these spirits, too. Lange, *Prädestination,* 169.

and blasphemers. Other Israelites received a better assessment. By repentance and making a commitment to keep the law the Israelites were able to avoid damnation and find their place in the congregation of the saved – provided they did not fall again.[14]

A solution to the menacing determinism of predestination theology was thus to be found in sapiential soteriology.[15] The children of Righteousness were actually not obedient to the law from their very childhood. They, too, had been misguided in this world. The call to repentance had been issued to precisely this kind of Israel. Only membership in the new community made the convert a child of Light. This ambivalent situation was justified by the concept of a government of two spirits or two angels fighting against each other.[16]

"Due to the Angel of Darkness all the sons of justice stray, and all their sins, their iniquities, their failings and their mutinous deeds are under his dominion... and all the spirits of their lot cause the sons of light to fall. However, the God of Israel and the angel of his truth assist all the sons of light" (1QS III, 21-25, Martínez).

Since the Israelites who had an opportunity of being saved were in an ambivalent position, we can say that the soteriology of Qumran is not based on a straightforward kind of double predestination. In other words, the Qumran sectarians did not think that God had predestined all men either to salvation or to damnation. It was always possible to find salvation by repentance. This is why the idea of repentance was so important in the soteriology of Qumran.[17]

A basic feature of the theology of Second Temple Judaism was the problem of theodicy. It was solved by using the idea of God's judgment which would fall on godless rulers. Since God was Almighty and the rule of the apostates was only transient, judgment had to be predestined. No sinner could avoid it. Normative Judaism, centred on the Temple, was perhaps able to live according to the traditional covenantal religion and reject such polarization. From Wisdom theology onwards the theology of religious movements was centred around the idea of predestination, however. Practically all Second Temple texts

---

[14] See especially 1QS III, 21-25

[15] The connection between the theology of Qumran and sapiential theology has been investigated e.g. by Hengel, *Judentum*, 400ff.; Hengel, *Qumrân*, 352; Kuhn, *Enderwartung*, 141ff., 154-162; modern discussion especially in Lange, *Prädestination*, 297ff.

[16] Sanders has noted this tension and mentions it in his study. Even though the mercy of God is the basis for election, it is man's task to choose the way that he wishes to walk. Perhaps due to his theory Sanders cannot, however, integrate this notion into predestinarian theology, but concludes that it would be anachronistic to speak of actual predestination in this context. *Paul*, 261. Sanders denies double predestination and in this respect his comment is justified. This prevents him, however, from explaining the soteriology of the sect with the aid of apocalyptic predestinarian theology.

[17] See e.g. Garnet, *Salvation*, 116.

contain these basic features and Qumran is no exception. This soteriology is not a simple covenantal nomism. It is based on soteriological dualism where the predestination of judgment is the key concept. We have to speak of a "weak" predestination, though, because the fallen Israelites were able to avoid the coming wrath. Repentance and commitment to the law of God were the conditions of eschatological salvation.

5.2. The call to repentance

The ambivalent nature of the Qumran concept of predestination becomes evident when we compare more closely the theoretical soteriology and the daily practice of the community. The greatest problems of Israel, namely sin, disobedience and apostasy, were treated practically and without deterministic belief. Every Israelite was able to repent and follow God in obedience to the law. This could be done solely by joining the community.[18] The call to repentance has several features which reveal a connection with sapiential theology.

As regards the texts of Qumran, the concept of free will and synergistic nomism appear in a clearly apocalyptic context. The teaching of the sect was based on soteriological dualism. It was not possible to enter the community without deep repentance.[19] Taking such a step involved submission to the commandments of the law and the authority of the priests.[20]

"Whoever enters the council of the Community enters the covenant of God in the presence of all who freely volunteer. He shall swear with a binding oath to revert to the Law of Moses with all that it decrees, with whole heart and whole soul, in compliance with all that has been revealed concerning it to the sons of Zadok, the priests who keep the covenant and interpret his will" (1QS V, 7-9; Martínez).

The allusion to Deuteronomy (Deut. 30) is made in accordance with the teaching of sapiential theology. Every repentant Israelite must of his own free will turn to God and fulfil his law. Later the sincerity of the convert and the perfectness of his obedience to the law was strictly inspected. "And when someone enters the covenant to behave in compliance with all these decrees, enrolling in the assembly of holiness, they shall test their spirits in the

---

[18] This tension in the theology of predestination has led to a new assessment of the whole concept, as was noted above. "Naturally these statements which presuppose man's cooperation are from a strictly logical point of view irreconcilable with the teaching of predestination. But they are not impossible because of this. Within the frame of a living religious experience these two ideas may coexist." Ringgren, *Faith,* 110; cf. Merrill, *Predestination,* 23.

[19] Cf. Jos. Bell. 2.137.

[20] On the demand of obedience, see Ringgren, *Faith,* 105-106; Yadin, *Message,* 118-119.

Community (discriminating) between a man and his fellow, in respect of his insight and of his deeds in law" (1QS V, 20-21).[21]

The call to repentance at Qumran does not, in principle, differ from that of the book of Sirach. There is a similar concept of man and a similar view of the law behind both of them. In a soteriological analysis it must be defined as synergism, and the first feature of this is that a man is guided to commit himself to strict obedience to the law of Moses.[22] This view is not one-sidedly legalistic, since the assembly regarded itself as a saving community. Its members believed that they were able to deliver God's grace. As regards eschatological salvation, it was in the hands of God. This view is an example of synergistic nomism, though, because one could not enter the saving community without committing oneself to a nomistic life by taking solemn oaths.[23]

Repentance was related to the idea of free will.[24] This becomes evident when we read the Community Rule: "This is the rule for the men of the Community who freely volunteer to convert from all evil and to keep themselves steadfast in all he prescribes in compliance with his will." (1QS V, 1, Martínez). On several occasions the members of the sect are said "freely to volunteer" to carry out God's commandments (1QS I, 7).[25]

The importance of repentance is even greater when we consider covenantal theology. In the context of synergistic nomism the traditional markers of the covenant, such as circumcision and association with the Temple cult, were not

---

[21] In the Damascus Rule background information is given. The first members of the covenant had sinned. This is why the covenant concerned only those who obeyed the commandments of God (CD III, 10-14). By these keepers of the law the writer presumably means members of the community. Garnet, *Pauline Studies,* 21.

[22] See Martínez-Barrera, *The People,* 68. Winston has endeavoured to solve the tension between predestination and free will by using a concept of voluntarism. God seems to have determined the psyche of man with the two spirits, but nevertheless a certain freedom to engage in voluntary acts remains. In his psychological explanation Winston has to be content with the conclusion, however, that in the theology of Qumran these two features are in disagreement. Winston, *Wisdom,* 50. In spite of his ambivalence he has come close to the idea of synergism.

[23] Garnet has noted that the demand for repentance is presented as a condition for salvation and the restoration of Israel in several Second Temple texts, such as Tob. 13:5, TJud. 23 and Jubilees 23:17-31. Garnet, *Pauline Studies,* 20-21.

[24] This can be seen in the Qumran Hymns, too. "1QH is replete with references to 'voluntarism', to the notion that as a moral agent man must decide for or against God and the Covenant. Soteriologically, he has the opportunity, even the full responsibility, to repent as a condition for his being admitted among the Sons of Light." Merrill, *Predestination,* 42.

[25] Cf. 1QS I, 11; 1QH XV, 10. The Mishnah presents a view such as this in a timeless way: "Everything is foreseen, yet freedom of choice is given." Abot 2,19.

considered sufficient to provide eschatological salvation.[26] At Qumran one could enter the community of the saved only by obeying strict rules and commandments. These conditions were probably – at least in some respects – results of the opposition towards the loose religiosity of the Temple.[27]

The rigorous obedience of a life of sanctification, and criticism of the Temple, were not set as conditions merely for the novices of the community. Essenes throughout the country, in towns and villages, were obligated by similar rules. In the midst of everyday life these rules could probably not be so strict as in the community of Qumran, where a priestly order was followed. The basic nature of religious life was the same, however. Because Jerusalem was under the rule of darkness, only separation from the ungodly could lead to salvation (CD VI, 11-17; XV, 5-10; XIII).[28]

The problem of theodicy was first of all a general principle behind the theology of Qumran, directing the details of soteriology. In addition, we must recognize that the book of Habakkuk, which is a primary writing on the issue of theodicy, and has been analyzed in previous chapters, was quite important for the theologians of the Dead Sea sect, too. In the commentary on Habakkuk (1QpHab) the writer tries to explain the basic crisis which led to the founding of the sect. It is easy to see that in such a situation the pattern of interpretation followed the lines of common Jewish interpretation at that period.

In the commentary on Habakkuk the ungodly comprise the priests of the Temple. They are the ones who persecute the righteous of Qumran. Their leader, the high priest, is the "Wicked Priest", who is behind all the persecution (1QpHab II, 2; V, 11; VIII, 7-13, 16; IX, 9; XI, 4-5; XII, 8-9).[29] The prophecies of the book of Habakkuk are being fulfilled in detail in the life

---

[26] In the soteriology of Qumran, even the members of the covenant could not attain salvation without perfect obedience to the law of God (CD XX, 25-27). See especially Garnet, *Pauline Studies*, 20.

[27] Sanders has naturally admitted that at Qumran the members of the new community had not always been "inside". Due to his theory he has been unable, however, to recognize the importance of repentance and free will as regards admission to the community. In this question he is somewhat inconsistent because, on the other hand, he speaks of the importance of the idea of free will in the predestinarian theology of the community. As his final interpretation Sanders presents a theory that God would, through an "interior" way of knowing, reveal knowledge concerning election to those who were to be saved: "the members of the sect were not born into the covenant. Thus they had to account for how they came to be in it. They thought of themselves, as we have seen, as predestined by God. But since those who were predestined were not marked by birth or by an external sign of the covenant such as circumcision, there had to be an *interior* way of *knowing* that they were predestined." *Paul*, 260-261. Fortunately, Qumran soteriology is not in reality as complex as this.

[28] Cf. Jos. Bell. 2.134-161.

[29] On the discussion about the identification of the Wicked Priest with the Man of Lies, mentioned also in the commentary (1QpHab II,1-2), see Collins, *ABD II* (1992) 98-99.

of the community, according to the writers. The righteous are once again suffering oppression. Only God can help them, because after all it is He who acts behind every incident that takes place in Israel.[30]

This is why the problem of theodicy is solved in the commentary on Habakkuk in accordance with the original proclamation of the prophet. "Its interpretation concerns all observing the Law in the House of Judah, whom God will free from punishment on account of their deeds and of their loyalty to the Teacher of Righteousness" (1QpHab VIII, 1-3, Martínez). The members of the Qumran community were those righteous ones who had begun to observe the law perfectly in their lives.[31] Following a synergistic principle, they were the ones who had attained the mercy of God, and consequently, attained salvation.

At Qumran the solution to the problems of predestination was found in the demand for repentance. The children of righteousness were scattered around the country and most of them had been lost. They had to find their way back to the community of the saved. In practice this must have meant membership in the Essene movement. A condition for admission both at Qumran and in the Essene movement around the country was, according to the principles of synergism, a commitment to the keeping of the law of Moses. In this way novices ensured their lot in the community of salvation and attained the grace of God. In addition, the community provided atonement for their sins, as we shall see in the following chapter.

5.3. Atonement by obedience

In addition to the demand for repentance there is another trait in the theology of Qumran which in a substantial way affects the relationship between the concepts of predestination and free will. In the community it was necessary to re-define the concept of atonement, because they lived in a situation where contact with the Temple had been severed. The solution of the Qumran pious was, here too, to follow the tradition of sapiential theology: atonement was linked to obedience.

Synergistic soteriology usually includes the teaching that man can find forgiveness through a community of salvation. Furthermore, it is usually God himself who grants absolution. Moreover, in the concept of atonement of the Qumran community we can find the idea that salvation rests on the mercy of

---

[30] Historical connections of the commentary of Habakkuk have been studied e.g. by Jeremias, *Lehrer der Gerechtigkeit*, 144-145.

[31] Ringgren, *Faith*, 247.

God or on the righteousness (צדקת אל) of God.[32] Due to the nature of synergism the responsibility of man is emphasized at the same time. For this reason it is small wonder that the basic concept of atonement rested on the idea of obedience. It was an essential part of synergistic soteriology, not in any sense an antithesis to it.

Traditional Jewish soteriology was interpreted quite freely at Qumran. The Zadokite priests who had left the Temple of Jerusalem had been prepared to change their concept of atonement and to apply it to the new eschatological situation in which they now found themselves. Atonement was part of the fight for survival of the remnant of Israel which had fled into the desert. It could no longer be considered a part of the traditional temple service of Israel.[33]

Furthermore, the concept of atonement in the community of Qumran includes a feature which strengthens the status of obedience in their soteriology. The community was led by a council of three priests and twelve men who all had to be "perfect in everything that has been revealed about all the law to implement truth" (1QS VIII, 1-2; Martínez).[34] Since the community was a new Temple in the wilderness, the council provided atonement for all who were inside. "They shall preserve the faith in the Land with steadfastness and meekness and shall atone for sin by the practice of justice and by suffering the sorrows of affliction" (1QS VIII, 2f, Vermes). Members of the council were certain that they had access to the means of atonement.[35]

The titles by which the council is called, reveal how it was esteemed in the community.[36] It is identified as an "everlasting plantation", and a "holy house for Israel", and a "holy of holies for Aaron" (VIII, 5-8). According to these

---

[32] The most optimistic scholars considered that the Qumran community had accepted a complete concept of mercy resembling that of New Testament teaching. See e.g. Marx, *RQ 6/22* (1967) 180-181.

[33] The use of temple symbolism in the sect is understandable for historical reasons. There is a good consensus among the scholars that the emphasis of the Zadokite priesthood in the sect was due to the priestly background of the founders of the community. One would expect a priestly movement to use temple symbolism in their theology. Cf. Milik, *Discovery*, 78; Gärtner, *Temple*, 4.

[34] Discussion of the status of the council in the community is given in Collins, *ABD II* (1992) 87. It is probable that the status changed at the time of the expansion of the sect, about 100 B.C. This has little to do with the functions of the council, however.

[35] On the council, see Gärtner, *Temple*, 16ff.

[36] Temple terminology is analyzed especially by Gärtner: "But at the same time the community is expressly stated to be a 'sanctuary', meaning that the community has replaced the Jerusalem temple and its functions." Gärtner, *Temple*, 24. Black, on the other hand, has proposed that the cultic meal of the sect was related with the priestly meal in the Temple, where sacrificial food was eaten. Black, *Scrolls*, 103, 108; also Kuhn mentions the priestly nature of the cultic meal but explains it primarily in relation to eschatology, Kuhn, *Scrolls*, 71-72.

titles, the council is actually the Temple itself and the place where God dwells.
The Temple symbolism reaches its climax in the teaching that the council of the
community had replaced the Temple of Jerusalem in several respects and
functioned in a similar way, even in details which had previously been
exclusively restricted to the service of the Temple. This, in particular, concerns
the act of atonement.

"For, by the spirit of the true counsel concerning the paths of man all his sins are atoned so
that he can look at the light of life. And by the spirit of holiness which links him with his
truth he is cleansed of all his sins. And by the spirit of uprightness and of humility his sin is
atoned. And by the compliance of his soul with all the laws of God his flesh is cleansed by
being sprinkled with cleansing waters and being made holy with the water of repentance"
(1QS III, 6-9; Martínez).

The community was not attempting to imitate the Temple of Jerusalem by
providing an alternative sacrificial service conducted in a similar manner.
Sacrifices were understood in a metaphorical sense. Atonement was produced
without the help of whole burnt offerings at Qumran.[37]

"When these exist in Israel in accordance with these rules in order to establish the spirit of
holiness in truth eternal, in order to atone for the fault of the transgression and for the guilt
of sin and for approval for the earth, without the flesh of burnt offerings and without the fats
of sacrifice – the offering of the lips in compliance with the decree will be like the pleasant
aroma of justice and the correctness of behaviour will be acceptable like a freewill offering –
at this moment the men of the Community shall set themselves apart (like) a holy house for
Aaron, in order to enter the holy of holies, and (like) a house of the Community for Israel,
(for) those who walk in perfection."

(1QS IX, 3-6).[38]

The Teacher of Righteousness, who with his followers had fled to Qumran,
had built a new sanctuary there. The group believed that they had been faithful
to God and obedient in observing the law of Moses, and now the promises of
God, as well, were fulfilled for them. The priestly nature of the community is
thus closely connected with its strict asceticism. As a movement dedicated to
sanctification, the sect was engaged in obeying the prescriptions of the Lord in
every detail.

A perfect life and the "works of the law" compensated for the stumbling of
the nation. In addition, they atone for the transgressions of the members of the
sect. The obedient community had taken the identity of the remnant of Israel,

---

[37] "The Community itself was to be the sacrifice offered to God in atonement for Israel's
sins." Vermes, *Qumran in Perspective,* 163.

[38] Gärtner says that obedience in keeping the law and in service was believed to replace the
service of the Temple of Jerusalem and the sacrifices. Precisely in this context belonged the
idea that the works of law brought atonement. Gärtner, *Temple,* 20-21; cf. Klinzing,
Umdeutung, 105; Janowski, *Sühne,* 264.

an elect nucleus, which would be God's instrument in the restoration of Israel.

The defence of the law was an essential feature of the Zealot movement, which stood in the Maccabean tradition. As an ideology it had exercised a strong influence on Second Temple Judaism. Being zealous (קנא / ζηλόω) for the law of Moses meant struggling against all ungodliness and idolatry in Israel.[39] The concept of atonement in the Qumran community seems to fit into this tradition.

One of the most important themes in the soteriology of Zealotism was that obedience atones for the sins of Israel, which lives under the wrath of God. The starting-point of this kind of theology was to be found in the Old Testament. The person of Phinehas is of the utmost importance here.

Aaron's grandson Phinehas, a priest as well, resisted idolatry in the wilderness and by his actions brought reconciliation for all Israel: "he showed his zeal for his God and made expiation for the Israelites" (Num. 25:13).[40] By killing two sinners he atoned for the transgressions of the people.

The obedience of Phinehas is unique since it provided for atonement. For this reason he became a prototype for the kind of zeal which atones for transgressions. In later Jewish writings Phinehas is remembered as a great leader of the nation, side by side with Moses and Aaron. The act of Phinehas was also the basis for a new priestly covenant. All this is later noted in Ps. 106:30 and Sirach 46:23-24.[41]

In the Hasidic revival of the Hasmonean period this kind of zeal and obedience to the law was indeed necessary. This is evident in the speech of Mattathias in the first book of Maccabees.[42]

"Arrogance and scorn have now become strong; it is a time of ruin and furious anger. Now, my children, show zeal for the law, and give your lives for the covenant of our ancestors. Remember the deeds of the ancestors... Was not Abraham found faithful when tested... Phinehas our ancestor, because he was deeply zealous, received the covenant of everlasting priesthood" (1 Macc. 2:49-54).

The Essene theology of the Qumran community evidently built on this kind of tradition. Their opposition to the Temple was analogous to that of Mattathias to the fallen priests of Jerusalem and to all apostates.[43] The covenant of priesthood was based on obedience to the law, and it was also a means of

[39] Stumpff, *ThWNT II* (1990) 886-887; Rhoads, *ABD* 6 (1992) 1051.

[40] On Phinehas, see Hengel, *Zealots,* 149-150; Rhoads, *ABD* 6 (1992) 1044.

[41] In the theology of Qumran the connection between obedience, atonement and Phinehas has been studied by Garnet, *Salvation,* 59-60.

[42] The example of Phinehas was important both for rabbinic theology and for the Zealots in their struggle against the Romans. Hengel, *Zealots,* 156ff., 171ff.

[43] Hengel connects the "zeal" mentioned in the book of Hymns with Maccabaean tradition (1QH II, 15; XIV, 14). Hengel, *Zealots,* 179.

atonement for Israel. A reformatory movement of priestly origin could desire no better argument in support of their rebellious acts and their new situation. Precisely such a concept of atonement was accepted at Qumran. The council of the sect believed that this was the reason why they were able to atone for everyone entering the community.[44]

The idea that obedience would bring atonement was compatible with the synergistic nomism of the community. The Law was to be observed in every detail. This concept would result, however, in a teaching which would no longer fit in with the beliefs of so-called normative Judaism, i.e. Temple circles. At Qumran the atonement of sins was not connected with the traditional cult. The mercy of God was not presented in the context of "covenantal nomism". Reconciliation was based on an act of obedience and was thus governed by synergistic soteriology.[45]

The concept of atonement of the Qumran community helps us to understand the synergistic soteriology of the sect. Precisely in this way a belief in a merciful God could be united with a rather legalistic nomism, with all its demands of obedience. In the theory of covenantal nomism the grace of God was emphasized in an appropriate manner. Righteous Jews would never have ceased to trust in God's mercy.[46] In this respect the texts of Qumran make no exception. They are filled with beautiful descriptions of forgiveness and caring. In the context of synergistic theology, however, these clauses never contradict the demand of obedience.[47]

In the community no one would have boasted that he would be saved merely by keeping the commandments of the law, even though it was a condition for salvation. In the psalm which concludes the Community rule the grace of God is extolled and his righteousness is described as a gift. The hope of those who had entered the community of salvation was in the acts of God. "As for me, in God is my judgment (righteousness); in his hand is the perfection of my path

---

[44] In addition, there was even a more general concept of atonement at Qumran, which concerned the whole of Israel. According to Garnet, the eschatological condemnation of the wicked was seen as an act of atonement. The sin of Israel had to be dealt with through an act of atonement, and the destruction of the wicked was the ransom provided for Israel. Garnet, *Pauline Studies*, 31.

[45] This is noted by Ringgren: "Forgiveness is a gift of God, it is true, but at the same time, it is inseparably connected with repenting of sin and a proper frame of mind." Ringgren, *Faith*, 123.

[46] In this sense the new attitude demanded by Sanders is necessary. See the excursus above.

[47] Klinzing notes that in the concept of atonement, too, we can see an act of God. The obedience of members was always directed by the Spirit of God (e.g. 1QS III, 4-12). Klinzing, *Umdeutung*, 100-101.

with the uprightness of my heart; and with his just acts (righteousness) he cancels my sin" (1QS XI, 2-3).[48]

Even more beautiful is the section a little later where the expressions used remind one of a similar passage in the letters of Paul:[49]

"As for me, if I stumble, the mercies of God shall be my salvation always; and if I fall in the sin of the flesh, in the justice of God, which endures eternally, shall my judgment be; if my grief commences, he will free my soul from the pit and make my steps steady on the path... he will judge me in the justice of his truth, and in his plentiful goodness always atone for all my sins" (1QS XI, 11-14).

The council of the community provided for (vicarious) atonement for every member by its perfect obedience. One of the features of sapiential synergism is that sin can never exceed the atoning power of obedience.

There is a tension between the conditions of admission to the community and eschatological salvation. It is resolved by the theology of free will, described above, and a kind of "weak" predestination.[50] Sin was not considered to be so serious that it could have prevented man from entering the "chosen remnant" of Israel. The synergistic action of man was considered to be merely his response to the saving act of God in the last aeon.[51] The eschatological hope of the community was in the "justifying" righteousness, or judgment, of God. God had promised to forgive his obedient people.

The soteriology of Qumran belongs in the centre of Second Temple Jewish theology. The special circumstances under which the sect was living had not essentially changed the deep traits of the theology of the community, which was rooted in the sapiential tradition of the Second Temple period and in emerging apocalypticism. Fear often occurred in the community, and this fear was a justified one. During different periods of the history of the sect, godless rulers had persecuted them. This even strengthened the dualism of their soteriology. The righteous ones of Qumran believed steadfastly in the Lordship of God. This resulted in a firm eschatological hope in the salvation provided by God. A condition for salvation was submission to obedience to the law. In

---

[48] Cf. Ringgren, *Faith*, 121.

[49] In this respect we can agree with Betz: "In Qumran hat die *Gerechtigkeit Gottes absolute Priorität vor dem menschlichen Tun.*" Betz, in his "Rechtfertigung in Qumran", now in *Jesus*, 56 (italics his). Betz acknowledges the aspect of synergism, though, and does not indulge in any over-interpretation in the manner of Marx, as mentioned earlier; see (Betz) p. 58.

[50] Merrill did not consider this question deeply enough. This is why he is content to say that the concept of the community is "near" to double predestination, even though in a dogmatic sense it is not precisely so. Merrill, *Predestination*, 41.

[51] "Salvation is mediated by life in the Community and the attitude or spirit of submission which is manifested there is spoken of in terms of an atonement." Garnet, *Salvation*, 80.

addition, God was merciful, and what is of further importance, atonement was provided in the community. It was based on the perfect obedience of the council of the sect. In this synergistic context the basis of salvation was always to be found in the grace of God and in the righteousness of God. The members of the sect awaited the inauguration of God's Kingdom and the new age of salvation.

Summary

The occurrence of the problem of theodicy is well attested throughout Second Temple Jewish literature. The theologians of that period attempted to explain the crises into which Israel had drifted. Israel was the Chosen People, whom God had taken out of Egypt and led to the Promised Land. Now this nation had to suffer oppression under foreign rulers. This made them doubt their calling and even God's ability or at least his willingness to help his people.

Even though there were several branches within the diverse Second Temple literature, the theology of crisis can be found in most of them. It found its way into quite different circles of tradition. The solution given differs, though, with the nature of the text in question. Sirach, 1 Enoch, the Community Rule, the Psalms of Solomon and 4 Ezra each have a different historical context. This is why the theological setting, too, varies. Nevertheless, there are naturally common features, due to the common (Second Temple Hasidic) tradition and the Scriptures. There are certain fixed ways of interpreting the problem of theodicy.

As a theological question the problem of theodicy is important for the further reason that it usually occurs in the context of key factors of soteriology. The political crisis of Israel is at the same time a theological problem, or a crisis of salvation history. A crisis can be interpreted only as a breach in relations with God. This is why the primary reason for such a breach, according to the writers, is usually sin. Pondering on the problem of sin of Israel is in the centre of the soteriological aspect of the problem of theodicy.

There are several explanations of the nature of sin. The most traditional way to assess the causes of oppression is to refer to the sins of the people. The anguish of the nation is a result of the ungodliness of Israel. In addition, the responsibility of the (Israelite) rulers is also emphasized. According to most writers, a fallen ruler brings the wrath of God upon the whole nation. A third group consists of foreign rulers. On the one hand, they execute the punishments which God himself has prescribed. On the other hand, they are at the same time oppressors of the righteous, and they, too, must perish on the last day.

As regards judgment, we find two central features. Firstly, Israel will have to face the punishments of God in history. This concerns foreign nations too, because their fate also is in the hands of God. Secondly, there will be an eschatological judgment. Justice will eventually be revealed on the Day of the wrath of the Lord.

Future expectations usually imply some kind of concept of predestination. God is believed to have prescribed a sentence for transgressors. Sin will not be left unpunished. The ungodly have been predestined to be subject to the wrath of God. In this way justice will be brought to the suffering righteous on the last day. The concept of predestination was not deterministic, however. It was possible to repent and return to the path of salvation. Only the most ungodly oppressors found themselves in a different situation. According to several writers, they were "children of darkness" who could no longer repent. Their fate had been sealed and God's sentence only awaited its execution.

The reverse side of predestinarian theology was synergistic nomism. The only way to salvation was in repentance and returning to keeping the law of Moses. Only in this way could Jews return to covenantal grace and the mercy of God. Only in this way could the eschatological punishment be avoided.

The synergistic nature of Jewish soteriology can be seen in the belief that in spite of the prescribed sentence a way to salvation was possible. Instead of a deterministic double predestination we meet another kind of predestinarian theology. Salvation was united with a demand for repentance. From Sirach to the texts of Qumran the eschatological proclamation had a positive attitude towards the majority of Israelites. The hearers were almost children of God or children of Light – whatever the epithet. Without sincere repentance and obedience to the law they would not be saved, however. This was the belief of most eschatological groups of the Second Temple period.

When we move on to the soteriology of Paul, we must assess how he answers the crucial theological questions of his time. We can assume that Paul worked in close relation to the tradition which he had learnt as a pious Pharisee in Jerusalem. In the following an assessment will be given of the treatment of the problem of theodicy, and the content of predestinarian theology in particular, in the soteriology of Paul.

Chapter 2

The Problem of Theodicy and Predestination in Paul's Soteriology

Paul's way of treating the problem of theodicy differs from that of other Jewish writings. He does not attempt to give reasons for a national or political crisis or to explain the consequences. Roman occupation was painfully real to the people of Israel, but this is not what he focussed his attention upon. The starting-point of Paul's theology was a religious crisis and a crucial turning-point in salvation history – the execution and resurrection of Jesus Christ.

Such a different context does not mean, however, that in this matter Paul had rejected his Jewish roots. We can still find a typically Jewish setting in his theology. In fact, he seems to be bound up with Jewish tradition and constantly uses themes derived from Second Temple writings. His theology of predestination builds on Jewish presuppositions, and it was presented by Paul as a critical antithesis to traditional beliefs.

Paul and Jewish theology have several themes in common, such as the questions of sin and punishment, as well as that of divine judgment. In Paul's theology these themes are central for the definition of soteriology. Paul's concept of salvation, with all its original features and details, must thus be placed at the end of a long development which took place in Jewish theology during the Second Temple period.

§ 6   Will God Still Help His People?

It seems to be a widely-held opinion among modern readers that Paul does not speak much about the problem of theodicy itself. It is true that in his letters the righteousness of God is not often questioned. He does not usually cast doubt on the goodness of the will of God. The question is not totally absent, however. In Romans 3 we have an almost classical treatment of the problem of theodicy. The question of sin seems to be of special importance to Paul here. In Romans 8 a similar discussion appears in the context of predestinarian theology. This kind of reasoning is also the subject of chapters 9-11, where the problem of the fate of the Chosen People forms a classical crux in Pauline studies.

6.1. The faithfulness of God has not failed (Rom. 3:3-4)

In Romans 3 Paul treats the question of the unfaithfulness of Israel almost as a true sapiential theologian.

"What if some were unfaithful? Will their faithlessness nullify the faithfulness of God? By no means! Although everyone is a liar, let God be proved true" (Rom. 3:3-4a).

Considered in the context of Second Temple Judaism, Paul's teaching fits well in a situation where the relationship between God and Israel had been questioned over and over again. The chosen people had fallen; Israel had abandoned her God. God's promises could have been fulfilled true, had the nation not lived in sin. Now the only question that remained was, why did God not protect Israel from sin.[1]

τί γὰρ εἰ ἠπίστησάν τινες;

      μὴ ἡ ἀπιστία αὐτῶν   (unfaithfulness)

      τὴν πίστιν τοῦ θεοῦ καταργήσει;   (faithfulness)

μὴ γένοιτο·

      γινέσθω δὲ ὁ θεὸς ἀληθής,   (true)

      πᾶς δὲ ἄνθρωπος ψεύστης   (false)

(Rom. 3:3-4) [2]

Paul's answer to the problem of God's faithfulness is based on traditional terminology. We may note especially that his word-play on πίστις / ἀπιστία leads us to the theme of theodicy. Israel had been unfaithful, indeed, but this is not something of which one could accuse God.

Here Paul is using precisely those ideas of Jewish sapiential theology which we have analyzed in the previous chapters.[3] Sin is considered a problem of man himself – God is not to be blamed. Man lives under the power of sin, but

---

[1] Such a context is also referred to by Moo, *Romans*, 183. The question remains, however, whether Paul is speaking here of faithfulness in the old covenant or of faith in Christ. Dunn rightly remarks that Paul still has in mind the indictment outlined in 2:17-29, instead of the reasoning of the later chapters 9-11. (In spite of this he interprets the faithfulness as faith in Christ, see the discussion in the notes below.) Dunn, *Romans*, 131. Räisänen, however, has identified this section with the argumentation of chapters 9-11. Räisänen, *Torah*, 188f. Such a conclusion cannot be correct because Paul is certainly speaking here of the situation of the Jews in the "old" covenant. In such a situation the faithfulness of God is questioned.

[2] The structure has been analyzed e.g. in Wilckens, *Römer I*, 161-162; Dunn, *Romans*, 132-133.

[3] Cf. chapters 3.2. and 3.3.

God is righteous. He will judge the earth and bring sinners to account for their sins.[4]

But how should we understand the word "faithlessness"? Does it mean "not being obedient", or "unbelief", lack of faith?[5] Finnish Bible translations often give the latter alternative, while English translations in general prefer the former alternative: "Will their faithlessness nullify the faithfulness of God?" (NRSV v. 3; NIV however: "lack of faith"). Solutions to this problem are evidently dependent on one's general interpretation of Paul's message in this passage.

The word πίστις is quite an important term for Paul and we might imagine that he would let it dominate the thought throughout the whole section. On the other hand, the dynamics of the word-play lead us in another direction. If Paul is here treating the problem of theodicy, which is probable as regards the context, he is no doubt dealing with the question of obedience. According to this interpretation, Paul is here asking a typically Jewish question: now that Israel has fallen, is God still able to guide and protect his people?[6]

The aspect of obedience is also prominent when consideration is given to Paul's basic polarization in this section. He contrasts obedience with sin. He is not speaking of people's denial of Christ, as he would have done when speaking of unbelief. Nor is unfaithfulness to the covenant an issue here. This might have been the interpretation of those who accept the theory of covenantal nomism.[7] On the contrary, Paul is talking about Israel's sin. In the parallelism of verse 4, truth stands in antithesis to lies. And in the following verses Paul is speaking of injustice. Later, in verse 9, he summarizes all of this: the Jews too are under sin. One is obliged to draw the conclusion that in 3:3-4 Paul is speaking of the disobedience of Israel.

---

[4] The exact meaning of the word ἀπιστία is not easily defined. From a semantic point of view it could mean "unbelief", but in this context it is contrasted with God's faithfulness. Thus the meaning "faithlessness" is emphasized. Dunn underlines the basic difference in meaning between these alternatives, since he thinks that Paul speaks in covenantal terms. This would mean faithlessness towards the covenant. As Dunn, however, at the same time states that faithlessness means the Jews' unwillingness to confess Christ, there remains practically no difference whatsoever in meaning. Dunn, *Romans*, 131-132.

[5] Cranfield tries to include both of these meanings in his interpretation (in spite of the fact that he prefers 'unbelief'), Cranfield, *Romans*, 180; Black considers the description of their relationship to be a word-play, Black, *Romans*, 54.

[6] It is understandable that, according to Räisänen, Paul is here talking about unbelief. He uses the argument that in Paul's thought the breaking of the covenant is identified with unbelief. The basic reason was that Räisänen parallelled this passage with chapters 9-11. Räisänen, *Torah*, 188-190. The context of the problem of theodicy is too clear for such an interpretation.

[7] Cf. Dunn, *Romans*, 131f.; Ziesler, *Romans*, 96.

The scriptural quotation in verse 3 provides us with more information about Paul's argumentation. It is taken from the Psalms (Ps. 116: 11; 51:6). The first of these proof-texts is actually only an allusion which functions as an introduction (v. 3b). Afterwards there comes an explicit quotation (v. 4) where the wording follows the Septuagint (Ps. 50:6 LXX). "So that you may be justified in your words, and prevail when you are being judged" (NRSV translates: "in your judging"; LXX: καὶ νικήσεις ἐν τῷ κρίνεσθαί σε).[8]

We must note that in the original context of this Psalm the focus is on confession of sin. The Psalmist stands before a heavenly court and makes his confession. Juridical language is evident here. God is a Judge and his righteousness will be proved true (Ὅπως ἂν δικαιωθῇς) in his judgments.[9] By confessing their sins people also acknowledge God's right to judge them.[10]

Even though this Psalm does not itself come within the scope of the discussion about theodicy, it contains similar terminology. The idea of repentance implies the question of God's right to judge his creatures. If there were any doubts as regards God's power they are now blown away. God is just in his judgments and those under sentence must accept that fact.[11]

It seems clear that Paul needed to use this argument in his teaching about God's judgment.[12] This is what he actually says in verse 6. The aim of the whole train of thought is to assert God's right to judge the world. And if this could be proved, it would result in a negative assessment of Israel. This must have been in Paul's mind. He aimed at depicting Israel in all her wretchedness.

There is a tension between election and rejection here, and it is quite intense. Even though Israel, as the Chosen People, had possessed all the promises of God (v. 2), she had now lost them one by one. According to Paul, all the previously "elected" Jews were now covenant-breakers. Now they were

---

[8] Concerning the use of the quotation from the Psalms, see Fitzmyer, *Romans*, 328. A comparison between the methods of interpretation employed by Paul and other Jewish writers is presented by Wilckens, *Römer I*, 164-165.

[9] See e.g. Dunn, *Romans*, 133.

[10] In this way Michel, *Römer (1955)*, 79-81. He thinks that the theme of God's unconditional righteousness in verse 4 provides a basis for all Paul's teaching on justification.

[11] Dunn thinks that Paul used Psalm 51 because the words "transgresssion" and "sin" frequently occur there. In that case Paul would probably link the psalm with the idea of unfaithfulness. Dunn, *Romans*, 133. A better solution, however, can be found in the explanation that Paul needed a Scriptural basis for the idea of God's righteous judgment.

[12] Stuhlmacher, *Römer*, 49-50.

subject to the wrath of God.[13] This was a radical thing to say. In the eyes of traditional Jews Paul's teaching was plain blasphemy.

Paul turns the implicit claim of blasphemy around. When God's righteousness is understood as juridical justice, God must always have the right to judge his creatures. Thus God is not unjust when he inflicts his wrath (vv. 5,6).[14] Sin does not increase God's glory even if it proves him righteous! Sin will always dishonour God.

This assertion was necessary, however, in order to protect God's righteousness. With the aid of skilful rhetoric Paul presents antitheses in the form of questions and answers, where faithfulness and faithlessness, truth and falsehood are opposed to each other.[15] God is truthful (ἀληθής), but every man is a liar.[16] Therefore God's judgment will fall on mankind truthfully. It would be a false conclusion to say that God is responsible for sin, and thus unjust in his judgments. God is not unjust (ἄδικος)[17] when he allows his wrath to condemn sin (v. 5).[18]

For Paul, there is only one solution to the problem of the sinfulness of Israel, and consequently, to the problem of theodicy. It is the judgment of God. By his just judgment God will recompense those who suffer from injustice. At the same time all ungodliness will be punished. Paul actually treats the problem of theodicy in the same way as the Jewish sapiential theologians or other Jewish groups in the Second Temple period. The question is a traditional one: should the ungodliness and faithlessness of many prominent Jews be regarded as a sign of God's rejection of his people? In that case God would turn out to be a liar because it would mean that he had broken his promises.[19]

---

[13] The tension between election and judgment is discussed in Wilckens, *Römer I*, 168. In this respect there seems to be a connection with the later chapters 9-11. Dodd, *Romans*, 44; Dunn, *Romans*, 131. The basic setting is prepared here even though Paul does not yet give all his arguments.

[14] Cf. Wilckens, *Römer I*, 165.

[15] Paul's rhetoric is analyzed in Stowers, *CBQ 46* (1984), 707ff. Stowers thinks that the purpose of Paul's dialogue with his alleged Jewish partner is to show him that Israel has been unfaithful to the covenant, see p. 715.

[16] One should not exaggerate the tension between the words "some" (v. 4) and "everyone" (v. 5). Even though some scholars have asked whether Paul really thought that some people could fulfil the righteousness of the law, such a discussion is not appropriate here. The problem must be solved by theology, not by rhetoric. Cf. Schlier, *Römerbrief*, 92-93.

[17] The word ἄδικος is also used by Paul in a word-play. Firstly, it is an antithesis to the word "righteous". Secondly, the execution of a sentence, δίκη, cannot be entrusted to anyone who himself has been sentenced to punishment. This is one of those near-blasphemous arguments of which Paul has also been accused.

[18] Stuhlmacher, *Römer*, 50.

[19] Scholars rarely consider the theme of judgment from the point of view of the problem

The ideas of Jewish theology and Paul's thought differ from the modern philosophical problem of theodicy. The former do not call into question God's *ability* to help. God's sovereign power is not at issue as it is in modern discussion. Instead Paul and other Jewish theologians are concerned with God's *willingness* to help. They ask if God is still loyal to his people. This distinction is important, as we must remember that both the Jews and the first Christians never actually doubted the mighty Lordship of God. Every writer seems to acknowledge that God rules over this world and that he is capable of judging every man when the day of judgment comes. God's righteousness would be questioned only if old promises were to be denied whey the sentence is delivered.[20]

The first section of our analysis confirms the hypothesis that Paul is dealing with the problem of theodicy when he writes about soteriology. There is an interesting relationship between Paul and his Jewish background. On the one hand, Paul employs themes and even solutions previously found in Second Temple Jewish theology. On the other hand, Paul's perspective on this question has changed. He is writing in a new situation where the righteousness of God has been revealed to this world in Christ. Therefore there is a tension between traditional Judaism and the followers of Jesus. It is easy to see that the argumentation in Romans 3 points to the same subjects as will be treated in detail later in the letter, in chapters 9-11. The basic question in Paul's mind concerns the soteriological status of Israel. In Romans 3 this is explicit only intermittently, however.

Paul answers the question of theodicy and makes only a few preliminary statements. God is faithful, truthful and just. He will punish all injustice and faithlessness. He will judge sinners. Here Paul shares the tradition of the

---

of theodicy. They are content to analyse the eschatology, and at most connections with the Old Testament are referred to. See Michel, *Römer (1955)*, 81; Schlier, *Römerbrief*, 93-94; Fitzmyer, *Romans*, 325-328. Dodd briefly mentions the problem of theodicy. From the Jewish point of view the abandoning of Israel would at the same time have been a threat to God's justness. When solving this problem, all Paul could do was to appeal to the unconditional righteousness of God's judgment. Dodd, *Romans*, 45; cf. Wilckens, *Römer I*, 169, who says that the justification of a sinner eventually solves the problem of theodicy.

[20] Räisänen neglects the context of Jewish theology and gives a Christological interpretation even here. Räisänen, *Torah*, 201-202 (cf. analysis later in chapter 14.2.). He states that Paul did not actually consider the breaking of the covenant with the Jews to be a problem. The real problem was that they wanted to remain in the old covenant and did not accept Christ as the object of faith. Cf. Sanders, *Law*, 198-199. This kind of interpretation is a forced one because the context reveals that Paul is writing about the problem of sin. Sin was the reason for the punishments sent by God both during and after the Exile. This raises the problem of theodicy – and this is precisely what Paul was endeavouring to solve.

Jewish theology of his time. The judgment of God is at hand, and it will bring justice to this world.

6.2. *The righteous shall live by faith (Rom. 1:16-17)*

In Romans we find other passages where the problem of theodicy clearly affected Paul's theology. The developed predestinarian theology of the prophet Habakkuk (2:4), which was analysed in chapter 3, is referred to at the very beginning of the letter (1:17). The prophet's crucial answer to the cries of the suffering righteous could not occur in a more important passage of Paul's letter. It is used as a Scriptural argument in the climax of the introduction, where Paul describes the righteousness that comes from faith.[21] Why did he use precisely this Old Testament text to support his most important argument? Does the way he quotes the Old Testament have a direct connection with his theology of predestination?

In previous chapters we have already paid attention to the fact that in Habakkuk the fate and future of Israel were explained in terms of the problem of theodicy. In his prophecy the agony of the people was vented with the cry: why does God not help? The prophet solved the problem in a traditional way. God is faithful and keeps his promises. He will judge the godless, but the faithful will see a time of renewal and be granted a new life.

The quotation of Habakkuk is interesting enough, and not least for its later influence, its "Wirkungsgeschichte". This text was important for the identity of the righteous Jews at Qumran, as we have seen above. Paul quotes Hab. 2:4 twice, once in Galatians and once in Romans.[22]

"For I am not ashamed of the gospel; it is the power of God for salvation to everyone who has faith, to the Jew first and also to the Greek. For in it the righteousness of God is revealed through faith for faith; as it is written, 'The one who is righteous will live by faith.' (ὁ δὲ δίκαιος ἐκ πίστεως ζήσεται)."

(Rom. 1:16-17).[23]

This important quotation of Habakkuk 2:4 has been troublesome in scholarship because there are several different versions of it found elsewhere.[24] In the text of Paul we have a wording which differs both from the Masoretic Text and

---

[21] Besides the commentaries, the quotation of Habakkuk has been analyzed e.g. by Feuillet, *NTS* 6 (1959) 52-80; Cavallin, *StTh* 32 (1978) 33-43; Moody, *ExpT* 92 (1980) 205-208; and Koch, *ZNW* 76 (1985) 68-85.

[22] See also above chapters 3.1. and 5.2.

[23] NRSV gives also another alternative for the last lines: "The one who is righteous through faith will live." See below the discussion concerning these alternatives.

[24] Here the summarizing analyses of Fitzmyer and Moo are helpful, Fitzmyer, *Romans*, 262-265; Moo, *Romans*, 74-75.

from the Septuagint. So a comparison with the Masoretic Text gives us only
one alternative for the explanation of Paul's text: "Their spirit is not right in
them, but the righteous live by their faith/faithfulness."

According to the Masoretic Text, Habakkuk 2:4 speaks of the obedience/
faithfulness of a righteous Jew. The righteous one is given life on account of
his faithfulness (באמונתו). This is also the alternative followed by several
translations, such as the New English Bible ("the righteous man will live by
being faithful") and the modern Finnish translation (1992). [25]

The tradition of Qumran very likely confirms this textual form. Unfortunately
the text in the Habakkuk commentary is damaged in precisely the lines where
the actual word meaning faithfulness would have been written. The
interpretation itself is clear, however, and points to a certain alternative. "Its
interpretation concerns all observing the Law in the House of Judah, whom
God will free from punishment on account of their deeds and of their loyalty
(ואמנתם) to the Teacher of Righteousness" (1QpHab VIII, 1-3, Martínez). The
text of Habakkuk was a basis for exhorting the Qumran community to
obedience. Other texts make it clear, too, that such a belief was an important
part of the soteriology of the community. [26]

The Greek textual tradition contains an important detail, namely the Naḥal
Ḥever manuscript of the twelve minor prophets. The reading in this manuscript
at Habakkuk 2:4 is the oldest one in existence in Greek, and it follows quite
accurately the standard Hebrew wording. The Masoretic Text is in fact
followed word for word in the translation: [δί]καιος ἐν πίστει αὐτοῦ
ζήσετ[αι] (8HevXIIgr 17.29-30).[27] This reading strengthens our view that the
original form of the text spoke of the faithfulness of the righteous one.

The discovery of an old reading which follows the Masoretic Text is interesting enough, since the wording of the Septuagint differs from that of the
Masoretic Text. Actually, we cannot even speak of a single reading of the
Septuagint, because the manuscripts provide us here with a great number of
problems. There are three different readings, and each one of them seems at
first sight quite distant from the Masoretic Text or the Greek version of the
Naḥal Ḥever text.

The readings of the Septuagint are as follows:

---

[25] Hab. 2:4 MT: וצדיק באמונתו יחיה. NIV translates "by his faith" and NRSV gives us
both of these alternatives. Wilckens thinks that Paul, too, must have known the verse in
precisely this form when he used it in his letter, Wilckens, *Römer I,* 89; Cf. Kertelge,
Rechtfertigung, 93; Schlier, *Römerbrief,* 45-46.

[26] See above chapter 5.2. The basic idea of the Masoretic Text can later be detected in the
Targums and in rabbinic tradition, see Strack-Billerbeck, *Kommentar III,* 542ff.

[27] Cf. Fitzmyer, *Romans,* 264. This reading is found in Aquila and Symmachus, see
Koch, *ZNW* 76 (1985) 70.

1. ὁ δὲ δίκαιος ἐκ πίστεώς μου ζήσεται (e.g. W*, B)
2. ὁ δὲ δίκαιος μου ἐκ πίστεως ζήσεται (e.g. A, C)
3. ὁ δὲ δίκαιος ἐκ πίστεως ζήσεται (e.g. 763*)[28]

It is no easy task to decide between these readings. There is a solution, however, proposed by Koch. He has suggested, supported by rather good arguments, that the first of these (W*), in spite of some peculiarities, is a translation of the original Hebrew text of the verse. He points to the fact that in the same clause there is a change of subject. Instead of speaking of the soul of man, W* reads "my soul", denoting God. This change of subject then also affects the translation of the end of the verse. Here too the translator emphasizes God as the subject of the action and translates the word (באמונתו) as meaning God's faithfulness (ἐκ πίστεώς μου).[29] The righteous one will receive life through the faithfulness of God.[30]

As regards the other two variants, we need to consult the textual history of the Letter to the Hebrews. In the New Testament a similar discussion concerns the manuscripts of that letter. All the variant readings of the Septuagint can be found there, too (Heb. 10:38). The first of the readings (ἐκ πίστεώς μου) is found e.g. in manuscript D*; the second one (δίκαιος μου) e.g. in P[46], ℵ, A; and the third one (δίκαιος ἐκ πίστεως) e.g. in P[13] and D[2].

As we try to explain the second variant, we must ask: were there really several versions of the Septuagint behind the textual tradition of Hebrews? This is improbable. The text of the letter to Hebrews is itself older that variant 2 of the Septuagint. This is why it is better to explain the variant readings of the Septuagint with the aid of the text of Hebrews and not *vice versa*. In this case the actual LXX text behind the original text of Hebrews must be the oldest reading of the Septuagint (ἐκ πίστεώς μου), as we explained above.

Since the variant in P[46] is of primary value in the textual history of Hebrews, and in addition it is a "difficult" variant which would not be expected here, it must be considered the original form of the text of Hebrews 10:38. Variant 2 in Hebrews must thus be an intentional variant made for theological reasons.[31] This is understandable enough when we consider the text of Hebrews. In the teaching of the writer a free use of the Scriptural quotation well serves the

---

[28] Käsemann has suggested the wording: ὁ δὲ δίκαιος μου ἐκ πίστεώς μου ζήσεται. Käsemann, *Römer*, 28. This reconstruction in probably based on an erroneous interpretation of the information of textual criticism, see Koch, *ZNW* 76 (1985) 69 n. 4.

[29] Koch, *ZNW* 76 (1985) 70-73.

[30] The change has been explained by a misreading of *yod* for *waw*. Cavallin, *StTh* 32 (1978) 35; Fitzmyer, *Romans*, 264. The idea that the subject was changed intentionally is a better argument, however.

[31] Here I follow Koch, *ZNW* 76 (1985) 75; and Dunn, *Romans*, 45.

purposes of his dynamic parenesis.[32] The writer claims that his righteous readers (δίκαιος μου) must remain obedient to God and not give up in apostasy. As a consequence we must conclude that LXX variant 2 (A, C) arose due to the influence of the Letter to the Hebrews.

For the third variant we also need the help of Paul. Paul, as we well know, does not follow either of the two previous alternatives. The quotation from Habakkuk is in the third form (LXX 763*), and what is of great importance, the wording is exactly the same in two letters from different periods. The older one, Galatians, gives us the reading ὁ δίκαιος ἐκ πίστεως ζήσεται (Gal. 3:11). In Romans the same clause is repeated, only with an added conjunction ('Ο δὲ δίκαιος..., Rom. 1:17). We are justified in concluding that the version did not arise by chance.

Did Paul know a variant reading of the Septuagint, which he simply quoted here? This is improbable. The version of the Septuagint with a similar reading (LXX 763*) is again in this case a late one. As regards the text of Romans, we are most probably faced with Paul's original use of Habakkuk.[33] The clause Paul uses is so unique that it has become his trademark. This is why it is repeated in different letters when the same theme is under discussion.[34] The only reasonable conclusion is, then, that variant 3, both in Hebrews and in the Septuagint, has its origin in the letters of Paul.

As a result of this excursus we can say that both of the readings of the Septuagint which resemble those of the New Testament arose under the influence of the latter. In Paul's time there was but one reading of the Septuagint known in his churches: the one with the words ὁ δὲ δίκαιος ἐκ πίστεώς μου ζήσεται.[35]

In Romans Paul quotes the key-line of Habakkuk, but he does not use the wording of the Septuagint. This is why we must ask whether he changed the text intentionally or not. In attempting to answer this question we can firstly assume that Paul must have known the difference between the Septuagint and

---

[32] In the Scriptural quotation there are further echoes of Isa. 26:20 and Habakkuk 2:3.

[33] In this way Koch, *ZNW* 76 (1985) 83-85; Dunn, *Romans*, 45.

[34] As a curiosity we may mention the solution of Karl Barth, where the problems of the text have disappeared: "Denn die Gerechtigkeit Gottes enthüllt sich in ihr: auf Treue dem Glauben, wie geschrieben steht: Der Gerechte wird leben aus meiner Treue." Barth, *Römerbrief*, 10. Since Barth decided to translate the word πίστις by "faithfulness" (or: "Treue Gottes"), he in fact interpreted the quotation of Habakkuk following the Septuagint (see the introduction to the second edition, *Römerbrief*, XVII).

[35] Commentaries seldom discuss the textual variants, but in this case it has not done any harm, since the result happens to be the starting-point of most scholars when they quote the LXX.

the Masoretic text.[36] If this difference as such was significant, he could have used the Masoretic wording in the first place. The difference from the Septuagint would in this case easily have worked to his advantage in his theology.

Paul's version of the verse of Habakkuk, as far as linguistics are considered, could well-nigh be his own, a somewhat inaccurate translation of the Hebrew text. The Greek text differs from that of the Naḥal Ḥever manuscript, which was very accurate and literal in its translation. In this case we should further ask why the Hebrew suffix is left out, even if it is important for the original thought. This would, however, be the only difference to be noted. As regards the content, Paul's text would be quite near the original Hebrew source.[37]

On the other hand, it is obvious that the use of the text of the Septuagint as such would have been natural and useful. One would not have needed to work on the Greek wording, and the quotation would have been familiar to the Greek-speaking readers of Paul's letter, who used the Septuagint in their churches. If the text of the Septuagint could have served Paul's purposes he would not have needed to change the wording.[38] This is why we can assume that there had to be a special reason for using an exceptional quotation.[39]

Even when the context of Paul's verse is considered, the text of the Septuagint would seem logical and suitable to use here. Had Paul wished to quote the Septuagint, he could well have done so and nothing would have been changed.[40] He is talking about the righteousness of God, which appears now as a saving gospel. This idea is implicit in the LXX text. God's faithfulness brings righteousness and salvation. This would make perfect theology for Paul. When Paul later teaches about Abraham he in fact uses this kind of argument, in Romans 4:3. Now Paul has made a different choice, and we must

---

[36] This is a natural starting-point for the discussion. See e.g. Feuillet, *NTS* 6 (1959) 52; Dunn, *Romans*, 45; Black, *Romans*, 35. Scholars have not doubted that Paul was aware of the originality of the wording he was using. They have been interested in explaining the purpose of the change he makes.

[37] Feuillet thought that Paul made the change for theological reasons. He emphasized the term ἐκ πίστεως and connected it with the righteous one: the one who is righteous by faith finds life. Feuillet, *NTS* 6 (1959) 53. According to Moody, this was not Paul's purpose. In that case Paul would have used an expression more typical of him. Moody says that Paul was faithful to the Masoretic Text against the Septuagint. Moody, *ExpT* 92 (1980-1981) 205-206. Cavallin, *StTh* 32 (1978) 36, also uses typical Pauline expressions as an argument.

[38] This is why I would not agree with the conclusion reached by Ziesler, who says that Paul took the verse from the LXX but omitted the 'my' after 'faith'. Ziesler, *Romans*, 71.

[39] Against the old Sanday-Headlam commentary, which maintains that Paul intentionally followed the content of Habakkuk. Sanday-Headlam, *Romans*, 28.

[40] This problem has been noted by Campbell, too. Campbell, *JBL 113* (1994) 279f.

take it into account. One cannot help assuming that his choice was made for theological purposes.[41]

What was Paul's purpose in using the quotation of Habakkuk? In order to answer this question we must place the clause and the verse in their proper context. This quotation has a certain logical application in the course of Paul's rhetoric. What he is doing is presenting arguments for the right understanding of the "righteousness of God".[42]

The basic idea in 1:17 is a simple one. Paul says that the righteousness of God has been revealed in the gospel (ἐν αὐτῷ). For Paul, this divine revelation (ἀποκαλύπτεται) is by no means arbitrary.[43] It is based on the Scriptures, and on God's promise (καθὼς γέγραπται). So, first of all, the quotation of Habakkuk presents the proper content of the gospel and depicts the authentic way to salvation. The prophetic word concerning righteousness confirms the "good news" which, in verse 16, is "the power of God for salvation".[44]

Secondly, the quotation of Habakkuk is used as an argument for a proper understanding of faith. From this point of view it is justified to say that Paul intentionally inserted his beloved term "through/by faith" (ἐκ πίστεως) in the quotation.[45] In this way Habakkuk becomes a witness to righteousness by

---

[41] On the basis of the MT, Gaston reaches the conclusion that the quotation in the text of Paul should be translated "The righteous shall live by faithfulness". Furthermore he thinks that this point of departure affects the interpretation of the beginning of the verse. "For God's righteousness is revealed in it, from [his] faithfulness to [our] faithfulness..." Thus Gaston concludes that for Paul, the text of Habakkuk actually reads: "The righteous shall live by [God's] faithfulness". Gaston, *Paul*, 118-119, 170. This is too difficult a theory compared with the possibility that Paul could well have used the LXX for such a purpose. Cf. discussion below.

[42] The purpose of the quotation has been explained in several ways. Black thought that Paul wanted to reject Pharisaic legalism, Black, *Romans*, 37. According to Cranfield, he wished to express the deeper, religious content of the prophetic text. Cranfield, *Romans*, 101. Dodd's explanation comprises both of these notions. He thought that Paul changed the concept of *pistis* and by using the quotation taught both trust in God and righteousness by faith. Dodd, *Romans*, 14. In a similar way Michel said that Paul unites faith and obedience in his terminology. As at the beginning of the letter (1:5) here too the proper obedience in the context of eschatological soteriology is the obedience of faith, and this signifies righteousness by faith. Michel, *Römer (1955)*, 47.

[43] Following Wilckens we may further note that when Paul says that the righteousness of God is "revealed" (ἀποκαλύπτεται, present tense) in the gospel, he is actually posing an antithesis to the revelation in the Torah. Wilckens, *Römer I*, 88.

[44] Cf. Michel, *Römer (1978)*, 90. We could even write the clause in the form: δικαιοσύνη γὰρ θεοῦ ἐν (τῷ εὐαγγελίῳ) ἀποκαλύπτεται.

[45] In accordance with Koch, *ZNW* 76 (1985) 83; and Wilckens, *Römer I*, 90; but against Dunn, who says that Paul did not want to exclude the previous meaning but to extend and broaden the meaning. Dunn, *Romans*, 45.

faith.[46] As we noted above, Paul uses this technique elsewhere. For example, in Romans 4 Abraham becomes the father of righteousness by faith (4: 3).

The importance of faith is also emphasized by the complex expression in verse 17, "through faith for faith", NRSV ("from faith to faith" AV; Gr: ἐκ πίστεως εἰς πίστιν). Due to its originality it has caused problems for scholars. In principle Paul's teaching here is easy to understand. In the gospel we see the way to salvation which God has provided: faith. Only the expression which Paul uses is difficult. When the righteousness of God is revealed, the way to salvation becomes evident.

Because of the nature of the prepositions some scholars have thought that this expression is describing some kind of progress. The traditional explanation was that these words were divided into two parts. The first was said to mean God's loyalty, and the latter was said to mean the faith of man.[47] On the other hand, some writers have thought that Paul is here speaking of a development in the faith of man.

Because Paul on other occasions uses the first of these terms (ἐκ πίστεως) when he speaks of man's faith in general terms, the whole expression has been interpreted along these lines. In this case it would mean mere faith.[48] The explanations given above are most often based on a theological premise. Besides this we should remember a simple linguistic alternative. Linguistics open up a new perspective. We must note that the expression ἐκ πίστεως εἰς πίστιν is formulary. It is not simple prose which should be understood as the description of a progression.

Similar formulas occur in Paul's text elsewhere. One of the best examples is to be found in 2 Corinthians:

οἷς μὲν ὀσμὴ ἐκ θανάτου εἰς θάνατον,
οἷς δὲ ὀσμὴ ἐκ ζωῆς εἰς ζωήν. (2 Cor. 2:16).

---

[46] Feuillet, *NTS 6* (1959) 53-54. Wilckens, too, emphasizes this but does not make a difference between the Masoretic Text and the Septuagint. This is why the change of subject does not bother him, Wilckens, *Römer I*, 89. Moody, who wants to separate the terms "faith" and "righteousness", emphasizes the new life which is a consequence of faith. Moody, *ExpT 92* (1980-1981) 206. Such an interpretation goes beyond the soteriology of Paul.

[47] This is the classical explanation from Barth (*Römerbrief*, 16) to Dunn (*Romans*, 43) and Davies (*Faith*, 43). Wilckens adjusted the thought in a way that according to the text, the real righteousness (of God), on the one hand, is based on faith (instead of works), and, on the other hand, its goal is faith (that all men would believe). The latter term would now express the effect which is a result of proclaiming righteousness. Wilckens, *Römer I*, 88. We have also seen above the explanation of Gaston, in which the term "faithfulness" is exploited. "For God's righteousness is revealed in it, from [his] faithfulness to [our] faithfulness..." Gaston, *Paul*, 118-119, 170. This explanation does not fit the quotation, though.

[48] This is common in Schlatter's tradition, in which the Protestant theme "sola fide" is prominent. Schlatter, *Römer*, 15-16; cf. Dunn, *Romans*, 43.

This seems to be a double expression which aims at strengthening the main idea and the significance of the content: "to the latter it is a deadly fume that kills, to the former a vital fragrance that brings life" (2:16, NEB). This formula must be a Semitism which builds on the original prepositions מִן and אֶל. In Greek translation this reads ἐκ – εἰς.[49] In the Septuagint this formula is used when these prepositions are translated e.g. in LXX 83:8 (Ps. 84:7, NRSV): "they go from strength to strength" (LXX, πορευσόνται ἐκ δυνάμεως εἰς δύναμιν).[50]

These conclusions help us to explain the passage in Romans. Here the latter term εἰς πίστιν seems to be strengthening the content of the former. The latter phrase is not used primarily to express a change in the quality or basis of faith. We could as well present a dynamic translation of the passage as follows: "In the gospel the righteousness of God is revealed: it is by faith and solely by faith". The gospel of Christ is, for Paul, an expression of the fact that divine salvation is restricted to faith only.[51]

In the discussion concerning the quotation of Habakkuk there has been an ongoing debate as to whether Paul is here speaking of justification by faith at all.[52] As an alternative there has been an interpretation by which the clause is talking about the new life which faith produces. Scholars are asking whether the word "faith" should be connected with the word "righteous" or the verb "shall live". In the latter case Paul is talking either of the obedience of a believer or, rather, of the eschatological life of the saved.[53]

In spite of the generality of the discussion, the problem itself seems to be a secondary one. In the Habakkuk quotation there is no word for "justification". This is why an interpretation speaking of justification is always a conclusion which has been reached by relying on theological premises.

Furthermore, we must note that it would in fact be rather odd to translate the Greek expression ὁ δὲ δίκαιος ἐκ πίστεως as "anyone who is righteous

---

[49] In this way Schlier, *Römerbrief*, 45.

[50] Cf. the formula also in Jer. 9:2 (LXX).

[51] In this way Dodd, *Romans*, 14; Cranfield, *Romans*, 100. In modern commentaries cf. Fitzmyer, *Romans*, 263; Moo, *Romans*, 71. A linguistic explanation would seem the best alternative. On the other hand, we must admit that most explanations end up with quite a similar conclusion in any case. This is why there is not much diversity among different explanations.

[52] In his thorough article Cavallin provides an investigation of nearly every commentary of the older generation, and precisely from this point of view. Cavallin, *StTh 32* (1978) 33-35.

[53] This opinion is supported e.g. by Cavallin, *StTh 32* (1978) 33, 42; Moody, *ExpT 92* (1980-1981) 207-208; and Ziesler, *Romans*, 72. On linguistic grounds we must prefer the alternative of eschatological life to the alternative of the obedience of faith.

through faith".[54] Paul never uses such a wording in his letters. He speaks e.g. of "righteousness that comes from faith" (Rom. 3:22; 4:5; 4:13; 9:30) and of "justification by faith" (Rom. 3:26; 5:1; Gal. 2:16).

This is why the semantics of the Habakkuk quotation are necessarily directed by the Old Testament concept of a righteous person, a pious man. The prophet is speaking of the fate of a righteous one. In addition, Paul's version of Habakkuk is saying that a righteous person will receive (new) life through faith. We could paraphrase this as follows: "It is from faith that the righteous shall live (and not law, works, covenant, race etc.)". The word "life" quite clearly denotes salvation. So the only real question here is, how can one receive this new life?[55]

As Paul introduces the idea of receiving a new life, he is evidently teaching righteousness by faith. Verse 17 presents all that is needed for that righteousness. Paul is speaking of the revelation of God's righteousness (without the law). It is revealed to "faith, and solely to faith", and this is why it is righteousness by faith. This is at the same time the reason why the "righteous one", about whom Habakkuk had delivered his prophecy, now gained new life solely on the grounds of righteousness by faith.[56]

But who is the "righteous one"? Can we simply identify the term with a believer? The Habakkuk quotation has had an important role to play in the so-called ΠΙΣΤΙΣ ΧΡΙΣΤΟΥ discussion, where a messianic interpretation has prevailed. According to several scholars, we should consider Paul's teaching here as being Christocentric and identify the "righteous one" as Christ himself.[57]

How can one arrive at such an interpretation? There are several reasons for

---

[54] According to Hays, this might be the correct interpretation of the sentence in its original context in Habakkuk. Hays, *Faith*, 151. In his own interpretation he has abandoned this alternative, though, as we shall see below. Cf. Reumann, *ABD V* (1992) 765. This alternative can be found in RSV and NEB: "justified through faith".

[55] For example, Moo sees these connections. He concludes though that the verse should be translated "the one who is righteous by faith shall live". Moo, *Romans*, 72.

[56] Cf. Michel, *Römer (1978)*, 86; Hofius, *Paulusstudien*, 159.

[57] The modern discussion has been inaugurated by Hays with his book *The Faith of Jesus Christ*. (For a history of previous research, see Hays, *Faith*, 158-162). Hays has developed his ideas later in several articles, see Hays, *Apocalyptic* 191ff.; Hays, *SBL Seminar papers* (1991) 714ff. The last of these articles was answered and debated by Dunn, *SBL Seminar papers* (1991) 730ff. The interpretation of Hays has been accepted by Campbell, *Righteousness*, 204ff.; see also his recent article in *JBL 113* (1994) 265ff.

this. Firstly, the section is no doubt eschatological.[58] We can admit that in the first chapter of the Romans the gospel of God is a gospel of his Son Jesus. On a general level we could thus say that the eschatological revelation of God's righteousness in Christ could mean the appearance of the "Righteous One". This general statement is, however, not yet a valid reason for the conclusion that in verse 17 (and in the quotation from Habakkuk in particular) "Jesus Christ would be the means of the revelation of God's righteousness ἐκ πίστεως."[59]

The messianic interpretation has further been explained by the facts that the very text Hab. 2:2-4 is used as a messianic text even in Jewish literature, and that the term ὁ δίκαιος is a common messianic title (e.g. 1 Enoch 38:2; 53:6; Acts 3:14; 7:52).[60] This sounds convincing, but there are also several weaknesses in this reasoning. It is obvious that the preceding verse in Habakkuk, Hab. 2:3, is already interpreted in a messianic sense in the Septuagint.[61] This does not mean, however, that verse 4 has a similar meaning. In this context the "title" ὁ δίκαιος has never been interpreted as a messianic title. No one can deny that the title itself is used in 1 Enoch and in Acts, but that is of no importance here. One should be able to prove that there was at least one case where it it used as a messianic title in the quotation from Habakkuk.[62]

---

[58] Campbell opposes the "anthropocentric" reading with an "eschatological" reading, but he does so on strange grounds. He claims that the only proper way to understand the traditional reading in verse 17 leads to the interpretation: "The saving power of God within the gospel is being revealed by means of faith." Thus the expression ἐν αὐτῷ "functions adjectivally" within this reading. Campbell, *JBL 113* (1994) 271-272. Such an explanation is not valid. There is no reason why ἐκ should or even could be translated here by "by means of". Campbell goes on by presenting an appropriate eschatological interpretation: "God's eschatological salvation is being revealed *in it*, that is, in the gospel". I can fully agree with Campbell as regards the latter interpretation. He is wrong, however, when he maintains that the "traditional" interpretation of the clause *"is possible only if the first reading is the correct one"* (italics his). The weakness of Campbell's argument is probably in his original explanation of the expression ἐκ πίστεως.

[59] So Hays, *SBL Seminar papers* (1991) 719.

[60] See Hays, *Apocalyptic,* 193ff.; Hays, *SBL Seminar papers* (1991) 719.

[61] LXX reads "the Coming One". For the messianic interpretation of verse 3, see especially Strobel, *Untersuchungen,* 53ff.

[62] Scholars seem to have been too optimistic as regards Strobel's analyses on this question. Strobel has shown that Hab. 2:3 is widely used as a messianic text in Judaism, especially due to the influence of the Septuagint. He does not give examples of verse 4, however. See Strobel, *Untersuchungen,* 53ff., 175, 181f. Hays refers to Strobel quite too lightly, Hays, *SBL Seminar papers* (1991) 719, and also Campbell, who admits some problems with such an interpretation, does not hesitate to identify the expressions of Hab. 2:3 and 2:4. Campbell, *JBL 113* (1994) 283.

The parallel texts in Galatians and Hebrews create more problems still. In Galatians 3:11ff., where the quotation from Habakkuk also appears, Paul opposes obedience and faith. It is impossible to interpret this section as messianic. The righteousness that comes from the law (ὅτι δὲ ἐν νόμῳ οὐδεὶς δικαιοῦται παρὰ τῷ θεῷ) is here opposed to the righteousness that comes from faith. The latter is expressed simply by using a direct quotation of Hab. 2:4.[63] This is why in Galatians the righteous one who will find new eschatological life (salvation) in God's righteousness is the one who believes in Christ.[64]

In Galatians the function of the law is defined in the context of Paul's teaching on the righteousness by faith. The law guards people who are under the law "until faith would be revealed (εἰς τὴν μέλλουσαν πίστιν ἀποκαλυφθῆναι)" (Gal. 3:23). Obedience to the law could not be a medium for salvation, however, even though this is what Habakkuk had proclaimed. The law was merely a disciplinarian (παιδαγωγὸς ἡμῶν γέγονεν) until God revealed the righteousness that comes from faith (3:24, ἵνα ἐκ πίστεως δικαιωθῶμεν).

In Hebrews we find the quotation from Habakkuk once more (Heb. 10:35-39). In the parenesis of the writer Hab. 2:4 serves as an admonition to steadfast faith in times of temptation. "But we are not of those who shrink back and are destroyed, but of those who have faith and keep their souls." (Heb. 10:39). Faith, mentioned in Hab. 2:4 and referred to in this verse, can by no means be identified with the faithfulness of Christ. In Hebrews it is, even more

---

[63] This has also been noted by Howard, even though he sees no problem in speaking of justification by faith instead of the righteous one: "The one who is justified by faith will find eternal life." Howard, *Crisis*, 62.

[64] This against Hays, who forces even Galatians into his messianic interpretation. Hays, *Apocalyptic,* 210. We might further add that the discussion concerning the relation of the sections in Gal. and Rom. is rather confused. Campbell uses Gal. when criticizing the interpretation of Dunn, which he labels "theocentric". Campbell claims that, according to Dunn, in Romans Paul speaks of God's faithfulness referring to Hab. 2:4. Such an interpretation would mean that Paul has radically changed his use of the text between these two letters, because such an intepretation in Gal. would lead to "extraordinary hermeneutical acrobatics". Campbell, *JBL 113* (1994) 277-279. Dunn, however, denied precisely this kind of interpretation and emphasized that Paul dropped the personal adjective (my/his) in order to avoid the excluding of important features and in order to extend and broaden the meaning by referring both to man and to God. Dunn, *Romans*, 44-45; cf. Dunn, *SBL Seminar papers* (1991) 742. One must wonder at Campbell's remark for the further reason that his comment is in contradiction to his own explanation: he himself has to assume that Paul changed his use of the text between the two letters.

emphatically than in Paul, the "obedience of faith" which keeps believers on the right path.[65] The passage is completely parenetic.

The quotation from Habakkuk was of utmost importance to Paul. It was the most central scriptural proof he could find for his theology. Habakkuk had spoken of the fate of a pious Jew, the righteous one, and Paul was able to find a reference to faith in his prophecy.[66] It is justified to say that the expression ἐκ πίστεως has the same meaning in both 17a and 17b.[67] The righteousness of God that has been revealed in the gospel is the righteousness that comes from faith – and this is what Habakkuk had foreseen: it is from faith that the righteous one will receive his eternal life.[68] This interpretation of verse 17 is in line with the content of verse 16, too. We must remember that in that verse the gospel was "the power of God for salvation to everyone who has faith". In both verses gospel and faith are parallelled. This connection would be lost if the latter verse were considered messianic.

---

[65] Hays is quite aware of the parenetic nature of this section of Hebrews. In spite of this he returns to his own theory by making Christ an ideal type of steadfast obedience. "Thus, although the Habakkuk citation in Heb. 10.37-38 does not understand *ho dikaios* as a messianic title, it does project a vision of faithfulness for which Jesus is the prototype." Hays, *Apocalyptic* 202ff., especially 204. I cannot find such a denial of counter-arguments acceptable.

[66] There is no reason to think that Paul would have changed the meaning of Habakkuk's word "the righteous". The meaning in Habakkuk is clear, as Dunn comments: "The MT clearly has in view the *sadiq*, the righteous man." Dunn, *Romans*, 45. One should not be led astray by a Western scholastic mind, asking why a righteous man should be justified again. For Jews the "righteous one" is *sui generis*, and Paul is merely speaking of the reason for his justification.

[67] Such consistency is demanded by Campbell, but he thought that this would lead to a messianic interpretation. Campbell, *JBL 113* (1994) 273. Our conclusion is quite the opposite. Romans 1:17 is a parallel text to 3:21-22. Paul is convinced that the righteousness of God has been revealed apart from the law, and through faith it brings righteousness to "all who believe". This is the message in 1:17. Such an interpretation of the expression ἐκ πίστεως fits well with Paul's use of it in other sections in his letters. See the analyses of Dodd, *JBL 114* (1995) 471f.; Dunn, *SBL Seminar papers* (1991) 740ff.

[68] As regards the messianic interpretation of Hays we must note that, in spite of his bold statements, he has been rather cautious with his final conclusions. He says, for example, that he is merely making "suggestions", Hays, *SBL Seminar papers* (1991) 720; or a "first attempt" to think through some ideas, Hays, *Apocalyptic,* 211; or following Hanson admits that "it cannot be taken as proved" that Paul understood Hab. 2:4 as messianic, Hays, *Faith,* 154. We must also remember that his theory rests on his narrative interpretation of the section. According to Hays, Paul's gospel was founded upon the "story" of a Messiah who is vindicated/justified by God through faith. Thus all people are justified through *his* faith; and people's response, too, is faith. Hays actually claims that Hab. 2:4 functions on all these levels at once. Hays, *Faith,* 156-157. With such an interpretation Hays is quite near the explanation of Dunn – as we saw above – in spite of their disagreement in public. Both of them embrace both the faithfulness of God/Christ and man's response in faith – and use Paul's dropping of the "my" of LXX as a decisive argument for such an interpretation.

Our analysis concerning the quotation of Habakkuk and its context has resulted in the conclusion that Paul wanted to emphasize above all the *perspective of faith.*[69] On this basis we can also provide solutions to some of the most important problems concerning the quotation. First of all, we must ask why it was Habakkuk that Paul decided to quote when he was teaching about righteousness by faith.

We need not be content with the explanation that Paul was simply quoting Habakkuk in order to utilize the word "faith" (πίστις) for his own purposes.[70] This explanation does not fit in with the alternative of the Masoretic Text, because it contained an opposite soteriology from Paul's. On the other hand, that alternative cannot be supported by the text of the Septuagint, since its reading was different. Paul's readers, who were naturally using the Septuagint, would have been confused, because their "Bible" did not contain the same idea.

These notions raise a problem which has not been an easy one for modern scholarship to deal with. Why did Paul use a scriptural quotation even though he actually changed the content of the text? How could his readers and especially his Jewish opponents accept this kind of argument? Is not Paul writing here against himself?

As a solution to this problem some scholars have suggested that when changing the text of Habakkuk Paul was using a method of rabbinic interpretation.[71] This is why his Jewish opponents could well have accepted his arguments, assuming that he succeeded in his interpretation. It is true that Paul uses a similar interpretation elsewhere. Jewish texts, as well, contain such an interpretation. This we have seen above in the texts from Qumran.[72] An explanation such as this can perhaps be accepted on a general level, but it must be made more accurate in the details.

The most important of the conclusions to be reached here is that Paul intentionally wished to oppose the message of the Masoretic Text of Habakkuk with his teaching of righteousness by faith.[73] His version of the wording of Habakkuk has a significant theological purpose. This brings us right into the

---

[69] This only strengthens several previous explanations of scholars such as Michel, *Römer (1978)*, 90; Stuhlmacher, *Römer*, 30; Hofius, *Paulusstudien*, 154ff.; Moo, *Romans*, 73.

[70] For example, Fitzmyer seems to interpret the section in this way. Fitzmyer, *Romans*, 265.

[71] E.g. Nygren, *Till Romarna*, 96; Dunn, *Romans*, 45.

[72] See chapter 5 above.

[73] According to Wilckens, Paul opposes his interpretation to both the Old Testament tradition and the interpretation of Jewish Christianity which can be seen in Hebrews. The reason for this opposition is Paul's Christological starting-point which governs the teaching of Romans. Wilckens, *Römer I*, 89-90.

middle of a discussion of the problem of theodicy. We can assume that Paul, as a Jewish theologian, was quite familiar with the problem of theodicy in Habakkuk.[74]

Paul is both criticizing and reinterpreting the idea of Habakkuk.[75] Criticism can be seen in his claim that traditional obedience no longer brings salvation to Israel. But on the other hand, Paul answers the problem of theodicy in a similar way as does the prophet Habakkuk. The wrath of God is about to be revealed and judgment is at hand (Rom. 1:18). Only a certain difference remained. Man cannot appeal to his obedience, as Habakkuk had declared.

Here Paul presents a radical reinterpretation. The obedience mentioned in the Scriptures and demanded by the Old Testament prophets, has now been changed into faith (πίστις) in Jesus Christ.[76] Salvation will be provided by God's saving righteousness, which is being revealed in the gospel. The obedience of the people is replaced by the faithfulness of God. This is evidently an idea which the text of the Septuagint could have supported if Paul had decided to refer to it.[77]

Paul needed a different word however. He wanted to use a term denoting the faith of man. This is why he could not make use of the Septuagint. The real righteousness for Paul was righteousness by faith. Furthermore, faith in Jesus Christ was a real obedience of faith, where the salvation provided by God was realized.[78] This kind of obedience of faith was first presented at the beginning

---

[74] Moo describes the difference between the original text of Habakkuk and the purpose of Paul by emphasizing Habakkuk's complaint about God's inaction and injustice. Moo, *Romans,* 72.

[75] J.A. Sanders has remarked that it was customary for Jewish theologians to apply Scripture to contemporary events. Both at Qumran and in Paul we see a *pesher* interpretation, where the writers believed that the text had a dynamic relevance to their lives and to the Israel of their time. Sanders, *JR 39* (1959) 242.

[76] In this sense the traditional interpretation which has emphasized Paul's teaching on justification, has been on the right track, Michel, *Römer (1978),* 86-91; Dodd, *Romans,* 14; Wilckens, *Römer I,* 89-90; Stuhlmacher, *Römer,* 30; Moo, *Romans,* 72; Black, *Romans,* 35-36. Herold maintains that Hab. 2:4 was a suitable text for Paul to apply to the gospel concerning the eschatological revelation of the righteousness of God for the justification of individuals through faith. Herold, *Zorn,* 255.

[77] J.A. Sanders is quite right when he says that the basic difference can be found in the area of eschatological conceptions. "The difference is not in the call to obedience, it is in Qumran's view that obedience to the law will put off the day of judgment; or, rather, the distinction here, in view of the varieties of Judaism of the period, is Paul's." Sanders, *JR 39* (1959) 239.

[78] J.A. Sanders, again comparing Qumran and Paul, concludes that each "views the Old Testament phrase out of his eschatological perspective." When they wrote of the meaning of Habakkuk, they were certain that this was the eschatological message of the prophet. "Each believed that he had drawn from Habakkuk its true meaning." Sanders, *JR 39* (1959) 240.

of the first chapter of Romans: "to bring about the obedience of faith among all the Gentiles" (Rom. 1:5).[79]

Paul had an answer to the problem of theodicy. He knew why God's help seemed to be delayed, and why God Himself seemed to be powerless. *His answer was righteousness by faith. God had delayed His judgment, and salvation as well, because his purpose was to offer salvation to all sinners in Christ.*[80]

This claim would give the impression of being exaggerated, had not Romans given good arguments in favour of it. In chapter 3 the delay of judgment is explained by God's forbearance. "He did this to show his righteousness, because in his divine forbearance he had passed over the sins previously committed" (Rom. 3:25). The patience of God shows his righteousness, as well: "he himself is righteous and... justifies the one who has faith in Jesus" (3:26, καὶ δικαιοῦντα τὸν ἐκ πίστεως Ἰησοῦ).[81]

In chapter 9 we have similar teaching about the delay of judgment. Here the fate of Israel is again bound up with the problem of theodicy: "Why then does he still find fault? For who can resist his will?" (9:19). This problem will be solved by the plan God has laid concerning salvation.

According to Paul, in spite of her sufferings, Israel has been under the providence of God. He has "endured with much patience the objects of wrath that are made for destruction" (9:22). Here again the delay has taken place in order to leave room for salvation: "[A]nd what if he has done so in order to make known the riches of his glory for the objects of mercy, which he has prepared beforehand for glory." (9:23)

How did God show his mercy, then? In the text of Paul it is obvious. He did so by his own righteousness which was revealed in Christ (10:3-4), righteousness by faith (10:6), which is a gift of the kerygma concerning resurrection: "For one believes with the heart and so is justified" (10:10).

---

[79] On the obedience of faith, see Michel, *Römer (1978)*, 89.

[80] Hays has noted this feature in Habakkuk. Hab. 2:4 is a "response to the problem of theodicy, an implicit assertion of God's righteousness. The faithful community is enjoined to wait with patience for that which they do not yet see: the appearing of God's justice." Hays, *Apocalyptic*, 207f. This was the idea still at Qumran and even in Hebrews, but Paul sees the situation differently. The prophecy has been fulfilled and the "manifestation of the righteousness of God is present reality." This has resulted in – what Hays does not say directly but can be read out of his reasoning – the solving of the problem of theodicy: "Paul is claiming that Habakkuk's hope has at last received its answer through a revelation *ek pisteôs*." Hays, *Apocalyptic*, 208. This conclusion of Hays' is consistent and brilliant – its only problem is that it is not in agreement with his messianic interpretation. Here he has to work – to my understanding rightly – with terms such as obedience and faith. Later he begins to use messianic terminology and loses sight of Paul's dynamic interpretation.

[81] Cf. Rom. 3:30; 4:16; 5:11; 9:30-32; 10:6; 14:23.

Paul quite clearly connects his teaching concerning righteousness by faith with the problem of theodicy. His presentation can be compared with that of other Jewish writings in the Second Temple period. In all circles the problem of the delay in the arrival of God's help was pondered. Everyone sought to explain why the salvation of Israel had not yet come. Paul's soteriology is built on this kind of basis and point of departure. The history of Israel has been a history of waiting. But as Paul writes, God has not been silent without a purpose. His silence was not an expression of his wrath, either. On the contrary, God has been patient and restrained from revealing his wrath against sin. The goal of salvation history was the atoning work of Christ, and it eventually made righteousness by faith possible.

In the soteriology of Paul we find clear traits of predestinarian theology – even in the most crucial statements. He deals with the problem of theodicy both on a general level and in individual passages. Especially the reinterpretation of the message of Habakkuk reveals that Paul intentionally wished to present his gospel as an answer to the most difficult problems of Second Temple Jewish theology. The suffering of Israel was not a sign of the silence of God or of his weakness. The hope of those who had continued to wait was rewarded because eventually God gave the best of his gifts. The Gospel meant the revelation of the righteousness of God. God's saving work reached its climax in the appearance of Christ, and after that everything was seen in a new light. The obedience demanded by the prophets had become an obedience of faith. Righteousness, in turn, was mere grace, righteousness that comes from faith, and this was given to sinners in Jesus Christ.

6.3. The Day of Wrath will come (Rom. 1:18)

In Second Temple Jewish theology the most prominent feature in the discussion concerning the problem of theodicy was the description of God's judgment. The idea of a coming judgment answered the question why God had not yet punished sinners. In this matter Paul follows previous Jewish theology: the final consummation of salvation history will be reached when God appears on the heavenly judgment seat. The climax of eschatology explains both the unfortunate history of Israel and the problem concerning the omnipotence of God. In Paul's theology, judgment is a premise without which soteriology cannot be formulated.

The theme of judgment forms the background of soteriology in Paul's earliest letter. In *1 Thessalonians* the introductory part climaxes in a reminder of this theme as a key feature concerning the hope of believers:

"you turned to God from idols, to serve a living and true God,
and to wait for his Son from heaven,

whom he raised from the dead –
Jesus, who rescues us from the wrath that is coming" (1 Thess. 1:10).

Jesus, risen from the dead, had an eschatological mission. He was to save believers from the wrath (ἐκ τῆς ὀργῆς) of God. The day of judgment was a day when God's wrath would be revealed. On that day sin and ungodliness would be destroyed. The hope of the ekklesia was in the Son of God, who was able to protect his own from the wrath.[82]

The theme of judgment is a prominent feature in *Romans*, too. The theological argumentation of the letter begins with a description of doom immediately following greetings and the programmatic soteriological statement (vv. 16-17). The end of the first chapter (vv. 18-32) deals solely with judgment and the causes of God's punishment. In verses 16-18 the soteriology of Paul builds on a tension between two central concepts, the salvific righteousness of God and the wrath of God.[83]

As Paul sets the righteousness of God against God's wrath, he intentionally exploits prophetic language. There is again a strict polarization here. Gospel and faith are opposed to the revelation of God's wrath: "the righteousness of God is revealed... the wrath of God is revealed from heaven against all ungodliness and wickedness of those who by their wickedness suppress the truth."(Rom. 1:17-18). The antithesis between the righteousness of God and the wrath of God is underlined by the use of the same word denoting revelation (Ἀποκαλύπτεται γὰρ ὀργὴ θεοῦ).[84]

The revealing of God's wrath is an eschatological, and even apocalyptic theme.[85] This is why it is transcendental, since the wrath of God comes from "heaven". Further, in a historical sense, it is an eschatological climax of the last aeon. The judgment day itself is described by Paul by using Old Testament imagery and apocalyptic language (Rom. 2:5-6).[86]

In the passage in Romans 2, Paul describes the eschatological Day of Wrath in detail. "But by your hard and impenitent heart you are storing up wrath for yourself on the day of wrath, when God's righteous judgment will be revealed. For he will repay according to each one's deeds" (Rom. 2:5-6).

---

[82] Cf. Wanamaker, *Thessalonians*, 88.

[83] In this way Wilckens, *Römer I*, 101. Stuhlmacher has explained this tension by using his theory concerning the righteousness of God. Already in the Old Testament the righteousness of God and the wrath of God stand in opposition to each other. The former signifies God's just rule and goodwill towards his people. God's wrath will be directed towards those who abandon the mercy and love of God. Stuhlmacher, *Römer*, 35.

[84] Wilckens, *Römer I*, 101.

[85] Cf. the analyses in chapter 4.4.

[86] See e.g. Michel, *Römer (1955)*, 65f.; Dodd, *Romans*, 33; Schlier, *Römerbrief*, 72.

There are several key terms here, which are closely connected with Jewish tradition.

1. By sinning people *store up* the wrath of God for themselves.[87]

2. The moment of wrath was the climax of eschatology, the *"day of the wrath"* of God (ἐν ἡμέρᾳ ὀργῆς).[88]

3. In that day God's just *judgment* shall take place. (ἀποκαλύψεως δικαιοκρισίας τοῦ θεοῦ).

Judgment is described as God's wrath several times in the Old Testament. Already in the books of Moses God's attitude towards sin is described as 'wrath' (Num. 25:4; 32:14).[89] In the proclamation of the prophets this feature is even clearer (see Isa. 5:25; 9:11; 10:4; 30:30; 59:18). The books of Jeremiah and Lamentations tell how God in His wrath destroyed Jerusalem and expelled Israel into Exile (Jer. 4:8; 12:13; Lam. 1:12; 2:1, 3, 22; Ezek. 22:21). In the language of the Psalms the wrath of God is connected with several events in the history of the people and it has been directed both at the enemy and Israel (Ps. 30:6; 76:8; 78:49; 106:23).[90]

In the book of Jeremiah the wrath of God is clearly an eschatological theme (Jer. 25:15; 30:24; 51:45). It is connected with the concept of the "Day of Wrath", which is one of the most important terms in the eschatology of the Old Testament. The day of the destruction of Jerusalem was already in a sense a day of the wrath of God. According to the prophets, it was not the only day of wrath, however. The climax of eschatology was also to be a day of wrath (Isa. 13:9, 13; Ezek. 7:19; Zeph. 1:15, 18; 2:2, 3; Job 20:28; 21:20, 30).[91] Further the revealing of the wrath of God occurs in the royal ideology. In the royal Psalms the wrath of God is a guarantee of the power of the Davidide (Pss. 2:12; 110:5).[92]

The reasons for the revealing of God's wrath are quite obvious: wrath comes as a result of the sinfulness of men and the disobedience of Israel. In this

---

[87] There is a scandalous claim implied here, as Michel has noted. Paul asserts that the wrath of God will be directed to Jews, as well, and not only to the Gentiles, as most Jews would have believed at that time. Michel, *Römer (1978)*, 114-115; Moo, *Romans,* 134.

[88] Dunn remarks that in the teaching of Paul, "wrath" occurs several times as a description of God's final judgment on human rebellion. Dunn, *Romans,* 84.

[89] For the relation of God's anger and human sinfulness, see Herion, *ABD VI* (1992) 993.

[90] For the occurrences in the Old Testament, see Fichtner, *ThWNT V* (1990) 401ff., H-C. Hahn, *TBLNT* (1979) 1499f.

[91] Cf. Fichtner, *ThWNT V* (1990) 401; Hiers, *ABD II* (1992) 80; Cathcart, *ABD II* (1992) 85.

[92] Some prophets also mention a future Messiah or Davidic king when they speak of the Day of Yahweh (Isa. 11:10; Jer. 23:5-6; 30:8-9; 33:15-16; Hag. 2:23; Zech. 3:8-10; Amos 9:11). See Hiers, *ABD II* (1992) 83.

respect the theme of wrath is connected with covenantal theology. God is just and keeps his promises. This is why he will punish sin and help the oppressed. God's wrath cannot be separated from his everlasting love towards men.[93]

In Second Temple theology, too, the theme of the wrath of God is prominent. In sapiential theology it concerns both the punishments which God has prescribed for Israel (Wisd. 11:9; 16:5; 18:20) and the wrath of God against sin (Sirach 5:6; 36:8). In apocalyptic writings the eschatological judgment is described as the revealing of the wrath of God (1 Enoch 84:4; 91:7-9).[94]

When *Paul* speaks of the wrath of God (Rom. 1:18) his terminology echoes that of the Old Testament. He can speak either of a punishment by wrath (Rom. 3:5), or of being saved from wrath (Rom. 5:9). The theme of wrath is so common at that time that Paul did not consider it necessary to use Scriptural quotations to support it.

Paul speaks naturally of a future wrath, but in addition he also says that the wrath of God is already at work in this world.[95] God shows his wrath against the ungodliness of sinners.[96] In this respect it is only natural that before speaking of the gospel and the revealing of God's righteousness (Rom. 3:21ff.) Paul describes in a long section the reality of the wrath of God (1:18-3:20). The wrath of God is not merely a fact of the future. In the lives of many contemporary people it is actual reality. This wrath is a condition for the revealing of the righteousness in Christ.[97]

This point of view is evident also as the perspective of Jewish theology is considered. There we found the strong conviction that the wrath of God is being revealed in the middle of history. This is why all the signs of punishment by God which can be observed are at the same time proof of the reality of the

---

[93] As Fichtner says: "es ist Jahves verletzte heilige Liebe, die in ihm den Zorn erweckt". Fichtner, *ThWNT* V (1990) 404.

[94] The theme of judgment is also important in the Sibyllines, as we have seen in previous chapters (especially 4.4.), but there the idea of wrath is not of the essence.

[95] The word for revelation which Paul uses here is not solely of a future nature. In Jewish apocalyptic it also denotes the revealing of God's secrets in the last days. Wilckens, *Römer I*, 102. Such a double concept most probably lies behind the teaching of Paul.

[96] I do not agree with Fitzmyer, who provides a scheme for the first three chapters of Romans. He thinks that the first section (1:19-32) speaks of the godlessness of the Gentiles, the second one (2:1-3:8) of the sins of the Jews, and only in the third chapter does Paul reach the idea of the sinfulness of all people (3:9). Fitzmyer, *Romans*, 270. We must note that already in 1:20 Paul begins to speak of all people by mentioning the creation.

[97] See Wilckens, *Römer I*, 103; cf. Cranfield, *Romans*, 108-110.

coming judgment of God. This leads to Paul's conclusion: the two "revelations", the revealing of saving righteousness (1:17) and the revealing of wrath (1:18), are in reciprocal relation to each other. The reality of wrath also provides proof of the revealing of his righteousness.[98]

This is why right at the beginning of the letter (1:18), Paul refers to the revealing of the wrath of God in the present tense. He is once again explaining his theology of predestination. This world is already now living under sin and under judgment. There is an evident need for the revealing of God's saving righteousness. Without it this world would have to live without hope.[99]

According to Paul, God's wrath will be revealed from heaven (ἀπ' οὐρανοῦ, 1:18). This small detail may be an expression of a broader perspective of a transcendent dualism which is typical of Second Temple Jewish apocalyptic. We must not overemphasize the "present" tense of the (final) revealing of God's wrath. Paul locates the place of the revelation in heaven.

According to the apocalyptic world-view, God acts mainly in heaven and he has left people in this world to their own devices. This thought implied a criticism of the Temple, because normally the glory of the Temple would have been based on the belief that God was acting in the Temple of Jerusalem. In apocalyptic eschatology the most important task of God was to bring down the rule of the wicked and judge them in his wrath.[100]

In one sense the teaching of Paul fits this scheme. On the other hand, we must remember that the terminology he uses is rather commonplace. Even the prophets of Israel described the judgment as God's wrath revealed from heaven.[101] We should remember that, according to the eschatology of Isaiah in Isa. 63:15 – 64:11, pious Jews waited for God to open the heavens and make

---

[98] Schlier says that the word γάρ at the beginning of verse 18 confirms the reciprocal relation, which is suggested otherwise by the repetition of the word denoting revelation. Schlier, *Römerbrief*, 48. In addition, Herold has pointed out that there is an eschatological tendency throughout verses 16-18. Already in v. 16a there is an eschatological intention, which has usually been understood and translated incorrectly. Paul is not speaking of psychological shame, but of eschatological judgment. He is certain that he will not be left in shame (condemnation) with the gospel. This idea is in agreement with the teaching of the following clauses. Only the righteousness that comes from faith can free one from the wrath of God to be revealed on the day of judgment. Herold, *Zorn*, 231, 241, 302ff.

[99] Cf. Stählin: "gerade weil (γάρ v 18) Gott über alle Welt, nicht nur über die Heiden, auch über die Juden, ja über jeden einzelnen... zürnen muss, darum schenkt er Gerechtigkeit... und erweist sich in der Anerkennung dieser Gerechtigkeit als der gerechte Richter (3, 26)." Stählin, *ThWNT V* (1990) 427.

[100] For Jewish apocalyptic see especially chapter 4.4.

[101] Also, according to traditional Jewish thinking the judgment seat of God was in heaven, and this was the place where God pronounced his sentences (Ps. 76:9). This is why we need more evidence for a transcendental dualism. Cf. Stuhlmacher, *Römer*, 35.

his name known to his adversaries: "Oh that you would tear open the heavens and come down" (64:1).[102]

We should further note that the idea of God's judgment is prominent throughout Paul's theology. A good proof of this is the fact that in Romans 2:16 he says that the proclamation of judgment is an essential part of his *gospel*: "according to my gospel, God, through Jesus Christ, will judge the secret thoughts of all". This connecting of judgment with the gospel has been considered difficult.[103] We should not regard it as a problem, though, because right from the first chapter of Romans Paul teaches the gospel (1:16) by describing the tension between God's righteousness and his wrath.[104] Both condemnation and salvation are part of the gospel. This is why the gospel in 2:16 does not mean a criterion for judgment but the news of salvation which Paul is preaching.[105] His gospel contains a total eschatological scene, not merely individual roles without a plot and a performance. The predestination of judgment is a condition for righteousness by faith and this is why it forms the essence of the gospel as a saving revelation.[106]

In the theology of Paul the theme of judgment is, at least in a general sense, a solution to the problem of theodicy which lies behind the teaching on soteriology. The idea of predestination is prominent here, too. God has predestined and prescribed his judgment on all those who "suppress the truth" (1:18). In Paul's soteriology the hamartological aspect is important, because the judgment of God is described as the appearance of his wrath. The wrath of God is severe in its attitude to sin, and the ungodly will be punished. Israel has naturally already suffered from punishments during the course of history, but the final day of judgment is yet to come. As the wrath was also realized during

---

[102] See Herold, *Zorn*, 307-309.

[103] See the discussion in Schlier, *Römerbrief*, 80. The value of verses 14 and 15 has been under discussion, and some scholars have tried to enclose them in brackets. (Bultmann considered v. 16 an interpolation, but Michel has denied this. Michel, *Romans (1955)*, 70, n. 3.) Schlier is apparently right when he says that verse 16 does not fit the content of verse 13 any better than verse 14. As the textual tradition does not support the idea of any interpolations and the terminology is common to Paul (see Wilckens, *Römer I*, 137), the solution must be found with the help of the content of the text itself.

[104] Wilckens suggests that 2:16 should be interpreted according to the dynamics that exist between 1:16 and 1:18. Wilckens, *Römer I*, 137.

[105] Dunn thinks that the gospel, too, would be a criterion for judgment, but this idea does not fit the context where Paul treats judgment according to works, with law as a criterion. See Dunn, *Romans*, 103.

[106] Herold concludes that Paul's teaching implies even here the theology of the cross. Wrath is a judgment term to him, and that is why the actual revelation of God's wrath must have taken place in the event of the cross (Gal. 3:10; Rom. 4:15). Herold, *Zorn*, 304f. Such a wider context for the passage 1:16-18 is no doubt correct.

the lifetime of Paul himself, this was a sign of the fact that sin was still in control and salvation was desperately needed for everyone. Salvation was needed because the "Day of Wrath" would be a day when all humankind would be taken to the just judgment of God. On that day only the righteousness of God which had been revealed in Christ can save men from the terrible punishment.

6.4. God's judgment will bring justice

As the theme of eschatological judgment is being analyzed, a brief investigation of the language of judicial discourse is necessary. The text of Paul is full of juridical metaphors which have been taken from the life and practice of a court of law. They were naturally common in the Old Testament, but in the writings of Paul they seem to reveal several traits which were significant for his soteriology, too.

The day of the wrath of the Lord is, according to Paul, a day when the whole world will be taken to a court of law. God himself is a judge and human beings are defendants (πῶς κρινεῖ ὁ θεὸς τὸν κόσμον, Rom. 3:6, "how could God judge the world"). The verb κρίνω denotes especially acting as a judge in a court of law.[107] In the text of Paul this verb is used when the last judgment is being described. That day is above all a day of just judgment (δικαιοκρισία τοῦ θεοῦ).[108]

Paul further makes a distinction between judgment and punishment when it is of importance for his purpose. When he writes about the consequences of Adam's sin, in chapter 5, Paul makes a distinction between the judgment in general and the passing of the verdict: "For the judgment following one trespass brought condemnation" (5:16). Here we have a word-play which is not easily translated: τὸ μὲν γὰρ κρίμα ἐξ ἑνὸς εἰς κατάκριμα. The judgment (κρίμα) is mentioned first as a primary cause. It has been prescribed generally on every transgressor of the law. Due to the sin of Adam there is also a reason for a condemnation, and this is why a verdict has been passed

---

[107] See e.g. Acts 3, where the word occurs in the story about Pilate and Jesus (Acts 3:13).

[108] Wilckens points out that the word δικαιοκρισία also appears in old manuscripts when a common distribution of justice is described. Wilckens, *Römer I*, 125 (also footnotes 282, 283). In the texts of Jewish theology it is common, as well. In the Testament of Levi God's just judgment will be directed on fallen Jews, TLev. 3:2; 15:2. A similar term appears in the Hebrew texts from Qumran, as well (1QH 1:23; cf. 1:30; 10:36; 17:20. משפטי צדק). This is why the term is not solely typical of Hellenistic Judaism. It is used more widely. Michel is probably right when he says that the term which we have in the New Testament, δικαία κρισίς (2 Thess. 1:5; John 5:30) belongs to the same tradition. Michel, *Römer (1955)*, 66 (also n. 1).

(κατάκριμα).[109] It is an eschatological death sentence – but a present reality – under which all the descendants of Adam are at the present time (vv. 15, 17).

There is furthermore a code of laws, the law of God, νόμος. It is the code by which the works of men are assessed: "all who have sinned under the law will be judged by the law (διὰ νόμου κριθήσονται)." (Rom. 2:12).[110] The juridical nature of eschatological judgment is emphasized also when Paul teaches that men will be judged by their works (Rom. 2:6; 14:12; 1 Cor. 3:8; 2 Cor. 5:10).

In Romans 3 the law reveals the sinfulness and guilt of men (ὑπόδικος γένηται πᾶς ὁ κόσμος τῷ θεῷ, Rom. 3:19, "the whole world may be held accountable to God"; AV: "become guilty"). The guilt of men is here not merely a feeling or experience. It means that a verdict of guilty has been passed already. The word ὑπόδικος (*hapax legomenon*) denotes the passing of a verdict in court (<δίκη).[111] This denotation is evident also because there is no room for defence after the verdict of guilty has been passed: "every mouth will be silenced" (3:19; NEB: "so that no one may have anything to say in self-defence").[112]

As a heavenly judge God also has a judgment seat, and all people shall be brought before it. "For we will all stand before the judgment seat of God (πάντες γὰρ παραστησόμεθα τῷ βήματι τοῦ θεοῦ)... each of us will be accountable to God." (Rom. 14:10-12). The mention of the judgment seat brings us to a court of law where legal processes are conducted.

The judgment seat of God, βῆμα, is not a throne. The word denotes a judgment seat. The word is often used about the judgment seats of earthly rulers (see Matt. 27:19; John 19:13; Acts 18:12, 16; 25:6, 10, 17). Both Jewish theology and the New Testament teach that God has this kind of seat.[113]

The judgment seat of God is, according to Paul, also the judgment seat of

---

[109] In German scholarship the words Urteil - Verurteilung are used. See e.g. Michel, *Römer (1955)*, 125. In English the words judgment - condemnation have been helpful, see Dunn, *Romans*, 280.

[110] In Jewish texts the law of Sinai is several times mentioned as a criterion for judgment, see e.g. Jubilees 5:13; Pseudo-Philo 11:1-2; 2 Baruch 48:47, "your Law which they transgressed will repay them on your day".

[111] In Greek texts this word often gains a juridical meaning, see Liddell-Scott, s.v. ὑπόδικος.

[112] It is easy to agree with Maurer, who said that this word describes a sinner who is under judgment and facing condemnation, and no longer has anything to say in his favour. Maurer, *ThWNT VIII* (1990) 557-558.

[113] Concerning Jewish theology see Or.Sib. 2:218; 8:222, 242. Paul's theology was later developed in Polycarp 6:2.

Christ. "For all of us must appear before the judgment seat of Christ, so that each may receive recompense for what has been done in the body, whether good or evil." (2 Cor. 5:10). Here the judgment seat of Christ is not a "throne of grace", as in some texts of the New Testament, where the metaphor of throne has been taken from Temple terminology (Heb. 4:16; cf. Rom. 3:25). Instead the judgment seat, βῆμα, is the place of God's eschatological judgment.

According to Paul's Christocentric treatment, Christ accompanies God in the execution of the last judgment. This feature also occurs in the second chapter of Romans: "God, through Jesus Christ, will judge the secret thoughts of all" (Rom. 2:16b).

Metaphors taken from legal terminology concerning processes in the court of law emphasize the juridical nature of God's eschatological judgment. Judgment is unavoidable because transgressions have been evil. Here we can see that Paul is treating the problem of theodicy in the tradition of Jewish sapiential theology. Members of the Chosen People have abandoned God's law and transgress against God's precepts. The ungodliness of the people will arouse the wrath of God and lead to a just judgment. Only the final judgment and the revealing of God's wrath can renew this world which has been corrupted by sin.

§ 7 The Radical Anthropology of Paul's Soteriology

One of the principal questions of the theology of predestination concerns the problem as to who are the ones who will be left under the wrath of God. Who will be sentenced to damnation and who will be saved? Jewish theology in the Second Temple period answered this question with a strict soteriological dualism. The righteous were clearly separated from sinners. God's judgment had been ordained for apostates and the Gentiles. In the theology of Paul we meet another kind of polarization. He changed the traditional dualism in a significant and even radical way.

The consideration of anthropological questions is also important for methodological reasons. As we have seen in the introduction to this book, conceptions regarding predestination were connected with anthropology in general, and with the concept of sin in particular.

7.1. The total domination of sin

The most crucial difference between Paul and his Jewish tradition is that he radicalized his anthropology. He sharpened the concept of sin and taught that the whole of humankind was guilty and ripe for condemnation when the judgment of God arrives. No man could avoid the punishment of sins. Judgment would be according to one's deeds, and the result was considered negative.

Paul's concept of universal sinfulness is a common theme, naturally. It is so familiar that most scholars have accepted it. The integration of this concept into his theology is not so easy, however. It can best be done with the aid of predestinarian theology.[1]

The idea of universal sinfulness of the whole of humankind is, evident in all of Paul's letters. For example, the first part of Romans as a whole (1:18 – 3:20) is one long description of sinfulness and depravity.[2] This is a section where the righteousness of God and his wrath are antithetically opposed. According to Paul, humankind which lives under sin thus lives under the wrath of God. In verse 3:21 a new point of view opens up.[3] There the eventual realization of the righteousness of God is presented. So we can see that the

---

[1] For the pessimistic hamartology of Paul see e.g. Schoeps, *Paulus*, 198ff.; Eichholz, *Paulus*, 77f.; Goppelt, *Theologie*, 468; Kümmel, *Theologie*, 159f.; Ridderbos, *Paul*, 93ff.; Stuhlmacher, *Theologie*, 278f.; Witherington, *Paul's Narrative Thought World*, 11ff. The idea of universal sinfulness in Paul's theology has also aroused controversy in modern scholarship. This will be examined below in 7.2.

[2] See Cranfield, *Romans*, 191; cf. Schlier, *Römerbrief*, 48; Wilckens, *Römer I*, 92ff.; Dunn, *Romans*, 50ff.; cf. also Hofius' analysis in *Paulusstudien*, 121ff.

[3] This turning-point will be analyzed later, in chapter 13.2.

soteriological core in the third chapter (vv. 21-26) is related to the beginning of the letter and the letter must be interpreted accordingly.

At the beginning of Romans 3 Paul summarizes what he has been developing throughout the previous chapters, by using Scriptural quotations and giving examples: "all.. are under the power of sin" (3:9). Sin is actually a personified entity here. It is a power which rules over people and whose command every human being is subject to (ὑφ' ἁμαρτίαν).[4] The belief that sin is a cosmic power was common in Jewish theology (Sirach 21:2; 27:10; 1QH 1:27; 4:29-30). We must note, however, that in Paul's theology this concept is used in defining anthropology.[5] This is evident when the context of the introduction of the letter, as well as the catalogues of sin in the first chapter are considered.[6]

In soteriology the idea of the power of sin is of crucial importance. Later in the third chapter Paul states (Rom. 3:23):

"since all have sinned and fall short of the glory of God"
πάντες γὰρ ἥμαρτον καὶ ὑστεροῦνται τῆς δόξης τοῦ θεοῦ

This clause is closely connected with the themes of the first three chapters and in fact summarizes their intention.[7]

The dualism of Jewish soteriology was based on an expectation that the wrath of God would fall on sinners, but the righteous are under the providence of God. Paul here gives another kind of solution. Both God's wrath and his righteousness – as a saving act – have been directed to all humankind.[8] The idea that "all" are under sin is in verse 23, too, connected with the fall of Adam. Individual sins of Paul and his contemporaries are connected with the sin of the first man. This point of view can be detected from the aorist form of the verb 'to sin', which emphasized the unique character of the act (ἥμαρτον).[9]

The idea of the fall of the first man is expressed in a special way in the teaching of the falling short of "glory". Even though the word "glory" is not used in the story of the Fall in Genesis, in Jewish texts the Fall is often described as falling short of the glory of God (especially ApMos. 20; ApAdam

---

[4] Michel, *Römer (1978)*, 142; Cranfield, *Romans*, 191; Hofius, *Paulusstudien*, 123. Paul also describes mankind under sin in Galatians: "the scripture has imprisoned all things under the power of sin (ὑπὸ ἁμαρτίαν)" (3:22).

[5] Michel, *Römer (1978)*, 142; Dunn, *Romans*, 149.

[6] Cranfield has noted that Paul hardly ever uses the word ἁμαρτία when speaking of actual sins, but this does not affect our explanation. Cranfield, *Romans*, 191.

[7] Cf. Kümmel, *Theologie*, 160.; Stuhlmacher, *Römer*, 57.

[8] This controversy between Paul and Jewish theology is underlined by Wilckens, *Römer I*, 185.

[9] Dunn, *Romans*, 168; cf. Witherington, *Paul's Narrative Thought World*, 22.

1:5).[10] This loss of glory has its counterpart and opposition in the restoration and return of the glory in the last days with the arrival of the Messiah (LAE 39:2; 1 Enoch 50:1; 4 Ezra 7:122-125; 2. ApBar. 51:1, 3; 54:15, 21; 1QS 4:23; cf. CD 3:20).[11]

The glory of the first man cannot be identified with the description of him as being made in the image of God.[12] In Jewish theology 'glory' is the glory of God and this is the purpose in the teaching of Paul, as well. This glory was rather identified with the righteousness of the first man. This view is prevalent both in Jewish texts and in the theology of Paul (cf. ApcMos. 20f.).[13] In Paul's letters the word 'glory' often appears in opposition to "flesh", which denotes the corrupt man (Rom. 1:23; 6:2-4; 8:21; 1 Cor. 15:40-48).

The concept of predestination in Paul thus rests on the conviction that all humankind lives under the power of sin. Passages which express this thought are frequent in his letter. Man has been "sold into slavery under sin" (Rom. 7:14) and he lives in a "body of death" (7:24).[14] As regards God, man is already in his earthly life in fact dead: "the body is dead because of sin" (8:10). This is the pessimistic view of Paul, which has been summarized in the brief statement of 1 Corinthians: "all die in Adam" (1 Cor. 15:22).

When Paul describes the sinfulness of man he is not content with assessing individual acts. The significance of sin is greater still. Sin is an anthropological entity.[15] His anthropology speaks of essential sinfulness of an ontological

---

[10] Wilckens presents some parallel texts in Jewish literature, Wilckens, *Römer I*, 188, also note 509. Cf. Black, *Romans*, 58; Stuhlmacher, *Römer*, 57; Moo, *Romans*, 226. This kind of concept occurred in rabbinic theology, as well (see GenRabb. 12:5), Ziesler, *Romans*, 110.

[11] Concerning the parallels in Jewish theology see Cranfield, *Romans*, 204; Dunn, *Romans*, 168.

[12] Black, *Romans*, 59, against Dodd.

[13] Schlier, *Römer*, 107; Stuhlmacher, *Römer*, 57; cf. Betz, *TRE I* (1977) 418.

[14] In this respect Martin is right when he says that the teaching concerning the "I" of chapter 7 refers to Paul's and our involvement in Adam's disobedience. Martin, *Law*, 84. I shall later propose a somewhat different interpretation of the details of Paul's concept of the "I", however. See below, chapter 10.1.

[15] This has not been accepted by all scholars. For example, G. Davies argues that Romans 3:9-18 only proves that the *wicked* among the Jews and Gentiles are sinners and stand under God's condemnation. Davies, *Faith and Obedience*, 75, 80-104, especially 103f.; cf. Lichtenberger, *Paulus und das antike Judentum*, 371; Moyise, *ExpT 106* (1995) 369. Such a traditional polarization cannot be Paul's intention, however. Even the Old Testament catena he uses intends to prove that there are no exceptions to his indictment. Schreiner, *Law*, 69.

character.[16] This anthropological point of view is evident in two separate themes. The first of these can be found in Romans 3, where Paul speaks of falling short of the "glory" of God. The second is actually a consequence of the first. Man without glory is "flesh", and his nature has become corrupted.[17]

Stating this is no novelty, naturally. It has been a common conviction both in Protestant dogmatics and Biblical theology. More challenging in this respect is the questioning of the consistency of Paul's teaching, which we shall examine below. As regards the idea of universal sinfulness there is one interesting angle, however. There is a basic difference between Paul and Jewish soteriology. As Davies has noted, Rabbinic theology in particular underlined human freedom as a necessary condition for the choosing of obedience or disobedience.[18] This notion is in line with our previous analysis of sapiential theology. In a synergistic context a totally negative anthropology is impossible. This is why the original feature of Paul's theology is the radicalization of the concept of sin.

Paul's radical anthropology is the foundation on which he constructs his teaching concerning man's status before God. Because judgment has been prescribed for all sinners, the predestination of the whole of humankind is rightly justified. All humankind falls short of the glory of God and lives "in the flesh". This becomes the starting-point of soteriology. Thus hamartology reveals the first signs of the polarization which directs the theology of Paul. When the concept of sin is considered from the point of view of salvation history, it turns out to be different from the teachings of traditional Jewish theology. All of fallen humankind must face God before his judgment seat at the end of days.

---

[16] Winninge has noted that Paul's occasional terminology should not be confused with his general conviction. Paul uses Jewish terminology when speaking of apostate Jews. Here he states that Jews can be even worse than sinners from the Gentiles. Paul's basic conviction is, however, that no man is righteous before God. "Paul simply claims that there are no righteous persons whatsoever, because all Jews and Gentiles are sinners from the outset." Winninge, *Sinners and the Righteous*, 264, see also 258f.

[17] Cf. Kümmel, *Theologie*, 160-161.; Stuhlmacher, *Theologie*, 279; Beker, *Paul*, 215.

[18] W.D. Davies first calls the universal feature only a "solidarity of all mankind in Adam", but remarks then that there is a crucial difference between Paul and the Rabbis: "the Rabbis were always anxious to safeguard human freedom". Davies, *Paul*, 32-33. Paul's sin is related to that of Adam. Paul evidently thought that even he himself was tied to the negative heritage of Adam. Such a radicalization has been examined above and it is a prominent feature of Paul's theology of predestination.

7.2. The dynamics of Adam typology

Even though the idea of universal sinfulness seems to be rather clear in the theology of Paul, it has been a controversial issue in scholarship. In the existentialist tradition the discussion has been governed by a kind of hermeneutical bias, which is undeniably understandable as regards the basic dilemma of scientific research. How are we to understand the sinfulness of man? Did Paul assume that Adam was really a historical person? And if he did, what is the logic in the causality between the sin of Adam and the sinfulness of the whole of humankind? Do we have to take the dogmatic locus of "original sin" into account?[19]

These themes concern Paul's anthropology, and the Adam typology in particular. The latter no doubt directs his interpretation and really is a key to the understanding of his concept of sin. Paul uses cosmic language, and his speech is rooted in the Old Testament. Earlier we noted that in the third chapter of Romans Paul used the Genesis story of the Fall when martialling arguments for the sinfulness of humankind. In chapter five later, this argumentation becomes detailed and forceful.

From a thematic point of view the joining of two themes, those of sin and death, is essential. The theme of death, which is prominent in the Old Testament story, becomes in the text of Paul a real metaphor for the Fall.

"Therefore, just as sin came into the world through one man, and death came through sin (διὰ τῆς ἁμαρτίας ὁ θάνατος), and so death spread to all because all have sinned." (Rom. 5:12).

All have died in Adam,[20] and in this incident they have been predestined to

---

[19] This discussion has been inspired especially by Bultmann's existentialist interpretation in his *Theologie*, 252ff., as we shall see below. In modern discussion a developed version of this is the psychologizing interpretation of Räisänen's. For him sin is not a reality, and this is why Paul's theology both concerning law and sin is merely a matter of "secondary rationalization", motivated by his "personal experience of liberation". According to Räisänen, Paul had had "ecstatic experiences" in the "charismatic movement" of early Christianity. This is why the concept of sin, as well, must have been based on a deduction made from ecstatic premises. See Räisänen, *Law*, 233.

[20] In the Bultmannian tradition the theological content of this section has been totally reinterpreted. In his *New Testament Theology* Bultmann says that Paul's teaching cannot be identified with original sin. Man cannot be responsible for sins he has not committed. According to Bultmann, Paul tried to explain the origin of death, not the origin of sin. This is why he considers verse 13 totally incomprehensible. According to Bultmann, Paul runs into problems when he tries to explain the existence of sin before the giving of the law. This problem can be solved only by an existential interpretation. Bultmann thinks that in Adam only a "potential" of sin was created. This will be actualized only when individuals become responsible. Bultmann, *Theologie*, 252-253.

punishment.[21] The consequences described here are universal. In verse 19 Paul says accordingly that by the "one" man's disobedience the many were made sinners (ἁμαρτωλοὶ κατεστάθησαν οἱ πολλοί).[22] This is not traditional soteriological dualism. He is not merely expressing a confrontation between the old existence of man in slavery and the new life in Christ, but describing the essential sinfulness of all mankind.[23]

In verse 16 too Paul emphasizes that the act of Adam had crucial consequences as regards salvation history: "For the judgment following one trespass brought condemnation" (τὸ μὲν γὰρ κρίμα ἐξ ἑνὸς εἰς κατάκριμα). Paul's rhetoric here exploits a word-play on words denoting condemnation, and it is not easily reproduced in other languages. We cannot, however, neglect that word-play. Paul means that the judgment following the trespass of Adam, κρίμα, resulted in a condemnation to damnation for the whole world, κατάκριμα.[24]

The meaning of this clause is tied up with the latter part of the parallelism: "but the free gift following many trespasses brings justification". The effect of grace is contrary to that of sin. The free gift will produce righteousness (δικαίωμα) in spite of many trespasses.[25] Here we have a typical Pauline polarization between punishment and justification by grace.[26]

---

[21] Bultmann made, however, certain reservations as regards the applicability of these thoughts to Paul himself: "Ob man das als den eigentlichen Gedanken des Paulus ansehen darf, muss allerdings fraglich bleiben; für ihn steht jedenfalls die faktische allgemeine Verfallenheit der adamitischen Menschheit an Sünde und Tod ausser Frage." Bultmann, *Theologie,* 253. Later Paul's inconsistency in these verses has been maintained e.g. by Räisänen, *Law,* 145-147.

[22] Bultmann's ambivalence concerning the concept of sin, which we assessed above, is quite understandable. He explains this section with the help of a Gnostic theory. Paul was writing under the influence of Gnosticism: "unter dem Einfluss des gnostischen Mythos". Bultmann, *Theologie,* 251. Against this see e.g. Luz, *Geschichtsverständnis,* 196. Several later writers note that the opposition between Adam and Christ builds on a common (Jewish) "Messianological" theme, see e.g. Schoeps, *Paulus,* 199.

[23] Against Brandenburger, *Adam,* 262. We must further remember that, as Martin has pointed out, underlying humankind's solidarity with Adam in sin is its solidarity with him in the flesh (cf. 1 Cor. 15:42-50). Martin, *Law,* 108.

[24] Michel, *Römer (1987),* 125. Concerning the terminology, see 6.4. above. This is at the same time an eschatological condemnation, Wilckens, *Römer I,* 324. Judgment is here an immediate result of Adam's sin. Moo, *Romans,* 351. This emphasizes the idea of universality in this verse.

[25] As the existentialist interpretation only emphasized a renewed Creator-creature relationship, Barrett sought after a corrective: "along with the existentialist interpretation of Paul there must be a cosmological (or apocalyptic-mythical) interpretation." Barrett, *Adam,* 20-21.

[26] See Schlier, *Römerbrief,* 170, 171. According to Stuhlmacher, this is one of the most

A little later Paul makes a polarization by using the concept of a life-giving justification. "Therefore just as one man's trespass led to condemnation for all, so one man's act of righteousness leads to justification and life for all (εἰς δικαίωσιν ζωῆς /justification that brings life for all men, NIV)." (5:18, "justification of life", AV).[27]

The opposition between death caused by sin and eternal life occurs in Romans chapter 6, too. Here death is the determined consequence of sin: "For the wages of sin is death (τὰ γὰρ ὀψώνια τῆς ἁμαρτίας θάνατος), but the free gift of God is eternal life in Christ Jesus our Lord." (6:23). The free gift of God is emphasized here, as well as at the end of chapter 5 (v. 21), by using a *kyrios*-statement. This produces an allusion to a confession which is the basis of the faith of the missionary churches.[28]

In Romans 5 Adam and Christ are set in opposition to each other as representatives of two ages in salvation history. Sin has had a reign of its own and it has brought death upon people ever since the trespass of Adam. In Christ a new reign of grace has begun which leads to life (5:21).[29] Adam and Christ thus represent complete cosmic ages. The salvation of man is not dependent merely on the activity of an individual. It is directed by cosmic powers which determine the eternal fate of man.[30]

There are clearly two distinct ways of assessing Paul's radical anthropology. In the research of previous decades the Adam typology has usually been

---

essential themes in Paul's soteriology: "Nach Paulus kann und soll sich die Erlösungshoffnung der Sünder und der Schöpfung, die mit Adams Falls der Nichtigkeit verfallen ist (Röm 8,20), einzig auf Christus richten. Er hat durch seinen Gehorsam der Sünde Einhalt geboten und die Herrschaft der Gnade aufgerichtet (Röm 5,19.21). Stuhlmacher, *Theologie*, 271.

[27] Barrett reminds us that here we meet "not only the expected *parallels* between Adam and Christ", but also surprising contrasts (in verse 15). "The act of Jesus was the act of an obedient man, but at the same time it was the act of a gracious God." Barrett, *Adam*, 71-72 (italics his).

[28] See Michel *Römer (1987)*, 124.

[29] Cf. e.g. Jeremias, *ThWNT I* (1990) 143; Brandenburger, *Adam*, 261; Luz, *Geschichtsverständnis*, 57; Dunn, *Romans*, 287; Beker, *Paul*, 85; Stuhlmacher, *Theologie*, 279.

[30] On the idea of universal sinfulness, see Schlier, *Römerbrief*, 182. Wedderburn is here worried by the conservative tendency to maintain the literal truth of Gen. 1-3. He wishes to separate the discussion from this aspect of the subject: "In the first place, whether or not these chapters were literally true is probably not a question over which Paul would really have been consciously exercised; like most of his contemporaries he could simply assume it." Wedderburn, *Studia Biblica III*, 423. In spite of this Wedderburn, too, underlined the fact that Paul, along with his fellow Jews, insisted on the universality of sin.

considered a description of the total sinfulness of man.[31] In modern
discussion, however, this anthropological perspective has been abandoned
quite generally. It has been considered Paul's secondary rationalization which
is of no crucial importance for his theology. This has further resulted in a belief
that Paul's nomism was merely a guide to obedience. In this case the
anthropology of Paul has been left aside, even though it must always be one of
the conditions of soteriology.[32] This has produced problems in interpretation,
because it is not possible to investigate Paul's soteriology without his radical
anthropology. The latter is the basis on which Paul can rely when he says that
the predestination of judgment concerns all humankind.

But what is the real problem here? Is it the question whether or not modern
scholarship should take the (historical) Fall into account in its interpretation? I
reckon that Bultmann has already answered this question. He was cautious
enough to make a distinction between his own existential interpretation and the
convictions of Paul. If we are to understand the theology of Paul, we must
acknowledge that he undeniably believed in the total corruption of man.

There is another problem, however, and it concerns the consistency of Paul's
thinking. Several scholars have claimed that in spite of his pessimistic
anthropology Paul at the same time taught the freedom of man and the
possibility of keeping the law perfectly (especially in Romans 2). Some
scholars tend to interpret this as meaning that Paul never actually intended to
claim the total depravity of man.[33] There are others, however, who simply
state that Paul was eclectic due to his "human weakness", and that his mind
was ambivalent.[34]

This discussion mainly concerns the interpretation of Romans 2 and some
references have been made to Philippians, as well, where Paul remarks that, as
to righteousness under the law, he is blameless (3:6). Did he really think that
man could in principle fulfil the law?

In Romans 2 the context itself is rather clear as regards the treatment of sin.
All sinners will be punished. In verse 12 Paul declares that those without the

---

[31] See the examples in 7.1.

[32] This is probably due to the change of paradigm in scholarship which took place when
the theory of covenantal nomism became popular.

[33] Following the interpretation put forward by Räisänen and Sanders, Ziesler explains the
nomism in this section as indicating that Paul is making no attempt to demonstrate the
complete sinfulness of men here. This would be impossible, because in chapter 2 Paul
speaks positively of the law (and further in Philippians states that he himself has been
blameless). Ziesler thinks that Paul only wished to emphasize and oppose the sin of sinners
to the righteous. Ziesler, *Romans,* 41, 100. Such an interpretation does not fit the
anthropology of Paul, however.

[34] See e.g. Räisänen, *Law,* 107, 150; Wedderburn, *Studia Biblica III,* 424.

law will perish as well as those who have transgressed against the law. It is easy to see that the Adam typology is at work here. But why does Paul say that the Gentiles "by nature" do what the law requires (v. 14)? And how can he place transgressing Jews in opposition to a Gentile who keeps the law (vv. 26-27)?

The first of these questions is easy to answer. When referring to the universal knowledge of the law Paul merely repeats the teachings of Jewish sapiential theology. In Second Temple Judaism *Torah* was identified with the creative power of God. As a consequence of this the whole order of the created world was seen as an expression of God's will (Sirach 16:26–27; Bar. 3:32; 4:1).[35] This is why *Torah* could be further identified with Wisdom (Bar. 4:1; Sirach 15:17; SapSol. 1:12–15), and in this way there was a universal basis for the knowledge of the law. In Jewish thinking this naturally led to a demand for perfect obedience to God, as well, and resulted in a dualism between sinners and the righteous.

But knowledge of the law is one thing and the ability to keep it another. Did Paul think that the former actually led to the latter? The most difficult of the questions dealt with in this chapter is the one of the "righteous Gentile". In 2:26 Paul seems to assume that there undeniably are Gentiles who keep the law: "So, if those who are uncircumcised keep the requirements of the law (ἐὰν οὖν ἡ ἀκροβυστία τὰ δικαιώματα τοῦ νόμου φυλάσσῃ), will not their uncircumcision be regarded as circumcision?". This has been a key verse, for example, for Räisänen in his conclusion that Paul is inconsistent.[36]

The answering of the difficult questions arising from this text is a matter of interpreting Paul's rhetoric in this section. Räisänen is evidently right when he says that Paul does not mean merely the keeping of "some" precepts of the law. Neither is Paul here speaking of Gentile Christians who would keep the law in the new existence governed by the Spirit.[37] But there is another option in addition to the previous ones. In his rhetoric Paul uses hypothetical argumentation.[38]

As we consider the argumentation in verses 12-29 we first note that Paul's aim is to tell his readers that the "real" circumcision is the "circumcision of the

---

[35] Hengel calls this "Tora-Ontologie" (in: *Judentum*, 455ff., especially 456). For the nature of sapiential nomism see also Stuhlmacher, *Theologie*, 255ff., especially 258.

[36] "We thus have to accept that Paul is really speaking of Gentiles who fulfil the law outside the Christian community." Räisänen, *Law*, 105.

[37] See Räisänen's evaluation of traditional alternatives, Räisänen, *Law*, 103-4: against older scholars, such as Nygren, Zahn and Barth.

[38] For this see e.g. van Dülmen, *Theologie*, 77ff. This, too, is an alternative which Räisänen rejects.

heart" which is a result of the work of the Holy Spirit (2:29). In order to justify such a claim Paul has to prove that all men are equal before God. He has begun his argumentation by referring to the universality of the knowledge of the law. In addition, he has to prove that the Jews, as well as the Gentiles, trespass the law. If this were true, Paul's Jewish readers would have to admit that, as regards salvation, they no longer have a privileged status in respect to the Gentiles.

Such argumentation was under consideration when verse 26 was written. It contains a rather difficult clause which has usually been translated inaccurately. It should be read as follows:

"If one who is uncircumcised were to keep the righteous requirements of the law, would not his uncircumcision be counted to him as circumcision?"

This translation is inevitable for linguistic reasons. We have here a prospective conditional clause (ἐὰν οὖν) which is of an unreal nature.[39] The rhetorical power of the argument is not dependent on the possibility of man's fulfilling the requirements of the law in practice.[40] The rhetorical power is in the principle that obedience precedes circumcision.[41]

Paul evidently presented his arguments by conforming his thoughts and his terminology to the convictions of the reader. This is evident also from the fact that Paul is speaking of the circumcision in a positive sense: "will not their uncircumcision be regarded as circumcision?" This is possible only if we admit that Paul wishes to convince his readers by using *their own* arguments. What Paul is trying to say is that the intention of circumcision is fulfilled when the law is kept.[42]

Now we end up with two quite contrary interpretations. According to the theory of Räisänen, Paul has a split mind. Paul's thinking is deductive and eclectic, and he speaks of man's ability to fulfil the law whenever it seems necessary for his argumentation. According to our analysis of Paul's rhetoric, however, Romans 2 claims just the opposite. Instead of using arguments for man's ability to keep the law, Paul is describing the universal sinfulness of both Jews and Gentiles. Even the ethnocentric premise does not hold, because Jews have to admit that the principle of keeping the law also precedes this one.

---

[39] Against Schlier, *Römerbrief*, 88.

[40] Räisänen opposes such an explanation. He thinks that the arguments of Paul are effective only if he really meant that the Gentiles are able to fulfil the whole law. Räisänen, *Law*, 103, 105; see also Ziesler, *Romans*, 93.

[41] This conclusion is often reached even though the unreal nature of the clause is not recognized, see e.g. Wilckens, *Römer I*, 155; Moo, *Romans*, 165; Fitzmyer, *Romans*, 320.

[42] In other instances Paul always speaks of circumcision in a negative sense, 1 Cor. 7:18-19; Gal. 5:2-6. On the importance of the theme of circumcision, see Dunn, *Romans*, 122.

If one (a Gentile) kept the law, this alone should be reckoned as circumcision –
but because no one in fact does keep it, circumcision too is useless before the
judgment seat of God, "on the day when... God, through Jesus Christ, will
judge the secret thoughts of all" (v. 16).[43]

How should we decide between these alternatives? As we try to construct the
line of thought in Paul's theology in Romans 1-3, the latter is to be chosen. It
alone suits the theology of predestination that Paul is constructing throughout
these chapters. In Romans 1 he described the total depravity of man by
exploiting the Genesis story and then moving on to the Psalms and the other
Writings. In Romans 2 Paul begins to hammer away at the Jewish identity
using his opponents' weapons. His sole aim is to show that both Jews and
Gentiles are under the power of sin. This is also his conclusion in 3:9.

Were one to abandon this logic in Paul's argumentation, one would evidently
have to conclude that Paul "was either not all that logical in his thinking or at
least not logical in the sense in which we understand the term."[44] We should be
more careful with our analysis of Paul's rhetoric, however. It is not always
easy to comprehend the sort of argumentation he uses. Paul is certainly logical
in the "sense in which we understand the term", but the examples he uses are
not familiar to us.

Our aesthetic preferences cannot be used as the criteria here, however. Paul
only had to convince the Jews to whom he was addressing his speech. And in

---

[43] Snodgrass has tried to solve the problems of chapter 2 in a new way. He suggests that
Paul's text should be read as it is. Paul is not presenting negative examples but teaching
normal Christian obedience instead. "There is no doctrine of works righteousness in chapter 2
that is countered in 3. 20 and replaced by the grace of God in Christ. Rather, in chapter 2,
there is presented a gracious, acting God who judges righteously. His wrath awaits those who
reject him and do evil, but life awaits those who respond in obedience, and this granting of
life has its foundation in the death of Christ." Snodgrass, *NTS 32* (1986) 82. The reason for
such an interpretation was that Paul "took the judgment texts seriously and expected that by
God's grace, on the basis of the death and resurrection of Christ, salvation is to 'the doers',
those responding in godly obedience." (p. 86). Snodgrass has an interesting point of view,
but his solution still lacks the perspective of predestinarian theology. His version of Pauline
soteriology resembles a Christianized sapiential obedience. This was not enough for Paul,
however. He "took the judgment texts" so seriously that he ended up with a polarized
soteriology. This is why we must go beyond Snodgrass' suggestion. Paul is not speaking of
a positive "justification to the doers" here. On the contrary, he claims that even the obedience
that precedes circumcision is not enough.

[44] Wedderburn, *Studia Biblica III*, 424. Martin has suggested that Paul is here making a
"general statement in a vivid manner about the consequences of Gentiles obeying the law
without stating that they really do obey the law." Martin, *Law*, 93. He is here following the
line of interpretation that Paul's reasoning was hypothetical (for the discussion see his *Law*,
93, footnote 138). One need not be content with merely stating that Paul spoke in a general
manner. His rhetoric was persuasive and the linguistic analysis proves his point, as well, as
we have seen above.

this respect his argument was watertight. Obedience precedes circumcision, and when obedience fails (in Adam), even Jews become sinners.

In Romans 1-7 Adam typology is an effective tool for Paul's theology of predestination. It is a medium by which he was able to justify his claim that all mankind lives under the power of sin. He is evidently not answering the question of modern philosophy of religion, asking how the universality of sin was possible in principle. Paul just took it for granted.[45] In Adam sin entered this world and all human beings fell short of the glory of God. This is the basis of Paul's pessimistic anthropology. Sin also brought the wrath of God upon all mankind. "In Adam" all people were condemned to damnation. The scene is completed with a pattern of "Universalgeschichte" (Luz): Adam and Christ are identified in a typological sense with two aeons. The age of Adam is without hope as regards salvation. For the sake of God's mercy there have been individuals who have in the manner of Abraham and the patriarchs believed in the mercy of God and been justified by faith. Most Jews, however, have not followed Abraham, but died in their sins.

Scholars who have investigated Adam-typology have been consistent in their unanimity as to the importance of this theme for the anthropology and soteriology of Paul. Paul thought that the fate of all humankind is bound up with the trespass of Adam. It has been claimed that Paul did not hold to this view consistently in his letters, but according to our analysis these claims are based on false arguments. For Paul, the relationship between God and man was determined by Adam's fall. With this typology Paul justified his radical anthropology, which was stricter than that of Second Temple sapiential theology. By his underlining of the Fall Paul approached Jewish apocalyptic, even though he radicalized the assertions made in that tradition. Adam-typology makes the idea of polarization, typical of the soteriology of Paul, even more profound. The universality of sin is justified by using a proof which undeniably covers all the descendants of Adam on earth. This is confirmed by the idea of two aeons. The age of Adam is the age of death, and salvation from it is possible only when the new age of Christ has begun.

---

[45] There have been efforts to explain the origin of such a teaching, however. Schoeps thought that Paul's thinking must be based on Jewish – mostly Rabbinic – teaching of the evil tendency or will of man, *yetzer hara'*. This evil *yetzer* is a cosmic power which lives in the hearts of men, and the life of an individual is an inner struggle due to this reality. This is what, according to Schoeps, Paul is describing in Romans 7. Schoeps, *Paulus*, 193ff. For such a tradition in 4 Ezra, see Thompson, *Theodicy*, 332ff. Even though there is no room for a detailed analysis of this theory here, it is proper to say that we should avoid simplistic identifications between Rabbinic theology and Paul, and take note of the differences which Schoeps too underlines in his study, see e.g. pp. 194f.

7.3. *The principle of paradoxical polarization in soteriology*

The extreme dualism of Paul has one significant consequence which becomes a dominating feature in his theology. Because of universal sinfulness and strict predestination there is no essential difference between the Jews and other peoples as regards salvation. When presenting this idea Paul employs the formula "Jews and Greeks" which he used in the context of salvation history. Now these groups are described as equal before God. Jews no longer receive anything "first". As regards salvation they are under the power of sin along with all the other nations of the world.[46]

This radical predestination is explicit in the third chapter of Romans: "we have already charged that all, both Jews and Greeks, are under the power of sin" (Rom 3:9). This clause continues the judgment speech which was interrupted in verse 2:29. When Paul returns to the subject he presents a summary of the whole previous section of the Romans (1:18-2:29).[47]

As we saw earlier, Paul taught the total domination of sin. Romans 3:9 was a key text of that teaching and it is only logical that he mentions Jews and Greeks on that occasion, too. The traditional Jewish ethnocentric principle has been here confronted with hamartology.[48]

In all the first three chapters of Romans the purpose of Paul is to show that the judgment of God concerns both Jews and Greeks without exception. This argumentation began in chapter one, verse 16, where the gospel of Christ was presented as a message of salvation for the Jews, too. Behind this concept of salvation there is a strict predestination: all are under sin and under the wrath of God. God has prescribed a punishment for sin, but at the same time his saving righteousness has been revealed in the gospel.

This concept of predestination has produced a special principle of interpretation in Paul's theology. He uses it constantly in the predestinarian sections of his letters. It can be called the principle of *paradoxical polarization*. Paul means that, on the basis of universal sinfulness and the unconditional judgment of God, our understanding of salvation must be rethought. Israel as the Chosen People had no special advantage as regards eschatological salvation. As God made his plan for the salvation of mankind, he decided to consign all under judgment so that, accordingly, he can show his mercy to all in the atoning work of Christ.[49]

---

[46] Wilckens, *Römer I*, 172.

[47] The idea of a summary has been noted by several scholars. Schlier, *Römerbrief*, 98; Wilckens, *Römer I*, 172; Ziesler, *Romans*, 102; Schreiner, *Law*, 67.

[48] See above chapter 7.1.

[49] This theme is to be analyzed in detail later, in chapter 8.1.

Such a principle is to be seen in chapter 3. When we proceed further in this chapter we meet even more evidence of a tendency to summarize. In 3:22 we again have the righteousness that comes from faith, referring to the "from faith to faith" locus in 1:17. The idea of the sinfulness of all (πάντες) is repeated here (cf. 1:18; 3:9). Further the Adam-typology from chapter 5 finds its place in the idea of falling short of glory (v. 23).[50]

This summary highlights the predestinarian theology of the third chapter of Romans. By summing up his previous claims Paul prepares the way for the crystallized presentation of the core of his soteriology. As regards sin, there is no "distinction" (διαστολή) between Jews and Greeks. All are under sin: "all have sinned and fall short of the glory of God" (3:22-23, οὐ γάρ ἐστιν διαστολή· πάντες γὰρ ἥμαρτον).[51] This is a sufficient argument for the rejection of ethnocentric claims.[52]

One would expect διαστολή to be a significant and widely-used term because it has such a crucial function in this key sentence. It probably was one, too, as it appears in Exodus 8:19 (LXX) with an identical function.[53] One cannot call it a proper technical term, however, since in the Septuagint three different Hebrew words are translated by διαστολή and the section of Exodus is the only one where the meaning of the word is similar to that in Romans. At least we know that the διαστολή was certainly observed in Jewish theology. So the "distinction" must refer to an exclusive identity in a more general sense.

There are two especially important theological features in verse 3:23. Firstly, we must note that the polarization is made on the ground of universal sinfulness. So there is no question of the fact that Paul's soteriology is totally dependent on the idea of universal sinfulness. His rejection of the traditional

---

[50] Stuhlmacher, *Römer*, 57; Schlier, *Römerbrief,* 106f.; Wilckens, *Römer I,* 188; Fitzmyer, Romans, 345f.

[51] In Romans 10:12 διαστολή appears with a similar function, with the only difference that there is no "distinction" as regards salvation. So 10:12 is a "positive equivalent" of 3:22. Dunn, *Romans,* 610. As regards Romans 3, according to Seifrid, Paul makes this negatively: "Negatively, Paul claims that universal sinfulness means that God makes no distinction on the basis of *Torah* observance in his dispensation of this gift." Seifrid, *Justification,* 220.

[52] In this case Dunn's interest in Paul's rejection of Jewish ethnocentric idealism is appropriate. "The familiarity of the assertion to present-day readers should not be allowed to dull the shocking character of what Paul says: the established character of the phrase 'Jew and Gentile/Greek'... expressed the axiomatic nature of the Jewish self-understanding of the people of Israel as different. The object of 1:18–3:20, however, had been precisely to destroy the Jewish presumption of special prerogative and defence even before the faithful covenant God (the point reiterated in v. 23)." Dunn, *Romans,* 167.

[53] Dunn is evidently right when he refers to Exodus 8:19 (LXX), where διαστολή is used for the distinction between Israel and the Gentiles. Dunn, *Romans,* 610.

"distinction" is not understandable without this premise.[54] Secondly, we note that the polarization Paul makes is of a paradoxical nature. Israel should have been *the* Chosen People, but now pious Jews were made equal with Gentile sinners. As regards Judaism, this was naturally a blasphemous claim. Paul was not content with the idea that we see in 4 Ezra: that fallen Jews had no privilege by virtue of their nationality.[55] Paul claimed that even the righteous were under the wrath of God.

In his teaching Paul touched on one of the most important convictions of Jewish identity. Separation from the Gentiles was made on several grounds. First of all, the Gentiles were called "sinners".[56] This is already part of the teaching of the Old Testament (Isa. 14:5; Ps. 9:6-18; 1 Macc. 2:48). The reason for such a description was more often than not the fact that the Gentiles did not know the Law and lived immorally.[57] In addition, they were, for rather obvious reasons, idolaters as well.[58]

Jewish purity regulations reveal other features of the Jewish attitude towards the Gentiles. Because the Gentiles were regarded as impure (mToh. 7:6; mNid. 10:4), this had several consequences in everyday life. Gentiles were forbidden

---

[54] Without the context of predestinarian theology Paul's claims would seem to be exaggerations. This is actually how e.g. Räisänen explains this section. "Paul's argument is here simply a piece of propagandist denigration." Räisänen, *Law*, 101; cf. Sanders, *Law*. 125: "Paul's case for universal sinfulness, as it is stated in Rom. 1:18–2:29, is not convincing; it is internally inconsistent and it rests on gross exaggeration." Both writers appeal to Paul's "empirical" arguments concerning the complete sinfulness of man. Instead of such reasoning we must see that Paul is writing predestinarian theology. It is precisely due to universal sinfulness that Paul is justified in giving his "empirical" proof-texts which expose the sinful actions of men under the power of sin.

[55] When comparing Paul's theology and 4 Ezra, B. Longenecker saw that in both directions the traditional, covenantal ethnocentricity was rejected on the grounds of the reality of sin. "Moreover, the manner by which both authors facilitate the breakdown of ethnocentricism is precisely the same; that is, they both dwell on the Jewish commonplace that all are guilty of sin." Longenecker, *Eschatology and Covenant*, 270.

[56] This also in Gal. 2:15; see the analysis later, in chapter 11.1.

[57] Cf. Pseudo-Philo 12:2; Ps.Sol. 17:24. An overview is given by Longenecker, *Eschatology and Covenant*, 27-31. See also Rengstorf, *ThWNT I* (1990) 329-330. There was usually a conflict behind such statements. In 1 Maccabees 2 it is the defilement of the Temple. One could almost say that Gentile sinners were considered to be at war with God Himself. For the strict conceptions of the Qumran community, see Deines, *Die Heiden*, 59ff., especially 78ff.

[58] See e.g. Encyclopaedia Judaica, s.v. Gentile, *EJ 7* (1971-) 410f. We must remember that this was linked with the extended prohibition of marriage in the Second Temple period. Cf. Heckel, *Die Heiden*, 283f., 287.

entry to the Temple rampart (mKelim 1:8),[59] and when Jewish people were in a state of ritual purity, they were required to avoid foreigners (Jos. Ant. 14.285).[60] For a pious Jew even meeting Gentiles in the market-place was sufficient reason for immersion in a *miqveh* at home.[61]

In such a context Paul's teaching was paradoxical, indeed. The Gentiles had been considered sinners and the διαστολή had been real and visible. Now the new revelation of God altered Paul's previous convictions. All the children of Adam were sinners and their only hope was in the righteousness of Christ. This was the basis for equality in Paul's teaching, as previously expressed in Romans. "There will be anguish and distress for everyone who does evil, the Jew first and also the Greek" (Rom. 2:9). Judgment does not ask a person's nationality. Paul's polarization was repeatedly directed against ethnocentricity.

Statements such as this call into question the Jewish religious identity in a radical way. The status of Israel as the Chosen People, distinct and separate from other peoples, had been changed.[62] As regards salvation, every man is equal before God. Everyone falls short of the glory of God and true righteousness. This is why everyone is in need of the righteousness which God gives through faith in Christ.[63]

Paul's concept of soteriological polarization affects the formation of his theology in many ways. In Romans 2 he crosses the boundaries of Jewish identity and makes a clear distinction between ethnocentric idealism and the reality of salvation history. "For a person is not a Jew who is one outwardly, nor is true circumcision something external and physical."(2:28).[64] Real

---

[59] In 1 Macc. 14 we have the "inscription of Simon", where Simon is praised for removing the defilement of the Temple which the Gentiles had been guilty of, 1 Macc. 14:36ff. As regards the prohibition of entry, among the archaeological finds we, of course, have the famous fragment of a warning inscription from Herod's Temple. As Josephus too testifies, this inscription was a warning "prohibiting the entrance of a foreigner under threat of the penalty of death". Jos. Ant. 15.417. For an overview, see Finegan, *Archeology*, § 182 (p. 197); cf. the informative footnote in the Loeb edition of Jos. Ant. 15, footnote *d,* pp. 202-203.

[60] Cf. Jub. 22:16ff.: "Separate yourself from the gentiles... and do not perform deeds like theirs... Because their deeds are defiled, and all their ways are contaminated". See also Encyclopaedia Judaica, s.v. Purity and impurity, ritual, *EJ 13* (1971-) 1409.

[61] Cf. Mark 7:3ff. Such an attitude was common at Qumran and among the Essenes, as well. See e.g. CD 11:2f., 14ff.; 1QH 6:24-28. Deines, *Die Heiden*, 85.

[62] This has been emphasized especially by Dunn, *Romans,* 167.

[63] Cf. Wilckens, *Römer I*, 187f.; Stuhlmacher, *Römer*, 57; Beker, *Paul*, 82.

[64] This, of course, is a conclusion of Paul's treatment of the status of circumcision (see above 7.2.). When Paul summarized his critique of ethnocentric idealism he was able to use the Jewish parenetic tradition and in this way again appeal to the premises of his opponents. Cf. Wilckens, *Römer I*, 158; Schlier, *Römerbrief,* 89; Dunn, *Romans,* 123.

"Jewishness" in salvation history concerns all those whom the Spirit grants adoption and bears witness that they are children of God by his mercy (2:29).[65] This is why the boundaries of the Chosen People, the people of promise, fall down (cf. Rom. 9:6).

Since the only thing that matters in salvation is the question of how God reveals his righteousness, the righteousness that comes from faith is the only criterion in soteriology. This is why the justification of both circumcised and uncircumcised is based on a similar principle (Rom. 3:30).[66] On this basis we may conclude that Paul's understanding of circumcision is dictated by his theology of predestination.

A similar pattern of soteriology is to be detected in other letters of Paul, for example in 1 Corinthians.

"For Jews demand signs and Greeks desire wisdom, but we proclaim Christ crucified, a stumbling block to Jews and foolishness to Gentiles, but to those who are called, both Jews and Greeks, Christ the power of God and the wisdom of God" (1 Cor. 1:22-24).

We see that Paul has already here stated that the Jews have not "submitted" to God's plan of salvation. They have not accepted God's saving acts but quite to the contrary considered the new teaching a heresy (cf. Rom. 10:3). This is why they do not know the saving power of God.

The equality of the Jews and the Greeks similarly concerns the gospel and salvation. This can best be seen in the thesis of Romans 1, and the same idea occurs throughout his letter. "For I am not ashamed of the gospel; it is the power of God for salvation to everyone who has faith, to the Jew first and also to the Greek." (Rom. 1:16; cf. 9:24; 15:8-9). In 1 Corinthians we meet this parallelism in the context of the metaphor of the body of Christ: "For in the one Spirit we were all baptized into one body – Jews or Greeks, slaves or free" (1 Cor. 12:13). In Galatians such equality is a consequence of adoption to new childhood. "There is no longer Jew or Greek, there is no longer slave or free, there is no longer male and female; for all of you are one in Christ Jesus" (Gal. 3:28).

These passages which speak of the relationship between Jews and Greeks

---

[65] Moo reminds us of the fact that the contrast between outward circumcision and circumcision 'done to the heart' is well known in the Old Testament and Judaism. "From the earliest history of Israel, God called on the people to manifest the kind of heart response to Him that was characterized as a 'circumcision of the heart' (Deut. 10:16; cf. Jer. 4:4). Significantly, it is also recognized equally early on that it is God Himself who must intervene to bring about this response (Deut. 30:6)." Moo, *Romans*, 171. For parallel texts in Jewish theology, see e.g. Jub. 1:23; Odes Sol. 11:2.

[66] Cf. Seifrid, *Justification*, 223: "Appealing to the quintessentially Jewish theme of the unity of the sovereign God, Paul claims that boasting is excluded and that God will justify the uncircumcised through faith."

confirm the view that, in the theology of Paul, soteriological dualism is directed by the concept of predestination. His conception cannot be identified with that of Jewish apocalyptic. Paul accepts the basic Jewish claim of the difference between sinners and the saved, but the nature of his soteriology is new.[67] The righteousness of God is realized only in Christ.[68] This is why the previous eschatology has lost its value.[69]

Paul's understanding of the relationship between Jews and Gentiles is based on a strict polarization. In God's plan of salvation Israel no longer has a special function, by which the whole nation could be identified with the kingdom of God. The previous soteriological dualism has been replaced by a new paradoxical polarization. The true Israel is comprised only of those who belong to Christ. All others are under the wrath of God and condemned to death. This polarization is paradoxical as regards traditional Jewish soteriology, because it cannot be justified without the new, radical concept of predestination. As a consequence of the polarization Paul's pessimistic anthropology results in the rejection of Jewish ethnocentricity.

---

[67] This is also the conclusion of Winninge after a comparison of Paul's teaching and the beliefs of the Psalms of Solomon. Paul's radicalism is in his concept of universal sinfulness. This is a view unparalleled in the Jewish theology of his time. Winninge, *Sinners and the Righteous*, 308f.

[68] Most scholars agree, at least partly, on the idea that Paul teaches such a soteriology. The main difficulty has been rather the question, why does Paul teach this? – as we have already seen in the course of the discussion. It seems that modern scholarship is in danger of ignoring Paul's anthropology and not regarding it as essential. The perspective of predestinarian theology helps us to keep anthropology in the centre of Paul's soteriology, where it rightly belongs.

[69] Cf. Wilckens, *Römer I*, 150-153.

§ 8 *Mankind Imprisoned Under the Power of Sin*

Several of the themes which had traditionally been prominent in the treatment of the problem of theodicy, also occur in the theology of Paul. The concepts of the wrath of God, and the consequent judgment, were of crucial importance to him. When these themes were combined with a radical anthropology, Paul's soteriological setting was almost complete. What was lacking was a basic hermeneutical standpoint which would justify this new polarization in opposition to traditional Jewish soteriology. This necessary factor was found in the idea of divine predestination.[1]

8.1. Sold into slavery

In Jewish sapiential theology the theme of predestination occurred in the context of the idea of free will. The free will of man gave sufficient anthropological conditions for his responsibility with regard to ungodliness. This is why the predestination of judgment seemed to be justified. Judgment would fall on those who had themselves, from their own free will and malice, chosen ungodliness.

At Qumran predestinarian theology was somewhat stricter than in traditional sapiential theology. In the dualism of the sect people were divided into two groups, the children of light and the children of darkness. Their fate was determined by spirits and every man had his share of these spirits. From the practical solutions of the teaching of Qumran we may conclude, however, that soteriological dualism could never supersede the theology of free will. The soteriology of the sect was based on the possibility of repentance. If most Israelites were totally predestined and predetermined children of darkness, they would never have been able to repent. This is why most people had to be defined as "misguided" children of light.[2]

In Paul's theology the predestination of judgment occurs in quite a different context, and it gains another kind of status. The power of sin, according to

---

[1] When treating the question of predestination we must remember that in this study the concept is not deterministic. We have earlier noted (e.g. 3.3., 5.1.) that in Jewish theology there was a clear predestination of doom for the wicked. In the sapiential tradition, however, the fate of the Israelites was hardly ever considered deterministic. There was usually room for repentance and renewed obedience. In fact, this was most often seen as a basis for the restoration of Israel.

[2] See especially 5.2. We must remember that this means a crucial difference with respect to the idea of double predestination. This cannot be explained as a "widening" of such predestination, because according to the theologians of Qumran, the "misguided" Israelites were condemned to damnation if they did not join the new community. Predestinarian theology was unable to displace traditional soteriological dualism.

Paul, is complete. Separation from God began with the fall of Adam. The damnation of the disobedient has been ordained, accordingly, but it does not concern only a few ungodly individuals. It concerns all mankind, because all are equal before the judgment seat of God.

In the letters of Paul the concept of absolute predestination of judgment occurs in two kinds of contexts. The first group comprises actual predestinarian statements which in one way or another speak of God's deliberate action in determining the fate of sinners.[3] In addition, there are in Paul's letters several descriptive predestinarian statements in which the state of the wicked is described and the reality of the power of sin is explained in detail.

When the letters of Paul are investigated with respect to the above-mentioned definition, we find some clauses which could be defined as "actual" predestinarian statements:

"For his sake I have suffered the loss of all things (ἐζημιώθην) [all is far outweighed, NEB]" (Phil. 3:8, literally: "made loss")

"But the scripture has imprisoned (συνέκλεισεν) all things under the power of sin" (Gal. 3:22)

"I am of the flesh, sold (πεπραμένος) into slavery under sin" (Rom. 7:14)

"For God has imprisoned all in disobedience so that he may be merciful to all."(συνέκλεισεν)" (Rom. 11:32).

Both the argumentation and the purpose of these statements are rather uniform. Due to the radical concept of sin, man's relation to God has been changed and God has consigned all people under sin and condemnation. A similar content occurs in descriptive predestinarian statements, such as the following:[4]

"all, both Jews and Greeks, are under the power of sin" (Rom. 3:9)

"the whole world may be exposed to the judgment of God " (Rom. 3:19, NEB)

"all have sinned and fall short of the glory of God" (Rom. 3:23)

"sin came into the world through one man,
and death came through sin" (Rom. 5:12)

---

[3] As we speak of "actual" predestinarian clauses we must remind ourselves of the definition given at the beginning of this study with regard to the concept of predestination. In this case we are speaking merely of the predestination of judgment. It is possible to call other predestinarian clauses "actual", even though they speak of election and salvation. This was the solution proposed by Mayer, as we have seen. Further, as regards the question concerning the hardening of Israel (Rom. 9-11), this must be examined separately later (8.2.).

[4] Several of these sections have been examined in previous chapters. They all occur in the context of soteriological teaching and usually also bring the presentation to a climax, as we have seen. For Paul's negative hamartology, see e.g. 7.1.

"the judgment following one trespass brought condemnation" (Rom. 5:16)
"I see in my members another law... making me captive to the law of sin that dwells in my members " (Rom. 7:23)

Among the actual predestinarian statements, the one in Romans 11 is probably the clearest and most helpful. Here Paul gives almost a formal definition of the predestination of judgment: "For God has imprisoned all in disobedience so that he may be merciful to all" (11:32).[5]

Here we have a cosmic summary of salvation history regarding the fate of mankind in God's world.[6] Even though Paul is speaking of Israel in the previous verses, this statement cannot be restricted to Israel solely. It is in total agreement with the argumentation which Paul has been building throughout the letter. God's predestination concerned all people (ὁ θεὸς τοὺς πάντας...). Jews and Greeks are equal as regards divine salvation history (cf. Rom. 3:9). As verse 11:32 presents a summary of the pondering of Israel's status, it actually gives a summary of the main theme of Romans.[7]

Disobedience was a problem both to the Gentiles and Israel (vv. 30-31). This disobedience can be identified with submission to the power of sin, which Paul previously described by using Adam as a type. All mankind was left under a death sentence in Adam (Rom. 5). The divine predestination of judgment falls on sin and concerns all humankind. All people have been "imprisoned" (συν-έκλεισεν γὰρ ὁ θεὸς) in disobedience. The powerful metaphor of prison highlights Paul's predestinarian theology.[8]

Paul writes of God's judgment and preparation of salvation from the pers-

---

[5] Kr.: συνέκλεισεν γὰρ ὁ θεὸς τοὺς πάντας εἰς ἀπείθειαν ἵνα τοὺς πάντας ἐλεήσῃ.

[6] According to Michel, this is a crucial statment of Paul concerning his theology of history and connected with his theology of aeons. It is teleological, and aims at the climax of eschatology, i.e. salvation in the last days. Michel, *ThWNT VII* (1990) 746.

[7] The great importance of this verse as a climax of Paul's argumentation has often been noted in research, see Michel, *Römer (1955)*, 253; Schlier, *Römerbrief*, 344; Wilckens, *Römer*, 262; Dunn, *Romans*, 695: "the summary of the summary"; Hübner, *Law*, 81: "the climax of Paul's whole argument on justification". Cf. Stuhlmacher, *Gerechtigkeit*, 92: "V. 32 aber ist der Zentralsatz des von Paulus wahrgenommenen und mitgeteilten eschatologischen μυστήριον über Gottes Geschichtswalten und zugleich die grundlegende Maxime für die gesamte paulinische Rechtfertigungslehre und Rechtfertigungstheologie".

[8] Even though this theology of Paul's is not usually called predestinarian theology by scholars, they do emphasize that for Paul it was crucial to mention total disobedience when presenting his theology of justification. Dunn, *Romans*, 696: "God has confined human beings to disobedience precisely because it is only to the disobedient that he can show mercy." Beker, in turn, thinks that 11:32 is the climax of the whole letter and that its emphasis is "on the universal embrace of God's mercy". Beker, *The Romans Debate*, 329-330.

pective of salvation history.[9] In this scheme, too, the fate of Israel is treated in Romans 11. The positive history of the Chosen People under the providence of God has naturally been a sign of God's remarkable salvation, but this is also true as regards the abandonment of Israel. The predestination of the judgment day, when the whole world shall stand before God, has been a preparation for a unique salvation which God will give in his Son Jesus Christ.[10]

As we compare this teaching of Romans with that of Galatians, we must not forget the theory of the development of Paul's theology. Such a theory was namely based on the very sections we are examining here. According to the theory, in these two letters Paul wrote differently concerning soteriology and nomism.[11] This theory must be reassessed because, as regards predestinarian theology, Paul's teaching seems to be exactly the same in both instances.

The predestinarian statement of Galatians connects the themes of imprisonment and sin (Gal. 3:22):

"But the scripture has imprisoned all things under the power of sin"

συνέκλεισεν ἡ γραφὴ τὰ πάντα ὑπὸ ἁμαρτίαν

The one who captures is here "the scripture" and consequently nomism forms the context. The Law has the power to put all people in prison and accuse them of sin.[12] This theme is frequent in Paul's letters. The Law awakens sin and puts people to death (Rom. 5:20-21; 7: 10). The Law makes all people guilty before God (Rom. 3:19).

In Galatians Paul explains primarily the function of the law in God's plan of salvation. The scripture has imprisoned all people under sin. This does not mean, however, that the law could do this all by itself. The imprisonment is

---

[9] This is how Michel understands Paul's teaching on "imprisonment". It is of an eschatological nature and has a teleological aim in God's plan of salvation. Michel, *ThWNT VII* (1990) 746.

[10] Käsemann rightly remarks that the predestinarian statement of Paul's must not be explained by determinism. Käsemann, *Römer,* 302. Besides, he is content with giving an existential interpretation about a divine word which attempts to restore man to the original state of creation. This describes only vaguely the radical soteriology of Paul. In this context Käsemann regards the word for imprisonment only as a metaphor for the confinement of man (p. 303).

[11] See especially Hübner, *Law,* 57, 81, 124.

[12] In this respect Hübner explains this verse in a similar way: "The *nomos* has the function of serving as the sphere of enslavement for man." Hübner, *Law,* 33; cf. Dunn, *Galatians,* 194. Schlier and Betz want to differentiate scripture from the law here, but this is quite unnecessary. See Schlier, *Galater,* 164-165; Betz, *Galatians,* 175.

here, too, an act of divine predestination.[13] Its aim is the preparation of salvation. This is why the predestinarian statement combines these two features: "But the scripture has imprisoned all things under the power of sin, so that what was promised through faith in Jesus Christ might be given to those who believe" (3:22).[14]

When we later, in Romans 7, find the teaching that men are sold into slavery, it is easy to see how closely these two letters are related. "Being under the power of sin" means complete slavery. It is not possible to be freed from it without divine intervention and God's deliberate action. In Philippians (3:8) we also have a predestinarian statement, but it is more developed that the other ones described above. There Paul is speaking of good becoming real harm for believers. This idea is developed into the principle of "counting as loss", which is also very important to Paul.[15]

The closest parallel text to Galatians (3:22) can be found in Romans 11. Both of these texts speak of binding man to sin and disobedience. In this respect it is not possible to discern a principal change or development between Galatians and Romans. Even though there are changes in terminology and the examples used are different, the basic theology of predestination is the same in both of these letters.[16]

As regards the descriptive clauses, they most often occur in the context of the anthropological themes which we examined earlier in chapter 7. In these clauses Paul describes above all the all-embracing power of sin. In this respect also these clauses deny the ethnocentric ideal and emphasize the absolute nature

---

[13] As Eckstein writes, God himself is behind the "scripture". "Somit ist es also Gott selbst, der durch die Schrift qua Gesetz die Sünder bei ihrer Sünde behaftet, in der Absicht, ihnen die von der Schrift qua Verheissung bezeugte Rechtfertigung in Christus frei zu schenken." Eckstein, *Verheissung*, 211.

[14] The relation of these two "strands" has been quite a puzzle in the history of the Church, and at the Reformation it was interpreted along the dynamics of "law and gospel". Modern scholars speak e.g. of "different levels in the divine economy", see Longenecker, *Galatians*, 145. The perspective of predestinarian theology helps us to define the function of the law more clearly.

[15] This theme in Paul's letters will be analyzed later in chapter 11, and the section of Philippians especially in chapter 11.2.

[16] It is no wonder that Hübner, who speaks of a development in the theology of Paul, has to make reservations to his theory precisely on the grounds of the evident connection described above: "Rom 11.32... may seem to present the most serious difficulties for the thesis we are trying to develop, for do we not have here the 'final' statement, the lack of which in 4.15 made it possible to differentiate this passage from Gal 3?" Hübner, *Law*, 81. Hübner tries to solve this problem by commenting that Paul does not seem to mean predestination but merely an imprisonment of people in their "own" disobedience. Such strained explanations can be avoided by locating this verse within Paul's predestinarian theology – where it belongs, according to our analysis.

of the Fall. In addition, the descriptive clauses speak of God's judgment and the curse that falls on sin.

The dynamics of predestinarian statements are thus based on a causality between sin and punishment. As a starting-point in his anthropology Paul uses the story of the Fall in Genesis. The state of mankind has been predetermined in a cosmic event. In a holistic interpretation Paul claims that all died in Adam. This is why condemnation falls on all mankind. After Adam all men have in principle been "sold" or "imprisoned" under the slavery of sin.[17]

On this basis Paul presents his predestinarian theology in effective *contrast formulas*. They do not have a strict pattern, but a similarity in content is obvious:
"all have sinned and fall short of the glory of God;
            they are now justified by his grace as a gift"
            (Rom. 3:23-24).
"Therefore just as one man's trespass led to condemnation for all,
            so one man's act of righteousness
            leads to justification and life for all"
            (Rom. 5:18; cf. v. 19).
"For the wages of sin is death,
            but the free gift of God is eternal life in Christ Jesus
            our Lord" (Rom. 6:23).
"For God has imprisoned all in disobedience
            so that he may be merciful to all."
            (Rom. 11:32).
"But the scripture has imprisoned all things under the power of sin,
            so that what was promised through faith in Jesus Christ
            might be given to those who believe"
            (Gal. 3:22).

With the help of contrast formulas Paul can briefly express the tension which he has, from the very beginning of the Romans, been describing as a dynamic relation between God's righteousness and God's wrath.[18] The aim of his predestinarian theology is not merely the proclamation of God's judgment. The

---

[17] This feature is noted by most scholars, even though some of them attempt to explain the theme by detecting non-Jewish influence on the subject. See e.g. Bultmann, *Theologie,* 250f.; Bornkamm, *Paulus,* 143f. Several scholars accept the negative anthropology as a basic element of Paul's theology, Schoeps, *Paulus,* 193ff.; Luz, *Geschichtsverständnis,* 197, 204; Beker, *Paul,* 215f.; Stuhlmacher, *Theologie,* 270-271.

[18] Such contrast formulas are typical of Paul, even though he probably also uses traditional material on these occasions. Usually it is not possible to find a unanimous answer concerning the limits of the traditional material, as the discussion by Käsemann on Rom. 3:23-24 shows, see Käsemann *Römer,* 88-89; for the syntactical problems concerning this passage, see Dunn, *Romans,* 168.

predestination of judgment is the background and the first stage in God's plan for the salvation which will be prepared for all people.[19] The revealing and appearance of God's righteousness is his predetermined gospel. The vicarious death of Christ concerns precisely the same humankind that has been imprisoned under the power of sin. "But God proves his love for us in that while we still were sinners Christ died for us" (Rom. 5:8).[20]

Paul's "descriptive" predestinarian clauses emphasize the perspective of salvation history. They give a picture of humankind struggling under the power of sin. In this struggle there is no difference between Jews and Gentiles. All people belong eventually to one and the same family, because they are all descendants of Adam. Only a salvation which relates to godless sinners can really help the human race as it is.[21]

In summary, we may note that Paul, following Jewish theology in general, believes that the eschatological judgment is predestined. The judgment of God will unavoidably fall on godless people. The soteriological dualism of Second Temple Jewish texts stands in contradiction to Paul's radicalized concept, however. According to the predestinarian statements of Paul, the eschatological judgment with its punishments concerns all people. All the descendants of Adam are under sin and under condemnation. In Paul's soteriology the strict polarization resulted in a new understanding of the nature of salvation: God has imprisoned all people under the power of sin. This is the only way to prepare salvation for all people through atonement. The sacrificial death of Christ is the only possible means of salvation in this fallen world where the descendants of Adam have fallen short of the glory of God. This is the scheme that Paul repeats over and over again in several contrast formulas in his letters.

8.2. The hardening of Israel

As we have analyzed Paul's predestinarian statements and examined his concept of judgment, we have consciously avoided the question concerning the evident predestination of a person's fate, i.e. the problem of the hardening of Israel. In Romans 9-11 Paul explains the fate of Israel in a way which reminds one of the classical idea of predestination: God seems intentionally to predetermine the future of his people. God "hardens the heart of whomever he

---

[19] Concerning Rom. 5:18, cf. Wilckens, *Römer I,* 326; Moo, *Romans,* 354f.

[20] Paul's predestinarian theology is part of his Christology. This subject will be treated in detail below, in chapter 9.

[21] Cf. Witherington, *Paul's Narrative Thought World,* 22ff. "There are three universals that Paul believes all experience. *All* live in this present age and are subject to its spiritual and even supernatural wickedness and problems... *All* are in bondage to sin, both Jew and Gentile, so none can be justified by their works... *All* are subject to death... Thus, outside Christ there is only lostness and a complete inability so save oneself" (p. 29).

chooses" (Rom. 9:18), and guides world history as he pleases in a sovereign way.[22]

What is Paul teaching here, then? Has he abandoned his great discovery concerning the righteousness of God? Is he lost in an endless scholastic debate, where he is trying to apply his new soteriology to traditional Jewish covenantalism? Or is he reaching for the climax of his soteriology instead? Could chapters 9-11 reveal the crown of Paul's argument in the whole letter?

Some scholars think that Paul's theology of predestination should be defined solely on the grounds of these chapters. We have chosen another way. The teaching of these chapters will be compared with the basic concept of predestination as defined in the context of the problem of theodicy, especially in the Second Temple period. When we do this, we must ask, however, if there is any inconsistency in the teaching of Paul. Is this section not a clear example of double predestination?[23]

Firstly, we must note that the argumentation in Romans 9-11 shows that in this section, too, Paul applies the principle of paradoxical polarization. Soteriological dualism, which we have examined already, is an integral part of the teaching where Israel and the Gentiles are opposed to each other in a new way.

Paul's criticism is directed above all against ethnocentric ideology.[24] The traditional teaching concerning God's election is no longer sufficient for Paul. He is convinced that it has been replaced by a new dualism. The opposition is between those saved in Christ and those outside this new salvation. This new polarization is paradoxical in the sense that it does not seem to be quite

---

[22] The section 9-11 has most often been studied from the point of view of the question of Israel's fate, and the aspects of predestination and determinism have been treated as part of that discussion. There is a vast amount of literature on this subject, including Munck, *Christ and Israel*; Plag, *Israels Wege*; Müller, *Gottes Gerechtigkeit*; Stendahl, *Paul Among Jews and Gentiles;* Hübner, *Gottes Ich;* and the collection *Israelfrage,* ed. De Lorenzi. There are also some fairly recent dissertations on the subject, such as Schmitt, *Gottesgerechtigkeit*; Siegert, *Argumentation*; Lübking, *Paulus und Israel;* and Röhser, *Prädestination.* Several themes in modern research have further been analysed in Räisänen, *Social World,* 178-206; and Räisänen, *Texts and Contexts,* 743-765.

[23] As regards the consistency of Paul's teaching, there are two questions that have been under discussion. The first of these concerns the problem of double predestination, as was mentioned above. In addition, there has been discussion on the relation between chapters 9 and 11. According to Hübner, Paul presents two solutions to the problem of Israel's destiny. Hübner, *Gottes Ich,* 122; cf. Lüdemann, *Paulus und das Judentum,* 30-35; Watson, *Paul,* 168-170. In the context of the "new perspective" on Paul this alleged tension has been considered an example of Paul's inconsistency as regards the fate of Israel. See Räisänen, *Law (2nd ed.),* xvii, xx.

[24] Cf. Hofius, *Paulusstudien,* 177. In this respect also the analysis by B. Longenecker is appropriate, see Longenecker, *Eschatology and the Covenant,* 253.

consistent with the promises of the old covenant. Only the idea of radical predestination makes it understandable and sensible. When such a principle is applied in defining the status of Israel in God's plan of salvation, a question arises concerning the fate of the Chosen People. In Romans 9-11 we see that this problem was a difficult one. When Paul explained it he had to approach the problem of predestination from different angles. What is the status of Israel as the Chosen People? What is the status of Israel in God's plan of salvation? What is the relation of the Chosen People to their Messiah?[25]

These questions are answered in Romans 9-11. We are evidently faced with predestinarian theology here, but the nature of these chapters is quite complex. It is no wonder that the general interpretation of this section has always affected the entire explanation of its details.

In previous scholarship Romans was most often divided into two parts. The first part was considered to be teaching on the subject of justification, and it comprised chapters 1-8. It was regarded as the main part of the letter. According to this interpretation, chapters 9-11 were but a separate addition to the important and consistent dogmatic letter.[26]

In modern scholarship the significance of these chapters is seen in a different light. The section is regarded as a consistent consequence of the previous chapters. Paul is here developing the very themes he has been dealing with throughout the letter. This is no excursus, not to mention a path of error, but an integral part of the theological teaching, and even the climax of his presentation.[27] This point of view is confirmed by the contextual analysis. The letter was addressed to Jewish Christians, and so the content of chapters 9-11

---

[25] Beker has presented this problem in a clear way: "Is the gospel the abolition of or the fulfillment of Israel's election and salvation-history?" The basic problem concerns the consistent continuity of salvation history. Beker, *Paul*, 77.

[26] In the commentary of Sanday-Headlam we see an explanation typical of the era: that Rom. 9-11 is an "appendix" to Paul's teaching; Sanday-Headlam, *Romans*, 226. Dodd, in turn, here used his famous principle of interpretation, that Paul used several sermons in his letters. To him chapters 9-11 formed "a compact and continuous whole, which can be read quite satisfactorily without reference to the rest of the epistle." Thus the sudden "new" themes of Paul are explained by his additional "sermon". Dodd, *Romans*, 148f. Beker criticized these interpretations and asserted that they are too often based on the Baurian pattern of the history of the early Church. Because Paul always had to be presented as an opponent of Jewish Christianity, he was described as a "lonely revolutionary", who turned his back on Israel and proclaimed a universal gospel of liberty. Beker, *Paul*, 64.

[27] See e.g. Cranfield, *Romans*, 445f.; Wilckens, *Römer II*, 181; Dunn, *Romans*, 519; Stuhlmacher, *Römer*, 129; Beker, *The Romans Debate*, 329-330; Becker, *Paulus*, 362; Schmitt, *Gottesgerechtigkeit*, 71; Wright, *Climax of the Covenant*, 235; Siegert, *Argumentation*, 113f.

was essential as regards the aims of Paul.[28] The question of the salvation of Israel is easily explained as the climax of the whole letter. This is due to the fact that the sharpest point of Paul's theology comes in chapter 10. There Paul eventually reveals the heart of his gospel, "the word of faith", the content of the message of salvation (10:9-10).

On a general level we could say that even the basic theme of Romans, i.e. the gospel as God's saving righteousness, leads one to expect the problem of Israel to be dealt with in the course of the letter.[29] This is only natural because the gospel, according to Paul, is based on eschatological salvation and on God's election which aims at the redemption of Israel and the salvation of the entire creation.[30] As we examine predestinarian theology this becomes even more clear. If both Jews and Gentiles are equal as regards the eschatological salvific act of God (Rom. 2:28; 3:9; 3:22), then the question of the salvation of Israel must be a burning issue.[31]

When Paul answers the implicit questions arising from his soteriology, he puts forward theses which further his argumentation. His *first thesis* concerns the basis of soteriology in the promises of God: there has been no change in God's promises in any way.[32] The "word of God" has not failed, and his promises have not been left unfulfilled (Rom. 9:6).[33] God's saving righteousness also concerns Israel all the time. God has had "children of the promise" at every stage of salvation history (9:8).[34] Similar teaching is continued at the beginning of chapter 11.

Even this first thesis is an outstanding expression of predestinarian theology. Paul simply states that Israel has actually never been given a promise without certain conditions.[35] The fulfilment of promise in the middle of the dark history

---

[28] So Beker, *Paul*, 72, 74f., 92; cf. Jervell, *Romans Debate*, 60-61.

[29] See Cranfield, *Romans*, 446.

[30] This is the way the setting of chapters 9-11 is explained by Stuhlmacher, *Römer*, 129.

[31] See above, chapter 7.3.

[32] Cf. e.g. Davies, *NTS* 24 (1977) 29, 34; Hofius, *Paulusstudien,* 178f.

[33] Here Paul is again treating the problem of theodicy. The question itself remains the same. Räisänen defines it as follows: "What sort of God does not see to it that his promises to Israel come true?" Räisänen, *Social World,* 180. Jervell has noted that this question connects several chapters of Romans and forms a considerable theme within the whole teaching of Paul. Jervell, *Romans Debate,* 61.

[34] See Stuhlmacher, *Römer*, 134.

[35] This is quite another thing from the claim that, according to Paul, God never actually chose "all Israel". See e.g. Räisänen, *Social World,* 182: "The implication is clear. *The majority of Israel... have never been elected.*" Such a view must be based on the conviction that Paul accepted the concept of double predestination and was here attempting to solve the dilemma of divine election.

of Israel has always concerned a minority instead of the whole people. Salvation concerns only a remnant, as the prophet Isaiah had already proclaimed (Rom. 9:27; 11:4). God's punishments have fallen on the nation in history, and God has provided salvation in the way he himself has chosen.[36]

We must remember that such teaching did not separate Paul from his Jewish predecessors. In the Second Temple period soteriological dualism was the rule, not the exception, as we have seen in the first chapters of this study. This was actually the very reason for the emergence of the problem of theodicy. The unfaithfulness of sinners was never interpreted as a sign of the unfaithfulness of God. When Paul taught that only a part of Israel would be saved, he was merely exploiting Jewish tradition.[37]

What is exceptional in Paul's teaching is his claim that the borderlines of Judaism had been changed. This is one of the key themes in the whole letter, and once again based on paradoxical polarization. In the novel eschatological situation one was not accepted as a true Jew merely by possessing external markers or even on the grounds of nationality. One had to be a Jew inwardly (Rom. 2:28f.). So the "eschatological Jew" was not necessarily a member of the historical people. He could also be a Gentile.[38] The promises of God were steadfast, but they were applied to a new group – those who believed in Christ.[39]

According to Paul's *second thesis,* God furthermore had a sovereign right to election. In the eyes of men this seems to be deterministic, but to Paul it is something else. "So then he has mercy on whomever he chooses, and he hardens the heart of whomever he chooses" (9:18). To Paul such a hardening did not, despite all its implications, mean an actual determinism. He employs the theme here as a kind of metaphor. This is evident when we look at how he uses the theme. Paul is consistent with his theology of predestination and says that the reason for the "obduracy" of Israel was actually its fall and its sin.[40]

Israel "stumbled over the stumbling stone" (9:32). It was a "disobedient and contrary people" (10:21). Israel killed the prophets sent by God and demolished God's altars (11:3). The Israelites have stumbled ($\pi\tau\alpha\acute{\iota}\omega$) and are in danger of falling ($\pi\acute{\iota}\pi\tau\omega$) outside the scope of salvation: "So I ask, have they

---

[36] Cf. Westerholm, *Mosaic Law,* 219.

[37] Cf. chapter 3.2.

[38] See Dinkler, *JR 36* (1956) 111. According to Dinkler, such a principle is employed by Paul in Romans 9-11 in a special way: "Paul's answer is that the promises refer not to the *empirical-historical* Israel but to the *eschatological* Israel" (p. 114).

[39] Cf. Vischer, *Judaica 6* (1950) 92.

[40] Contra e.g. Räisänen, who considers the idea of hardening to be deterministic, Räisänen, *Social World,* 183.

stumbled so as to fall?" (11:11). The members of the fallen people were dry branches which had to be "broken off because of their unbelief" (11:20) and be separated from the true olive tree, the Israel of the promises (11:20).[41]

All this is common Second Temple Jewish theology, as we have seen above. Israel had been in crisis for centuries. The nation as a whole cannot be the Israel of the promises. Israel's own sin is first and foremost the reason why she has a hardened heart. This is why she has to face God's punishments. In this respect not even here does Paul's teaching differ from Jewish teaching in general. Most Jews made a distinction between natural Israel and the "remnant", the community of the saved.[42] Further, the variety in conceptions was so wide that Paul the Jew would easily fit in this group, too.[43]

The section 9:18-23 is somewhat more complex than merely a description of stumbling Israel, however. It has often been explained as teaching double predestination, and this is why it has created problems for scholars.[44] Hardening is here clearly a result of God's action and it seems to raise an actual problem of determinism, familiar from the philosophy of religion: if God determines the fate of men, how can he accuse them on the day of judgment? [45] "You will say to me then, 'Why then does he still find fault? For who can resist his will?" (9:19).

If no man can resist God's will, is God Himself not then responsible for evil?[46] This is the timeless question of determinism and it is interesting that

---

[41] The interpretation of chapters 9-11 in 20th-century Europe is not without dramatic implications, as the article of Reichrath shows. During the post-war period it became necessary to emphasize the continuity between the historical Israel and the Church. Romans 9-11 was no longer an example of anti-Semitic propaganda (as it really had been), but an expression of God's plan of salvation instead. Reichrath, *Judaica 23* (1967) 162f., 170ff., 175. The correction made at that time was a right one. To Paul the Jews are never the only ones under sin. The whole world has fallen in Adam. The emphasis is on the fact that *both* Jews and Gentiles are under the power of sin. This is why the salvation of Israel, too, is tied up with the question of the salvation of the whole world.

[42] Cf. Westerholm, *Mosaic Law*, 221-222: "And remnant theology – by which the majority of Jews at given points of history are declared faithless and bound for judgment while the community of survivors, prior to a dramatic turning to God in the 'last days', is effectively limited to a minority of Israelites – was no Pauline innovation."

[43] This interpretation is dependent on the "new approach" on Second Temple Judaism, made according to the principle of "multiple Judaisms", see chapters 2.6., 3. *Excursus.*

[44] Cranfield leaves the question unanswered, even though he desires to reject the predestinarian theology of Calvin in principle. Cranfield, *Romans*, 489.

[45] And as Dodd puts it: "mechanical determinism annihilates morality." Dodd, *Romans*, 158.

[46] There is a close inner continuity with similar thoughts presented earlier in 3:5. See Wilckens, *Römer*, 201. This is additional proof of the fact that Paul is here presenting his familiar predestinarian theology.

Paul, too, paid attention to it.[47] One cannot understand Paul's answer unless one takes into account the fact that it is based on a new way of defining soteriological dualism.

Divine predestination must not be defined as double predestination, according to which God chose certain individuals for salvation.[48] On the contrary, God has shown forbearance towards all sinners until now.[49] Life after the Fall has been possible only because God has *not* shown his wrath (9:22).[50] This forbearance has produced an age of mercy for all Israelites who have stumbled. "What if God, desiring to show his wrath and to make known his power, has endured with much patience the objects of wrath that are made for destruction" (κατηρτισμένα εἰς ἀπώλειαν, 9:22).[51]

Paul's theology of predestination is of an apocalyptic nature. He is speaking of an eschatological judgment where sin will be punished. This is why predestinarian theology is based on anthropology, too. And this anthropology is quite negative in Romans. Sinful mankind has been left under punishment, "made for destruction", and as regards the coming of God's judgment, this predetermination is unconditional.[52]

According to Paul, the whole of mankind, descended from Adam, was destined for judgment (cf. Rom. 3:5-9; 5:16). In chapter 9 he reminds his

---

[47] For example, Röhser concludes that here we have teaching of double predestination "in the very sense of the word". Röhser, *Prädestination,* 128.

[48] As we saw earlier, Käsemann rejected the idea of deterministic predestination. Here he rightly concludes that in order to understand the teaching of Paul one has, however, to connect it with some kind of concept of predestination. This is true, but Käsemann himself is unconvincing as he emphasizes only the existential responsibility of the individual before his Creator. Käsemann, *Römer,* 256.

[49] Paul is not speaking merely of Jews here (contra e.g. Schlier, *Römerbrief,* 303). We must note that in verse 24 he mentions both Jews and Gentiles.

[50] Wilckens explains these rather complex clauses in such a way that verses 22 and 23 should be understood separately and antithetically. God has been patient towards the sins of Israel, but these sins will be punished eventually. In this way the condemnation is directed against Israel and salvation is promised to the Gentiles. Wilckens, *Römer,* 204f. To my understanding this was not Paul's purpose. We should understand Paul's argument in such a way that God has withheld his judgment in order to reveal his righteousness, i.e. mercy and salvation in Christ.

[51] This is a theme which we also meet in Rom. 3:25. See above chapter 6.2.

[52] Cf. Mattern, *Verständnis des Gerichtes,* 62-64. Caird, who is wrestling with Calvin and Arminius, does not even wish to solve the paradox of free will and determinism. "The doctrine on predestination forbids us to say that all men will in fact be saved... The doctrine of free will reminds us that no man can be saved without his consent or without his free acceptance of God's offer of mercy." Caird, *ExpT 68* (1957) 327. To my understanding, Caird is tied up with the problems of modern dogmatics, and this prevents him from finding the radical predestinarian theology of Paul.

readers that God in his mercy has always left a remnant of the fallen people. Over the generations there have always been "objects of mercy" to whom God has shown his grace. Paul emphasizes that God's glory is made known by his willingness to grant his righteousness solely by grace and through the gospel (cf. 9:23). This is the key point when we search for an answer to the problem of determinism. God's judgment is not unfair or unjust, because it has been preceded by his mercy (cf. 2:4-5; 3:25-26; 5:8-10).

We may further conclude that Paul's soteriological dualism does not concern the obedient and the ungodly in a traditional sense. His dualism is universal. It concerns fallen mankind and reconciled sinners. Therefore it is justifiable to say that according to Paul the whole of mankind belongs to the "objects of wrath", even though this has not actually been said in this section.[53]

The justification for our conclusion comes from Paul's use of the term "objects of mercy". It is true that these objects have been "prepared beforehand" for glory (ἃ προητοίμασεν εἰς δόξαν, 9:23). Paul is not claiming, however, that they were chosen for salvation, one by one, as in the doctrine of double predestination. Instead, they have been called (καλέω) to salvation. This calling takes place in the proclamation of the word of the gospel (9:24). It does not concern only a small group of people who had been elected beforehand. It concerns all descendants of Adam.[54]

Such teaching is completed in chapter 10. God's election is Christological. It will be implemented through the gospel (10:9-10). No "object of wrath" or man under God's condemnation is subject to determinism. Paul's gospel is universal: "Everyone who calls on the name of the Lord shall be saved" (10:13).[55]

We meet a similar concept of mercy in chapter 11, where Paul reaches the final conclusions of his argumentation (11:26, 30-31). The disobedience of Israel is a fact. It does not determine the fate of the nation, however, despite

---

[53] Contra Davies, who also with regard to Romans 9-11 maintains that Paul had in fact accepted and employed traditional Jewish soteriological dualism. Paul would thus have been speaking of sinful Jews and righteous Jews (as well as of sinful Gentiles and righteous Gentiles), not of the universal sinfulness of both Jews and Gentiles. Davies, *Faith*, 96, 177ff.; cf. Sanders, *Law*, 37.

[54] Müller says this straightforwardly: "Prädestination in der Wortverkündigung geschieht". Müller, *Gottes Gerechtigkeit*, 78. For him Paul's teaching is part of his eschatological theology of creation: "Die paulinische Prädestinationslehre überhaupt ist sinnvoll nur als äusserste Radikalisierung des *Schöpfungsgedankens* zu verstehen" (italics his). Cf. Schmitt, *Gottesgerechtigkeit*, 84.

[55] Cf. Dinkler, *JR 36* (1956) 124: "The essential connection of chapters 9-11 with 8:28ff. makes evident that God's *election* comes to us as grace *in and through Christ Jesus,* that God's election and predestination are Christological-soteriological categories, concrete in divine grace and in human faith."

the severity of their stumbling. Paul is certain that Israel, too, will find the mercy of God in the end: "all Israel will be saved" (v. 26).

This analysis concerned Paul's second "thesis". For Paul, God is sovereign, and He is able to direct world history as he pleases. He hardened the hearts of the Israelites in the same manner as he hardened the heart of Pharaoh. However, Paul's argument was not centred around the act of hardening, but he was rather explaining the election of the Gentiles (9:13, 18, 25, 33; 10:16-21; 11:11, 20, 25, 31). Thus the hardening is not meant to be deterministic but is rather a description of Israel's sin and stumbling. Israel has rejected its Messiah in the same manner as it had rejected God Himself over the centuries. The true Israel is always merely a remnant. Despite the temporary rejection, Paul is optimistic as to the salvation of all Israel in the end.

"Just as you were once disobedient to God but have now received mercy because of their disobedience, so they have now been disobedient in order that, by the mercy shown to you, they too may now receive mercy" (Rom. 11:30-31).

After this examination we shall conclude with Paul's *third thesis* in chapters 9-11. It concerns election by grace: "So too at the present time there is a remnant, chosen by grace" ("according to the election by grace", κατ᾽ ἐκλογὴν χάριτος, 11:5). In the context of Paul's soteriology this election by grace must be the saving righteousness of God which has now been made known apart from the law (3:21; cf. 11:6). It is justification by faith which is the power of God for salvation (1:16).[56]

We are thus entitled to conclude that due to predestination theology chapters 9-11 do not form a separate "appendix" in the teaching of Paul. In this way we confirm the notion expounded above. This section is rather the climax of Paul's soteriology.[57] Paul believes that God revealed his righteousness in the

---

[56] See also Dinkler, *JR 36* (1956) 115. He takes note of the fact that in verse 11:6 Paul opposes "works" to the "call" of God. G. Wagner has paid attention to the broad outline, according to which the epistle begins with a Christological statement that relates the mission of Christ to God's chosen people Israel (1:1-4). In 1:16-17 this statement is interpreted soteriologically: for salvation to everyone who has faith, to the Jew first and also to the Greek. In Romans 9-11, then, it becomes clear that "justification, rooted in Christ, has a historical dimension." Wagner, *Eschatology*, 99.

[57] Räisänen has reached quite the opposite conclusion: "In a synthesis of 'early Christian religion,' Romans 9-11 would not primarily belong to a section on 'soteriology'." Räisänen, *Texts and Contexts,* 756. Instead, he emphasizes the "identity of the new sect and the battles, external and internal, connected with it". I cannot agree with Räisänen, as such a separation between identity and soteriology fails to recognize the essence of the message: Paul is convinced that God through the gospel calls men to a new "identity", i.e. new sonship.

suffering and resurrection of his Son.[58] This righteousness was the fulfilment of God's plan of salvation, and it should also have been the redemption of Israel. The nation was living with a hardened heart, however, as it had done so often throughout history. Therefore Israel had to face the fact that only a remnant will be saved. By his election by grace God has reserved "for himself" a group that will assure the continuity of salvation history. The remnant of Israel consists now of those who believe in Christ.

Paul is thus addressing himself to the whole of Israel, his "own people", which is so dear to him and whose fate makes him grieve (9:2-3). Israel should understand the manner in which God has made his righteousness known and the fact that salvation has been granted. It was necessary to see that behind election by grace there lies humankind which has died in Adam. Israel, too, is part of this humankind and thus stands under the condemnation of God.[59] Only the completed election by grace can save human beings. This election has been realized in the righteousness that comes from faith and which is granted by the gospel of Christ.[60]

In chapter 11 predestinarian theology is expressed by elaborating the theme of the revelation of God's "mystery".[61] Paul exposes the salvific plan of God:

---

[58] Cf. Lübking, *Paulus und Israel,* 155. K. Stendahl is famous for his suggestion concerning the centrality of chapters 9-11 in the letter. "The real center of gravity in Romans is found in chapters 9-11, in the section about the relation between Jews and Gentiles, the mystery of which had been revealed to Paul." Stendahl, *Paul,* 28ff. The curiosity of his explanation is, however, in his claim that this theme should be separated from Paul's teaching on justification (see p. 40). Contrary to this, we have seen above that most of Paul's central theological themes are also present in chapters 9-11.

[59] Cf. Wright, *Climax of the Covenant,* 249.

[60] Such reasoning on Paul's part has to do with the problem concerning the relation between chapters 9 and 11. According to Watson, there are two separate views in Romans. In chapter 9 and elsewhere, too, Paul sets his view of the salvation of the Gentiles in polemical opposition to the Jewish theology of the covenant. In chapter 11 Paul argues that "his view of the salvation of the Gentiles is *compatible with* the Jewish theology of the covenant, and may be incorporated into it". Watson, *Paul,* 170 (italics his); cf. Räisänen, *Law (Preface to the second edition),* xx; Räisänen, *Social World,* 192ff. As Pauline predestinarian theology is considered, there is no such opposition in Romans 9-11. Paul is presenting a new interpretation of the traditional soteriological dualism of Second Temple Jewish theology. The New Israel comprises those human beings who believe in Christ and have in this way become "Jews inwardly". This paradoxal polarization is a key theme in Paul's soteriology.

[61] Bultmann considered this mystery to be only a part of mythology and a result of Paul's speculative imagination, Bultmann, *Theologie,* 484. Müller, however, has interpreted this theme with the aid of the tradition behind Revelation 11. He maintains that in Romans 11:25ff. there are three aspects which agree with that tradition: Israel will be subjected to the Gentiles; there is a limitation to that subjection, however; and eventually a restoration of Israel will take place. Müller, *Gottes Gerechtigkeit,* 42.

through the hardening of Israel God has made the basis of salvation evident to everyone. There is but one way to salvation for every human being.

But why does Paul suddenly speak of "all Israel" that will be saved? Does this contradict his previous conviction that part of Israel has been hardened and part of it will be saved?[62] Paul is evidently using an apocalyptic theme in his theology of predestination. This is not an exception to his soteriology, however. He is convinced that the promises given by the prophets will be fulfilled. The "remnant" forms an element of continuity until the time of great revival comes.[63] Even though the expression "all Israel" must be considered an apocalyptic hyperbole, it reveals Paul's hope that Israel, too, will turn to its Saviour (11:26).[64]

It is only natural that Paul concludes his argument in Romans 9-11 with a crystallized predestinarian statement: "God has imprisoned all in disobedience so that he may be merciful to all" (11:32).[65] Predestinarian theology implies a new polarization, and this also concerns Israel.[66] The Chosen People belong to the family of Adam. Israel is the "elect" of God, however, and has enjoyed a special status because of that. No man – not even Abraham – has been saved

---

[62] Some scholars think that there is a contradiction here. Plag suggests that 11:25-27 must be an interpolation originating in some other Pauline letter. Plag, *Israels Wege,* 60, 65. Lüdemann, in turn, considers 11:11-36 an independent theme which Paul added to his usual teaching due to the failure of the Jewish mission. Lüdemann, *Paulus und das Judentum,* 34-35. Räisänen, in turn, suggests a psychological explanation: "The revelation vocabulary of 11:25-26 notwithstanding, Paul is wrestling with a burning personal problem, attempting to 'square the circle,' trying different solutions." Räisänen, *Social World,* 196.

[63] Some scholars maintain, however, that Paul is not expecting an "end-time conversion" of Israel. They believe that God has a different plan of salvation for Israel. See e.g. Gaston, *Paul,* 148; Mussner, *Kraft,* 63-64. From this point of view it is, however, quite impossible to understand why Paul throughout the letter to the Romans emphasizes that "all" are under the power of sin, both Jews and Gentiles.

[64] Plag gives a decent analysis of such a tradition, beginning with Isa 2:1-4, and treating texts such as TBenj. 10:11. Plag, *Israels Wege,* 56-59; cf. Haacker, *Judaica 33* (1977) 172. Wright maintains that Paul is speaking of two different Israels in chapter 11. He says that there is no "large-scale, last-minute salvation of Jews". Wright, *Climax of the Covenant,* 251. To my mind, Paul's apocalyptic hope is more concrete, and he really believes that the Jews will have a time of revival.

[65] Cf. the rhetorical analysis of Siegert: "Mit diesen kunstvoll entfalteten und auch wieder bis zur grösstmöglichen Fasslichkeit vereinfachten Schlussthesen hat Paulus inhaltlich (semantisch) sein Ziel erreicht." Siegert, *Argumentation,* 175. See also Hofius, *Paulusstudien,* 200.

[66] According to Jeremias, verse 32 is a final example of the revelation of God's mystery. Jeremias, *Israelfrage,* 203. As we have noted earlier, Beker considers this verse 11:32 the climax of the whole letter. Beker, *The Romans Debate,* 329-330; cf. Munck, *Christus und Israel,* 105; Müller, *Gottes Gerechtigkeit,* 48. Such an interpretation is justified, since this parallelism surely summarizes the basic ideas of Paul's predestinarian theology.

without the mercy of God, however. If Israel now rejects the Son of God, it will not find life.[67] It is bound to be left under the wrath of God.[68]

Romans 9-11 is not a separate appendix to the "dogmatic" letter of Paul. Quite to the contrary, this section highlights Paul's argumentation in the entire letter. He is here explaining why the Gentiles were chosen before the people of the promise. In this explanation he quotes examples from the Old Testament. In the course of history God has always elected a mere remnant. Those who have fallen have been left in their sins. Their hearts have been hardened as regards accepting the gracious gift of God. This presentation of Paul's does not differ from his predestinarian theology, however, but follows it in every detail. The idea of hardening is submitted to radical predestinarian theology. Paul is not teaching double predestination here. As regards salvation, God does not choose certain individuals from the mass of sinners, leaving others behind. Paul's anthropology is pessimistic even in this section. God has imprisoned all people under the power of sin. The only way out can be found through the gracious gift of God. Here we see a consequent continuity with the previous chapters of Romans. God has shown his mercy by making his righteousness known in the work of Christ. Thus the gospel of the death and resurrection of Jesus is the saving message which calls people to salvation from the prison of death – and it needs to be preached to all people. The freely granted righteousness in Christ is an instrument for the election of grace which applies to everyone who calls on the name of the Lord.

8.3. The predestination of judgment

As the theme of judgment has been examined in this study, we have reached one of the basic elements of Paul's predestinarian theology. Predestinarian theology usually has two sides to it, and we have attempted to discern their basic features. The first aspect concerns the condemnation that has been prescribed for sinners. The second aspect presents the way to salvation. The latter aspect contains the principles of the election of God and the conditions for salvation.

As a brief summary we may at this stage give an account of some of the most important features of Paul's predestinarian theology. Firstly, he is evidently following Second Temple theology, and employs themes of Jewish

---

[67] Cf. Käsemann, *Exegetische Versuche 2*, 191. Stauffer argued the idea of *apokatastasis* by quoting this verse. Stauffer, *Theologie*, 203. For a criticism, see Schmitt, *Gottesgerechtigkeit*, 115. There is no room for "universalism" in Paul's theology.

[68] Vischer comments that this is not actually a "Theodizee", since it is not the task of man to justify God. "Gott hat das nicht nötig." All Paul needed to do was to explain the righteousness of God, i.e. that it is God who declares his fallen creatures righteous. Vischer, *Judaica 6* (1950) 131. In an academic sense I would still call it Paul's theodicy, however. It is the righteousness of God, revealed in Christ, that solves the problem of theodicy.

eschatology, but he changes and reinterprets their content according to his own premises and aims. One of the most important themes in this tradition is the problem of theodicy, which has directed Jewish theology almost without exception in every line of tradition. In Paul's theology the idea of divine judgment solves the problem of theodicy and restates the belief that God is just. God is faithful, and he will fulfil all the promises he has given to previous generations.[69] No man needs to doubt God's goodwill and providence. God is just and faithful and He is guiding his plan of salvation in history.

In Paul's theology the problem of theodicy does not concern merely the injustice which the righteous of Israel have had to endure, or the agony of the people under the power of godless rulers. Soteriological dualism can no longer be defined in the same way as it had been earlier. Paul wants to answer the problem of theodicy on a universal level. The reason for this is the new, crucial phase of salvation history. Paul is determined to explain how the justice and righteousness of God are realized in the work of Christ on the earth.[70]

When Paul explained the status of the predestination of judgment, he based his arguments on a pessimistic anthropology. His view was radical as regards the traditional Jewish teaching of sapiential theology, but it was justified with scriptural proofs from the Old Testament. According to Paul, the whole of mankind since Adam has lived under the wrath of God. When the eschatological judgment comes there is no distinction between Jews and Gentiles. On this basis Paul makes a radical polarization of soteriology. God has imprisoned all men to disobedience and under the power of sin.[71]

Paul's predestinarian theology thus differs essentially from Jewish soteriology. Soteriology is always dependent on anthropology, and this was what had

---

[69] The conception that judgment brings perfect justice is quite common in Pauline studies, and even Bultmann did not deny it, see *Theologie*, 263. Nowadays reference is often made to it in Pauline studies. See e.g. Stuhlmacher, *Theologie*, 308f; Beker, *Paul*, 190-192; Becker, *Paulus*, 468f.

[70] This point of view is important, especially as we consider the analysis of Romans 9-11. The predestinarian theology of Paul cannot be explained solely on the ground of Jewish discussion of the problem of theodicy. For this reason the analysis of predestinarian theology by some scholars, e.g. Röhser, is bound to remain rather narrow. Röhser attempted to solve the problems of Pauline predestinarian theology primarily by analysing the themes of divine determination and hardening. Röhser, *Prädestination*, 173f. In addition, Paul's theology of predestination is an essential factor in his teaching on justification.

[71] As regards anthropology, the idea of strict predestination is in agreement with several previous investigations. This does not concern all scholarship, however. As we have seen above, it was mostly the existentialist interpretation that tended to change the focus from divine predestination to human decision (see above, e.g. chapter 7.2.). In Bultmann's explanation Paul's anthropology was centred around existential experience, and descent from Adam provided only the possibility of sin ("die Möglichkeit der Sünde"), Bultmann, *Theologie*, 227, 253.

changed in the teaching of Paul. Jewish eschatology, which built on the sapiential tradition, based its views on an autonomous anthropology. Sapiential theologians believed that man had been created free to choose his own pathway. Therefore the guilt and burden of sin could never be shifted onto God. The responsibility belonged to man. God had never made any man a sinner. It was in man's power to obey the will of God, if only he so wished.[72]

Especially at Qumran, as well as in later apocalyptic, the soteriological dualism was defined more sharply and it actually included a deterministic feature. Since the whole world was under God's power, he must have created both the ungodly and the righteous. Such a determinism was not very profound, however. The fault of apostates lay ultimately in their rejection of God. They were disobedient of their own free will. Their wickedness was condemned from the very beginning, and God had prescribed a judgment for them.[73]

Such an autonomous anthropology helped theologians to avoid the problem of theodicy in a convenient way. God could never be made responsible for evil. God was truthful and just, a fact no one could deny. This is why eschatological groups usually presented a simple way to salvation. Every fallen Israelite was called to repentance and perfect obedience to the law of God.[74]

When compared with such a soteriology, Paul's teaching appears to be quite radical. He builds his anthropology on the Genesis story. All mankind died in Adam. Men have been imprisoned under the power of sin ever since. In accordance with Jewish theology, Paul believes that there is a judgment for the wicked. But due to his pessimistic anthropology this paints a terrifying scene: the problem of theodicy would be solved by apocalyptic destruction. There is not much hope for humankind here. All the children of Adam belong to the multitude of the condemned.

---

[72] Even though there have been suggestions that e.g. the nomism of 4 Ezra presents a similar pessimistic soteriology to Paul's, the differences between these two remain essential. In 4 Ezra, namely, nomism is connected with the idea of autonomy, as it is in the theology of Qumran. See e.g. B. Longenecker *Eschatology and the Covenant,* 270ff.; cf. chapter 4.3. above.

[73] For the ambivalent treatment of determinism, see chapter 5.2.

[74] Seifrid finds a "significant difference between the soteriology of 1QS and that of the Pss. Sol." He claims that "the stress on divine predestination shields Qumran soteriology from locating the ultimate cause of salvation in the atoning conduct of the community." In Pss. Sol., however, the "exclusivistic soteriology... implicitly attaches salvific value to the behaviour of the 'pious'." Seifrid, *Justification,* 132-133. Seifrid thinks that only in the latter text is there mercy because of piety. This is not the case, however. The synergism of both of these texts is based on an autonomic anthropology, and both of them belong in the tradition of Second Temple sapiential theology. There is no justification of the wicked at Qumran, even though the grace of God is emphasized in a good synergistic manner. That grace was preserved exclusively for the repentant members of the community.

The traditional soteriological dualism of Jewish theology is totally altered in the theology of Paul. According to his teaching, there is no such thing as a righteous Jew who could be saved on account of his obedience and faithfulness to the law. God's mercy cannot be attained by such means. Here Paul opposed Second Temple synergism, even though God's grace was important here, too. Obedience was but a condition for the gracious gift of God. In Paul's soteriology there is no room for synergism. The whole of humankind is fallen. The judgment applies to every man.[75]

Paul describes this human situation as being in prison and as being sold into slavery. Man lives without the glory of God, he is under a curse, subject to condemnation and predetermined to death. In this strict predestinarian theology the future of man is completely determined. Eschatology will reach a climax on the Day of the Wrath of God, and all the world will be brought before God then. All humankind has been placed under condemnation, and this is the fate of every descendant of Adam. Only a new salvation prepared by God can save people from this future.

The basic structure of Paul's soteriology can thus be explained with the aid of his predestinarian theology. There is a judgment for the descendants of Adam, and the reason for it is sin. God's judgment will be just, and thus it also solves the problem of theodicy. The last judgment will take vengeance on ungodliness and reveal the ultimate power of God to the whole world.[76]

The predestination of judgment, according to Paul, is unconditional and unavoidable in principle. It cannot be escaped by obedience, as the sapiential teachers of Israel and the righteous sectarians of Qumran had believed. The principles of soteriology must be reconstructed. On the one hand was God's terrible wrath, but on the other hand the righteousness that had been made known without the law. Soteriology had to be constructed on a sharpened

---

[75] This line of reasoning has been rather common in Pauline studies, even though it has not often been connected with predestinarian theology. The idea of a radical soteriological dualism has been accepted by scholars from rather different backgrounds, see e.g. Dodd, *Romans*, 50ff.; Wilckens, *Römer I*, 200ff.; Stuhlmacher, *Theologie*, 326, 334; Schlier, *Römerbrief*, 106ff.; and Dunn, *Romans*, 178-179.

[76] Predestinarian theology is thus a structural element in Paul's teaching. It is not merely a heuristic tool with which one can analyze the themes of hardening and divine omnipotence. The concept of predestination provides a basic category for soteriology. As regards the discussion of the methodology of Pauline studies, we need to remark that the idea of predestination is *not* presented here as a "doctrinal centre" for Paul's theology, replacing e.g. the theology of justification or participation. Instead, we are speaking of a structural element which helps to explain the relation of Paul to the tradition he has been using. This is why it leads us further to the dynamics of contemporary application, which is so typical of Paul's soteriology.

polarization.[77] This is also the message of the contrast formulas which Paul uses constantly.

There is a watershed between the saved and the fallen, but it must be located in a new place. It can no longer be found between those who possess the promises and Gentile sinners. The reason for condemnation is the fall of Adam. This provides the basis for salvation history. God has prepared but one way of salvation for this world, which lives under sin. He sent his own Son, who atoned for sin on behalf of the whole world. And because Christ was the embodiment and fulfilment of the promises of the old covenant, he was the only salvation for the Jews, as well.[78]

Eventually we are led once more to Christology. In contrast formulas Paul opposes the predestination of judgment with the work of Christ. This is why the perfect righteousness that comes from Christ through faith must be closely connected with the idea of election. In the next chapter we shall examine in detail how Paul understands this connection.

In his predestinarian theology Paul opposes both autonomic anthropology and the traditional soteriological dualism which had prevailed in Second Temple Jewish theology. Paul's own conception is simple and even black-and-white. The predestination of judgment has been confirmed and applies to all mankind. God imprisoned all men to disobedience so that he could be merciful to all. God's judgment is predetermined and man cannot change it or alter his own situation as regards the day of wrath. Therefore salvation, too, must be based on God's determination and God's own action.

---

[77] This is, to my understanding, also the reason why Paul seems to neglect the concept of grace that already existed in the old covenant, especially in the Temple service and the sacrifices. The criticism of Sanders and Räisänen was that Paul had to exclude some essential aspects of Judaism in order to be able to present the fate of humankind as completely hopeless. We have seen above that such an antithesis is erroneous. The predestinarian theology of Paul was based on the Scriptures and on the promises of God. We shall return to this question later in chapter IV.

[78] A further remark on the study of Paul's soteriology is necessary here. Most of the main features of Paul's theology are so common and so familiar to scholars that there is a temptation to neglect them in the constructive work of the general interpretation of Paul's soteriology. This problem concerns, for example, the treatment of the themes of sin, atonement and grace. We need to keep them constantly within the argumentation so that we do not distort the picture we are giving of Paul's teaching – despite the sometimes annoying fact that these things have been written in all general introductions over the centuries and that they occur in the writings of the Reformation period.

§ 9 *Predetermination and Election*

We have stated above that the basic structure of Paul's soteriology can be explained with the aid of his predestinarian theology. This claim was based on a comparison between Paul's teaching and Second Temple Jewish theology, especially as regards the treatment of the problem of theodicy. In the theology of Paul soteriological dualism, prevailing in contemporary Jewish theology, was re-interpreted according to the principles of paradoxical polarization. This was furthermore the reason why both anthropology and hamartology became essential in the elaboration of soteriology. Paul's theology of predestination is primarily a theology of the judgment of God. The revelation of divine justice is one of the directive principles concerning the teaching of salvation.

As predestinarian theology is of the essence in Pauline soteriology, it is quite consistent that we should search for the principles of election and actual salvation in the same contexts. We have above investigated several contrast formulas which Paul used, and they, too, point in a similar direction. When Paul speaks of judgment, he usually also mentions the opportunity to avoid that judgment. In this way we are led to several Christological statements which are of a predestinarian nature. This is how we can link our previous analyses with the theme of Christocentric predestination, which in itself has been a traditional subject of Pauline research.[1] In the letters of Paul there are several soteriological passages in which he uses explicit predestinarian terminology.[2]

The subject of election by grace is not a new one as regards the investigation of predestinarian theology. On the contrary, even from the times of the Church Fathers it has been a central theme in the area of soteriology. The basic setting comes from the teaching of Augustine. When writing, for example, of Romans 9-11, Augustine spoke about election by grace, *electio gratiae*. According to Augustine, election to salvation is made by the Almighty, who by his will chooses those whom he wills. The basis for soteriology is in anthropology. Because all people are under the power of sin and death, only God's free gift of grace can make them free and call them to a new life.[3]

With such a view, however, Augustine laid the basis for a difficult dogmatic problem. If it is God who alone elects those who will be saved, it must also be

---

[1] For example, the analyses of Mayer and Luz have concentrated on the theme of election by grace as regards Paul's theology of predestination. Mayer, *Heilsratschluss*, 11; Luz, *Geschichtsverständnis*, 227, 263.

[2] These questions have already been treated in the Introduction, see chapter 1.2.

[3] On Augustine, cf. Mayer, *Heilsratschluss*, 115-17. See especially Augustine, *Enchiridion (Faith, Hope and Charity)*, 98-103.

God Himself who predestines ungodly sinners to damnation. This problem concerning double predestination has directed almost all discussion about the theology of predestination ever since.[4]

9.1. Calling and election (Rom. 8:28-30)

As regards election, the teaching of the Old Testament is of primary importance. Israel as the Chosen People has naturally always been the object of God's gracious acts. She was privileged, as she had been chosen to be God's own people. This is why it was Israel as a nation that possessed the promises which have always been the basis of eschatological soteriology – both in the old and the new covenants.

The subject of election evokes several theological problems, however, which have been under discussion in Pauline scholarship. It is not easy to link Paul's radical polarization with the concept of election as we find it in the Old Testament. When Paul, in addition, happens to write complex clauses concerning predestination, a point of disagreement has been unavoidable.[5]

In Jewish theology, the theme of predestination was a normal part of the soteriology of different groups and sects. These groups taught eschatological salvation, and therefore they needed a reason for teaching soteriological dualism. Despite threatening judgment the elect had hope, because they had been converted to God and committed themselves to the keeping of God's precepts. In the tradition of sapiential theology such an opportunity was considered possible on the grounds of the free will of man. The righteous ones of Qumran had a somewhat more complex conception, however. There conversion meant freedom from the power of the spirit of falsehood. In this pattern, as well, predetermination was only conditional.[6]

---

[4] Primarily, Augustine wished to construct a universal soteriology. As Paul had written, humankind was totally corrupted (*massa perditionis*). And so only God can save man and by his love bring him within the sphere of salvation. The salvation of sinners is thus totally in the hands of God and his will. Even though Augustine never stated that God would determine any man to damnation, his concept evidently leads to the teaching of double predestination. In this conception, condemnation to damnation must be based on *not* being saved by God Almighty. See e.g. Hägglund, *History*, 136-139; McGrath, *Theology*, 450-451; Lohse, *Christian Doctrine*, 116; Jewett, *Predestination*, 5ff., 74. In its historical context the soteriology of Augustine is very consistent and proper, as it was directed against the synergism espoused by Pelagius.

[5] This question concerns above all the problem of covenantal theology, as we have stated before. For example, Sanders had to suggest complex explanations in order to explain the idea of predestination in Jewish theology and especially in the teaching of Qumran. The reason for this was his attempt to link traditional covenantal theology with the eclectic elements of several sectarian texts. See Sanders, *Paul*, 260f., 333.

[6] Dinkler links Qumran's view of justification with the sect's conception of predestination

In the theology of Paul the concept of predetermination was based, on the one hand, on his strict understanding of predestination, and, on the other hand, on his Christocentric soteriology. These premises were used in his teaching concerning eschatological salvation. Even though the theme of the wrath of God is central in Paul's predestinarian theology, we must not forget other kinds of predestinarian statements that occur in his writings. Paul also employs predestinarian terminology in his Christology and Christocentric soteriology. The teaching of the vicarious atonement of Christ is thus not merely a conclusion drawn from, or an addition made to, predestinarian theology, but an essential part of the theology itself.

But how does Paul connect God's election with salvation in Christ? Is there any continuity with the previous Jewish teaching or does his theology break with all tradition? And what is the relation of the new Christocentric election to the election of Israel?

According to Paul, God is active in the act of election. It is God Himself who calls the "elect" to Himself. In this connection Paul also uses the term denoting predestination, but in his theology this word acquires quite an original meaning which has little to do with previous Jewish theology.

One of the most important, but at the same time difficult, passages dealing with predestination and calling, is Romans 8:28-30.[7] This section contains a summary of salvation history, and both divine election and calling are linked here with justification and glorification.

"We know that all things work together for good for those who love God, who are called according to his purpose. For those whom he foreknew he also predestined to be conformed to the image of his Son... And those whom he predestined he also called..." (Rom. 8:28-30).

As to its terminology and theology, this passage is evidently part of Paul's predestinarian theology. This is why it has been considered over the centuries

---

and suggests that these theologians taught justification through grace. He assumes that the idea of strict predestination co-existed without contradiction side by side with the theology of justification. Dinkler, *RGG* 5 (1986) 481. In our previous analysis we have stated, however, that due to their synergistic theology the sect had a consistent view of the relation of righteousness to predestination, and one does not need to separate these conceptions in the manner of Dinkler (see chapter 5.1.).

[7] In spite of the fact that there is a clear structure in this passage, I do not agree with Luz that Paul was using tradition material here. Luz, *Geschichtsverständnis*, 251. Paul often writes poetic clauses, uses rhythm and builds chiastic constructions. Thus Luz's conclusions concerning Paul's additions to tradition material are too hasty. A further problem lies in the suggestion that, due to the use of tradition materials, the passage is coherent and contains progressive argumentation (cf. discussion below).

one of the most important passages of Paul on this subject. Even in the history of dogma it has been a key section according to which Paul's conception of divine predestination has been defined.[8] The nature of the divine election is far from clear in these verses, however. Quite to the contrary, we are able to explain Paul's teaching only after a detailed analysis.

One of the most common mistakes made in earlier research was the implicit claim that the section presents a progressive pattern where Paul's argument proceeds stage by stage, and forms a "chain" throughout verses 28-30. Such an assumption proves to be problematic, even as the wording of the section is considered. The same words appear in new verses without any sign of evolutive continuity. Also, their "logical" order changes from verse to verse. Instead of one overall scheme, there seem to be two parts to this section. Only the latter (v. 30b) contains a sort of chain of inference.[9]

The context of these verses reminds us of the purpose of Paul in this chapter. In the course of the chapter he has been speaking of the suffering of believers. Paul reminds his readers that even in the midst of hard times they can put their trust in the eschatological hope of the gospel.[10] It is this theme that comprises the message in verse 28: "We know that all things work together for good for those who love God...". Paul is not merely consoling people in their difficulties. He desires to lift their eyes to the future life and emphasize the greatness of the glory which in the end will replace the present suffering.[11] This is what he had said in verse 18: "I consider that the sufferings of this present time are not worth comparing with the glory about to be revealed to us." Paul's

---

[8] Augustine had already considered this passage to be of importance, see Hägglund, *History*, 139; as well as Calvin, *Institutes*, 3.22.10.

[9] So also Schlier, *Römerbrief*, 271. The analysis of the structure of the section is of crucial importance, as regards the explanation of the content of the clauses. In the context of Calvinist theology there has been one primary interpretation: the passage is evolutive and presents stages which describe the divine predestination in terms of foreknowledge, foreordination and election. For example, Cranfield discerns five separate steps in Paul's argumentation. Cranfield, *Romans*, 430ff. Five steps are mentioned also by Fitzmyer, who understandably is not content with the Calvinist interpretation itself (see also below), Fitzmyer, *Romans*, 524f.

[10] Cf. Michel, *Römer (1978)*, 274: "*Gott führt sein Werk durch trots menschlichen Leidens, menschlicher Vergänglichkeit und menschlicher Schwachheit*" (italics his); see also Röhser, *Prädestination*, 95; Beker, *Paul*, 364-365.

[11] This kind of explanation is rather commonly accepted. Behind Paul there no doubt is a theme already familiar in Jewish theology, that even painful things in the lives of the righteous eventually arrive at a good conclusion by the will of God. Cf. TReub. 3:6; TIss. 3:7; TDan. 1:7; TGad 4:5; TBenj. 4:5; see Michel, *Römer (1978)*, 275; Cranfield, *Romans*, 429; Dunn, *Romans*, 481. We must note, however, that Paul is not merely repeating such Jewish teaching, based on soteriological dualism, but instead he exploits it in his Christocentric soteriology.

perspective is that of salvation history. It was God's plan "to produce good" (πάντα συνεργεῖ εἰς ἀγαθόν) for the people he had called.

This passage is of an eschatological nature. The "good" about which Paul is speaking can be identified with eschatological "good". In short: he is speaking of salvation. God will grant a good future to believers, and this is how God performs his saving acts.[12] The content of this "good" becomes evident from the teaching that follows, i.e. the teaching concerning Christ.

Before we are able to deal with the theological content of the passage we must pay attention to the terminology of Paul, as well as to the structure of the section. Paul's terminology seems to belong to the discussion concerning (dogmatic) predestinarian theology. On the other hand, the structure of the passage has been an important argument as regards the interpretation of the message of these verses.

1. Problems concerning terminology. In this section there are several words which seem to denote divine foreknowledge. The most important of these words, προτίθημι, προορίζω, and προγινώσκω all begin with a προ- prefix. On this basis it is natural to explain the meaning of the words by referring to God's (temporally) predestined election. The question is not that simple, however. These words are not similar as to their meanings and they are not used with a similar function either. Therefore a more detailed analysis is needed in order to explain their denotations.

As we investigate verses 28-29 we must first of all note that Paul is speaking of believers. The grammatical object is not humankind before election but the ones who have already been called, those "who are called according to his purpose (κατὰ πρόθεσιν)". The verb προτίθημι here has the very same meaning as a little later in verse 9:11. God has made a plan and He will also carry it out in the course of history. In this respect the word denotes God's plan of the history of salvation.[13] Such a plan is aimed at calling men and women to salvation. As the verb "to call" appears in this context, its meaning is highlighted. The act of calling becomes crucial in God's history of salvation.[14]

The first clauses have usually been rather easy to explain and there has been

---

[12] Michel, *Römer (1978),* 276: "das Heil selbst." See also Schlier, *Römerbrief,* 270; Stuhlmacher, *Römer,* 124-125. Cf. Mayer, *Heilsratschluss,* 160; Luz, *Geschichtsverständnis,* 254.

[13] Concerning the linguistic background of the term, see Michel, *Römer (1978),* 276, especially footnotes 4,5. Moo underlines that Paul is here speaking of the "purpose" of God, not the purpose of man. Moo, *Romans,* 567.

[14] Cf. Röhser: "[Gott] hat sie [die Christen] *zur Berufung, zum Christ-Sein (und darin zum Heil) vorherbestimmt."* Röhser, *Prädestination,* 95-96. His weakness is that at this point he does not define his relation to the idea of double predestination, which in other instances he has accepted.

some degree of consensus as to the meaning of the details. Verse 29, however, is more difficult, because one's presuppositions begin to influence the interpretation to a greater extent. The essential problems concern the words "foreknow" and "predestine".

The verb προγινώσκω would seem to denote foreknowledge more evidently than the previous term. If we explain the word with the aid of traditional etymology, such a conclusion is logical. In spite of this we must note that this word has a special meaning both in the Old Testament and in Paul.

In the teaching of the Old Testament the verb "to know" (ידע) often denotes election by God. When God announces that He "knows" Abraham or one of the prophets, he expresses their election.[15] Precisely this shade of meaning can be detected in Paul's use of the word. Paul calls believers in this context "those whom he has chosen" (οὓς προέγνω). Believers are chosen ones in a similar manner as Israel was the chosen people. This interpretation is confirmed by the fact that a little later, in 11:2, Paul employs the same word when speaking of the chosen people. In this respect the word even has a covenantal meaning.[16]

It is necessary to emphasize that a "temporal" interpretation of election is not primary in these texts. Paul does not explicitly state that God knew beforehand the individuals who would later be saved.[17] Instead he teaches that the new faith can be described as a new covenant which is parallel to that of the old covenant with Israel. This new covenant is the one that God has given to Israel so that it could be a way to salvation for many.

The only way for an individual to enter this new covenant is by being called into it. This feature is quite evident because the election and calling are completely identified in this passage. In verse 28 Paul first mentions the calling and afterwards describes those who have been called as 'the elected ones' (v. 29a).[18]

---

[15] In this sense it is justified to parallel the term with the election of Abraham (Gen. 18:19) or the election of Jeremiah (Jer. 1:5). Michel, *Römer (1978),* 277; Cranfield, *Romans,* 431f.

[16] Moo acknowledges the denotation of choosing here, but he tends to interpret this temporally: "1 Pet. 1:20 and Eph. 1:4 suggest rather that Paul wants to place this choosing of us ' before the foundation of the world'." Moo, *Romans,* 570.

[17] Such an aspect has been emphasized even in translations, however: "For God knew his own before ever they were" (8:29, NEB). This problem cannot be solved simply by Mayer's suggestion that Paul is here using apocalyptic language and teaching Christ's predetermination to the office of Saviour. Mayer, *Heilsratschluss,* 158-159. A Christocentric interpretation, which no doubt fits the explanation of 1 Cor. 2:7, is not possible here. The eschatological aspect of the passage leads to the idea of the believer's predestination to resurrection.

[18] According to Luz, *Geschichtsverständnis,* 253, the calling is: "den schöpferischen Ruf Gottes".

The prefix προ- is thus not in itself a sign of a temporal eclectic election, which took place "beforehand".[19] If one wishes to speak of an election that was made beforehand, one can refer only to God's plan, which is ready for mankind.[20] The terms which we have analyzed above do not confirm Calvinist double predestination, but refer only to God's will, which aims at the salvation of men.[21]

As a result of this investigation we can explain the content of the clauses in verses 28 and 29. Paul is here speaking of those "called ones" whom God has elected (through the gospel). In verse 29 Paul then speaks of the eschatological hope of these chosen ones: they are the ones whom God has predestined to resurrection, where they are "conformed to the image" of Christ.

In verse 29 we then have a third term, προορίζω, which by any standard seems to be a word denoting predestination. It means that something is preordained and determined to some foreknown status. The meaning of the word is not a problem here. On the contrary, the meaning is quite certain. As regards the interpretation of the passage there is a problem, however, that concerns the question of the object of predestination. Who has been predestined and for what?

As we attempt to find an answer to these questions, we must define the nucleus of the verse. This is a section where God's plan of salvation is explained using original concepts. Firstly, Paul speaks of an "image" and thus brings connotations from Adam-typology. Secondly, his actual purpose is to teach about resurrection, and here he refers to Christology. "For those whom he foreknew he also predestined (καὶ προώρισεν) to be conformed to the image of his Son (συμμόρφους τῆς εἰκόνος τοῦ υἱοῦ αὐτοῦ), in order that he might be the firstborn within a large family" (8:29).[22]

Adam is in Paul's thoughts because he mentions the "image" that man bears. According to Paul, man always bears some kind of image in this world. The

---

[19] Dogmatic tradition affects the explanation of this subject. For example, supralapsarism has been an influential conception for the interpretation of this subject. See Jewett's analysis of this influence, Jewett, *Predestination*, 83ff.

[20] Cf. Beker, *Paul*, 366: "The predestination language in Rom. 8:29-30 is not philosophical speculation about 'beginnings,' or a theory of speculative theodicy; instead, it functions as a retrospective grounding of the apocalyptic glory of God. The End, announced in Christ, manifests the eternal faithfulness of the God of the Beginning."

[21] Cranfield, in his somewhat Calvinist interpretation, uses the same argument in favour of the idea of foreknowledge: "it took place before the world was created." Cranfield, *Romans*, 431. We must note, however, that in Romans 11 Paul does not say that all the "elected" members of the (old) covenant would now be heirs of salvation. He feels free to use the term in a dynamic way.

[22] Cf. Beker, *Paul*, 365.

descendants of Adam have a share in "the image of the man of dust" (1 Cor. 15:49; cf. Gen. 5:3 "son in his likeness, according to his image"). Christ, in turn, is a new Adam, and the firstborn in a new creation (cf. 1 Cor. 15:23). In the coming resurrection believers will bear "the image of the man of heaven" (1 Cor. 15:49).[23]

The reality of the new being begins only in the resurrection. For this reason the theology of the image is part of eschatology. Man will become the image of Christ at his coming. This is the teaching of Paul in 1 Corinthians, and it explains the ideas of Romans, as well. "[F]or as all die in Adam, so all will be made alive in Christ. But each in his own order: Christ the first fruits, then at his coming those who belong to Christ" (1 Cor. 15:22-23).[24]

As Paul in Romans writes that believers have been "predestined to be conformed to the image of his Son", he is speaking of an eschatological hope. Therefore we must conclude that this is not a clause where Paul speaks of an eclectic predestination of the elect beforehand. Paul means that believers have an assurance of the coming resurrection.[25] In saying this he is merely continuing the teaching which he has given above (in verse 11). "If the Spirit of him who raised Jesus from the dead dwells in you, he who raised Christ from the dead will give life to your mortal bodies also through his Spirit that dwells in you" (Rom. 8:11). For Paul, the Spirit is an assurance of his future life, even though he is still living in "the image of Adam". The body of Paul is mortal because of sin (8:10) but God will create a new body in the resurrection. This will be the day when all believers will bear the image of Christ.[26]

This eschatological point of view is linked with the resurrection Christology of Romans. Already at the beginning of the letter Paul writes that the resurrection of the dead has begun in the resurrection of the Davidide (1:3,4). Later, in chapter 8, he writes that in the resurrection this Davidide has sat down

---

[23] A parallel section to this passage is without doubt 1 Cor. 15, where Paul writes about his eschatological theology of resurrection. Similar themes are repeated in Romans 8, as we have noted above. Cf. Thüsing, *Gott und Christus,* 123; Moo, *Romans,* 571f.

[24] Cf. Schlier, *Römerbrief,* 272; Stuhlmacher, *Römer,* 124-125.

[25] Röhser, too, says that Paul is here speaking of the positive predestination of believers, which aims at the likeness of Christ, "die eigentliche 'positive Prädestination' der Christen." Röhser, *Prädestination,* 97. Several writers even here leave room for a Calvinist interpretation, emphasizing the word "before", see e.g. Dodd, *Romans,* 140f., Moo, *Romans,* 570f.

[26] Michel identifies Paul's teaching with the early Christian baptismal liturgy (Eph. 1:5; Col. 1:14-18) and suggests that Paul on that basis teaches about the process in which believers are engaged. Phil. 3:21 must in that case be seen as a parallel passage: "He will transform the body of our humiliation that it may be conformed to the body of his glory." Michel, *Römer (1978),* 277.

at the right hand of God, just as Psalm 110 predicted, and is now praying there for his people. The resurrected Christ, who is the awaited Davidide and Son of God, is now the "firstborn" (εἰς τὸ εἶναι αὐτὸν πρωτότοκον, Rom. 8:29; cf. Ps. 89: 4, 20-29), whose resurrection from the dead has become the basis of Christian hope.[27]

2. The structure of the passage. Secondly, we need to pay attention to the analysis of the structure of the passage. We have seen above that a simple assumption of a five-step inference in the section has no basis in the texts. In verse 29 Paul describes the new reality of the resurrection from the dead, but in verse 30 he returns to the themes of calling and justification. These subjects must not be compelled to fit a schematic temporal order.

In verses 28-29 Paul describes primarily the future resurrection that has been promised to believers. These ideas have no link with the otherwise popular discussion over double predestination. Paul's concept of predestination is Christocentric. Believers have been "predestined" to be conformed to the image of Christ in the resurrection of the dead.[28] Such an argument is completed in verse 30a, which forms a *chiasmus* with the preceding verses. Here Paul repeats the words "predestination" and "calling": "those whom he predestined he also called." In other words, those who have been predestined "to be conformed to the image of his Son" have also been called to have a share in the saving gospel.[29]

As God elects people, his only instrument is, according to Paul, the call (οὓς δὲ προώρισεν, τούτους καὶ ἐκάλεσεν).[30] It is an historical act, not one before the beginning of "history". The emphasis on calling underlines the message which creates anew. New salvation can be reached through the word of the

---

[27] See Stuhlmacher, *Römer*, 124-125.

[28] Cf. Thüsing, *Gott und Christus,* 124: "Die Sinnrichtung von Röm 8,29 zielt auf die Beziehung der leiblich auferstandenen Christen zu Christus – also *auf die Christozentrik der Vollendung.*" (italics his). Contra Wilckens, who thinks that Paul is speaking of transformation into the image of Christ in a more general sense; see Wilckens, *Römer II,* 164.

[29] Scholars who speak of the five "steps" in Paul's inference explain this chiastic form in quite the opposite way. They think that the pattern proceeds from predetermination to calling and only thereafter to justification. See e.g. Luz, *Geschichtsverständnis,* 252 ("Der Reihenfolge der Verben liegt sicher ein zeitliches Schema zugrunde."); Fitzmyer, *Romans,* 525f. Wilckens, too, thinks that Paul's argument proceeds from predestination (v. 29) to calling (v. 30). Wilckens, *Römer II,* 163. Within this kind of interpretation it is impossible to explain the evident chiastic structure of the passage. The verbs cannot be juxtaposed in such a consistent manner as several scholars would like to see.

[30] Cf. Althaus, *Römer,* 84: "bei Paulus ist die Berufung also die Durchführung der Erwählung, die Berufenen sind die Erwählten."

gospel.[31] People who have been "dead" in the eyes of God will now receive the Spirit of God and be adopted into a new sonship (8:15).

This is a further reason why, for Paul, it is the calling which becomes an eschatological task in the service of God. He is here speaking at the same time about his personal ministry as a messenger of God's good news (cf. 2 Cor. 5:18). The word of the gospel creates life and righteousness in all who receive the message of salvation.[32]

As regards the structure of the passage (vv. 28-30), it is not until the next clause (30b) that there begins a new "chain" of inference. The first clause in verse 30 ends the chiastic structure and inspires Paul to expand the idea of calling. In this section with three parts or steps we finally find the following structure: calling - justification - glorification:

"(And those whom he predestined he also called;) and those whom he called he also justified; and those whom he justified he also glorified" (Rom. 8:30).

The three steps ἐκάλεσεν - ἐδικαίωσεν - ἐδόξασεν describe the salvation of man in a universal manner. Here the justification of the elect is parallelled with their glorification. Also, the word for glorification is in the aorist tense, even though Paul must be speaking of a future event.[33]

As regards the content, verse 30b is in fact parallel to the preceding section (28-30a). Both of these passages have the same message, namely consolation for believers who are suffering in this world. The "sufferings of this present time" are minor as compared with the everlasting glory that will be attained in the resurrection. Unity with Christ in the resurrection is so certain that Paul can say that it is predestined for all those who have been adopted into new sonship in Christ.

Similar teaching is continued in the following verses. By referring to the death of Jesus Paul reminds his hearers that no distress or persecution can

---

[31] Against Cranfield, who maintains that the passage is based on the idea of double predestination. Cranfield asserts that each of the five steps in Paul's argument describes one aspect of predestination. He places emphasis on "calling", which in his modernized Calvinistic interpretation means "call effectually". The predestination of salvation is in the new creation which the word effects – but only in those "elected" whom God has foreknown. "When God thus calls effectually, a man responds with the obedience of faith." Cranfield, *Romans*, 432. A similar view is supported by Dunn, *Romans,* 485: "The thought is not of an invitation which might be rejected; God does not leave his purpose to chance but puts it into effect himself."

[32] Schweitzer, too, spoke of double predestination, and ended up with quite another kind of explanation. He asserts that the calling is here a crucial term for predestination and implements the election of God. So he concludes that, according to Paul, God will help only those whom he has called according to his predestination. Schweitzer, *Mystik,* 104.

[33] Several commentators pay attention to this, see e.g. Michel, *Römer (1978),* 278; Dunn, *Romans,* 485f.; Mayer, *Heilsratschluss,* 164-165.

separate the believer from the love of Christ (8:31-39). In the midst of all hardship God will make his own "more than conquerors" (v. 37). This word of consolation provides the basis for eschatological hope and assurance for believers until the last day.

3. The theological purpose of the section. The detailed analysis of the passage 8:28-30 shows that the common arguments concerning double predestination vanish as the analysis proceeds.[34] The section does not turn out to be a progressive explanation which proceeds step by step, verse by verse. This is why it is no longer possible to maintain that here was a scheme of pre-determinative election, or a description of the predestination of an individual elected to salvation.[35]

Paul did not yet ponder the question which has become popular over the years: did God know those individuals who would receive the gospel and salvation in due time.[36] This kind of argument cannot be found even in Romans 9-11, where the hardening of Israel is explained.[37] The hardening of Israel was eventually identified with the sin of the people. Hardness of heart had been the problem of Israel during all the centuries before the appearance of the Messiah. This is why it was also a sufficient reason for the rejection of the Messiah. But as regards the Israel of Paul's time, he never excluded the possibility that the Israelites could repent and come to their Messiah, even now.

Instead of speculating over individual election, Paul aims at two central points here. The verses which we have investigated belong in the context of verses 18-39 where Paul comforts those who have to suffer in this time. He

---

[34] It is good to remember that interpretation has been directed by a long tradition, commencing with Augustine. His view, which led to the concept of double predestination, was based mainly on Rom. 8:30. See Hägglund, *History*, 139.

[35] Luz is more uncertain here: "Offen bleibt, ob Paulus in erster Linie an die Prädestination des einzelnen oder der Gemeinde denkt: die meisten Begriffe finden sich in beiden Verwendungen, und die alternative stellte sich für Paulus wohl gar nicht, denn der einzelne Christ ist nur als Glied der Gemeinde erwählt." Luz, *Geschichtsverständnis*, 253.

[36] This is Fitzmyer's conclusion, too, even though he interprets the passage according to five progressive steps. "He [Paul] does not have in mind the predestination of individuals (either to glory or to damnation). Such an interpretation of these chapters began with Augustine in his controversy with the Pelagians, and it has distracted interpreters of Romans from the main thrust of Paul's discussion in these chapters ever since." Fitzmyer, *Romans*, 522.

[37] Ziesler, too, admits this, but he employs quite a different argument. Ziesler is building on an over-emphasized covenantal theology. "Chapters 9-11 confirm that Paul is concerned not with the salvation or damnation of individuals, but with the choice of a people to further his purposes." Ziesler, *Romans*, 226. This kind of explanation makes one ponder the same kind of question which was formulated by Sanders: if this was the case, what really is the difference between Judaism and Christianity?

encourages believers with the message that the oppressed will in the end be resurrected to eternal life. In the context of such a general purpose Paul defines two separate themes which highlight the same idea.

Firstly, Paul reminds believers that God's call and his justification are God's own work and come as a free gift to sinners. In his goodwill God has given the gospel by which the children of Adam can be set free from the bondage of death.

Secondly, Paul emphasises that those who have been elected through the gospel and adopted to a new sonship, and whom God himself has made righteous, may be certain of their future renewal.[38] God has predestined them to be conformed to the image of Christ in the last day, and in this conviction Paul can assure his hearers that they have already been glorified.[39]

The terms 'election' and 'calling' occur several times in Romans, especially after this passage. In Romans 9 Paul speaks of God's call which applies to all the descendants of Adam. It must be proclaimed to all people with no exception: "[objects of mercy]... including us whom he has called, not from the Jews only but also from the Gentiles" (9:23-24). In chapter 10 this calling is identified with the proclamation of the gospel, the "word of faith" (10:8). There is no distinction between Jews and the Greeks, but: "Everyone who calls on the name of the Lord shall be saved" (10:13). "So faith comes from what is heard, and what is heard comes through the word of Christ" (10:17). The call of God must be proclaimed to all people with no distinction.

Paul's Christological concept of predestination is universal. He does not claim that God merely elected certain individuals to salvation from the midst of fallen mankind. Nor does he revive the Jewish teaching concerning soteriological dualism between the righteous and sinners. Paul's Christological soteriology is much more radical: it concerns the justification of sinners through faith in Christ Jesus. This is why in Romans 8 Paul says that the divine predestination is centred on Christ. All people, the descendants of Adam, have been predestined to find salvation in him. For this reason, too, the instruments of salvation are few. Only God's gospel of the unique Saviour can call men to salvation and bring them into the Kingdom of God.

---

[38] Beker makes this passage the climax of his interpretation of Paul's theology. These verses speak to him of God's final triumph, which will take place, notwithstanding our weakness, and also in the midst of and because of our sufferings. "In Paul, God's triumph is not located in the doctrine of creation, because creation is not the place where the question of theodicy and the origin of evil in the created order are solved. God's triumph is centered not protologically but eschatologically, because the end will manifest the glorious majesty of God in the defeat of evil and death in the kingdom of God, when 'the glory of the Lord shall be revealed and all flesh shall see it together'." Beker, *Paul*, 366.

[39] Cf. Schlier, *Römerbrief*, 274.

Thus the gospel itself is universal. It concerns every descendant of Adam, both Jews and Greeks. We must not abandon such a universalism in the soteriology of Paul on the ground of a biassed concept of predestination. Paul is certain that everyone "who calls on the name of the Lord" will be saved (Rom. 10:13). This promise is not given merely to certain individuals elected beforehand, but to all who would hear the gospel.[40]

Paul's concept of predestination was focussed on Christ. He was convinced that God has decreed only one way for salvation – namely that of gaining new sonship through the gospel of Christ and being predestined "to be conformed to the image of his Son" in the resurrection. This is the message of the crucial passage of Romans 8:28-30. The analysis has shown that Paul is not speaking here of temporal predestination, which would lead to double predestination. There is no progressive pattern in the section. Instead, there is a chiastic structure which underlines the Christocentric soteriology of Paul's teaching. The act of election can be found in the call of God. This calling takes place in the proclamation of the gospel. God's good news give believers a new hope which aims at final resurrection and eternal life.

9.2. Christocentric predestination

The primary features of Paul's Christocentric predestinarian theology lead us to undertake a more thorough investigation of his soteriology from this angle. Paul often interprets the themes of election and calling by focussing on Christ and his gospel. In Paul's letters there are furthermore several passages where predestinarian language occurs directly in the service of Christology.

In 1 Thessalonians Paul teaches that believers have been ordained for salvation through their faith. "For God has destined us not (οὐκ ἔθετο ἡμᾶς) for wrath (εἰς ὀργὴν) but for obtaining salvation through our Lord Jesus Christ" (1 Thess. 5:9).

This passage is eschatological and it focusses on the advent of the day of the wrath of the Lord. Those who believe in Christ have been destined for salvation. They are no longer under the wrath of God. Such an antithesis between wrath and salvation is perfect predestinarian theology.

If we ask, who are those who have been ordained for wrath, we are led once again to Paul's apocalyptic eschatology. Paul is undoubtedly speaking of

---

[40] Dunn attempts to rescue universal soteriology by concluding that in the interpretation of the theology of Paul, one cannot use traditional concepts such as determinism or free will. According to Dunn, Paul "deliberately sets the whole process of cosmic and human history between its two poles". "His thought is simply that from the perspective of the end it will be evident that history has been the stage for the unfolding of God's purpose." Dunn, *Romans*, 486. This conclusion does not resolve the discrepancy between double predestination and universal soteriology, however.

people who are the object of divine predestination.[41] But we do not need to speculate on the question whether some foreknown individuals have been destined for God's anger or not.[42] Already in this early letter, written at the beginning of Paul's missionary activity, we see the radical polarization of Paul's soteriology. All humankind has been destined to be under God's wrath, and there is but one way of escape from this prison. Those who are in Christ, and only they, have been destined to salvation through his grace.

In connection with this divine predestination Paul uses the verb τίθημι. In God's salvation history both the final judgment and salvation in Christ have been decreed as permanent orders. Ungodly mankind has been destined for the wrath of God, but one can find salvation through faith in Christ.[43]

The idea of Christocentric predestination is evident in this passage. Faith in Jesus (cf. 1 Thess. 1:3, 10) is the criterion for eschatological election. Those who believe in Christ await salvation on the last day through Christ. In this respect we can say that 5:9 expands the message of 4:4 into predestinarian theology: "For since we believe that Jesus died and rose again, even so, through Jesus, God will bring with him those who have died" (4:14).[44]

The object of divine predestination is actually Christ and the salvation he brings.[45] As a consequence, those who believe in him are decreed for salvation when Christ appears at the end of time.[46] In 1 Thessalonians this message is proclaimed as a consolation for those who fear the coming of the day of the Lord. Paul assures them that their salvation is certain. God has destined them for salvation through their faith in Jesus Christ.[47]

---

[41] Against Holtz, who actually denies the possibility that Paul was at all talking of those who are destined to wrath. "Die negative Aussage hat keine selbständige Bedeutung, sie dient der akzentuierenden Hervorhebung des positiven Satzes." Holtz, *Thessalonicher*, 228.

[42] For such speculation see Best, *Thessalonians*, 217: "Does our passage teach that some are destined for God's anger? Paul does not draw this apparently obvious logical deduction. There is of course no need for him to do so since he is writing about unbelievers, but equally there is no need for him to deny it."

[43] Cf. Mayer, *Heilsratschluss*, 62ff.; Wanamaker, *Thessalonians*, 186-187.

[44] Synofzik has suggested that 5:9-10a refers to baptismal catechesis and contains "vorpaulinisch" tradition. I do not agree with him as regards the vocabulary and the theology of vv. 9-10a, since they seem to fit quite well in the teaching of Paul. His conclusion, however, is acceptable: "Die in der Taufe sichtbare Erwählung wird auf das Prädestinationshandeln Gottes zurückgeführt und mit dem eschatologischen Ziel der Rettung (negativ ausgedrückt: nicht des Zorngerichtes) verbunden. Synofzik, *Vergeltungsaussagen*, 96-97.

[45] This even more clearly in Eph. 1:5: "He destined us for adoption as his children through Jesus Christ, according to the good pleasure of his will."

[46] Thüsing, *Per Christum*, 204; Mayer, *Heilsratschluss*, 65f.

[47] Mayer, *Heilsratschluss*, 68.

A similar example of Christocentric predestination appears in 1 Cor. 2:7, which is a passage that echoes Jewish sapiential theology. "But we speak God's wisdom, secret and hidden, which God decreed before the ages for our glory (ἣν προώρισεν ὁ θεὸς πρὸ τῶν αἰώνων εἰς δόξαν ἡμῶν)." Paul's gospel which (especially in this context) concerns the crucified Christ (cf. 1:23-24, 2:2) is the secret which God has foreordained. God elects people solely through the gospel. It is the good news which Paul preaches, the "wisdom" which has been foreordained for the glory of men.

Paul's text is filled with apocalyptic, predestinarian language. He speaks of historical aeons (πρὸ τῶν αἰώνων) which point to the consummation of eschatology.[48] The salvific work of Christ is presented as a cosmic plan which God has predested (ἣν προώρισεν) for the salvation of men.[49]

Predestinarian theology is here focussed on the gospel. This emphasizes the interplay between God's predestined plan of salvation and the actual calling in history, which takes place in the proclamation of the message.[50] This is the theme which Paul later developed in Romans 8, as we have seen above.

When we read Romans we find similar passages in which Paul speaks of Christocentric election. God has decreed Christ to be the one who brings the righteousness of God to this world and atones for the sins of the whole world. The Christocentric passages of Thessalonians and Corinthians thus confirm our previous suggestion that Paul's theology of justification is guided by predestinarian theology. It comprises the aspects of both predestination of judgment and divine election.[51]

We do not need to repeat all the relevant passages here, but some brief points are useful to make. In Romans 3 Paul claims that all people, both Jews and Greeks, are under the power of sin (Rom. 3:9, 23). On this basis divine election can be nothing but election by grace.[52] God's saving righteousness is God's gift which is given freely on the ground of the atoning death of Christ and through the righteousness that comes from faith (3:24).

---

[48] Barrett, *Corinthians,* 71; Fee, *Corinthians,* 105.

[49] Cf. Schrage, *Korinther,* 251-252. "Formal entspricht προορίζειν Aussagen der Apokalyptik, wonach Gott schon in der Urzeit die Heilsgüter bereitet hat und sie bis zur Endzeit im Himmel verborgen bereithält. Die als Geheimnis charakterisierte göttliche Weisheit aber zielt auf die Verherrlichung der Erwählten" (p. 252). For a parallel idea concerning Moses, see AssMos. 1:14; cf. also Acts 4:28, where the fate of Jesus is explained by divine foreordination.

[50] Here I agree with Conzelmann, *Corinthians,* 62; cf, Schmidt, *ThWNT V* (1990) 457.

[51] Cf. above chapters 6.2. and 8.1.

[52] See chapters 7.1. and 7.3. This is also the message of the Adam-typology in Romans 5, which aims at exclusive redemption in the "Second Adam". In Romans 8:3 it is expressed by a theology of atonement, and in 10:9-10 by resurrection Christology.

As regards the aspect of election, Paul's predestinarian theology is exclusively Christocentric. The basis of divine election is solely the atoning work of Christ, his death and resurrection. God himself justifies the ungodly through faith in Christ. Christocentric predestination is thus a key element in Paul's soteriology. Several passages which speak of such a predestination describe the eschatological hope which believers have in Christ. This hope is based on the calling of believers, which is the true *electio gratiae* of God. Those who have been called through the gospel have been destined for salvation in the last day.

9.3. The problem of double predestination

The analysis which we have made above has shown that conceptions regarding Paul's soteriology are often dependent on the view which the scholar holds on the question of predestination. Such a hermeneutical dependence is understandable because of the long history of theology and the influential dogmas of different churches. Even a brief acquaintance with exegetical literature on predestination reveals a close dependence between exegesis and dogmatic questions. In respect of Pauline studies, one of the most influential of the traditional doctrines is that of Calvin.[53]

It is probably justified to say that Calvin, with his teaching of double predestination, drew the ultimate conclusions from the predestinarian statements of Augustine. According to Calvin, God has foreordained certain individuals, i.e. the elect, to salvation and others to damnation. This "awesome decree", *decretum horribile,* was carefully defined in his writings. "For all are not created in equal condition; rather, eternal life is foreordained for some, eternal damnation for others."[54]

This kind of double predestination is inevitably deterministic. In the beginning God elected those individuals who would be saved.[55] In this scheme eschatology is planned entirely beforehand, and people's predetermined fate will come true in the course of history. Salvation is predestined, and God will call only those whom he has foreordained to eternal life.[56] Those who have

---

[53] As regards the problems of predestination, in several commentaries scholars discuss dogmatic problems and refer e.g. to Calvin. See Dodd, *Romans,* 141; Cranfield, *Romans,* 428ff, 488ff. Also, some modern monographs in the field of systematic theology have been influential in the field of exegesis, too, for instance one by Jewett (see Jewett, *Predestination*).

[54] Calvin, *Institutes,* 3.21.5. See also the Introduction of the present study. An introduction to Calvin's theology is found e.g. in McGrath, *Theology,* 451f.

[55] Cf. the analyses of Mayer, *Heilsratschluss,* 28-29; and Jewett, *Predestination,* 79ff.

[56] Such a view has been applied to the interpretation of Paul's theology by e.g. Schweitzer, *Mystik,* 102-104. For further examples cf. the discussion below.

been foreordained to damnation do not have any opportunity, or even the possibility, of being saved – even though theologians refrain from stating that any individual might actually be conscious of his horrible fate.

In the area of New Testament exegesis and Pauline studies the conception of double predestination has affected the investigation of two separate subjects. Firstly, it has directed the interpretation of Second Temple Jewish soteriology. According to several scholars, double predestination was a common feature of Jewish soteriology at that time.[57] Secondly, it has affected the interpretation of Paul's concept of predestination, which we shall deal with later.

As regards the first subject, our analysis in this work has led to quite the opposite conclusion. The concept of predestination in Second Temple Jewish texts, and in the sapiential tradition in particular, is not deterministic. One cannot provide a sufficient explanation of Jewish soteriology by appealing to double predestination. Not even the sect of Qumran held a deterministic view, even though the soteriological dualism of the sect was strict, and Israel was divided into the children of light and the children of darkness.[58]

The hymns from Qumran provide an interesting parallel in this matter. They show us how the sect's opposition to the Temple placed emphasis on divine judgment. The Temple was no longer considered a focus of salvation in Israel. Therefore God's covenant had to find some other manifestation. This led to a new notion of election. The ungodly were predestined to damnation and the righteous to life. This teaching was accompanied by the conviction that God "knows" the fate of this world and has also revealed it to his elect.[59] It is small wonder that predestinarian language is prominent in these texts.[60]

Despite the fact that there was a deterministic element in Qumran's concept of history, the soteriology of the sect was still based on synergism. The election of God was not deterministic in itself. If a Jew wished to live a life of repentance it was possible for him to apply for membership in the community

---

[57] See the discussion in chapters 4 and 5 above.

[58] Cf. Flusser, who assesses the soteriology of Qumran with reference to double predestination, Flusser, *Judaism*, 28-29.

[59] This word occurs 56 times in the Hymns. Merrill, *Predestination*, 25.

[60] Cf. 1QH VII (= XV and frags. 10,32,34,42), 16-22: "I have known, thanks to your intellect, that it is not by a hand of flesh that the path of man [is straightened out,]... You, you alone, have created the just man... But the wicked you have created for the time of wrath." (Martínez).

of the children of light.[61] This feature essentially diminished the deterministic nature of their soteriology.[62]

We have earlier seen that this kind of soteriology was dependent on the tradition of Second Temple sapiential theology. The strong impact of synergism was only confirmed as we observed that it was influential even in a strict sect like that of Qumran.[63] In this setting the theology of free will was a counterpart to the idea of predestination. Even though foreordination and election were decreed by God, the future life of men was, nevertheless, dependent on their obedience.[64]

As regards our second subject, namely the interpretation of the theology of Paul, it is easy to see that he preserved the conviction that God is sovereign in his decrees. God can harden "the heart of whomever he chooses" (Rom. 9:18). In spite of this, Paul provided quite a different solution to the problem of the relation between determinism and free will. A radicalized concept of predestination led his soteriology towards a new polarization pointing to Christocentric predestination.[65]

The concept of double predestination maintains that God has elected only part of humankind to salvation. Such an idea is not compatible with the teaching of Paul. Paul was convinced that the atonement relates to the whole world.

---

[61] Merrill, too, notes that, despite the fact that in the theology of Qumran there are features which are "something very close" to double predestination, there is also room for the idea that Jews can apply for membership and enter into the covenant in that way. Merrill, *Predestination,* 41. The abovementioned tension in the teaching of the community led Ringgren to remark that there is a "certain inconsistency" in the conception of the sect. Ringgren, *Faith,* 74. This problem can be resolved when we assess the concept of predestination with the aid of sapiential anthropology. In Second Temple Judaism predestination was dependent on the obedience of a "free" man. See chapter 3.3.

[62] Luz, too, pays attention to the tension which in Qumran theology occurs between strict predestination and voluntary obedience. He denies the possibility of a relativizing predestinarian theology ("relativen Prädestinationslehre") on that ground. This is why he suggests that the reason is double predestination. Luz, *Geschichtsverständnis,* 230f. To my understanding, the solution is not in the teaching concerning the two spirits, however, as Luz suggests. Instead, we need to concentrate on anthropology. When the latter is assessed, the conception of the sect remains ambivalent.

[63] See e.g. chapters 3.3. and 5.2.

[64] Even Sanders – despite his different interpretation in general – has noted that in Jewish theology predestinarian statements occur side by side with statements concerning man's free choice. Sanders, *Paul,* 446.

[65] Ziesler, who follows Sanders in his interpretation, says that in Jewish theology conceptions of "human responsibility (and freedom) and divine decision could go hand in hand". This idea is naturally based on covenantal theology, which was assumed to form the basis of both Jewish and Pauline theology. Ziesler, *Romans,* 226. This subject reminds us of the ambivalence of Sanders' theory. He could not find a solution to the synergism of Jewish theology. We shall treat the problem later, in chapter 14.1.

Therefore he was able to say that "one man's act of righteousness leads to justification and life for all" (Rom. 5:18), even though he did not mean universal restoration. Paul would never have said that the whole world will be saved on the last day.[66]

Uncertainty over the definition of predestinarian theology has led some scholars to an ambivalent interpretation of Paul. One of the main reasons for this has been an erroneous explanation of the concepts of Second Temple Jewish theology. As we have seen, some scholars have thought that the theology of free will occurred side by side with the concept of double predestination. Against such a background, Paul's theology, too, becomes incomprehensible. These premises led to an evident discrepancy between Romans 8 and 10. According to this kind of interpretation, in chapter 8 Paul says that God will save only those whom he has elected beforehand, while in chapter 10 he suddenly says that the saving gospel must be preached to the whole world.

Some scholars have attempted to solve this problem by saying that God has also foreknown those who will in the future hear the gospel and be saved through it.[67] Such an interpretation ends with complete determinism and is not acceptable. There are no grounds for it in the letters of Paul.

As we have noted before, the basic problems here once again concern the doctrines of systematic theology which derive from the heritage of the Reformation. Some of the most influential doctrines were laid down by Reformed orthodoxy. As regards the Calvinist concept of predestination, we encounter the "Five Points of Calvinism", which have been very influential in

---

[66] It is good to remember the introductory questions of Jewett: "[I]s the problem that some have conceived the electing will of God *casually,* so that the 'pre' of *predestination* becomes the initial segment on the time line that reduces everything that follows to meaninglessness? Or yet again, does the problem consist in the fact that many have misunderstood the *object* of predestination, that when they should have thought of the object of election as Christ, the chosen Servant of the Lord, they have instead thought of a fixed number of individuals, the 'roll of the elect,' and have thus been driven to the inescapable inference that there is also a fixed number of nonelect for whom there is no hope." Jewett, *Predestination,* 2 (italics his).

[67] So Sanders, following Schweitzer (see chapter 2.2.), Sanders, *Paul,* 446f. "Here [Rom. 10.13-17] the sequence preaching, hearing, faith leaves out of account the very predestination which was insisted on two chapters earlier. The lists could be harmonized: God chooses who shall hear and believe the message and, on the basis of faith, he justifies and glorifies them." In addition, Sanders underlines the fact that Paul did not feel compelled to make the harmonization. On the contrary, Paul felt free to employ predestinarian terminology. As an example, Sanders' explanation shows that, in the end, the concept of double predestination leads to a dead end in the interpretation of Paul's soteriology. Instead of such ambivalence, we need a concept of radical predestination when we explain the theology of Paul.

all Reformed theology.[68] As regards the theology of Paul, some principles of Reformed orthodoxy can be considered as being in total agreement with it.

During our investigation we have seen that Paul's theology is guided by his radical anthropology. His soteriology is based on the conviction that both Jews and Gentiles are under sin. This is also the conviction of Five-Point Calvinism: the total depravity of sinful human nature. A disagreement arises when this premise is applied to soteriology in general. In Reformed orthodoxy the concept of double predestination governed soteriology in all its details. Therefore it was rather consistent that Reformed theology also applied the principle of "limited atonement". On the basis of predestinarian theology theologians were convinced that Christ died solely for the elect.[69] This is where this kind of theology departs from the teaching of Paul. Paul is quite certain that Christ died for the sins of all the descendants of Adam.

In this respect Calvinism had been led in the opposite direction from Augustine. On the basis of predestinarian theology, Calvinism abandoned universal soteriology. Augustine, on the other hand, had attempted to define universal soteriology with his concept of predestination. Perhaps we should think that Calvinist orthodoxy drew the right kind of conclusions from the premises of Augustine, and in this sense their conclusion was really a *reductio ad absurdum*. Thus the result of this argumentation should lead us to initiate a search for new solutions. In Calvinism the conclusion drawn was quite the opposite, as we have seen.[70]

This is where the new analysis of Paul's concept of radical predestination can help us to find new alternatives in the interpretation. We have seen that Paul constantly used soteriological contrast formulas in his teaching (chapter 8.1.). They prove without doubt that in the theology of Paul the "total depravity" of man was opposed to the atoning work of Christ. Paul's soteriology becomes understandable only when it is placed in the context of strict predestination.

---

[68] The term refers to the five central principles of Reformed soteriology, as they were laid down by the Synod of Dort (1618-1619): total depravity, unconditional election, limited atonement, irresistible grace, final perseverance of the saints. See McGrath, *Theology,* 453; Jewett, *Predestination,* 15, 79ff.

[69] This was one of the principles of Five-Point Calvinism; see above. Cf, McGrath, *Theology,* 453.

[70] There is a hermeneutical problem here. The analysis turns out to disagree with some basic principles of modern Calvinism on this question. This creates the danger of being led into a conflict with Calvinist scholars, and the scholarly discussion may be replaced by dogmatical (denominational) disagreement. I hope that this can be avoided and that the focus might be on the analysis of Paul, instead.

Due to sin, God has consigned all men to disobedience, so that he could be merciful to all in Christ.[71]

According to the preceding passages, predestination, for Paul, is not an eclectic act of pre-history. As regards both the judgment of sinners and atonement for sins, the predestination of God, which can be identified as the salvific plan of God, concerns the whole of humankind – all the descendants of Adam. Christ is predestined to be the way to salvation for all people. The ideas of universal atonement and Christocentric salvation are united here. It is the gospel of Christ alone that can bring salvation to the descendants of Adam.[72]

If we accept the perspective of dogmatic theology, we are most often led to consider temporal or logical causality. God must elect a man before he can call him. The election must be based on the will of God and the decree of God, not the acts of men.[73] Such reasoning does not fit in with the theology of Paul, however. He teaches radical predestination, instead. All human beings have first been predestined to damnation. In this sense we could even say that God "wants" the condemnation of the ungodly.[74]

On the basis of this first predestination, Paul's universal soteriology is Christocentric. In a general sense, all men have been "elected" to find salvation in Christ. Paul makes a distinction between atonement and election, however. The election in history takes place in the calling. This is logical, too. It is only the gospel of the righteousness revealed in Christ that can make men free from the predestination of judgment.

How does this conception differ from the belief in "restoration of all things" (*apokatastasis*) which was somewhat popular in the early Church and later elaborated in Reformed theology, too? The basic difference can be found in the principle that Paul's concept is Christocentric, not anthropocentric. The death of Christ gains atonement for sins, but it does not yet deliver salvation to

---

[71] The lack of this notion weakens the conclusions of Röhser, who, on the other hand, has presented a useful explanation as regards the problem of theodicy. He emphasizes the unrestricted power and presence of God when attempting to solve the problem of the rejection of Israel. Röhser, *Prädestination*, 171-173.

[72] In the area of dogmatics one is too easily led to emphasize the "secret" of God's grace. This is also done by Jewett at the end of his valuable analysis, where he refers to Romans 11:32ff. Jewett, *Predestination,* 138f. Similarly Dodd, when explaining Rom. 8, notes that Augustine and Calvin were wrong when they made the theology of predestination a matter of dogmatics. He suggests the exaltation of a mystery, instead. Dodd, *Romans*, 140-141. Exegetical analysis picks up verse 11:32 and reminds us that, for Paul, predestinarian theology was the basis for universal grace.

[73] For such a view, see Jewett, *Predestination*, 66.

[74] This is where I suggest a correction to Mayer's interpretation. As he opposes the idea of double predestination, he remarks that Paul does not mention a "negative predestination" of the ungodly. Mayer, *Heilsratschluss*, 320. I claim just the opposite. On a general level there is a predestination of judgment for all the descendants of Adam.

individuals. These two are carefully separated from each other in Paul's theology.[75]

The analysis has shown that Paul's concept of predestination belongs to the core of his soteriology. One might expect this because the idea of predestination is most often mentioned when election to salvation is taught. Paul uses predestinarian language and terminology, especially in passages where he defines his teaching on justification. They are key terms in his teaching on how the righteousness of God has been revealed in Christ.[76] Only a concept of radicalized predestination provides a sufficient basis for his universal soteriology.

The problem of double predestination can be resolved by Paul's radical concept of predestination. Paul does not think that God elected merely a few individuals beforehand to salvation. As he begins with a pessimistic anthropology, where all the descendants of Adam have been subjected to death and damnation, he can also conclude by teaching universal soteriology on the basis of the work of Christ. Soteriological dualism is, in the theology of Paul, directed by a Christocentric principle.

Summary

The problem of theodicy, which was so typical of Second Temple Jewish theology, also occurs behind several soteriological passages in Paul. Thus he made use of predestinarian theology when giving his response to the great questions of soteriology. It is easy to discern predestinarian terminology in the respective passages, too. For Paul, God's faithfulness can, on the one hand, be seen in his promise that the righteous judgment will come on the last day.

---

[75] As regards *apokatastasis*, see e.g. Origen, *De Principiis*, 3.6.4-5. Later, for example, Barth came to a similar conclusion. For him the message of Romans came to a climax in 11:32f., in a universal solution of predestinarian theology. Barth thought that God would in the end bring all humankind to salvation in his amazing goodwill. Barth, *Römerbrief*, 407. A similar teaching can be found in his dogmatics, see McGrath, *Theology*, 455-456.

[76] Contra Luz, who thinks that in the theology of Paul we can find a similar conception of double predestination as at Qumran (see above). He is not able to explain the meaning of this concept of predestination in the soteriology of Paul, however. In order to avoid a contradiction, he says that the subject is merely a "horizon" of soteriology for Paul, not a leading theme. *"Allemal sind also die Prädestinationsaussagen bei Paulus nur Horizont seines Denkens, nicht Thema; in irgend einer Weise dienen sie immer dazu, Aspekte der eschatologischen Gnadentat Gottes zu beleuchten, aber ihre Verwendung im einzelnen ist entsprechend ihrer verschiendenen Herkunft verschieden."* Luz, *Geschichtsverständnis*, 263 (italics his). Such an ambivalence in the interpretation of the meaning of the theme of predestination is a result of insufficient definition of the concept. On the basis of the analysis given above we may say that predestination is a primary theme in Pauline soteriology. Luz has also been criticized by Röhser, *Prädestination*, 172 ("mehr als bloss eine Denkdimension"); who, on the other hand, also accepts the idea of double predestination.

God's wrath will be revealed and the ungodly will perish. On the other hand, there is also a significant meaning in the delay of the judgment. In his divine forbearance God has "passed over the sins previously committed" (Rom. 3:25). This patience of God shows his righteousness. God's plan was to reveal his saving righteousness in the atoning death of Christ. This is how the righteousness that comes from the law was replaced by the righteousness that comes from faith. Justification by faith was thus a solution to the problem of (dis)obedience, as it had been separating Jews from God.

Paul's reinterpretation of the message of Habakkuk 2:4 (in Rom. 1:17) confirms the notion that Paul intentionally presented his gospel as an answer to the greatest problems of the Jewish theology of his time. The silence of God, which Israel had experienced, had a purpose – the revealing of the final righteousness of God in Christ. This is furthermore the reason why the obedience demanded by the prophets had now become an obedience of faith.

As regards the last judgment, Paul is convinced that God will punish sinners in the end. God will condemn the ungodly in a just judgment. As Paul writes about this judgment he uses several judicial metaphors which emphasize the juridical aspects of his soteriology.

The anthropology of Paul is, respectively, based on the idea of universal sinfulness. According to his radical anthropology, the whole of humankind has been living under the power of sin since Adam. This principle alters the (traditional Jewish) interpretation of salvation history. As the problem of theodicy is provided with an answer in this situation, Paul is led to adopt a new paradoxical polarization. There is no difference between Jews and Greeks, as regards salvation. All men are in an equal position. The basic opposition is between God and sinful humankind.

When Paul explains the fate of humankind he concludes with the idea of the predestination of judgment. God has imprisoned all men in sin and disobedience. This is why soteriology can no longer be based on traditional sapiential synergism. One cannot solve the problem of sin by increasing the responsibility of man. For this reason, too, why God has revealed his saving righteousness without the law. The imprisonment was obligatory, so that God may be merciful to all. The new paradoxical polarization above all concerns Israel. Previous soteriological dualism has been abandoned. The true Israel comprises those who belong to Christ. Paul's pessimistic anthropology results in a rejection of Jewish ethnocentricity.

This new polarization can also be detected behind Paul's treatment of the fate of Israel in Romans 9-11. The idea of the hardening of Israel is submitted to radical predestinarian theology. Even Jewish theologians had taught that not all Jews can attain salvation. Eternal life was promised only to the faithful. In

Paul's theology this concerns Israel in a new way. The only way to salvation
can be found in the righteousness of God, which has now been revealed in
Christ. This is why the new paradoxical polarization of soteriology also
dictated the fate of temporal Israel in the time of Paul.

The predestinarian theology of Paul is completed by his Christocentric
statements. Paul teaches that the election of God is an election by grace. It
takes place in the calling when the gospel of Christ is proclaimed. This gospel,
and all its content, including the work of Jesus at Easter, is God's foreordained
plan of salvation. Therefore it is the gospel which has been predestined for
salvation to all mankind. There is an important distinction between this
universal soteriology and the concept of double predestination, since the latter
inevitably implies the acceptance of the idea of limited atonement and eclectic
soteriology. Paul, however, teaches that everyone "who calls on the name of
the Lord" shall be saved (Rom. 10:13).

Chapter 3

Predestination, Law and Justification

Paul's concept of predestination directs his soteriology. It is also quite evidently a structural factor in his theology. This is why several details in his soteriology differ essentially from the teachings of other Jewish writers of his time. For example, Paul's understanding of the meaning and function of law in soteriology is very original when compared with almost any Jewish teaching in the Second Temple period. As a solution to the problem of theodicy the idea of predestination altered the soteriological scheme and re-defined the function of law in this context.

Predestinarian theology is an important context for the investigation of the Pauline concept of law, because his nomism is usually considered a part of soteriology. For him, law is a factor which affects salvation. When teaching about practical applications of the law in everyday life Paul seldom uses the words "law" or "righteousness". On this ground some scholars have even said that in his letters Paul does not actually discuss the application of the law, *halakha*.[1] An analysis of some of his letters, such as 1 Corinthians, reveals, however, that Paul is very accustomed to reflecting on matters of *halakha*.[2]

There are indeed differences between Paul and other Jewish literature. As the Pharisees and later Rabbinic Judaism discussed at great length how everyday life should be ordered in accordance with the law, Paul is primarily interested in the aspect of salvation history.[3] He is not discussing the *right way* to observe purity regulations, the *details* of Sabbath restrictions, the *treatment* of illnesses, *principles* to be followed in the punishment of crimes – only sporadically the *status* of women in everyday life, and on no account the

---

[1] As W.D. Davies says: "there are few strictly 'legal' discussions in Paul", Davies, *Paul and Paulinism*, 4.

[2] Tomson, in his thorough analysis, has shown that there are several examples of *halakha* in the letters of Paul. Details which reveal a reference to Jewish tradition are detected in cases where *halakha* is "reflected in behaviour or speech". Tomson, *Paul*, 260.

[3] Paul naturally taught about several practical questions concerning everyday life and ethical behaviour. Especially the letters to the Corinthians evidence this kind of teaching. Paul's argumentation in these letters differs, however, from that of traditional Jewish theology. This is why Tomson concludes that in Paul's letters *halakha* is a part of Christian exhortation. His examples are the kind of *halakha* which appeals to the words of Jesus and apostolic *halakha*. Tomson, *Paul*, 262.

correct *action* of Temple priests or the correct manner of performing sacrifices. The difference with regard to Rabbinic Judaism is crucial, because it is precisely these features which are significant in the Mishnah and can be detected even in the list of contents of the tractates.[4]

A direct connection with the traditional treatment of the law can be found in the area of moral issues. Paul forbids, for example, stealing, fraud, lying, unchastity and immorality.[5] Most of these comments appear in a soteriological context, as well. This is why they too can help us in defining Paul's concept of law.

§ 10   The Paradoxical Function of the Law

First and foremost, predestinarian theology helps us to understand why Paul gives God's good law of love a rather paradoxical function in soteriology. He does say that the law is good in itself. It is a good guide, especially in the area of ethics (Rom. 7:12; 13:9-10). In this respect, Paul is in agreement with the teaching of Jewish sapiential theology. Nevertheless, there is a difficult problem concerning the relationship of the essence of the law and the soteriological function of the law. Why does God's good law kill men instead of giving them life?[6]

A traditional solution to the difficulties in explaining Paul's complex concept of law was to make a distinction between moral law and ritual law. According to several scholars, the moral law was still valid. In the new eschatological

---

[4] Some scholars are of the opinion that the law was not a problem to Paul before the crisis in Galatia, which concerned a disagreement with Jewish-Christian preachers. See e.g. Hübner, *Law,* 20-21, 86-87. This is an over-statement which has been criticized, for example, by Lührmann, *JSNT 36* (1989) 76. Hübner accepts the old theory of Bultmann, according to which Paul was totally separate from Palestinian Judaism (and Jewish Christianity). Paul's theology can no longer be explained by a narrow Hellenistic interpretation.

[5] Cf. Rom. 1:22-32; 3:11-18; 13:9; Gal. 5:19-21. We must remember this when we assess Tomson's explanation. He emphasized that the Gentiles as proselytes were required to observe only part of the law, the so-called Noachide code. Tomson, *Paul,* 269-272; cf. Kruse, *Paul,* 49. On this question we must also note the warning of J. A. Sanders, who reminds us that Christianity cannot be regarded as "a kind of Reform Judaism subject only to the Noachide Laws". Sanders, *God's Christ,* 137.

[6] The Pauline theology of law has been one of the most highly investigated themes of his theology over the past two decades, as we have noted earlier. For the discussion, see chapter 2.5. Concerning details, see e.g. the new introduction in Räisänen, *Law (2nd ed.)*; Westerholm, *Law,* 15-101; Martin, *Law,* 39-67.

situation, however, the ritual law was re-interpreted.[7] The appearing of Christ was an eschatological event which had changed Paul's attitude towards the details of ritual law, such as circumcision and purity regulations. Paul did not depreciate these in a religious sense, but he was convinced that their status had been altered in a new eschatological situation.

The traditional setting no longer seems to be a fruitful way of explaining the Pauline concept of the law. For Paul, the law was a single vast entity.[8] In soteriological contexts he makes no clear distinction between moral law and ritual law.[9] The distinction is rather in the question as to whether law produces life or death. The law aims at providing the basis for a good life, but as regards the eternal salvation of men it cannot produce the desired result. This is why the function of law must be defined on a different basis.

It is characteristic of the Pauline concept of law that law and sin are closely connected. The word law, νόμος, often appears in a hamartological context. In the same context he uses the word 'precept' or 'commandment' (ἐντολή) as a synonym for law. In Romans we can find several such occurrences. From this we may conclude that in several cases Paul's concept of law gains its meaning precisely from the concept of sin.[10] The meaning of law in the context of salvation history is bound up with Paul's concept of the sinfulness of man.

10.1. The Law which brings death

One of the most important claims that Paul makes as concerns the function of law is that law brings damnation and death to men and women. This statement

---

[7] In the Calvinist tradition, the distinction between moral law and ritual law has naturally been one that has long been drawn. It was believed that Christ is the end of the latter, while leaving the former still in effect. See the discussion in Martin, *Law,* 32. In modern scholarship this distinction has been accepted e.g. by the Lutheran Hübner, *Law,* 82-86; and by the Anglican Cranfield, *SJT 17* (1964) 67. Cf. also Dunn, *Law,* 224, and – with certain reservations – Sanders, *Law,* 101.

[8] This is the conclusion reached by Winger after detailed linguistic analysis, Winger, *By What Law,* 86-87. Cf. also the discussion in the long footnote by Hengel in his *Sohn Gottes,* 106, n. 123. In Second Temple Jewish theology there is no significant distinction to be found between moral law and ritual law.

[9] So also Gutbrod, *ThWNT IV* (1990) 1072; Longenecker, *Paul,* 119-120, Schreiner, *Law,* 40; Moo, *WTJ 45* (1983) 82-84.

[10] Even though this notion concerns exegesis, it is of great methodological significance. In old etymological studies Paul's concept of law was often defined without an assessment of the relevant context of the occurrence. In this case the semantic field of the word "law" has been narrowed and even distorted in the theology of Paul. For such an etymological study, see as recent an example as Räisänen, *Jesus, Paul and Torah,* 69-94. Modern semantics are exploited consistently in Winger, *By What Law;* concerning methodology see especially pp. 15-20.

usually appears in anthropological contexts, where Paul ponders the significance of sin. The relationship between sin and law is thus essential in nomism, the guiding principle of which is predestinarian theology.

Especially in Romans Paul emphasizes that without the law one has no knowledge of sin. He underlines this by saying that sin is "dead" without the law. When we attempt to provide an explanation of this somewhat enigmatic statement we are led once again to investigate the relationship between the Fall and the giving of the law.

There is an interesting polarity between Adam and Moses, and Paul wishes to define their relationship in a new way. Adam is a prototype of unfaithfulness, while Moses is an example of obedience. Adam is the one who transgresses the commandment given by God, but Moses is the obedient one who hands on God's law. These two persons become prominent figures in salvation history. Paul defines their relationship cautiously and in detail.

The event of the giving of the law, according to Paul, did not occur in a vacuum. It was preceded by a long history which began with the fall of Adam. This is why it must be interpreted from this perspective. The law had a special function in this context: it became the exposer of sin. In a hamartological context νόμος is not merely the law of Moses in a general sense. It is at the same time a juridical code of law, by which people are judged before the judgment seat of God.[11] On the basis of the code of law one was found guilty and on that basis sentence was pronounced. This scheme is especially evident in the teaching of Romans 5.[12]

In this chapter the polarity between Adam and Moses is clear. Sin gains its actual meaning only after the giving of the law. Sin has been in the world since Adam (5:12), but there has not been a code of law by which it could have been judged. Because the Law is such a basis for evaluation, sin was not "reckoned":

"Sin was indeed in the world before the law, but sin is not reckoned when there is no law" (5:13).

Paul's starting-point is simple: *sin is of primary importance and it is an essential factor in anthropology. Every man's relation to law is determined by it.*

---

[11] The hamartological context is investigated e.g. by Moo, *NTS 32* (1986) 122; Martin, *Law,* 69-70; Thielman, *Plight,* 99-100; Schreiner, *Law,* 65ff.

[12] The basic problem here, as Luz has pointed out, is the question of the purpose for which Paul needed these claims. Firstly, he most evidently did not need to prove to any Jew that sin was in this world even before Moses. Secondly, we must ask whether Paul's sole purpose was to say that without the law sin could not be proven and condemned. But if this was the case, what ever happened to the basic problem: what was the fate of men before Moses? See Luz, *Geschichtsverständnis,* 198-199.

We must note that Paul is not pondering on the nature of sin but on the meaning and status of law.[13] The term "reckoning" which Paul uses here:

$$\dot{\alpha}\mu\alpha\rho\tau\dot{\iota}\alpha\ \delta\dot{\epsilon}\ o\dot{\nu}\kappa\ \dot{\epsilon}\lambda\lambda o\gamma\epsilon\tilde{\iota}\tau\alpha\iota\ \mu\dot{\eta}\ \ddot{o}\nu\tau o\varsigma\ \nu\dot{o}\mu o\nu$$

is a juridical concept. Evil works are recorded when there is a juridical reason for doing so. This was possible only when law could be used as a code by which men could be accused of sin. After Moses the sin of Israel was a transgression of a commandment of the law (παράβασις, verse 14).[14] Sin, naturally, had been in this world ever since Adam.

The word "reckon" (ἐλλογέω) belongs to the same semantic field as the verb λογίζομαι, which Paul uses in other instances when describing both the reckoning of sin and righteousness. Both of these terms have a juridical meaning and the latter one is common in Pauline terminology.[15]

The defining of the relation between law and sin also poses some problems. Why does Paul say that sin is not "reckoned" (οὐκ ἐλλογεῖται), even though in chapter 2 he has said that judgment also concerns those who do not have the law? Some scholars are content to say that Paul is simply inconsistent.[16] He wrote here with a different purpose and his previous argumentation was

---

[13] Luz does not pay enough attention to this fact. He is content to say: "Das entscheidende Fazit: 'Also hat Adams Sünde allen den Erbtod gebracht' ist von Paulus gerade nirgends ausgesprochen; der Leser muss es erraten. Luz, *Geschichtsverständnis*, 198-199. Such an interpretation is astonishing. Verse 12 underlines the fact that all die in Adam. It is not in any sense a mere inference. Furthermore this is in line with the thought in 1 Cor. 15:21, ἐν τῷ Ἀδὰμ πάντες ἀποθνῄσκουσιν. This bypath of Luz is somewhat strange, especially as regards his other (quite fine) conclusions below. His argument that 1 Cor. 15 differs too much from Rom. 5 as regards its context in a struggle against gnosticism is not an assuring one. The similarities in soteriology are obvious enough.

[14] Wilckens, *Römer I*, 317.

[15] Paul often uses the word λογίζομαι in juridical contexts when he speaks of reckoning something for someone's benefit or finding a person guilty. "Counting" as righteous is common, especially in Romans 4 (4:3, 5, 9, 11, 22; cf. Gal. 3:6). Reckoning of sin occurs in Rom. 4:8 and 2 Cor. 5:19.

[16] For example, Bultmann considered verse 13 totally incomprehensible, "vollends unverständlich", because sin did not originate as a contravention of the Law. He asks how it can have brought death if it was not "counted". Bultmann, *Theologie*, 252f. Räisänen's solution here, too, was that Paul is simply inconsistent in his thinking (see below). Räisänen, *Law*, 147. Räisänen says that Paul has one simple point of departure here. Paul speaks of heavenly book-keeping where sins are counted. According to Räisänen, Paul encounters difficulties, though, because he simultaneously has to operate with the theme of the giving of the law.

forgotten.[17] Paul's thought is not that simple, however. We must remember that there is always a pessimistic anthropology in the background of his theology. It is always a sufficient reason for the damnation of man. "All who have sinned apart from the law will also perish apart from the law"(Rom. 2:12). Fallen mankind is destined to perish. A similar understanding of the consequences of sin can be found in chapter 5. "Yet death exercised dominion from Adam to Moses, even over those whose sins were not like the transgression of Adam" (5:14). The generations which followed Adam had no special status in the eyes of God. They had been exiled from Paradise and subjected to the power of death.[18]

Paul's presentation remains unclear if one assumes that he is here evaluating conditions for salvation. It seems that some scholars attempt to find an answer to the difficult question, familiar from the philosophy of religion, as to whether people who lived before Moses will have a chance of being saved. Such a question cannot have been in Paul's mind. He was writing solely about the status of the law. This is why the question concerning the "reckoning" of sins is to be solved in the context of nomistic theology.

It would be erroneous to think that Paul's anthropology would have changed in between different chapters of Romans. Under no circumstances would he consider people sinless.[19] This point of anthropology has been expressed even

---

[17] Räisänen considers Paul's statements incompatible with the presentation of chapter 7, where Paul states that sin was "dead" before the giving of the law (7:7-13). This disagrees with the teaching that sin was a strong power ever since Adam (5:13f.). Räisänen, *Law,* 147. This criticism of Räisänen's is rather strange. Paul never states that sin would be counted without the law. Instead, in Romans 5, Paul explains the cosmic status of sin before God, beginning from the Fall. In Genesis the factual punishment of sin was exile (and death). Here Paul has a strong argument for his claim that sinners will be destroyed even without the law. A real wonder in this situation was the possibility that some people could be saved in spite of sin.

[18] Cf. Schlier, *Römerbrief,* 165. Räisänen, too, notes this teaching of Paul's, but in spite of this he does not find any consistency in Paul's thought. "If the law was given merely an informative function, the use of ἐλλογεῖν becomes very strange. If Paul's statement can be filled with any concrete sense at all, it would seem to refer to a technical trifle. Until the law sin had been punished because it was sin; since the law, the very same punishments are imposed because of 'transgression'. Räisänen, *Law,* 146. Räisänen seems to argue as if man had never been exiled from Paradise. Luz gives quite a brilliant analysis here, by contrast. As he investigates Paul's concept of (salvation) history, he says that Paul is here actually writing a "history of sin", *Unheilsgeschichte.* "*Entscheidend ist nun, dass dieser einzige Gesamtentwurf der Geschichte bei Paulus nicht ein Entwurf der Heilsgeschichte, sondern gerade ein Entwurf der Unheilsgeschichte ist.*" Luz, *Geschichtsverständnis,* 204 (italics his).

[19] This is Westerholm's criticism of Räisänen. "The law, by implication, effects a change from sin to transgression, but hardly one from innocence to guilt." Westerholm, *Law,* 180.

more sharply: Paul does not know of "innocent sinners".[20] The question concerning the reckoning of sins cannot be treated by separating the problem from Paul's anthropology.

The period before the Law, according to Paul, was special in the sense that at that time the relationship between God and man could not be evaluated according to the precepts of the Law. *Sin was not reckoned in the period between Adam and Moses, because the relationship of God and men had not yet become a juridical one. That relationship was determined rather by a cosmic dualism.*[21]

Even though sin as such was not exposed – and in a juridical sense was even "dead" – man, too, was dead as regards God. "[M]any died through the one man's trespass" (Rom. 5:15). Adam-typology is here again a prominent premise for Paul. The giving of the law did not change the eschatological status of man. It merely added one new feature for its assessment.[22]

The period between Adam and Moses is thus in Paul's scheme a *period of transition*. He emphasized this idea by saying that the transgression of people before Moses was not similar to that of Adam: "not like the transgression of Adam" (μὴ ἁμαρτήσαντας ἐπὶ τῷ ὁμοιώματι τῆς παραβάσεως 'Αδάμ, 5:14). The quality of transgression is once again an argument for theology concerning the law, not an argument explaining the fate of Adam's descendants.[23]

The transgression of Adam is here called a trespass (τὸ παράπτωμα, 5:17), in a similar way as in Genesis (cf. παραπίπτω, to fall beside). In addition, it meant disobedience (παρακοή, 5:19). The trespass had taken place in a situation where fellowship with God existed. Adam had opposed God and disobeyed his commandment.[24] The descendants of Adam no longer enjoyed this fellowship and the precise commandment of God had been lost until Moses gave the law of God to Israel.

---

[20] This comical opposition is presented by Cranfield, *Romans*, 282; see also Westerholm, *Law*, 181.

[21] Cf. Stuhlmacher, *Römer*, 81.

[22] Martin tried to solve the problem of the relation of sin and law by maintaining that what Paul says literally is that sin was in the world even before Moses. Because sin is not counted without the law, the law, too, must have been in the world before Moses. Such an explanation is incorrect since Paul is here intentionally using the argument that when it came, law revived the transgression. See Martin, *Law*, 74-75.

[23] See Moo: "But Paul uses *parabasis*, as we have seen, not to draw a distinction between personal and original sin but between personal transgression of a direct law and personal sin without the presence of such law." Moo, *Romans*, 345.

[24] Dunn emphasizes that the sin of Adam is a special trespass, because it transgresses the commandment of God. Dunn, *Romans*, 276.

Paul's aim in chapter 5 is to define the status of law in the anthropological context which was governed by the fall of Adam. Because all mankind after Adam lived under the power of sin and under the power of death, the law of God became an exposer of that sin.[25]   God's word to Moses at Sinai corresponded to God's word to Adam in Paradise. Paul develops this thought in verse 5:20. Here he says that the law made the transgression "complete": But law came in, with the result that the trespass was multiplied (νόμος δὲ παρεισῆλθεν ἵνα πλεονάσῃ τὸ παράπτωμα, Rom. 5:20; "that the offence might abound", AV).[26]

Paul's scheme in chapter 5 clearly concerns salvation history.[27]   He is describing different phases of God's action and pondering on their purposes. The giving of the law becomes an important event in this scheme, because it is precisely here that the law gains its negative function.[28] When law came the trespass became serious. The law brought a *juridical* relation between God and man. In this respect the idea of verse 13 is similar to that of verse 20.[29]

In the context of chapter 5 "sin" becomes almost identified with punishment. This becomes evident when we look at the antithesis at the end of verse 20. When the trespass was increased (completed), the grace of God exceeded even that. In this opposition the juridical nature of the word "grace" is emphasized, denoting release from punishment. Sin which had been reckoned on the basis of law will no longer lead to punishment, because the grace of God rescinds the sentence.

Paul's theology of law is always a part of soteriology, and for this reason his writings often contain such antithetical clauses. The relation of sin and grace becomes understandable only when both of these factors are taken into

[25] Stuhlmacher, *SEÅ 50* (1985) 98-99: "the Law does not have the power to make sinners righteous in the sense of the innocence of paradise. The Law can do only one thing over against sinners: it can make them conscious of their sin and brand them as sinners".

[26] In modern translations the idea of "increasing" (NIV) is common, but it leads the interpretation astray. The problem of "qualitative vs. quantitative" interpretation will be treated in the next chapter. Moo uses both of these qualifications when explaining the "reckoning" of sins. He says first that law is a "stimulant" of sin. In addition, however, "the law brings a qualitative difference". Moo, *Romans*, 345.

[27] For this see also van Dülmen, *Theologie*, 97.

[28] The negative function of the law is noted also by Sanders, *Law*, 70, even though his theory deals normally with positive nomism. Thielman criticizes Brandenburger for claiming that Paul "sharply devalues the law by calling into question the Jewish teaching on its eternality and assigning it a negative and therefore outmoded place in salvation history." Thielman, *Plight*, 100; cf. Brandenburger, *Adam*, 248-254. Such a criticism is needed in the sense that we must note that the negative function of the law is merely the reverse side of the positive essence of the law.

[29] Cf. Michel, *Römer (1955)*, 126; Wilckens, *Römer I*, 318f., 328f.; Stuhlmacher, *Römer*, 82; Moo, *Romans*, 360-362. Against Käsemann, *Römer*, 148.

account.[30] This point of view will become even clearer in those sections where Paul describes sin as a personified power. Sin is a king who reigns (ὥσπερ ἐβασίλευσεν ἡ ἁμαρτία, Rom. 5:21) and who is armed (Rom. 6:13). On the other hand, Paul describes sin as a master whom its slaves serve (Rom. 6:6, 17, 20) and into whose power they have been sold (Rom. 7:14).[31] The opposition of this personified sin is Christ, who frees people from slavery.

According to Paul, the power of sin is absolute. Man is totally subject to its despotism. This thought is a consequent result of Paul's theology of predestination. Sin and Christ are dramatically opposed. We could even say that hamartology is a negation of Christology. Salvation from the power of sin means that Christ is allowed to be man's Master, King and Lord. This is why it is natural that it is exactly this antithetical position which makes Paul's argument complete in 5:21: "so that, just as sin exercised dominion in death, so grace might also exercise dominion through justification leading to eternal life through Jesus Christ our Lord."[32]

A juridical perspective is evident also in the famous summary of Romans 3, where Paul writes on the essence of righteousness (3:19-20). Once again the context here is that of hamartology. The law brings knowledge (ἐπίγνωσις) of sin: "for through the law comes the knowledge of sin" (3:20). This knowledge is no neutral information, but is of a juridical nature. Sin is recognized as sin by the fact that it will be followed by punishment.

This knowledge of sin thus also becomes a reason for the "reckoning" of sins and the exposure of the guilty. Verse 19 proclaims that the whole world will be "held accountable to God" ("become guilty", AV). The expression ὑπόδικος γένηται means literally that people have been subject to judgment and they have already been sentenced to damnation. They can no longer expect to be found "not guilty" and be acquitted.[33] They will be found guilty without doubt.

"Every mouth may be silenced," because there is no more room to put up a

---

[30] Davies points out that one of the dangers of Pauline studies is the separation of the discussion concerning the law from Paul's faith in Jesus as Messiah. This notion is important, even though Davies' conclusions differ from those reached above. Davies, *Paul and Paulinism*, 7.

[31] Paul's concept of personified sin is analyzed by Martin, *Plight*, 69-70.

[32] In the Greek text the idea of the rule of Christ is clearer than in most translations: διὰ Ἰησοῦ Χριστοῦ τοῦ κυρίου ἡμῶν. In this respect Käsemann's interpretation concerning 'dominions' is correct, Käsemann, *Römer*, 149; cf. Moo, *Romans*, 363.

[33] Cf. Michel, *Römer (1955)*, 86; Stuhlmacher, *Römer*, 53-54. This verse is obviously parallel to Gal. 3:19. Already in Galatians it is salvation history that defines Paul's concept of the law, even though his example differs from that of Romans. Paul's conclusion in Galatians is similar to that in Romans. The law was needed in order to expose trespasses.

defence. The law has said the last word: it has given the knowledge of sin. These sections give us a good background when we move on to chapter 7, where Paul states that sin is "dead" without the law,

χωρὶς γὰρ νόμου ἁμαρτία νεκρα, Rom. 7:7.

Paul does not mean here that only those who hear the law will be sentenced to damnation. Sin, of course, is not powerless without the law. For all the descendants of Adam sin has been a cosmic reality which has resulted in damnation and destruction. Without the law sin is not a transgression against God's revealed commandment. It is of a different nature. This was the case dealt with in Romans 2.

In Romans 7 Paul uses the metaphor of death in a similar way as in the preceding chapters, but here it occurs in a somewhat astonishing context. Now the law causes death to the "I" of the letter (Rom. 7:7-13). This section has been considered especially difficult, because Paul is here speaking as an "I" of things which in no sense fit into his biography.[34] Instead we seem to be in a situation where Paul's life and the whole history of Israel are united in a mysterious way. Because of this unity Paul can use quite courageous comparisons, and these help him expound his theology of predestination.

"I was once alive apart from the law, but when the commandment came, sin revived and I died, and the very commandment that promised life proved to be death to me" (Rom. 7:9-10)

Paul is speaking of a time when the "I" was living without the law (7:9). As a Jew, he himself had never actually been able to live without the law. The theory that Paul is speaking of his youth, and of his becoming a *"bar mitzvah"*, would be an overstatement.[35] There seems to be another kind of identification here. In the larger context of Romans, Paul's life is identified collectively with Israel. The nation had been living without the law before Moses, and at that time sin was not reckoned as there was no law (5:13).[36]

The fate of Paul's collective "I" is similar to that of Israel. When the commandment of God (here: ἐντολή) came, sin was revived and "I" died, i.e.

---

[34] Traditional alternatives in the explanation of the section are presented in Moo, *NTS 32* (1986) 122. A good summary of the solutions of modern scholarship can be found in Kruse, *Paul*, 209f. The most common alternatives are the following: "I" refers to Paul himself, to Adam or to mankind in Adam, to Israel, or to man in general. The last one includes the famous study by Kümmel, who assumed that "I" is merely a rhetorical device without any personal reference. See Moo, *Romans*, 452.

[35] This has been suggested in previous research e.g. by Deissmann, *Paulus*, 73; Davies, *Paul*, 24-25. For criticism, see Wedderburn, *Studia Biblica III*, 422.

[36] Stauffer, *ThWNT II* (1990) 356; van Dülmen, *Theologie*, 102, 109; Moo, *NTS 32* (1986) 129. In the existentialist tradition Paul's perspective of salvation history has naturally been replaced by a subjective interpretation, see Bornkamm, *Studien*, 59.

Israel died (7:9). With its juridical function law condemned transgression and accused people of sin. This is the function which Paul earlier ascribed to the law in Romans (cf. 5:13-14).[37]

In the middle of chapter 7 the discourse comes to a climax and Paul makes a central statement of his theology of law. The tension between Adam and Moses needs a solution. The law can be ascribed a proper meaning and function only in the context of that tension. And the solution is this: the law was given to a people who were already under sin and destined for damnation.

This is why nothing remains but *the great paradox of the Torah*:

"the very commandment that promised life proved to be death to me" (7:10).

The law which had been given to the chosen people became, due to sin, a code of law which exposed transgressions and brought death. This paradoxical conclusion is a consequent result of a radicalized concept of predestination.[38] Man has been sold under the power of sin and can no longer gain the righteousness that one needs before God (7:14). This is why it is the "good", i.e. God's perfect law of love, that brings death (7:13).[39]

Already these analyses confirm the assumption that Paul is treating the problem of the relation of law and sin from the point of view of his concept of predestination. Man is totally under sin and "falls short of the glory of God". This is why the function of the law has to do with the sin of men. God has

---

[37] Moo, *NTS 32* (1986) 127. Luz connects the fate of the "I" with the Fall and identifies "I" with Adam. Adam, too, had to face the revival of sin and was sentenced to death as a punishment for his trespass. See Smend-Luz, *Gesetz*, 101. Kruse thinks that in the interpretation of the section, the "combination of the redemptive-historical and autobiographical approaches is best." "In this case, the 'I' of Romans 7:7-25 is not simply Israel, but Paul in solidarity with Israel." Kruse, *Paul*, 211, following Moo, *Romans*, 456. In such an interpretation we must note that Paul means an existential identification with the fate of Israel. Further, there is naturally an analogy with the Genesis story and the fall of Adam. This is why such an interpretation cannot be seen as an opposition to the one given above. In verses 7:10-13 there are no doubt echoes from Genesis. See e.g. Stuhlmacher, *Römer*, 99-100; Schlier, *Römerbrief*, 224-227.

[38] According to J.A. Sanders, Paul "apparently contradicts himself" when in Rom. 3:31 he affirms the law, and in 7:22 delights in it, even though e.g. in 7:1-10 he says clearly that the law has been abolished. Sanders, *God's Christ,* 132. Sanders tries to solve this problem by maintaining that the positive attitude towards the law in Paul is only *haggadah*, the story of divine election and redemption in Christ. Sanders, *God's Christ,* 138. Such a distinction does not do justice to Paul's claim concerning the great paradox of the Torah.

[39] Several authors underline the fact that it is actually sin which brings death as it uses the law as its instrument. Schlier, *Römerbrief*, 227; Wilckens, *Römer II,* 83. Even though this is true in principle, we must be accurate in interpreting Paul's finesses. The purpose of his polarization is to expose the paradoxality of law. This was actually based on his view that the law in itself was good. It is a conviction that Paul never abandoned, cf. Reicke, *ThZ 41* (1985) 242.

prescribed his judgment for the wicked and sinners. This is why the law of Moses functions as a means of exposing sin and revealing God's judgment. In such a setting law can never have a neutral meaning. Paul's claims of the function of the law have been produced from his radical theology of predestination.[40] Paul's soteriology is governed by a scheme of salvation history and this is why the law is given a function which has not been produced by the essence and implicit aim of the law. The law in itself is good and just, without doubt, but its function is to be defined by the anthropology and hamartology which precede it: simply the relationship of God and man before the giving of the law.

Our first topic on the theme of sin and the law leads us to a notion of the *juridical nature* of their relationship. For Paul, the law is a code by which transgressions can be judged.[41] Sin, on the other hand, is a negative reality. On the ground of the sinfulness of man the juridical function of the law becomes frightening. In defining this task Paul employs his theology of predestination. Law makes people aware of sin and exposes their guilt. Before the heavenly judgment seat there is no longer room for a defence. Man must keep silence before the expositions of the law.

This juridical feature is a further proof for the conclusion that Paul's theology of law mainly concerns anthropology and only to a small extent Christology. This distinction is crucial in soteriology. The juridical element should not, however, be pressed too hard so that Paul's theology is too closely connected with the theme of morality. He is dealing with man's whole relationship to God and his perspective reaches from the Fall to the Day of Wrath.

For Paul, the law is good in itself. This is why we must make a distinction between the essence and the function of the law. In this world of sin law is given a judicial function. This is why the law which is essentially good and strives for righteousness has a negative function in salvation history. In this respect Paul is not so far from the Jewish theology of his time. In sapiential theology, too, the law was expected to expose sin. Paul, in his radicalized view, thought that because of the universality of sin this function concerned all men. In his theology of predestination it was only natural that the law would expose the guilt of men before God. In conclusion, he had to maintain further that the law could no longer be considered a neutral exhortation to lead a life of obedience. This resulted in the great paradox of the Torah: as the good law exposed sin, it brought death to the chosen people.

---

[40] The basic motivation of Paul's juridical concept of law is to be found in eschatology. In this sense Paul is following the tradition of Second Temple Jewish apocalyptic. Paul's eschatology is quite radical, however: when God gave the Torah, he at the same time exposed the sin of Israel. This is why the law brought the wrath of God with it (Rom. 4:15).

[41] In this juridical interpretation I follow e.g. Stuhlmacher, *Theologie*, 260ff, 278ff.

10.2. Does the law produce sin?

The analyses made above have led us to a problem which has puzzled several scholars for the past two decades. On the one hand, the law, especially in the context of salvation history, seems to be a paradoxical concept for Paul. As regards man, it is really a destructive power. On the other hand, Paul presents us with a developed, positive concept of the essence of law. Here the law is a basic element of the whole existence of man and a cohesive force in this world.

How does this tense setting fit in with Paul's theology of predestination? We must approach this problem anew from a proper perspective. Now we must ask whether Paul really thought that the law could produce sin. How radical a change and polarization was he ready to make on the basis of his theology of predestination?

The negative function of the law is, in the context of Paul's theology of predestination, admittedly quite polarized. The function of the law has changed to its antithesis, as we have seen above. The principle of paradoxical polarization functions in the theology of law so that, according to Paul, the law leads people to damnation. The simple belief that the law gives life has been essentially changed.[42]

This new principle of polarization can help us solve the seemingly difficult problem of the Pauline concept of law. The law which in principle is good and positive as regards its essence, receives a negative function on the basis of predestinarian theology. Due to strict predestination the traditional function of the law has been totally changed. The law becomes a prosecutor who accuses men in the last judgment and is authorized to sentence people to death.

Here we must further remember that both in the Old Testament and in the tradition of Jewish sapiential theology the law was always seen as an exposer of sin, too. In this respect the function of the law has always been defined according to the anthropology adopted. Even though the law, in the Pentateuch, is given as a way of life, it is at the same time an exposer of transgressions – in other words: sin. In this respect Paul did not alter the Jewish concept of law. The change of function concerned the status of law in Jewish piety. The law had been a positive goal for the righteous and now it became a negative factor on the basis of predestinarian theology. Due to the new polarization the value of obedience to the law had to be denied.

But how far was Paul prepared to go in defining the new function of the law?

---

[42] Our starting-point in the assessment of the theology of law is the dynamics of Paul's soteriology, which produces paradoxal conclusions, especially as regards traditional Jewish soteriology, cf. chapters 7.3., 8.1., 10.1. Here we shall investigate how radical this change was considered to be. The discussion has been set in motion above all by Räisänen with his suggestion regarding the negative function of law, see Räisänen, *Law*, 140ff.

Did he really think that the law would actually produce and bring about sin in the life of men? We have seen some suggestions concerning this kind of interpretation above. In practice this concerns the explanation of certain sections of Paul's letter. In what follows we shall investigate some of the most significant of these texts.

Some scholars have interpreted Romans 5:20 as if Paul were here speaking about the increase of sin in the sense that law would multiply the trespass.[43]

"But law came in, with the result that the trespass multiplied"
νόμος δὲ παρεισῆλθεν ἵνα πλεονάσῃ τὸ παράπτωμα, 5:20

The word 'trespass' (τὸ παράπτωμα) occurs here in the singular. Therefore it can mean either the specific trespass of Adam or trespasses of men in general, in an abstract sense.[44] If Paul is speaking of the trespass of Adam – which naturally was an important subject in the preceding verses – he would probably mean the increase in the number of trespasses. We could even simplify this: when the trespasses can be "counted", there is a greater number in the world.

It is more probable, though, that Paul is speaking here of the role which law plays in salvation history. In the preceding verses he maintains that the fall of Adam resulted in condemnation (κατάκριμα, v. 16). The law had a negative, eschatological task to reveal this condemnation to men. This is why the law places sin conclusively under the condemnation of God in the universal history of humankind.[45]

Thus Paul is not speaking of the increase in the number of single transgressions, but of the change of the quality of trespass.[46] When law is present, sin can be an object of accusation. At the same time condemnation becomes

---

[43] This interpretation has become rather popular, especially in the context of Romans 5 and 7, see Räisänen, *Law,* 144, "5.20 refers to an 'objective' increase of sin: an increase of transgressions."; cf. Sanders, *Law,* 71. In the same tradition of interpretation Ziesler is more cautious, however. He says that "the Law turns potential or implicit sinfulness into concrete acts of sin, i.e. trespasses". Ziesler, *Romans,* 152. Räisänen opposed his view with the traditional explanation which spoke of an increase of legalism and self-righteousness. For such a view, see Brandenburger, *Adam,* 252f.

[44] Schlier refers to the trespass of Adam, Schlier, *Römerbrief,* 177. Hübner remarks that the word is in the singular form, and should thus be identified with sin. Hübner, *Law,* 80.

[45] For such an interpretation, see Wilckens, *Römer I,* 329.

[46] The change in quality concerns the objective interpretation of the law. Räisänen is right when he says that Paul does not mean a subjective and cognitive change. Several scholars suggest, namely, that through law man becomes aware of sin and in this sense the knowledge of sin multiplies. Räisänen, *Law,* 144; contra e.g. Dodd, *Romans,* 83; Hübner, *Law,* 80; cf. Kruse, *Paul,* 243: "in the sense that it increases culpability by making sin known." In this respect Räisänen has abandoned the existentialist interpretation of Bultmann, according to which the law increases sin by guiding people to trust the false "security" which the keeping of the law gives. Bultmann, *Theologie,* 266.

real to transgressors. In this case sin means a transgression against a specific commandment of God, παράπτωμα, which, on the other hand, also means disobedience to the will of God. As regards the verse in question, this would result in a translation which leaves room for a change in quality, such as that of NIV: "The law was added so that the trespass might increase".[47]

A juridical interpretation is best in this section.[48] The change concerning trespasses is that it is set in a juridical relation as regards God. In this way a trespass becomes an act of disobedience to God's actual commandment.[49] The principle of paradoxicality is here at work in a simple sense: the law is said to produce a result contrary to the one expected, as regards its very essence.

A similar setting, according to Räisänen, faces us in Romans 7. When the commandment comes, sin actually springs to life (7:9, ἐλθούσης δὲ τῆς ἐντολῆς ἡ ἁμαρτία ἀνέζησεν). This is another section where Paul seems to maintain that only the law brings about actual sinning.[50] Behind the interpretation of Räisänen is the idea of Paul's empirical reasoning. The commandments of the law awaken in man the desire to transgress them. In this way the law promotes sin. Such an "empirical claim" is, according to Räisänen, absolutely impossible in Judaism in the time of Paul.[51]

There is a problematic weakness in the argumentation of Räisänen, and this

---

[47] This interpretation is in agreement with the immediate context of verse 20b. The increase of trespass is parallel to the increase of sin: "But where sin increased, grace increased all the more." On the basis of this correspondence Schreiner too abandons the cognitive interpretation. He is content, however, with explaining the "increase" merely as a multiplication of transgressions. See Schreiner, *Law*, 74, 91.

[48] "Die von Gott erlassene Weisung macht die Sünde gerichtlich einklagbar (V.13) und lässt sie in ihrer ganzen Schwere erscheinen." Stuhlmacher, *Römer*, 82.

[49] Sanders thinks that in chapter 5 Paul is consistent in his teaching on the relation of sin and law. Here we have, however, only the first version of this relationship in Paul's writings. Because the law was not able to produce righteousness, Paul ascribed to it a negative function in God's plan of salvation. "It produces sin, so that salvation would be on the basis of faith." Sanders, *Law*, 73. According to Sanders, Paul later abandoned this view, see p. 75.

[50] Räisänen, *Law*, 144: "According to ch. 7, it is only the law with its commandments that *brings about* actual sinning." Räisänen suggests that this verse is parallel to Gal. 3:19 (τῶν παραβάσεων χάριν), at least if it is taken in a "radical causative sense: the law was added to bring about... transgressions". He admits, though, that the "pedagogical" function of the law (3:24) "suggests rather the notion of preventing transgressions". Räisänen, *Law*, 144-145, also footnote 84. He clearly follows Bultmann here, even though he does not mention it. See Bultmann, *Theologie*, 266.

[51] "In Rom 7.7f. Paul sets forth an empirical claim: the commandments of the law awaken in man the desire to transgress them." Räisänen, *Law*, 148.

is the lack of analysis of the positive essence and function of the law.[52] He seems to think that law only awakens the willingness to transgress against the commandments of God – as he says: "law *causes...* men to sin" (italics his).[53] Paul sees the situation differently. For his argumentation it is essential to maintain that, in principle, the law is good (7:12) and that it was what is good that brought death through sin (7:13):[54]

"Did what is good, then, bring death to me? By no means! It was sin, working death in me through what is good (διὰ τοῦ ἀγαθοῦ), in order that sin might be shown to be sin, and through the commandment might become sinful beyond measure."

Paul's radical anthropology leads him here to give an actual definition of polarization. The commandment is good and aims at life. Man, however, lives in a situation where this aim is not reached. Sin came in between. This is why it is sin which brings death through what is good. Paul's final conclusion comes in a new final clause which emphasizes that this is how the commandment of God made the quality of sin even worse: "sin... through the commandment might become sinful beyond measure" (7:13, ἵνα γένηται καθ' ὑπερβολὴν ἁμαρτωλὸς ἡ ἁμαρτία διὰ τῆς ἐντολῆς).[55]

Räisänen's explanation leads in another direction, however, and one that gives a rather existential impression. He speaks solely of the willingness of an individual to transgress against the commandment. We have pointed out above that this is not Paul's intention in this chapter. He is dealing with the problem of Israel's relation to the law, instead. A subjective interpretation is in this case insufficient. The point of departure in the presentation of Paul, in a symbolic way, must be the Genesis story of Adam in the Garden of Eden. There the commandment of God revives sin when it exposes it. As regards Israel, this recurred at Sinai, when the Law of God was given to the people. At that

---

[52] When pondering on the possible positive meaning of the law, all Räisänen finds is once again a contradiction. "There are thus two lines of thought in Paul. According to one, the possibility that the law could lead to life is excluded already in principle. According to the other, that possibility is shown to be irrelevant merely on empirical grounds. Either God did not want the law to be a way to salvation, or the actual law did not suit that purpose and another means had to be provided. Clearly these two lines contradict each other." Räisänen, *Law*, 152. This quotation shows that Räisänen does not give any constructive definition of the essence of law at all.

[53] Räisänen, *Law*, 142.

[54] Dunn remarks that Paul consciously avoids the identification of sin and law. This would in fact lead to a rejection of the law in the manner of Marcionism. "As he rejected the equation between the law and sin so he refuses absolutely to accept that the law is to be blamed for death... The law may have condemned to death, but the real cause of death is *sin.*" Dunn, *Romans*, 403 (italics his).

[55] In this way already Käsemann, *Römer*, 188; cf. Stuhlmacher, *Römer*, 102; Moo, *Romans*, 479f.; concering a change in quality, see Dunn, *Romans*, 386-387.

moment sin revived "anew", as the verb ἀναζάω, taken literally, describes the event.[56]

This is why Paul's argumentation is in no sense "empirical". His interpretation is once again directed by the principle of paradoxical polarization. The law as to its essence is positive, but because of the essential sinfulness of the descendants of Adam it cannot produce what is good. This is why sin, which has been in the world ever since Adam, sprang to life in opposition to God when the commandment was given to Israel.[57]

When Paul then remarked that through the law sin became "sinful beyond measure" (7:13: ἵνα γένηται καθ' ὑπερβολὴν ἁμαρτωλὸς ἡ ἁμαρτία διὰ τῆς ἐντολῆς), he was merely emphasizing the same subject. Sin which was in this world becomes an actual problem in a juridical context.

In conclusion, we must state that in this section Paul does not teach that the law would actually produce sinful actions. He is speaking of a change in the quality of sin. There is a hermeneutical perspective behind his thinking, concerning the status of law in God's salvation history.[58] When the law enters the stage of world history it makes sin even more sinful. The law does not give birth to sin because the whole world after Adam has lived totally under the power of sin.

Sanders' problem concerning the relation between law and sin was of a different kind. He proposes that Paul gave two different interpretations concerning their relation. The first of these is in Romans 5, where the negative function of the law was a necessary condition for salvation history. In this section the relation of law and sin (transgression) is simple. Sin was seen as a transgression of God's law.[59]

In Romans 6, however, according to Sanders, Paul uses another kind of anthropology. The free and active man is no longer only tempted and tested by sin. He is now totally under the power of sin and he can escape sin only

---

[56] Dunn rightly pays attention to the Genesis story of the Garden of Eden but separates it then from the actual aim of Paul, i.e. from the definition of the relation of Israel and the law. Dunn, *Romans*, 383. The law of Sinai is taken up by Althaus, *Römer*, 75; van Dülmen, *Theologie*, 109-110; Moo, *NTS 32* (1986) 123f. Luz considers it possible to interpret the text by appealing to "I" as a personification of Israel, but finally chooses the identification with Adam, *Geschichtsverständnis*, 165-166.

[57] It is hardly necessary to point out that before Sinai sin was not totally powerless. See Dunn, *Romans*, 383. Paul is not speaking of the existence of sin but of the juridical status it has received.

[58] Cf. Moo, *NTS 32* (1986) 124; Luz, *Geschichtsverständnis*, 167.

[59] Sanders, *Law*, 73, 75.

through death. In this case the law could no longer be said to produce sin or to multiply transgressions, because the realm of sin was outside God's plan.[60]

According to Sanders, such a tension is perceptible in Romans 7. In 7:7-13 Paul still declares that the law is good and that it was meant to bring life. Its only problem was that it was used by a foreign power, i.e. sin (7:8, 11, 13). This is why law plays a negative role in God's plan of salvation. Later in section 7:14-25, according to Sanders, Paul had to alter the setting. There Paul regards the law merely as God's good will and connects the trespass solely to "another law", namely sin. In the "second line of thought... the law does not even provoke sin. Its 'fault', rather, is that it does not bear within itself the power to enable people to observe it."[61]

The problem of Sanders' explanation, as of Räisänen's, too, is especially that he treats the main concept of sin in a very abstract sense. He does not ponder on the essence of sin or its status in Pauline anthropology. In fact he states that in these contexts the very word 'sin' means for Paul merely a cosmic power, which has not been given an exact definition. Sanders' conception as regards the human possibilities of man differs crucially from the teaching of Paul. In the middle of his analysis he even remarks: "The human plight, without Christ, is so hopeless in this section that one wonders what happened to the doctrine that the creation was good."[62]

The problems of such a statement are evident. Our analysis of the first few chapter of Romans in the previous chapters of this book (especially chapter 7) has shown that Paul's hamartology depends heavily on the Genesis story of the Fall. For him, sin is the sin of Adam, and it continues its victorious progress in the lives of the contemporaries of Paul. The sin of the world fallen in Adam is not abstract, either. It can be described with all the detailed examples that Paul gives in Romans 1 and 2.[63]

The modern scholar is tempted to treat Paul's theology merely as an abstract systematic structure, in which Paul could add almost any concept insofar as it is convenient for his Christological argument. This is how Sanders in fact explains the way Paul ascribed a negative function to the law. It was negative merely on the ground that, after the appearance of Christ, the law could no

---

[60] Sanders, *Law*, 73. "*The law could no longer be said to produce sin or to multiply transgression as part of God's overall plan,* since *the realm of sin is now considered entirely outside that plan.*" (italics his).

[61] Sanders, *Law*, 74-75.

[62] Sanders, *Law*, 75.

[63] Sanders has naturally noted these sections, but he is content to conclude that " The statements of universal sinfulness are remarkably inconsistent." Sanders, *Law*, 35. By this remark he refers mainly to the discussion concerning Romans 2 and the problem as to whether the keeping of the law is possible in principle.

longer bring righteousness.[64] In a similar way Sanders thought that Paul had a "tendency" to alter his concept of universal sin on the account of his Christology.[65] With such ambivalent reasoning one is in real danger of assuming that, in "reality", sin was for Paul almost a secondary tool formed after the principle of Christology.[66]

It is evident that we need to remember the teaching of the Old Testament and the tradition of Second Temple Judaism.[67] Paul did not need to invent the Fall. The concept of sin already existed and he was able to teach hamartology by using Scriptural proof-texts and allusions. Such argumentation was further quite natural in Jewish theology, and we are familiar with it. This is why it was easily accepted by Paul's fellow-Jews.

The idea that sin was universal can be found in the Old Testament and it was common in Second Temple texts, as well. This has become evident in our analyses above.[68] In the theology of Paul it is a firm basis upon which he builds several themes. It is important as regards his anthropology, which in no sense changes between different "chapters" of Romans.[69] Paul's difference as regards Jewish theology is mainly in the fact that in Judaism sin was hardly ever considered to be as serious as in Paul. The reason for this was the synergistic nomism which we investigated in chapter 3.3.

In Paul's theology of predestination the universality of sin became highly important. His concept of sin is radical. When all the children of Adam were imprisoned by sin and left under judgment, all the basic factors of soteriology had to be altered. This is why we simply cannot investigate Paul's theology of law without noting that he himself firmly believed in the Fall of Adam.

As a summary we may propose some reservations with regard to the suggestions made in recent scholarship. The idea that the law as such could produce sin, needs to be defined more precisely. Paul did not think that the law as to its essence would have produced sin. This would infer an argument ad

---

[64] Sanders, *Law,* 73: "Paul was in a dilemma, since he thought, as a good Jew, that God gave the law, while he also was convinced, on the basis of the revelation of Christ to him, that the law could not produce righteousness. We saw that he responded to the dilemma by giving the law a negative role in God's plan of salvation."

[65] Sanders, *Law,* 72: "his general tendency... was to universalize the human plight."

[66] This kind of view can also be found in Räisänen: "If what I have said before is on the right track, it follows that this picture represents a radicalization in retrospect, triggered off by Paul's Christological conviction. He does not consistently hold that man apart from Christ is a helpless victim of sin, and this very inconsistency betrays the secondary character of the radicalism." Räisänen, *Law,* 150.

[67] Here we may refer to the analysis made in chapter 4.

[68] Cf. Bar. 2:6-7; 1QS XI; 1 Enoch 98:10; 4 Ezra 7:117-118; TLev. 18:7-11.

[69] We should not forget that Paul never dictated "chapters".

absurdum. God's commandment as such naturally does not command men to sin, i.e. to transgress the will of God. As to its essence the law is good and just   (Rom. 7:12; cf. 13:8-10). It is obvious, however, that in Pauline soteriology the law has a negative function. The law does something that is destructive as regards the salvation of man. In this sense we must accept the basic problem of Paul's concept of the law that has been highlighted by Sanders and others: even though the law was given to produce life, it was not able to produce righteousness. Instead it confirmed the guilt that comes from transgression. In the context of his theology of justification Paul's concept of the sinfulness of man was sharpened further still. He was ready to make such a radical polarization that righteousness from the law itself became sin.

10.3. Avodat Israel and the "works of the law"

The idea of paradoxicality can be detected further in another area, namely that of Paul's negative attitude towards the "works of the law".[70] As regards Jewish tradition, we are dealing with a positive term denoting a life of obedience in accordance with the will of God. In the theology of Paul, however, this term becomes utterly negative in respect of salvation. There is evident paradoxicality in the use of the term. This is a result of Paul's soteriology and therefore this example, too, is closely connected with the theology of predestination.

In the writings of Paul this question becomes acute, for example in Romans 3: "For no human being will be justified in his sight by works of the law (ἐξ ἔργων νόμου οὐ δικαιωθήσεται πᾶσα σάρξ, Rom. 3:20). Here "works of the law" is a key term in Paul's debate with his hypothetical opponents. There is little doubt that soteriology is what is at issue. Paul certainly believed that for some people the works of law meant a way to righteousness. This idea is significant only if it met with some kind of relevant opposition.

This example brings us to the very heart of modern discussion concerning Paul's theology. Did Jewish theologians in Paul's time use the term "works of the law" in the meaning of attaining righteousness, or is Paul intentionally distorting their beliefs when confronting them? The discussion has been coloured by a strong tension between Judaism and Christianity – or by a denial of that tension. In most cases the true identity of both of these religions has been lost behind attacks and counter-attacks by different scholars.[71]

As we have noted earlier, Paul has been pictured as a passionate opponent of

---

[70] As the title reveals, I shall refer below to Jewish service to God, of which I have, in most cases, chosen to use the term *Avodat Israel* in the popular form still in use in the Siddur, the Jewish prayer-book. In some cases, whenever it seems appropriate, I use the proper transliteration, ^cabodah.

[71] The same problem has been noted, e.g., by Snodgrass, *JSNT 32* (1988) 98.

Jewish legalism. In several modern interpretations, on the other hand, there seems to be little difference between Paul and Jewish soteriology, as regards the works of the law. In traditional exegesis the works of the law were an example of Jewish self-righteousness. Paul was believed to oppose the pertinent Jewish striving after self-righteousness by works of the law.

This interpretation was criticised by Sanders, who thought that Paul's term "works of the law" denoted life according to the law precisely in the context of covenantal nomism. This resulted in a covenantal interpretation: the abandoning of the works of the law was in fact a criticism of the old covenant and the previous election of Israel.[72] This is why in his writings Paul never really attacked Jewish legalism, but rather covenantal soteriology in its entirety.[73] Paul denied that works could be a condition for "getting in" the new covenant.[74]

It is quite obvious that both of these interpretations must have had some kind of evidence to back up their assertions. There is no doubt a perceptible tension between Paul and Jewish or Jewish-Christian theologians. On the other hand, Paul's attack was not concerned merely with a problem of petty legalism. These were the preliminary explanations, but we must not be content with them. The question concerning the law is evidently a more difficult one, and it cannot be answered simply by replacing the old controversy with a new concept of mainstream nomism.

Sanders' solution, for example, was one of reaction. He himself thought that his approach revealed the real nature of the theology of Second Temple Judaism. He was searching after the "pattern of religion" of Judaism. This legitimate purpose was endangered, though, because at the same time he was intentionally launching an attack on earlier German scholarship.[75]

J. Dunn attempted to solve the problems raised by his predecessors by concentrating on the social dimensions of the two religions. He thinks that the

---

[72] On the discussion, see Sanders, *Law,* 46-47; cf. the excursus concerning the theory of covenantal nomism, above.

[73] As Lührmann has noted, this kind of explanation is similar to the interpretation of Bultmann and his school. Recent debate gives the impression that Paul became aware of the law as a problem only when he encountered Jewish-Christian missionaries, e.g. in Galatia. See Lührmann, *JSNT 36* (1989) 76; against Hübner, *Law,* and Räisänen, *Law.* Such assertions would be logical only if we were to separate Paul totally from Palestinian Judaism and accept the narrow concept of Hellenistic Judaism proposed by Bultmann.

[74] Sanders, *Law,* 105.

[75] Moule has in fact criticised Sanders for misunderstanding Jewish theology: "I am asking whether 'covenantal nomism' itself is so far from implicit 'legalism'. Moule, *Jesus, Judaism, and Paul,* 48.

works of law were a boundary between Judaism and other systems of belief.[76] By adopting this kind of approach he hoped to pass over the problematic and prejudiced controversy of earlier scholarship. New dimensions are indeed necessary in the study of this difficult theme. Research should be undertaken with an attitude of respect towards the respective religions.

As a first step we may conclude that in the earlier debate concerning the meaning of the "works of the law" scholars did discover some new insights, but the discussion was biassed by a controversy of too intense a nature as to provide a balanced treatment of the question. We have learnt something, though. Judaism cannot be defined as a religion of petty legalism. On the other hand, Paul is hardly a simple covenantal nomist, who did not really mean what he said about the law – or did not even know what the works of the law meant for Israel. We require a contextual analysis which maintains a respectful attitude towards both Jewish theology and Christian teaching. This is why we first need to evaluate the explanation given by Dunn. Could the problem be of a social nature?

Dunn, who saw the evident importance of the law for Israel, was not satisfied with Sanders' explanation. He desired to find a new status for the "works of the law" in the Jewish concept of salvation. He thought that in Jewish theology the law began to express the *distinctiveness* of Israel as the "chosen people". "In sociological terms the law functioned as an 'identity marker' and 'boundary', reinforcing Israel's sense of distinctiveness and distinguishing Israel from the surrounding nations."[77] This distinctiveness also created the privileged position of the people and resulted in pride in the law as the mark of God's special favour towards Israel.[78]

According to Dunn, the sociological point of view helps us to understand how election and covenantal nomism were realized in religious behaviour and rituals. Within covenantal nomism the Jews performed several acts (identity markers) which ensured their religious identity. These were circumcision, the dietary laws and the Sabbath. Dunn thinks that it was precisely these acts which Paul called the "works of the law".[79] Paul's criticism of the law would

---

[76] The contribution of Dunn has been published in his book *Jesus, Paul and the Law*, which is a compilation of essays on the theme. For his assessment of the discussion in general, see the Introduction, pp. 1ff.

[77] Dunn, *Romans*, lxix; cf. Snodgrass, *JSNT 32* (1988) 102.

[78] Dunn, *Romans*, lxx.

[79] Dunn, *Law*, 194, 196. It is interesting to note that later on this view was accepted by Sanders, too. He makes particular mention of circumcision, the dietary laws and the Sabbath, and remarks that they "created a social distinction between Jews and other races in the Greco-Roman world." Sanders, *Law*, 101-102. He does not here refer to Dunn, though.

thus concern only the social function of the law.[80] This explanation is problematic because in the text of Paul the law clearly has a wider meaning and a greater number of functions.[81]

Paul's main endeavour, thought Dunn, was to "free both promise and law for a wider range of recipients, freed from ethnic constraints which he saw to be narrowing the grace of God."[82] Thus the most important part of God's salvation was passed over – Christ himself. The actual antithesis, according to Dunn, was not between covenantal nomism and faith in Christ.[83] Paul's point was that justification by works of law and justification by faith are antithetical.[84] This kind of "novelty" in the antithesis was based on Dunn's idea that the works of law (identity markers) were parallelled with faith as a means of realizing covenantal nomism. This is why faith in Christ was the opposite of circumcision and the ritual law.

In Romans 2, according to Dunn, Paul was directly criticizing details of the Jewish concept of covenantal nomism. This concerned features such as the law as an emblem of nationalistic zeal, the law as a boundary-marking ritual and circumcision as a sign of national distinctiveness. In other parts of Romans, however, Paul criticizes the narrow and distorted misuse of the law (Rom. 3:27-31; 7:14-25; 9:30-10:4).[85] Here Dunn attempted to find a new application for the theory of covenantal nomism in the interpretation of the theology of Paul. Several scholars had come to the conclusion that there was inconsistency in Paul's concept of the law.[86] Dunn, however, concluded that for Paul the concept of law was a central factor and an integrating strand in soteriology. It justified the Christological re-interpretation of Jewish covenantal nomism.[87]

---

[80] Dunn, *Law*, 224. According to Dunn, this was also a solution to the problem why Paul treated the law in one case negatively and in some other cases positively.

[81] The critique by Westerholm of Dunn's explanation of the "works of the law" is worth considering. Paul does not mention works of the law only when speaking about the visible features of the covenant. To Paul the works of the law are constantly considered in the context of God's commands. Westerholm, *Law*, 118. Even though Dunn later defined his assertions with greater precision, declaring that the entire law of Moses is to be considered when analyzing the works of the law, his emphasis on the social function of the law seems to be too pronounced. See Dunn, *Law*, 238.

[82] Dunn, *Romans*, lxxi-lxxii.

[83] Dunn, *Law*, 196. This was his criticism of Sanders' assertion; see also Sanders, *Paul*, 551-552.

[84] Dunn, *Law*, 195.

[85] Dunn, *Romans*, lxxii.

[86] Here see especially Räisänen, *Law*, 210. Räisänen has been one of the most active participants in this debate.

[87] Dunn, *Romans*, lxxii.

Dunn was no doubt on the right track when he emphasized that Paul renewed and re-interpreted the themes of Jewish covenantal theology. Even Paul's terminology reveals this endeavour. The weakness of Dunn's approach, however, is in his narrowing of Paul's theology of the law.[88] Dunn cannot, or at least does not, explain the fact that Paul also uses the law when he speaks of the judgment of God. This is why the concept of sin does not receive its proper place in his analysis of the function of the law. For Dunn the soteriology of Paul is merely a theology of renewal of the covenant.[89]

The advantage of Dunn's approach was that he was able to suggest a relevant context for the term "works of the law" within Jewish theology. He developed his explanation by endeavouring to imagine how Jewish theologians treated the theme of obedience to the law in the cases which Paul was criticizing. Such a point of view is necessary in any attempt to expound the identity of Jewish faith.

There remains an interesting question to be asked: where did Dunn find this idea about the social nature of the "identity markers"? He himself mentions two scholars, E. Lohmeyer and J. B. Tyson, who wrote about the connection between the cultic practices of the Old Testament and the important term "works of the law". When we turn to investigate the backgrounds of the term "works of the law" and the themes of work and service in the Old Testament, we are led to an interesting new field where the social aspect is but one small detail in a wide spectrum of cultic service.

Jewish identity involved more than a kind of covenantal nomism. It was centred on an obedient 'service of the law' ("Dienst des Gesetzes")[90] or "nomistic service".[91] In our analysis we must remember that in the Old Testament all kinds of service to God are described as "work" or "acts/works". The task of fulfilling God's will was the "work of Israel", *Avodat Israel,* to which the people of Israel had been elected from among all peoples.

In the Old Testament the service of priests in the Tabernacle was designated in this way, in Exodus (MT עבדה, LXX ἔργα τῆς σκηνῆς, ἔργα τῆς κατασκευῆς).[92] In the book of Joshua this work (עבדה) of Israel, service to God in the Tabernacle, testified to the people's will to serve God and thus secured their relationship to the Lord (Joshua 22:27).

---

[88] For a similar criticism of Sanders, see Schreiner, *NovT 33* (1991) 226.

[89] In this sense the notions and criticism presented by Westerholm are quite valid. Westerholm, *Law,* 118-120. 148-149. Cf. the detailed analysis by Hübner, *Werke,* 127ff.

[90] Lohmeyer, *Probleme,* 33-74; 67.

[91] A term used by Tyson, *JBL 92* (1973) 424-425, following Lohmeyer.

[92] Ex. 35:21, 24. See Kaiser, *Theological Wordbook* (1980) § 1553; Hahn, *TBLNT* (1979) 1387.

This service was not a task restricted to the priests, however. It was not merely an ordinance concerning service in the Tabernacle. In the story about the first Passover God commands "this work/rite/service" (עבדה)", i.e. the Passover meal, as an ordinance which Jewish families should obey "for ever".[93]

According to Lohmeyer, there is a connection between "work" and *Torah*. When God commanded the service as a work for Israel, he actually gave the people the command which became the law, i.e. the law of Moses in the books of Moses. God's command was the *Torah*, which Israel was to obey. In this way the "work" of Israel was identified with the law.[94] In practice, the work (עבדה) meant the fulfilling of the precepts of the law of Moses.[95]

This kind of thinking is evident in several Jewish texts from the Second Temple period. Already in sapiential literature the works of men are identified with obedience to the law. In most cases the writers denounce wrong deeds, which are bound to be subject to the judgment of God. For example, the writer of the Wisdom of Solomon warns kings whose works (ἔργα) will be tested according to their willingness to obey the law   (Wisd. 6:3-4; cf. 12:4, 19; Sirach 10:6; 11:20-21; 15:19). According to Sirach, the judgment of God will concern precisely the "works" of men (16:12). In the Wisdom of Solomon the law is, moreover, the wisdom of God, and the dedicated pious ones choose its works (ἔργα, Wisd. 8:4).[96]

In the *Testaments of the Twelve Patriarchs*, too, the Testament of Levi parallels obedience to the law with work, the opposite of which are the works of Beliar: "Choose for yourselves light or darkness, the Law of the Lord or the works (ἔργα) of Beliar'. And his sons replied, 'Before the Lord we will live according to his Law'" (TLev. 19:1,2).

The work of Israel was the keeping of the law, and this, naturally, was one

---

[93] Ex. 12:24-26.

[94] Lohmeyer, *Probleme,* 39. This identification is only natural, because the content of the *Avodat Israel* is the *Torah* itself.

[95] Here Tyson directed the interpretation by emphasizing merely those issues which were mentioned by Paul (in Galatians). He mentioned circumcision and the dietary laws and suggested that Paul associated only these with nomistic service. Tyson, *JBL 92* (1973) 430-431. This view was later adopted by Dunn, as we have seen. Tyson's identification is a hasty one, however, and clearly erroneous. These are not the only important characteristics of (Jewish) nomistic service.

[96] Kaiser has noted that the Hebrew word עבדה does not appear in ethical teaching in Wisdom literature. Kaiser, *Theological Wordbook* (1980) § 1553. In Greek texts the case is quite the opposite with the word ἔργα. It is directly identified with obedience to God's precepts.

of the main themes in Second Temple sapiential theology in general.[97] The admonition to such obedience was given in a good synergistic sense typical of this sapiential tradition.[98] So the choice between the works of the law and the works of Beliar is, in TLev. too, a choice of a person's own free will and a choice one is obliged to make. In the Testament of Benjamin, in turn, the good works of a devout man are praised as an example of a life lived according to God's will:

"If you continue to do good, even the unclean spirits will flee from you and wild animals will fear you. For where someone has within himself respect for good works (φόβος ἀγαθῶν ἔργων) and has light in the understanding, darkness will slink away from that person" (TBenj. 5:2,3).

In Jewish theology the concept of righteousness according to works is thus based on the Old Testament. In the theology of the Second Temple period, the proper context for this kind of theology was the problem of theodicy, which provides an interesting additional feature for one's analysis of the question. Examples from the *Psalms of Solomon* prove this affirmation. In PsSol. 9 the writer first mourns the horrors of exile, but at the same time he praises God for his just judgments. Israel has suffered because of her sins, because no sinner can avoid God's judgment (PsSol. 9:3). In this psalm, too, the theological solution of the writer follows a synergistic concept of the meaning of the law.[99]

The subject of reconciliation is naturally God himself, but it is the task of men to ensure this grace with their good works. "Our works [ἔργα] (are) in the choosing and power of our souls, to do right and wrong in the works of our hands, and in your righteousness you oversee human beings" (PsSol. 9:4). Obedience to the law surely brings life and salvation:[100] "The one who does what is right saves up life for himself with the Lord" (9:5).

---

[97] See e.g. Sirach 15:16-17; 21:1-6; Wisd. 6:17-19; cf. 1 Macc. 2:49-54.

[98] E.g. Sirach 15:14-15; 17:6-7. For the synergistic tradition see Maier, *Mensch und freier Wille*, 93-94; Skehan - DiLella, *Ben Sira*, 271; Laato, *Paulus*, 83, 91.

[99] Sanders, who explains this passage in line with his theory of covenantal nomism, has rightly emphasized that there is a belief in mercy in the soteriology of the writer. His problem is that he ignores the synergistic clauses in the text and mishandles the thought of the writer: "When speaking of one's own treatment by God... one would hesitate to attribute good treatment by God to one's own merit." Sanders, *Paul*, 395. The information in verse 4 is quite the opposite. Winninge attempted to bypass the problem of free will by saying that the grace of God "came first". Winninge, *Sinners and the Righteous*, 74-75. Moreover, he has not recognized the synergistic nature of this psalm.

[100] Seifrid thinks that this text is the sign of a new tension between individualism and covenantal theology. "The conception of divine righteousness as a *iustitia distributiva* introduces a strong element of individualism and universalism into the soteriology of the Pss. Sol. Thus the destiny of the individual can be said to be contingent upon behavior, and not merely membership in the nation." Seifrid, *Justification*, 119-120.

After these examples it is easy to say that in Jewish theology obedience to *Torah* was described as "working", as fulfilling the precepts of the Lord. This is evident when we examine the Septuagint and Greek texts from the Second Temple period. The same kind of theology and terminology can be found in Hebrew and Jewish Aramaic texts, as well. This is most clearly demonstrated by the manuscripts from Qumran.

We must remember that at Qumran, too, the term מעשי תורה – "works of law" – appeared in the context of the proper application of the law in the life of the pious. This belief was based on the Scriptures. In the Old Testament, as well, the law is occasionally called works which the people were required to perform (המעשה).[101]

Obedience to the law was naturally an inseparable part of the identity of the Dead Sea Sect. Even the existence of the group was justified with promises from the Old Testament and the promises of God himself, as we have learnt above in chapter 5.[102] The bold, modernizing interpretation of these promises led to the idea that the sect was a new temple replacing the Temple in Jerusalem.[103]

There was a pre-condition for salvation in the community of Qumran: commitment to the law of Moses. Every new member was examined especially in this respect.[104] Perfect obedience had its blessing, too. It resulted in atonement and righteousness for the members of the assembly.[105]

This kind of trust in salvation can be seen in the pesher known as Florilegium. There the existence of the community and the fulfilling of the works of the law are interpreted as fulfilments of God's promises.[106]

"He has commanded that a Sanctuary of men be built for Himself, that there they may send up, like the smoke of incense, the works of Law (מעשי תורה)" (4QFlor. 1, 6-7).

Among the texts of Qumran there is also an interesting fragment of a letter, 4QMMT, which is believed to be a letter to the "Wicked Priest" of the

---

[101] "You shall teach them the statutes and the decisions, and make them know the way in which they must walk and what they must *do*." Ex. 18:20.

[102] This concerns the origin of the sect. The first members of the assembly had come from the Jerusalem Temple itself, following a conflict of a serious nature. A few devout priests had fled into the desert in order to assure the survival of the obedient "remnant" of Israel at the time of apostasy. Cross, *Qumran*, 100 ff.; Milik, *Discovery*, 44ff.

[103] See especially Gärtner, *Temple*, 4ff.; Cross, *Qumran*, 118.

[104] 1QS V,8-10. There is an interesting tension in the sect between the concept of predestination and the demand of obedience. See e.g. Hengel, *Judentum*, 397-402.

[105] 1QS VIII, 1-5. See Garnet, *Salvation*, 59-60; Gärtner, *Temple*, 20-21; Klinzing, *Umdeutung*, 105.

[106] See Schreiner, *NovT 33* (1991) 230.

Jerusalem Temple. In this document the reader is reminded of proper service of God (in the Temple) and of a proper notion of the precepts of the *Torah*. When the "works of the law" (מעשׂי התורה) are duly performed, the welfare of the ruler and his people is assured (4QMMT c, 27; b, 2ff.).[107]

This text is evidently in a central position when we attempt to understand the origins of the Qumran community. Some scholars think that the MMT was a letter sent by the Teacher of Righteousness to the Hasmonean ruler, probably Jonathan.[108] Fragments of several copies were found in the caves. This does not, however, mean that it was a text written merely for didactic purposes in the community, because the document has all the characteristics of a letter.

4QMMT contains comments on a number of themes which were undoubtedly of significance for Jewish priests. It begins with a religious calendar, which is identical with the Essene solar calendar. This is followed by comments on the holiness of certain sacrifices. The main purpose of these comments seems to be the guarding of the ritual purity of priestly ceremonies. These comments were not made in a light-minded manner, but are accompanied by warnings of the wrath of God. For the writer of the letter, Old Testament history is full of examples of the horrific fate of apostate priests and kings.

The "works of the law" which are mentioned concern those interpretations of the *Torah* which were important for the protesting priests – and presumably for the Teacher of Righteousness himself. They were factors in the separation between the Qumran priests and the priests of the Temple. This is why it is possible to reach a conclusion as to the significance of the works of the law for the rebellious priests. For them it was a matter of being obedient to the word of God. Works of the law signified perfect obedience to and fulfilment of the precepts of the *Torah*. In MMT the ritual purity of the priests was considered to be of particular importance. This, of course, was of vital consequence as regards the service in the Temple.

Because the works of the law fulfilled the precepts of the law of Moses, they were a guide to the perfect life. As we read the texts of the community we see that this obedience to law produces righteousness. And as we have seen above, the obedience of the leaders of the sect even produced atonement for the sins of the members of the community.

---

[107] VanderKam, *Dead Sea Scrolls,* 60; cf. Stuhlmacher, *Theologie,* 260. For the background of the term, see Qimron - Strugnell, *DJD X,* 139.

[108] In the Qumran texts we can find a hint concerning the existence of a letter of this kind. In the commentary on Psalm 37 it is mentioned that the Teacher of Righteousness sent a note to the Wicked Priest. This resulted in serious conflict between the two, and the Wicked Priest attempted to kill the Teacher of Righteousness. This short episode has often been left without proper evaluation. The nature of the text as a letter (to a ruler) is discussed in Qimron - Strugnell, *DJD X,* 113-114, 117-118.

The Qumran texts show us that the idea of the *Avodat Israel* was expressed as the demand of a right observance of "works of the law". So it was not only the Greek-speaking Jewish community which identified obedience to the law with "works". This was also done in Hebrew-speaking Israel, and above all in Temple circles, where the devout Essene priests were in conflict with the High Priest.

It is easy to see that the "works of the law" were not merely "identity markers" for devout Jews. The *Avodat Israel* concerned the whole *Torah* and this is why it needs to be borne in mind when defining the term. It contained all the precepts of the *Torah*. If any of these was called into question, devout theologians initiated a debate which might – in some cases – lead to extreme consequences.[109]

It is quite evident that before becoming a Messianic believer, Saul the Pharisee had laboured with the *Avodat Israel* in his own search for the devout life. The keeping of the law must have been the principal task of his life, as it had been to the writers of the Psalms of Solomon and the devout covenanters of Qumran.

Such an endeavour can still be seen in Paul's letters. He often writes of his intentions before his conversion. He was a "Hebrew born of Hebrews; as to the Law a Pharisee, as to zeal a persecutor of the church, as to righteousness under the law blameless" (Phil. 3:5-6). In this context the righteousness which is connected with law is most clearly the *Avodat Israel*. It is the righteousness which Saul had sought within his Jewish tradition and following his honoured teachers.[110] Keeping the law had been easy for him (κατὰ δικαιοσύνην τὴν ἐν νόμῳ γενόμενος ἄμεμπτος) and it had resulted in a good life.[111]

Saul's "zeal" does not imply that he had been a severe legalist in his relationship with God. Naturally the grace of God was provided for all those who followed the law wholeheartedly. Saul's zeal meant primarily that he had

---

[109] In scholarship there is a clear trend of development between the ideas of Lohmeyer, Tyson, Dunn, Sanders and Snodgrass. (See Snodgrass, *JSNT 32* (1988) 102.) In this tradition the notions of Lohmeyer have been interpreted following an ethnocentric principle (the identity markers). This has further led to a juxtaposition of the alleged Jewish concept and Paul's theology of participation in Christ. Snodgrass, *JSNT 32* (1988) 98. In my view this explanation has weaknesses concerning both the nature of Jewish nomism and Paul's soteriology.

[110] See especially Gal. 1:14: "I advanced in Judaism beyond many of my own age... so extremely zealous was I for the traditions of my fathers."

[111] As we noted above, according to Lührmann, the study of Paul has been strongly affected by the 'history of religions' school and especially by Bultmann, who located Paul almost totally in the sphere of Hellenistic Judaism. In this explanation Paul's Palestinian background was neglected and his understanding of the law was treated in contrast with "Palestinian" Judaism and Jewish Christianity. Lührmann, *JSNT 36* (1989) 75-76.

been proud of the law – as any devout Jew would be – and he would have done almost anything for the protection of the will of God.[112]

This attitude resulted in what was later to become the most difficult trauma experienced by Paul the Christian. In his *ͨabodah* he had been zealous in the manner of the Maccabaean warriors mentioned earlier (1 Macc. 2:49-54). He had been ready to fight till the bitter end – and became a persecutor of the church (κατὰ ζῆλος διώκων τὴν ἐκκλησίαν, Phil. 3:6; cf. Gal. 1:13). Defending the law was the highest possible form of the *Avodat Israel*. It was "zeal" in the footsteps of Phinehas, the son of Aaron, who killed apostates in the wilderness and saved Israel from the wrath of God.[113]

All of these examples show us that the law had been especially important to Saul. But what about the content of the law? Was Saul interested in the cultic service or perhaps even in the aspect of a social boundary? What kind of law did he defend? And what did he maintain when he seemingly rejected the law upon becoming a follower of Jesus?

There has been a long tradition in scholarship that the law which Saul talked about – i.e. the *Avodat Israel* we are now analysing – was primarily the cultic law of Moses. In soteriology the ritual law and the moral law were separated from each other and a distinction was made between them.[114] The moral law was considered to be of continued validity in the theology of Paul, but the ritual law was explained as having been re-interpreted in a new eschatological situation.[115] This was seen as the reason for the rejection of circumcision and the laws of purity in the New Covenant. They were not despised, but they did not seem to have any soteriological value after Easter. [116]

This discussion very evidently leads us astray. According to both the Jewish identity and the soteriology of Paul, the main purpose of the whole law is to maintain a good relationship with God – and only after that with one's fellow men. "Loving one's neighbour" is only a secondary result of that primary purpose. Transgressions are primarily offences against God, even though they at the same time hurt our neighbours. This is why the purpose of the moral law is primarily religious, not social. This should not be confused with the fact that

---

[112] Cf. Lührmann, *JSNT 36* (1989) 77; Donaldson, *CBQ 51* (1989) 672-673.

[113] See Num. 25:13; Ps. 106:30; Sirach 46:23-24. This "zeal" and model was very important to both the devout covenanters of Qumran and the Zealots in the time of Jesus. See Hengel, *Zealots,* 149-150; Garnet, *Salvation,* 59-60.

[114] See the discussion at the beginning of chapter 10.

[115] On the discussion concerning the Calvinist tradition, see Martin, *Christ and the Law,* 32.

[116] According to Dunn, who emphasized the social function of the law, the right understanding of the works of the law confirmed the traditional distinction between ritual law and moral law; Dunn, *Law,* 224.

the keeping of the law naturally has positive social consequences and that many prescripts are naturally written from the human point of view. The conclusion of all this is that in theology the nature of the so-called "moral" law was considered to be quite "ritual".

There are several passages in Paul where this kind of concept of law is explicit. In Gal. 3:10 Paul cites Deuteronomy in a very holistic sense: "Cursed be every one who does not abide by all things written in the book of the law, and do them." The book of the law prescribes the "work" for Israel and so the people must obey God in all that is written. If they do not do so, they cannot approach God.[117]

This analysis confirms the suggestion made in chapter 10, that in Jewish theology and in Paul there was no distinction made between ritual law and moral law. The law of Moses was a single entity and the *Avodat Israel* required wholehearted obedience to it.[118] Ritual prescripts had their own function, naturally, and in practice it was usually different from that of the moral code. A sharp distinction between, or even a separation of these two is, however, a result of the analytical Western mind and there is no reason for anything of this sort in the texts themselves.[119]

The observance of the works of the law, *Avodat Israel*, was based on a holistic view of life and service. Its purpose was the keeping of the law "in all that is written". This attitude can be detected in practically all Second Temple Jewish texts, from sapiential theology to the texts of Qumran.

An interesting and crucial question arising from this conclusion is: why then did the law pose problems for Paul? Why should the law come to an end? Why did the positive works of the law, which were the sign of honest obedience, become negative works which lead to self-righteousness? What justified the unexpected polarization made by Paul the Christian in his letters?

As we begin to look for answers to these questions, we must go back to the letter to the Romans, which was quoted at the beginning. In that context the term "works of the law" should now be interpreted according to the new concept of law which we have expounded here. "For no human being will be justified in his sight by works of the law" (Rom. 3:20). For Paul, the works of the law must have meant the service and righteousness which God had

---

[117] Cf. Gal. 5:3. "The logic of Paul's argument prohibits a neat distinction of moral and ceremonial law." Moo, *WTJ 45* (1983) 84.

[118] See e.g. Longenecker, *Paul*, 119-120, Schreiner, *Law*, 40; Moo, *WTJ 45* (1983) 82-84.

[119] Martin suggested that Paul made an implicit distinction between ritual law and moral law for pragmatic reasons. This interpretation does not do justice to Paul's soteriology, where Christ is the fulfilment and end of the law. See Martin, *Christ and the Law*, 33-34.

prescribed to his people. "No human being will be justified by *Avodat Israel*."
This was the blasphemous claim made by Paul.

This means that we must not use the "works of the law" as a philosophical
term which would be merely an abstract symbol for the self-righteousness of
Israel. These works were works of obedience by which the Israelites were to
apply in practice all those precepts which God had given to Israel, and which
were to bring them life. This is why we must find another way to explain the
self-righteousness which Paul seems to be talking about.

From the point of view of Paul's predestinarian theology the question
whether the Jews regarded themselves as self-righteous legalists or not, is
rather secondary and irrelevant. Paul is constructing his soteriology on a
polarization which defines the nature of individual factors. Soteriology is
directed by a radicalized anthropology.[120] The assessment of the Avodat Israel
must be made in the context of predestinarian theology. This is why his
teaching concerning the works of the law is, as regards Jewish theology, quite
paradoxical.

The new polarization behind Paul's theology of law is perceptible also in his
way of opposing works of the law and saving faith. The term that he uses,
"works of the law", denotes obedience and service to the whole law of Moses.
This was a central part of Jewish identity, the Avodat Israel, the "work" of
Israel, and its aim was to serve God in everything that had been prescribed in
the law of Moses. Performing the works of the law was part of the synergistic
soteriology of Second Temple Judaism. On the other hand we must remember
that there was also a belief in God's grace and a confidence in God's covenant
prevailing in that faith. In the context of Paul's predestinarian theology,
however, the works of the law were identified with the old covenant which
could not be compared with salvation in Christ. This is why only Christ could
bring the salvation to which the law had pointed. In this new polarization the
works of the law became an antithesis to the true salvation prepared by God.

---

[120] Cf. Wilckens, *EKK Vorarbeiten 1*, 54.

§ 11 The Principle of "Counting as Loss" in Paul

In Paul's theology of predestination the principle of polarization is constantly applied to new cases. His teaching on the justification of man contains features in which the dynamics of the formation of his theology appear clearly. In these sections righteousness by faith and a Christocentric soteriology are set in opposition to the self-righteousness of corrupt man. This is why these examples reveal excellently how Paul applies the principle of paradoxical polarization to different details of his theology. Traditional Jewish dualism in soteriology was abandoned. God had given a new criterion for election. Paul called it righteousness by faith.

11.1. Abandoning the old religious identity (Gal. 2:15-16)

One of the most important features in Paul's theology of predestination was the altering of the previous dualism of salvation history. The radicalization of divine judgment had led him to polarize the field of God's saving acts in a new paradoxical way as regards the teachings of Jewish theology. The position of the Jews and the Gentiles was no longer regarded as different before God and in respect of the salvation he had accomplished.

In Galatians Paul makes a clear difference between the new salvation and the covenantal promises or previous election of God. Israel has possessed all the promises of God, but they alone are insufficient as regards eschatological hope. Salvation is tied up with justification. Proper righteousness is righteousness from Christ and this is what Paul sought in order to attain salvation (Gal. 2:15-16).

"We ourselves are Jews by birth and not Gentile sinners; yet we know that a person is justified not by the works of the law but through faith in Jesus Christ. And we have come to believe in Christ Jesus, so that we might be justified by faith in Christ, and not by doing the works of the law, because no one will be justified by the works of the law."

In this section Paul further gives his solution to the basic problem of salvation history. He opposes two interpretations concerning dualism in salvation history.[1] The teaching and faith of the Old Testament were naturally simple. Israel was the Chosen People before all other nations. The Gentiles were sinners and did not know the real God. This belief is evident in verse 15: "We

---

[1] The content of verses 15-21 has, after the rhetoric analysis of Betz, been usually explained according to the rules of the rhetoric of antiquity. The *narratio* at the beginning of the letter would in this case be followed by a *propositio*, where Paul would mention items on which he agrees with his opponents. Betz, *Galatians,* 114-116. Paul and his opponents in Jewish Christianity would thus agree on both the ethnic principle and the denial of Pharisaic soteriology.

ourselves are Jews by birth (φύσει Ἰουδαῖοι) and not Gentile sinners (ἐξ ἐθνῶν ἁμαρτωλοι)".[2]

This statement of Paul appeals to basic Jewish dualism as regards soteriology. Israel has always been the chosen people and the only people to whom God has revealed himself. Only this nation had a right relationship with God. Other nations worshipped idols. People from those nations were able to attain salvation only by entering Judaism as proselytes.[3]

Paul's new, paradoxical interpretation concerned this crucial point. Even though he himself was a Jew "by birth", he was no longer permitted to appeal to the covenantal promises of Israel. God had a plan in salvation history which was not fulfilled in the old covenant of Israel. God had chosen another way to salvation. Paul the Jew needed to believe in Christ in order to find justification. This is expressed by a final clause "so that we might be justified" (ἵνα δικαιωθῶμεν, v. 16).

This final clause reveals the principle of "counting as loss" in the thinking of Paul. Even though the term has now been borrowed from another context, it is characteristic of his teaching.[4] As a consequence of soteriological polarization, several such beliefs, positive in themselves, are now refuted.

Once again we find an antithesis between Jewish tradition and righteousness which comes from Christ. This is presented by introducing an ethnic principle and a consideration of the function of the law.[5] Paul's motive seems to be once again the concept of an unconditional, predestined judgment of God. Paul as a Jew had himself lived under the condemnation of God. This is why, in the new situation, he had to re-interpret his conception of the value of Jewish

---

[2] In fact the theme of law also concerns this subject, as Hahn has remarked. Hahn, *ZNW* 67 (1976) 59. The separation of the Jews from the Gentiles meant at the same time that the law did not mean anything to the latter. This is why everything that Paul here says about the law exclusively concerns Jews.

[3] As regards the Jewish assessment of the Gentiles, see R.N. Longenecker, *Galatians,* 83; Betz, *Galatians,* 115.

[4] See the analysis of Phil. 3:4-8 below.

[5] Schlier identifies the teaching of the opponents of Paul with the nomistic piety which is based on Jewish righteousness of the "works of law", and which can be detected in the Old Testament and Second Temple texts. Schlier, *Galater,* 55. According to Tyson, in turn, this section serves as a clear example of Paul's denial of all "nomistic service" as regards obedience to law, which was essential in Jewish piety. Tyson, *JBL 92* (1973) 426; cf. above, chapter 10.3.

tradition and the old promises.[6] This section contains above all a theology of righteousness. The word-group meaning 'righteousness' (δικ-) appears four times in verses 16-17.[7] This confirms our opinion that the abandoning of ethnocentricity is dependent on the concept of justification.

On the basis of predestination and the prescribed judgment of God Paul is certain that man cannot find righteousness by doing works of law (ἐξ ἔργων νόμου, v. 16). Obedience to the commandments of the law and zeal for the law were traditional Pharisaic virtues but they did not lead to proper righteousness. They cannot fulfil the promises concerning salvation. The promises of God are fulfilled solely in Christ and this is why the righteousness which Christ gives is the only way to salvation both for Jews and Gentiles.[8]

Paul's anthropological proof is exposed in the word "flesh", which is also here used as an expression for the basic reality of corrupt man. Paul exploits the double meaning of the word and tells that "all the world / all flesh" is under sin: "no one will be justified by the works of the law" (v. 16; ἐξ ἔργων νόμου οὐ δικαιωθήσεται πᾶσα σάρξ). Man who lives under the power of sin cannot find salvation by the works of the law.[9]

Paul's teaching in this section is thus similar to that of Romans later. As regards soteriology, there is no longer any difference between Jews and Greeks (Rom. 3:9, 22). The polarization has been changed at Easter.[10] This is why the Jews have to believe in Christ in the same manner as "Gentile

---

[6] Sanders is naturally right when he says that Paul radicalized his soteriology and his concept of sin only after encountering Christ. As a Jew, Paul had been zealous for the law because this had been the main element by which Judaism was separated from sinful Gentile nations. Sanders, *Paul,* 499. This notion of Sanders' is an evident concession, which is not quite compatible with his understanding of the nature of covenantal nomism. The connecting of nomism so clearly with sin and soteriology does not fit in well with his over-emphasized covenantalism. This problem will be treated later in chapter 14.1. In the footsteps of Sanders, Longenecker explains the passage by saying that here Paul opposes Judaism as a "Mosaic religious system". Longenecker, *Galatians,* 85.

[7] See e.g. Longenecker, *Galatians,* 84.

[8] If rhetorical analysis is allowed to dominate the whole interpretation of the section, this results in problems as regards the content. This has happened in the explanation by Longenecker, who all too often seeks after those elements which support the idea of Paul's agreement with Jewish Christianity. This purpose makes him, for example, translate the words "faith in Christ", in verse 16, with the words "the faithfulness of Jesus Christ". Longenecker, *Galatians,* 88. This interpretation is not dependent on Betz's rhetorical analysis, though, since Betz himself here emphasizes the object of faith (*fides quae creditur*). Betz, *Galatians,* 117.

[9] Flesh referring to all human beings here. For the quotation of Ps. 143:2 (LXX 142:2) see Burton, *Galatians,* 123-124.

[10] See above, chapter 7.3.

sinners", if they wish to find the salvation which God has provided. This is the only way to reach the righteousness of God.

In Pauline soteriology and in the concept of righteousness by faith there are strong dynamics in which we can detect two factors. On the one hand, the belief in a predestined judgment sets new conditions for the concept of righteousness. On the other hand, the belief that Christ brings salvation provides soteriology with a Christological basis. The final conclusion made of these two premises is the principle of "counting as loss". It is a principle which Paul uses in several sections when speaking of justification.

The relation between Paul's teaching and Judaism or Jewish Christianity has been considered somewhat problematic in modern scholarship.[11] Some scholars think that Paul here presents precisely those elements which separate him from Jewish Christianity.[12] One of the separating factors was the concept of the works of law – at least when these are defined as "identity markers" of Judaism.[13] In this case continuity has been found especially in the area of covenantal theology, and this continuity has been with Jewish theology. Justification, in this context, means in no sense an inauguration of something new (an initiatory act). It is rather a confirmation of the old covenant.[14]

This explanation has two weaknesses. Firstly, the works of law have been understood in too narrow a sense. Jewish nomism in the Second Temple period was holistic. It would be erroneous to separate some "markers" of the covenant from the unity of the law of Moses as an entity. This would in fact result in opposing them implicitly to each other.[15] Secondly, it is impossible to play down Paul's idea of abandoning ethnocentric soteriology. The new righteousness in Christ is, according to Paul, definitely the inauguration of a new reality. There is an evident discontinuity as regards the old covenant.[16]

In this section Paul evidently tries to find features in common between himself and the Jewish Christians who opposed him. Even his choice of words reveals this kind of aim. He wants to find a description of faith common to

---

[11] This discussion has grown on the basis of Sanders' theory of covenantal nomism, see especially Dunn, *Law*, 188ff., Räisänen, *Jesus, Paul and Torah*, 112ff., and Hübner, *Glaube und Eschatologie*, 123-133.

[12] Dunn suggests, against the theory of Betz, that in these verses we find disagreement instead of agreement. Paul is opposing Jewish Christians. Dunn, *Law*, 188.

[13] Dunn here repeats his theory of "identity markers". Dunn, *Law*, 191-192; cf. chapter 10.3. above.

[14] Dunn, *Law*, 190. He develops his interpretation so much that, on the grounds of covenantal theology, he eventually identifies justification by faith with Jewish soteriology. On this question Betz's interpretation was quite the contrary. Betz, *Galatians*, 119.

[15] The explanations of Dunn and his predecessors, such as Tyson have been analyzed critically above, in chapter 10.3.

[16] In this sense, for example, Räisänen's criticism of Dunn is appropriate. Räisänen, *Jesus, Paul and Torah*, 124; cf. Hübner, *Glaube und Eschatologie*, 127.

both him and his rivals: "Knowing that... even we have believed in Jesus..." (v. 16, AV; εἰδότες [δὲ] ὅτι... ἐπιστεύσαμεν)". The aorist tense emphasizes the birth of faith in Christ, and thus Paul wishes to remind his opponents of this and keep the discussion within the kingdom of salvation.[17]

Paul would hardly be Paul had he not at the same time desired to teach his opponents a lesson. It would be an exaggeration to say that this section is a document of unanimity.[18] One cannot understand the ideas of Paul without the hermeneutical perspective described above. Paul challenges his opponents to draw the right conclusions as to the new polarization which their own religion and principles of faith have laid before them.

In Galatians Paul uses his theology of predestination to justify his teaching concerning righteousness by faith. There was once a gulf between Jews and Gentiles, but now it was no longer to be found since all people must stand together before the judgment seat of God. Paul finds another polarization, instead. Jews, too, needed to believe in Jesus in order to find proper righteousness. Paul himself had done this and abandoned his previous hopes for the old Israel. The true Israel for him was now the assembly of the saved who had believed in Christ and in this way been brought within the sphere of God's saving acts.

11.2. Denying human efforts (Phil. 3:4-8)

Another section where Paul opposes his Jewish heritage with the righteousness which Christ brings, can be found in Philippians 3. Here Paul presents several details from his personal biography. He speaks of his Jewish background, which he is shamed of, as we know from other passages. Paul had the advantage of an exellent education and his status had accordingly been a prominent one in the Jewish community. This turned out to be a curse, as well, because he ended up persecuting the followers of Christ (cf. 1 Cor. 15:9; Gal. 1:13-14).

As regards the context of Paul's presentation, there is a similarity with that of the section of Galatians we have investigated above. Here, as well, Paul is most probably opposing Jewish-Christian preachers, who followed in his footsteps and taught another kind of soteriology.[19] This explains why Paul's

---

[17] At least in this respect the theory of Betz is justified.

[18] Dunn went even further than this, as we have see above. "Justification by faith, it would appear, is not a distinctively Christian teaching." Dunn, *Law,* 191.

[19] The section 3:1b-4:1, 8-9 has even been considered a separate letter due to its special nature. Here Paul would in this case be writing against his Jewish Christian opponents. See the discussion e.g. in Gnilka, *Philipperbrief,* 5-11, 184-185. The exclamation against "dogs" in verse 2 is extremely sharp.

answer resembles the one given in Galatians. After presenting his biography Paul once again mentions the promises of Israel and the hopes which had been attached to them:

"If anyone else has reason to be confident in the flesh, I have more: circumcised on the eighth day, a member of the people of Israel, of the tribe of Benjamin, a Hebrew born of Hebrews; as to the law, a Pharisee; as to zeal, a persecutor of the church; as to righteousness under the law, blameless" (3:4-6).

Paul's rhetoric is astonishing. Even though in other instances he emphasizes that no one can fulfil the law, he says here that as to righteousness he had been blameless. From a dogmatic perspective this would seem quite inconsistent with his general teaching.[20] From a rhetorical point of view Paul's statement becomes crucial, however, as regards his argumentation. He had possessed all the promises of Israel and been obedient to the law. In spite of this Paul had to seek salvation in Christ. He was not found publicly guilty of any sin. He would not face the judgment of God on the ground of transgressing Jewish tradition. In spite of all this his "own" righteousness was insufficient to bring salvation. God has chosen another way to salvation.[21]

Paul's description of his Jewish background corresponds to our view of the Jewish ideal of piety and the righteous life. The tradition of Jewish religion and obedient living which was analysed in the previous main chapter, i.e. the *Avodat Israel*, contained several of the features which are mentioned here.[22] Circumcision, ethnic priority and zeal for the law were prominent features of hasidic piety in the Second Temple period.[23]

Paul's argumentation is once again directed by his theology of predestination. The principle of paradoxical polarization leads him here to a denial and depreciation of his previous obedience and pious efforts. In the context of his theology of righteousness we have now a similar situation to the one we met previously in the context of nomism, when the works of law were considered.

---

[20] This is one of the sections which are referred to by Räisänen when he speaks of the inconsistency of Paul's teaching. Räisänen, *Law*, 106, 176.

[21] Lohmeyer is right when he says that Paul speaks here of human righteousness which can be achieved by ethical conduct, and not of perfect righteousness before God. Lohmeyer, *Philipper*, 130-131.

[22] Schreiner is right when he says that Dunn's interpretation is insufficient here. Paul goes beyond the mere listing of boundary markers. Schreiner, *Law*, 113.

[23] See above chapter 10.3. It is a little surprising that Sanders considers this the only section where Paul admits that the righteousness of law is a possible reality. On other occasions Paul usually says that the righteousness of law is not proper righteousness. His remark is surprising because it is not quite compatible with Sanders' theory. He presumably thinks that the righteousness which Paul means here was covenantal nomism. In this case the alleged covenantal nomism would be in strict opposition to righteousness by faith – but this is an explanation which in another instance Sanders denies. See Sanders, *Paul*, 505.

Avodat Israel must be re-assessed in the context of Paul's theology of predestination. It can no longer be regarded as a condition for proper piety.[24]

This principle of interpretation is quite radical as regards Jewish theology. The repudiation of the value of obedience to the law resulted in the "counting as loss" of piety, which as such should have been positive in the context of the old covenant. Paul had to repudiate the good in order to reach the perfect.[25]

One of the consequences of this new interpretation is a change in soteriological dualism. According to Paul, it, too, must be defined in a new way after Easter. Jewish tradition is insufficient. Paul himself cannot rely on his previous achievements. This is why he repudiates his previous obedience to the law and his good reputation: "Yet whatever gains I had, these I have come to regard as loss because of Christ (ταῦτα ἥγημαι διὰ τὸν Χριστὸν ζημίαν)"(3:7).[26]

The Christological motive in soteriology can be seen here clearly. Old hopes and previous tradition are now "loss" because of Christ. The literal meaning of this "loss" is harm done to someone.[27] Paul considered that his human efforts produced harm to him, because they led him in the wrong direction as regards salvation.[28]

Paradoxical polarisation is here so strong that it produced an actual predestination statement. Christ has *made* "everything" – i.e. Jewish piety – loss

---

[24] In this sense Paul's theology of righteousness is parallel to his theology of law.

[25] Sanders calls this a shift in dispensations, Sanders, *Law*, 140. This interpretation would agree with the theory of Dunn, as well. Gundry has criticized Sanders' interpretation by noting that Phil. 3:2-11 "climaxes with confidence in personal accomplishments". This is why Paul must be speaking of self-righteousness. "Zeal for the law was good, but not the self-righteousness that followed." Gundry, *Bib 66* (1985) 13-14. We must remember, however, the corrective remark of Thielman. The basic problem is not the self-righteous attitude but inadequate righteousness. Thielman, *Law*, 154-155.

[26] "But whatever was to my profit I now consider loss for the sake of Christ." (Phil 3:7, NIV; "counted loss for Christ", AV). Eichholz has rightly said that Paul here presents himself as an example of a converted Jew, whose Jewish conduct as such cannot be blamed: "Phil 3,4bff zugleich und primär ein *paradigmatischer* Text ist. Ich meine damit, dass Paulus sich selbst als Beispiel für die Begegnung des Juden mit Christus versteht. Er hat sich in Phil 4,4b-6 als den typischen Juden beschrieben, ja als den in jeder Weise integren Juden, dessen Judesein von keinem Juden sonst überboten werden kann." Eichholz, *Theologie*, 224.

[27] The lexical meaning of the word is above all "damage", see Bauer s.v. ζημία; cf. Liddell-Scott. The meaning of the respective verb contains the idea of actively producing damage, Bauer s.v. ζημιόω.

[28] Stumpff emphasizes the difference between objective content and a given significance. Paul denies the latter, i.e. the soteriological value of his merit. Stumpff, *ThWNT II* (1990) 892-893. Such a division may be useful in the context of traditional interpretation, but as regards Paul's radical soteriology it must not lead to a softening of the uncompromising denial of the value. On the opposition of merit and loss, see Schlier, *ThWNT III* (1990) 672.

(δι' ὃν τὰ πάντα ἐζημιώθην, v. 8), because real righteousness comes from another direction.[29] The polarisation is here similar to that in Paul's other letters. Only the term used for it is different.

In addition, the idea of paradoxicality can be easily detected in this section. Paul has above described his life as a pious Jew. This is why the polarization explicitly concerns the traditional Jewish concept of righteousness. Paul's predestinarian statement is here extremely paradoxical, since his conclusion is incomprehensible without a concept of strict predestination.

The statement in verse 8 is parallel to that of Romans 11:32, and one of the clearest predestinarian statements of Paul:

"Everything has been made loss through him" (Phil. 3:8).
"God has imprisoned all in disobedience" (Rom. 11:32).

Paul's argumentation behind his Christological soteriology has two sides to it. On the one hand, one must remember the Genesis story of the Fall and Paul's claim that all died in Adam. This is the background for the predestination of judgment. On the other hand, it was precisely the death and resurrection of the Son of God which justified strict predestination. All people have been imprisoned in disobedience, but simultaneously all righteousness in this world of sin has been made "loss" and even harm – because Christ has brought a perfect righteousness.

Paul constructed a complete salvation history around a simple core of reconciliation. His teaching here parallels that of Romans. Because Christ "was handed over to death for our trespasses", he was also "raised for our justification" (Rom. 4:25). In Philippians Paul desires to know the power of the resurrection of Christ and receive the righteousness which comes from him. This faith led to a hope and belief that Paul himself, too, would be resurrected. This would be the climax of eschatology for him personally.[30]

After finding the gospel of the work of Christ, Paul changed the views which he had accepted as a Jewish Pharisee and teacher. Because Christ had come, a zealous Jew, too, had to believe in him in order to attain salvation. This is emphasized once again by using a final clause. Paul is seeking after righteousness in Christ, so that he would "be found in him" (3:9; καὶ εὑρεθῶ ἐν αὐτῷ).

With the aid of final clauses Paul builds an antithesis between his previous

---

[29] Hawthorne explains this clause in a traditional way. Paul merely declared that he himself had lost everything. Hawthorne, *Philippians,* 138. In this case the purpose of the dynamic expression is ignored. The basic idea of this section is usually quite well explained in commentaries. Paul's emphasis is on the word "everything", and this brings the holistic interpretation to the fore. See e.g. Michael, *Philippians,* 146.

[30] Cf. Thielman, *Law,* 155.

life and the saving righteousness which Christ gives.[31] In such a scheme which
is governed by polarization, the righteousness that comes through faith in
Christ is unavoidably opposed to a righteousness of one's own that comes
from the works of law and a zeal for the law (μὴ ἔχων ἐμὴν δικαιοσύνην τὴν
ἐκ νόμου, v. 9b). Due to the power of sin and God's unconditional judgment
there is no room for a saving righteousness outside of Christ. This is why Paul
is searching after a righteousness given by God, which is righteousness
through faith in Christ (ἀλλὰ τὴν διὰ πίστεως Χριστοῦ, τὴν ἐκ θεοῦ
δικαιοσύνην ἐπὶ τῇ πίστει, v. 9c).[32]

This section is connected with Pauline soteriology in general by brief references to the Lordship of Jesus and his resurrection. When Paul mentions
knowing his "Lord" (τὸ ὑπερέχον τῆς γνώσεως Χριστοῦ Ἰησοῦ τοῦ κυρίου
μου, v. 8) he implicitly refers to confessing Christ as Lord, which is one of the
basics of faith (cf. Rom. 10:9). Resurrection power is a centre of both faith
and future hope (τοῦ γνῶναι αὐτὸν καὶ τὴν δύναμιν τῆς ἀναστάσεως
αὐτοῦ, Phil. 3:10). In Paul's theology this theme is essential both in baptismal
catechesis and in proclamation (cf. Rom. 6:3-5; 8:10-11; 10:8-10).

In Philippians Paul continues to underline the opposition between traditional
Jewish piety and righteousness by faith. This time Paul's own zeal for the law
becomes an example and point of departure for his argumentation. He is able to
present himself as a blameless representative of traditional Pharisaic Judaism.
This especially concerns obedience to the law of Moses. In that phase of his
life Paul/Saul must have solved the problem of theodicy in favour of his own
salvation. He was one of the righteous of Israel and had been fighting against
those who transgressed the traditions of the fathers. After conversion this

---

[31] Cf. Schreiner, *Law*, 113.

[32] We need to return to Sanders' suggestion that Paul was speaking of "dispensations"
here. First, he opposes the Mosaic dispensation to that of Paul. In Phil. 3 he sees proof for
the idea that Paul is merely offering another dispensation to replace the old one. Paul "does
not draw out the negative conclusion about the law by saying that it is a law which brings
only death. He continues, rather, by contrasting two righteousnesses. If he gains Christ, and
is found in him, he will have not his own righteousness, which was based on law, but
another righteousness, one which comes from God on the basis of faith in Christ... The only
thing that is wrong with the old righteousness seems to be that it is not the new one."
Sanders, *Law*, 140. Sanders is evidently on the right track when he says that Paul here
contrasts two kinds of righteousness. His heavy dependence on the idea of dispensations leads
him astray, however. It is somewhat astonishing that, after even describing the pessimistic
anthropology and hamartology of Paul, Sanders quickly shifts to quite another perspective
and treats the "Mosaic dispensation" as neutral in Paul. By reproducing the famous thesis of
his *Paul and Palestinian Judaism* he maintains that " the only thing that is wrong" with the
old dispensation is that it is not faith in Christ. In Paul's theology of predestination the
setting is quite the opposite. What is wrong with the old righteousness is that it is
insufficient before the judgment seat of God.

persecutor became a proclaimer of justification by faith, when he came to realize that divine predestination demanded the greatest sacrifice of them all: the life of the Son of God. As a result the principle of paradoxical polarization led him to deny the value of his previous righteousness. His previous merit became a loss to him, because it had prevented him from finding the true righteousness of God, that revealed in Christ.

11.3. Denying religious achievements (Rom. 3:27-28)

The third section where the influence of the theme of predestination is clearly seen in an explicit polarization of the theology of justification, is in Romans 3. Even though quite a long period of time had elapsed between the writing of Galatians and Romans, and years had passed since the sending of Philippians, Paul's teaching was still based on a rather unified theme. There is one great principle which induced Paul the Jewish Christian to conclude that righteousness by faith must be the only possible form of justification.

At the beginning of the chapter Paul had arrived at one of his most important conclusions and theses: there cannot be any difference between Jews and the Gentiles as regards salvation. All are under sin (3:9). This is why there can be but one basis for justification: the righteousness which God himself has elected and which he also presents to all those who believe, in and through the gospel of Christ (3:24).[33]

The antithesis is presented here in Paul by using new terminology. The law of Moses is opposed to the "law of faith". The law of faith has changed the traditional piety attached to Jewish identity. It has removed the only natural and reasonable argument from the righteousness of law, namely that of the pride of man in his blameless life. "Is there any reason for boasting?", asks Paul in 3:27. Modern translations of this section do not always follow the details of the text literally.

"Then what becomes of boasting? It is excluded. By what law? By that of works? No, but by the law of faith. For we hold that a person is justified by faith apart from works prescribed by the law" (Rom. 3:27-28).

The translation may give the impression of a superior boasting, but this is not the issue here. The object of Paul's question is simply traditional Jewish pride in the law (Ποῦ οὖν ἡ καύχησις;). This word belongs in the same semantic field with words denoting "rejoicing".[34] Even though there is no word for "zeal" in this section, Paul is evidently thinking of a traditional concept of law. This is why he is speaking of the "works of the law".

The word for boasting, καύχησις, it is true, appears in the Old Testament in

---

[33] See especially chapter 7.3.

[34] Cf. Bauer-Aland, s.v. καυχάομαι.

a negative sense in some cases. In those sections it describes the arrogant boasting of sinners (Hebrew *hithallêl,* Ps. 52:3/LXX 51:3; 94:3/LXX 93:3). Besides that, however, the term denotes with greater frequency the joy which the righteous experience in God (Ps. 5:12; 32:11/LXX 31:11; 89:18/LXX 88:18; the final doxology of the blessing of Moses, Deut. 33:29; and Jer. 17:14). Thus the "boasting" as rejoicing is an essential element of the positive identity of Israel.[35]

This positive pride is also attached to rejoicing about the law of God. This can be seen especially in Sirach, Ecclus. 39:8: "He will show the wisdom of what he has learned, and will glory in the law of the Lord's covenant (καὶ ἐν νόμῳ διαθήκης κυρίου καυχήσεται)." This kind of boasting/glorying cannot be identified with legalistic self-confidence, which has prevailed in the traditional explanation of Pauline texts. Pride in the law has to be understood in the context of Jewish synergism. The final object of boasting is always God himself.[36] In the context of synergism the "work" of Israel, *Avodat Israel,* is a source of constant joy for a pious Jew.

In the above text Paul once again opposes Jewish identity with Christ. The logic of the section is similar to that of Philippians. Here, too, Paul uses the principle of "counting as loss". Even blameless conduct of life and a perfect righteousness as regards human standards, i.e. the sapiential tradition and the aim of hasidic zeal, have lost their power. The predestination of judgment is final. This is why even justified pride in the law can no longer be regarded as a sign and proof of election. It is insufficient as regards eschatological salvation.[37]

There is an actual predestinarian statement in this section and it comprises a single word. Paul says that human possibilities, i.e. the righteousness by law has been totally excluded (ἐξεκλείσθη) as regards the attaining of salvation. Translations often need to expand the rhetorical answer of Paul in order to make a complete sentence. This is also true in English: "It is excluded." (3:27).

---

[35] See e.g. Hahn, *TBLNT II* (1979) 1052.

[36] Here we need to alter the traditional explanation. For example, Hahn thought that Jewish pride in the law was negative boasting and self-righteous pride based on one's ability to keep the law. Hahn, *TBLNT II* (1979) 1052; cf. Althaus, *Römer,* 35. In the Bultmannian tradition boasting has usually been explained as a false self-reliance, Bultmann, *ThWNT III* (1990) 649; Käsemann, *Römer,* 95; Hübner, *Law,* 116. Dunn's criticism of this explanation is quite justified, Dunn, *Romans,* 185.

[37] Paul's polarization concerns Jewish identity. Pride in the law was a positive attitude in the old covenant and its basic object was God himself. Pious Jews rejoiced in God's saving works and his good law. This is what Paul questioned in comparison with Christ. Cf. Michel, *Römer (1978),* 154-155, footnote 20. Cranfield too notes the positive significance of rejoicing but eventually he interprets the above-mentioned verse in line with the traditional opposition, *Romans,* 164, 219.

The verb ἐκκλείω means isolation and exclusion.[38] By using the aorist tense Paul emphasizes the unconditional and final nature of the exclusion. The subject of the act of predestination is God. This is expressed here by the passive form.[39]

The antithesis to the law of works is the law of faith. It presents righteousness solely by faith (Rom. 3:27, ἐξεκλείσθη. διὰ ποίου νόμου; τῶν ἔργων; οὐχί, ἀλλὰ διὰ νόμου πίστεως). Faith has become a new "law" which determines who will be given life.[40] This change concerns salvation history. God has given a new revelation. He has revealed his own righteousness which had been hidden – but to which the law and the prophets testify (cf. 3:21).

In this new situation righteousness is defined, also according to this section, by a polarization directed by the theology of predestination, and there is a certain logic to it. Righteousness by faith can be concluded from new premises, i.e. God's just judgment, God's new way to salvation and the reconciliation which Christ has brought. When expounding this theology of predestination Paul, in a quite courageous way, employs a term taken from rhetoric: "Therefore we *conclude* that a man is justified by faith without the deeds of the law" (Rom. 3:28 AV; λογιζόμεθα γὰρ δικαιοῦσθαι πίστει ἄνθρωπον χωρὶς ἔργων νόμου). The verb λογίζομαι is used here not for some abstract inference, but to denote a strong conviction.[41]

The idea of righteousness by faith is explained here with the aid of a strict polarity. Jewish tradition is not sufficient since the basic factors of soteriology have been changed. Solving the problem of theodicy has resulted in an uncompromising predestination. Only the death of the Son of God could rescue mankind from the wrath of God. This is why the law of works has been replaced by the law of faith.

One can no longer attain salvation by joining the old people of God and by performing traditional rites. Neither can circumcision be a condition of

---

[38] See Bauer s.v. ἐκκλείω.

[39] "In view of what follows it would seem that the reference is not simply to the fact that what has been said has demonstrated the absurdity of all such glorying, but to the exclusion effected by God Himself (the passive concealing a reference to a divine action), whether in the sense that God has rendered all such glorying futile and absurd by what He has done in Christ or – perhaps more probably, in view of the next few words – in the sense that He has shown it to be futile and absurd through the OT scriptures." Cranfield, *Romans,* 219.

[40] Winger, *Law,* 34-35, 85. In the word-play of Paul the word law becomes a principle. Even though this feature has aroused discussion, the dynamic change it expresses is not difficult to understand. Stuhlmacher, *Römer,* 63: the first readers must have understood this as follows: "das Gesetz, das durch den Glauben (an Jesus Christus) bestimmt ist".

[41] Paul uses this verb in important passages, such as Rom. 6:11 and 14:14. See Dunn, *Romans,* 187. NRSV is rather cautious here: "For we hold that a person is justified by faith apart from works prescribed by the law."

becoming a child of God, even though it was formerly a symbol of election. Now it is the passion and resurrection of the Son of God that show us that God "will justify the circumcised on the ground of faith and the uncircumcised through the same faith" (3:30).

Paul again uses the important term "works of the law". In this way this section is connected with the other texts we have investigated above. Firstly the ethnocentric setting has been polarized once again. The works of the law are factors which support Jewish identity, even though one cannot define them merely as "identity markers" of Judaism. Secondly, the works of the law give content to the concept of righteousness. This is why the presentation of Paul here is theology relating to righteousness.

This section presents us with an example of Paul's polarizing soteriology. In his theology of justification he applies a principle which is familiar to us from his other letters, namely that of "counting as loss". This dynamic helps us to explain this section of Romans. Paul is not here merely denying Jewish boasting about their privileged status among the nations.[42] Any explanation which appeals solely to the exclusion of a supercilious attitude and legalism is also too narrow.[43] Paul is here opposing faith to the very identity of Jewish faith.

The faith of pious Jews had centred on a natural joy over the law and its giver. Their obedience had been realized in the works of the law, in the keeping of God's commandments and a true zeal for those prescripts. In the new polarization this positive zeal was once again "counted as loss". God himself has excluded traditional piety from salvation. It has been replaced by Christ. This is why Paul can "conclude" that man is justified by faith alone.

All the examples that have been investigated in the previous chapters show us how Paul, due to his theology of predestination, claims that the dualism of traditional Jewish soteriology has lost its significance. As regards eschatological salvation, there is no longer a crucial difference between Jews and Gentiles. In the context of the theology of predestination the polarization is different. Man is under the wrath of God and only the righteousness of Christ can help him. This is why the righteousness that comes from faith is a logical consequence of the principles which Paul has proved to be valid. They are

---

[42] See e.g. Sanders, "against boasting in privileged status", *Law*, 33. Cf. Räisänen, *Law*, 170-171.

[43] Such an interpretation has been put forward in modern scholarship by e.g. Westerholm, *Law*, 170-171; Moo, *Romans*, 250: "It is not the Jew's pride in a covenant relationship with God but the pride in accomplishments, the tendency for the Jew to think that his obedience to the law constituted some kind of claim on God, that Paul here rejects."

valid because they resolve the problem of theodicy in the tradition of Jewish theology. As Paul teaches this righteousness of faith he employs a special principle of "counting as loss", and formulates his soteriology in accordance with a theology of predestination.

§ 12   Two Kinds of Righteousness

As regards the conception of law, Paul's polarizing predestinarian theology resulted in the view that there is a visible tension between the essence of the law and its soteriological function. A good law brought death to the descendants of Adam because of sin. For this reason the obedience of the old covenant, service to God, *Avodat Israel*, had to be considered negative works of the law once the proper righteousness of God had been revealed. This polarization also relates to justification. Because the *Torah* is not a proper channel for the realization of God's righteousness, the previous righteousness of the law must be "counted as loss". Therefore one needed to abandon the good brought by the law: zeal for the law and the ethnocentric election of Israel.

The polarization with regard to justification eventually leads to a question which has been waiting behind the discussions described above. On what grounds was Paul able to say that the Jews were relying on their own righteousness? Were not the Jewish beliefs in the mercy of God and in His salvific work sufficient to prove at least the basic conviction that the Jews themselves did not think that they were self-righteous in their striving to obey the law of God?

12.1. Submitting to God's righteousness (Rom. 10:2-3)

The problem with regard to self-righteousness is one of the most widely discussed issues in the modern study of Pauline soteriology. According to the covenantal nomism theory of Sanders, Second Temple Judaism was not a legalistic religion in itself. This basic thesis has in principle been accepted in the previous chapters. The Jewish religion was centred on the Temple of Jerusalem. People undoubtedly believed that Temple offerings provided atonement for sins and brought forgiveness. This belief in the grace of God was essential for Jewish sects, as well, even in a situation where they had been separated from the Temple.

The conclusions of this discussion are not quite clear, however. Sanders' theory contains a certain ambivalence, as we have noted earlier. He emphasizes that in theory Judaism cannot admit any legalism due to its basic "pattern". Nomism is submitted to the covenant. On the other hand, however, Sanders contents himself with saying that, in Judaism, grace and works are "in the right perspective". He actually directs his criticism at the theory that the Jewish religion was merely "petty legalism".[1] We have noted already that Sanders' theory in fact defines synergism, even though Sanders himself does not describe the Jewish faith in these terms.[2]

The theme of self-righteousness is more prominent in the writings of Sanders' followers. Several scholars think that Paul gave a distorted picture of Jewish identity. He is said to have depicted Jews as archetypes of self-righteousness merely in order to be able to justify his own preaching.[3] In this case Paul's teaching on self-righteousness would be but a piece of religious propaganda and an addition to his negative, black-and-white soteriology.

What, then, is Paul's relation to his Jewish heritage on this question? Several passages show that Paul described his pre-conversion life according to the same standards of piety as normative Judaism, i.e. according to the picture we can see in most sapiential, sectarian or pseudepigraphical texts of that time. A zeal for the law was the highest criterion of piety. Obedience to the law was sufficient piety before God, as well, since disobedience left men under the wrath of God. As regards his personal attitude, this obedience was hardly considered the one and only merit to be relied upon.[4]

In the age of synergistic nomism the grace of God was essential and of utmost importance for pious Jews. Salvation was naturally believed to come from God. The keeping of the law was merely a condition for participation in the salvific work of God. One of the basic features of synergism was, however, that obedience to the law was not merely a neutral act of voluntary "response" by men to God's actions. Already in sapiential theology it was considered a condition for the mercy of God and even for eschatological salvation.

---

[1] At the end of his book Sanders becomes more cautious and announces that he has actually rejected the idea that Judaism was *merely* governed by casuistic legalism: "the Judaism of before 70 kept grace and works in the right perspective, did not trivialize the commandments of God and was not especially marked by hypocrisy... By consistently maintaining the basic framework of *covenantal nomism,* the gift and demand of God were kept in a healthy relationship with each other, the minutiae of the law were observed on the basis of the large principles of religion..." Sanders, *Paul,* 427. This statement confirms the doubts that there is a basic ambivalence in the principles applied by Sanders. This problem will be treated in detail below, in chapter 14.1.

[2] See especially the excursus in chapter 3.

[3] Räisänen, *Law,* 176, 178-179. Sanders himself does not hold this view, however. He thinks that Paul does not really claim that the Jews were self-righteous – because Paul did not need such an argument in his theology. See e.g. a critical comment against Räisänen in Sanders, *Law,* 19-20, especially footnote 16 (p. 51). "Neither side sees the law as a possible means of salvation in the sense of producing sufficient *merit.* Paul's opponents take the standard Jewish view that to enter into the Biblical promises one has to accept the Biblical condition: the law of Moses." (footnote 16).

[4] Cf. above, chapters 4.1., 5.2. and 11.2.

The latter feature later became more prominent in the teaching of apocalyptic groups. In his theology of predestination Paul interpreted this tradition in a new way. This can be seen especially in the climax of Romans chapter 10, where he describes the situation of the Jews as follows:

"I can testify that they have a zeal for God, but it is not enlightened. For, being ignorant of the righteousness that comes from God, and seeking to establish their own, they have not submitted to God's righteousness" (Rom. 10:2-3).

The Jews, as regards their tradition, had a proper zeal for the law (ζῆλον θεοῦ ἔχουσιν, Rom. 10:2) in the very best sense of the word. Here we see echoes of Maccabaean piety and Zealot enthusiasm.[5] Paul praises his Jewish brothers for the same "zeal" which he himself had shown for the law of God before his conversion (Phil. 3:6).[6] This traditional zeal was not enough, though. The status and function of the law had changed, the relation between Jews and Gentiles had changed – as regards eschatological salvation – and at the same time the concept of saving righteousness, too, had changed.

When describing the situation of the Jews Paul speaks here without hesitation of a righteousness of their "own" (τὴν ἰδίαν). In addition, he seems to say that the Jews strove for this righteousness in a very conscious way (ζητοῦντες στῆσαι). This does not mean, however, that Paul aimed to blacken Jewish legalism. He explains what was meant by this Jewish "zeal".[7] It was precisely this zeal (ζῆλος) of the Jews which was changed into self-righteousness.

This righteousness of their own had several features: it was zeal for the law and for God; it did not recognize the righteousness of God, however, and it

---

[5] Cf. Michel, *Römer (1978)*, 325, especially footnote 4; Wilckens, *Römer II*, 219; Cranfield, *Romans*, 514. In such a context zeal is not an epithet for a state of mind but rather a description of Jewish piety. This is how the term is most usually explained by scholars.

[6] Paul gives a real "testimony" to this. "Paul solemnly testifies to his fellow-countrymen's zeal for God." Cranfield, *Romans*, 513.

[7] Dunn, *Romans*, 587; cf. the discussion in Thielman, *Law*, 299, n 51. Dunn is over-interpreting the word στῆσαι, however, in order to be able to interpret the section according to his ideal of covenantal nomism. By allusion to the Hebrew word קים he introduces the idea of God's covenant into the interpretation: [στῆσαι] "usually of God's "establishing" his covenant". On these grounds proper righteousness becomes covenantal nomism: "Clearly it is this kind of loyalty to the covenant which Paul has in mind, the concern to maintain covenant righteousness as Israel's peculiar obligation... Here is a good expression of 'covenantal nomism'..." (p. 588). This can hardly be justified on the basis of a single word. Dunn's explanation has relevance, however, as regards the idea that the "zeal" of the Jews was an expression of their obedience to God.

did not submit to God's acts.[8] The basic dynamic of Paul's teaching here is the opposition between a person's own righteousness and God's righteousness.[9]

Paul is still using the main theme of Romans, i.e. the idea of the revelation of God's righteousness (cf. Rom. 3:21). Paul is certain of the fact that the righteousness from the law cannot do what the righteousness of God is doing: making a sinner righteous. In modern Pauline studies this section has sometimes been totally separated from the idea of the righteousness from the law.[10]

The text of Paul shows clearly that such a restriction cannot be made. Some verses earlier (9:32) he mentioned "works" explicitly. In this sense self-righteousness is identified with a person's own righteousness, which unavoidably means righteousness of works. In this respect the parallelism with the teaching of Philippians is evident:[11]

---

[8] Stuhlmacher, *Römer*, 140. This section shows that Paul did speak of the self-righteousness of the Jews. Sanders optimistically thought that Paul would neither have mentioned it nor have needed this theme in his argumentation. This is evidently erroneous. Cf. the quotations from Sanders' writings above. When explaining these verses Sanders attempts to show that Paul did not speak of "self-righteousness" but of "their own righteousness". The latter would in this case be common Jewish "zeal", which for Paul, too, was a positive thing in itself: "the peculiar result of being an observant Jew, which is *in and of itself a good thing* ('zeal,' Rom. 10:2; 'gain,' Phil. 3:7) but which is shown to be 'wrong' ('loss,' Phil. 3:7f.) by the revelation of 'God's righteousness,' which comes by faith in Christ." Sanders, *Law*, 44-45 (italics his). As he tries to reject the claim of a self-righteous *attitude* Sanders at the same time waters down Paul's polarization. According to Paul, self-righteousness becomes "works of law", which oppose the righteousness of God, whether it is done consciously or not.

[9] Wilckens, *Römer II*, 220, emphasizes that it is still the righteousness of God revealed in Christ that Paul regards as the antithesis. Cf. Michel, *Römer (1978)*, 325f.; this is also accepted by Ziesler in his dissertation, Ziesler, *Righteousness*, 206 (cf. an altered view in his commentary, presented in the next footnote).

[10] In his commentary, which follows the theory of covenantal nomism, Ziesler abandons his previous view and explains the "own" righteousness in a rather mild way. If one's only premise is that the Jews did not know Christ – and in Sanders' interpretation this was their only fault – there is not much substance for their own righteousness. For Ziesler the content is ethnocentricism: "Christ-rejecting and for Jews only". Ziesler, *Romans*, 256-257. A similar explanation can naturally be found in the work of Dunn, who has a tendency towards ethnocentric interpretation (cf. "identity markers"). Dunn, *Romans*, 588. Paul has much more to say, however. We have seen that according to his interpretation Jewish piety as such had turned into self-righteousness.

[11] Cf. e.g. Schlier, *Römerbrief*, 307; Michel, *Römer (1978)*, 325f.; Stuhlmacher, *Römer*, 139-140. Dunn thinks that the problem of the parallelism with Phil. 3:9 can be solved by using the concept of covenant: "the righteousness of a covenant-keeper, as opposed to the righteousness from God". Dunn, *Romans*, 588. In the context of covenantal nomism, however, Ziesler ended up with a strict opposition and one cannot change this into agreement within one and the same theory of interpretation.

"not having a righteousness of my own that comes from the law, but one that comes through faith in Christ, the righteousness from God based on faith" (Phil. 3:9).

Secondly, we must note that Paul underlines a certain passivity on the part of the Jews in opposing true righteousness. He says that the Jews do not "know" God's righteousness (ἀγνοοῦντες γὰρ τὴν τοῦ θεοῦ δικαιοσύνην).[12] Pious Jews would never oppose God consciously.[13] They themselves were convinced that they were serving God in the best possible way. They even defended God's honour against threats – just as Paul had done when persecuting the followers of Jesus (Phil. 3:6). So Paul is here again, at least implicitly, an example of a converted pious Jew whose life is compared with that of other Jews.

A third feature in Paul's argumentation is that those Jews who have heard the gospel have not submitted (οὐχ ὑπετάγησαν) to God's righteousness.[14] They did not accept the way of salvation which God himself had chosen and given to his people. Therefore it is justifiable to say that Paul was not claiming that Judaism is a consciously self-righteous religion. He was well aware – and this was only self-evident for a Pharisee – that Israel had its promises and covenants and cult with sacrifices at the heart of its faith. Paul was not trying intentionally to distort this picture but instead to present another kind of salvation history. He claimed that in the history of Israel (and the history of the whole world) a crucial border-line had been crossed. Now that Christ has come and Easter has passed, all the promises of Israel have been fulfilled in Christ. It is the Son of God who has brought real righteousness.

We must further note the seriousness of Paul's teaching. He warns the Jews with prophetic authority and proclaims that they have not been obedient to God after all.[15] But even when he blames his fellow countrymen, Paul at the same time grieves over the fate of Israel, just as he did at the beginning of chapter 9. When the Jews oppose Christ and reject the righteousness that he has brought,

---

[12] Against Schlier, who connects this word with the expression "have not submitted". Schlier, *Römerbrief*, 310.

[13] This is why I do not accept the traditional explanation expressed by Cranfield: "their stubborn determination to establish their own righteousness". Cranfield, *Romans*, 515.

[14] Black remarks that here too one can see an antithesis to Jewish piety, since the Jews did "submit" to the righteousness of the law, cf. 2 Bar. 54:5. Black, *Romans*, 141. I am inclined to think that Paul used the term in order to describe a somewhat different tension.

[15] Michel, *Römer (1978)*, 326: "*Die Anklage auf Ungehorsam... ist also stark betont*".

they actually reject God himself.[16] This is the proper context for the interpretation of the climax of Paul's theology of the law in chapter 10: "For Christ is the end of the law so that there may be righteousness for everyone who believes." (10:4). Christ as the *telos* of the law is above all the end of the righteousness that comes from the law. God's righteousness has been revealed in Christ and he himself is righteousness (εἰς δικαιοσύνην) for everyone that believes in him.

There has never been any other righteousness that was perfect as regards the will of God. Paul's argument does not need any such premise. The essence of the law in itself implies an ideal of perfect righteousness. This ideal was impossible to attain, however. In this respect we could make an application and say that "Christ is the end of the demand of the law". Such an interpretation would be controversial in modern discussion, however, because as regards its terminology it is related to a dogmatic tradition which has recently been openly rejected.[17]

The paradoxical feature of predestinarian theology is evident in this section, too. An adherent of Jewish tradition cannot submit to the righteousness of Christ unless he changes several of his previous beliefs. It is only faith in the Resurrected One that makes predestinarian theology acceptable.

It is evident that Paul's polarization between the revelation of God's true righteousness and Jewish zeal for the law is similar to that in the previous chapters of Romans and to that in Galatians and Philippians, which we have investigated before. Paul's concept of self-righteousness is part of his theology of predestination, but not necessarily the experience of a pious Jew himself. It must be regarded as a consequent inference of paradoxical polarization, which in turn is a result of Paul's strict understanding of predestination.[18]

---

[16] Fitzmyer assumes that Paul is building a linguistic bridge with the previous clauses (9:33), which speak of the "stumbling" of Israel, Fitzmyer, *Romans*, 584: "Paul uses here 2nd aor. pass. *hypetagêsan*, but in the middle sense. See BDF § 76.2. The use of the 3rd pl. aor. here echoes that of *prosekopsan* in 9:32."

[17] This verse and especially the idea of Christ as the end of the law has aroused much discussion. A history of interpretation is given by Badenas, *Law*, 7-37. The main lines of interpretation, as regards the word τέλος, can be called temporal, teleological and an interpretation of fulfilment. This is not the place to comment on all such investigation, suffice it to say that the solution given here confirms the explanation where the "end" of the law is considered temporal. At the same time teleological interpretations lose their probability.

[18] Cf. Seifrid, *Justification*, 249: "No longer is the theme of forensic justification by faith used solely in regard to Jew-Gentile relations. As we have seen above, in Rom 5:1-11 it has become the means for assuring Gentile readers of deliverance from the apocalyptic manifestation of God's wrath. In Rom 9-11, through Israel's example, it has become the reason for excluding boasting in any religious pride."

We could even say that Paul's concept of righteousness is the culminating point of his predestinarian theology. He is describing the whole of divine salvation history. There is a dark background, i.e. the sinfulness of all men and their complete separation from the presence of God. When this background is connected to belief in the uniqueness of Christ, Paul arrives at his concept of one true righteousness. This righteousness comes from God and is given as a free gift in Christ.

This is why Paul can state that in this new polarized situation there are, in principle, but two different kinds of righteousness: one is the righteousness from God and the other is man's "own" righteousness. Outside Christ and outside the righteousness from faith man is unavoidably left in the sphere of his own righteousness. Thus Paul's concept of man's self-righteousness is naturally a logical consequence of his theological premises.[19]

Paul's concept of the self-righteousness of the Jews was formed according to the basic antithesis by which the righteousness of God is set against the ideal righteousness from the law. In the context of a theology of predestination, righteousness from the law is completely impossible, because in the new polarization it has become the antithesis of God's saving righteousness. This is why the obedience of men becomes self-righteousness, even though it was probably never conscious legalism. When the Jews did not submit to God's righteousness, but instead rejected Christ, they fell within the sphere of their own righteousness. Therefore, paradoxically enough, in their zeal for God they became enemies of God.

12.2. *"As if based on works" (Rom. 9:31-32)*

When we investigated the consequences of soteriological polarization as regards the theology of justification, our first conclusion concerned the nature of self-righteousness. This was defined as an antithesis to God's righteousness. Next we must ask whether the same dynamic can be detected in Paul's concept of the works of the law. We have already seen some evidence of this in chapter 10, where the *Avodat Israel* was analysed. Now we must approach the question from another angle. Does Paul mean that he has defined "works" as loss merely on the grounds of theological reasoning and logical inference?

---

[19] When we make this inference we must remember the basic difference between polarisation and deduction. In the context of the theory of covenantal nomism Paul's theology is defined merely as a deduction without valid reasons. In that case all the roots of Paul's theology are being cut off. As an example we could name the narrowing of the concept of self-righteousness. If there is nothing more left than the emphasis on ethnocentricism, one does not really grasp the radical claim of Paul concerning righteousness by works.

In this analysis we shall remain in the context of the previous section of Romans. In Romans 9 Paul treats the question of the righteousness that Israel is striving after.

"Israel, who did strive for the righteousness that is based on the law (NIV: the law of righteousness, διώκων νόμον δικαιοσύνης), did not succeed in fulfilling that law (NIV: has not attained it). Why not? Because they did not strive for it on the basis of faith, but as if it were based on works (ὅτι οὐκ ἐκ πίστεως ἀλλ' ὡς ἐξ ἔργων)." (9:31-32).

Israel's zeal for the law was an honest effort to obey the will of God. Now it has turned out to be futile, because the Israelites have not accepted the way of faith.

As regards exegesis, this section is not a simple one. Instead of speaking of the righteousness from the law, Paul uses the term "law of righteousness" (νόμος δικαιοσύνης). It is a complex expression and can refer either to the demand of the law or to the promise of the law.[20] The word 'righteousness' has a positive tone in the clause as regards the law. So it cannot have been meant as an antithesis here. The law of righteousness is obviously the law that, as to its essence, strives at righteousness.

This is the law which Israel never achieved (εἰς νόμον οὐκ ἔφθασεν). First of all, we may say that Israel never achieved the right kind of righteousness, and this is why it never achieved the right law. Only the perfect keeping of the law is a proof of righteousness.[21] In this sense Paul is speaking directly of an ability to keep the law.[22]

The word for 'achieving' (φθάνω) can be connected with athletic imagery. In a sense it means "to arrive first", "to precede someone".[23] Paul seems to apply here the principle "the first will be the last". Israel had received all the promises

---

[20] The discussion on this term has been lively, see the analysis in Martin, *Law*, 135-138; as regards older scholarship, see Käsemann, *Römer*, 265. For Schlier law is a demand, Schlier, *Römerbrief*, 307. Most scholars connect it with promise, however, in one way or another. The essence of the law is one that promises righteousness to all who fulfil its precepts, see Stuhlmacher, *Gerechtigkeit*, 92; Käsemann, *Römer*, 265; Wilckens, *Römer II*, 212; Badenas, *Law*, 194.

[21] "εἰς νόμον οὐκ ἔφθασεν besagt nicht nur, dass Israel die Gerechtigkeit nicht erlangt hat, sondern schärfer, weil grundsätzlicher: Es hat damit auch *das Gesetz* nich 'erreicht'. Die Tora ist eben nicht eine Heilsgabe, die als solche Bestand hat, ob Israel sie erfüllt oder nicht erfüllt, sondern wer das Gesetz nicht *tut,* verfehlt auch die Zugehörigkeit zu ihm als Signum der Erwählung." Wilckens, *Römer II*, 212.

[22] Against Ziesler: "he is not saying that they did not keep the Law. He is instead saying that in their pursuit of the goal of righteousness they failed to find the Law that would lead to it. They were bound to fail, because such a Law did not exist." Ziesler, *Romans*, 253. This explanation of Ziesler's is quite strange because one then has to ask what Paul did oppose. It is no wonder that Ziesler does not explain the word "works" at all. It most evidently does not fit his interpretation, as it provides an antithesis to faith, see p. 254.

[23] Badenas, *Law*, 104.

of God and the law of God, but she did not reach the goal. The Gentiles preceded them and attained salvation through the righteousness that comes from faith in Christ.[24]

It may be that Paul at the same time meant a larger view of salvation history: Israel which had been striving after the law, i.e. obedience to the law, had not in fact been obedient to the law (or the prophets, cf. 3:21) as a promise, because she had not understood that this very law testified to Christ. Paul said here explicitly that the "law of righteousness" can only be strived after by faith.

Paul's argument aims at describing the righteousness that comes from works. He says that the righteousness which is left outside righteousness by faith is unavoidably righteousness from works for theological reasons. Israel who strove for the righteousness that is based on the law did not find it, because it was not done on the basis of faith (ὅτι οὐκ ἐκ πίστεως). A striving for righteousness that is done without faith is done "as if it were based on works" (9:32, ὡς ἐξ ἔργων).

The little word ὡς that Paul uses here becomes surprisingly crucial as regards the understanding of his purpose. Most commentators pass over the word without comment, or it is referred to merely by saying that it underlines Israel's own striving for works of the law.[25] Some scholars also maintain that Paul was possibly emphasizing the illusive nature of Israel's works of the law.[26] Such a view has further been proven by parallel texts where the word ὡς is used. Paul is said to accuse the Jews of striving at righteousness by using the wrong means, "as if by some kind of works – even though they do not really exist".[27]

Such logic is inconsistent, however. In 2 Corinthians Paul uses the word ὡς in a positive sense: "For we are not peddlers of God's word like so many; but in Christ we speak as persons of sincerity (ἀλλ' ὡς ἐξ εἰλικρινείας), as persons sent from God (ἀλλ' ὡς ἐκ θεοῦ), and standing in his presence" (2 Cor. 2:17). In 2 Thessalonians, on the other hand, a negative alternative is presented: "we beg you... not to be quickly shaken in mind or alarmed, either by spirit or by word or by letter, as though from us..." (2 Thess 2:1-2, μήτε δι' ἐπιστολῆς ὡς δι' ἡμῶν). In the latter case the letter itself is not genuine, even though it is presented as such. In both cases, however, the word ὡς refers to something which is valuable in itself.

This kind of rhetoric device is not employed in Romans 9. There Paul is not

---

[24] "What Paul says, then, is that in spite of Israel being first 'in the race', the Gentiles, the latecomers, have reached the goal while most Jews have not." Badenas, *Law*, 104.

[25] For example Michel, *Römer (1955)*, 220; Schlier, *Römerbrief*, 307.

[26] "Die Juden handeln aus einer Illusion." Käsemann, *Römer*, 266; Dunn, *Romans*, 583.

[27] See Bauer, *Wörterbuch*, s.v. ὡς III.3.; Badenas, *Law*, 105.

trying to distort something positive and turn it into an antithesis by using the word ὡς. In that case he would have written the clause differently: ὡς ἐκ πίστεως, "as if it were from faith". Only in this case could the linguistic opposition function. If we consider the text we have, Paul should have thought that the only proper way of reaching salvation is by works – but that the Jews were striving for it by "wrong" deeds. This explanation does not fit Paul's antithesis of works and faith.

What does the word ὡς mean, then? I suggest that Paul uses it in a rather general sense when opposing works to faith.[28] When striving at the righteousness from the law by being obedient to God's commandment, Israel made one crucial mistake. It rejected the faith which God himself gave to men to be their righteousness. This is why obedience remains mere works. And this is why righteousness itself is striven for "as if " it were by works. This is something other than conscious legalism. It is an evident conclusion: Outside Christ even positive obedience to the law turns into self-righteousness.

It is quite evident that Paul is again applying the principle of paradoxical polarization. The "work" of Israel (Ἰσραὴλ δὲ διώκων νόμον δικαιοσύνης) is evidently based on a positive axiom, but in the new polarization it must be regarded as a most shameful kind of self-righteousness, i.e. works. In this way Paul's term "as if" (ὡς) becomes crucial for the interpretation of the section. It is, in fact, a hermeneutical key to all his theology of the law. Paul is convinced that, in divine salvation history, *Avodat Israel* has lost its function. If it is performed as such after Easter, it becomes negative "works" that prevent people from coming to the Messiah.[29]

This is how Christ became a "stumbling stone" for the Jews (προσέκοψαν τῷ λίθῳ τοῦ προσκόμματος, v. 32). They did not submit to the righteousness that God himself offered. Therefore they walk in a state of blindness and they miss salvation, in spite of all the promises and covenants.

---

[28] This antithesis is noted in most commentaries, see e.g. Michel, *Römer (1955)*, 220; Schlier, *Römerbrief*, 307; Stuhlmacher, *Römer*, 138; Dunn, *Romans*, 583 (against Sanders, *Law*, 37); Fitzmyer, *Romans*, 579.

[29] This view has both similarities with and differences from the explanation by Sanders. He says, too, that Paul is interpreting the status of works according to a new principle. Because the Jews did not believe in Jesus, their zeal for the law became negative works. Sanders, *Law*, 36-37. The application of the theory of covenantal nomism led Sanders to adopt too narrow an interpretation, however. He explains the section merely according to a Christological principle: "Israel's failure is not that they do not obey the law in the correct way, but that they do not have faith in Christ." *Law*, 37. This is why the law, for Sanders, is only a marker of ethnocentricism and Paul becomes an opponent of this. *Law*, 38, 46-47. The narrowing of the theology of law occurs so often in the texts of Sanders that it must be a structural element in his theory. Our analysis above has shown, however, that Paul, when speaking of the works of the law, always implies that the Jews were unable to fulfil the commandments perfectly.

The analysis of this section confirms the conclusion that the righteousness from works need not be identified with conscious self-righteousness. In the context of predestinarian theology the status of human righteousness has been changed. One cannot refer to synergistic nomism when describing righteousness that comes from faith. Even good striving for the law, due to paradoxical polarization, must be considered "as if it were" by works. In the grand eschatological finale every human effort proves to be insufficient. The perfect righteousness of Christ has replaced it.

There is an interesting link between Romans and Philippians. In both of these letters the fates of Israel and Paul himself are identified. In Philippians Paul's own obedience and zeal was "loss" (3:7). According to his theological principle, it was considered loss as compared with true righteousness. In Romans the striving of Israel was considered to be a similar kind of effort. It was good in itself but it nevertheless had to be considered futile. It was done "as if" it were by works. In this world of sin obedience always remained insufficient.[30]

Behind Paul's polarizing presentation there is an explicit tendency to deny the value of Jewish piety. Synergistic nomism may have been accepted by most Jews, as Paul himself had accepted it before his conversion. Now it required to be reinterpreted, however. The new predestinarian theology had proved it to be insufficient as regards salvation.

A similar identification between Paul's life and Israel's history is explicit in Romans 7.[31] Paul's "I" had lived without the law in a similar manner as Israel had lived before Moses and Sinai. When the law came, sin revived and Paul died. In a similar way Israel died at Sinai. Israel is an heir of Adam and for this reason is under the judgment of God. This is why the law has become an instrument for exposing the sin of Israel. This identification is rather important to Paul and by using it he was able to explain the difference between traditional Jewish piety and the righteousness that comes from faith.

Paul's hermeneutical principle, which we have earlier called the principle of paradoxical polarization, results in a denial of the value of traditional piety. Such a principle can be called paradoxical because it produces perplexing conclusions. Positive human endeavours are changed into their opposites. In Paul's theology this principle works mainly in two areas. Firstly, the principle of "counting as loss" is a key to his polarized concept of righteousness. Secondly, such a hermeneutic helps us to understand Paul's radical concept of the law.

Paul's conception of justification is polarized, and it can best be interpreted in

---

[30] See chapter 11.2. above.

[31] See also chapter 10.4.

the context of predestinarian theology. In soteriology it helps us to define how Paul understood the claim of the self-righteousness of man. Outside the righteousness of Christ all striving after righteousness is doomed to remain insufficient human effort, because when compared with the revelation of God's final righteousness, it is done "as if" it were by works. This polarized concept of righteousness occurs in several of Paul's letters. He often identifies his own life with the fate of Israel. Both of these must be interpreted by applying the principle of "counting as loss". This means that every effort in striving to keep the law must be regarded as loss. A consequent application of this principle to soteriology produces the seemingly paradoxical nature of Paul's theology, typical of all his letters.

12.3. The righteousness of Christ (Rom. 3:21-26)

In Paul's polarized theology of justification Israel's zeal (ζῆλος) for the law and their honest obedience in the keeping of the commandments were ascribed a negative function as they were compared with God's righteousness that had been revealed in Christ. As the last aspect of this theme we must further investigate how Paul describes the righteousness that comes from Christ and how that description fits the theory of polarization. The most important of the relevant texts here is Romans 3.

The point of departure in this treatment is Paul's concept of *God's righteousness* (δικαιοσύνη θεοῦ). We must remember that the study of Paul's theology of justification was essentially changed after the influential article by *E. Käsemann*, where the focus was precisely on that term.[32] In his search for a new interpretation of Paul Käsemann emphasized cosmic and theocentric features in several key texts of soteriology. According to Käsemann, Paul did not think of justification merely as an existential event in the life of an individual (against Bultmann). Paul taught of the revelation of God's righteousness as an eschatological climax. According to Paul, the Lordship and power (*Macht*) of God in this world was revealed in Christ.[33]

This theme was developed further by *P. Stuhlmacher*. According to Stuhlmacher, the term for righteousness did not denote merely God's righteous nature or holiness as an antithesis to sin. In the theology of Paul it has other

---

[32] Before Käsemann Bultmann's existential interpretation prevailed, especially in Europe. Justification was seen as an encounter with God, and man was said to find his authentic existence through justification. See e.g. Bultmann, *Theologie*, 284-285. The history of research is given in Seifrid, *Justification*, 1-77.

[33] In his article "Gottesgerechtigkeit bei Paulus" Käsemann presented this idea in a real thesis: "Alles Gesagte lässt sich dahin zusammenfassen, dass δικαιοσύνη θεοῦ für Paulus die sich eschatologisch in Christus offenbarende Herrschaft Gottes über der Welt ist". Käsemann, *Exegetische Versuche 2*, 192.

connotations connected with the Old Testament. In the Old Testament the righteousness of God is mentioned several times (see e.g. Deut. 33:21; 1 Sam. 12:7; Ps. 103:6). There it denotes *God's saving work*, his acts for the salvation of Israel. This is why it cannot be interpreted merely as a quality of God, but it also concerns his actions for the benefit of Israel.[34]

When explaining Paul's concept of justification, Stuhlmacher is not content with the mere theme of *Macht*, God's saving Lordship. According to Stuhlmacher, there is always the idea of God's wrath behind the belief in justification by faith in Christ. Thus the justification of the ungodly is always a juridical act and has to do with God's creative power. "Rechtfertigung des Gottlosen meint bei Paulus den Anbruch der Neuen Schöpfung über und in dem Täufling in Form einer seinsgründenden, worthaften Rechts-manifestation."[35]

The contribution of this line of study was that the Jewish belief in the justification of God became more clearly defined. Later in his commentary on Romans Käsemann concluded that the idea of justification by faith was typical not only of Paul but of Jewish theology as well. It was rooted in Jewish apocalyptic. "Auch bei äusserster Vorsicht wird man es nicht nur für möglich, sondern für wahrscheinlich halten dürfen, dass Paulus das für ihm so charakteristische Stichwort als bereits geprägte Formel aus jüdischer Apokalyptik übernahm."[36]

The weakness of Käsemann's approach was in the way he separated justifi-cation from its anthropological conditions. According to Käsemann, justifi-

---

[34] Stuhlmacher, *Gerechtigkeit Gottes,* 142f.; see also *Theologie,* 327-328; cf. Jüngel, *Paulus und Jesus,* 36f. This theme is especially important, for example, in the texts from Qumran, which we have investigated earlier, cf. 1QS 11, and in Jewish apocalyptic, Stuhlmacher, *Gerechtigkeit Gottes,* 154f. Bultmann's pupils disagreed as to the correct interpretation of the theology of justification. According to Lohse, Paul's concept of the righteousness of God must be understood against the background of the Old Testament and Jewish theology. In this case it means God's gracious work, because he is faithful to his covenant. God shows his mercy first, and then the saved sinner lives by the righteousness that God has given to him. Lohse, *Theologie,* 83f. In this way the new concept of the righteousness of God was united with the existentialist interpretation. By his interpretation Lohse wished to correct Käsemann, who had spoken of a righteousness that was merely a revelation of God's power. On the other hand, he also criticized Stuhlmacher, according to whom the righteousness of God meant his saving work within history.

[35] Stuhlmacher, *Gerechtigkeit Gottes,* 236; cf. 238. This is a correction of the explanation of Käsemann, even though the latter also mentioned this feature with reference to apocalyptic, Käsemann, *Exegetische Versuche 2,* 185.

[36] Käsemann, *Römer,* 27. Cf. Stuhlmacher, *Theologie,* 331: *"Gleichwohl kennt und bezeugt die alttestamentliche Tradition die Rechtfertigung der Gottlosen sehr wohl, und zwar als Tat Gottes, zu der er sich aus freier Liebe und Barmherzigkeit gegenüber seinem schuldbeladenen Eigentumsvolk Israel durchringt."* (italics his); cf. Seifrid, *Justification,* 41.

cation was merely an expression of God's power (*Macht*): the righteousness of God brought Israel (and the whole world) back under the rule of God.[37] For this reason he further concluded that in no letter of Paul can justification be separated from sanctification.[38] Faith, according to Käsemann, means obedience to God's righteousness.

In such an interpretation Paul's radical anthropology is left too much to one side. We must remember that Paul's concept of justification always implies the idea of the justification of the ungodly. In Käsemann's interpretation there is not enough room for the aspect of sin. For him, justification means some kind of existentialist "partnership" with God, though under the *Macht* of God. It is actually a little astonishing that Käsemann can at first appeal to on Jewish apocalyptic soteriology and speak of the Lordship of God, and then conclude with a rather mild concept of justification.[39]

It is consequently better to place the theme of the righteousness of God in the context of Paul's theology of predestination. This is the setting in which this theme occurs in Romans 3, which is rightly considered a key section for Paul's theology of justification. Here Paul opposes in a radical way the Old Testament promises to salvation in Christ.

The law and prophets testified to the righteousness of God, but "now, apart from law (χωρὶς νόμου), the righteousness of God has been disclosed" in this world (Rom. 3:21). New salvation is based on justification by faith, which God himself gives as a gift to men, because they "fall short of the glory of God" (3:22-23; πάντες γὰρ ἥμαρτον καὶ ὑστεροῦνται τῆς δόξης τοῦ θεου).

Behind Paul's teaching there is always this radical anthropology, which we

---

[37] "Gottes Macht greift nach der Welt, und Heil der Welt ist es, dass sie unter Gottes Herrschaft zurückgeführt wird." Käsemann, *Exegetische Versuche 2*, 193.

[38] Seifrid is right to criticize Käsemann for the error that, for him, Paul speaks of the righteousness of God (and justification accordingly) only as a revelation of God's power. For Paul, forensic justification is something other than mere sanctification and obedience to the righteousness of God. Seifrid, *Justification*, 43; cf. Käsemann, *Exegetische Versuche 2*, 184, 193. Seifrid seems to be right, too, when he says that Käsemann has been accepted by Catholic scholars precisely because of his "joining of *gerecht erklären* and *gerecht machen*" (p. 38). On this, see Kertelge, *Rechtfertigung*, 12, ("Durch die Interpretation Käsemanns ist in die bisherige Diskussion eine neue Terminologie eingeführt worden, die hilfreich sein kann, alte Missverständnisse bezüglich der Wirkung des göttlichen Rechtfertigungshandelns zu überwinden."); cf. 259.

[39] Compared with this Stuhlmacher's concept is different as regards Paul's teaching on justification. He thinks that there are two basic features in the soteriology of Paul, one that relates to atonement and one that relates to the law: "(1)... Gott versöhnt (versühnt) die Welt mit sich selbst durch Christus und gewährt allen Glaubenden aufgrund des Sühnetodes Jesu und seiner Fürsprache die endzeitliche Rechtfertigung... (2) Das Heilswerk der Rechtfertigung der Gottlosen... überbietet und erledigt die δικαίωσις aufgrund von Werken des Gesetzes." Stuhlmacher, *Theologie*, 334. Cf. Hofius, *Paulusstudien*, 35, 125ff.

have investigated previously. Because all have died in Adam, all fall short of the glory of God (v. 23). Therefore there is no longer any difference between Jews and Gentiles (v. 9 above). True righteousness can only be that attained by the justification of a sinner, because it is the only means that God presents to us.[40]

According to Paul, the righteousness of God has as its aim the justification of all human beings before God. It was not possible to reveal justice before, because it would have led to the destruction of all men. Justice would have had to take place in judgment, and no man could have survived it. Now the situation is different. In "his divine forbearance" God has "passed over the sins previously committed" (3:25). All the sins of men have been condemned in Christ, instead. For this reason Christ was "put forward as a sacrifice of atonement" for all people (v. 25).[41] It is impossible for man to attain a perfect righteousness of his own. God will justify all through faith in Christ (3:25-26).[42]

The theology of predestination culminates in the idea of God's forbearance. The classical solution to the problem of theodicy demanded a punishment for "the sins previously committed". This was the point of Jewish soteriology in apocalyptic circles and in Second Temple literature. God's righteousness will be realized only when sinners are destroyed as a "sacrifice" for the righteous of Israel.[43]

Paul's theology of predestination led to a totally new polarization. The whole of mankind lacks salvation, and so God chose to sacrifice his own Son for the

---

[40] See Jüngel, *Paulus und Jesus,* 40f., 46.

[41] The Day of Atonement is naturally referred to here, see Michel, *Römer (1955),* 94; Moo, *Romans,* 246. Cf. the parallel passage 2 Cor. 5:14ff., and Hofius, *Paulusstudien,* 45ff.

[42] According to Lohse, the Jewish concept of righteousness found its way into the early church, where even before Paul people believed that it meant God's faithfulness to his covenant. Paul emphasized somewhat differently the justifying action of God. Paul declares that without this grace man is lost, but within the scope of justification he can rely on God's compassion. The existentialist view of Lohse's has two aspects. On the one hand, he admits that Christ is the righteousness of men because he has been "made to be sin" for them (2 Cor. 5:21). The power of sin has been defeated and sinners will be made righteous. On the other hand, this justification is only an existential experience: it is merely a hope that faith provides. Lohse, *Theologie,* 85-86.

[43] Verse 25b has been a "puzzle" (Dunn, *Romans,* 174) for scholars, since it has not been connected with Paul's theology of predestination. The word πάρεσις (*hapax legomenon*) is difficult. It means "passing over", but not "overlooking". "Rather it has the more strictly legal sense of 'letting go unpunished, remission of penalty", Dunn *Romans,* 173. This puzzle can be solved by considering Paul's theology of predestination. In his divine forbearance God has left sins unpunished. Now the time of πάρεσις has ended, however, as Schlier rightly points out, *Römerbrief,* 113. The only thing that counts is one's relation to Christ, in whom the righteousness of God has been revealed.

sins of the descendants of Adam. This is how God was able to reveal his own righteousness, his own saving work in this world. And this is why the righteousness of Christ is the righteousness that comes from faith.

Paul's concept of the righteousness of God thus contains all the most important features of predestinarian theology. He was able to use this term in order to bring forth the essence of his soteriology. The saving acts of God helped Israel over the centuries, but the final goal of the righteousness of God was the sending of Christ. This goal can never be considered a change in God's plan. Rather it underlines God's forbearance. Sin should have been punished. Through the sacrifice of Christ, however, God has reconciled the whole world before him.

The righteousness of God is one of the leading themes in Pauline soteriology. He elaborates it in his teaching on God's saving righteousness. In this teaching Paul's view is governed by his theology of predestination. Mankind has lived under sin and under the wrath of God ever since the days of Adam. Therefore no man can ever have had perfect righteousness before God in reality. The mercy of God can be seen in his forbearance. The wrath of God has not yet fallen on men. However, in Christ the course of history has changed. Now the righteousness of God has been revealed. So there are only two kinds of righteousness before God. One is the incomplete righteousness of the children of Adam, and the other is the righteousness from God, which comes through faith in Christ.

Summary

Paul's conception of justification is directed in a special way by his theology of predestination. To some extent he has accepted the views of previous Jewish theology, but for the most part he gives a novel reinterpretation of the tradition. This points soteriology in a new and, as regards Jewish theology, paradoxical direction.

As a teacher of the law, Paul differs from other Jewish teachers. His letters do not contain the common themes of *halakha,* even though he seems to use some of the principles of Jewish interpretation of the law. In Paul's letters the law occurs mostly in a soteriological context. His teaching concerning the function of the law is clearly governed by the ideas of a theology of predestination. The law, which is good as to its essence and in this sense aims at righteousness, is given a new function in divine salvation history. This function is based on Paul's radical anthropology. Due to the sin of Adam all men are under the wrath of God. As a result the good law is transformed into a horrifying power. It brings death to every one who is left under its sway. This results in the great paradox of the Torah as regards Israel: the law that was given for life, ultimately brings death to the chosen people.

Following the same principle, Paul teaches about the works of the law. Old Testament faith was based on obedience to the will of God. It found its best expression in service to God, *Avodat Israel*, which meant the keeping of all the precepts of the Lord. This "work" was the pride and joy of all Israel. In the new polarity of the theology of Paul this piety became mere works of the law, the significance of which had to be defined in the context of predestinarian theology. The works of the law could never be true righteousness, even though they had a good intention.

In the predestinarian theology of Paul the principle of "counting as loss" became a leading feature. It is a consequent conclusion of the application of paradoxical polarization to the theology of justification. When compared with the righteousness of God that has been revealed in Christ, the value of all human piety must be denied. The salvation that God has prepared does not seem to fit in every detail the expectations of most Jewish theologians.

In Galatians Paul employed a theology of predestination as a proof for his concept of justification by faith. By emphasizing the judgment that was upon all mankind he was able to conclude that there is no difference between the Jews and the Gentiles as regards salvation. There is another kind of polarization, instead. The Jews, too, must believe in Christ in order to find proper righteousness. The true Israel is that group of the saved who have believed in Christ.

In Philippians Paul lays down the principle of denying the value of previous achievements. Such a denial was based on the idea of paradoxical polarization. This also concerned Paul's own piety and his obedience to the law as a Pharisee. His previous achievements and perfect life had now become a source of 'harm' to him, because they had prevented him from finding the righteousness of God in Christ.

This polarization, produced by predestinarian theology, defines Paul's concept of justification and makes it dualistic. In principle there are but two kinds of righteousness. One is the kind that comes from God. This is the righteousness that comes from faith in Christ. The other is human righteousness, and this must be regarded "as if" it were by works. This is why it becomes self-righteousness. If the hearers of the gospel do not submit to God's righteousness, they are left on their own, i.e. under the power of the law. In this case they are unavoidably left under the wrath of God because they are under the predestination of judgment. The righteousness that comes from Christ, on the other hand, is a free gift of God. It is revealed to faith and through faith, and it produces life.

Chapter 4

Paul's Universalist Soteriology

Our investigation of predestinarian theology leads eventually to a general interpretation of Paul's soteriology. This is only natural, because questions relating to the restricted freedom of man are crucial as regards the teaching about salvation. Here too the problem of theodicy has its proper place. In previous chapters we have already seen that, in the letters of Paul, predestinarian theology occurs in important passages which speak of the revelation of God's righteousness and the justification of man. This is how our topic is connected with the more general theme: how Paul understands the salvific message which concerns all mankind. In scholarly discussion of this theme the Christological principle used by Paul has been the focus of interest. For this reason we must pay special attention to its nature.

§ 13 The Christological Argument in Soteriology

Since the beginning of the 1960s scholars have been discussing the primacy of Christology in Paul's soteriology.[1] According to some scholars, his universalist soteriology is based solely on theological reflection on the Easter event. If God decided to bring salvation to men by sending Christ into this world, then the whole of God's plan of salvation – even before Easter – must be interpreted in line with this centre.[2] As the result of such reasoning the soteriology of Paul appears to be based on a radical reinterpretation and even arbitrary use of tradition.[3]

This kind of discussion has given birth to a difficult problem with regard to

---

[1] See e.g. Schoeps, *Paulus,* 177; van Dülmen, *Theologie,* 212-213.

[2] "Denn die ganze "Theologie" des Apostels is ja zunächst nichts anderes als ein Umdenken aller überkommenen Vorstellungen und Begriffe auf dieses Ereignis hin... " Schoeps, *Paulus,* 177.

[3] "Christus ist das Zentrum und der Angelpunkt der paulinischen Theologie; einzig aus ihm erhellt sich die tatsächliche Bedeutung alles Vorausgegangenen... Hat Gott tatsächlich in Christus das Heil gewirkt, so ist sein früheres Handeln nur von hier aus richtig zu verstehen und einzuordnen. Nur das von Christus retrospektive Denken erfasst das Heilshandeln Gottes in der Zeit vor Christus. So ist auch die Frage des Gesetzes für Paulus einzig ein christologisches Problem." van Dülmen, *Theologie,* 213.

Paul's Christological soteriology. This is the claim that Paul produced theology mainly by deductive inference – and that this unavoidably led to discretion and contradiction as regards Second Temple Jewish theology in general. If Paul had formulated his teaching merely in terms of Christology, he apparently needed to distort traditional Jewish teaching to some extent.

The harsh opposition and antagonism in respect of Jewish theology which is evident in Paul's letters, has been explained on the same principle. This kind of reasoning has further led to the conception that Paul's own relation to his Jewish heritage was a rather tense and contradictory one. It is precisely this aspect of Pauline studies which has led some scholars to suggest that Paul actually gives a false and even distorted picture of the Judaism of his time.[4] In such a situation we have good reason to ask what is the status of the Christological argument in Paul's soteriology.

13.1. Paul and his Jewish heritage

The explanation of Paul's relation to his Jewish heritage, and Second Temple Jewish soteriology in particular, is not an easy task. On the one hand, it is clear that Paul renewed and reinterpreted Jewish teaching. His statements troubled the leaders of traditional Judaism, and some Jewish Christians, too. In addition, his teaching differs from the conceptions of most religious sects and groups in Second Temple Judaism. We have earlier analyzed some of Paul's principles in his reinterpretation of traditional Jewish theology. They changed the content of theology, sometimes even in the direction of a paradoxical antithesis.

On the other hand, however, we have to admit that Paul constantly uses themes which derive from Jewish theology. He makes use of the Old Testament, but, in addition, his soteriology is widely based on conceptions which prevailed in Second Temple theology in general. The traditional subjects which Paul treats are not in contradiction with contemporary Jewish theology. Only his interpretation is new.

For example, Paul shares with several Jewish texts the conviction that God will ultimately punish the ungodly.[5] He also proclaims that God himself will solve the problem of sin by granting his righteousness to the elect – a concept which was common in the teaching of many Jewish groups, even though their

---

[4] The debate initiated by Sanders and Räisänen has been necessary. It requires new contributions, however, since the relation between the Christological argument and tradition has not been investigated sufficiently – even though most scholars would agree on its importance.

[5] This is a general feature of Second Temple Jewish Theology, see analyses in chapters 3-5. Cf. Mattern, *Verständnis des Gerichtes,* 19ff.; Winninge, *Sinners and the Righteous,* 42f.; Seifrid, *Justification,* 118-119.

understanding of election and justification differed from that of Paul.[6] In this respect the statements of Paul remind one of those made in Second Temple writings, such as the Testaments of the Twelve Patriarchs or the Qumran texts.

"And after this there shall arise for you a Star from Jacob in peace: And a man shall arise from my posterity like the Sun of righteousness... and in him will be found no sin... and he will pour the spirit of grace on you. And you shall be sons in truth" (TJud. 24:1-4).[7]

"And he shall open the gates of paradise; he shall remove the sword that has threatened since Adam, and he will grant to the saints to eat of the tree of life. The spirit of holiness shall be upon them." (TLev. 18:10-11).

"Blessed be the God of Israel who keeps mercy towards His Covenant, and the appointed times of salvation with the people He has delivered" (1QM XIV, 4–5; Vermes).

In this respect Paul's soteriology can be considered a consistent interpretation of Jewish tradition. Even though he most probably did not know all the writings that we mentioned above, he was evidently familiar with similar themes deriving from common Jewish theology and the Old Testament. Such a conclusion is further confirmed by Paul's way of employing quotations from the Scriptures.[8]

As regards detail, Paul's soteriology is much more radical than previous Jewish conceptions. Despite such radicalness we must remember that most groups interpreted God's promises and especially the teachings of the prophets by applying them to their own historical situation.[9] *Even a radical contemporary application, as such, is not contrary to the common principles of interpretation of Second Temple Jewish theology.*[10]

---

[6] The basic idea of synergism contained these two aspects, as we have stated in this study. Salvation comes from God – but only for the righteous.

[7] I am of the opinion that the quoted part of this passage belongs to Jewish tradition. The messianology of the text is traditional and the adoption formula is common to most Second Temple Jewish writings.

[8] For the relation between Jewish pseudepigrapha, early Judaism and early Christian theology cf. Charlesworth, *Old Testament,* 68. The principles of eschatological interpretation have been investigated by Ellis, *Old Testament,* 101ff.

[9] This authoritative reinterpretation can be detected in the pages of the Old Testament, see Fishbane, *Biblical Interpretation,* 538f. As regards rabbinic teaching, there was also a principle of authority, and this is a feature common to both rabbinic theology and Jesus. Daube, *New Testament,* 218f.

[10] Sanders, who has proposed the priority of the Christological principle, fails to recognize this. For him, Paul's soteriology is antithetical only in a deductive way. "Paul seems to ignore (and by implication deny) the grace of God toward Israel as evidenced by the election and the covenant... *Paul in fact explicitly denies that the Jewish covenant can be effective for salvation, thus consciously denying the basis of Judaism.*" Sanders, *Paul,* 551 (italics his). This is where I find his explanation erroneous. A contemporary application takes full account of tradition. The idea of fulfilment does not mean a denial of "the basis of Judaism".

On the contrary, Paul seems to construct his theology quite in the manner of Second Temple Jewish tradition. The dynamics of this interpretation are simple. Traditional themes are used in the interpretation of contemporary events.[11] The interpretation itself introduces new elements into the message, but the basic material and the main subjects remain the same. This is why we can find several subjects which are common to many different writings of the Second Temple period.[12] One can find features in common as regards the theology of the law, the expectation of judgment, the interpretation of the tradition of promise and messianology. All of these themes build a bridge between Second Temple Jewish theology and Paul's soteriology.

As regards Paul's concept of righteousness from the law, there is a counterpart in Jewish theology relating to the very identity of Jewish piety (in *Avodat Israel*), as we have seen earlier.[13] Jewish nomism was not, however, left in the sphere of mere legalism, as scholars have rightly noted. In a synergistic context there is a strong belief that it is God who acts for the salvation of man. The righteous, too, fall into sin. Most Jewish writers are convinced that man is a sinner by nature.

We must remember, however, that Jewish theologians do not teach the justification of sinners.[14] We must make a distinction between the Temple service with its atoning sacrifices and Second Temple soteriological dualism. Even though several writers speak of God's righteousness almost in terms of forensic justification, in these texts it is the righteous – though fallen in some respect – who are declared righteous by the mercy of God. This is the belief, for example, in the Psalms of Solomon.[15]

A similar conviction can also be found in the texts from Qumran, where the mercy of God was exalted in an extraordinary way:

---

[11] Cf. Barrett, *Cambridge History of the Bible,* 407ff.

[12] This was evident, for example, as regards the teachings on eschatology among different groups of that period; see analyses in chapter 4.

[13] See chapter 10.3.

[14] In the covenantal interpretation, however, such an identification was made as we have already seen in chapter 11.1. According to Dunn, Jewish covenantal theology was based on the idea of "justification by faith", and this belief was thus something that Jews and Christians had in common. Dunn, *Law,* 190-191.

[15] Lührmann totally identifies these concepts: "Nor, finally, was Paul the first to understand human righteousness in a forensic sense of 'being justified by God' – the *Psalms of Solomon* have the same idea when the righteous ones are those whom the Lord will cleanse, will declare clean (3.8)." Even though Lührmann's explanation seems to be somewhat anachronistic, it reveals the basic analogy between these views. Lührmann, *JSNT 36* (1989) 89.

"As for me, if I stumble, the mercies of God shall be my salvation always; and if I fall in the sin of the flesh, in the justice of God, which endures eternally, shall my judgment be" (1QS XI,12, Martínez).

There is no doubt a covenantal ideology behind this kind of belief, but it cannot be identified with traditional covenantalism.[16] The Qumran community taught exclusivistic, apocalyptic covenantalism where most Jews of that time were condemned under the power of the Spirit of Falsehood.[17]

The question of the righteousness that comes from God is more complex than this, however. At Qumran a claim that God would also justify ungodly outsiders by faith alone, would have been mere blasphemy.[18] The soteriology of the sect concerned only those obedient righteous ones who had proved their validity in the strict ascetic system of the community. They were – and this is not to be denied – the ones who were objects of God's everlasting mercy and his irresistible providence.

In this kind of historical and theological context we can further discern some of the special features of Paul's soteriology. Firstly we may note that the references of his contemporary applications are unique. He gives a theological explanation of the death of a religious leader, and what is most peculiar, his resurrection from the dead. One can naturally find no parallel for such a hermeneutic in Second Temple Judaism. Even though there were candidates for the messianological office, they were primarily political and their campaigns were short-lived. After their revolts were put down, there was no

---

[16] Seifrid refers to the predestinarian nature of such a concept of grace which, according to him, is common to both Qumran and Paul. Nevertheless he emphasizes that there is a difference, too: "Paul never attaches an atoning value to the behaviour of believers in Christ." Seifrid, *Justification,* 181; cf. Röhser, *Prädestination,* 75.

[17] It is good to note that even scholars who accept the covenantalist theory admit this. Sanders himself writes about the admission of novices: "We have previously noted that members are purified on entry. One of the most basic views of the Qumran community was that all outside the sect were damned. Since one cannot be born into the Qumran covenant, it follows that there must be purification at the time of admission." Sanders, *Paul,* 318.

[18] Some scholars identify the Qumranic conception optimistically as righteousness through faith, as we have seen in earlier chapters. See e.g. Marx, RQ 22 (1967) 181. Most scholars perceive the difference, however, and this can be found in Paul's radical concept of justification by faith alone. See Jüngel, *Paulus und Jesus,* 41. Cf. Benoit: "It should be noted that at Qumran the sinner is never said to be 'justified'." Benoit, *Paul and the Dead Sea Scrolls,* 26-27; cf. Ringgren, *Faith,* 120f., 144f. Grundmann finds an explanation to this problem in covenantal theology. The Teacher of Righteousness renewed the alliance of God with Israel: "election and alliance are acts of God's grace and free will, but they oblige the elect to observe the treaty of alliance given in the Torah; God's goodness makes the fallen and sinful men of Israel just through the renewal of the spirit of truth in them." In the theology of Paul the place of the Law is taken by Christ. This is why Paul's teaching of justification differs crucially from that of Qumran. Grundmann, *Paul and the Dead Sea Scrolls,* 97-98; 114.

one to proclaim their resurrection.[19] In the sapiential tradition we have more points of contact with Paul's soteriology.

The predestinarian theology of the books of Maccabees is interesting since here we find teaching concerning the fate of martyrs.[20] This message was directed against ungodly rulers who had persecuted the righteous. In such a situation it was necessary to formulate a theology explaining the fate of martyrs. The problem of theodicy was now solved by promising resurrection to the righteous and prescribing condemnation to the ungodly.[21]

"But the souls of the righteous are in the hand of God, and no torment will ever touch them. In the eyes of the foolish they seemed to have died, and their departure was thought to be a disaster... but they are at peace. For though in the sight of others they were punished, their hope is full of immortality... They will govern nations and rule over peoples, and the Lord will reign over them forever... But the ungodly will be punished as their reasoning deserves..." (SapSol. 3:1-10).

A similar conviction can be seen in 2 Maccabees, in the response of a freedom fighter as he stands before his persecutors: "One cannot but choose to die at the hands of mortals and to cherish the hope God gives of being raised again by him. But for you there will be no resurrection to life" (2 Macc. 7:14).

Such predestinarian theology, explaining the fate of the martyrs, has some parallel features with the teaching of Paul. There is a firm conviction that the suffering of the innocent will be avenged and that the martyrs will be exalted in the resurrection. This was not a messianological belief, however. The main aim of such teaching was to assure the pious that God was on their side, and to promise them compensation for the sufferings which they have to face at the hands of their persecutors. This would eventually be fulfilled in their exaltation by God.

Paul's radical predestinarian theology changed this pattern, too.[22] It was

---

[19] As Benoit concludes, a complete change had taken place when Paul formulated his soteriology. "The Christian attains to his new justice through faith in Christ (Rom 3:22ff.). There is nothing comparable to this in Qumran, where it is not even conceivable. The Teacher of the Hodayoth never proclaims belief in his own person which would bring salvation to his disciples... The faith in Christ, which saves a Christian, is not merely faith in his teaching, but faith in his death and resurrection." Benoit, *Paul and the Dead Sea Scrolls,* 27. In addition, we must remember that the eschatological hope of Israel in general was focussed on the restoration of the Davidic monarchy. See e.g. Collins, *Scepter and the Star,* 23, 51ff., 57.

[20] See above chapter 3.2.

[21] Cf. Nickelsburg, *Resurrection,* 48ff.

[22] According to Lührmann, Paul differs from other Jewish theologians especially when he radicalizes what, for example, the Psalms of Solomon teach about salvation or about the promises given to Abraham's seed. Lührmann, *JSNT 36* (1989) 89f. The reason for such a radicalization is simply Christ himself.

based on a new interpretation of divine judgment. The whole of mankind is held accountable for the passion of the Son of God. The sins of entire mankind are laid on Christ and he atones for them, thus bringing redemption to all men (see e.g. Rom. 3:25; 4:25; 5:18; 8:3).

The uniqueness of Paul's theology lies, then, in the very same feature which we are investigating here: the Christocentric interpretation. On this ground Paul abandons the optimistic anthropology of sapiential theology and refuses to appeal to the will of man. Instead of referring to a person's free will and to repentance he speaks of death and man's complete inability to fulfil God's precepts.[23]

For Paul, the problem of theodicy cannot be solved by increasing the responsibility of man. One cannot escape the awaiting judgment and condemnation merely by committing oneself to perfect obedience. Thus the setting is crucially different from that of the traditional Jewish theology of predestination. Paul is not treating the problem of how the sufferings of the righteous ones (the Jews) would finally be recompensed.[24] Instead of these traditional subjects Paul teaches radical predestination to eternal damnation.

The problem of theodicy cannot be explained merely by referring to the antithesis between the righteous and the ungodly. According to Paul, humankind is facing a universal crisis. The relationship between God and man is totally corrupted and needs a major solution. Christocentric soteriology presents a brand-new solution here. The problem of theodicy will not be solved by God's compensatory act of exalting the persecuted righteous on the last day. Instead, the whole world will be brought before the judgment seat of God when the last day comes. In the context of this kind of eschatology the unique atoning act of Christ becomes the only possible sacrifice that can bring redemption to sinners.[25]

It is Christ alone who has suffered for the guilt and punishment of the

---

[23] We can apply to Paul what Rogerson said with regard to the whole New Testament: "Whatever else it may be, Christianity is a unique interpretation of the OT." Rogerson, *ABD III* (1992) 425.

[24] The suffering of Christians is naturally a common theme for him, see e.g. Rom. 8:18ff.

[25] Cf. Seifrid as regards the explanation of Romans 3:25f. "If sins prior to Christ's death... had already received forgiveness in God's covenantal faithfulness, Christ's death could scarcely be interpreted as an atonement. Paul's reference to God's restraint... points in this direction as well, since Paul refers to it elsewhere in Romans as a divine forestalling of punishment which allows for repentance. In this case, the reference to God's righteousness as his covenantal faithfulness signifies his determination to punish those who because of transgression are outside of his covenant." Seifrid, *Justification,* 221. This leads to a complete reinterpretation of the covenantal theory, even though Seifrid does not himself say so.

collective sinfulness of mankind and atoned for sins before the Mighty God who is the true judge of the whole world.

Our first notion concerning the status of the Christological argument in soteriology focusses on Paul's relation to his Jewish heritage. It seems that modern scholarship has partly over-simplified the dynamics which direct Paul's use of tradition. In several themes relating to salvation or judgment Paul uses Jewish tradition quite in the manner of other writers in the Second Temple period. He makes a radical contemporary application in his teaching – but so did most religious groups of his time, albeit on different subjects. This conclusion leads us to further questions. How does Paul view his time, and how does he interpret the events which form the basis of his gospel?

13.2. The centre of salvation history

The basic idea of the primacy of Christology in the soteriology of Paul is in itself rather old in Pauline scholarship. As regards New Testament interpretation, it is a theme which has been prominent for at least as long as scholars have considered the divine plan of salvation to be a central theme of Paul's soteriology.[26] The modern discussion differs from the earlier one only in its emphasis that Paul's nomism should be treated in a novel way. According to the previous interpretation, called by the term 'history of salvation,' Paul made Christ the centre of world history – and especially the centre of God's plan of salvation.[27] This was furthermore the reason why Paul's interpretation of Jewish theology was explained with the aid of this "centre".

Such a pattern of interpretation is quite a useful one. One cannot explain Paul's soteriology satisfactorily unless one takes his conception of history into account. Even a short glimpse at Paul's treatment of history and eschatology justifies such an approach.[28] Such a perspective with regard to salvation history gives us a fresh point of departure when we attempt to answer the

---

[26] The term 'salvation history' comes especially from the writings of O. Cullmann, see Cullmann, *Heil als Geschichte*. We need to bear in mind this line of interpretation because this is precisely where the Christological interpetation of Paul's soteriology has been prominent in the history of Pauline studies.

[27] Cullmann, *Heil als Geschichte*, 85-86. According to Cullmann, the awareness of salvation history was constantly in the minds of New Testament writers, and thus it becomes a primary principle of interpretation in New Testament scholarship, too, see Cullmann, *Heil als Geschichte*, 54, 97f., 104f.

[28] Such a view is supported, for example, by Schoeps, who speaks of an eschatological theology of aeons, Schoeps, *Paulus*, 96ff.; Luz, who writes of theology concerning history, Luz, *Geschichtsverständnis*, 222ff.; and Beker, whose interpretation of history is of an apocalyptic nature, Beker, *Paul*, 144ff. A complete pattern of salvation history is also accepted by Goppelt, *Theologie*, 386-388, and Stuhlmacher, *Theologie*, 269ff.

question, to what amount the Christological premise affected the formation of Paul's soteriology. In this task it is useful to analyse the points where Paul opposed traditional Jewish theology with his new soteriology.

Here we can make use of the analyses made in previous chapters. Paul's antitheses are based on his predestinarian theology, because it was precisely this aspect which was used as a basis for the new polarization. According to the principle of polarization, the judgment of God was universal. The fall of Adam concerned all humankind. Thus every man, whether Jew or Gentile, was predestined to be left under the wrath of God. There was no longer any distinction between the chosen people and the Gentiles. And the basic reason for this was God's salvific act in the death of Christ.[29]

"For there is no distinction, since all have sinned and fall short of the glory of God; they are now justified by his grace as a gift, through the redemption that is in Christ Jesus" (Rom. 3:22-24).

This new antithesis occurs constantly in the writings of Paul. Mankind is not merely under sin (Rom. 5:8) but more: it is actually God's enemy. "For if while we were enemies, we were reconciled to God through the death of his Son, much more surely, having been reconciled, will we be saved by his life" (5:10).

In the history of salvation Adam and Christ are in opposition to each other. The fall of Adam brought death which could be overcome only by redemption through the death of Christ. "For if the many died through the one man's trespass, much more surely have the grace of God and the free gift in the grace of the one man, Jesus Christ, abounded for the many" (5:15). Paul further emphasized such an antithesis by describing the results of sin: "For the wages of sin is death, but the free gift of God is eternal life in Christ Jesus our Lord" (6:23).[30]

Paul's soteriology is centred around the death and resurrection of Christ. His message is simply the act of God in Christ, and this act has taken place in history. In this respect Easter is inevitably the centre of salvation history. All

---

[29] Even though the predestinarian theology of Paul has rarely been investigated from this point of view, his teaching on atonement has been treated in a similar manner as here. Cf. e.g. Wilckens, *Römer I*, 199ff.; Stuhlmacher, *Römer*, 58ff. It is probably useful to remark that this is not merely a quest for a "centre" of Pauline theology. As Beker has noted, there is a certain "coherence" in Paul's theology which is based on an apocalyptic scenario of his thought: "my definition of the term coherence points to a field of meaning, a network of symbolic relations which constitutes Paul's 'linguistic world'. The master-symbolism of this coherent field, or its substratum, is Jewish apocalypticism..." Beker, *NTS 34* (1988) 369. Paul's predestinarian theology is part of his apocalyptic scenario and he can employ it in several "contingent" applications without losing the basic content.

[30] Adam-typology is suggested here e.g. by Luz, *Geschichtsverständnis*, 206-207.

other stages of that history or scenario must be inferred from that primary event.[31]

In the writings of Paul there are passages where the Christological principle is opposed to Jewish tradition. The most important of these is in Romans 3. Paul considers it essential that God disclosed his salvation and righteousness in the atonement which Christ has achieved. "But now, apart from law, the righteousness of God has been disclosed, and is attested by the law and the prophets" (Νυνὶ δὲ χωρὶς νόμου δικαιοσύνη θεοῦ πεφανέρωται)" (Rom. 3:21). The word "now" which begins the clause emphasizes the appearance of Christ as a crucial moment in salvation history, and in fact makes it once again the centre of the whole of history.

The disclosure of God's righteousness is an eschatological event and it took place in the work of Christ.[32] Instead of speaking of revelation (cf. 1:17,18) Paul here uses a word meaning "disclosing" (φανερόω). So he can underline that the righteousness of God which has "now" been disclosed has also been completely fulfilled in history.[33] God's saving action has been fulfilled in the righteousness which Christ brings, and the promises of the law and the prophets must be interpreted according to this principle and projected to this centre.

The centrality of the appearance of Christ is furthermore an important factor as regards Paul's understanding of the revelation of God. Paul is convinced that the righteousness of God which has been disclosed in Christ is God's final revelation of the salvation he has provided for the whole of humankind. The new righteousness is in this sense unique and different from all other aspects of divine revelation. This is why Paul makes the suffering and resurrection of Christ a hermeneutical principle by which all Scripture and the whole of soteriology must be interpreted.

This led to a total reinterpretation of Jewish theological tradition. Paul renewed conceptions concerning the Law, righteousness, and especially the nature of faith in respect to faithfulness. They all had to be conformed to the

---

[31] In monographs on New Testament theology this principle has been described in several ways. Goppelt emphasizes the event of the cross and the cultic interpretation connected with it, Goppelt, *Theologie,* 416, 423. According to Beker, the message of Easter is based on "an apocalyptic horizon in the impending triumph of God". Beker, *NTS 34* (1988) 373. Stuhlmacher uses the term gospel, which for Paul means the Easter message as the final salvific will of God, Stuhlmacher, *Theologie,* 315.

[32] Eschatological interpretation is suggested e.g. by Schlier, *Römerbrief,* 104; Stuhlmacher, *Römer,* 57.

[33] For the "watershed of history", see especially Wilckens, *Römer I,* 185.

Christological principle. This is why the righteousness of God is basically righteousness that comes from faith (Rom. 1:17; 3:22; 4:24-25; 10:3,6).[34]

For Paul, justification became an important principle of interpretation in soteriology. It was an instrument with which he could reinterpret traditional Jewish theology. On the other hand, however, we must remember that Paul consistently based his teaching of the righteousness of God on the Scriptures.[35] Just like other religious groups at that time, Paul did not think that his reinterpretation abrogated God's promises in the Scriptures or nullified Jewish tradition as such. On the contrary, he was convinced that he was now witnessing the fulfilment of salvation history which God himself had been conducting throughout the history of Israel. The new which Paul was experiencing and interpreting was never in opposition to the old, but rather built on its foundation.

Paul seems to be trying to say that a Jew does not need to become a "Christian" before he can see and accept the very meaning of the righteousness of God as his saving action. In practice, however, there was a tense contradiction. So we might say that eventually the acceptance of the righteousness of God would, according to Paul, change one's relation to traditional Judaism, as well.

The use of the Christological principle in the theology of Paul can be seen especially in his concept of history. The work of Christ at Easter is, for Paul, the centre of God's history of salvation. It is a watershed of God's work in this world, and therefore it is also the fixed point by which the reinterpretation of previous tradition must be made. We must note, however, that this re-interpretation was made according to the principle of contemporary application. This is why an analysis of this principle is essential as we attempt to solve the problems of Paul's Christocentric soteriology.

13.3. The principle of contemporary application

As we attempt to explain how Paul applied the Christological principle, we need to define the relation between contemporary application and soteriological polarization. Christology has a primary function in Paul's soteriology precisely because he believed that Christology was based on God's saving acts in contemporary history. The death and resurrection of God's Son formed the centre of God's plan of salvation, as well as the centre of history. Therefore Paul was determined to project all Jewish tradition onto Christology and make the application to soteriology from that point of view.

How does this application relate to the radical polarization of soteriology? Are we speaking of mere deduction? It seems evident that Christological

---

[34] Cf. Goppelt, *Theologie,* 470-471; Stuhlmacher, *Theologie,* 326-330, 334.

[35] For questions concerning the righteousness of God, see chapters 12.1. and 12.3.

soteriology served as a justification for the radicalization of the concept of predestination. It was precisely because God's Son had had to face death that this death had to be a crucial factor in salvation history.

We have already referred to the idea that the Easter message implied several subjects of soteriology even on the basis of its normal content. As the Son of God had died, the whole of humankind must also have been under the power of death. And when this death had from the very beginning been explained as an atoning death for people's sins, it had to be essential, too, as regards anthropology – and consequently our conception of the eschatological future of man.

After such a conclusion Paul could no longer teach that man's relation to God was dependent only on the principles of traditional Judaism. The promises of God were not enough, and the Temple service was no longer sufficient. As the whole world was under the power of sin, a right relation to God could be attained only through Christ who has become the Saviour of the world.[36]

It is easy to understand that due to such an argumentation several scholars have concluded that Paul's soteriology was deductive. But should we consider Paul's relation to Jewish theology as being that simple? We have already seen above that the principles of interpretation which Paul applied were similar to those of Second Temple Jewish theology. Contemporary application did not mean the rejection of tradition – which actually never happened among Jewish religious groups either.[37]

Those scholars who emphasize the primacy of Christology have felt it easy to say that most themes in Paul's theology were formed merely on the Christological principle. This concerned, for example, his conception of the law.[38] Such explanation was an over-interpretation and must be assessed in detail later.

This kind of interpretation was further influenced by the views which

---

[36] Cf. e.g. chapter 8.1.

[37] Talmon has suggested that the identity of the Qumran sect was based on a "prophetically inspired belief-system". "It is my thesis that the Community of the Renewed Covenant should be viewed as the third- or second-century crystallization of a major socio-religious movement which arose in early post-exilic Judaism. The movement was prophetically inspired and inclined to apocalypticism. It perpetuated a spiritual trend whose origins can be traced to the prophets of the First Temple period." Talmon, *Community*, 22. There is a prophetical validity in the reinterpretations by the Qumran community, and this is most probably one important aspect in Pauline reinterpretation, too.

[38] See e.g. Schoeps: "Die Aufhebung des Gesetzes ist für die Theologie des Apostels Paulus ein messianologisches Lehrstück. Sie ist akut geworden durch die gemäss urchristlichem Glauben kürzlich erfolgte Auferstehung Jesus von den Toten." Schoeps, *Paulus*, 177; and van Dülmen: "So ist auch die Frage des Gesetzes für Paulus einzig ein christologisches Problem." van Dülmen, *Theologie*, 213.

scholars held about the historical context of Paul's theology. After Bultmann Paul was explained in the context of pagan Hellenism and even Gnosticism. In such a scholarly tradition it was easy to maintain that Paul's concept of the law was not directed by Jewish tradition but by Christology. This is no longer the point of departure in modern Pauline studies. We have seen that, before his conversion, Saul had accepted a "zealous" view of the Law which was common in Second Temple Judaism.[39]

When we attempt to explain the relation between contemporary application and soteriological polarization, we must place Paul once more in his natural theological – as well as historical – environment. Here again we can make special use of Qumran, even though Paul, as far as we know, did not have direct contact with that sect. Qumran provides us with a relevant example of a soteriology which had been formed apart from the Temple of Jerusalem and in opposition to its cultic service.

As we have seen in chapter 5, the sacrifices of the new "temple" of Qumran were prayer and perfect obedience.[40] They were able to make the sect a proper temple replacing the corrupt Temple of Jerusalem. The righteous ones of Qumran went so far as to describe their own council as the holy of holies, the place were God Himself lived (1QS IX, 5-6).

In Florilegium (4QFlor.) we see a description of how God would re-plant Israel and build her a new "house".[41] The interpretation reads as follows:

"This (refers to) the house into which shall never enter [...] either the Ammonite, or the Moabite, or the Bastard, or the foreigner, or the proselyte, never, because there [he will reveal] to the holy ones, eternal [glory] will appear over it for ever; foreigners shall not again lay it waste as they laid waste, at the beginning, the tem[ple of Is]rael for its sins. And he commanded to build for himself a temple of man, to offer him in it, before him, the works of the law" (4QFlor 3-6).

At Qumran the Teacher of Righteousness had founded a new "temple". The community believed that they had been obedient to the will of God and now the promises of God were fulfilled in their lives, as they submitted themselves to keeping the precepts of the law of Moses. At Qumran the priestly nature of the sect and their strict asceticism as regards the obedience to the law, were closely connected with each other.[42]

As a holiness sect the group were obliged to fulfil the demands of the law in

---

[39] Cf. Lührmann, *JSNT 36* (1989) 77.

[40] See especially chapter 5.2.

[41] There was a reference to Exod. 15:17-18.

[42] Gärtner, *Temple,* 20ff.; Klinzing, *Umdeutung,* 80ff. It should be emphasized once again that this was the primary reason for the strict synergism of the sect. The soteriology of the sect cannot be interpreted in terms of "Deuteronomistic" covenantal nomism; contra Sanders, *Paul,* 241, 248.

every detail. Devout living, the doing of the "works of law" (the perfect *Avodat Israel*) atoned for the sins of the elect.[43] The community which lived in obedient devotion was convinced that it was the elect "remnant" which was chosen to lead Israel to eschatological glory.

Qumran theologians thus had had the courage to reinterpret the holiest centre of Judaism which throughout history had been the core of (the priestly) Jewish religion: the primacy of the Temple. By contemporary application Qumran theologians made their own sect the community of salvation and God's promises were projected onto it.[44] Even the act of making atonement was transferred from the temple to the community.[45]

Paul exploits a similar pattern of contemporary application in his Christological interpretation. He, too, is convinced that atonement and salvation no longer come through the Temple service. They can now be found in the gospel of the resurrected Christ, instead. This is undeniably a courageous reinterpretation and unique in content, but as a procedure not unparalleled in Second Temple theology. According to certain extraordinary principles of Jewish theology, it was possible to consider salvation possible apart from the Temple and on the ground of the atoning work of a new Saviour and Messiah, whom God sent into this world.[46]

The differences between the conceptions of Qumran and Paul's Christological soteriology are crucial. Paul believed in the Son of God who atones for the sins of Israel and actually for the sins of the whole of humankind.[47] At Qumran, atonement was still sought after through obedience. In this sense, for Paul, Christology is a primary and directive factor in soteriology. He no

---

[43] Cf. Garnet, *Salvation*, 116: "One of the reasons for the existence of the Community was to study the Law and thus prepare the way of the Lord. Knowledge and trust were intended to issue in obedience, which is seen as a *sine qua non* for salvation. For the sinner this involves repentance, for the saint patience. The Community member accepts the punishment of his sins and knows that in so doing he is benefiting from the remedial effect that is intended." See also Seifrid, *Justification*, 96.

[44] According to Gärtner, Qumran theologians interpreted Messianic terms – such as *Ebed Yahweh,* Son of man etc. – collectively when they taught about the atonement. "Part of the self-consciousness of the community was made up of the idea that they were a group who were called to fulfil the Old Testament prophecies connected with these terms." Such a collective interpretation extended to the question of temple symbolism, as well. "In the Qumran texts it is the community that is the temple." Gärtner, *Temple*, 137.

[45] For the "applied exegesis" of Qumran, see e.g. Vermes, *Qumran in Perspective*, 148ff.; Martínez-Barrera, *People*, 112. Cf. Barrett: "It is however particularly important that the Qumrân sectaries saw scripture being fulfilled in themselves and in the event that befell them." Barrett, *Cambridge History of the Bible*, 387.

[46] Cf. Barrett, *Cambridge History of the Bible*, 407.

[47] This simple point of departure must be borne in mind. "God had made atonement apart from the provisions of *Torah* in the crucifixion of the Messiah." Seifrid, *Justification*, 178.

longer thought it possible to return to the traditional principles and traditional service to God without faith in the Son of God. Christ had renewed the whole pattern of service to God.[48]

In addition, the radicalness of Paul's contemporary application is relative. At Qumran their dualistic soteriology was so polarized that the Temple priests were considered "children of darkness".[49] Paul, on the other hand, radicalized his soteriology with a stricter polarization still: all men die in Adam. Despite such a black-and-white polarization Paul did not abandon the terminology of Jewish theology, as little as did the theologians of Qumran. According to Paul, the new community was the "remnant" of Israel. It was the "true" Israel which comprised the new people of promise. Paul's polarization never distorted the basis of soteriology, which lay in the promise tradition of the Old Testament.

The focus on Christological argument in Paul's soteriology is fruitful as regards the explanation of the relation between Paul and his Jewish heritage. For him, Christ was the centre of God's history of salvation. In Paul's soteriology one can find evident inferences from Christ to different aspects of the teaching of salvation. Modern scholarship seems to have been too quick, however, to define this principle in a merely deductive way. By contrast, Paul uses a principle of contemporary application, which was a common principle in Second Temple Jewish theology. In such a context Christology is a consistent conclusion of a re-interpretation of Jewish tradition. This crucial status of Christology has led some scholars further to raise another difficult question. As Paul had focussed his theology on Christ and the events of Easter, was he compelled to reconstruct an antithesis for Christology – an antithesis which actually did not exist in Jewish theology itself?

---

[48] See e.g. Grundmann, *Paul and the Dead Sea Scrolls,* 114.

[49] Klinzing, *Umdeutung,* 12ff.; Ringgren, *Faith,* 32ff., 216f.

§ 14 A Solution Before the Plight?

As the nature of the Christological soteriology of Paul was analyzed in the context of nomistic theology, some scholars began to ask whether his new theology was actually providing a response to any real problem of Jewish theology. If soteriology was based on the death and resurrection of Jesus, was it not merely an additional task for Paul to seek – or even invent – a human plight which could be solved by this new salvation? Discussion of this theme centred around the covenantal nomism theory of E.P. Sanders and the claims of H. Räisänen that Paul's thought was inconsistent.

14.1. Paul and the alleged "covenantal nomism"

With his theory of covenantal nomism, Sanders has probably been the most efficient of those who have promoted and developed the notions of van Dülmen and Schoeps with regard to the primacy of Christology in Paul's soteriology. The main idea in covenantal nomism was that the keeping of the law in Judaism was, on behalf of men, merely a response to God's election and mercy – within the covenant. Nomism in itself was not a condition of "getting in" but a condition of "staying in".[1]

If this idea of covenantal nomism in Judaism is true, says Sanders, Paul could never have really considered Judaism to be a legalistic religion. Instead, Paul must have known Judaism *as* covenantal nomism. The concept of legalism must be of later origin. Most probably it is just a poor interpretation of Protestant Biblical theology. Therefore we must now consider it erroneous.

When this is the point of departure, Paul's concept of the law must have been developed in accord with soteriology. Paul had to find a solution to the burning question as to the extent to which non-Jewish Christians were obliged to keep the law. Due to his all-embracing soteriology he ended up rejecting the law. Sanders says that the law was not rejected because there had been a common misunderstanding of it in Judaism. Neither was the reason in the alleged soteriological function of the law in Jewish theology.[2] The one and only reason for the rejection of the law was Christology, which for Paul became more important than the law.

Sanders attempted to re-assess especially the understanding of the nature of Judaism. Any application concerning the theology of Paul was thus merely of a

---

[1] For related literature, see 2.5., and especially the *Excursus* in chapter 3. Overviews have been provided e.g. by Westerholm, *Law*, 15-101; Hagner, *BBR 3* (1993) 111-130, Seifrid, *TyndB 45* (1994) 75ff.

[2] Sanders, *Paul*, 497.

secondary nature.[3] According to Sanders, the tradition of interpretation in Protestant scholarship was on the wrong track. Thus the interpretation of Paul, too, must have been based on false premises. This concerned above all the emphasis on Paul being an enemy of Jewish legalism, righteousness by works.[4] Sanders' Paul was a kind of covenantal nomist, who built a Christological soteriology on a Jewish foundation.

We must note, however, that Sanders does not explain Paul's theology simply by parallelling it with his concept of covenantal nomism. As in the analysis of Jewish theology, in the analysis of Paul, too, he wishes to give "a presentation of Paul's 'pattern of religion'."[5] The claims with regard to legalism are thus a result of this kind of analysis.

According to Sanders, Paul did not want to present primarily a "renewed" covenantal nomism. We have already seen that Sanders borrowed a participatory interpretation from Schweitzer and put emphasis on Christ-mysticism.[6] Sanders claims that a subjective element prevails over other features. Consequently, the core of Paul's teaching is the theology of "being in Christ", i.e. "participatory eschatology".[7]

According to Sanders, Paul's theology is totally governed by Christology. Paul's concept of salvation is based on his convictions about the resurrection and Lordship of Christ. Since Christ and the Jewish tradition must be set against each other, Paul rejects the belief that the election of Israel and the covenant with God were unique indications of God's grace. Circumcision is not a sign of God's covenant, either.[8]

The final conclusion reached by Sanders is that Paul was not initially trying to criticize the conduct of Jewish faith, such as nomism, but the central elements of the religion, such as election, covenant and law. Because these elements had turned out to be false, the conduct of faith must be wrong, too. Not a negation of Jewish beliefs but new Christology dictated the soteriology of Paul. This led Sanders to utter his famous slogan: "In short, *this is what Paul finds wrong in Judaism: it is not Christianity.*" [9]

---

[3] Sanders, *Law,* 46-47, also n. 142.

[4] Sanders, *Paul,* 59.

[5] Sanders, *Paul,* 433. As Hagner points out in his analysis, there was a tendency to reassess traditional Protestant understanding of Paul. This led to a radical reassessment of Paul's soteriology: "justification by faith is not the center of Paul's theology but instead represents a pragmatic tactic to facilitate the Gentile mission." Hagner, *BBR 3* (1993) 112.

[6] See chapter 2.5. and Sanders, *Paul,* 459.

[7] Sanders, *Paul,* 552.

[8] See especially Sanders, *Paul,* 551.

[9] Sanders, *Paul,* 552 (italics his).

Naturally no one would deny that Christ is the centre of Paul's soteriology. The main questions concerning his theology are, however, what is the basic structure in his thinking, and how does it relate to the teachings of other writings of Second Temple Judaism? On this question Sanders initiated a long discussion concerning the relation of the "plight" and the "solution" in Paul's soteriology. He was convinced that Paul was inferring "backwards", beginning with a solution that Christ has brought.[10] Now we must ask whether Paul's theology is merely a deduction from a Christological starting-point or a reaction to his own theological background in a more comprehensive way. [11]

Sanders thinks that Paul's soteriology is built upon a rather neutral Jewish covenantal theology. Because his concept of salvation is governed by a Christological argument, it is only an unfortunate coincidence that Jewish soteriology drifts into conflict with the new soteriological principle.

As we assess Sanders' interpretation of Paul's soteriology, we must pay attention to several rather difficult problems.

1. Paul and his Jewish background. Firstly, we must return to the discussion and criticism presented in the *Excursus* (chapter 3) above. Sanders' theory has been criticized over the years for its one-sided approach to Second Temple Jewish writings.[12] His perspective has been governed by certain concepts of rabbinic theology, and this has also affected his attitude towards other writings. Our analysis has confirmed such suspicions. Furthermore, the problem is more complex than merely a question of choosing texts. Our analysis in the first part of the work has shown that Jewish apocalyptic soteriology has little in common with the concept of covenantal nomism. The picture Sanders gives of the nature of Second Temple Jewish theology is rather incomplete.[13]

As regards Sanders' criticism of earlier "Protestant" scholarship, he has no doubt found a problematic bias in the traditional description of Judaism in

---

[10] See Sanders, *Paul*, 474.

[11] In international discussion there has been much debate about the relationship between the "plight" and the "solution" in Paul's theology. Sanders thought that the solution was there first. Hagner in turn considers that we can use such an order even though we must change the point of view to synergistic soteriology. Hagner, *BBR 3* (1993) 122. This question will be treated in detail in chapter 14.3.

[12] One cannot really overlook the criticism that has sometimes been quite negative, as the words of G. Brooke reveal: "The book is highly problematic." Brooke, *JJS 30* (1979) 247.

[13] There is a rather wide consensus among scholars on this problem, see e.g. Porton, *Diversity,* 73; Overman-Green, *ABD III* (1992) 1038f.; Hagner, *Interp. (1997)* 26. This concerns both Sanders' view of rabbinic theology and his overall view of Judaism. Avemarie, *Tora und Leben,* 579-583; cf. the review of Hengel and Deines on Sanders' more recent monograph *Judaism,* in *JTS 46* (1995) 39, 42, 68f. As regards Sanders' book *Jesus and Judaism,* cf. Allison, *JSNT 29* (1987) 57ff.

European biblical criticism.[14] His own analysis of Jewish theology does not seem to have gone deep enough, however. A description of the Jewish theology of that time should begin with an analysis of how different writers attempt to answer the difficult question of theodicy. Jewish soteriology is usually based on the idea of predestination. One cannot understand the concept of eschatological "getting in", or salvation, without this perspective.[15]

We have to pay attention to the strict soteriological dualism which is evident in most writings from the Second Temple period. In fact: as far as textual evidence is considered, it is difficult to find even one text which explicitly represents "Sadducean" covenantalism that could be rightly called covenantal nomism. Nomism appears in a synergistic context. It is an essential element in most soteriological concepts of Second Temple writings.[16]

As regards the relation between Paul and Jewish theology, there are both points of continuity and points of discontinuity. A comparison between Paul and Second Temple Jewish writings reveals many themes which are common to them both.[17] Paul's soteriology is not merely a function of Christology which had been fused into normative covenantal nomism. To be exact: an alleged covenantal nomism is not the background of Paul's theology.

Paul is answering the question of theodicy as enthusiastically as earlier generations had done. Soteriological dualism is an important theme for him.[18] He worked on predestinarian theology and provided his own solution to it.

---

[14] Cf. the analysis in the Excursus, in chapter 3.

[15] This was a time of "crisis and reaction", as Scott has dubbed it. Scott, *EQ 64* (1992) 197ff.

[16] In the discussion of the nature of Jewish faith there is an interesting comment from a Jewish scholar, B.S. Jackson. In his article "Legalism" Jackson tries to prove that the charge of legalism, laid on the Jews, originates in internal Christian theological debate. He finds the analysis of Sanders very helpful in his criticism and agrees with the latter that one should not accept negative Christian criticism of Judaism and consider it truthful. Jackson, *JJS 30* (1979) 2-3. Jewish identity does not rest on legalism. "The reason for observing the law could only lie in faith in its divine author; observance of the law thus itself presupposed faith in God" (pp. 4-5). Such an attitude is no doubt sincere and it need not be questioned. We must note, however, that for Jackson, "Judaism was an earthly religion" (p. 6). He does not accept eschatological soteriology but projects it onto Christianity. In this he must at the same time reject most of Second Temple Jewish theology, as well, even though he does not say so. Thus it is no wonder that he closes his article by quoting a synergistic poem (p. 22).

[17] Brooke reminds us that Sanders has himself revealed many agreements between Paul and some Palestinian Jewish literature, especially as regards matters of reward and punishment as required by divine justice. According to Brooke, such a result points to the unsatisfactory nature of the author's methodology. Brooke, *JJS 30* (1979) 249; cf. Beker, *TToday 35* (1978) 110.

[18] Flusser, who has also debated with Sanders, lists as central features in sectarian Jewish theology dualism, predestination and election. Flusser, *Dead Sea Sect,* 72.

Paul has a new concept of election and takes a stand on his Jewish background.

In Sanders' theory there is a difficult ambivalence which becomes evident when he deals with some problematic details. He is well aware of a tension between free will and election but does not resolve it.[19] Furthermore, it is clear to him that in most of the texts the concept of belonging to the covenant was not "deuteronomistic". According to many groups, not all Jews belonged to the covenant automatically.[20] Several texts mention "getting in" to the covenant and Sanders himself has noted the strict demands of keeping the law laid down as conditions for getting in. This did not affect his theory, however. And lastly, Sanders has noted the problem of predestination and discussed it in the introduction of his book but he is not able to work out the theme in the context of covenantal thinking.[21]

In addition, Sanders' treatment of the concept of predestination is ambivalent. On the one hand, he assesses Jewish teaching in line with a rather deterministic double predestination. On the other hand, he has to admit the important role of free will in sapiential theology, because in the source texts there is evidently room for independent human action and responsibility.[22] It is evident that one cannot solve such an ambivalence in the context of the theory of covenantal nomism.

As regards this first subject, we must conclude that Sanders' interpretation does not explain the relation between Paul and Second Temple Jewish theology. A theory should be able to explain why Paul gives negative assessment of the law – especially when a positive covenantal nomism is presupposed.[23] This does not happen in the explanation given by Sanders. Paul's theology must be assessed against the diversity of Second Temple Judaism. We must note the points of both continuity and discontinuity in Paul's theology.

2. Legalism or synergism? Our analysis has led to the statement that the ambivalence behind the study of Sanders has in fact resulted in a tension in his definition of covenantal nomism. His own definition contains the idea of a synergistic religion even though he never explicitly says so in his book. Keeping the law is necessary for "staying in" and without it there is no

---

[19] Sanders, *Paul,* 261.

[20] Sanders, *Paul,* 147; 243; 404; 414.

[21] Sanders, *Paul,* 15.

[22] See Sanders, *Paul,* 261, 333, 345.

[23] Cf. M.D. Hooker: "Clearly we cannot speak of 'covenantal nomism' in Paul's case, since that would run counter to Paul's basic quarrel with the Law." Hooker, *Paul and Paulinism,* 52.

salvation.[24] At this point, though, Sanders is destined to be left in an ambivalent position because his main purpose is the negation of legalism.[25]

How should we understand covenantal nomism from such a perspective? If we were to interpret the theory as a description of synergistic Jewish theology, it might be more useful. Sanders is no doubt right in his assertion that the Jews were not consciously striving after self-righteousness. Every religious group thought that God's saving acts are necessary. In that case we would be left with the problem that the theory could not make a distinction between non-eschatological Sadducean covenantalism and eschatological soteriology of different apocalyptic and Zadokite groups of that period.[26]

Moreover, we would see that Paul himself could never accept synergistic nomism as a basis for his soteriology. "Synergistic" covenantal nomism would rather be the antithesis against which he would fight. Paul's soteriology cannot be explained merely as a combination of "normative" covenantal Judaism and Christological argumentation.[27] This is, however, what Sanders would have had to state in principle. If the only problem with Judaism was that it was not Christianity, there are not many other options. [28]

3. Can soteriology be a "pattern"? As regards the general thrust of Sanders' theory, there have been critical voices raised against his attempt to identify soteriology with the "pattern" of religion. A religion cannot be reduced to one scheme of attaining salvation. A "pattern", if one can be produced, should comprise several areas and functions of a religion.[29]

One of the weaknesses of Sanders' arguments has been the use of socio-

---

[24] This is a problem noted by many scholars, see Gundry, *Bib 66* (1985) 35; Cooper, *WTJ 44* (1982) 137; Moule, *Tradition,* 48.

[25] At the end of the book the ambivalence of Sanders' theory is stated as follows: *"works are the condition of remaining 'in', but they do not earn salvation".* Sanders, *Paul,* 543.

[26] Cooper also maintains that the basic difficulty lies in the ambivalence of Sanders' own statements. Sanders has admitted that, for Paul, the universality of condemnation is the situation from which man must be saved. If Sanders had acknowledged this, he could have related Paul's forensic categories to his participationist eschatology. Cooper, *WTJ 44* (1982) 135.

[27] In this respect the radical solution proposed by Räisänen (discussed in 2.5.) is understandable. He tried to solve the problem of Sanders' theory and concluded that Paul must have written merely a caricature of Jewish theology. This has also been noted by Moo, *SJT 40* (1987) 292.

[28] Caird expected a bolder hypothesis from Sanders, where Paul would be said to reject the corrected "genuine" Judaism as expounded by Moore and Sanders himself. See Caird's book review in *JTS 29* (1978) 542. Gundry in turn has pointed out that in comparing the patterns of religion Sanders is not very consistent. On the one hand, he says that they are "essentially different" (*Paul,* 543) but, on the other hand, he maintains that Paul and Palestinian Judaism agree on grace and works. Gundry, *Bib 66* (1985) 5-6, n. 14.

[29] See the criticism of Saldarini *JBL 98* (1979) 302f.; McNamara, *JSNT 5* (1979) 72.

logical categories in his reasoning. This has narrowed his theory even more. It is justifiable to question his approach in this respect. There has been an error in the use of the categories of soteriology. Even soteriology – not to mention a whole "pattern" – is more than an act of "joining a club". Sanders has presented an explanation of the method of conversion in Paul's theology. In this respect his participatory interpretation is not very explanatory or convincing.[30]

As we analyze Paul's soteriology we must pay attention to his radicalized concepts of universal sinfulness and divine predestination. Paul's "pattern", even in a narrow sense, comprises several themes, such as the function of the law, the meaning of redemptive atonement, and the dynamics of justification.

4. Paul, predestination and justification. There are several problems in Sanders' interpretation of the major themes of Paul's theology, as well. Paul's soteriology can hardly be a Christological deduction without other premises. Even though such a polarization is something of an over-simplification, it has been considered a consistent consequence of Sanders' theory. Against this setting we can already here say that Paul did not need to invent the ideas of theodicy, predestination and judgment. He did not invent sin. There was a "plight" even though synergistic Judaism provided different solutions to it. It is evident that Paul is not making up a "plight" only in order to place Christ in the structure of covenantal nomism.[31]

Paul's theology is a remarkable construction where he answers the burning questions of his time. Christ is the solution to the problem of theodicy. This results in a concept of "strong" predestination according to which no man on earth can be saved without the Son of God.[32] Law, justification and reconciliation find their natural places in this soteriological structure. It is not an imaginative construction but an interpretation of Messianic Jewish soteriology within the scope of Second Temple Jewish theology.[33]

---

[30] According to Hooker, Sanders has fallen into the very trap which he attempted to avoid, "in that he has taken something which in only a part of Paul's theology – central though that may be – and compared and contrasted it with a pattern of religion which he has traced in Judaism." Hooker, *Paul and Paulinism,* 53.

[31] We shall treat these questions in detail below, in chapter 14.3.

[32] In a forthcoming article in *JSJ* I have used the concept of "strong" predestination in opposition to the "weak" predestination of synergistic theology. The basic difference between these two concepts lies in the different anthropology behind them. In synergistic teaching one is always able to alter one's fate by an act of one's free will. Paul considers this impossible.

[33] According to Hooker, Sanders fails to bring out the inner logic which leads Paul to argue that the death and resurrection of Christ mean the end of the reign of the Law. The

Pauline scholars working inside the "new perspective" have usually rejected several of the great themes of Paul's theology. This concerns especially the teaching about justification. When Paul's soteriology is considered deductive, and there seems to be no problem with Jewish covenantal nomism, one does not really need the concept of justification. It is classified in the group of other subjects produced by Paul's "secondary rationalizations" and forgotten.[34]

The covenantal nomism factually defined by Sanders turns out to be the antithesis of the soteriology of Paul. Had there been a situation where Paul encountered such teaching he would have refuted it harshly. It could never be the basis for his own theology. But as we have stated during the analysis, the whole theory does little to explain the main corpus of Second Temple Jewish writings and can by no means be considered a proper way of interpreting their soteriology. Therefore the key factors in both Jewish and Pauline soteriology call for an unprejudiced re-assessment.

By way of summary we may note that Sanders' theory of covenantal nomism does not help us in our explanation of Paul's soteriology. The theory in itself is ambivalent and full of inner tensions. Even if we were to re-define it for a theory of Jewish synergism, it would be too narrow to explain Second Temple Jewish theology, and its contribution to the interpretation of Paul's theology would be minimal. A similar negative assessment concerns Sanders' definition of Paul's nomism as traditional covenantal nomism. If covenantal nomism were to be regarded as synergism, it would be in opposition to Paul's theology instead of its premise. Paul would have opposed it strongly. In the light of our analysis we must conclude, however, that Paul's relation to his Jewish background is much more complicated. There are both points of continuity and points of discontinuity. And in addition we must note that participatory theology does not explain Paul's soteriology satisfactorily. It is unable to include central Pauline themes, such as universal sin, divine judgment, atonement and justification – which together are eventually linked with the theme of participation. To Paul, Christ was an answer to the problem of

---

answer, says Hooker, "is surely that the inadequacy of the Law is seen in the fact that one who was *condemned by the Law* has been *pronounced righteous by God*. Christ has been declared righteous, not only *apart from the Law*, but *in spite of the Law*. In the resurrection, the Law's verdict has been overthrown. This is why the righteousness of the Law is not an alternative route to salvation but a blind alley." Hooker, *Paul and Paulinism*, 55 (italics his).

[34] See especially the criticism made by Seifrid. His complaint is that most modern scholars neglect the justification theology of Paul and obscure his teaching of righteousness. Seifrid, *Justification*, 55, 62ff. 76f.; Cf. Cooper, *WTJ 44* (1982) 138.

theodicy. This resulted in a conception of strict predestination, where Christ was considered the only possible way to salvation, both for the Jews and for the Gentiles.

14.2. Paul's consistency questioned

In his monograph *Paul and the Law* H. Räisänen accepted the view of Sanders concerning covenantal nomism as a basic definition of Second Temple Jewish soteriology.[35] In his assessment of Paul's theology, however, Räisänen did not follow Sanders. He thought that Paul was not simply exploiting Jewish covenantal nomism in his new theology, but attacking Jewish theology, instead. For personal reasons Paul gave his readers a biassed picture of Jewish nomism.[36] He turned covenantal theology into legalism. This was wrong, says Räisänen, because in Judaism the Law was never presented as a way to salvation.[37]

In the preceding chapters we have seen several of Räisänen's explanations of Paul's treatment of the function of the law. Paul could not really decide whether the law is still valid or whether it has been abolished. The possibility of keeping the law seemed to be ambiguous, too. Paul's attitude towards the law was both positive and negative.[38] Only in certain passages does Paul state that it is impossible to keep the law – namely when he is trying to prove that

---

[35] Räisänen, *Law*, 179f. His book provoked a debate which is well known among New Testament scholars. Even though the problem of the complexity of Paul's terminology and some of Räisänen's other questions were considered justified, most scholars could not accept his pessimistic and even destructive conclusions. The dispute can easily be followed by reading the long preface to the second edition of Räisänen's book. Cf. the overviews in Moo, *SJT 40* (1987) 287-307; Westerholm, *Law*, 93-101; Thielman, *Law*, 37-47; Schreiner, *Law*, 18-28.

[36] There were, as I have maintained, two different ways of assessing the consequences of Sanders' theory, the other being a positive attitude. Cf. Dunn: "Seen from the perspective of Jewish Christianity at that time, the most obvious meaning is that *the only restriction on justification by works of law is faith in Jesus as Messiah.* The only restriction, that is, to covenantal nomism is faith in Christ. *But,* in this first clause, covenantal nomism itself is not challenged or called in question – restricted, qualified, more precisely defined in relation to Jesus as Messiah, but not denied." Dunn, *Law*, 195-196.

[37] Räisänen, *Law*, 187. Scholars were divided into two camps as regards the acceptance of this view. Some scholars welcomed Räisänen's explanation, see von Dobbeler, *NT 26* (1984) 374-376; Wedderburn, *SJT 38* (1985) 613ff.; Getty, *CBQ 47* (1985) 561-563; Watson, *Paul,* 18, 179f.; and in fact Sanders himself, cf. Sanders, *Law*, 15 n. 26, 51 n. 16 Negative criticism has been presented e.g. by Hübner, *ThLZ 110* (1985) 894-896; Hays, *JAAR 53* (1985) 513-515; Stuhlmacher, SEÅ 50 (1985) 102; Beker, *NTS 34* (1988) 365ff.; Westerholm, *Law*, 99f., 215ff.; Weima, *NT 32* (1990) 235; Schreiner, *Law*, 120.

[38] See Räisänen, *Law* , 82, 199-200.

the Jews too are under the power of sin.[39] On other occasions he does not think that it is impossible to fulfil the precepts of the law, even for the Gentiles.[40]

What is of importance in Räisänen's explanations is that these examples are not merely individual problems concerning Paul's theology of the law. Paul's main coherent idea behind all his reasoning was the Christological motif which governed his theology. Because of this Christological "bias" Paul, according to Räisänen, often gave a distorted picture of Judaism and presented conflicting statements about theology.[41]

This leads us to the question concerning the Christological principle. Räisänen maintains that this principle has negative consequences in theology. When soteriology is governed by this premise, the definition of nomism, too, must be conformed to it.[42] This again is not possible unless one does violence to Jewish tradition.[43] Therefore, says Räisänen, the result is necessarily contradictory.

"The starting point of Paul's thinking about the Torah is the Christ event, not the law. This structure of thought he fully shares with other early Christian writers. No other writer, however, is led to such radical and negative conclusions with respect to the law as Paul: the law incites man to sin and increases transgressions; the law ought to be fulfilled 100 per cent; Jews do not fulfil the law whereas the Christians do; the law was given through angels, not by God. All these negative statements are made problematic because other Pauline statements contradict them. Paul's most radical conclusions about the law are thus strangely ambiguous."[44]

Such an interpretation has two important consequences. Firstly, Paul is separated from Jewish theology and his teaching is treated as a result of rather psychological motives. When Räisänen says that Paul's concept of nomism is not consistent with Jewish theology, he has to imply that Paul's teachings concerning the function of the law and the belief in divine judgment must also differ from those of common Judaism. In the theory of Räisänen, Jewish theology must be totally different from the picture that Paul presents.[45]

Secondly, Paul's soteriology is reduced to a nomistic scholasticism where the aspects of divine judgment, the day of wrath and eternal punishment have

---

[39] Räisänen, *Law*, 95; 97.

[40] Räisänen, *Law*, 106.

[41] Räisänen, *Law*, 150, 187.

[42] Räisänen, *Law*, 176.

[43] Räisänen, *Law*, 178; 187.

[44] Räisänen, *Law*, 201(italics his); accepted later e.g. by Wedderburn, *SJT 38* (1985) 622.

[45] Räisänen does compare the teachings of Paul to Jewish theology in the course of his study, but he finds more discontinuity than continuity.

no place or significance.[46] This results in neglect of the aspects of sin and judgment in Paul's theology.[47] Thus the description of Paul's soteriology remains one-sided. The Christological factor has no other reason or purpose than Paul's personal, spiritual experience.

As a result of all this Räisänen defines the characteristics of Paul's theology from a *psychological* point of view. He maintains that Paul's thinking is a product of "secondary rationalization".[48] Having the Christ–event as a starting-point Paul's argument runs "backwards". This special feature of Räisänen's theory deserves closer treatment.[49] In scholarly discussion there has been disagreement and even confusion concerning Räisänen's final treatment of Paul's soteriology. Räisänen has been accused of a lack of constructive approach. His conclusions have been claimed to reduce Paul's statements to meaningless fragments of subjective thinking.[50] This is an important discussion per se, but it cannot be conducted successfully without an analysis of Räisänen's theory of hermeneutics. It has too often been overlooked in Pauline studies, though it alone provides the arguments for the psychological interpretation of Paul.[51] The theory as such is familiar at least to those who have become acquainted with Räisänen's writings on biblical theology.

---

[46] Räisänen does write about the relation between law and sin when he investigates the first five chapters of Romans, but he finds no basis in Jewish tradition for the idea of universal sinfulness. Furthermore, Paul's concept of judgment is to Räisänen just an example of Paul's superficial and distorting attempt to justify the claim of universal sinfulness. Räisänen, *Paul*, 97ff. "Paul's argument is here simply a piece of propagandist denigration" (p. 101).

[47] Räisänen, *Law*, 108; 150. This has naturally been noted in international scholarship, see e.g. Westerholm: "Though Sanders and Räisänen both concede that Paul argues for universal sinfulness in Romans 1-3, the tenet is dismissed to the periphery of Paul's thought." Westerholm, *Law*, 160; cf. Weima, *NT 32* (1990) 235.

[48] "It is tempting to see in all this the mechanism at work which is called *secondary rationalization* in depth psychological theory... Paul has, for all practical purposes, broken with the law, and he is now concerned to put forward 'rationalizations': it is, against all appearance, *he* who really upholds the law; and insofar as this is not the case, the fault lies with the law itself...The very inadequacy of these arguments betrays their secondary origin. Paul's argument runs 'backwards', having the Christ event as its starting point." Räisänen, *Law*, 201.

[49] Cf. Seifrid: "Räisänen's description very much represents a return to the psychological portraits of Paul popular in the last century, in which intuition and experience are played off against any theological element in Paul's motivations." Seifrid, *Justification*, 69.

[50] I refer especially to the discussion between Räisänen, Hübner and Hays (see below). Räisänen's answers have been presented in the introduction of *Law (2nd ed.)*.

[51] I consider a short description of this theory of interpretation to be useful here, as it probably is not as well known elsewhere as it is in Finland. For the understanding of Räisänen's interpretations it is of crucial importance, however.

Firstly, Räisänen's theory of interpretation is based on cognitive psychology. Its basic elements were borrowed from the theories of Peter Berger. A key term here is, as Räisänen himself also calls it, the "sociology of knowledge". A person who perceives the world tries to understand and analyze it according to the "symbolic universe" he has been taught in his community. This "symbolic universe" is a social construction – even though religious in content – and consists of symbols and ideas with which the community has traditionally interpreted life and theology. These "symbols" naturally comprise all common theological concepts, such as those expressed by cultic, legal or royal terminology.[52]

Räisänen considers the creation of theology a process where man attaches meaning to his personal experiences by using "symbols". This does not happen in a vacuum. Everyone lives in a community which has a wide range of symbols at hand. This is why, according to Räisänen, the interpretation of an individual is always based on a *dialectic* between tradition, experience and interpretation.[53]

In his book *Beyond New Testament Theology*, Räisänen attempted to create a method for the "early Christian history of religion". This method was based on the idea of the dialectic mentioned above.[54] For Räisänen, early Christianity was full of different and often contradictory theological ideas. They were based on personal experiences of this world. How, then, should one understand the nature of the Bible? Räisänen opposes incoherency and revelation. The Bible cannot be a source of divine revelation. One cannot and must not search for "universal" truth in it.[55]

Instead, the Bible is a document of diverse experiences which form a chain of interpretations, each made in a different context. For Räisänen, the possibility of a coherent biblical theology is ruled out even in principle. This was applied to the theology of Paul, as well. Only psychological factors can, according to Räisänen, explain Paul's ambivalent and inconsistent statements

---

[52] Räisänen, *Beyond*, 129-130. As early as 1972 Räisänen published an article where he explained the principles of his theory (in Finnish, *TAik* [1972] 76-86). In that article he identified the chain of interpretations as "natural theology".

[53] Räisänen, *Beyond*, 131. There seems to be an inner relationship with the interpretative theory of Bultmann. Räisänen uses "symbols" for "myths". The "existential interpretation" has been replaced by an unending chain of interpretations, where every new personal interpretation in a new context is an expression of man's efforts to interpret his experiences.

[54] Räisänen, *Beyond*, 122f.

[55] Such an approach must also be the reason why denying inspiration remains important for Räisänen. For Räisänen this has further been a central aspect in the analysis of the consistency of Paul: "As it has become increasingly difficult to regard Paul's ideas as literally 'inspired' or 'revealed', Christian s[c]holars often stick to the second-best alternative of having in him at least a nearly-inspired, first-class thinker." Räisänen, *Law (2nd ed.)*, xiii.

in his letters.[56] This kind of hermeneutics in Pauline studies results in a "historical-psychological" interpretation of Paul.

When at the end of *Paul and the Law* Räisänen wrote the chapter entitled *The origins of Paul's conception of the law,* he referred, for example, to Paul's psychological prehistory, and after that treated the whole theology of Paul from a psychological perspective. "We have of course very little hope of being able to penetrate into the psychic life of a person of the ancient world 2000 years later. Nevertheless, some psychological commonplaces are probably applicable."[57] In Räisänen's theory interpretation focusses on the subjective experience of the writer. Thus a psychological analysis is considered a proper way to explain Paul's writings.

Räisänen's interpretation is based on the idea of an inner conflict in the mind of Paul: "It is one such commonplace that the unconscious can break through in opposition to the conscious belief to which one clings." Paul's theology reveals such an "unconscious struggle". His soteriology can be explained only by a "pneumatic experience", which Paul experienced in a new charismatic Christian movement. Such an experience of freedom later resulted in a radical theology with respect to the law. According to Räisänen, Paul was a spiritualist whose theology was directed by his personal experiences. This is why his theology was in practice produced by the aforementioned "secondary rationalization".[58]

There is evident causality between Räisänen's interpretation of Paul and his hermeneutics. Due to his cognitive theory Räisänen treats Paul as an individual thinker who tries to find theological explanations for his religious experiences. *In this process Paul is obliged to use "secondary rationalization", because the dialectic between tradition and interpretation had been disrupted by the Christological principle.*

This point of view must be taken into account in any discussion of Räisänen's approach. Some scholars have criticised Räisänen for his lack of "constructive" exposition of Paul's thought – even though they would agree on his view of the "new perspective" on Paul. Räisänen considers such claims unjustified, since the psychological treatment is a logical consequence of his

---

[56] In the "Preface to the second edition" of his *Law,* Räisänen maintains that his approach to Paul is that of "an historical-psychological account of the growth of Paul's thought" (pp. xiii-xiv). In his *Theology* he identifies this approach with the "history-of-religions perspective", which is also mentioned in the new preface (p. xv).

[57] Räisänen, *Law,* 232.

[58] Räisänen, *Law,* 232-233.

theory of interpretation.[59] This horizon of psychology is for Räisänen the final explanation why no consistent system of theology can be found in the letters of Paul.

When H. Hübner criticized Räisänen for a lack of synthesis in his Pauline studies, Räisänen answered by accusing Hübner of not reaching the conclusions required by the results of his own analyses. For example, with respect to Romans 9-11 Hübner has stated that, as regards Israel, these chapters stand in an unresolvable, logical contradiction to each other. According to Räisänen, there is but one way to explain such an inner contradiction: that of psychological analysis.[60]

Even though we can see that the criticism of Räisänen's explanation has not really hit the target, there is room for reassessment. The justification of the quest for a synthesis cannot be denied by referring to a compilation of certain inconsistencies in Paul's letters. This at least seems to be the reason why several scholars have asked Räisänen to do some constructive work instead of collecting contradictions.

The hermeneutics of Räisänen explain why a synthesis is impossible. For Räisänen, theology was mainly the result of interpreting religious experiences. There is no need to expect a consistent system in such a process.[61] The contradictions which Räisänen has found in the letters of Paul are not considered just some accidental flaws in his teaching. Instead they are signs of a deeper reality: that of the basic arbitrariness of his theology.

The lack of constructive synthesis separates Räisänen from Sanders, too. He no longer attempts to formulate a "pattern" of Paul's theology or soteriology, as Sanders did. Participatory interpretation has no special value for Räisänen – neither do other individual theological themes, such as universal sinfulness or the juridical concept of justification, not to mention the cultic conception of

---

[59] Such a constructive approach was requested e.g. by Hays in his review of Räisänen's monograph, Hays, *JAAR 53* (1985) 514. A reply by Räisänen was given in the new preface of the *Law (2nd ed.)*, where he said that "there *is* a level on which Paul's statements cease to be meaningless fragments... and fall into an intelligible pattern." pp. xxi-xxii (italics his). His critics do not seem to understand, however, that the "level" he means is the "psychological-historical" level (p. xxii), on which Räisänen is able to show that only an "unconscious struggle" explains the otherwise "meaningless fragments".

[60] Hübner, *ThLZ 110* (1985) 896; Räisänen, *Law (2nd ed.)*, xiii. This discussion concerns Hübner's treatment of Romans 9-11 in his *Gottes Ich,* 122. The question was referred to above, in chapter 8.2. When Räisänen accuses Hübner of not reaching the conclusions that should be evident, he is actually accusing him of not admitting that Paul's theology is inconsistent in principle. Hübner never accepted such a view but insisted on the need for a synthesis in all Pauline study, instead.

[61] One should perhaps wonder why in Jewish theology there was, according to Räisänen, one consistent soteriological "system", namely that of covenantal nomism.

atonement.[62] They are merely separate interpretations of personal experiences among other interpretations. For Räisänen, there is no "core" in Paul's theology.[63]

This was actually the reason for Hübner's criticism, who accused Räisänen of dissolving Paul's theology into "meaningless fragments".[64] Räisänen did not reject this accusation. He answered that a scholar can only try to understand Paul amidst of all his conflicts and struggles. A synthesis of Paul's theology is impossible, because in reality there is no such theology. There are only contextual *ad hoc* interpretations which occasionally contradict each other.[65]

Such an analysis of Räisänen's theory of interpretation helps us to evaluate the discussion concerning the consistency of Paul's theology. As Paul's consistency is being questioned, we should pay attention to the arguments which are used as proof. In Räisänen's interpretation of Paul, the Christological principle affects the 'plight-solution' discussion rather differently than in the case of Sanders. Räisänen is not describing any particular teaching of Paul which could be compared with or opposed to the teaching of Jewish theology. Paul is merely a propagandist whose twisted purpose is to give a distorted picture of Judaism – whenever it suits his missionary work.[66]

The 'plight-solution' discussion is thus, according to Räisänen, not a question of finding a proper way of describing of the relation between Paul and Jewish theology. He is convinced – on the level of history of religion and psychology – that the only plight that exists, even in principle, is in the mind of Paul. It is quite evident that no comment on such a theory in academic

---

[62] Räisänen is, more than Sanders, dependent on modern presuppositions on the hermeneutical level. We should remember, however, that modern beliefs never prevent *Paul* from believing e.g. in universal sinfulness or atonement. We shall return to this question in the next chapter.

[63] This, as well, is a feature which has its basis in Räisänen's analysis of biblical theology. He rejects the "pure" (universal) biblical theology of Gabler and chooses the history-of-religion approach of Wrede. See Räisänen, *Beyond*, 4, 16. He considers universal biblical theology dangerous, because it harmonizes the inconsistencies in the Bible. This method has been used in the interpretation of Paul's theology, too.

[64] Hübner, *ThLZ 110* (1985) 896.

[65] Räisänen, *Law (2nd ed.)*, xv. "*Fair comparison*, or fairness to the *others*, is one of the reasons why one should *not* try *excessively* hard to synthetize Paul's thought into a consistent whole" (italics his).

[66] Räisänen explicitly uses terms such as "propagandist denigration" and "distorted picture of Judaism" (*Law*, 101, 188). The significance of Paul's missionary purpose is especially investigated in *Law*, 256-263.

discussion can rely on analyses of Paul's texts. Such claims can be encountered only on the level of hermeneutics and the theory of religion.[67]

According to Räisänen, the Christological principle produced great problems for Paul. As Paul attempted to explain the function of the law in soteriology, he had to give different answers on different occasions. Since he was working backwards deductively from the Christological principle, the answers he gave contradict each other. This kind of inference Räisänen calls "secondary rationalization". Räisänen's explanation was based on his hermeneutics. He suggested a "historical-psychological" interpretation of Paul's theology. The basis for this kind of interpretation was to be found in the sociology of knowledge: theology in general must be defined as a subjective attempt to interpret religious experiences in certain social contexts. As Paul had rejected his Jewish background and replaced Jewish tradition with Christology, his theology was unavoidably in disagreement with Jewish teachings. This resulted in a contradiction with normative Judaism, and this was furthermore the reason why Paul, according to Räisänen, intentionally gave his readers a distorted picture of Judaism.

14.3. What is the "plight" of man?

The problem concerning the relation of "plight and solution" is admittedly a difficult one. What Sanders had primarily maintained was that Saul/Paul did not consider his salvation uncertain before he found Christ. This notion can easily be confirmed by Philippians 3, where Paul describes his successful life "under the law". Accordingly, the Jews who opposed Paul, most probably never doubted the legitimacy of their own eschatology. In other words – as Sanders said – Saul did not anticipate a universal Saviour who would be the only one who could save him from the curse of the law. It was only after he found this Saviour that he found the "answer": Jesus Christ must be the Messiah of God and the Saviour of the whole of humankind.[68]

This much is simple in this picture. One could also interpret this kind of primacy in a neutral way in the context of traditional soteriology. It is a different thing to say that Christology directs Paul's soteriology than to maintain that Paul invented the plight of man. How should we assess the dynamics of this relation?

The first aspect in this discussion concerns the nature of the alternatives. The problem lies in the fact that *these alternatives are not exclusive*. In the context

---

[67] Cf. my analysis of contemporary Finnish theological discussion in Eskola, *EJTh* 5 (1995) 27-35.

[68] Sanders, *Paul*, 443. In the international scholarly community there has been much debate about the relationship between the "plight" and the "solution" ever since. See the overview in Thielman, *Plight*, 1-27.

of Paul's rich theology both aspects are possible in principle. The Christological argument as such is naturally valid. Without Easter Jewish soteriology produced quite another kind of soteriology than the one we see in the teaching of Paul. Suffice it to refer to the conceptions in texts such as the Psalms of Solomon, the Dead Sea Scrolls or 4 Ezra. On the other hand, one can also justify the primacy of the plight. Our analysis has shown that precisely the above-mentioned texts describe the plight of man almost in the manner of Paul. The differences are relative and concern the nature of the radicalization of these conceptions.[69]

On the other hand, the "solution" of Christology was very "Jewish", as well. Paul and other writers in the early Church were convinced that the Scriptures were full of prophecies about the Messiah and that Jesus was the fulfilment of those prophecies. Even though Jews and Christians have always disagreed over the *manner* in which Christology could mean a fulfilment of divine prophecies, one cannot doubt the *fact* that the apostles believed in such a fulfilment.[70]

In this study we shall concentrate especially to the problem concerning the "plight". During our analysis we have stated that it was precisely the "plight" of Israel that formed the basis of Second Temple Jewish theology. The soteriological dualism of that period was based on a theology of crisis.[71] In the sapiential tradition Israel's problems were identified with Israel's sins.[72] As regards the discussion concerning Pauline soteriology it would be erroneous to maintain that Paul was the first theologian to proclaim that sin leads to damnation. Quite on the contrary, this was the message of all eschatological groups of that time.

As Paul declaims against the sinful living of mankind he makes good use of Jewish theology. His terminology does not differ from that of Jewish theology

---

[69] Cf. chapter 4 above.

[70] We must remember that the nature of Second Temple Jewish Messianism was mostly political. In this sense the anticipation of a Davidide was linked to the basic experience of crisis. This is why one cannot separate Messianism from the problem of theodicy: it was the Davidide who was expected to be God's instrument in the final vindication and restoration of Israel.

[71] This was the thesis of Scott, for example, see *EQ 64* (1992) 197ff., 211; and our examination of Second Temple texts in part I has confirmed such a hypothesis.

[72] Thielman has proposed a "plight-solution pattern" as a solution to the dilemma of Paul and Palestinian Judaism, the plight being simply sin which was an important theme in Jewish eschatology, too. Thielman, *Plight*, 28ff., 46ff.; cf. Martin. *Law*, 69ff. This is a good starting-point, but the structural elements of soteriology are somewhat more complex than this.

and he needs no "Christian" presuppositions in his teaching.[73] This also concerns Paul's conception of the judgment. Sin was to be feared precisely because God's divine judgment would fall on sinners. This is another theme which Paul did not need to invent and teach as a novelty to his Jewish readers.[74]

It was precisely the problem of sin which led Jewish theologians to ponder the problem of theodicy. The texts which we have analysed in chapters 3-5 above confirm our conclusion that Jewish theology in the time of Paul was filled with a theology of crisis – theology grown from the problem of theodicy. The Pharisees who held to the sapiential tradition, taught it, apocalyptic groups based their identity on it and the righteous ones of Qumran justified their existence by it.

The original feature of Paul's theology is the radicalization of predestinarian theology. This radicalization was most probably based on principles of Christology. Paul gave a new answer to the problem of theodicy after he saw the fate of the Son of God. This is how he became convinced that God's final righteousness has been revealed to humankind. This kind of radicalization cannot, however, be identified with an artificial, deductive invention of the plight itself.[75]

As we have seen, the problem which Paul was dealing with had been alive in Jewish theology for centuries. Several Jewish theologians had given different answers to it on different occasions. The common principle used in these answers was the principle of contemporary application. Jewish sects were certain that God's punishments were taking place in history and God's promises were being fulfilled in the life of the sect. This kind of contemporary application frequently led to quite radical reinterpretations of previous tradition – even as regards the Temple and Jewish piety around the Temple service.[76]

---

[73] In his analysis of the Psalms of Solomon, Winninge has noted that in most radical passages Jewish apostates are considered to be worse than Gentile sinners (PsSol. 1:8; 2:11f.; 8:13; 17:15). Winninge, *Sinners and the Righteous*, 194. According to Winninge, however, the radicalization of Jewish belief to a concept of universal sinfulness was merely deductive, "Paul's argument in reality moved backwards". Winninge, *Sinners and the Righteous*, 312-313.

[74] Cf. Mattern, *Verständnis,* 213; Gundry, *Bib 66* (1985) 7-8.

[75] This is an aspect that one cannot find in the explanations given by Sanders and his followers. The reason for this is probably the fact that the concept of idealistic soteriology had prevented them from giving proper significance to the soteriological dualism apparent in Second Temple Jewish writings.

[76] It is not sufficient to make a slight correction to covenantal nomism and define it as a synergistic tradition which Paul opposed, see e.g. Hagner, *BBR 3* (1993) 122. As we have

As regards the "plight-solution" discussion, it seems that *no sufficient distinction between contemporary application and deduction has been made in the analysis of Paul's soteriology.* At its worst Paul's theology has been considered an etiological deduction where he would violently attempt to find an explanation for his religious experiences. This leads to psychological argumentation, as we have seen above.[77]

The Christological argument was but one premise for Paul when he created his soteriology. In the preceding chapter 13 we have seen that what Paul has in common with other Jewish writers in the Second Temple period is the principle of contemporary application. Paul's theology is not a mere deduction, but a radical re-interpretation of his own *Jewish* tradition. The problem of theodicy had been a burning issue for centuries. Predestinarian theology had found several expressions in different Jewish writings. Paul saw these subjects in a new light and therefore his soteriology differs from the teachings of his contemporaries.

It is no doubt true that Saul/Paul did not consider his salvation uncertain before his conversion - at least in a different manner as did pious Jews in different eschatological groups at that time.[78] He most probably accepted the soteriological dualism which had been common to all theology circulating within the sapiential tradition. The radicalization of predestinarian theology was based on a new polarization, however, and therefore there was a precise aspect of discontinuity in his soteriology.[79]

The "plight" of Israel was the plight which Paul was speaking about. He

---

stated in previous analyses, it is proper to refer to synergism, but this new aspect falsifies the whole theory of covenantal nomism – especially when its eschatological dimension is taken into account.

[77] Cf. the analysis of Räisänen's theory in the previous chapter.

[78] In this respect one can agree with Seifrid, even though he follows the theory of Sanders. Seifrid, *Justification*, 177-178. He suggests that the "idea of a crucified Messiah challenged the validity of the whole of apocalyptic Jewish piety."

[79] Points of discontinuity have been detected in modern study, as well. It is worth noting that there are several scholars who claim to work according to the "new perspective on Paul", but whose conclusions in fact make that theory implausible. B. Longenecker investigated "ethnocentric covenantalism" instead of nomism, and found strict polarization, see *Eschatology and the Covenant*, 34. He further placed emphasis on differences of anthropology, as did Laato, *Paulus*, 194. Seifrid, on the other hand, underlined that Paul's claim for the relevance of the Gospel was predicated upon a universal need for salvation. Seifrid, *Justification*, 219. All of these notions disagree with the interpretation based on Sanders' theory.

only saw that, as regards God's history of salvation, it was the plight of all mankind. It was a plight that had been there all the time. One did not need to invent it deductively. What was new was the solution. Paul proclaimed that salvation can be attained solely through faith in Christ.

This is where we must pay further attention to Paul's argumentation. As we analyze the dynamics of Paul's soteriology, it is in fact not the "plight" that is reached through a deductive inference. On the contrary, it is the *solution*. Paul's argument is simple: as the Son of God has died on the cross, his death must mean atonement for the sins of men. The plight had been there for centuries. Paul agreed with Second Temple Jewish apocalypticism that the wrath of God was hanging over all sinners. What Paul did here was that he radicalized the soteriological polarization on the basis of his deductive *solution*.

Discussion of the problem of "plight and solution" seems to have been on the wrong track. No sufficient distinction has been made between contemporary application and deduction. Paul's soteriology has been considered an inference going backwards, and as a result doing violence to Jewish theology in general. This is not what Paul does. Instead, he produces special theology concerning the plight of Israel. He uses this quite important theme of Second Temple Jewish theology and radicalizes the traditional idea. The plight is a universal one and so is the solution. As regards the direction of Paul's inference, it is in fact the solution which Paul has found by "deductive" inference from the Easter message.

Excursus: A Hermeneutical Problem – Lutherans, Calvinists and Dispensationalists study Jewish Christianity

In our investigation of Paul's theology we have encountered a somewhat original problem as regards the hermeneutical background of scholars. It has been strongly suggested that the views and theology – even confessions – of modern churches have affected the interpretation of Paul's theology. This discussion was initiated by Sanders with his rather dogmatic analysis at the beginning of his book *Paul and Palestinian Judaism,* which we have analysed and discussed in several respects in previous chapters. His suggestion was that the distorted picture of Judaism had arisen in Protestant scholarship – mainly in Germany. As regards Jewish theology, the views of Weber and numerous scholars after him were coloured by a black-and-white attitude. Judaism was seen as the antithesis of Christianity, and its soteriology was regarded as being legalistic.[1]

The idea of confessional hermeneutical influence was sharpened by J. Dunn in his comments on Sanders' interpretation. According to Dunn, in the Protestant and Lutheran tradition soteriology and faith have usually been explained in terms of a theology of justification. Because Paul had described Jewish soteriology as righteousness by works, in Lutheran interpretation this was seen as merit based on good works. In this context the relation between Paul and Judaism began to resemble "the Reformation rejection of a system where indulgences could be bought and merits accumulated". So the protest against the Roman Catholic teaching of the Middle Ages produced the conception of a cold, legalistic Judaism.[2]

Such criticism is of some value. Protestant biblical criticism has been centred on the theology of justification. This is naturally not an error as such, but it undeniably defines the opposition to alleged legalism. The polarity between legalistic Judaism and Paul's teaching on grace has been evident in most

---

[1] See the previous description in chapters 2 and 3. "With F. Weber, however, everything changed. For him, Judaism was the antithesis of Christianity. Judaism was a legalistic religion in which God was remote and inaccessible. Christianity is based on faith rather than works and believes in an accessible God." Sanders, *Paul,* 33. Also Sanders calls this "Protestant" interpretation, and maintains that it has given us a distorted picture of Judaism. Sanders, *Paul,* 35.

[2] Dunn, *Romans,* lxv. "The antithesis to 'justification by faith' – what Paul speaks of as 'justification by works' – was understood in terms of a system whereby salvation is *earned* through the *merit* of *good works.* This was based... partly on the Reformation rejection of a system where indulgences could be bought and merits accumulated... the hermeneutical mistake was made of reading this antithesis back into the NT period, of assuming that Paul was protesting against in Pharisaic Judaism precisely what Luther protested against in the pre-reformation church..." Cf. Watson, *Paul,* 2-22.

modern Protestant studies which cling to the traditional interpretation.[3] One is often blind as regards the awareness of one's own premises and this has no doubt resulted in a caricature of Second Temple Judaism.[4]

At the same time we must beware, in a critical examination, of falling into a black-and-white antithesis, where a whole tradition of interpretation is abandoned because of a few problems. Protestant scholarship has for a long time been able to define synergism in Jewish theology. This feature has been accompanied by a theology of free will, which is a theme that probably no expert in Jewish studies would question today.[5]

As we assess Sanders' theory, we must also investigate his background, which forms the basis for his hermeneutical setting. The theory of covenantal nomism seems to have several features in common with both Calvinism and dispensationalism, and especially with their concepts of soteriology. Sanders' soteriology is governed by covenantal thinking and his nomism bears a close relation to the idea of double predestination – even though the idea of predestination itself remains in the background.[6]

Calvinist soteriology is based above all on the idea of God's "glory" and his majestic power. This basic feature dictates the structure of soteriology, which is primarily covenantal. God has established a covenant of grace, both with Israel and with the whole world. Therefore salvation must be dependent on this covenant which God has confirmed. Fallen man can play no active role in the act of salvation.[7]

This covenantal element in Calvinism is linked with the idea of double pre-destination. God himself has elected those who will be saved. He also calls them. For this reason the saved do not themselves effect their salvation at any stage in the process. Salvation is pure grace, and their faith is only a response to the covenantal faithfulness of God.[8]

In Calvinist teaching the concepts of law and obedience are employed in line

---

[3] In this respect the references to e.g. Bultmann (Sanders, *Paul,* 3) or his pupils are justified. Cf. Bornkamm, *Paulus,* 145.

[4] This idea is supported by the analysis made previously, for example in chapters 3 and 10.

[5] The critique of Sanders' theory in the previous chapters has shown that the theory of covenantal nomism contains several weaknesses which are crucial as regards the fruitful application of the theory in the interpretation of different traditions in both Second Temple Jewish soteriology and Pauline soteriology.

[6] Sanders' terminology, for example, is close to that of dispensationalism, see especially Sanders, *Law,* 137ff.

[7] On Calvinism in general, see Hägglund, *History,* 259-265; McGrath, *Theology,* 69f.

[8] In my analysis this view has affected, for example, Barth's and Schweitzer's interpretations of Paul.

with predestinarian theology.[9] Obedience to the law on the part of the elect is not merit in any sense. Their obedience cannot affect their salvation because it is dependent solely on the election of God. Therefore obedience is merely a moral obligation for Christians. Faith itself will direct believers in their moral obedience. It is not a condition for salvation, because, according to Calvinist theology, the elect cannot fall into apostasy. God's election keeps them in the covenant of grace and in perseverance, and they can be certain of their salvation.

The Calvinist concept of law is basically directed by a precise distinction between law and gospel. The righteousness of law was regarded as real righteousness, but it was based on God's conditional promise. By contrast righteousness by faith was considered the only certain and unconditional way to salvation. For this reason in Calvinism obedience to the law has its reward on the grounds of the conditional promises attached to it.[10]

Adherents of the doctrine of double predestination are evidently in danger of interpreting soteriology from the perspective of final perseverance. This is only natural because the idea is always implicit in the doctrine itself. Our analysis here shows that in assessing both Jewish theology and the theology of Paul we should beware of being influenced by strong presuppositions. The Jewish concept of predestination has proved to be quite different from that of Calvinism. In Jewish theology it is connected with the concept of free will – and such a relation is totally incomprehensible in the context of Calvinism.

Another feature in covenantal nomism, namely that of the soteriological function of the law, leads one's thoughts towards American *dispensationalism*.[11] This is a theological tradition which has been promoted especially by the popular Scofield Reference Bible. According to dispensationalists, God has implemented his plan of salvation in this world through different dispensations and covenants.[12]

Abraham, for example, was given the covenant of promise, Moses the

---

[9] I am not attempting to give a detailed analysis of Calvinism here. It is sufficient for our present purpose to make a reference to "five-point Calvinism" on a general level. The basic tenets have been introduced above, in chapter 9.3.

[10] Fuller, *Gospel & Law*, 65, 115-117. The law is thus submitted to the covenant in this pattern, too.

[11] A detailed description of dispensationalism in the context of the Pauline theology of law is given by Fuller, *Gospel & Law*, 1-64. In this comparison of dispensationalism and Sanders' theory I am following the suggestion of D.A. Carson, who introduced this possibility to me in our discussion of the influence of Sanders on American scholarship.

[12] See Robertson, *Christ of the Covenants*, 203.

covenant of law and David the covenant of the kingdom.[13] According to dispensationalism, these dispensations are never in conflict with one another. This is why in the Scofield Bible the covenant of law is described only as an addition to and complement of the covenant of promise. There cannot be different ways to salvation. So the comments in the Scofield Bible emphasize that the law was not actually given as a real way to salvation, but only as a rule of living for those who were already in the covenant of Abraham and under the atonement provided by the Temple sacrifices.[14]

In dispensationalism the keeping of the law is further defined as obedience. The law is not seen as a means to salvation. Instead it is a means by which Israel, which has already been saved, can "through obedience fulfill her proper destiny".[15] In dispensationalism, nomism is thus governed by the concept of covenant. The covenant of law cannot be in conflict with the covenant of promise. Therefore the law has no soteriological function (at least in strict dispensationalism). The keeping of the law is merely obedience to God within the covenant.[16]

The 'covenantal nomism' of Sanders is not actually a brand new explanation in North American theology. In the dispensations of salvation history dispensationalism has introduced a similar concept of nomism governed by covenant. Law was submitted to a covenant of grace. Obedience to the law was intended to lead Israel towards the goal which had already been given to the

---

[13] Robertson, *Christ of the Covenants,* 210, 215.

[14] "[The law] was not given as a way to life (i.e. a means of justification, Acts 15:10-11; Gal. 2:16, 21; 3:3-9, 14, 17, 21, 24-25) but as a rule of living for a people already in the covenant of Abraham and covered by blood sacrifice." The New Scofield Reference Bible, a comment on Ex. 19:1 (NSB, p. 94 explanation 1). In this passage there is a disagreement with the previous edition of the Scofield Bible. In the earlier edition, Israel changed grace into law at Sinai. In the next edition (1967) this statement was corrected by linking these covenants together. See Robertson, *Christ of the Covenants,* 215. According to another stream of dispensationalism, there are also two different ways to salvation in these two covenants, namely righteousness according to works and righteousness according to faith. This dualism was taught in the early phase of the discussion, for example by C.I. Scofield and J.W. Bowman. See Fuller, *Gospel & Law,* 22, 33.

[15] "[L]aw is not here proposed as a means of salvation but as a means by which Israel, already redeemed as a nation, might through obedience fulfill her proper destiny." The New Scofield Reference Bible, a comment on Ex. 19:3 (NSB, p. 94 explanation 2).

[16] Fuller has noted that some of the later adherents of dispensationalism identified the faith of the old covenant with righteousness by faith: "salvation in every age is simply by faith through grace." This concept was developed especially by L.S. Chafer and it was confirmed in the so-called Dallas Seminary Statement of Faith (1952). Fuller, *Gospel & Law,* 35-36.

nation in the election of grace.[17] Sanders' theory is essentially covenantal. In his theory the election of God comes before everything else, because it alone is the reason for salvation. In addition, the status of the law is defined in relation to the covenant. Success in obedience to the law could not actually affect a person's salvation because the law had been given merely as a moral obligation within the covenant.[18] Salvation depended on God's election alone.

In the previous chapters we have noted several times that, in covenantal nomism, the law had been subordinated to the covenant, and this was the reason why Sanders had been able to make a methodological distinction between the "getting in" and the "staying in". Thus we may conclude that even the methodological structure of Sanders' theory is compatible with dispensationalism – no matter whether or not the writer was conscious of this while developing his theory.

In his monograph *Paul, the Law and the Jewish People* Sanders also investigates Paul's concept of the role of the law in salvation history.[19] Here his terminology follows precisely that of dispensationalism. Sanders calls the old dispensation "the Mosaic dispensation". Paul's Christological soteriology is based on a black-and-white dualism and thus the first dispensation is in

---

[17] Snodgrass maintains that this background has also directed several scholars' interpretation of Paul's theology. He accuses e.g. Räisänen of maintaining that Paul believed that the Jews regarded the law as a real way to salvation. "Dispensationalism traditionally has held such a view, and various New Testament scholars also have fallen into this language." Snodgrass, *JSNT 32* (1988) 94, also footnote 2 (p. 108). We must be accurate here, however. Snodgrass's statement applies only to a sharpened dispensationalism, which can hardly be used as a premise in this discussion. Räisänen does not argue that the law really was a way of salvation for the Jews. In the footsteps of Sanders he actually denies this, because the law was subject to the covenant. In this respect Räisänen's view corresponds to general dispensationalism. Paul is accused by Räisänen of holding quite another view. He claims that Paul depicts the Jews as legalists even though they were 'covenantal nomists'. Räisänen, *Law*, 178. This is why Räisänen's interpretation of Paul's theology of the law cannot be regarded as a product of dispensationalism, as Snodgrass thought. Räisänen's own covenantal theology, however, seems to be closely connected with it.

[18] Here Sanders' argumentation is rather ambivalent, as we have stated in the previous analysis. He had to admit that, according to most Jewish groups, transgression of the law was a hindrance to salvation. This problem did not lead him to change his understanding of the basic concept of covenantal nomism. See chapter 17.1.

[19] Sanders, *Law*, 137: "the role of the law in *Heilsgeschichte*". This was noted above. See also chapter 11.2.

inevitable opposition to the second one.[20] Where did dispensationalism find its rationale? In Sanders' theory, the answer seems to be in the description of traditional Judaism. The dynamics of dispensationalism can probably be further seen in the fact that in the tradition of interpretation which Sanders initiated, the soteriology of Judaism began to resemble that of Christianity in many respects.[21]

Moroever, the problems posed by this kind of premise must be considered in the study of the subject. Second Temple Judaism must be studied in the light of its own premises, concentrating on its own theology. This does not mean that we should now deny the importance of covenantal theology for Jewish teaching as such. Every reasonable and justified claim made in the context of the theory of covenantal nomism must be taken seriously. What it does mean is that we must try to be aware of our premises and be careful to recognize their influence in our interpretation of texts. We must not force Jewish soteriology into the pattern of our hermeneutics – whether it be of Lutheran, Calvinist or dispensationalist origin.

---

[20] "[H]e came to relegate the Mosaic dispensation to a less glorious place *because* he found something more glorious... I cannot see how the development could have run the other way, from an initial conviction that the law only condemns and kills, to a search for something which gives life, to the conviction that life comes by faith in Christ, to the statement that the law lost its glory because a new dispensation surpasses it in glory." Sanders, *Law,* 138 (italics his). The concept of dispensation is evidently the reason why Sanders ends up considering Paul's concepts of both the law and righteousness in an astonishingly neutral way. According to Sanders, Paul at the same time finds almost nothing wrong with the law/old righteousness, and regards the law as a demonic power and old righteousness inadequate before God.

[21] We must remember the conclusion reached by Sanders: according to Paul, there was no essential fault in Jewish soteriology. It was just not Christianity. Dunn developed this interpretation further, as we have seen earlier. "Justification by faith, it would appear, is not a distinctively Christian teaching." Dunn, *Law,* 191. Dunn does not himself reveal whether or not his conception is based on dispensationalism. In our analysis, at least, it proves to be completely compatible with it.

§ 15 The Principles of Predestinarian Soteriology

During the history of scholarship Paul's theology has been assessed following several different principles. In our overview of the history of research we have seen that some scholars have located the theology of Paul in Hellenism and others in traditional Judaism. There has furthermore been rivalry between interpretations centring on Christ-mysticism and on a juridical theology of justification. The contribution of the present work is in the widened analysis of the relation of Paul to Second Temple Jewish soteriology. This has proven to be the proper context of Paul's thinking. Paul's soteriology cannot be explained correctly without a detailed analysis of its dependence on Paul's Jewish heritage. His theology of predestination has further confirmed the importance of the juridical aspect of soteriology.

15.1. Providing a solution to the problem of theodicy

Second Temple Jewish theology was directed by the problem of theodicy, which remained a burning issue throughout the centuries. The tenets of soteriology took shape according to the ways in which this problem was solved. In the sapiential tradition most Jewish groups and sects accepted synergistic nomism as a basic principle of soteriology. Paul's theology of predestination quite evidently opposes precisely this kind of teaching.

Paul too formulated a theology of crisis. He was convinced that the crisis which he was explaining concerned the unique core of Jewish faith: the Son of God had entered this world, had died and been resurrected from the dead. It was most probably this setting which led Paul to quote especially the prophet Habakkuk of all the books of the Old Testament.[1]

In Second Temple Jewish theology the book of Habakkuk was sometimes a real symbol of the theology of theodicy. In Qumranic teaching the prophecies of Habakkuk were applied to the resolving of a crisis concerning the Temple priesthood. They were regarded as a prophecy of the work of the Teacher of Righteousness. Paul, on the other hand, applied the same verses to the work of Christ.

In Jewish theology the problem of theodicy concerned above all the problem of the suffering of Israel. God's help seemed to be delayed, while the power of godless rulers seemed to be unrestricted. It is small wonder that many Jews

---

[1] Herold is no doubt right when he says that Rom. 1:17 is a passage where Paul emphasizes the "forensic existence" of man before God. In this sense the quotation from Habakkuk serves the idea of justification by faith. Herold, *Zorn*, 256ff. In addition, we must note that there is a deeper dimension of predestinatory theology which is dependent on the discussion over theodicy.

lost their faith in the goodwill of God and the eternal election of Israel.[2] Paul responded to this agony in a new way. He underlined the fact that the suffering of the people had been temporary. God's help had been on its way all the time. God is faithful to his people. His saving will is an eternal decree which he has ordained for his people from the very beginning.

The perspective of the problem of theodicy is a wider one, though. It always extends to the problem of evil. It is not only the despotic rule of evil kings that is in question here. Theologians desire to speak of the existence of evil itself – in other words: sin. In the sapiential tradition these problems were constantly expressed in terms of sin and transgression, as we can read in texts from Sirach to Qumran and 4 Ezra. This seems to be the reason why, in the theology of Paul, this subject became a theology of justification and why it occurs in contexts where sin and atonement are taught.[3]

According to Paul, the crucial intervention of God took place when the righteousness of God was revealed to this world. Paul thought that God was not unconcerned about the sinful living of ungodly humankind. In his forbearance, however, God had restrained the revealing of his wrath. Instead of executing a relentless judgment, God has revealed his saving righteousness as grace.[4]

This is the message of the key verse of Romans, 1:17. By altering the original wording of the text of Habakkuk Paul opposed the traditional obedience of the old covenant to a new obedience of faith. The salvation that comes from faith is righteousness from faith. Faith in Christ is the only thing that can provide a perfect salvation for all those who "call on the name" of this Saviour (Rom. 10:13).[5]

Due to the nature of the problem of theodicy, the theology of predestination turns out to be judicial. Theodicy has to do with the justness of God, and this is why it concerns the themes of evil and sin, and of right and wrong. Is God completely righteous and just? In his predestinatory theology Paul wishes to

---

[2] In this sense Scott's hypothesis concerning the dynamic relation of "crisis and reaction" in intertestamental Judaism seems to be valid and has been confirmed during our analysis in the present study. Scott, *EQ 64* (1992) 199f.

[3] For example, Thompson, who has made a study of 4 Ezra – a perfect example of a treatment of the problem of theodicy – concluded that the real concern of the author of that work was the problem of moral evil. Thompson, *Theodicy*, 355.

[4] Cf. Stuhlmacher, *Gerechtigkeit*, 236.

[5] Cf. especially chapter 6.2. For the concept of "obedience of faith" see Garlington, *Obedience*, 254ff. I agree with Garlington as regards the emphasized aspect of faith in the soteriology of Paul. To my understanding, however, it is not only the "nationalistic bias" which Paul opposes with his teaching, as Garlington suggests. Paul's theology of predestination is based on a completely new soteriological polarization.

answer the question concerning universal – and even cosmic – justice. This is why the emphasis is on the last judgment, which is the climax of eschatology. In God's court men are put on trial on the criterion of perfect righteousness.[6]

In Paul's theology juridical features are obvious and central. In his eschatology he retains Jewish descriptions of the last judgment. The revealing of God's wrath is part of the solution to the problem of theodicy. He also gives a *pesher* interpretation of some Old Testament texts which speak of theodicy. In addition, his text is filled with judicial metaphors, such as the judgment-seat, the juridical process and the pronouncing of sentences.[7] These judicial features of Paul's soteriology have probably never been denied in Pauline scholarship, even though several scholars neglect them in their final explanation of Paul's theology.[8]

Even though the idea of divine judgment is evident both in Jewish texts and in the letters of Paul, it is not easy to relate it to the interpretation of the theology of either one. This must be due to the erroneous perspective of the theme of predestination. Through the decades predestination has been defined as double predestination, as we have seen above. In this scheme predestination means that God has divided humankind and predetermined the fate of every individual.[9]

Such a confusion is easy to understand. Second Temple Jewish texts emphasize soteriological dualism. The righteous ones were separated from the wicked, and this was a crucial difference. In eschatological contexts this dualism was often interpreted by employing rather deterministic terminology.

All this would be quite simple, insofar as the division between sinners and the righteous is a clear one. There is a problem, however, which arises from the fact that even within predestinatory theology all Israel is called to repentance. This creates an inner tension within the theology of predestination. This problem has two sides to it. If one wishes to preserve the idea of predestination, the call to repentance does not have a great deal of relevance. On the other hand, if one takes seriously the call to repentance, the idea of predestination must be reinterpreted in some way. This has also resulted in a

---

[6] In this respect I agree with Seifrid's conclusion as regards the centrality of the theme of justification in Paul's theology, Seifrid, *Justification*, 255, 270.

[7] Cf. the analysis of Paul's juridical metaphors in chapter 6.4.

[8] Juridical features have also been noted by scholars who in other instances emphasize the aspect of Christ-mysticism, see e.g. Schweitzer, *Mystik*, 64f., or who tend to interpret Paul's theology according to the principles of Gnosticism, see Bultmann, *Theologie*, 295. In commentaries on Romans the juridical aspect is usually a self-evident fact. It is referred to by quite different kinds of scholars, see Wilckens, *Römer I*, 186; Dunn, *Romans*, 70; and Fitzmyer, *Romans*, 278, 347-348.

[9] Cf. the analysis of the Calvinist theology of predestination in chapter 9.3.

situation where the idea of predestination has become isolated from other aspects of soteriology.[10]

When we investigate Jewish texts, most writers do not consider divine election to be deterministic, despite the fact that it was believed that the final justification of the suffering righteous would take place through God's judgment. Jewish theologians proclaim the call to repentance for the precise purpose that their hearers might have an opportunity to be saved. The judgment was real, but there was an opportunity to avoid it. Such a hope is prominent both in Sirach and in other sapiential literature, too.[11]

In the interpretation of Paul's theology it is essential to remember that Jewish soteriological dualism was based on synergism. Not only in Sirach but also in several other Jewish texts the theme of predestination occurred side by side with the idea of free will and the call to repentance. We have earlier called this view synergistic nomism. Nomism is here a soteriological factor equal to covenantal promises, not merely a moral code that can be subjected to covenantalism.[12]

On the grounds of the above-mentioned features, Paul's theology has been connected with two different kinds of background. According to the former interpretation, Paul is criticizing the deterministic concept of predestination prevailing in Jewish theology. According to the latter, Paul himself accepted the covenantal concept of nomism and resolved the principles of soteriology without any real emphasis on nomism or even justification. According to the analysis made in this study, however, both of these interpretations are erroneous.

Paul is opposing the synergistic nomism which was taught by most groups in the Second Temple period, almost without exception. His own soteriology also forms an antithesis to such a theology. He radicalizes soteriological polarization and teaches full predestination. Paul's concept is not deterministic, however, but forms a basis for his Christological interpretation of the

---

[10] Sanders attempted to provide a solution to the above-mentioned problem and tension. He suggested that election was to be identified with covenant. This is why actions concerning "staying in" were secondary as regards salvation. In the context of the theory of covenantal nomism the admonition to repentance is merely an admonition to "stay in". The election itself and salvation were accordingly based solely on the covenantal promises of God. The problem of this interpretation was the logical inconsistency between election and obedience, as we have seen in chapter 14.1.; cf. the Excursus in chapter 3.

[11] Cf. chapters 3.2. and 3.3.

[12] This was Maier's analysis, *Mensch und freier Wille*, 85ff., 113; and it was later exploited e.g. by Laato, *Paulus*, 210f.

revelation of God's saving righteousness.[13] According to Paul's radicalized concept of predestination, the judgment of God relates to all ungodliness, and every sinner is consigned to judgment and punishment. Due to the fall of Adam no human being can avoid this judgment. Instead, all men resemble Adam in that they live under the power of death even while they are still alive. Paul's soteriology builds on pessimistic anthropology. All men die in Adam, and this is why no man can have hope without the righteousness that comes from God.[14]

Several of Paul's predestinarian statements are holistic: all humankind has been imprisoned under the power of sin and all men have fallen short of the glory of God. This view leads to a Christocentric soteriology: the descendants of Adam have but one possibility of escape - the new righteousness that is given through Christ.[15]

Predestinarian theology led Paul's soteriology towards a strict polarization. The traditional synergistic nomism typical of Jewish theology was impossible, because the basic principles of God's history of salvation was in opposition to it. Since Adam, all humankind had lived under the power of sin. The history of salvation must take this premise into account.[16]

Israel enjoyed a special status in this history of salvation. According to Paul,

---

[13] In this respect we must correct the explanations of Luz and Röhser concerning the importance of the theme of predestination in the theology of Paul. Luz suggested that this is not an independent theme, but merely a dimension of thought: "Prädestination is für Paulus eine Denkdimension, die für konkrete Aussagen fruchtbar gemacht werden kann... Prädestination is für Paulus aber kein eigenes theologisches Thema und darum auch kein Ansatzpunkt für geschichtstheologische Erörterungen." Luz, *Geschichtsverständnis*, 258. Against this we must note that, for Paul, the concept of predestination was a crucial premise for the soteriological polarization. This is why it was further essential as regards the reinterpretation of the history of salvation. Röhser, on the other hand, restricts the concept of predestination too much when he says that Paul teaches a somewhat deterministic view. Röhser, *Prädestination*, 172ff. If we consider, for example, Paul's teaching in Romans 9-11, it has proven to be identical with the soteriological polarization in chapter 3.

[14] As regards anthropology, this study confirms those explanations which consider Paul's radical concept of sin a crucial element of his theology. Cf. Brandenburger, *Adam*, 159, 262; Eichholz, *Paulus*, 76-78; Stuhlmacher, *Theologie*, 273ff.; Winninge, *Sinners and the Righteous*, 333.

[15] The theme of forensic justification has been under discussion for decades. Käsemann altered the status of the forensic aspect in his interpretation of Paul's apocalyptic soteriology (see chapter 12.3.), and Sanders stated that justification was not a central term in Paul's soteriology at all, Sanders, *Paul*, 506. This view has been contested later e.g. by Seifrid, who reintroduces a juridical interpretation and forensic justification in the explanation of Paul's soteriology. Seifrid, *Justification*, 255ff.

[16] This subject has been prominent, for example, in Laato's critical examination of the theory of covenantal nomism, Laato, *Paulus*, 194, 210.

the faith of Abraham was proper faith which led to salvation, because its essence was the righteousness of God. Paul never denies that the Jews had a proper and real unity with God and his redemptive mercy even in the time of the old covenant.[17]

The power of sin could not be defeated, however, without the sacrifice of the Son of God. This is a further reason why the time of the old covenant was terminated when Christ came. With Christ the righteousness of God was disclosed "apart from law". Paul was convinced of the perfect righteousness of Christ because he believed that Christ's death and resurrection meant the revealing of God's own righteousness. This was not merely a new "rabbinic" interpretation or a novel opinion of old teachings. Paul was convinced that God himself had entered this world and that the age of salvation had begun. Apart from Christ there was no longer any righteousness of God.

Such a conviction concerning the final disclosure of God's righteousness also led Paul to the principle of paradoxical polarization. Due to this principle Paul gave a radical re-interpretation of both the status of the law and the essence of righteousness.

The concept of "works of the law" was no doubt a positive one in Judaism. It can be identified with the *Avodat Israel,* 'service to God', which was considered to be the most important task of the people. We are not speaking only about sociological identity-markers, but about the whole service. This leads to a holistic interpretation of the law, and of the term "works of the law", too.[18]

This kind of interpretation may also help us to avoid the problems met with in earlier debates. We hope to be able to do justice to the identity of both Judaism and Christianity. Judaism, in the Second Temple period, was conducting the *Avodat Israel* in the cult and in everyday life. There were evidently differences in detail and in conception, but the general basis of faith was common to all groups.

Early Christianity and Paul, in turn, introduced a radical reformation. They did not cut their roots in the Old Testament, but they aimed at a Messianic and

---

[17] In this matter scholars have proposed original explanations. For example, Schoeps maintained that Paul did not know or at least did not properly describe the status of Israel in the old covenant, because he did not pay attention to the covenantal grace of God. Schoeps, *Paulus,* 224. Such a claim is erroneous, because there are several passages in Paul's letters where he describes how the grace of God has been active and powerful ever since the days of Abraham. Schoeps' problem seems to be that he was never able to explain the strict soteriological polarization in Paul's theology.

[18] For this purpose we are in fact led backwards from the theories of Dunn, as we have stated before. In the holistic interpretation of the keeping of the Law we must investigate the Temple service and the individual piety of Israel in line with to the suggestions of Lohmeyer, *Probleme,* 33-74; see chapter 10.3.

Christological renewal in the tradition of the Fathers.[19] In Paul's interpretation, the works of the law had to be assessed from the point of view of a new polarization. After Easter there was but one way to salvation and it is for this reason that all tradition needed to be re-interpreted. In this interpretation the *Avodat Israel* too became a negative matter of human effort. We can see that Jewish nomism was no petty legalism, as many scholars have noted, but that it was based on synergism. This had to be set to one side. Paul presented a polarization which was based on a radical concept of predestination. After the fall of Adam all humankind was under sin and could not be saved without the Messiah.[20]

When Paul formulated his solution to the problem of theodicy he agreed on the problem of sin, which had been a prominent question in Jewish theology, especially in the sapiential tradition. Paul differs from his predecessors, however, as regards the conception of soteriological dualism. In his soteriology Paul opposes synergistic nomism and draws a holistic picture instead: all humankind lives under sin and under God's condemnation. In this situation the soteriological polarization is something new. Salvation comes only through faith in Christ.

15.2. Paul's apocalyptic eschatology

According to our analysis, the theme of predestination is further related to several aspects of Jewish apocalyptic. In Jewish theology the anticipation of the last judgment and the expectation of restoration were part and parcel of apocalyptic soteriology. The proclamation of judgment and salvation was aimed at the inauguration of the age of salvation. The final restoration of Israel was expected to come through an eschatological upheaval.[21]

---

[19] This is where a corrective to the interpretation of Dunn and his followers is apposite. Paul is not speaking merely against "ethnocentric" works which form the basis of religious identity, as B. Longenecker has maintained. Longenecker, *Eschatology and the Covenant*, 270f. It is the whole *Avodat Israel* that must be submitted to a new polarization. This does not mean, however, that the ethnocentric aspect was totally absent from Paul's theology. As Christiansen has shown, Paul no longer accepts ecclesiological identity defined in covenantal terms. Belonging to the Christian community is defined in categories of a professed faith in Christ. Christiansen, *Covenant*, 323.

[20] I cannot agree with G. Davies, who claims that Paul's intention was merely to point out Israel's lack of faith. Davies bases his views on an insufficient distinction between sinners and the righteous. Davies, *Faith*, 70, 138. Paul did not accept the traditional soteriological dualism which Davies assumes. There was a strict polarization instead.

[21] As regards the influence of Jewish apocalyptic in the theology of Paul, I prefer the suggestions of Beker to those of Käsemann (for their views see chapter 2.6). The language that Paul employs is based on apocalyptic terminology. There is a network of symbolic relations, a real symbolic universe of Jewish apocalypticism. Beker, *NTS 34* (1988) 369.

Such traits are obvious in Paul's theology, too. In his eschatology the day of the wrath of the Lord is a key point in the future. It is, in addition, crucial for the theology of predestination, because the new dualism would be futile without the conviction that there will be a judgment for the wicked.[22]

Several features of the world-view of apocalyptic eschatology can be detected in Paul's soteriology. They are so obvious that usually no scholar would deny them. The situation is similar to that concerning the juridical features of Paul's soteriology mentioned above. Individual features have been conformed to the general view of eschatology presented above.

Firstly, Paul thought that the last days were at hand. In his writings he employs eschatological terminology when he speaks of aeons which form the primary stages of the history of salvation. Paul's eschatology is not merely a question of individual terms, however. His overall picture of eschatology, too, is apocalyptic. There has been a crucial moment and turning-point in the divine history of salvation and the age of salvation has actually begun.[23]

In this sense apocalyptic fundamentally affected Paul's conception of the history of salvation. The appearance of Christ is not merely an occasional event in the history of mankind. It must be treated as the climax of God's plan of salvation. It was precisely through the work of Christ that God revealed to men his saving righteousness.

The apocalyptic setting furthermore contained a clear vision of the eternal fate of sinners and the righteous. In Paul's soteriology these features are so common that it may be a little difficult for scholars to devote special attention to them. The theme of eschatological judgment is a basic premise, however, and the hope of the followers of Christ is pictured against the dark background of judgment: Christ will rescue his people from the wrath that is to come (1 Thess. 1:10).[24]

Moreover, the soteriology of Romans is based on an apocalyptic tension.

---

[22] Schweitzer already paid attention to this aspect in his studies. His interpretation was based on the theory of "consistent eschatology", however, and this restricts its usefulness for Pauline studies. In Schweitzer's interpretation Paul's eschatology was turned into a polarized futuristic eschatology. Only his concept of Christ-mysticism distorted the harmony of this futuristic perspective. Schweitzer, *Mystik*, 90-91. For example, Conzelmann has criticized this kind of apocalyptic eschatology in the interpretation of Paul. Conzelmann, *Theologie*, 207. As this kind of criticism is proposed, we must beware of completely neglecting the apocalyptical perspective. This is the danger in Conzelmann's existential interpretation.

[23] This theme was of special importance for Schoeps' interpretation. He thought that Paul exploited the teaching of Jewish soteriology, according to which the age of the law would come to an end when the messianic age began. This is why the power of the law could no longer reach the followers of Christ. As these participate in the resurrection life of Christ they have been transferred to the sphere of a new aeon. Schoeps, *Paulus*, 177-178.

[24] See especially chapter 6.3. above.

The disclosure of God's righteousness is God's gracious act to a world which lives under the threat of God's wrath (1:18). The appearance of divine wrath is the premise of soteriology, determining the final solution for the promise of salvation.[25]

The teaching of the resurrection of the dead, too, is a theme which must be located in the world-view of apocalyptic.[26] In Paul's theology, faith, justification and participation in Christ are always united with the belief in the resurrection of the body on the last day. In Romans 8, for example, he teaches that the Spirit of God has been given to every believer as an assurance of the new life in a new body at the resurrection (8:11). In fact even faith itself is said to be born out of God's resurrection power, and this is why it is capable of giving believers the hope of salvation (Rom. 6:5).[27]

In apocalyptic and eschatological texts we find furthermore a doctrine of new creation, which is shared by Paul, too. He describes Christ as the new Adam, in whom the whole world will be created anew. Thus the resurrection becomes an event of new creation. The previous world will disappear and the new world with God's people will appear with new bodies (1 Cor. 15: 22, 45-50).[28]

The world-view of apocalyptic thus firmly directs Paul's theology of predestination. This is only natural because a teaching concerning the determination of an individual's fate requires a framework in which God powerfully directs the life of man. In traditional Jewish sapiential theology, as well as in the old deuteronomistic theology, the benefit of man was interpreted in terms of this visible world. After one's death only one's reputation and fame remain, and their quality is dependent on one's righteousness. In apocalyptic this scheme was altered. Man's fate was considered from the perspective of eternity.

Paul's predestinarian soteriology is based on an apocalyptic world-view. The predestination of judgment is an eschatological climax and it will consummate the soteriological dualism which is a reality even in this world. Paul's gospel is a gospel of a crucial change in the old covenant made with Israel. In God's history of salvation there are aeons which have been ordained from the very beginning. The final aim of the gospel is resurrection and salvation to eternal

---

[25] As Stuhlmacher writes, even Paul's conception of justification is determined by this eschatological "Erwartungshorizont". Stuhlmacher, *Theologie*, 327; cf. Herold, *Zorn*, 329ff.

[26] As Collins analyses the "legacy of Jewish apocalypticism", he refers especially to resurrection. See Collins, *Apocalyptic Imagination*, 207f.

[27] One should not forget that the resurrection which is referred to is the eschatological resurrection of the dead. Beker speaks of God's sovereignty which is "manifest in our predestination to glory through Christ's resurrection." Beker, *Paul*, 365.

[28] This is naturally a common theme in the study of New Testament theology, cf. Stuhlmacher, *Theologie*, 271ff.; Childs, *Theology*, 393f.

life with Christ. The hope of believers is in the resurrection of their own bodies when the last day comes. This is also the predestined future of the followers of Christ: God has decreed a resurrection for them.

15.3. Divine coercion and Christocentric universalism

As we have seen during this study, most interpreters of Paul's theology have concluded that his soteriology is of a mystical nature. Ever since the theses of Deissmann and Schweitzer, Paul's soteriology has been defined as Christ-mysticism. Later this perspective was developed into a participatory interpretation. The content of soteriology remained the same, however. This participatory interpretation has exercised great influence in Pauline studies and it has eventually resulted in a new conception of Paul's thinking. The aspects of justification and Paul's theology of the law have been displaced as central factors in his soteriology. This has sometimes even led to an opposition between the theology of justification and participatory soteriology.

The perspective of Paul's theology of predestination has shown, however, that the juridical theology of justification is an essential factor in his soteriology. One cannot understand Paul's teaching properly without the basic structure of predestinatory soteriology. Moreover, his Christocentric conception of the diffusion of the saving message is firmly dependent on his theology of predestination. This is why we must pay special attention to this theme in defining the basic structure of Paul's universal soteriology.

Firstly, we must once more pay attention to the basic features of Paul's pre-destinarian theology. In his predestinarian statements Paul radicalizes traditional Jewish soteriological dualism. He abandons the previous dichotomy between sinners and the righteous. Paul's anthropology underlines the universal sinfulness of the whole of humankind. The children of Adam live under sin and for that reason the basic tenets of soteriology must agree with this great principle.[29]

Secondly, Paul's theology of predestination is located in the context of the problem of theodicy. Here Paul's purpose is similar to that of Second Temple Jewish theologians. They attempted to show that the power of ungodly rulers is eventually subjected to the sovereignty of God. The problem of theodicy is solved by God's final intervention on the last day, when universal justice will be dispensed. This kind of theology is an example of absolutism, expressing

---

[29] See especially chapters 7.1., 7.3. This is also what Winninge has underlined in his recent studies. Winninge, *Sinners and the Righteous,* 333-334. One can also see Paul's close connection with Old Testament theology, as Hofius has shown. Hofius, *Paulusstudien,* 146.

the absolute rule of Almighty God.[30] Only after pointing out these premises can we correctly define the nature of Paul's predestinarian theology.

Paul's radical soteriology is based on the idea of *divine coercion*. In his interpretation the history of salvation becomes a story about predestination. *Predestination is God's coercive act where the whole of humankind is imprisoned in disobedience.*

This theology of divine absolutism has been expressed above all in several contrast formulas (Gal. 3:22; Rom. 11:32). God has imprisoned all humankind in disobedience *so that* he may be merciful to all. The purpose of these contrast formulas is Christocentric. This reveals that the ultimate purpose of Paul's predestinarian theology is Christocentric universalism.[31]

Paul's answer to the problem of evil and his solution to the traditional theology of crisis is but one side of the coin. Paul uses the conception of divine coercion as proof of the fact that God's saving righteousness has truly been revealed in Christ. This is why Paul's concept of salvation is basically predestinatory soteriology.[32]

Once more, however, a note is required on the use of the term predestination. Paul's theology of predestination is not deterministic. He is not teaching fatalism. Paul's soteriology is based on divine absolutism and this makes all the difference. As all human beings are under condemnation, every one of them has an equal possibility to be saved through the gospel – if only they have the opportunity to hear it (Rom. 10:14).[33]

In spite of this, Paul's soteriology is actually a theology of predestination. It is not merely an analogous idea with similar features. The first premise is clear: the fate of the ungodly, i.e. of all descendants of Adam, has been foreordained by God. The wages of sin is death. God is an absolute ruler who will punish sin. Paul is convinced that all sinners are predestined to damnation. Even

---

[30] We must further remember the clear insight of Crenshaw. Such pondering on the problem of theodicy did not mean that Jews in Sirach's day were enslaved by a doctrine of righteousness on the basis of works and were guilt-ridden because of their inability to achieve perfection. Crenshaw, *JBL 94* (1975) 63. Paul opposed Jewish soteriological dualism which was based on the idea of synergism.

[31] This was Mayer's conclusion, too, even though he did not concentrate on the theme of judgment and divine coercion, but analyzed the aspect of *electio gratiae* instead. Mayer, *Heilsrathschluss,* 319ff.

[32] Our conclusions here confirm the theses of Stuhlmacher, who analyzed the nature of God's righteousness in the theology of Paul. As Paul teaches that God's righteousness means his saving work among men, he justifies his teaching with the theology of divine absolutism. Cf. Stuhlmacher, *Gerechtigkeit,* 222ff., 238.

[33] The lack of determinism led Davies more or less to abandon the whole concept of predestination. Davies, *Paul,* 100. We must note, however, that Paul's soteriology in general fulfils the conditions of predestinarian theology.

though this belief should logically lead to a deterministic soteriology, God has in his sovereignty provided a paradoxical solution to the problem. He has revealed his saving righteousness precisely to sinners and without the law.[34]

This is how *Christocentric universalism* is justified. Divine coercion has resulted in the imprisonment of the whole of humankind. Salvation, however, has been given to sinners in Christ and this results in acquittal and redemption. For Paul there is thus also a Christocentric predestination. All those who believe in Jesus Christ as Lord have been predestined to resurrection and new life.[35]

This is a further reason why proper justification is justification by faith. It comes through faith in Christ, whose redemption has become universal righteousness for the benefit of all sinners. As this righteousness is, for sinners, righteousness that comes from faith, it is solely the gospel of Christ which can dispense this grace to people. Paul also identifies divine election with calling: the gospel presents God's righteousness to sinners as a free gift, without the works of the law.[36]

But what is the actual relation of this Christocentric universalism to participatory soteriology? Do they disagree at any specific point? In our analysis we have seen that one of the basic factors in Paul's participatory soteriology is Adam-typology. Paul teaches that the children of Adam bear the image of Adam, and the children of the second Adam – namely Christ – bear the image of Christ (1 Cor. 15:45, 49; Rom. 8:29; 2 Cor. 3:18; 4:4).

Paul's participatory conception is thus based on the theology of creation, the new creation of God, to be exact. He speaks of a new creation which is centred on resurrection. All believers are created in the image of Christ. As people participate in Christ they participate in the new creation as well, and their hope is in the resurrection of the body (Rom. 8:10-11, 23). This teaching concerning two Adams and two creations is good apocalyptic thinking which is closely connected with the scheme of two aeons, as we have seen.

We are justified in concluding that the participatory theme is actually based on the juridical aspect and can in no sense be opposed to it. Participation in Christ is possible only through justification by faith. The children of Adam are

---

[34] See especially chapter 9.3. In addition, it is good to remind ourselves that this is what separates Paul from other Second Temple Jewish theologians. The righteous ones of Qumran taught the overwhelming grace of God – but only to the obedient members of the sect. In 4 Ezra eschatological hope is real, but only on synergistic conditions.

[35] This soteriological predestination is not deterministic, either. As salvation is based on faith, there is always the danger of apostasy. This is why Paul constantly admonishes his readers to remain in the grace of Christ. Cf. 1 Thess. 3:5; Phil. 3:17; Gal. 1:6, 5:1, 4; 1 Cor. 3:17, 5:11, 16:13; 2 Cor. 7:1, 10, 13:5; Rom. 13:11.

[36] Cf. Seifrid, *Justification*, 255.

freed from the condemnation which the "one man's trespass" has brought with it. By faith believers bear the image of Christ and live "in Christ" (Gal. 3:26; 1 Cor. 1:30; 2 Cor. 5:17; Rom. 8:1).[37]

This relation has naturally been detected previously by scholars.[38] On the other hand, abandoning of the juridical aspect has happened for several reasons. In the studies of the 'history-of-religions' school the participatory element was located in pagan mystery religions.[39] The covenantal nomism theory, on the other hand, rejected the juridical aspect because it was considered an unfortunate side-track of proper Pauline studies.[40]

Finally, we may proceed to give a definition of the nature of Paul's predestinarian soteriology. In his various explanations Paul above all emphasizes the sovereignty of God. This is also the tradition which he had inherited from Second Temple Jewish theology. Israel was the chosen people of God. This is why every pious Jew expected that Almighty God would guide his people through providence. The theology of crisis had been an attempt to cope with the historical problems which seemed to nullify the very basis of Judaism and bring God's faithfulness into question. In such a flow of tradition the theology of Paul was centred on the theme of God's absolute faithfulness.[41]

As a theodicy basically aims at an apology for the omnipotence and faithfulness of God, this theology makes an extraordinary theodicy. In Paul's predestinarian soteriology divine coercion is an instrument of God's absolute faithfulness. All humankind has been imprisoned to disobedience so that salvation could be of justification by faith. Thus also the atonement of Christ is a proof of God's ultimate faithfulness:

---

[37] On this question I prefer the participatory interpretation of Davies to that of Sanders, because the former does not cut the roots of Paul's theology in Jewish thinking. See Davies, *Paul,* 86ff.

[38] For example, Schweitzer never regarded these themes as contradictory, even though he himself emphasized the primacy of Christ-mysticism, see chapter 2.

[39] In this way e.g. Schoeps, who altered the interpretation of Schweitzer in a Hellenistic direction, Schoeps, *Paulus,* 163.

[40] This is the general interpretation of Sanders and his followers, see Sanders, *Paul,* 506f.

[41] Beker emphasized the apocalyptic nature of Paul's soteriology and concentrated on the "triumph of God" as the eschatological scheme of Paul's theology. Beker, *Paul,* 362ff. This is undeniably a proper description of Paul's teaching as regards the aspect of resurrection theology. In addition, we must further bring to the fore the predestinarian aspect, which helps us to define the basic difference between Paul and his Jewish heritage and provide a justification for his universal soteriology.

"that he himself is righteous
and that he justifies the one
who has faith in Jesus"
(Rom. 3:26).[42]

In Second Temple soteriology we must make a distinction between Sadducean covenantalism, sapiential synergistic nomism and Paul's theology of divine coercion. In Paul's soteriology Jewish predestinarian theology still finds its place in the emphasis on God's absolute faithfulness, but in the new paradoxical polarization the solution is solely that of Christocentric universalism. Christ alone is God's secret wisdom which he decreed before the ages for our glory. This is why the gospel, in which the righteousness of God is disclosed, is the power of God for salvation to everyone who has faith, to the Jew first and also to the Greek.

---

[42] Stuhlmacher has proposed that Paul's theology in its entirety can be described and interpreted by the term ' righteousness of God'. Stuhlmacher, *Theologie,* 337. Our analysis can contribute to this by providing a theological perspective to the disclosure of God's righteousness. In Paul's predestinarian soteriology the disclosing of God's righteousness is an expression of God's absolute faithfulness which solves the problems of sin and suffering in God's creation.

Conclusion

Paul's theology of predestination is an essential and irreplaceable factor in his soteriology. The definition of his concept of predestination has turned out to be a somewhat more complex task than scholars have usually thought in earlier research. Not one of the different methods of definition assessed at the very beginning of this study has proved to be sufficient on its own for a proper definition of Paul's teaching. This concerns the narrow teleological aspect, the theme of divine hardening, and the concept of double predestination. None of these can help us solve the mystery of Paul's conception. A proper answer can be found only through a comprehensive theological analysis where Paul's soteriology is compared with the Jewish theology of crisis that was prominent in the Second Temple period.

Part I

First, we need to pay attention to the fact that Second Temple Jewish theology was to a large extent directed by the problem of theodicy. A survey of the literature of that time revealed that behind different soteriological presentations there is almost without exception a tension between the promises of God and the historical reality of Israel. The Israel of God suffered under ungodly rulers. Jewish theologians attempted to solve this tension in terms of the problem of theodicy. The solution was usually conformed to the theology of predestination.

Predestinarian theology has further resulted in a synergistic soteriology. As the concept of religion became more and more individualized, obedience was emphasized accordingly. And when the apocalyptic conception of history became commonly accepted soteriological dualism was united with nomism by all groups from the Pharisees and the Qumran community to the community of 4 Ezra. We may call the result an era of *synergistic nomism*. This notion questions the popular theory of covenantal nomism, according to which nomism in Second Temple Jewish theology should be totally subordinated to covenantal theology.

The corrected view of nomism in Jewish theology has also helped us to interpret the soteriology of the community of Qumran in a consistent way. The community's doctrine of predestination is ambivalent. On the one hand, sapiential soteriological dualism is utterly polarized in the writings of the sect. The world is divided into the children of darkness and the children of light. The former are assigned to terrible damnation following the judgment of God. On the other hand, the community taught strict nomism. Every novice was required to submit to the rules of the community and to wholehearted obedience to the Law. Without this no man could be accepted into the community of the saved. Synergistic nomism dictated even the concept of atonement at Qumran. The sect taught that the council of the community was so perfect in its obedience to the Law that by its conduct it was able to atone for the sins of the members.

Part II

Paul's theology is closely connected with both the Old Testament and Jewish theology. In his letters we can find direct references to previous discussion of the problem of theodicy. The most important of these is the scriptural quotation of Habakkuk (Hab. 2:4) which Paul employs in the climax of a soteriological statement in Romans 1:17. According to the analysis, we can state that Paul *consciously opposes* the previous synergistic theology of predestination with the theme of justification by faith. In order to make this clear he intentionally alters the text of Habakkuk. In addition, we must remark, against the Messianic interpretation of this passage (the ΠΙΣΤΙΣ ΧΡΙΣΤΟΥ debate), that Paul here especially underlines the faith of the believer.

Paul believes that the faithfulness of God is expressed especially in the act of the last judgment and the revealing of God's wrath. In that event God will punish sin and remove ungodliness from his creation. As God until now has in his forbearance restrained from punishing sin, his grace must necessarily break the determinism of the predestination of judgment. Thus *God's righteousness which is disclosed in Christ is a proper answer to the problem of theodicy.* Here this study confirms such an interpretation of Paul's theology as emphasizes the judgment of God and concentrates on the juridical aspect of soteriology.

Paul's predestinarian theology also teaches radical anthropology. In his view, the whole world since Adam had been living under the power of sin, and so God's plan of salvation must be seen in a new light. Paul's answer to the problem of theodicy generates a *principle of paradoxal polarization.* As regards salvation, there is no distinction between Jews and Greeks. The polarity is between God and fallen humankind. Therefore Paul constantly refers to the beginning of Genesis and the story of the Fall when writing on soteriology. Our study confirms the idea that anthropology is an essential part of Paul's soteriology and one not to be neglected in the final interpretation of his theology.

Concerning the judgment of God, Paul is of the opinion that it falls on the whole of humankind. God has actually imprisoned all men in disobedience. According to the *predestination of judgment,* all men are under the power of sin and under God's condemnation. For this reason, in soteriology, there is no room for synergistic nomism. The solution to the problem of sin cannot be found by increasing man's responsibility. All human beings have been imprisoned in disobedience so that God might also be merciful to all. According to Paul, God has in Christ disclosed his saving righteousness in a new way. This is a feature which connects Galatians and Romans on an issue where previous scholarship had seen differences and development of thought.

The theory of Paul's radical theology of predestination also solves some of the problems concerning the exposition of Romans 9-11. There Paul treats the issue of the fate of Israel quite in accordance with the principles which he employs elsewhere in his soteriology. The promises of God have never been fulfilled in the lives of all Israelites. Quite on the contrary, God has constantly punished people for their sins. Paul maintained that the situation was similar at the time when he wrote his letter. Israel is part of God's creation and belongs to the children of Adam. Therefore it can be rescued from the state of disobedience solely through God's final righteousness disclosed in Christ.

In the second part of this work we have paid further attention to the inseparable *unity of the themes of election and calling.* According to Paul, the descendants of Adam can enter the community of the elect only through the gospel of God. The same God who has prescribed the condemnation is now calling men and women to salvation through the message of reconciliation. This perspective also proves that Paul's conception of election is not deterministic (Rom. 8). Paul sees predetermination as the will of God only when Christ is predestined to be the Saviour of this world. In this respect Paul teaches Christocentric predestination.

God's election is thus not eclectic, as the adherents of the theory of double predestination would maintain. The basic election has been made in Christ. He has been decreed to be the bearer of saving righteousness. Thus the gospel concerning the risen Christ, which the community proclaims, really transfers people from the prison of sin to the community of the saved. In the analysis we have stated that the idea of *double predestination is an erroneous interpretation* of both Jewish theology and Paul's soteriology.

Part III

The soteriological polarization which is a result of predestinarian theology produces *a paradoxical situation concerning the theology of law*. The law, which both Jewish teachers and Paul himself consider good as regards its essence, now becomes a destructive power. Even the attempt to obey the law becomes a negative effort, a "work of law", which leads human beings to damnation. The new status of the law in the history of salvation is explained especially in Romans 7, where Paul parallels his own life to the fate of Israel. The Law had been given to Israel so that she might know the will of God. But when this law came it resulted in a paradoxical situation: it brought death to Israel (and in a symbolic way to Paul as well).

Paul's teaching of the works of law has been a subject of study for several decades. Some scholars have proposed a sociological interpretation according to which Paul is speaking merely of Jewish "identity markers". According to the present analysis, such an interpretation is too narrow. In Paul's writings the works of law concern the relation of God's Law and human conduct. The denial of works of law is not directed against ethnocentric "markers".

The paradox produced by the theology of predestination in Paul's thinking is profound. In the Old Testament God had prescribed obedience to the Law for Israel as regards both the cult and everyday life. It was the *Avodat Israel,* the work of Israel, which every pious Jew was to perform in his life. In the context of Paul's theology of predestination this ideal became negative self-righteousness, which in reality was still under the wrath of God. In the theology of Paul the function of the law was altered completely. The good law became a servant of sin and death. There is no longer room for synergistic nomism or the concept of free will. Only God's righteousness in Christ can bring salvation.

In the theology of justification the principle of paradoxal polarization also produced significant alterations. In several of his letters Paul applies the *principle of "counting as loss"*. In comparison with the perfect righteousness that Christ has brought, the value of all other human righteousness had to be denied. Traditional Jewish obedience to God had to be considered real harm if it prevented men from finding the righteousness of God in Christ.

According to Paul, there are only *two kinds of righteousness*. The righteousness of God is righteousness from faith and it is given as a free gift to repentant sinners. All human righteousness apart from this divine righteousness thus becomes self-righteousness, whether it was consciously intended for that purpose or not. According to Paul, all men without Christ are under the unconditional, predestined judgment of God.

Part IV

One of the most popular conceptions of modern Pauline studies is that Paul's soteriology is based solely on a Christological principle. The death and resurrection of Christ were such significant events for Paul that he formulated his whole conception of the divine history of salvation on this basis. Some scholars thought that Paul did not even need to justify his arguments but that he inferred backwards when inventing deductively all the other aspects of his soteriology. This interpretation of the soteriology of Paul has further affected the understanding of the relation between Paul and his Jewish heritage. According to one solution, the only problem that Paul had with Judaism was that it was not Christianity. According to another suggestion, Paul's Christological point of departure resulted in a distortion of the picture of Jewish faith. According to a milder version, Paul only reinterpreted Jewish covenantalism and conformed it to Christology.

The analysis of Paul's use of the Christological principle has revealed that he fits in well in his Jewish environment. Most texts from that period use the *principle of contemporary application,* which is of primary importance for Paul, too. Paul does not distort his Jewish tradition but applies it in the situation where he lives. Other writings confirm that even a radical contemporary application is not opposed to the common principles of interpretation of Second Temple Jewish theology. An application does not distort Jewish identity. On the contrary, it was usually made as an apology for the authentic Jewish identity. For Paul the work of Christ was the centre of the history of salvation. Thus it became the fixed point for the reinterpretation of tradition.

As regards the "plight" of man, we have argued that it was precisely this concept which Paul *shared* with other Second Temple theologians. The general form of theology of that time was the theology of crisis. According to practically all theologians of that period, the plight of Israel was sin, because it was sin that brought the wrath of God on the people from one century to another.

Academic discussion of the problem of "plight and solution" has also been on the wrong track on another issue. Most scholars have concentrated their investigation merely on the aspect of deduction. In Paul's theology, however, we see another principle at work. Quite in agreement with other Jewish theologians, Paul writes theology by applying the principle of contemporary application. Thus we must make a *distinction between deduction and contemporary application.* In addition, we must remark that in any case, in Paul's theology it is not the plight that is reached by deduction. It is the *solution* which Paul, with other early Christian theologians, inferred from the events of Easter. The Christological solution was a novel answer to an old plight.

During the analysis we have paid special attention to studies by two scholars, E.P. Sanders and H. Räisänen. Sanders has proposed that Paul's soteriology should be interpreted as participatory eschatology. The more traditional emphasis on a theology of justification has been wrong, according to Sanders, because the theory of covenantal nomism shows that nomism cannot be a crucial factor in soteriology. As the theory of covenantal nomism has turned out to rest on weak premises, according to the present study, we must re-assess the relation between the participatory element and the juridical conception of justification in Paul's soteriology. The explanation by Räisänen, on the other hand, cannot help us in this re-assessment. He has developed the ideas of Sanders in the direction of a psychological-historical interpretation of Paul. Such an interpretation no longer works with the theological structure of Paul's writings but concentrates on biographical psychology and the inner conflicts of the writer.

In addition to these conclusions we can make some remarks on the problem concerning a scholar's dependence on denominational identity. The "new perspective on Paul" began as a critique of the views of Protestant (Lutheran) scholarship concerning the nature of Jewish faith. As an antithesis to this, the theory of covenantal nomism was not without denominational identity, either. It has turned out to resemble some Calvinist principles in general, and the ideas of *dispensationalism* in particular. The analysis of such dependences clarifies the discussion and helps us to encounter different views.

Finally, in the final chapter a general outline of Paul's soteriology is drawn. There are several important principles in Paul's predestinarian soteriology. Firstly, *Paul is quite consciously responding to the problem of theodicy.* He uses biblical quotations (especially Hab. 2:4) which bear the tradition of the theology of crisis. Furthermore, he employs predestinarian ideas in order to solve the problem of evil, which he identifies with the problem of sin. In his writings Paul uses juridical metaphors and binds the structure of soteriology in this way with the perspective of justification. His opposition is to Jewish synergistic nomism, which appears to be a false interpretation of the situation of man before God.

Paul further plants this theology of predestination in an *apocalyptic world-view.* The predestination of judgment is an eschatological climax, and it will consummate the strict soteriological dualism which is a reality even now. The acts of divine predestination can be parallelled with and located in the aeons of God's history of salvation. A completely new era of salvation was inaugurated when the righteousness of God was disclosed in Christ. And further still, the final aim of the gospel is resurrection, which has been predestined for the followers of Christ.

In a final definition of Paul's radical soteriology we have stated that it is based on the idea of *divine coercion.* In his interpretation the history of salvation becomes a story about predestination. Predestination is God's coercive act where the whole of humankind is imprisoned in disobedience. In this sense Paul's teaching is properly a theology of predestination. The fate of the ungodly has been determined, even though this view does not result in a deterministic soteriology.

In Paul's predestinarian soteriology divine coercion was an instrument of God's absolute faithfulness. All humankind has been imprisoned in disobedience so that salvation might be through justification by faith. Thus the atonement of Christ, too, is a proof of God's ultimate faithfulness: "that he himself is righteous and that he justifies the one who has faith in Jesus" (Rom. 3:26). Paul's focus is thus on *Christocentric universalism.*

As a theodicy basically aims at providing an apology for the omnipotence and faithfulness of God, this theology makes an extraordinary theodicy. With his teaching concerning justification by faith Paul gives an answer to the greatest problem of Second Temple Judaism: why does God not help? Paul answers that the reason for the delay of God's judgment is actually God's forbearance towards sinners. The problem of theodicy is solved by grace – the revealing of God's righteousness in Christ. Therefore the gospel, in which the righteousness of God is disclosed, is the power of God for salvation to everyone who has faith, to the Jew first and also to the Greek.

Bibliography

1. Sources, texts

Allegro. J.H. (ed.), *Qumrân Cave 4: I (4Q158-4Q186).* DJD 5. Oxford: Clarendon.1968.

Augustine, *Faith, Hope and Charity (Enchiridion).* Transl. L.A. Arand. Ancient Christian Writers 3. New York: Newman. s.a.

Baillet, M. (ed.), *Qumrân Grotte 4: III (4Q482-4Q520).* DJD 7. Oxford: Clarendon. 1982.

Baillet, M. - Milik, J.T. - Vaux, R. de (eds.), *Les 'Petites Grottes' de Qumrân. Exploration de la falaise. Les grottes 2Q, 3Q, 5Q, 6Q, 7Q à 10Q. Le rouleau de cuivre.* DJD 3. Oxford: Clarendon. 1962.

Barthélemy, D. - Milik, J.T. (eds.), *Qumrân Cave 1.* DJD 1. Oxford: Clarendon. 1955.

Burrows, M. (ed.), *The Dead Sea Scrolls of St. Mark's Monastery.* 2 vols. New Haven: ASOR. 1950/1951.

Biblia Hebraica Stuttgartensia, Ediderunt K. Elliger et W. Rudolph. Textum Masoreticum curavit H.P. Rüger. Masoram elaboravit G.E. Weil. Stuttgart. 1977.

Biblia sacra iuxta vulgatam versionem, Recensuit et brevi apparatu instruxit Robertus Weber osb. Tomus II. Stuttgart. 1969.

Calvin, J., *Auslegung des Römerbriefes und der beiden Korintherbriefe.* Übersetzt und bearbeitet von G. Graffmann, H.J. Haarbeck, O. Weber. Johannes Calvins Auslegung der Heiligen Schrift. Neue Reihe 16. Hrsg. O. Weber. Neukirchen. 1960.

– *Institutes of the Christian Religion 2.* Ed. J.T. McNeill. LCC 21. Philadelphia: Westminster. 1960.

Charlesworth, J.H. (ed.), *The Old Testament Pseudepigrapha. Volume 1. Apocalyptic Literature and Testaments.* New York: Doubleday. 1983.

Charlesworth, J.H. (ed.), *The Old Testament Pseudepigrapha. Volume 2. Expansions of the "Old Testament" and Legends, Wisdom and Philosophical Literature, Prayers, Psalms, and Odes, Fragments of Lost Judeo-Hellenistic Works.* New York: Doubleday. 1985.

Charlesworth, J.H. (ed.), *The Dead Sea Scrolls. Hebrew, Aramaic, and Greek Texts with English Translations. Vol. 1. Rule of the Community and Related Documents.* The Princeton Theological Seminary Dead Sea Scrolls Project. Tübingen: Mohr / Louisville: Westminster. 1994.

Charlesworth, J.H. (ed.), *The Dead Sea Scrolls. Hebrew, Aramaic, and Greek Texts with English Translations. Vol. 2. Damascus Document, War Scroll, and Related Documents.* The Princeton Theological Seminary Dead Sea Scrolls Project. Tübingen: Mohr / Louisville: Westminster. 1995.

Danby, H., *The Mishnah. Translated from Hebrew with Introduction and Brief Explanatory Notes.* Oxford: University Press. Repr. 1980.

Fischer, J.A., *Die Apostolischen Väter. Griechisch und Deutsch.* 9., durchgesehene Auflage. München: Kösel. 1986.

Geffcken, J., *Die Oracula Sibyllina.* GCS 8. Leipzig: Hinrichs. 1902.

Holm-Nielsen, S., *Hodayot: Psalms from Qumran.* AThD 2. Aarhus: Universitetsforlaget. 1960.

Jonge, M. de (ed.), *Testamenta XII Patriarcharum. Edited According to Cambridge University Library MS Ff I.24 fol. 203a-262b. With Short Notes.* PVTG 1. Leiden: Brill. 1964.

Kittel, B., *The Hymns of Qumran. Translation and Commentary.* SBL diss. 50. Scholars Press. 1981.

Knibb, M.A., *The Qumran Community.* CCWJCW 2. Cambridge: Cambridge University Press. 1987.

Kurfess, A., *Sibyllinische Weissagungen.* Berlin: Heimeran. 1951.

Lohse, E. (hrsg.), *Die Texte aus Qumran.* München: Kösel. 1986.

Neusner, J., *The Mishnah. A New Translation.* New Haven/ London: Yale University Press. 1988.

Maier, J., *The Temple Scroll. An Introduction, Translation & Commentary.* JSOTS 34. Sheffield: JSOT Press. 1985.

Martinez, F.C., *The Dead Sea Scrolls Translated. The Qumran Texts in English.* ET: W.G.E. Watson. Leiden: Brill. 1994

Nestle - Aland (26), *Novum Testamentum Graece.* Post Eberhard Nestle et Erwin Nestle communiter ediderunt K. Aland, M. Black, C.M. Martini, B.M. Metzger, A. Wikgren. 26. Auflage, nach dem 7. revidierten Druck. Stuttgart: Deutsche Bibelgesellschaft. 1983.

Nestle - Aland (27), *Novum Testamentum Graece.* Post Eberhard et Erwin Nestle communiter ediderunt B. Aland, K. Aland, J. Karavidopoulos, C.M. Martini, B.M. Metzger. 27. revidierte Auflage. Stuttgart: Deutsche Bibelgesellschaft. 1993.

Newsom, C., *Songs of the Sabbath Sacrifice. A Critical Edition.* Harvard Semitic Studies. Atlanta : Scholars. 1985.

Origen, De Principiis. ANFa 4. 239-384. Peabody, Mass.: Hendrickson. 1994.

Qimron, E. - Strugnell, J. (eds.), *Qumran cave 4. V. Miqsat ma^{c}a´se ha-torah.* DJD X. Oxford: Clarendon. 1994.

Rahlfs, A. (ed.), *Septuaginta id est Vetus Testamentum graece iuxta LXX interpretes.* 2 vols. Stuttgart: Deutsche Bibelgesellschaft. 1979.

Sanders, J.A. (ed.), *The Psalms Scroll of Qumrân Cave 11 (11QPs^a).* DJD 4. Oxford: Clarendon. 1965.

Smend, R., *Die Weisheit des Jesus Sirach: Hebräisch und Deutsch.* Berlin: Reimers. 1906.

Scofield, C.I., *The New Scofield Reference Bible.* Holy Bible Authorized King James Version. With introductions, annotations, subject chain references, and such word changes in the text as will help the reader. Oxdord: Oxford University Press. 1967.

Thackeray, H.St.J., *Josephus. The Jewish War.* LCL. Cambridge, Mass./London: Harvard University Press. Repr. 1989.

Thackeray, H.St.J. - Marcus, R. - Wikgren, A. - Feldman, L.H., *Josephus. Jewish Antiquities.* LCL. Cambridge, Mass./London: Harvard University Press. Repr. 1991.

Tov, E. (ed.), *The Greek Minor Prophets Scroll from Nahal Hever (8HevXIIgr).* DJD 8. Oxford: Clarendon. 1990.

Vaux, R. de - Milik, J.T. (eds.), *Qumrân Grotte 4: II. Tefillin, Mezuzot et Targums (4Q128-4Q157).* DJD 6. Oxford: Clarendon. 1977.

Vermes, G., *The Dead Sea Scrolls in English.* Revised and Extended Fourth Edition. Sheffield: Sheffield Academic Press. 1995.

Violet, B., *Die Esra-Apokalypse (IV. Esra).* GCS 18. Leipzig: Hinrichs. 1910.

Whiston, W., *The Works of Josephus. Complete and Unabridged.* New Updated Edition. Peabody, Massachusetts: Hendrickson. 1987.

2. Subsidia

Aland, K. – Werner, H., *Computer–Konkordanz,* Zum Novum Testamentum Graece von Nestle–Aland, 26. Aufl. und zum Greek New Testament 3rd Edition. Herausgegeben vom Institut für Neutestamentliche Textforschung und vom Rechenzentrum der Universität Münster, unter besonderer Mitwirkung von H. Bachmann, W.A. Slaby. Berlin/New York: de Gruyter. 1980.

Balz, H. – Schneider, G. (hrsg.), *Exegetisches Wörterbuch zum Neuen Testament.* 3 vols. Stuttgart: Kohlhammer. 1980/1981/1983.

Bauer, W., *Griechisch–deutsches Wörterbuch.* 6., völlig neu bearbeitete Auflage. Hrsg. K. Aland und B. Aland. Berlin/New York: de Gruyter. 1988.

Blass, F. – Debrunner, A. – Rehkopf, F., *Grammatik des neutestamentlichen Griechisch.* 15. durchgesehene Auflage. Göttingen: Vandenhoeck & Ruprecht. 1979.

Botterweck, G.J. – Ringgren, H. (hrsg.), *Theologisches Wörterbuch zum Alten Testament.* Stuttgart: Kohlhammer. 1970ff.

Brown, F. – Driver, S.R. – Briggs, C.A. – Gesenius, W., *The New Hebrew and English Lexicon.* Peabody, Mass.: Hendrickson. 1979.

Davidson, B., *The Analytical Hebrew and Chaldee Lexicon.* London. 1970.

Fitzmyer, J.A., *The Dead Sea Scrolls: Major Publications and Tools for Study.* SBLSBS 8. Missoula: Scholars. 1975.

Hatch, E. – Redpath, H.A., *A Concordance to the Septuagint and other Greek Versions to the Old Testament (Including the Apocryphal Books).* 2 vols. Oxford: Clarendon. 1897. (= Grand Rapids: Baker 1987).

Kittel, G. – Fiedrich, G. (hrsg.), *Theologisches Wörterbuch zum Neuen Testament.* 10 vols. Stuttgart: Kohlhammer. 1933-1979.

Kuhn, K.G., (hrsg.) *Konkordanz zu den Qumrantexten.* Göttingen: Vandenhoeck & Ruprecht. 1960.

Koehler, L. – Baumgartner, W., *Hebräisches und Aramäisches Lexicon zum Alten Testament.* Dritte Auflage. 2. vols. Leiden: Brill. 1967/1974.

Koehler, L. – Baumgartner, W., *The Hebrew and Aramaic Lexicon of the Old Testament I-II.* Rev. by W. Baumgartner and J.J. Stamm. Leiden: Brill. 1994/1995.

Liddell, H.G. – Scott R., *A Greek–English Lexicon.* Revised and Augmented throughout by H.S. Jones. With a Supplement. New (ninth) edition. Reprinted. Oxford. 1973.

Metzger, B.M., *A Textual commentary on the Greek New Testament.* London/New York: United Bible Societies. 1975.

Reicke, B. – Rost. L. (hrsg.), *Biblisch-historisches Handwörterbuch.* 4 vols. Göttingen: Vandenhoeck & Ruprecht. 1962-1979.

Roth, C. – Wigoder, G. (eds. in chief), *Encyclopaedia Judaica* 1-16. Jerusalem: Keter. 1971–.

Stemberger, G., *Der Talmud. Einführung - Texte - Erläuterungen.* München: Beck. 1982.

Strack, H.L. - Billerbeck, P., *Kommentar zum Neuen Testament aus Talmud und Midrasch.* 1-6. München: Beck. [6]1986.

3. General bibliography

Allison, D.C.Jr., Jesus and the Covenant: A Response to E.P. Sanders. *JSNT 29* (1987) 57-78.

Althaus, P., *Der Brief an die Römer.* NTD 6. Göttingen. 1932.

Avemarie, F., *Tora und Leben. Untersuchungen zur Heilsbedeutung der Tora in der frühen rabbinischen Literatur.* TSAJ 55. Tübingen: Mohr. 1996.

Avi-Yonah, M., The Hasmonean Revolt and Judah Maccabee's war against the Syrians. – *The World History of the Jewish People I/6.* The Hellenistic Age. Political History of Jewish Palestine from 332 B.C.E. to 67 B.C.E. Ed. A. Schalit. London: Allen. 147-182. 1976.

Badenas, R., *Christ the End of the Law. Romans 10.4. in Pauline Perspective.* JSNTS 10. Trowbridge: JSOT Press. 1985.

Balz, H.R., *Methodische Probleme der neutestamentlichen Christologie.* WMANT 8. Neukirchen-Vluyn. 1967.

Barrett, C.K., *From First Adam to Last. A Study in Pauline Theology.* London: Black. 1962.

– *A Commentary on the Epistle to the Romans.* 2. Edition. BNTC. London: Black. 1967.

– *A Commentary on the First Epistle to the Corinthians.* 2. Edition. BNTC. London: Black. 1968.

– The Interpretation of the Old Testament in the New. – *The Cambridge History of the Bible. Volume 1.* Ed. P.R. Ackroyd, C.F. Evans. 377-411. Cambridge: Cambridge University Press. 1987.

Barth, K., *Der Römerbrief.* Zürich: EVZ-Verlag. [10]1967.

Baur, F.C., *Paulus, der Apostel Jesu Christi.* Stuttgart. 1845.

Becker, J., *Untersuchungen zur Entstehungsgeschichte der Testamente der zwölf Patriarchen.* Arbeiten zur Geschichte des Antiken Judentums und des Urchristentums 8. Leiden: Brill. 1970.

– *Paulus. Der Apostel der Völker.* Zweite, durchgesehene Auflage. Tübingen: Mohr. 1989.

Beker, J. Chr., E.P. Sanders, Paul and Palestinian Judaism. (Review). *TToday 35* (1978) 108-111.

– *Paul the Apostle.* Edinburgh. 1980.

– Paul's Theology: Consistent or Inconsistent? *NTS 34* (1988) 364-377.

– The Faithfulness of God and the Priority of Israel in Paul's Letter to the Romans. – *The Romans Debate.* Revised and Expanded Edition. Ed. K.P. Donfried. Peabody, Massachusetts. 327-332. 1991.

Benoit, P., Qumran and the New Testament. – *Paul and the Dead Sea Scrolls.* Ed. J. Murphy O'Connor, J.H. Charlesworth. New York: Crossroad. 1-30. 1990.

Berger, K., *Exegese und Philosophie.* SBS 123/124. Stuttgart: Katholisches Bibelwerk. 1986.

Berger, P.L., *The Sacred Canopy. Elements of a Sociological Theory of Religion.* New York: Doubleday. 1967.

Best, E., *A Commentary on the First and Second Epistles to the Thessalonians.* BNTC. London: Black. 1977.

Betz, H.D., *Galatians.* A Commentary on Paul's Letter to the Churches in Galatia. Hermeneia. Philadelphia: Fortress. 1979.

– Hellenism. *ABD III* (1992) 127-135.

– Paul. *ABD V* (1992) 186-201.

Betz, O., Adam. I. Altes Testament, Neues Testament und Gnosis. *TRE I* (1977) 414-424.

– Rechtfertigung in Qumran. *Festschrift für Ernst Käsemann zum 70. Geburtstag. –* Betz, O., *Jesus Der Messias Israels. Aufsätze zur biblischen Theologie.* WUNT 42. Tübingen: Mohr. 39-58. 1987.

Black, M., *The Scrolls and Christian Origins. Studies in the Jewish Background of the New Testament.* London: Nelson. 1961.

– *The Book of Enoch or 1 Enoch. A New English Edition with Commentary and Textual Notes.* In Consultation with J.C. VanderKam. SVTP VII. Leiden: Brill. 1985.

– *Romans.* Second Edition. NCeB. London. 1989.

Bornkamm, G., *Paulus.* Stuttgart: Kohlhammer. 1969.

– Wandlungen im alt- und neutestamentlichen Gesetzesverständnis. – Bornkamm, G., *Studien zum Neuen Testament.* München: Kaiser. 25-71. 1985.

Bousset, W., *Kyrios Christos.* Dritte Auflage. Göttingen. 1926.

– *Die Religion des Judentums im späthellenistischen Zeitalter.* 3. verbesseter Auflage, hrsg. Gressmann. HNT 21. Tübingen: Mohr. 1926.

Brandenburger, E., *Adam und Christus. Exegetisch-religionsgeschichtliche Untersuchung zu Röm. 5,12-21 (1. Kor. 15).* WMANT 7. Neukirchen-Vluyn: Neukirchener. 1962.

– *Die Verborgenheit Gottes im Weltgeschehen. Das literarische und theologische Problem des 4. Esrabuches.* AThANT 68. Zürich: Theologischer Verlag. 1981.

Brooke, G., E.P. Sanders, Paul and Palestinian Judaism. (Review). *JJS 30* (1979) 247-250.

Bruce, F.F., *New Testament History.* New York: Doubleday. 1980.

– *Paul: Apostle of the Free Spirit.* Revised Edition. Exeter: Paternoster. 1980.

Bultmann, R., *Theologie des Neuen Testaments.* UTB 630. 8., durchgesehene, um Vorwort und Nachträge wesentlich erweiterete Auflage, hrsg. O. Merk. Tübingen: Mohr. 1980.

– *Theology of the New Testament. Vols. 1-2.* ET K. Grobel. London: SCM. 1983.

– *Neues Testament und Mythologie. Das Problem der Ent-mythologisierung der neutestamentlichen Verkündigung.* Nachdruck der 1941 erschienenen Fassung hrsg. E. Jüngel. München. 1985.

– καυχάομαι, κ.τ.λ. *ThWNT III* (1990) 646-653.

Burton, E. De Witt, *A Critical and Exegetical Commentary on the Epistle to the Galatians.* ICC. Edinburgh: Clark. 1988.

Caird, G.B., Predestination - Romans ix.-xi. *ExpT 68* (1957) 324-327.

– Paul and Palestinian Judaism by E.P. Sanders. (Review). *JTS 29* (1978) 538-543.

Campbell, D.A., *The Rhetoric of Righteousness in Romans 3.21-26.* JSNTS 65. Sheffield: JSOT. 1992.

– Romans 1:17 – a *Crux Interpretum* for the ΠΙΣΤΙΣ ΧΡΙΣΤΟΥ Debate? *JBL 113* (1994) 265-285.

Cathcart, K.J., Day of Yahweh. *ABD II* (1992) 84-85.

Cavallin, H.C.C., 'The Righteous Shall Live by Faith' A Decisive Argument for the Traditional Interpretation. *StTh 32* (1978) 33-43.

Charlesworth, J.H. *The Old Testament Pseudepigrapha and the New Testament. Prolegomena for the Study of Christian Origins.* MSSNTS 54. Cambridge: Cambridge University Press. 1985.

Childs, B.S., *Biblical Theology of the Old and New Testaments. Theological Reflection on the Christian Bible.* London: SCM. 1992.

Christiansen, E.J., *The Covenant in Judaism and Paul. A Study of Ritual Boundaries as Identity Markers.* AGJU 27. Leiden: Brill. 1995.

Collins, J.J., Apocalyptic literature. – *Early Judaism and its Modern Interpreters.* 345-370. Ed. R.A. Kraft and G.W.E. Nickelsburg. The Bible and Its Modern Interpreters 2. Atlanta: Scholars Press. 1986.

– Was the Dead Sea Sect an Apocalyptic Movement? – *Archaeology and History in the Dead Sea Scrolls.* The New York University Conference in Memory of Yigael Yadin. Ed. L. Schiffman. Worcester. JSOT/ASOR Monograph Series 2. / JSPS 8. 25-51. 1990.

– *Apocalyptic Imagination.* An Introduction to the Jewish Matrix of Christianity. New York: Crossroad. 1992.

– Dead Sea Scrolls. *ABD II* (1992) 85-101.
– Early Jewish Apocalypticism. *ABD I* (1992) 282-288.
– *Daniel: A Commentary of the Book of Daniel.* Hermeneia. Minneapolis: Fortress. 1993.
– *The Scepter and the Star: The Messiahs of the Dead Sea Scrolls and Other Ancient Literature.* The Anchor Bible Reference Library. New York: Doubleday. 1995.
Colpe, C., *Die religionsgeschichtliche Schule.* FRLANT 60. Göttingen: Vandenhoeck & Ruprecht. 1961.
Conzelmann, H., *Grundriss der Theologie des Neuen Testaments.* EETh 2. Studienausgabe. München: Kaiser. ³1967.
– *1 Corinthians. A Commentary on the First Epistle to the Corinthians.* Hermeneia. Philadelphia: Fortress. 1988.
Cooper, K.R., Paul and Rabbinic Soteriology. A Review Article. *WTJ 44* (1982) 123-139.
Cranfield, C.E.B., *The Epistle to the Romans.* Volume I. (With corrections.) ICC. Edinburgh. 1982.
– St. Paul and the Law. *SJT 17* (1964) 43-68.
Crenshaw, J.L., "The Problem of Theodicy in Sirach: On Human Bondage" *JBL 94* (1975) 47-64.
– *Old Testament Wisdom. An Introduction.* Atlanta: John Knox. 1981
– Introduction: The Shift from Theodicy to Anthropodicy. – *Theodicy in the Old Testament.* Ed. J.L. Crenshaw. Issues in Religion and Theology 4. London: SPCK / Philadelphia: Fortress. 1-16. 1983.
– *Old Testament Story and Faith. A Literary and Theological Introduction.* Peabody: Hendrickson. 1992.
– Theodicy. *ABD VI* (1992) 444-447.
Cross, F.M., *The Ancient Library of Qumran.* 3rd Edition. The Biblical Seminar 30. Sheffield: Sheffield Academic Press. 1995.
Cullmann, O., *Heil als Geschichte. Heilsgeschichtliche Existenz im Neuen Testament.* Tübingen: Mohr. 1965.
Daube, D., *The New Testament and Rabbinic Judaism.* Peabody, Massachusetts: Hendrickson. 1956.
Davies, G.N., *Faith and Obedience in Romans. A Study of Romans 1-4.* JSNTS 39. Sheffield: JSOT. 1990.
Davies, P.R., *The Damascus Covenant. An Interpretation of the Damascus Document.* JSOTS 25. Sheffield: JSOT. 1983.
Davies, W.D., *Paul and Rabbinic Judaism. Some Rabbinic Elements in Pauline Theology.* London 1948.
– Paul and the People of Israel. *NTS 24* (1977) 4-39.
– Paul and the Law. Reflections on Pitfalls in Interpretation. – *Paul and Paulinism.* FS C.K. Barrett, eds. M.D. Hooker and S.G. Wilson. London: SPCK. 4-16. 1982.
– Paul and the Dead Sea Scrolls: Flesh and Spirit. – *The Scrolls and the New Testament.* Ed. K. Stendahl. With a new Introduction by J.H. Charlesworth. New York: Crossroad. 157-182. 1992.
Deines, R., Die Abwehr der Fremden in den Texten aus Qumran. Zum Verständnis der Fremdenfeindlichkeit in der Qumrangemeinde. – *Die Heiden, Juden, Christen und das problem des Fremden.* Hrsg. R. Feldmeier und U. Heckel, mit einer Einleitung von M. Hengel. WUNT 70. 59-91. Tübingen: Mohr. 1994.
Deissmann, A., *Paulus. Eine kultur- und religionsgeschichtliche Skizze.* 2. Auflage. Tübingen: Mohr. 1925.
De Lorenzi, L., *Die Israelfrage nach Röm 9-11.* SMBen.BE 3. Rom. 1977.

DiLella, A., Sirach. – *The New Jerome Biblical Commentary.* Ed. R.E. Brown, J.A. Fitzmyer, R.E. Murphy. Englewood Cliffs: Prentice Hall. 496-509. 1990.
– Wisdom of Ben Sira. *ABD VI* (1992) 931-945.
Dinkler, E., The Historical and the Eschatological Israel in Romans chapters 9-11: A Contribution to the Problem of Predestination and Individual Responsibility. *JR 36* (1956) 109-127.
– Prädestination. II. Im NT. *RGG 5* (1986) 483.
Dobbeler, A. von, H. Räisänen, Paul and the Law. (Review). *NovT 26* (1984) 374-376.
Dodd, B., Romans 1:17 – a *Crux Interpretum* for the ΠΙΣΤΙΣ ΧΡΙΣΤΟΥ Debate? *JBL 114* (1995) 470-473.
Dodd, C.H., *The Epistle of Paul to the Romans.* MNTC. London. 1947.
Donaldson, T.L., Zealot and Convert: The Origin of Paul's Christ-Torah Antithesis. *CBQ 51* (1989) 655-682.
Dülmen, A. van, *Die Theologie des Gesetzes bei Paulus.* SBM 5. Stuttgart: Katholisches Bibelwerk. 1968.
Dunn, J.D.G., *Romans 1–8, 9–16.* Word Biblical Commentary 38a, 38b. Dallas: Word Books. 1988.
– *Jesus, Paul, and the Law.* Studies in Mark and Galatians. Louisville, Kentucky: Westminster/ John Knox Press. 1990.
– *The Partings of the Ways. Between Christianity and Judaism and their Significance for the Character of Christianity.* London: SCM / Philadelphia: TPI. 1991.
– Once More, ΠΙΣΤΙΣ ΧΡΙΣΤΟΥ. *SBL.SP* (1991) 730-744.
– *The Epistle to the Galatians.* BNTC 9. Peabody, Massachusetts: Hendrickson. 1993.
Dupont-Sommer, A., *The Essene Writings from Qumran.* Oxford: Blackwell. 1961.
Eckstein, H-J., *Verheissung und Gesetz. Eine exegetische Untersuchung zu Galater 2,15 - 4,7.* WUNT 86. Tübingen: Mohr. 1996.
Eichholz, G., *Die Theologie des Paulus im Umriss.* Neukirchen-Vluyn: Neukirchener. [6]1988.
Eichrodt, W., *Ezekiel. A Commentary.* OTL. Philadelphia: Westminster. 1970.
– Faith in Providence and Theodicy in the Old Testament. – *Theodicy in the Old Testament.* Ed. J.L. Crenshaw. Issues in Religion and Theology 4. London: SPCK / Philadelphia: Fortress. 17-41. 1983.
Eissfeldt, O., *The Old Testament. An Introduction including the Apocrypha and Pseudepigrapha, and also the works of similar type from Qumran.* ET P.R. Ackroyd. Oxford: Blackwell. 1974.
Ellis, E.E., *The Old Testament in Early Christianity. Canon and Interpretation in the Light of Modern Research.* WUNT 54. Tübingen: Mohr. 1991.
Eskola, T., *Messias ja Jumalan Poika. Traditiokriittinen tutkimus kristologisesta jaksosta Room. 1:3,4. [Messiah and Son of God. A Tradition-Critical Study of the Christological Clauses in Romans 1:3,4.* English Summary.] SESJ 56. Helsinki: Suomen eksegeettinen seura. 1992.
– Biblical Theology versus the History of Early Christian Religion – Finnish Scholarship in a Debate. *EJTh 5* (1995) 27-35.
– An Era of Apologetical Hermeneutics – Detecting a Neo-Kantian Paradigm of Biblical Interpretation. *EQ 68/4* (1996) 329-344.
– Paul, Predestination and "Covenantal Nomism". Re-assessing Paul and Palestinian Judaism. *JSJ 28 (1997) Forthcoming.*
Fee, G.D., *The First Epistle to the Corinthians.* NICNT. Grand Rapids: Eerdmans. 1988.

Feuillet, A., La Citation d'Habacuc II.4 et les huit premiers chapitres de l'Épître aux Romains. *NTS* 6 (1959) 52-80.

Fichtner, J., ὀργή. Der Zorn Gottes im AT. *ThWNT* V (1990) 395-410.

Finegan, J., *The Archeology of the New Testament. The Life of Jesus and the Beginning of the Early Church.* Revised Edition. Princeton: Princeton University. 1992.

Fischer, Th., Maccabees, Books of. First and Second Maccabees. *ABD IV* (1992) 439-450.

Fishbane, M., *Biblical Interpretation in Ancient Israel.* Oxford: Clarendon. 1991.

Fitzmyer, J.A., *Romans. A New Translation with Introduction and Commentary.* AncB 33. New York: Doubleday. 1993.

Flusser, D., The Dead Sea Sect and Pre-Pauline Christianity. – *Judaism and the Origins of Christianity.* 23-74. Jerusalem: Magnes Press. 1988.

– Melchizedek and the Son of Man. – *Judaism and the Origins of Christianity.* 186-192. Jerusalem: Magnes Press. 1988.

– *The Spiritual History of the Dead Sea Sect.* Tel Aviv: MOD Books. 1989.

Fuller, D.P., *Gospel & Law. Contrast or Continuum? The Hermeneutics of Dispensationalism and Covenant Theology.* Grand Rapids, Michigan: Eerdmans. 1980.

Garlington, D.B., *'The Obedience of Faith'. A Pauline Phrase in Historical Context.* WUNT 2. Reihe 38. Tübingen: Mohr. 1991.

Garnet, P., *Salvation and Atonement in the Qumran Scrolls.* WUNT 2. Reiche 3. Tübingen: Mohr. 1977.

– Qumran Light on Pauline Soteriology. – *Pauline Studies.* FS F.F. Bruce. Eds. D.A. Hagner, M.J. Harris. Exeter: Paternoster/ Eerdmans. 19-32. 1980.

Gaston, L., *Paul and the Torah.* Vancouver: University of British Columbia Press. 1987.

Getty, M.A., H. Räisänen, Paul and the Law. (Review). *CBQ 47* (1985) 561-563.

Gnilka, J., *Der Philipperbrief.* Herder X 3. Freiburg: Herder. 1987.

Goppelt, L., *Theologie des Neuen Testaments.* Hrsg. J. Roloff. Unveränderter Nachdruck der dritten Auflage. UTB 850. Göttingen: Vandenhoeck & Ruprecht. 1991.

Greenberg, M., *Ezekiel 1-20. A New Translation with Introduction and Commentary.* AncB 22. New York: Doubleday. 1986.

Gruenler, R.G., *Meaning and Understanding. The Philosophical Framework for Biblical Interpretation.* Foundations of Contemporary Interpretation 2. Grand Rapids: Zondervan. 1991.

Gruenwald, I. *Apocalyptic and Merkavah Mysticism.* AGJU 14. Leiden/Köln: Brill. 1980.

Grundmann, W., The Teacher of Righteousness of Qumran and the Question of Justification by Faith in the Theology of the Apostle Paul. – *Paul and the Dead Sea Scrolls.* Ed. J. Murphy O'Connor, J.H. Charlesworth. 85-114. New York: Crossroad. 1990.

Gundry, R.H., Grace, Works and Staying Saved in Paul. *Bib 66* (1985) 1-38.

Gutbrod, W., νόμος. B. Das Gesetz im Alten Testament. C. Das Gesetz im Judentum. D. Das Gesetz im Neuen Testament. *ThWNT IV* (1990) 1029-1077.

Gärtner, B., *The Temple and the Community in Qumran and in the New Testament.* SNTS 1. Cambridge: Cambridge University press. 1965.

Haacker, K., War Paulus Hillelit? – *Das Institutum Judaicum der Universität Tübingen in den Jahren 1971-1972.* Hrsg. O. Betz. Tübingen. 106-120. 1972.

– Paulus und das Judentum. *Judaica 33* (1977) 161-177.

Hagner, D.A., Paul and Judaism. The Jewish Matrix of Early Christianity: Issues in the Current Debate. – *Bulletin for Biblical Research* 3 (1993) 111-130.

– Balancing the Old and the New. The Law of Moses in Matthew and Paul. *Interp.* (1997) 20-30.

Hahn, F., Das Gesetzesverständnis im Römer- und Galaterbrief. *ZNW 67* (1976) 29-63.

Hahn, H.-Chr., ἔργον. *TBLNT II* (²1979) 1386-1390.
– Ruhm. *TBLNT II* (²1979) 1051-1053.
– ὀργή. *TBLNT II* (²1979) 1498-1503.
Hanson, P.D., "Rebellion in Heaven, Azazel, and Euhemeristic Heroes in 1 Enoch 6-11". *JBL 96* (1977) 195-233.
– *The Dawn of Apocalyptic. The Historical and Sociological Roots of Jewish Apocalyptic Eschatology*. Revised Edition. Philadelphia: Fortress. 1979.
Harnisch, W., *Verhängnis und Verheissung der Geschichte. Untersuchungen zum Zeit- und Geschichtsverständnis im. 4. Buch Esra und in der syr. Baruchapokalypse*. FRLANT 97. Göttingen: Vandenhoeck & Ruprecht. 1969.
Hawthorne, G.F., *Philippians*. Word Biblical Commentary 43. Waco, Texas: Word Books. 1983.
Hays, R.B., *The Faith of Jesus Christ. An Investigation of the Narrative Substructure of Galatians 3:1-4:11*. SBL.DS 56. Chico, CA: Scholars. 1983.
– Paul & Law by H. Räisänen. (Review). *JAAR 53* (1985) 513-515.
– 'The Righteous One' as Eschatological Deliverer: A Case Study in Paul's Apocalyptic Hermeneutics. – *Apocalyptic and the New Testament. Essays in Honor of J. Louis Martyn*. Eds. J. Marcus, M.L. Soards. JSNTS 24. Sheffield: JSOT. 1989.
– ΠΙΣΤΙΣ and Pauline Christology: What Is at Stake? *SBL.SP* (1991) 714-729.
Heckel, U., Das Bild der Heiden und die Identität der Christen bei Paulus. – *Die Heiden, Juden, Christen und das problem des Fremden*. Hrsg. R. Feldmeier und U. Heckel, mit einer Einleitung von M. Hengel. WUNT 70. 269-296. Tübingen: Mohr. 1994.
Hengel, M., *Der Sohn Gottes. Die Entstehung der Christologie und die jüdisch-hellenistische Religionsgeschichte*. Tübingen: Mohr. 1975.
– Qumran und der Hellenismus. – *Qumrân. Sa piété, sa théologie et son milieu*. Ed. M. Delcor. BEThL XLVI. Paris-Gembloux: Duculot/Leuven University Press. 1978.
– *Judentum und Hellenismus*. 3., durchgesehene Auflage. WUNT 10. Tübingen: Mohr. 1988.
– The Political and Social History of Palestine from Alexander to Antiochus III (333-187 B.C.E.). – *The Cambridge History of Judaism*. Eds. W.D. Davies, L. Finkelstein. Vol 2. The Hellenistic Age. Cambridge: Cambridge University Press. 35-78. 1989.
– *The Zealots. Investigations into the Jewish Freedom Movement in the Period from Herod I until 70 A.D.* ET D. Smith. Edinburgh: Clark. 1989.
– Psalm 110 und die Erhöhung des Auferstandenen zur rechten Gottes. – *Anfänge der Christologie*. FS F. Hahn. Hrsg. Breytenbach und Paulsen. Göttingen: Vandenhoeck & Ruprecht. 43-73. 1991.
– Der vorchristliche Paulus. – *Paulus und das antike Judentum*. Hrsg. M. Hengel, U. Heckel. Tübingen-Durham-Symposium im Gedenken an den 50. Todestag Adolf Schlatters (19. Mai 1938). Tübingen: Mohr. 177-293. 1991.
Hengel, M. – Deines, R., E.P. Sanders' 'Common Judaism', Jesus, and the Pharisees. Review Article of *Jewish Law from Jesus to the Mishnah* and *Judaism: Practice and Belief* by E.P. Sanders. *JTS 46* (1995) 1-70.
Hengel, M. – Schwemer, A.M. (hrsg.), *Königsherrschaft Gottes und himmlischer Kult im Judentum, Urchristentum und in der hellenistischen Welr*. WUNT 55. Tubingen: Mohr. 1991.
Herion, G.A., Wrath of God. Old Testament. *ABD VI* (1992) 989-996.
Herold, G., *Zorn und Gerechtigkeit Gottes bei Paulus. Eine Untersuchung zu Röm. 1,16-18*. EHS.T 14. Bern: H. Lang / Frankfurt/M.: P. Lang. 1973.
Hiers, R.H., Day of Judgment. *ABD II* (1992) 79-82.

– Day of the Lord. *ABD II* (1992) 82-83.

Hofius, O., *Paulusstudien.* WUNT 51. Tübingen: Mohr. 1989.

Hollander, H.W. - de Jonge, M., *The Testaments of the Twelwe Patriarchs. A Commentary.* SVTP 8. Leiden: Brill. 1985.

Holm-Nielsen, S., *Hodayot. Psalms from Qumran.* AThD 2. Aarhus: Universitetsforlaget. 1960.

Holtz, T., *Der erste Brief an die Thessalonicher.* EKK XIII. Zürich: Benziger/Neukirchener. 1986.

Hooker, M.D., Paul and 'Covenantal Nomism' – *Paul and Paulinism.* FS C.K. Barrett, eds. M.D. Hooker and S.G. Wilson. London: SPCK. 47-56. 1982.

Howard, G., *Paul: Crisis in Galatia. A Study in Early Christian Theology.* Second Edition. MSSNTS 35. Cambridge: Cambridge University Press. 1990.

Hurtado, L.W., New Testament Christology: A Critique of Bousset's Influence. *TS 40* (1979) 306-317.

– *One God, one Lord: early Christian devotion and ancient Jewish monotheism.* London: SCM. 1988.

Hübner, H., *Law in Paul's Thought.* Edinburgh: Clark. 1984.

– *Gottes Ich und Israel. Zum Schriftgebrauch des Paulus in Römer 9-11.* FRLANT 136. Göttingen: Vandenhoeck & Ruprecht. 1984.

– Was heisst bei Paulus "Werke des Gesetzes". – *Glaube und Eschatologie.* FS W.G. Kümmel. Hrsg. E. Grässer, O. Merk. Tübingen: Mohr. 123-133. 1985.

– H. Räisänen, Paul and the Law. (Review). *ThLZ 110* (1985) 894-896.

Hägglund, B., *History of Theology.* Saint Louis: Concordia. 1968.

Isaac, E., 1 (Ethiopic Apocalypse of) ENOCH. A New Translation and Introduction – *The Old Testament Pseudepigrapha. Volume 1. Apocalyptic Literature and Testaments.* Charlesworth, J.H. (ed.), New York: Doubleday. 5-89. 1983.

Jackson, B.S., Legalism. *JJS 30* (1979) 1-22.

Janowski, B., *Sühne als Heilsgeschehen: Studien zur Sühnetheologie der Priesterschrift und zur Wurzel KPR im Alten Orient und im Alten Testament.* WMANT 55. Neukirchen-Vluyn: Neukirchener. 1982.

Jeremias, G., *Der Lehrer der Gerechtigkeit.* StUNT 2. Göttingen: Vandenhoeck & Ruprecht. 1963.

Jeremias, J., Paulus als Hillelit. – *Neotestamentica et semitica.* FS M. Black. Eds. E.E. Ellis, M. Wilcox. Edinburgh: Clark. 88-94. 1969.

– Einige vorwiegend sprachliche Beobachtungen zu Röm 11, 25-36. – *Die Israelfrage nach Röm 9-11.* Hrsg. L. De Lorenzi. SMBen.BE 3. Rom. 193-205. 1977.

– *Jerusalem in the Time of Jesus. An Investigation into Economic and Social Conditions during the New Testament Period.* Philadelphia: Fortress. [8]1989.

– ᾿Αδάμ. ThWNT I (1990) 141-143.

Jervell, J., The Letter to Jerusalem. – *The Romans Debate.* Revised and Expanded Edition. Ed. K.P. Donfried. Peabody, Mass.: Hendrickson. 53–64. 1991.

Jewett, P.K., *Election and Predestination.* Grand Rapids, Mich.: Eerdmans. 1985.

Jüngel, E., *Paulus und Jesus. Eine Untersuchung zur präzisierung der Frage nach dem Ursprung der Christologie.* HUTh 2. Tübingen: Mohr. 1962.

Kaiser, W.C., עבד. § 1553, *Theological Wordbook of the Old Testament.* Eds. R.L. Harris, G.L. Archer, B.K. Waltke. Chigago: Moody. 1980.

Kertelge, K., *"Rechtfertigung" bei Paulus. Studien zur Struktur und zum Bedeutungsgehalt des paulinischen Rechtfertigungsbegriffs.* NTA.NF3. Münster: Aschendorff. 1967.

Kim, Seyoon, *The Origin of Paul's Gospel.* 2. Edition. WUNT 2. Reihe 4. Tübingen: Mohr. 1984.

Klausner, J., The First Hasmonean Rulers: Jonathan and Simeon. – *The World History of the Jewish People I/6.* The Hellenistic Age. Political History of Jewish Palestine from 332 B.C.E. to 67 B.C.E. Ed. A. Schalit. London: Allen. 183-207. 1976.

Klinzing, G., *Die Umdeutung des Kultus in der Qumrangemeinde und im Neuen Testament.* SUNT 7. Göttingen: Vandenhoeck & Ruprecht. 1971.

Koch, D.-A., Der Text von Hab 2,4b in der Septuaginta und im Neuen Testament. *ZNW 76* (1985) 68-85.

Kraft, R.A., The Multiform Jewish Heritage of Early Christianity. – *Christianity, Judaism and Other Greco-Roman Cults.* FS M. Smith, ed. J. Neusner. Part III, Judaism before 70. SJLA 12/3. Leiden: Brill. 175-199. 1975.

Kraus, H.-J., *Psalmen. I-II. Teilband.* BKAT 15/1-2. Neukirchen: Neukirchener. 1960.

Kreitzer, L.J., *Jesus and God in Paul's Eschatology.* JSNTS 19. Worcester: Sheffield Academic Press. 1987.

Kruse, C.G., *Paul, the Law and Justification.* Leicester: Apollos. 1996.

Kuhn, H.-W., *Enderwartung und gegenwärtiges Heil. Untersuchungen zu den Gemeindeliedern von Qumran mit einem Anhang über Eschatologie und Gegenwart in der Verkündigung Jesu.* StUNT 4. Göttingen: Vandenhoeck & Ruprecht. 1966.

Kuhn, K.G., The Lord's Supper and the Communal Meal at Qumran. – *The Scrolls and the New Testament.* Ed. K. Stendahl. With a new Introduction by J.H. Charlesworth. New York: Crossroad. 65-93. 1992.

– New Light on Temptation, Sin, and Flesh in the New Testament. – *The Scrolls and the New Testament.* Ed. K. Stendahl. With a new Introduction by J.H. Charlesworth. New York: Crossroad. 94-113. 1992.

Käsemann, E., Gottesgerechtigkeit bei Paulus. – *Exegetische Versuche und Besinnungen II.* Göttingen: Vandenhoeck & Ruprecht. 181-193. 1964.

– Zum Thema der urchristlichen Apokalyptik. *-Exegetische Versuche und Besinnungen II.* Göttingen: Vandenhoeck & Ruprecht. 105-131. 1964.

– *An die Römer.* HNT 8a. Tübingen. 1973.

Kümmel, W.G., *The New Testament. The History of the Investigation of its Problems.* London : SCM. 1978.

– *Die Theologie des Neuen Testaments nach seinen Hauptzeugen. Jesus, Paulus, Johannes.* GNT 3. Göttingen: Vandenhoeck & Ruprecht. [5]1987.

Laato, T., *Paulus und das Judentum. Anthropologische Erwägungen.* Åbo. 1991. [ET *Paul and Judaism.* USF Studies in the History of Judaism 115. Atlanta: Scholars Press. 1995]

Lange, A., *Weisheit & Prädestination. Weisheitliche Urordnung & Prädestination in den Textfunden von Qumran.* StTDJ 18. Leiden: Brill. 1995.

Lichtenberger, H., Paulus und das Gesetz. – *Paulus und das antike Judentum. Tübingen-Durham-Symposium im Gedenken an den 50. Todestag Adolf Schlatters (19. Mai 1938).* Hrsg. M. Hengel – U. Heckel. WUNT 58. Tübingen: Mohr. 361-374. 1991.

Lohmeyer, E., *Probleme paulinischer Theologie.* Stuttgart: Kohlhammer. (n.d.)

– *Der Brief an die Philipper.* KEK 9. Göttingen: Vandenhoeck & Ruprecht. 1961.

Lohse, B., *A Short History of Christian Doctrine. From the First Century to the Present.* Philadelphia: Fortress. 1966.

Lohse, E., *Grundriss der neutestamentlichen Theologie.* Dritte, durchgesehene und ergänzte Auflage. ThW 5. Stuttgart: Kohlhammer. 1984.

Longenecker, B.W., *Eschatology and the Covenant. A Comparison of 4 Ezra and Romans 1-11.* JSNTS 57. Worcester: Sheffield Academic Press. 1991.

Longenecker, R.N., *Paul: Apostle of Liberty.* New York: Harper & Row, 1964.

– *Galatians.* Word Biblical Commentary 41. Dallas, Texas: Word Books. 1990.

Luz, U., *Das Geschichtsverständnis des Paulus.* BEvTh 49. München: Kaiser. 1968.

Lübking, H-M., *Paulus und Israel im Römerbrief. Eine Untersuchung zu Römer 9-11.* EHS.T 260. Frankfurt am Main: Lang. 1986.

Lüdemann, G., *Paulus und das Judentum.* TEH 215. München: Kaiser. 1983.

Lührmann, D., Paul and the Pharisaic Tradition. *JSNT 36* (1989) 75-94.

Maier, G., *Mensch und freier Wille. Nach den jüdischen Religionsparteien zwischen Ben Sira und Paulus.* WUNT 12. Tübingen: Mohr. 1971.

Marböck, J., *Weisheit im Wandel. Untersuchungen zur Weisheitstheologie bei Ben Sira.* BBB 37. Bonn: Hanstein. 1971.

Martin, B.L., *Christ and the Law in Paul.* NT.S. 62. Leiden: Brill, 1989.

Martinez, F.G., *Qumran and Apocalytic. Studies on the Aramaic Texts from Qumran.* STDJ IX. Leiden: Brill. 1992.

Martinez, F.G. – Barrera, J.T., *The People of the Dead Sea Scrolls. Their Writings, Beliefs and Practices.* Leiden/New York/Köln: Brill. 1995.

Marx, A., Y a-t-il une prédestination à Qumrân? *RQ 6* (1967) 163-181.

Mattern, L., *Das Verständnis des Gerichtes bei Paulus.* AThANT 47. Zürich/Stuttgart: Zwingli. 1966.

Maurer, Chr., ὑπόδικος. *ThWNT VIII* (1990) 556-558.

Mayer, B., *Unter Gottes Heilsratschluss. Prädestinationsaussagen bei Paulus.* FzB 15. Würzburg: Echter. 1974.

McGrath, A.E., *Christian Theology. An Introduction.* Second Edition. Oxford: Blackwell. 1997.

McKenzie, J.L., *Second Isaiah. Introduction, Translation and Notes.* AncB 20. New York: Doubleday. 1986.

McNamara, M., E.P. Sanders, Paul and Palestinian Judaism. (Review). *JSNT 5* (1979) 67-73.

Merrill, E.H., *Qumran and Predestination.* StTDJ VIII. Leiden: Brill. 1975.

Michael, J.H., *The Epistle of Paul to the Philippians.* Moffatt. London: Hodder and Stoughton. [6]1954.

Michel, O., *Der Brief an die Römer.* KEK IV. 10. Auflage. Göttingen: Vandenhoeck & Ruprecht. 1955.

– *Der Brief an die Römer.* KEK IV. 12. Auflage. Göttingen: Vandenhoeck & Ruprecht. 1963.

– *Der Brief an die Römer.* KEK IV. 14. Auflage. 5., bearb. Aufl. dieser Auslegung. Göttingen: Vandenhoeck & Ruprecht. 1978.

– συγκλείω. *ThWNT VII* (1990) 744-747.

Milik, J.T., *Ten Years of Discovery in the Wilderness of Judaea.* Studies in Biblical Theology. London: SCM. 1959.

– Milkî-Ṣedeq et Milkî-reˇsaᶜ dans les anciens écrits juifs et chrétiens. *JJS 23* (1972) 95-144.

– *The Books of Enoch. Aramaic Fragments of Qumrân Cave 4.* With the Collaboration of M. Black. Oxford: Clarendon. 1976.

Moo, D.J., "Law", "Works of the Law", and Legalism in Paul. *WTJ 45* (1983) 73-100.

– Israel and Paul in Romans 7.7-12. *NTS 32* (1986) 122-135.

– Paul and the Law in the Last Ten Years. *SJT 40* (1987) 287-307.

– *Romans 1-8.* The Wycliffe Exegetical Commentary. Chigago: Moody. 1991.

Moody, R.M., The Habakkuk Quotation in Romans 1,17. *ExpT 92* (1980-1981) 205-208.

Moore, G.F., Christian Writers on Judaism. *HTR 14* (1921) 197-254.

– *Judaism in the First Centuries of the Christian Era II. The Age of Tannaim.* Cambridge: Harvard University Press. 1955.

Moule, C.F.D., Jesus, Judaism, and Paul. – *Tradition and Interpretation in the New Testament.* FS E.E. Ellis, Ed. Hawthorne and Betz. Grand Rapids: Eerdmans / Tübingen: Mohr. 43-52. 1987.

Moyise, S., The Catena of Romans 3:10-18. *ExpT 106* (1995) 367-370.

Munck, J., *Christus und Israel. Eine Auslegung von Röm 9-11.* Acta Jutlandica. TS 7. Aarhus: Universitetsforlaget. 1956.

Mundle, W., Das religiöse Problem des IV. Esrabuches. *ZAW 47* (1929) 222-249.

Murphy, F.J., *The Religious World of Jesus. An Introduction to Second Temple Palestinian Judaism.* Nashville: Abingdon. 1991.

Murphy, R.E., *The Tree of Life. An Exploration of Biblical Wisdom Literature.* AncB Reference Library. New York: Doubleday. 1990.

Murphy-O'Connor, J., E.P. Sanders, Paul and Palestinian Judaism. (Review). *RB 85* (1978) 122-126.

Mussner, F., *Die Kraft der Wurzel. Judentum - Jesus - Kirche.* Freiburg: Herder. 1987.

Müller, Chr., *Gottes Gerechtigkeit und Gottes Volk. Eine Untersuchung zu Römer 9-11.* FRLANT 86. Göttingen: Vandenhoeck & Ruprecht. 1964.

Müller, K., Apokalyptik/Apokalypsen. III. Die jüdische apokalyptik. Anfänge und Merkmale. *TRE III* (1978) 202-251

Neill, S. - Wright, T., *The Interpretation of the New Testament 1861-1986.* Oxford/New York: Oxford University Press. 1988

Nickelsburg, G.W.E., *Resurrection, Immortality, and Eternal Life in Intertestamental Judaism.* HThS XXVI. Cambridge: Harvard University Press. 1972.

– Apocalyptic and Myth in 1 Enoch 6-11. *JBL 96* (1977) 383-405.

– *Jewish Literature Between the Bible and the Mishnah. A Historical and Literary Introduction.* London: SCM. 1981.

Nickelsburg, G.W.E. – Kraft, R.A., Introduction: The Modern Study of Early Judaism. – *Early Judaism and its Modern Interpreters.* 1-30. Ed. Kraft and Nickelsburg. (The Bible and its modern interpreters 2) SBL. Atlanta: Scholars. 1986.

Nickelsburg, G.W.E. – Stone, M.E., *Faith and Piety in Early Judaism. Texts and Documents.* Philadelphia: Trinity Press International. 1991.

Nygren, A., *Pauli brev till Romarna.* Tolkning av Nya testamentet VI. Stockholm. 1944.

Osten-Sacken, P. von der, *Gott und Belial. Traditionsgeschichtliche Untersuchungen zum Dualismus in den Texten aus Qumran.* StUNT 6. Göttingen: Vandenhoeck & Ruprecht. 1969.

Overman, J.A. – Green, W.S., Judaism. Judaism in the Greco-Roman period. *ABD III* (1992) 1037-1054.

Philonenko, M. (ed.), *Le Trône de Dieu.* WUNT 69. Tübingen: Mohr. 1993.

Plag, C., *Israels Wege zum Heil. Eine Untersuchung zu Römer 9 bis 11.* AzTh I/40. Stuttgart: Calwer. 1969.

Pohlenz, M., *Die Stoa. Geschichte einer geistigen Bewegung.* Göttingen: Vandenhoeck & Ruprecht. 1948.

Porton, G.G., Diversity in Postbiblical Judaism – *Early Judaism and its Modern Interpreters.* 57-80. Ed. Kraft and Nickelsburg. (The Bible and its modern interpreters 2) SBL. Atlanta: Scholars. 1986.

– Sadducees. *ABD V* (1992) 892-895.

Prato, G.L., *Il problema della teodicea in Ben Sira. Composizione dei contrari e richiamo alle origini.* AnBib 65. Rome: Biblical Institute Press. 1975.

Puukko, A.F., Paulus und das Judentum. – *Studia Orientalia II.* Societas Orientalis Fennica. Helsinki: Finnischen Litteraturgesellschaft. 1928.

Rad, G. von, *Theologie des Alten Testaments.* Band 1. 9. Aufl. München: Kaiser Verlag. 1987.
– *Theologie des Alten Testaments.* Band 2. 4. Aufl. München: Kaiser Verlag. 1965.
– *Wisdom in Israel.* ET J.D. Martin. Worcester: SCM. 1972.
Rajak, T., Hasmonean dynasty. *ABD III* (1992) 67-76.
Reichrath, H., Römer 9-11. Ein Stiefkind christlicher Theologie und Verkündigung. *Judaica 23* (1967) 160-181.
Reicke, B., Paulus über das Gesetz. *ThZ 41* (1985) 237-257.
Rengstorf, K.H., ἁμαρτωλός. *ThWNT I* (1990) 320-337.
Reumann, J., Righteousness. New Testament. *ABD 5* (1992) 745-773.
Rhoads, D., Zealots. *ABD 6* (1992) 1043-1054.
Ridderbos, H.N., *The Epistle of Paul to the Churches of Galatia.* NIC. Grand Rapids, Michigan: Eerdmans. [5]1968.
– *Paul. An Outline of His Theology.* Grand Rapids: Eerdmans. 1975.
Riesner, R., *Die Frühzeit des Apostels Paulus. Studien zur Chronologie, Missionsstrategie und Theologie.* WUNT 71. Tübingen: Mohr. 1994.
Ringgren, H., Apokalyptik. II. Jüdische Apokalyptik. *RGG I* (1986 [3]) 464-466.
– *The Faith of Qumran. Theology of the Dead Sea Scrolls.* Expanded Edition with a New Introduction by J.H. Charlesworth. New York: Crossroad. 1995.
Robertson, O.P., *The Christ of the Covenants.* Phillipsburg, New Jersey: Presbyterian and Reformed Publishing. 1980.
Rogerson, J.W., Interpretation, history of. History of OT interpretation. *ABD III* (1992) 424-433.
Rowland, C., *The Open Heaven. A Study of Apocalyptic in Judaism and Christianity.* New York: Crossroad / London: SPCK. 1982.
– *Christian Origins. An Account of the Setting and Character of the Most Important Messianic Sect of Judaism.* London: SPCK. 1985.
Rudolph, W., *Micha-Nahum-Habakuk-Zephanja.* KAT XIII/3. Gütersloh: Mohn. 1975.
Räisänen, H., Raamatun auktoriteetista. *TAik 77* (1972) 76-86.
– Legalism and Salvation by the Law. Paul's portrayal of the Jewish religion as a historical and theological problem. – *Die Paulinische Literatur und Theologie. The Pauline Literature and Theology.* Anlässlich der 50. jährigen Gründungs-Feier der Universität von Aarhus. Hrsg. S. Pedersen. Teologiske Studier 7. Århus: Aros / Göttingen: Vandenhoeck & Ruprecht. 63-83. 1980.
– Zum Verständnis von Röm 3,1-8. – *The Torah and Christ. Essays in German and English on the Problem of the Law in Early Christianity.* H. Räisänen. SESJ 45. Helsinki: Finnish Exegetical Society. 185-205. 1986.
– *Paul and the Law.* Philadelphia: Fortress. 1986.
– *Paul and the Law.* 2nd Edition, revised and enlarged. WUNT 29. Tübingen: Mohr. 1987.
– Paul, God and Israel: Romans 9-11 in Recent Research. – *The Social World of Formative Christianity and Judaism.* Essays in Tribute to H.C. Kee. Ed. J. Neusner, E.S. Frerichs, P. Borgen, R. Horsley. Philadelphia: Fortress. 178-206. 1988.
– *Jesus, Paul and Torah. Collected Essays.* JSNTS 43. Sheffield: JSOT Press. 1992.
– Romans 9-11 and the "History of Early Christian Religion". – *Texts and Contexts. Biblical Texts in Their Textual and Situational Contexts.* FS L. Hartman. Eds. T. Fornberg, D. Hellholm. 743-765. Oslo: Scandinavian University Press. 1995.
Röhser, G., *Prädestination und Verstockung. Untersuchungen zur frühjüdischen, paulinischen und johanneischen Theologie.* TANZ 14. Tübingen: Francke. 1994.
Saldarini, A.J., E.P. Sanders, Paul and Palestinian Judaism. (Review). JBL 98 (1979) 299-303.

– *Pharisees, Scribes and Sadducees in Palestinian Society.* Edinburgh: Clark. 1989.

– Pharisees. *ABD V* (1992) 289-303.

Sanday, W.– Headlam, A.C., *A Critical and Exegetical Commentary on the Epistle to the Romans.* Fifth edition. Reprinted. ICC. Edinburgh: Clark. 1945.

Sanders, E.P., *Paul and Palestinian Judaism.* Philadelphia: Fortress. 1977.

– The Genre of Palestinian Jewish Apocalypses. – *Apocalypticism in the Mediterranean World and the Near East. Proceedings of the International Colloquium on Apocalypticism.* 447–459. Ed. D. Hellholm. Tübingen: Mohr. 1983.

– *Paul, the Law, and the Jewish People.* Second printing. Minneapolis: Fortress. 1989.

– *Judaism: Practice and Belief 63 BCE - 66 CE.* London: SCM / Philadelphia: Trinity Press International. 1992.

Sanders, J.A., Habakkuk in Qumran, Paul, and the Old Testament. *JR 39* (1959) 232-244.

– Torah and Paul. – *God's Christ and His People.* FS N.A. Dahl. Eds. J. Jervell, W.A. Meeks. Oslo: Universitetsforlaget. 132-140. 1977.

Schade, H–H., *Apokalyptische Christologie bei Paulus. Studien zum Zusammenhang von Christologie und Eschatologie in den Paulusbriefen.* GTA 18. Göttingen: Vandenhoeck & Ruprecht. 1981.

Schiffman, L.H., *From Text to Tradition. A History of Second Temple & Rabbinic Judaism.* Hoboken, New Jersey: Ktav. 1991.

Schimanowski, G., *Weisheit und Messias. Die jüdischen Voraussetzungen der urchristlichen Präexistenzchristologie.* WUNT 2. Reihe 17. Tübingen: Mohr. 1985.

Schlatter, A., *Der Brief an die Römer. Ausgelegt für Bibelleser.* Erläuterungen zum Neuen Testament 5. Stuttgart: Calwer. 1962.

Schlier, H., *Der Brief an die Galater.* KEK 7. Göttingen: Vandenhoeck & Ruprecht. 1949.

– *Der Römerbrief.* Dritte Auflage. HThK VI. Freiburg: Herder. 1987.

– κέρδος, κερδαίνω. *ThWNT III* (1990) 671-672.

Schmidt, K.L., προορίζω. *ThWNT V* (1990) 457.

Schmitt, R., *Gottesgerechtigkeit - Heilsgeschichte - Israel in der Theologie des Paulus.* EHS.T 240. Frankfurt am Main: Lang. 1984.

Schmithals, W., *Der Römerbrief: ein Kommentar.* Gütersloh: Mohn. 1988.

Schnabel, E.J., *Law and Wisdom from Ben Sira to Paul. A Tradition Historical Enquiry into the Relation of Law, Wisdom, and Ethics.* WUNT 2. Reihe 16. Tübingen: Mohr. 1985.

Schoeps, H.-J., *Paulus. Die Theologie des Apostels im Lichte der jüdischen Religionsgeschichte.* Tübingen: Mohr. 1959.

Schrage, W., *Der erste Brief an die Korinther I-II.* EKK VII/1 - VII/2. Düsseldorf: Benziger / Neukirchen-Vluyn: Neukirchener. 1991/1995.

Schreiner, T.R., 'Works of Law' in Paul. *NT 33* (1991) 217-244.

– *The Law and its Fulfillment. A Pauline Theology of Law.* Grand Rapids: Baker. 1993.

Schrey, H.-H., Theodizee. II. Dogmengeschichtlich. *RGG VI* (^{3}1986) 740-743.

Schüpphaus, J., *Die Psalmen Salomos. Ein Zeugnis Jerusalemer Theologie und Frömmigkeit in der mitte des vorchristlichen Jahrhunderts.* ALGHJ 7. Leiden: Brill. 1977.

Schürer, E., *The History of the Jewish People in the Age of Jesus Christ (175 B.C. - . A.D. 135).* I-III. Revised and edited by G. Vermes, F. Millar and M. Black. Edinburgh: Clark. 1987.

Schweitzer, A., *Paul and His Interpreters. A Critical History.* New York: Macmillan. 1951.

– *Die Mystik des Apostels Paulus.* Tübingen: Mohr. ^{2}1954.

Schäfer, P., *Hekhalot–Studien.* TSAJ 19. Tübingen: Mohr. 1988.

Scott, J.J., Jr., Crisis and Reaction: Roots of Diversity in Intertestamental Judaism. *EQ 64* (1992) 197-212.

Segal, A.F., *Paul the Convert: The Apostolate and Apostasy of Saul the Pharisee.* New Haven: Yale University Press. 1990.

Seifrid, M.A., *Justification by Faith. The Origin and Development of a Central Pauline Theme.* NT.S 68. Leiden: Brill. 1992.

– Blind Alleys in the Controversy Over the Paul of History. *TyndB 45* (1994) 73-95.

Siegert, F., *Argumentation bei Paulus gezeigt an Röm 9-11.* WUNT 34. Tübingen: Mohr. 1985.

Skehan, P.W. - DiLella, A.A., *The Wisdom of Ben Sira.* AncB 39. New York: Doubleday. 1987.

Smend, R. - Luz, U., *Gesetz.* Kohlhammer Taschenbücher 1015. Stuttgart: Kohlhammer. 1981.

Smith, R.L., *Micah-Malachi.* WBC 32. Waco, Texas: Word Books. 1984.

Snodgrass, K.R., Spheres of Influence. A Possible Solution to the Problem of Paul and the Law. *JSNT 32* (1988) 93-113.

– Justification by Grace – To the Doers: An analysis of the Place of Romans 2 in the Theology of Paul. *NTS 32* (1986) 72-93.

Stauffer, E., *Die Theologie des Neuen Testaments.* ThW. Stuttgart: Kohlhammer. 1941.

– ἐγώ. *ThWNT II* (1990) 341-360.

Stemberger, G., *Jewish Contemporaries of Jesus. Pharisees, Sadducees, Essenes.* Minneapolis: Fortress. 1995.

Stendahl, K., *Paul among Jews and Gentiles and other essays.* Philadelphia: Fortress. 1976.

Stowers, S.K., Paul's Dialogue with a Fellow Jew in Romans 3:1-9 *CBQ 46* (1984) 707-722.

Strobel, A., *Untersuchungen zum eschatologischen Verzögerungsproblem auf Grund der spätjüdisch-urchristlichen Geschichte von Habakuk 2,2ff.* NT.S 2. Leiden: Brill. 1961.

Stuhlmacher, P., *Gerechtigkeit Gottes bei Paulus.* FRLANT 87. Göttingen: Vandenhoeck & Ruprecht. 1965.

– *Das paulinische Evangelium. I Vorgeschichte.* FRLANT 95. Göttingen: Vandenhoeck & Ruprecht. 1968.

– Paul's Understanding of the Law in the Letter to the Romans. *SEÅ 50* (1985) 87-104.

– *Der Brief and die Römer.* NTD 6. Göttingen: Vandenhoeck & Ruprecht. 1989.

– *Biblische Theologie des Neuen Testaments.* Band 1. Göttingen: Vandenhoeck & Ruprecht. 1992.

Stumpff, A., ζηλόω, ζηλωτής. *ThWNT II* (1990) 884-890.

– ζημία, ζημιόω. *ThWNT II* (1990) 890-894.

Stählin, G., ὀργή. Der Zorn des Menschen und der Zorn Gottes im NT. *ThWNT V* (1990) 419-448.

Sweeney, M.A., Habakkuk, Book of. *ABD III* (1992) 1-6.

Synofzik, E., *Die Gerichts- und Vergeltungsaussagen bei Paulus. Eine traditionsgeschichtliche Untersuchung.* GTA 8. Göttingen: Vandenhoeck & Ruprect. 1977.

Talmon, S., The Internal Diversification of Judaism in the Early Second Temple Period. – *Jewish Civilization in the Hellenistic-Roman Period.* Ed. S. Talmon. Philadelphia: Trinity Press International. 16-43. 1991.

– The Community of the Renewed Covenant: Between Judaism and Christianity. – *The Community of the Renewed Covenant. The Notre Dame Symposium on the Dead Sea Scrolls.* Ed. E. Ulrich, J. VanderKam. Notre Dame: University of Notre Dame Press. 3-24. 1994.

Tcherikover, V., The Political Situation from 332 B.C.E. to 175 B.C.E. – *The World History of the Jewish People I/6.* The Hellenistic Age. Political History of Jewish Palestine from 332 B.C.E. to 67 B.C.E. Ed. A. Schalit. 53-86. London: Allen. 1976.

Thielman, F., *From Plight to Solution. A Jewish Framework for Understanding Paul's View of the Law in Galatians and Romans.* NT.S 61. Leiden: Brill. 1989.

– *Paul and the Law. A Contextual Approach.* Downers Growe: IVP. 1994.

Thiselton, A.C., *The Two Horizons. New Testament Hermeneutics and Philosophical Description with special reference to Heidegger, Bultmann, Gadamer and Wittgenstein.* Exeter: The Paternoster Press. 1980.

Thompson, A.L., *Responsibility for Evil in the Theodicy of IV Ezra.* SBL.DS 29. Missoula: Scholars Press. 1977.

Thüsing, W., *Gott und Christus in der paulinischen Soteriologie. Band I. Per Christum in Deum. Das Verhältnis der Christozentrik zur Theozentrik.* 3., verbesserte und um hermeneutisch-methodische Vorüberlegungen zum Gesamtwerk sowie um einen Anhang erweiterte Auflage. Münster: Aschendorff. 1986.

Tomson, P.J., *Paul and the Jewish Law. Halakha in the Letters of the Apostle to the Gentiles.* Compendia Rerum Iudaicarum ad Novum Testamentum III.1. Assen: Van Gorcum / Minneapolis: Fortress. 1990.

Tyson, J.B., "Works of the Law" in Galatians. *JBL 92* (1973) 423-431.

VanderKam, J.C., *The Dead Sea Scrolls Today.* Grand Rapids: Eerdmans/SPCK. 1994.

Vermes, G., *The Dead Sea Scrolls. Qumran in Perspective.* Revised Edition. London: SCM. 1994.

Vielhauer, Ph., Ein Weg zur neutestamentlichen Christologie. *EvTh 25* (1965) 24-72.

Vischer, W., Das Geheimnis Israels. Eine Erklärung der Kapitel 9-11 des Römerbriefs. *Judaica 6* (1950) 81-132.

Wagner, G., The Future of Israel: Reflections on Romans 9-11. – *Eschatology and the New Testament. Essays in Honor of G.R. Beasley-Murray.* Ed. W. Hulitt Gloer. Peabody, Massachusetts: Hendrickson. 77-112. 1988.

Wanamaker, C.A., *The Epistles to the Thessalonians. A Commentary on the Greek Text.* NIGTC. Grand Rapids: Eerdmans. 1990.

Watson, F., *Paul, Judaism and the Gentiles. A Sociological Approach.* MSSNTS 56. Cambridge: Cambridge University Press (repr.). 1989.

Wedderburn, A.J.M., Paul and the Law. *SJTh 38* (1985) 613-622.

– Adam in Paul's Letter to the Romans. – *Studia Biblica III. Papers on Paul and Other New Testament Authors.* Sixth International Congress on Biblical Studies, Oxford 3-7 April 1978. Ed. E.A. Livingstone. JSNT.S 3. Sheffield: JSOT. 413-430. 1980.

Weima, J.A.D., The Function of the Law in Relation to Sin: An Evaluation of the View of H. Räisänen. *NT 32* (1990) 219-235.

Westerholm, S., *Israel's Law and the Church's Faith. Paul and his Recent Interpreters.* Grand Rapids: Eerdmans. 1988.

– Paul and the Law in Romans 9-11. – *Paul and the Mosaic Law.* Ed. J.D.G. Dunn. The Third Durham-Tübingen Research Symposium on Earliest Christianity and Judaism. (Durham, September, 1994). WUNT 89. Tübingen: Mohr. 215-237. 1996.

Westermann, C., *Isaiah 40-66. A Commentary.* OTL. Philadelphia: Westminster. 1969.

Whitehorne, J., Antiochus. *ABD I* (1992) 269-272.

– Ptolemy. *ABD V* (1992) 541-544.

Wilckens, U., *Der Brief an die Römer. Röm 1-5.* 2., verbesserte Auflage. EKK VI/1. Neukirchen – Vluyn: Benziger/Neukirchener. 1987.

– *Der Brief an die Römer. 2. Teilband. Röm 6–11.* 2., verbesserte Auflage. EKK VI/2.
   Neukirchen – Vluyn: Benziger/Neukirchener. 1987.
– Was heisst bei Paulus: "Aus Werken des Gesetzes wird kein Mensch gerecht"? – *EKK
   Vorarbeiten Heft 1.* 51-78. Neukirchen: Neukirchener / Zürich: Benziger. 1969.
Winger, M., *By What Law? The Meaning of* Νόμος *in the Letters of Paul.* SBL.DS. 128.
   Atlanta: Scholars. 1992.
Winninge, M., *Sinners and the Righteous. A Comparative Study of the Psalms of Solomon
   and Paul's Letters.* CB.NT 26. Stockholm: Almqvist & Wiksell International. 1995.
Winston, D., *The Wisdom of Solomon. A New Translation with Introduction and
   Commentary.* AncB 43. New York: Doubleday. 1979.
Witherington (III), Ben., *Paul's Narrative Thought World. The Tapestry of Tragedy and
   Triumph.* Louisville: Westminster/John Knox. 1994.
Woude van der, A.S., *Die messianischen Vorstellungen der Gemeinde von Qumran.* SSN 3.
   Assen: Van Gorcum. 1957.
Wright, A.G., Wisdom. – *The New Jerome Biblical Commentary.* 510-522. Ed. R.E.
   Brown, J.A. Fitzmyer, R.E. Murphy. Englewood Cliffs: Prentice Hall. 1990.
Wright, N.T., *The Climax of the Covenant. Christ and Law in Pauline Theology.*
   Edinburgh: Clark. 1991.
Yadin, Y., *The Message of the Scrolls.* With a new Introduction by J.H. Charlesworth. New
   York: Crossroad. 1992.
Ziesler, J.A., *The Meaning of Righteousness in Paul. A Linguistic and Theological Enquiry.*
   SNTSMS 20. Cambridge: Cambridge University Press. 1972.
– *Paul's Letter to the Romans.* TPI New Testament Commentaries. London: SCM /
   Philadelphia: Trinity. 1989.

Index of Passages

1. Old Testament

Genesis
1-3   131
5:3   172
18:19   170

Exodus
8:19   138
12:24-26   213
15:17-18   264
18:20   215
19:1   290
19:3   290
35:21-24   212

Numbers
25:4   118
25:13   90 , 218
32:14   118

Deuteronomy
10:16   141
24:1   32
30   45, 84
30:1-3   46
30:6   141
30:15-16   46
33:21   247
33:29   231

Joshua
22:27   212

1 Samuel
12:7   247

Ezra
9:13-14   33

Nehemiah
9   33

Job
20:28   118
21:20   118
21:30   118

Psalms
1:5   31
2:12   118
4:4   31
5:12   231
7:9   31
9:6-18   139
30:6   118
31:24   31
32:10   31
32:11   231
51:6   98
52:3   231
64:11   31
76:8   118
76:9   120
78:49   118
84:7   108
89:4   173
89:18   231
89:20-29   173
94:3   231
97:10   31
103:6   31, 247
106:23   118
106:30   90, 218
109:31   31
110   173
110:5   118
116:11   98
140:17   31
143:2   223

Isaiah
2:1-4   159
5:25   118
9:11   118
10:4   118

11:10	118	11:3	35
13:9	118	11:31-33	63
14:5	139	12:1-3	63
26:20	104		
30:30	118	*Amos*	
40:9	33	9:11	118
41:17	33		
42:24	33	*Habakkuk*	
43:15	33	1:2-3	30
44:6	33	1:13	30
50:1-2	32	2:1ff	
52:7	78	2:2-4	110
59:18	118	2:3	104, 110
63:15-64:11	120	2:4	31, 101, 102, 110, 111, 112, 114, 115, 187, 312
64:1	121		
		2:20	31
Jeremiah			
1:5	170	*Zephaniah*	
4:4	141	1:15f.	118
4:8	118	2:2f.	118
9:2	108	3:3-4	31
12:13	118	3:5	31
17:14	231		
23:5-6	118	*Haggai*	
25:15	118	2:23	118
30:8-9	118		
30:24	118	*Zechariah*	
33:15-16	118	3:8-10	118
51:45	118		
		8HevXIIgr	
Lamentations		17.29-30	102
1:12	118		
2:1f.	118		
5:7	32		
		2. Jewish Literature	
Ezekiel			
7:19	118	A. Apocrypha	
18:2-4	32		
18:5-8	32	*Tobit*	
18:23	32	13:5	85
22:21	118		
34:23	32	*Additions to Esther*	
36:25	32	4:6f.	74
37:5	32		
		Baruch	
Daniel		1:15-20	33
7:7	35	2:6-7	74, 207
7:14	76	3:32	133
9:4-19	76	4:1	133
8:5-21	35		

Greek Daniel
3:26-46   74

1 Maccabees
1:2-3   35
1:41-54   63
1:48   64
2   139
2:39-48   65
2:48   139
2:49-54   90, 214, 218
2:64   64
13:41-42   66
14:30-39   66

2 Maccabees
6:5   63
7:9-19   65
7:14   74, 257

Sirach
1:11-20   37
1:25-30   46
2:7, 11   46
2:9   43
5:5-6   37
5:6   119
5:8   42
7:17   43
8:7   42
10:6   213
10:8-9   37
10:12   46
10:12-13   42
11:20-21   213
11:28   43
15:11   44
15:12   38
15:14-15   45, 214
15:16-17   45, 214
15:17   133
15:19   213
15:20   46
16:11-12   42
16:12   213
16:26-27   133
17:1-6   38
17:6-7   45, 214
17:25   46
17:25-26   42

21:1-6   46, 214
21:2   126
27:10   126
33:11-15   44
33:14-15   41
36:8   119
39:8   231
39:16   38
40:10   38
41:11   43
46:23-24   90, 218

Wisdom of Solomon
1:12-15   133
1:15   43
1:15-2:1   38
2:12   38
2:19-20   65
3:1-10   257
3:10   39
4:7-11   65
4:17   43
4:19-20   43
5:15-16   65
6:3-4   213
6:17-19   48, 214
8:4   213
11:9   119
11:23   48
12:4, 19   213
12:19   48
16:5   119
18:20   119

B. Pseudepigrapha

Apocalypse of Abraham
31:2-8   71

Apocalypse of Adam
1:5   127

Apocalypse of Moses
20   126
20f.   127

Life of Adam and Eve
39:2   127

Assumptio Mosis/
Testament of Moses
1:14   179

Testament of Abraham
12-14   75

2 Baruch/Apocalypse of Baruch
5:2-4   71
13:2-6   71
48:47   123
51:1,3   127
54:5   239
54:15,21 127
78:5-7   71

1 Enoch
see also: 11, 23, 61, 62
1-5   74
6-11   35, 61
7:1-5   35
7:6   35
8:3-4   35
9:3-5   35
9:4-5   36
10:2   36
10:2-4   35
10:12   36
10:12-13   35
10:16-17   36
37-71   76
38:2   110
50:1   127
53:6   110
62:5-9   76
84:4   119
85-90   63
90:2   35
90:9   64
90:24ff.   64
91:7-9   119
94-102   62
98:8-16   62
98:10   75, 207
100:4-5   75

4 Ezra
see also: 11, 23, 56, 61, 62, 69,
                139
1:4-6   70

2:1-14   71
3:8   71
3:20   71
3:21   73
3:32-33   70
4:7-12   71
4:25   71
4:30   73
5:30   71
6:25-28   71
6:57-59   70
7:10-15   73
7:19-22   72
7:28-42   75
7:33-35   71
7:37   71
7:60   76
7:117-118 73, 207
7:122-125 127
9:7-8   72
9:15-25   62, 76
9:19   73
9:30-34   72

Jubilees
1:23   141
5:13   123
15:33-34 64
22-23   62
22:16ff.   140
23:17-31 85
23:24,26,30 64
30:21-23 64
36   62

Psalms of Solomon
see also: 11, 23
1:8   284
2   39, 40, 43
2:1-5   39
2:3-5   43
2:10   40
2:11f.   284
3:1-12   75
3:8   255
8   39
8:6-17   43
8:13   284
9:3-5   214
12   43

12:4-6	43		*TGad*	
14:1-4	75		4:5	168
14:6-9	75			
15:10-30	75		*TBenjamin*	
17:15	284		4:5	168
17:24	139		5:2-3	214
			10:11	159
Pseudo-Philo				
11:1-2	123		C. Dead Sea Scrolls	
12:2	139			
			CD	
Sibylline Oracles			I,7-11	64
2:218	123		III,10-14	85
3:669-673	75		III,20	127
3:670-700	62		VI,11-17	86
3:741-750	62, 76		XI,2f.	140
4:80-96	35		XI:14ff.	140
4:40-43	76		XIII	86
4:180-190	76		XV,5-10	86
8:222-224	123		XX,22-27	86
Testaments of the Twelwe			*1QH*	
Patriarchs			I,23	122
			I,27	126
TReuben			I,30	122
3:6	168		II,15	90
			II,23-24	80, 81, 82
TLevi			IV,29-30	126
3:2	122		VI,24-28	140
15:2	122		VII,16-22	181
18	62		X,36	122
18:2-3	76		XIV,14	90
18:7-11	207		XV,10	85
18:10-11	62, 77, 254		XV,12-21	81
19:1-2	213		XV,17	81, 82
			XVII,20	122
TJudah				
23	85		*1QM*	
24:1-4	254		I,1ff.	68
			XIV,4-5	254
TIssachar				
3:7	168		*1QS*	
			I,11	85
TDan			III,4-12	91
1:7	168		III,6-9	89
			III,17-21	81
TNaphtali			III,21-25	83
8:2-3	77		IV,12	81
			IV,23	127

V,1	85
V,7	85
V,7-9	84
V,8-10	215
V,20-21	85
VIII,1-2	88
VIII,1-5	215
VIII,2f.	88
VIII,5-8	88
VIII,6-8	68
VIII,14-15	68
IX,3-6	62, 89
IX,5-6	264
IX,9-11	77
XI	207, 247
XI,12	256

1QSa
II,11ff.	77
II,17-21	77

1QpHab
see also:	31, 86
II,1-2	86
II,2	86
V,11	86
V,11-12	67
VIII,1-3	87, 102
VIII,7-13	86
VIII,8-13	62
VIII,16	86
IX,4-6	62
IX,9	86
XI,4-5	86
XII,8-9	86

4Q 285	77

4QAaronA	77

4QFlor
3-6	264
6-7	215
10-13	77

4QMMT
see also:	67
b, 2ff.	216
c, 27	216

4QPatr
1-4	77

11QMelch
1-5	77
15-16	78
25	77

D. Josephus
Antiquities
11.297-301	34
11.304ff.	34
11.321-328	34
12.129-144	36
12.248-256	63
12.253	63
12.319, 386	63
12.414	65
13.46	66
13.172	49, 79
14.176	40
14.285	140
15.417	140
18.12-15	49

Jewish War
2.134-161	86
2.137	84
2.162-163	49
2.164-166	69
5.398	40

E. Rabbinic

mAboth
2:19	85

mKelim
1:8	140

mTohorot
7:6	139

mNiddah
10:4	139

GenRabb
12:5	127

3. New Testament

Matthew
27:19 — 123

Mark
7:3ff. — 140

John
5:30 — 122
19:13 — 123

Acts
3:13 — 122
3:14 — 110
4:28 — 179
7:52 — 110
15:10-11 — 290
18:12 — 123
25:6-17 — 123

Romans
1-3 — 135
1-8 — 151
1:3-4 — 172
1:5 — 106, 115
1:16 — 106, 112, 120, 121, 137, 141, 157
1:16-17 — 1, 101ff., 117
1:16-18 — 117, 120
1:17 — 31, 104, 106, 107, 109, 110, 112, 120, 138, 187, 261, 262, 293, 294
1:18 — 114, 116, 119, 120, 121, 138, 261, 301
1:18-32 — 117
1:18-2:29 — 137, 139
1:18-3:20 — 119, 125, 138
1:19-32 — 119
1:20 — 119
1:22-32 — 190
1:23 — 127
2 — 132
2:1-3:8 — 119
2:4-5 — 156
2:5-6 — 117
2:6 — 123
2:9 — 140
2:12 — 123, 132, 194

2:12-29 — 133
2:14 — 133
2:16 — 121, 124, 135
2:17-29 — 96
2:26 — 133
2:26-27 — 133
2:28 — 140, 152, 153
2:29 — 134, 137, 141
3 — 95, 100, 179
3:2 — 98
3:3 — 98
3:3-4 — 96, 97
3:4 — 97, 98, 99
3:5 — 99, 119
3:5-6 — 99
3:5-9 — 155
3:6 — 98, 122
3:9 — 97, 119, 126, 135, 137, 138, 144, 145, 152, 179, 223, 228, 230, 249
3:11-18 — 190
3:19 — 123, 144, 146
3:19-20 — 197
3:20 — 135, 208, 219
3:21 — 125, 157, 232, 238, 243, 248, 261
3:21-22 — 112, 119
3:21-26 — 126, 246
3:22 — 109, 138, 152, 223, 262
3:22-23 — 248, 257
3:22-24 — 260
3:23 — 126, 138, 144, 249
3:23-24 — 148
3:24 — 179, 230
3:25 — 115, 124, 155, 187, 249, 258
3:25-26 — 156, 249
3:26 — 109, 115, 120, 306
3:27 — 231, 232
3:27-28 — 230
3:27-31 — 211
3:28 — 232
3:30 — 115, 141, 233
3:31 — 199
4:3 — 105, 107, 193
4:5 — 109, 193
4:8 — 193
4:9 — 193

4:11	193	8	95, 179, 183, 185
4:13	109	8:1	305
4:15	200	8:3	179, 258
4:16	115	8:10	127, 172, 304
4:24-25	262	8:11	172, 301, 304
4:25	228, 258	8:15	174
5:1	109	8:18	168
5:1-11	240	8:18-39	175, 258
5:8	149, 260	8:20	131
5:8-10	156	8:21	127
5:9	119	8:23	304
5:10	260	8:28-29	169, 171, 173
5:11	115	8:28-30	166, 167, 168, 174, 175, 177
5:12	129, 144, 192, 193		
5:13f.	194, 198, 199	8:29	170, 171, 173, 304
5:14	195, 193, 194	8:30	173, 174, 175
5:15	123, 195, 260	9-11	4, 6, 23, 95, 96, 97, 99, 100, 149ff., 150, 151, 156, 161, 175, 187, 240, 280
5:16	122, 130, 145, 155, 202		
5:17	123, 195	9:2-3	158
5:18	131, 148, 258	9:6	141, 152
5:19	130, 131, 195	9:8	152
5:20	202	9:11	169
5:20-21	146	9:13	157
5:21	131, 197	9:18	150, 153, 157, 182
5:23	138	9:18-23	154
6:2-4	127	9:19	115, 154
6:5	301	9:22	115, 155
6:6-20	197	9:23	115, 156, 176
6:11	232	9:24	141, 155, 156
6:13	197	9:25	157
6:23	131, 148, 260	9:27	153
7	147, 198, 245	9:30	109
7:1-10	199	9:30-32	115
7:7	198, 203	9:30-10:4	211
7:7-13	194, 198, 206	9:31-32	241, 242
7:7-25	199	9:32	153, 238, 240, 243, 244
7:8	206		
7:9	203	9:33	157, 240
7:9-10	198, 199	10	183
7:10	146	10:2	238
7:10-13	199	10:2-3	235, 237
7:11	206	10:3	141
7:12	190, 204, 208	10:3-4	115
7:13	199, 204, 205	10:3-6	262
7:14	127, 144, 197, 199	10:4	240
7:14-25	206, 211	10:6	115
7:22	199	10:8	176
7:23	145	10:9-10	152, 156, 179
7:24	127		

10:10	115
10:12	138
10:13	156, 176, 177, 188, 294
10:14	303
10:16-21	157
10:17	176
10:21	153
11	146, 147, 158
11:2	170
11:3	153
11:4	153
11:5	157
11:6	157
11:11	154, 157
11:11-36	159
11:20	154, 157
11:25	157, 158
11:25-27	159
11:26	156, 157, 159
11:30-31	145, 156, 157
11:31	157
11:32	144, 145, 148, 159, 185, 228
13:8-10	208
13:9-10	190
13:11	304
14:10-12	123
14:12	123
14:14	232
14:23	115
15:8-9	141

1 Corinthians

1:22-24	141, 172
1:23-24	179
1:30	305
2:2	179
2:7	170, 179
3:8	123
3:17	304
5:11	304
7:18-19	134
12:13	141
15	172
15:9	225
15:21	193
15:22	127, 301
15:23	172
15:40-48	127

15:42-50	130
15:45	304
15:45-50	301
15:49	172, 304
16:13	304

2 Corinthians

2:16	107, 108
2:17	243
3:18	304
4:4	304
5:10	123, 124
5:17	305
5:21	249
7:1	304
7:10	304
13:5	304
15:18	174
15:19	193

Galatians

1:6	304
1:13	218, 225
1:14	217, 225
2:15	139, 221
2:15-16	221, 222
2:16	109, 225, 290
2:16-17	223
2:21	290
3:3-21	290
3:6	193
3:10	219
3:11	104, 111
3:16-4:9	225
3:19	197, 203
3:22	144, 146, 147, 148, 303
3:23	111
3:24	111, 203
3:24-25	290
3:26	305
3:28	141
5:1	304
5:2-6	134
5:3	219
5:4	304
5:19-21	190

Ephesians		*2 Thessalonians*	
1:4	170	1:5	122
1:5	172, 178	2:1-2	243

Philippians		*Hebrews*	
3:2-11	227	4:16	124
3:4-6	226	10:35-39	111
3:4-8	222, 225ff.	10:37-38	112
3:5-6	217	10:38	31, 103
3:6	132, 218, 237, 239	10:39	111
3:7	227, 238, 245		
3:8	144, 228	*1 Peter*	
3:9	239	1:20	170
3:17	304		

Colossians	
1:14-18	172

1 Thessalonians		4. Early Christian	
1:3	178		
1:10	117, 178, 300	*Odes of Solomon*	
3:5	304	11:2	141
4:14	178		
5:9	178	*Polycarp*	
5:9-10	178	6:2	123

Index of Authors

Allison, D.C.Jr., 269
Althaus, P., 173, 205, 231
Avemarie, F., 23, 55, 269
Avi-Yonah, M., 63
Badenas, R., 240, 242, 243
Balz, H.R., 9
Barrett, C.K., 130, 131, 179, 255, 265
Barth, K., 104, 133, 186, 288
Bauer, W., 227, 230, 232, 243
Baur, F.C., 8, 9, 25, 27
Becker, J., 77, 151, 161
Beker, J. Chr., 8, 10, 22, 24, 25, 128, 131, 140, 145, 148, 151, 152, 159, 161, 168, 171, 176, 259, 260, 261, 270, 275, 299, 301, 305
Benoit, P., 256, 257
Berger, K., 9, 13
Berger, P.L., 33
Best, E., 178
Betz, H.D., 27, 34, 146, 221, 222, 223, 224, 225
Betz, O., 92, 127
Black, M., 35, 68, 88, 97, 105, 106, 114, 127, 239
Bornkamm, G., 148, 198, 288
Bousset,W., 8, 9, 10, 18
Bowman, J.W., 290
Brandenburger, E., 69, 70, 130, 131, 196, 202, 297
Brooke, G., 269, 270
Bruce, F.F., 39, 48, 66, 69
Bultmann, R., 12, 13, 14, 15, 25, 27, 28, 129, 130, 148, 158, 161, 190, 193, 202, 203, 209, 217, 231, 246, 247, 288, 295
Burton, E. de Witt, 223
Caird, G.B., 52, 155, 272
Campbell, D.A., 105, 109, 110, 111, 112
Carson, D.A., 289
Cathcart, K.J., 118
Cavallin, H.C.C., 101, 103, 105, 108
Chafer, L.S., 290
Charlesworth, J.H., 254
Childs, B.S., 301

Christiansen, E.J., 299
Collins, J.J., 24, 55, 61, 62, 63, 67, 76, 77, 78, 79, 86, 88, 257, 301
Colpe, C., 9
Conzelmann, H., 179, 300
Cooper, K.R., 52, 56, 57, 272, 274
Cranfield, C.E.B., 97, 106, 108, 119, 125, 126, 127, 151, 152, 154, 168, 170, 171, 174, 180, 191, 195, 231, 232, 237, 239
Crenshaw, J.L., 30, 32, 33, 37, 41, 43, 50, 51, 303
Cross, F.M., 67, 68, 79, 80, 215
Cullmann, O., 259
Daube, D., 254
Davies, G.N., 107, 127, 156, 299
Davies, P.R., 64
Davies, W.D., 15, 16, 81, 128, 152, 189, 197, 198, 303, 305
Deines, R., 139, 140
Deissmann, A., 9, 10, 15, 22, 198, 302
De Lorenzi, L., 150
DiLella, A., 37, 38, 42, 46, 48
Dinkler, E., 3, 153, 156, 157, 167
Dobbeler, A. von, 275
Dodd, B., 112
Dodd, C.H., 99, 100, 106, 108, 114, 117, 127, 151, 154, 163, 172, 180, 185, 202
Donaldson, T.L., 218
Dülmen, A. van, 133, 196, 198, 205, 252, 263
Dunn, J.D.G., 22, 29, 96, 97, 98, 99, 103, 104, 105, 106,109, 111, 112, 113, 118, 121, 123, 125, 126, 127, 131, 134, 138, 140, 145, 146, 148, 151, 163, 174, 177, 191, 195, 204, 205, 209, 210, 211, 212, 213, 217, 218, 224, 225, 226, 227, 231, 232, 237, 238, 243, 244, 249, 255, 275, 287, 292, 295, 298, 299
Dupont-Sommer, A., 80
Eckstein, H-J., 147
Eichholz, G., 125, 227, 297

Eichrodt, W., 30, 32, 33
Eissfeldt, O., 29
Ellis, E.E., 254
Eskola, T., 13, 14, 282
Fee, G.D., 179
Feuillet, A., 101, 105, 107
Fichtner, J., 118, 119
Finegan, J., 140
Fischer, Th., 66
Fishbane, M., 254
Fitzmyer, J.A., 98, 100, 101, 102, 103, 108, 113, 119, 134, 138, 168, 175, 240, 244, 295
Flusser, D., 80, 82, 181, 270
Fuller, D.P., 289, 290
Gabler, J., 10, 281
Garlington, D.B., 23, 294
Garnet, P., 52, 56, 57, 59, 74, 83, 85, 86, 90, 91, 92, 215, 218, 265
Gaston, L., 22, 106, 107, 159
Getty, M.A., 275
Gnilka, J., 225
Goppelt, L., 17, 125, 259, 261, 262
Greenberg, M., 32
Gruenler, R.G., 13
Gruenwald, I., 24
Grundmann, W., 256, 266
Gundry, R.H., 44, 52, 53, 56, 57, 58, 72, 227, 272, 284
Gutbrod, W., 191
Gärtner, B., 68, 79, 88, 89, 215, 264, 265
Haacker, K., 27, 159
Hagner, D.A., 44, 267, 268, 269, 285
Hahn, F., 222
Hahn, H.-Chr., 118, 212, 231
Hanson, P.D., 36, 61
Harnisch, W., 69, 70
Hawthorne, G.F., 228
Hays, R.B., 109, 110, 111, 112, 115, 275, 277, 280
Heckel, U., 139
Heidegger, M., 13, 25
Hengel, M., 24, 27, 30, 34, 35, 36, 37, 38, 45, 46, 49, 50, 55, 65, 67, 68, 76, 81, 83, 90, 133, 191, 215, 218
Hengel, M. – Deines, R., 269
Hengel, M. – Schwemer, A.M., 24
Herion, G.A., 118
Herold, G., 114, 120, 121, 293, 301
Hiers, R.H., 74, 118

Hofius, O., 18, 109, 113, 125, 126, 150, 152, 159, 248, 249, 302
Hollander, H.W. - de Jonge, M., 77
Holm-Nielsen, S., 80
Holtz, T., 178
Hooker, M.D., 52, 271, 273, 274
Howard, G., 111
Hurtado, L.W., 9, 24, 76, 78
Hübner, H., 145, 146, 147, 150, 190, 191, 202, 209, 212, 224, 231, 275, 277, 280, 281
Hägglund, B., 166, 168, 175, 288
Isaac, E., 35
Jackson, B.S., 270
Janowski, B., 89
Jeremias, G., 64, 67, 80, 87
Jeremias, J., 27, 48, 66, 69, 131, 159
Jervell, J., 152
Jewett, P.K., 1, 166, 171, 180, 183, 184, 185
Jüngel, E., 15, 247, 249, 256
Kaiser, W.C., 212, 213
Kertelge, K., 102, 248
Kim, S., 18
Klausner, J., 66
Klinzing, G., 79, 89, 91, 215, 264, 266
Koch, D.-A., 101, 102, 103, 104, 106
Kraft, R.A., 28
Kraus, H.-J., 31
Kreitzer, L.J., 24
Kruse, C.G., 190, 198, 199, 202
Kuhn, H.-W., 83
Kuhn, K.G., 80, 88
Käsemann, E., 24, 103, 146, 148, 155, 160, 196, 197, 204, 231, 242, 243, 246, 247, 248, 299
Kümmel, W.G., 8, 9, 22, 125, 126, 128, 198
Laato, T., 20, 23, 44, 45, 214, 285, 296, 297
Lange, A., 80, 81, 82, 83
Lichtenberger, H., 127
Liddell, H.G.- Scott, R., 123, 227
Lohmeyer, E., 70, 212, 213, 217, 226, 298
Lohse, B., 166
Lohse, E., 247, 249
Longenecker, B.W., 21, 22, 23, 69, 72, 73, 139, 150, 162, 285, 299
Longenecker, R.N., 147, 191, 219, 222, 223

Luz, U., 130, 131, 148, 165, 167, 169, 170, 173, 175, 182, 186, 192, 193, 194, 205, 259, 260, 297
Lübking, H-M., 150, 158
Lüdemann, G., 150, 159
Lührmann, D., 27, 28, 75, 190, 209, 217, 218, 255, 257, 264
Maier, G., 17, 37, 45, 46, 214, 296
Marböck, J., 34, 38, 41, 44
Martin, B.L., 22, 127, 130, 135, 190, 191, 192, 195, 197, 218, 219, 242, 283
Martinez, F.G., 24, 102
Martinez, F.G. – Barrera, J.T., 81, 85, 265
Marx, A., 80, 88, 92, 256
Mattern, L., 61, 155, 253, 284
Maurer, Chr., 123
Mayer, B., 1, 5, 17, 144, 165, 169, 170, 174, 178, 180, 185, 303
McGrath, A.E., 2, 166, 180, 184, 186, 288
McKenzie, J.L., 32
McNamara, M., 52, 56, 59, 272
Merrill, E.H., 47, 80, 82, 84, 85, 92, 181, 182
Michael, J.H., 228
Michel, O., 98, 100, 106, 109, 113, 114, 115, 117, 118, 122, 123, 126, 130, 131, 145, 146, 168, 169, 170, 172, 174, 196, 197, 231, 237, 238, 239, 243, 244, 249
Milik, J.T., 35, 80, 81, 88, 215
Montefiore, C., 15, 18
Moo, D.J., 52, 56, 96, 101, 108, 109, 113, 114, 118, 127, 130, 134, 141, 149, 169, 170, 172, 191, 192, 195, 196, 197, 198, 199, 204, 205, 219, 233, 249, 272, 275
Moody, R.M., 101, 105, 107, 108
Moore, G.F., 18, 19, 23, 61, 272
Moule, C.F.D., 52, 56, 57, 209, 272
Moyise, S., 127
Munck, J., 150, 159
Mundle, W., 61, 69, 70
Murphy, R.E., 37, 38, 41, 42, 47
Murphy-O'Connor, J., 52, 56
Mussner, F., 159
Müller, Chr., 150, 156, 158, 159
Müller, K., 61, 64
Neill, S. - Wright, T., 21
Neusner, J., 54

Nickelsburg, G.W.E., 29, 35, 39, 64, 65, 257
Nickelsburg, G.W.E. – Kraft, R.A., 56
Nickelsburg, G.W.E. – Stone, M.E., 48, 63, 65, 69, 74, 75
Nygren, A., 113, 133
Osten-Sacken, P. von der, 68, 81
Overbeck, F., 22
Overman, J.A. – Green, W.S., 23, 28, 56, 269
Philonenko, M., 24
Plag, C., 150, 159
Pohlenz, M., 81
Porton, G.G., 28, 55, 69, 269
Prato, G.L., 37, 45
Puukko, A.F., 16
Qimron, E. - Strugnell, J., 216
Rad, G. von, 30, 31, 32, 33, 47
Rajak, T., 65, 66
Reichrath, H., 154
Reicke, B., 199
Reitzenstein, R., 8
Rengstorf, K.H., 139
Reumann, J., 109
Rhoads, D., 90
Ridderbos, H.N., 125
Riesner, R., 27
Ringgren, H., 47, 62, 68, 80, 84, 87, 91, 92, 182, 256, 266
Robertson, O.P., 289, 290
Rogerson, J.W., 258
Rowland, C., 22
Rudolph, W., 30, 31
Räisänen, H., 10, 22, 53, 54, 56, 72, 96, 97, 100, 129, 130, 132, 133, 134, 139, 150, 152, 153, 157, 158, 159, 164, 190, 191, 193, 194, 201, 202, 203, 204, 206, 207, 209, 211, 224, 226, 233, 236, 253, 272, 275-282, 285, 291, 312
Röhser, G., 1, 4, 23, 24, 150, 155, 161, 168, 169, 172, 185, 186, 256, 297
Saldarini, A.J., 49, 50, 52, 53, 55, 56, 58, 60, 272
Sanday, W.– Headlam, A.C., 105, 151
Sanders, E.P., 3, 5, 18, 19, 20, 21, 22, 23, 25, 27, 29, 40, 42, 47, 51, 52-60, 63, 71, 72, 83, 86, 91, 100, 132, 139, 156, 164, 166, 175, 182, 183,

191, 196, 202, 203, 205, 206, 207, 209, 210, 211, 214, 217, 223, 224, 226, 227, 229, 233, 235, 236, 238, 244, 253, 254, 256, 264, 267-275, 281, 282, 284, 285, 287, 288, 289, 291, 292, 296, 297, 305, 312
Sanders, J.A., 114, 190, 199
Schade, H–H., 24
Schiffman, L.H., 63, 66, 69, 74
Schimanowski, G., 22, 23
Schlatter, A., 107
Schlier, H., 99, 100, 102, 108, 117, 120, 121, 125, 127, 131, 134, 137, 138, 140, 145, 146, 155, 163, 168, 169, 172, 176, 194, 199, 202, 222, 227, 238, 239, 242, 243, 244, 249, 261
Schmidt, K.L., 179
Schmitt, R., 150, 151, 156, 160
Schmithals, W., 15
Schnabel, E.J., 23, 45
Schoeps, H.-J., 15, 16, 17, 125, 130, 136, 148, 252, 259, 263, 298, 300, 305
Schrage, W., 179
Schreiner, T.R., 22, 127, 137, 191, 192, 203, 212, 215, 219, 226, 229, 275
Schrey, H.-H., 33
Schüpphaus, J., 75
Schürer, E., 18, 33, 39, 66
Schweitzer, A., 5, 8, 11, 12, 15, 16, 17, 19, 24, 25, 174, 180, 183, 288, 295, 300, 302, 305
Schäfer, P., 24
Scofield, C.I., 290
Scott, J.J., Jr., 30, 32, 41, 50, 56, 270, 283, 294
Segal, A.F., 24
Seifrid, M.A., 22, 23, 39, 54, 75, 141, 162, 214, 240, 246, 247, 248, 253, 256, 258, 265, 267, 274, 277, 285, 295, 297, 304
Siegert, F., 150, 151, 159
Skehan, P.W. - DiLella, A.A., 38, 41, 43, 45, 46, 48, 214
Smend, R. - Luz, U., 199
Smith, R.L., 30
Snodgrass, K.R., 135, 208, 210, 217, 291
Stauffer, E., 160, 198
Stemberger, G., 49, 69
Stendahl, K., 150, 158
Stowers, S.K., 99

Strack, H.L. - Billerbeck, P., 16, 102
Strobel, A., 110
Stuhlmacher, P., 15, 17, 18, 74, 98, 99, 113, 114, 117, 120, 125, 126, 127, 128, 131, 133, 138, 140, 145, 148, 151, 152, 161, 163, 169, 172, 173, 195, 196, 197, 199, 200, 203, 204, 216, 232, 238, 242, 244, 246, 247, 248, 259, 260, 261, 262, 275, 294, 297, 301, 303, 306
Stumpff, A., 90, 227
Stählin, G., 120
Sweeney, M.A., 30
Synofzik, E., 178
Talmon, S., 28, 32, 55, 263
Tcherikover, V., 34, 35, 36
Thielman, F., 21, 22, 31, 40, 192, 196, 227, 228, 237, 275, 282, 283
Thiselton, A.C., 13
Thompson, A.L., 61, 69, 70, 71, 72, 73, 136, 294
Thüsing, W., 172, 173, 178
Tomson, P.J., 19, 28, 189, 190
Tyson, J.B., 212, 213, 222, 224
VanderKam, J.C., 67, 80, 216
Vermes, G., 89, 265
Vielhauer, Ph., 9
Vischer, W., 153, 160
Wagner, G., 157
Wanamaker, C.A., 117, 178
Watson, F., 150, 158, 275, 287
Weber, F., 18, 287
Wedderburn, A.J.M., 131, 132, 135, 198, 275, 276
Weima, J.A.D., 275, 277
Weinel, H., 8
Westerholm, S., 20, 21, 22, 50, 153, 154, 190, 194, 195, 211, 212, 233, 267, 275, 277
Westermann, C., 32
Whitehorne, J., 35, 36, 63
Wilckens, U., 96, 98, 99, 100, 102, 106, 107, 113, 114, 117, 119, 121, 122, 125, 126, 127, 130, 134, 137, 138, 140, 142, 145, 149, 151, 154, 155, 163, 173, 193, 196, 199, 202, 220, 237, 238, 242, 260, 261, 295
Winger, M., 22, 191, 232
Winninge, M., 23, 40, 43, 54, 75, 128, 142, 214, 253, 284, 297, 302

Winston, D., 38, 39, 47, 48, 85
Witherington (III), B., 125, 126, 149
Woude van der, A.S., 77
Wrede, W., 10, 281
Wright, A.G., 39, 43

Wright, N.T., 151, 158, 159
Yadin, Y., 84
Zahn, Th., 133
Ziesler, J.A., 97, 105, 108, 127, 132, 134, 137, 175, 182, 202, 238, 242

Index of Subjects

Aaron, 88, 90, 218
Abraham, 105, 107, 136, 170, 289, 298
Adam, 45, 73, 122, 126, 128, 130, 144, 192, 193, 195, 198, 202, 204, 206, 260
Adam-typology, 127, 129ff., 133, 136, 138, 145, 148, 158, 170, 176, 179, 260, 304
Aeons, 136, 179, 259, 300, 304
Alcimus, 63, 65
Alexander Balan, 66
Alexander the Great, 34, 35
Anthropocentricism, 50
Anthropology, 14, 15, 46, 47, 125ff., 129, 131, 132, 136, 143, 147, 161, 192, 204, 220
Antiochus III the Great, 36, 37
Antiochus IV Epiphanes, 37, 62, 63, 64, 65
Antiochus Eupator, 63
Apocalyptic
- literature, 24, 61, 62, 74
- theology, 61ff., 74, 78, 120
Apokatastasis, 160, 185, 186
Apostasy, 68, 82, 84, 90, 104, 128, 289
Arminius, 155
Atonement, 76, 116, 167, 182, 184, 248, 249, 258, 263, 265, 305
Augustine, 165, 166, 168, 175, 184, 185
Authentic existence, 13, 14
Autonomic anthropology, 162, 164
Avodat Israel, 208ff., 212, 217, 219, 220, 226, 227, 231, 235, 241, 244, 251, 255, 265, 298, 299, 310

Babylon, 30, 31
Bagoses, 34
Bar mitzvah, 198
Being in Christ, 9, 11, 16, 19, 268
Ben Sira
- biography, 36, 37
- creation, 38, 44, 45, 47
- dualism, 41, 43
- eschatology, 38, 42, 47, 48
- law, 38, 45
- nomism, 37, 42, 46

- synergism, 44, 48
Boasting, 230f., 233
Boundary, *see*: Identity markers

Calvin, 2, 154, 155, 168, 180, 185
Calvinism, 5, 58, 168, 171, 172, 174, 183, 184, 191, 218, 287, 288ff., 292, 295
Chaldeans, 30
Christ
- cross, 121, 286
- death of, 232, 256
- resurrection, 115, 117, 158, 173, 228
- and Torah, 240
Christology, 13, 124, 164, 224, 252, 263
Christocentric predestination, 177ff., 185, 258, 302
Circumcision, 49, 54, 59, 64, 85, 133, 134, 140, 141, 210, 211, 218, 226
Consequent eschatology, 11
Contrast formulas, 148ff., 303
Cor malignum, 73
Covenant, 40, 96, 119, 175, 211, 221, 256, 288
Covenantal nomism
- Christological premise, 22, 254
- criticism of, 20, 21, 52, 59, 267ff.
- and dispensationalism, 229, 290
- and diversity, 40, 55
- functional feature, 58
- "getting in" and "staying in", 53, 59, 267, 291
- inconsistency of, 57, 59
- legalism, 52, 56, 58, 91, 209, 236
- pattern of religion, 18, 19, 20, 53, 59, 60, 272f.
- and Paul, 273f.
- and sociology, 53, 54, 58, 59, 60, 273
- theory of, 19, 22, 26, 52, 132, 224, 226, 235, 241, 267ff., 280, 290
Creation, 42, 46, 47, 304
Crisis, theology of, 19, 33, 50, 61, 66, 93, 95, 154, 283, 293

Day or Wrath, 74, 75, 116ff., 122, 177, 200, 276

Deification, 11

Desecration of the Temple, 63ff.

Determinism, 5, 32, 42, 45, 47, 146, 154, 181, 295

Diadochi, 35

Dietary laws, 210

Dispensations, 227, 229, 289, 290, 291

Dispensationalism, 287, 289ff., 312

Divine coercion, 302ff., 305, 313

Divine hardening, 149, 154, 157, 158, 175, 182

Double predestination, 2, 5, 12, 82, 83, 92, 150, 156, 166, 169, 171, 173, 174, 177, 180ff., 271, 288, 289

Dream visions, 63

Dualism, 39, 40, 43, 49, 61, 81, 137, 150, 221

Dualistic soteriology, 41, 51, 64, 71, 75, 78, 80, 82, 126, 142, 143, 153, 156, 163, 166, 186, 227

Ebed Yahweh , 265

Ecclesiasticus, see Ben Sira

Egypt, 35

Election, 4, 5, 33, 41, 152, 155, 157, 158, 165ff., 169, 170, 172ff., 182, 185, 221, 231, 254, 271, 309

Enoch, 1st Book of
- eschatology, 63, 74, 119
- dualism, 36, 75
- soteriology, 35, 75

Entmythologisierung, 12, 13

Eschatology
- Judaism, 50, 58, 76
- Paul, 116, 118, 168, 172, 299ff., 301

Essenes, 49, 90, 140

Ethnocentricism, 137, 140, 147, 150, 217, 223, 224, 238

Existential interpretation, 13, 14, 15, 25, 161, 202

Existentialism, 12, 13, 249

Ezra, 4th Book
- eschatology, 71, 72
- methodological problems, 70
- nomism, 72
- relation to apocalyptic, 70, 72
- soteriology, 71, 73, 136, 139, 162
- synergism, 72

Faith, 97, 105, 106, 107, 108, 110, 111, 112, 113, 114, 223, 228, 247

Faithfulness (of man), 102, 103

Five-point Calvinism, 183, 184, 289

Flesh, 127, 223

Foreknowledge
- and calling, 169, 173
- and Christocentricism, 176, 177ff.
- covenantal meaning of, 170
- and determinism, 170, 178, 183
- terminology, 169

Foreordination
- and determinism, 4, 181
- and predestination, 2, 3, 171, 175ff.,, 301
  180

Free will, 19, 20, 45, 46ff., 73, 84ff., 92, 155, 166, 182, 258, 271

Gabinius, 39

Gentiles/Nations, 133, 134, 135, 139, 140, 223, 276

Gerizim, 34

Giant story, 35

Glory, 126, 127, 128

Gnosticism, 12, 14, 25, 130, 264

God
- creator, 51, 304
- faithfulness, 7, 32, 95, 96, 97, 103, 161, 187, 305
- forbearance, 115, 249
- justice, 30, 98, 122, 123
- lordship, 33, 49, 62
- mercy, 115
- righteousness, 18, 95, 98, 99, 102, 104, 105, 109
- wrath, 117ff., 125, 148, 300, 301

Halakha, 189, 250

Hardening, *see*: Divine hardening

Hasidic piety, 90

Hasmoneans, 39, 65, 66, 90

Hellenism, 34, 35

Hellenistic cult, 9

Hellenistic Judaism, *see*: Judaism

History-of-religions school, 8, 9, 13, 14, 15, 25, 28, 217, 278, 281, 305

Holy war, 68

Hyrcanus II, 39

Idolatry, 64
Individualism, 50
Identity, religious, 54, 135, 233, 262
Identity markers, 22, 210, 211, 212, 217, 224, 233, 238
"Innocent sinners", 195
Israel
- and Christ, 239
- disobedience of, 6, 21, 31, 39, 90, 96, 97, 153
- faithfulness of, 31
- promises to, 33, 152, 154, 161, 221, 233
- rejection of, 62, 70, 82, 83, 98, 146, 157
- restoration of, 40, 63, 65, 90, 116, 157, 159
- in Romans 9-11, 149ff., 160, 175, 187
Iustitia distributiva, 214

Jerusalem
- capture, 39
- destruction, 69ff., 118
Jesus, 9, 122
- *see also*: Christ
Jewish theology
- diversity, 25, 56, 93
- eschatology, 11, 24, 162
- post-exilic situation, 32
- Second Temple period, 6, 15, 17, 18, 21, 22, 25, 27, 40, 44, 49, 90, 119
Jews
- and Gentiles/Greeks, 137, 138ff., 145, 177, 221ff., 225ff., 230ff.
- *see also*: Israel; Judaism
Jonathan Maccabaeus, 66, 67
Josephus, 34, 36, 40, 48, 49, 55, 63, 65, 69, 79, 140
Judas Maccabaeus, 64, 65, 66
Judaism
- Hellenistic, 9, 16, 34, 37, 38, 55, 122
- Second Temple period, 28, 39, 41, 63
Judgment
- eschatological, 62, 74, 94, 100, 114, 130, 155, 253, 295, 300
- final judgment, 42, 75, 121, 124, 146, 187
- of God, 98, 115ff., 122, 302
Judgment seat, 123, 124
Juridical metaphors, 122ff., 295
Justification
- by faith, 101, 108ff., 116, 222, 233, 247, 251

- God's power (*Macht*), 246ff.
- in Judaism, 28, 30f., 37, 78, 91, 249, 255
- juridical nature, 98, 193, 196, 197, 200, 203, 294, 300
- in Paul, 101ff., 130, 167, 239, 246ff.
- of the wicked, 162, 176, 238, 249, 255, 256

Kerygma, 14
Kyrios, 9, 131

Law
- Christ the end of, 240
- and death, 191ff.
- keeping of, 132, 134, 219
- moral law, 190, 191, 218
- obedience, 47, 49, 102, 110, 213, 218, 220, 236
- paradoxical function, 190ff., 201
- and righteousness, 132, 189, 203, 226, 230, 289
- of righteousness, 242ff.
- and sin, 135, 191, 192, 193, 196ff., 200, 201ff., 204, 277
Law of faith, 232
Legalism, 43, 52, 71, 91, 209, 217, 233, 235f., 268, 271, 275, 299
Limited atonement, 184
Lutheranism, 52, 287, 292

Maccabees, 65, 237
Manasseh, 30, 34
Marcionism, 204
Martyrs, 257
Mattathias, 64, 90
Melchizedek, 77
Menelaus, 63
Merkavah literature, 24
Messiah
- of Aaron, 77
- eschatological atonement, 76
- priestly Messiah, 76, 77
- king, 76, 77
- Son of David, 76, 118
- Son of Man, 76
Messianic expectations, 62, 110, 150, 256, 283
Michael (archangel), 63, 78
Mishnah, 85
Miqveh, 140

Monergism, 20
Moses, 192, 193ff., 289
Mystery religions (Hellenistic), 9, 10, 11, 17, 305
Myth, 13, 14, 278

Nationalism, *see*: Ethnocentricism
Neo-Kantian philosophy, 13
New covenant, 218
Noachide code, 190
Nomism, 41, 46
Nomistic service, 212, 222

Obedience, 41, 50, 110, 128, 162, 214, 219, 220, 236, 290
Obedience of faith, 108, 110, 114, 115, 294
Oral law, *see*: Halakha
Origen, 186

Paradoxical polarization, 137ff., 139, 142, 151, 153, 187, 199, 201, 204, 219, 222, 226, 227, 228, 240, 245, 251, 260, 262, 266, 298, 308f.
Participationist eschatology, 19, 268
Participationist soteriology, 9, 11, 12, 16, 26, 217, 304, 305
Paul
- apocalyptic, 10, 24, 25, 117, 120, 155, 162, 177, 247, 260, 299
- biography, 27, 217, 218, 225, 226, 285
- Christocentric theology, 124, 252ff., 258, 259, 261, 265, 297, 303
- Christological principle, 253, 261, 263, 266, 267, 274, 276, 282ff., 285, 311
- Christology, 113, 167, 207
- covenant, 224
- alleged inconsistencies of, 132, 133, 135, 193, 275ff., 280
- and Judaism, 21, 27, 253, 268, 275, 285
- justification, 8, 113, 152, 174, 225, 250, 254, 273, 297, 304
- and legalism, 202, 275
- and Israel, 149ff., 198
- and Jewish theology, 128, 133, 161, 190, 207, 208, 211, 253, 262, 265, 274, 283, 296, 298, 305
- and mysticism, 8, 9, 11, 16, 17
- Pharisaism, 16, 28, 217, 225, 228
- predestinarian soteriology, 17, 95ff., 125, 141f., 145, 160ff., 260, 284, 296f., 305

- problem of the "I", 127, 198ff., 245
- radical anthropology, 125ff., 131, 248
- righteousness, 113, 130, 152, 226, 241, 245, 250
- theology of the law, 20, 21, 132, 147, 189ff., 194, 200ff, 207, 245, 250, 263, 267, 275ff., 279, 310
- zeal, *see:* Zeal
Paulinismus, 10
Pelagius, 166, 175
Persian religions, 80
Persians, 34
Pharisees, 48, 49, 189
Philo, 55
Phinehas, 90, 218
Pilate, 122
ΠΙΣΤΙΣ ΧΡΙΣΤΟΥ debate, 109ff.
Plight and solution debate, 267ff., 269, 273, 281, 282ff., 286, 311
Pompey, 39
Predestination
- definition of, 3, 49, 183
- and determinism, 48, 50, 156, 176, 303
- and soteriological dualism, 142, 143, 270
- in Paul, 19, 95ff., 137, 142, 144ff., 149, 172, 175, 186, 199, 256, 273, 296f., 305
- at Qumran, 79ff., 84, 92, 143, 181
Predestinarian theology, 1, 6, 17, 23, 50, 101, 116, 125, 128, 135, 139, 141, 143ff., 149, 150, 155, 158, 160, 163ff., 182, 186, 188, 220, 228, 230ff., 232, 237, 240, 241, 248ff., 257, 260, 270, 284, 293ff., 302, 305, 306, 308f.
Predestinarian statement, 144, 145ff., 159, 228, 231, 302
Predestination of judgment, 121, 132, 143, 160ff., 187, 228, 309
Predetermination, 165ff., 301
Priesthood, 65, 66
Principle of counting as loss, 147, 221ff., 233, 245, 310
Principle of contemporary application, 254ff., 262ff., 284, 285, 311
Problem of theodicy
- concept of God, 95
- determinism, 162
- obedience, 97
- *see also*: Theodicy
Prospective predestination, 47
Protestant theology, 128, 268, 269, 288

Psychological interpretation, 277ff., 281
Ptolemaic rule, 35, 36
Ptolemy V Epiphanes, 36
Purity regulations, 139, 140, 189, 216

Qumran community
- admittance, 84
- apocalyptic, 83
- atonement, 87ff., 91, 92, 216, 264, 265
- council, 88, 89, 92
- covenant, 85, 90, 263
- creation, 68, 80
- determinism, 81, 82, 83, 84, 181
- dualism, 68, 162
- election, 82, 86, 166, 256
- eschatology, 28, 68, 69, 77, 78, 81, 86, 92
- Essenes, 67, 79
- history, 67, 68, 79, 86
- justification, 91, 92, 256
- Man of lies, 67, 86
- oaths, 85
- obedience, 84ff., 90, 215, 264
- offerings, 89, 264
- priesthood, 67, 79, 84, 89, 216
- repentance, 81, 83, 84, 85
- righteousness, 83, 88, 91, 256
- Sadducees, 68, 69
- salvation, 77, 82, 83, 86, 87, 92, 152, 166, 265
- synergistic soteriology, 82, 87, 91, 92, 143, 181, 265
- Teacher of Righteousness, 66, 67, 80, 87, 88, 216, 256, 264
- Temple, 67, 79, 80, 86, 88, 216, 264, 265
- Temple symbolism, 88, 89, 215, 264
- Two spirits, 81, 82, 83
- Wicked Priest, 67, 77, 86, 215, 216
- works of law, 215, 216
- Zadokite priesthood, 79, 88

Rabbinic theology, 15, 16, 18, 21, 23, 90, 136, 189
Rabbis, 128
Reformation, 1, 8, 164, 183, 287
Reformed orthodoxy, 183, 184
Remnant, 40, 88, 153, 154, 159, 265
Responsibility of man, 42, 44, 46, 49, 182, 258
Resurrection, 172, 257, 301

- *see also:* Christ
Righteousness of God, 18, 98, 106, 107, 112, 117, 119, 141, 158, 224, 235ff., 246ff., 250, 261, 294, 306
Righteousness
- Judaism, 30, 46, 71f., 84ff., 214
- Paul, 101, 111, 116, 222, 223, 226, 228, 232, 235ff., 239, 242, 244, 255, 310
Ritual law, 190, 191, 211, 218, 219
Roman rule, 39, 40
Rome, 40, 90

Sabbath, 210
Sadducees, 28, 68
Samaria, 34, 36
Sanballat, 34
Sanhedrin, 67
Sapiential literature, 23
Sapiential theology, 14, 28, 36, 38, 43, 84, 87, 96, 133, 214, 294
Salvation, 40, 78, 141, 164, 176, 189
Salvation history, 130ff., 145ff., 149, 158, 169, 187, 196, 202, 204, 221, 243, 259ff., 291, 300
"Secondary rationalization", 277, 279
Second Temple Judaism
- diversity of, 23, 25, 26, 27, 28, 54, 253, 268
Seleucids, 35, 36, 66
Self-righteousness, 237f., 241, 244, 245, 272
Septuagint, 104, 113, 114
Simon II, 36, 37
Simon Maccabaeus, 66, 67, 140
Sin
- Judaism, 31, 37, 64, 72, 84
- Paul, 122, 123, 125ff., 129, 135, 137, 143, 146, 147, 194, 195, 205, 283
- personified power, 197
Sinners and the righteous, 127, 133, 139, 258
Sirach, *see*: Ben Sira
Sirach, Hebrew, 38, 41, 48
Sociology of knowledge, 278
Sola fide, 107
Son of Man, 76
Soteriological dualism, 41, 51, 64, 71, 75, 78, 80, 82, 126, 142, 143, 153, 156, 163, 166, 186, 227, 270, 283, 284, 295, 302, 307

Soteriology
- soteriological synergism, 48, 78, 87, 88, 91
- in Paul, 128, 140, 161, 163, 252ff., 260ff., 263, 265, 282
Stoicism, 47, 81
Suffering, 30, 31, 33, 43, 87, 99, 101, 115, 168, 174, 257, 258
Supralapsarism, 171
Symbolic structure, 24
Synergism, 20, 44, 46, 48, 56, 58, 85, 87, 88, 128, 163, 231, 254, 271, 296
Synergistic nomism, 44, 57, 72, 85, 91, 93, 214, 245, 272, 296. 307
Synod of Dort, 184
Syria, 35, 63

Tabernacle, 212, 213
Temple, 34, 39, 62, 63, 65, 88, 90, 120, 140, 235, 265
Theocentricism, 50
Theodicy
- in apocalyptic, 29, 65, 257, 294
- in Ben Sira, 37, 47
- in 4 Ezra, 69ff., 72, 73
- in Paul, 95ff., 114, 115, 150, 152, 160, 162, 186, 232, 258, 293ff., 305, 308f., 312
- problem of, 2, 6, 27, 28, 30, 33, 40, 50, 78, 93, 95, 100, 101, 160, 214, 384, 293, 307ff.
- at Qumran, 68, 83, 86, 87

Torah, 18, 29, 51, 133, 200, 213, 215, 217, 265
Torah, paradox of, 199, 200
Tora-Ontologie, 133
Total depravity, 135, 184

Unbelief, 97
Universalgeschichte, 136
Universalism, 185
Universalistic soteriology, 166, 177, 185, 302ff., 312
Universal sinfulness, 125ff., 130, 132, 136, 137ff., 142, 187, 200, 207, 260, 280, 296

Voluntarism, 47, 85

Works of the Law, 22, 58, 89, 208ff., 212, 217, 219, 220, 222, 230, 231, 233, 241, 242, 243, 244, 298
- *see also: Avodat Israel*
Worship, 212, 213
Wrath of God, *see:* God

Yahweh, *see*: God
Yezer hara^c, 136

Zadokite priesthood, 67, 68, 79, 88
Zeal, 90, 217, 218, 223, 226, 228, 231, 237, 238, 240, 245, 264
Zealots, 90, 218, 237

Wissenschaftliche Untersuchungen zum Neuen Testament

Alphabetical Index of the First and Second Series

Anderson, Paul N.: The Christology of the Fourth Gospel. 1996. *Volume II/78.*
Appold, Mark L.: The Oneness Motif in the Fourth Gospel. 1976. *Volume II/1.*
Arnold, Clinton E.: The Colossian Syncretism. 1995. *Volume II/77.*
Avemarie, Friedrich und *Hermann Lichtenberger* (Ed.): Bund und Tora. 1996. *Volume 92.*
Bachmann, Michael: Sünder oder Übertreter. 1992. *Volume 59.*
Baker, William R.: Personal Speech-Ethics in the Epistle of James. 1995. *Volume II/68.*
Balla, Peter: Challenges to New Testament Theology. 1997. *Volume II/95.*
Bammel, Ernst: Judaica. Volume I 1986. *Volume 37* – Volume II 1997. *Volume 91.*
Bash, Anthony: Ambassadors for Christ. 1997. *Volume II/92.*
Bauernfeind, Otto: Kommentar und Studien zur Apostelgeschichte. 1980. *Volume 22.*
Bayer, Hans Friedrich: Jesus' Predictions of Vindication and Resurrection. 1986. *Volume II/20.*
Bell, Richard H.: Provoked to Jealousy. 1994. *Volume II/63.*
Bergman, Jan: see *Kieffer, René*
Betz, Otto: Jesus, der Messias Israels. 1987. *Volume 42.*
– Jesus, der Herr der Kirche. 1990. *Volume 52.*
Beyschlag, Karlmann: Simon Magus und die christliche Gnosis. 1974. *Volume 16.*
Bittner, Wolfgang J.: Jesu Zeichen im Johannesevangelium. 1987. *Volume II/26.*
Bjerkelund, Carl J.: Tauta Egeneto. 1987. *Volume 40.*
Blackburn, Barry Lee: Theios Anēr and the Markan Miracle Traditions. 1991. *Volume II/40.*
Bockmuehl, Markus N.A.: Revelation and Mystery in Ancient Judaism and Pauline Christianity. 1990. *Volume II/36.*
Böhlig, Alexander: Gnosis und Synkretismus. Teil 1 1989. *Volume 47* – Teil 2 1989. *Volume 48.*
Böttrich, Christfried: Weltweisheit – Menschheitsethik – Urkult. 1992. *Volume II/50.*
Bolyki, János: Jesu Tischgemeinschaften. 1997. *Volume II/96.*
Büchli, Jörg: Der Poimandres – ein paganisiertes Evangelium. 1987. *Volume II/27.*
Bühner, Jan A.: Der Gesandte und sein Weg in 4. Evangelium. 1977. *Volume II/2.*
Burchard, Christoph: Untersuchungen zu Joseph und Aseneth. 1965. *Volume 8.*
Cancik, Hubert (Ed.): Markus-Philologie. 1984. *Volume 33.*
Capes, David B.: Old Testament Yaweh Texts in Paul's Christology. 1992. *Volume II/47.*
Caragounis, Chrys C.: The Son of Man. 1986. *Volume 38.*
– see *Fridrichsen, Anton.*
Carleton Paget, James: The Epistle of Barnabas. 1994. *Volume II/64.*
Crump, David: Jesus the Intercessor. 1992. *Volume II/49.*
Deines, Roland: Jüdische Steingefäße und pharisäische Frömmigkeit. 1993. *Volume II/52.*
– Die Pharisäer. 1997. *Volume 101.*
Dietzfelbinger, Christian: Der Abschied des Kommenden. 1997. *Volume 95.*
Dobbeler, Axel von: Glaube als Teilhabe. 1987. *Volume II/22.*
Du Toit, David S.: Theios Anthropos. 1997. *Volume II/91*
Dunn, James D.G. (Ed.): Jews and Christians. 1992. *Volume 66.*
– Paul and the Mosaic Law. 1996. *Volume 89.*
Ebertz, Michael N.: Das Charisma des Gekreuzigten. 1987. *Volume 45.*
Eckstein, Hans-Joachim: Der Begriff Syneidesis bei Paulus. 1983. *Volume II/10.*
– Verheißung und Gesetz. 1996. *Volume 86.*
Ego, Beate: Im Himmel wie auf Erden. 1989. *Volume II/34.*
Eisen, Ute E.: see *Paulsen, Henning.*
Ellis, E. Earle: Prophecy and Hermeneutic in Early Christianity. 1978. *Volume 18.*
– The Old Testament in Early Christianity. 1991. *Volume 54.*
Ennulat, Andreas: Die ›Minor Agreements‹. 1994. *Volume II/62.*
Ensor, Peter W.: Jesus and His ›Works‹ . 1996. *Volume II/85.*
Eskola, Timo: Theodicy and Predestination in Paul's Soteriology. *Volume II/100*
Feldmeier, Reinhard: Die Krisis des Gottessohnes. 1987. *Volume II/21.*
– Die Christen als Fremde. 1992. *Volume 64.*
Feldmeier, Reinhard and *Ulrich Heckel* (Ed.): Die Heiden. 1994. *Volume 70.*

Fletcher-Louis, Crispin H.T.: Luke-Acts: Angels, Christology and Soteriology. 1997.
Volume II/94.

Forbes, Christopher Brian: Prophecy and Inspired Speech in Early Christianity and its
Hellenistic Environment. 1995. *Volume II/75.*

Fornberg, Tord: see *Fridrichsen, Anton.*

Fossum, Jarl E.: The Name of God and the Angel of the Lord. 1985. *Volume 36.*

Frenschkowski, Marco: Offenbarung und Epiphanie. Volume 1 1995. *Volume II/79* – Volume 2
1997. *Volume II/80.*

Frey, Jörg: Eugen Drewermann und die biblische Exegese. 1995. *Volume II/71.*

– Die johanneische Eschatologie. Volume I. 1997. *Volume 96.*

Fridrichsen, Anton: Exegetical Writings. Hrsg. von C.C. Caragounis und T. Fornberg. 1994.
Volume 76.

Garlington, Don B.: ›The Obedience of Faith‹. 1991. *Volume II/38.*

– Faith, Obedience, and Perseverance. 1994. *Volume 79.*

Garnet, Paul: Salvation and Atonement in the Qumran Scrolls. 1977. *Volume II/3.*

Gräßer, Erich: Der Alte Bund im Neuen. 1985. *Volume 35.*

Green, Joel B.: The Death of Jesus. 1988. *Volume II/33.*

Gundry Volf, Judith M.: Paul and Perseverance. 1990. *Volume II/37.*

Hafemann, Scott J.: Suffering and the Spirit. 1986. *Volume II/19.*

– Paul, Moses, and the History of Israel. 1995. *Volume 81.*

Hartman, Lars: Text-Centered New Testament Studies. Hrsg. von D. Hellholm. 1997.
Volume 102.

Heckel, Theo K.: Der Innere Mensch. 1993. *Volume II/53.*

Heckel, Ulrich: Kraft in Schwachheit. 1993. *Volume II/56.*

– see *Feldmeier, Reinhard.*

– see *Hengel, Martin.*

Heiligenthal, Roman: Werke als Zeichen. 1983. *Volume II/9.*

Hellholm, D.: see *Hartman, Lars.*

Hemer, Colin J.: The Book of Acts in the Setting of Hellenistic History. 1989. *Volume 49.*

Hengel, Martin: Judentum und Hellenismus. 1969, [3]1988. *Volume 10.*

– Die johanneische Frage. 1993. *Volume 67.*

– Judaica et Hellenistica. Volume 1. 1996. *Volume 90.*

Hengel, Martin and *Ulrich Heckel* (Ed.): Paulus und das antike Judentum. 1991. *Volume 58.*

Hengel, Martin and *Hermut Löhr* (Ed.): Schriftauslegung im antiken Judentum und im
Urchristentum. 1994. *Volume 73.*

Hengel, Martin and *Anna Maria Schwemer* (Ed.): Königsherrschaft Gottes und himmlischer
Kult. 1991. *Volume 55.*

– Die Septuaginta. 1994. *Volume 72.*

Herrenbrück, Fritz: Jesus und die Zöllner. 1990. *Volume II/41.*

Herzer, Jens: Paulus oder Petrus? 1998. *Volume 103.*

Hoegen-Rohls, Christina: Der nachösterliche Johannes. 1996. *Volume II/84.*

Hofius, Otfried: Katapausis. 1970. *Volume 11.*

– Der Vorhang vor dem Thron Gottes. 1972. *Volume 14.*

– Der Christushymnus Philipper 2,6–11. 1976, [2]1991. *Volume 17.*

– Paulusstudien. 1989, [2]1994. *Volume 51.*

Hofius, Otfried and *Hans-Christian Kammler:* Johannesstudien. 1996. *Volume 88.*

Holtz, Traugott: Geschichte und Theologie des Urchristentums. 1991. *Volume 57.*

Hommel, Hildebrecht: Sebasmata. Volume 1 1983. *Volume 31* – Volume 2 1984. *Volume 32.*

Hvalvik, Reidar: The Struggle for Scripture and Covenant. 1996. *Volume II/82.*

Kähler, Christoph: Jesu Gleichnisse als Poesie und Therapie. 1995. *Volume 78.*

Kammler, Hans-Christian: see *Hofius, Otfried.*

Kamlah, Ehrhard: Die Form der katalogischen Paränese im Neuen Testament. 1964.
Volume 7.

Kieffer, René and *Jan Bergman (Ed.):* La Main de Dieu / Die Hand Gottes. 1997. *Volume 94.*

Kim, Seyoon: The Origin of Paul's Gospel. 1981, [2]1984. *Volume II/4.*

– »The ›Son of Man‹« as the Son of God. 1983. *Volume 30.*

Kleinknecht, Karl Th.: Der leidende Gerechtfertigte. 1984, [2]1988. *Volume II/13.*

Klinghardt, Matthias: Gesetz und Volk Gottes. 1988. *Volume II/32.*

Köhler, Wolf-Dietrich: Rezeption des Matthäusevangeliums in der Zeit vor Irenäus. 1987. *Volume II/24.*

Korn, Manfred: Die Geschichte Jesu in veränderter Zeit. 1993. *Volume II/51.*

Koskenniemi, Erkki: Apollonios von Tyana in der neutestamentlichen Exegese. 1994. *Volume II/61.*

Kraus, Wolfgang: Das Volk Gottes. 1996. *Volume 85.*

– see *Walter, Nikolaus.*

Kuhn, Karl G.: Achtzehngebet und Vaterunser und der Reim. 1950. *Volume 1.*

Laansma, Jon: I Will Give You Rest. 1997. *Volume II/98.*

Lampe, Peter: Die stadtrömischen Christen in den ersten beiden Jahrhunderten. 1987, [2]1989. *Volume II/18.*

Lau, Andrew: Manifest in Flesh. 1996. *Volume II/86.*

Lichtenberger, Hermann: see *Avemarie, Friedrich.*

Lieu, Samuel N.C.: Manichaeism in the Later Roman Empire and Medieval China. [2]1992. *Volume 63.*

Loader, William R.G.: Jesus' Attitude Towards the Law. 1997. *Volume II/97.*

Löhr, Gebhard: Verherrlichung Gottes durch Philosophie. 1997. *Volume 97.*

Löhr, Hermut: see *Hengel, Martin.*

Löhr, Winrich Alfried: Basilides und seine Schule. 1995. *Volume 83.*

Maier, Gerhard: Mensch und freier Wille. 1971. *Volume 12.*

– Die Johannesoffenbarung und die Kirche. 1981. *Volume 25.*

Markschies, Christoph: Valentinus Gnosticus? 1992. *Volume 65.*

Marshall, Peter: Enmity in Corinth: Social Conventions in Paul's Relations with the Corinthians. 1987. *Volume II/23.*

Meade, David G.: Pseudonymity and Canon. 1986. *Volume 39.*

Meadors, Edward P.: Jesus the Messianic Herald of Salvation. 1995. *Volume II/72.*

Meißner, Stefan: Die Heimholung des Ketzers. 1996. *Volume II/87.*

Mell, Ulrich: Die »anderen« Winzer. 1994. *Volume 77.*

Mengel, Berthold: Studien zum Philipperbrief. 1982. *Volume II/8.*

Merkel, Helmut: Die Widersprüche zwischen den Evangelien. 1971. *Volume 13.*

Merklein, Helmut: Studien zu Jesus und Paulus. 1987. *Volume 43.*

Metzler, Karin: Der griechische Begriff des Verzeihens. 1991. *Volume II/44.*

Metzner, Rainer: Die Rezeption des Matthäusevangeliums im 1. Petrusbrief. 1995. *Volume II/74.*

Mittmann-Richert, Ulrike: Magnifikat und Benediktus. 1996. *Volume II/90.*

Niebuhr, Karl-Wilhelm: Gesetz und Paränese. 1987. *Volume II/28.*

– Heidenapostel aus Israel. 1992. *Volume 62.*

Nissen, Andreas: Gott und der Nächste im antiken Judentum. 1974. *Volume 15.*

Noormann, Rolf: Irenäus als Paulusinterpret. 1994. *Volume II/66.*

Obermann, Andreas: Die christologische Erfüllung der Schrift im Johannesevangelium. 1996. *Volume II/83.*

Okure, Teresa: The Johannine Approach to Mission. 1988. *Volume II/31.*

Paulsen, Henning: Zur Literatur und Geschichte des frühen Christentums. Hrsg. von Ute E. Eisen. 1997. *Volume 99.*

Park, Eung Chun: The Mission Discourse in Matthew's Interpretation. 1995. *Volume II/81.*

Philonenko, Marc (Ed.): Le Trône de Dieu. 1993. *Volume 69.*

Pilhofer, Peter: Presbyteron Kreitton. 1990. *Volume II/39.*

– Philippi. Volume 1 1995. *Volume 87.*

Pöhlmann, Wolfgang: Der Verlorene Sohn und das Haus. 1993. *Volume 68.*

Pokorný, Petr and *Josef B. Souček:* Bibelauslegung als Theologie. 1997. *Volume 100.*

Prieur, Alexander: Die Verkündigung der Gottesherrschaft. 1996. *Volume II/89.*

Probst, Hermann: Paulus und der Brief. 1991. *Volume II/45.*

Räisänen, Heikki: Paul and the Law. 1983, [2]1987. *Volume 29.*

Rehkopf, Friedrich: Die lukanische Sonderquelle. 1959. *Volume 5.*

Rein, Matthias: Die Heilung des Blindgeborenen (Joh 9). 1995. *Volume II/73.*

Reinmuth, Eckart: Pseudo-Philo und Lukas. 1994. *Volume 74.*

Reiser, Marius: Syntax und Stil des Markusevangeliums. 1984. *Volume II/11.*

Richards, E. Randolph: The Secretary in the Letters of Paul. 1991. *Volume II/42.*

Riesner, Rainer: Jesus als Lehrer. 1981, [3]1988. *Volume II/7.*

Wissenschaftliche Untersuchungen zum Neuen Testament

– Die Frühzeit des Apostels Paulus. 1994. *Volume 71.*
Rissi, Mathias: Die Theologie des Hebräerbriefs. 1987. *Volume 41.*
Röhser, Günter: Metaphorik und Personifikation der Sünde. 1987. *Volume II/25.*
Rose, Christian: Die Wolke der Zeugen. 1994. *Volume II/60.*
Rüger, Hans Peter: Die Weisheitsschrift aus der Kairoer Geniza. 1991. *Volume 53.*
Sänger, Dieter: Antikes Judentum und die Mysterien. 1980. *Volume II/5.*
– Die Verkündigung des Gekreuzigten und Israel. 1994. *Volume 75.*
Salzmann, Jorg Christian: Lehren und Ermahnen. 1994. *Volume II/59.*
Sandnes, Karl Olav: Paul – One of the Prophets? 1991. *Volume II/43.*
Sato, Migaku: Q und Prophetie. 1988. *Volume II/29.*
Schaper, Joachim: Eschatology in the Greek Psalter. 1995. *Volume II/76.*
Schimanowski, Gottfried: Weisheit und Messias. 1985. *Volume II/17.*
Schlichting, Günter: Ein jüdisches Leben Jesu. 1982. *Volume 24.*
Schnabel, Eckhard J.: Law and Wisdom from Ben Sira to Paul. 1985. *Volume II/16.*
Schutter, William L.: Hermeneutic and Composition in I Peter. 1989. *Volume II/30.*
Schwartz, Daniel R.: Studies in the Jewish Background of Christianity. 1992. *Volume 60.*
Schwemer, Anna Maria: see *Hengel, Martin*
Scott, James M.: Adoption as Sons of God. 1992. *Volume II/48.*
– Paul and the Nations. 1995. *Volume 84.*
Siegert, Folker: Drei hellenistisch-jüdische Predigten. Teil I 1980. *Volume 20* – Teil II 1992. *Volume 61.*
– Nag-Hammadi-Register. 1982. *Volume 26.*
– Argumentation bei Paulus. 1985. *Volume 34.*
– Philon von Alexandrien. 1988. *Volume 46.*
Simon, Marcel: Le christianisme antique et son contexte religieux I/II. 1981. *Volume 23.*
Snodgrass, Klyne: The Parable of the Wicked Tenants. 1983. *Volume 27.*
Söding, Thomas: Das Wort vom Kreuz. 1997. *Volume 93.*
– see *Thüsing, Wilhelm.*
Sommer, Urs: Die Passionsgeschichte des Markusevangeliums. 1993. *Volume II/58.*
Souček, Josef B.: see *Pokorný, Petr.*
Spangenberg, Volker: Herrlichkeit des Neuen Bundes. 1993. *Volume II/55.*
Speyer, Wolfgang: Frühes Christentum im antiken Strahlungsfeld. 1989. *Volume 50.*
Stadelmann, Helge: Ben Sira als Schriftgelehrter. 1980. *Volume II/6.*
Strobel, August: Die Stunde der Wahrheit. 1980. *Volume 21.*
Stuckenbruck, Loren T.: Angel Veneration and Christology. 1995. *Volume II/70.*
Stuhlmacher, Peter (Ed.): Das Evangelium und die Evangelien. 1983. *Volume 28.*
Sung, Chong-Hyon: Vergebung der Sünden. 1993. *Volume II/57.*
Tajra, Harry W.: The Trial of St. Paul. 1989. *Volume II/35.*
– The Martyrdom of St.Paul. 1994. *Volume II/67.*
Theißen, Gerd: Studien zur Soziologie des Urchristentums. 1979, [3]1989. *Volume 19.*
Thornton, Claus-Jürgen: Der Zeuge des Zeugen. 1991. *Volume 56.*
Thüsing, Wilhelm: Studien zur neutestamentlichen Theologie. Hrsg. von Thomas Söding. 1995. *Volume 82.*
Tsuji, Manabu: Glaube zwischen Vollkommenheit und Verweltlichung. 1997. *Volume II/93*
Twelftree, Graham H.: Jesus the Exorcist. 1993. *Volume II/54.*
Visotzky, Burton L.: Fathers of the World. 1995. *Volume 80.*
Wagener, Ulrike: Die Ordnung des »Hauses Gottes« . 1994. *Volume II/65.*
Walter, Nikolaus: Praeparatio Evangelica. Hrsg. von Wolfgang Kraus und Florian Wilk. 1997. *Volume 98.*
Watts, Rikki: Isaiah's New Exodus and Mark. 1997. *Volume II/88.*
Wedderburn, A.J.M.: Baptism and Resurrection. 1987. *Volume 44.*
Wegner, Uwe: Der Hauptmann von Kafarnaum. 1985. *Volume II/14.*
Welck, Christian: Erzählte ›Zeichen‹. 1994. *Volume II/69.*
Wilk, Florian: see *Walter, Nikolaus.*
Wilson, Walter T.: Love without Pretense. 1991. *Volume II/46.*
Zimmermann, Alfred E.: Die urchristlichen Lehrer. 1984, [2]1988. *Volume II/12.*

For a complete catalog please write to the publisher
Mohr Siebeck, P.O.Box 2040, D–72010 Tübingen, Germany.